DEVELOPMENTAL SOCIAL PSYCHOLOGY

The first comprehensive presentation of theory and research based on recent efforts to integrate social psychology and developmental psychology, the present volume provides an excellent introduction to developmental social psychology as a distinct field of inquiry. Written by leading scholars in the area, each of fourteen original contributions offers an extensive review of relevant conceptual models and empirical findings.

The topics discussed in this book reflect the breadth and innovation characteristic of this emerging new field. Organized around the three major themes of Internal versus External Determinants of Behavior, Interpersonal Perception, and Applications to Individual and Social Problems, this collection should serve as a stimulating source book for students and professionals in both developmental and social psychology.

The Editors

Sharon S. Brehm received her Ph.D. from Duke University and is currently Associate Professor of Psychology at the University of Kansas. Author of *The Application of Social Psychology to Clinical Practice* and *Help for Your Child: A Parent's Guide to Mental Health Services,* her recently completed book with J. W. Brehm, *Psychological Reactance: A Theory of Freedom and Control,* will be published in 1981.

Saul M. Kassin received his Ph.D. from the University of Connecticut and is currently Assistant Professor of Psychology at Purdue University. His research interests include developmental processes in attribution, and he has published a number of papers in scholarly journals on this and other research areas.

Frederick X. Gibbons received his Ph.D. from the University of Texas at Austin and is currently Assistant Professor of Psychology at Iowa State University. His research interests include attitudes of and towards stigmatized individuals, and he has published a number of papers in scholarly journals on this and other areas.

Oxford University Press, New York

Jacket design by Joy Taylor   ISBN 0-19-502840-6

Developmental Social Psychology

THEORY AND RESEARCH

Edited by

SHARON S. BREHM
University of Kansas

SAUL M. KASSIN
Purdue University

FREDERICK X. GIBBONS
Iowa State University

OXFORD UNIVERSITY PRESS
New York   1981   Oxford

Library of Congress Cataloging in Publication Data
Main entry under title:
Developmental social psychology.
Includes index.
1 Social psychology—Addresses, essays, lectures.
2. Developmental psychology—Addresses, essays,
lectures. I. Brehm, Sharon S. II. Kassin, Saul M.
III. Gibbons, Frederick X. [DNLM: 1. Child
development. 2. Social behavior—In infancy and
childhood. WS105.5.S6]
HM251.D48 302 80–18740
ISBN 0–19–502840–6
ISBN 0–19–502841–4 pbk.

Printing (last digit): 987654321
Printed in the United States of America

Surgeons must be very careful
When they take the knife!
Underneath their fine incisions
Stirs the Culprit—*Life*!

Emily Dickinson

PREFACE

Many people regard Kurt Lewin as the father of modern social psychology. Lewin was a protean figure—indeed, a veritable Renaissance man—whose interests ranged easily and fruitfully over a variety of topics. He studied traditional content areas of social psychology such as attitude change and group interaction, but he also had a strong interest in developmental processes, the application of psychological knowledge to real-world problems, and deviant psychological functioning (such as the behavior of mentally retarded individuals). For Lewin, then, social, developmental, abnormal, and applied psychology were not separate domains of inquiry; instead, they were only arbitrary divisions of subject matter and professional allegiance that he felt free to ignore. In terms of his own theory, Lewin saw the boundaries between these areas of psychology as being distinctly permeable.

In view of this geneological history, one is surprised how the social psychology of the past generation has tended to honor Lewin's patrimony more in the breach than in the observance. Unfortunately, not only social psychology, but the entire field of psychology has become fragmented and parochial, and, on occasion, the fervor with which psychologists allied with one designated field defend themselves from intrusion from those identified with another area suggests a kind of professional chauvinism. Some of this narrow definition and protection of boundaries is understandable. After all, there is nothing more discouraging or irritating than witnessing an expert in another area of psychology come trampling into one's own field with little or no knowledge of the extant body of research.

While such *un*informed cross-disciplinary research may be counterproductive, we believe that well-informed and thoughtful cross-disciplinary endeavors can be exceedingly beneficial to each of the separate areas involved. From time to time, we all suffer from not being able to see the forest because of the trees; sometimes an "outsider" can offer a point of view that provides clarification and added scope. Moreover, we are all in need of good ideas and should be delighted to snatch one whenever we see it, regardless of its particular intellectual heritage.

In the last few years, the possibilities for productive cross-disciplinary efforts have been increasingly recognized. Perhaps the most dramatic example of this trend has been the application of learning theory and, to a lesser extent, social psychological principles to solving problems in the real world. This book seeks specifically to promote and expand this ongoing process in the interface of two other traditional areas: social psychology and developmental psychology.

Although developmental psychologists have always been interested in social phenomena, their orientation typically has isolated them from the research being conducted with adults by social psychologists. On the other hand, social psychologists have, until quite recently, rarely shown interest in developmental issues and, generally, were unaware of relevant research that had been conducted in that area. Children sometimes appeared as subjects in social psychological research, but this was usually because they simply provided an available subject population.

Fortunately, this situation appears to be rapidly changing. The two disciplines appear to be moving toward the creation of a common boundary area with complementary interests. This book bears testimony to how far we have come. We believe that a blend of the developmental and social traditions offers unique benefits to both areas. Each discipline contributes to the mix its theoretical orientations, methods, favorite substantive issues, applied problems, and controversies. Their respective differences, of course, occur in the context of social psychology's focus on fully developed processes in adults and developmental psychology's focus on growth and change.

Most of the contributors to this book identify themselves professionally as social psychologists. All of the authors, however, share a commitment to utilizing theories and empirical findings derived from both disciplines. Such integrative tasks are not easily accomplished, and the reader should expect to find at least as many questions raised as there are answers provided. Nevertheless, we believe that this volume delineates the complex and frustrating but potentially fruitful effort of attempting to combine social and developmental psychology in terms of both basic research and applications to the real world.

Plan and scope of the book. The chapters in this book cover a wide range of topics and are divided into three major areas: internal versus external determinants of behavior, interpersonal perception, and applications to individual and social problems. Preceding each of these sections, we have provided a brief introduction to and survey of the material to be covered. These separate sections should not imply that those chapters within any given section are relevant only to each other. Indeed, any one chapter may have implications for a number of other chapters throughout the book. We have, therefore, provided citations to other chapters whenever there appeared to be important cross-chapter relationships in the material being discussed.

At this point, we should note that the scope of this book is, by necessity, substantively limited in two respects. First, a glance at our table of contents reveals that the areas represented here are ones that have traditionally been of interest to social psychologists. As such, certain widely studied topics in mainstream developmental psychology, such as child rearing and parental authority, do not appear as the direct focus of any chapter in this book. Many of the chapters, however, contain significant material relevant to these issues. Second, although we use the generic term "developmental," our authors address only those age groups ranging from infancy through early adulthood. Our failure to cover later developmental periods, such as the social psychology of the aging individual, is a reflection of the limits of a single volume and in no way implies limited interest in, nor importance of, these periods of life.

We believe that this book will be of direct interest to both developmental and social psychologists. Specifically, it can serve two purposes. First, it provides 14 excellent and fairly comprehensive reviews that may prove to be invaluable bibliographic reference points to the interested reader who would like to become acquainted with an area. At the same time, the more advanced reader will enjoy the fact that those scholars who contributed chapters offer many new theoretical insights, empirical findings, and suggested directions for future research. In terms of the writing level and complexity of material presented, this book is directed toward an audience of advanced undergraduates, graduate students, and professionals. It is our hope that this collection will stimulate thought throughout a wide range of scholarly levels.

Acknowledgments. Any edited book is necessarily the joint product of the work of many people. As editors, we wish to thank our authors for their dedication to their individual projects and for their cooperative efforts with us in bringing their chapters from birth to maturity. We are also most grateful to Marcus Boggs of Oxford University Press, who has given us unfailing support and encouragement throughout this endeavor, and to the entire production staff at Oxford whose superb work is reflected, literally, on every page of this volume. Special thanks are due to Nancy Amy whose patience and competence played a major role in bringing this book to publication. Finally, we each have our own social support networks, including the other two editors of this book, and we thank our friends and relations for tolerating, or discreetly ignoring, the inevitable obsessiveness, fits of pique, and lost weekends that accompany the editing of a book.

Lawrence, Kansas	S.S.B.
West Lafayette, Indiana	S.M.K.
Ames, Iowa	F.X.G.
January 1981	

CONTENTS

DEVELOPMENTAL SOCIAL PSYCHOLOGY

one

INTERNAL VERSUS EXTERNAL
DETERMINANTS OF BEHAVIOR

The chapters in this section cover a wide variety of content areas. Topics that are discussed include the effects of obtaining a reward, the effects of delaying a reward, the motivation to achieve, the facilitation of prosocial behavior, and the creation of oppositional behavior. Each chapter stands quite well on its own, and the detection of an underlying theme throughout these chapters is neither necessary nor sufficient for an appreciation of the ideas presented in the following pages.

Such a theme, however, does seem to wind its way through the diverse phenomena and theoretical perspectives that are examined. Each chapter, in its own individual manner, pays attention to the comparison of, and the tension between, internal and external determinants of behavior. This tension is played out in different ways, depending on the focus of the particular chapter. In this introduction, we will describe briefly the various points of view taken in regard to this fundamental duality.

The chapter by Lepper and Gilovich can be seen as setting the tone for the entire section. These authors provide an intricate assessment of the ways in which external rewards can reduce subsequent interest in activities that, initially, were of high intrinsic interest. After reviewing the relevant literature on this topic, Lepper and Gilovich propose a model describing the multiple functions of external rewards. This model makes clear that external reward can have many different effects—on instrumental value, task performance, and evaluation of one's performance—that will not necessarily reduce intrinsic motivation. When, however, the facilitating effects of reward are held constant and its major effect is to serve a social control function over the person's behavior, then reward may, as the authors put it, turn "play" into "work."

Whatever their effects on subsequent behavior, not all rewards are immediately available. Often, in order to obtain a very important reward, one has to wait. The chapter by Karniol and Miller discusses the effects of delaying gratification and the ways in which coping with this delay can be made less aversive for the individual. Central to their approach is the distinction between delays that are self-imposed (where the individual has the power to terminate the delay) and delays that are externally imposed (where the individual does not have this power). Karniol and Miller suggest that the dynamics of these two types of delay situations are quite different and that individuals who cope well with one kind of delay may not be the same individuals who cope well with the other type.

The internal-external duality also plays an important role in Frieze's chapter on children's attributions for success and failure. Frieze points out that one of the major dimensions of attribution for academic performance is whether that performance is attributed to internal factors (such as ability and effort) or to external factors (such as task difficulty and luck). This distinction, however, represents only the broad beginnings of a classification scheme for achievement-related attributions; Frieze also explores a number of more finely delineated categorizations. Throughout her chapter, emphasis is placed on how initial expectancies about success and failure may influence attributions which, in turn, may influence expectations for future performance.

In Moore and Underwood's chapter on the development of prosocial behavior, both internal and external determinants of this type of behavior are considered. On the one hand, Moore and Underwood point to external factors such as social norms and the socialization practices of parents that may facilitate the development of prosocial behavior. On the other, they examine in some detail possible internal determinants such as perspective-taking and empathy. For both kinds of determinants, the authors attend carefully to the ways in which cognitive variables may interact with more situational and social factors in promoting prosocial behavior.

The final chapter in this section focuses on how external influence attempts may create the internal motivational state of psychological reactance. Reactance arousal is, then, postulated to motivate the person to act in opposition to the source of the influence and to attempt to reestablish the behavioral freedom that was threatened. Brehm's chapter on oppositional behavior in children is clearly consistent with the position elucidated by Lepper and Gilovich: Strong social influence attempts may obtain immediate compliance, but in the long run fail to maintain the desired behavior.

All of these chapters are based on a developmental social approach to their content areas. Social psychological *and* developmental theories are considered; research conducted with both adults *and* children is reviewed. The integrative theoretical formulations that emerge seek to provide general theoretical principles that may extend throughout development, but that are mediated at any specific developmental point by relevant cognitive and experiential factors.

The combination of a developmental social approach with a focus on the interplay between internal and external determinants of behavior virtually guarantees that issues of some considerable complexity will be examined. These chapters fulfill that guarantee, but we believe that they do so with clarity and precision. It is unlikely that readers of these chapters will come away convinced of the simplicity of the formulations that are offered. We hope, however, that readers will derive the satisfaction of significantly expanding their understanding of a number of crucial issues in psychological development.

1

THE MULTIPLE FUNCTIONS OF REWARD: A SOCIAL–DEVELOPMENTAL PERSPECTIVE

MARK R. LEPPER
THOMAS GILOVICH
STANFORD UNIVERSITY

> If [Tom Sawyer] had been a great and wise philosopher, like the writer of this book, he would have now comprehended that Work consists of whatever a body is *obliged* to do and that Play consists of whatever a body is not obliged to do. And this would help him to understand why constructing artificial flowers or performing on a treadmill is work, while rolling ten-pins or climbing Mont Blanc is only amusement. There are wealthy gentlemen in England who drive four-horse passenger coaches twenty or thirty miles on a daily line, in the summer, because the privilege costs them considerable money; but if they were offered wages for the service that would turn it into work and then they would resign.
>
> Mark Twain
> *The Adventures of Tom Sawyer*

As Mark Twain noted over a century ago, the definition of an activity as work or as play may depend importantly on the context in which we encounter it. Whether one is engaged in an activity either for its own sake or in order to obtain some extrinsic goal, for example, may have important consequences for the way in which we approach that

Preparation of this report was supported, in part, by Research Grants HD-MH-09814 from the National Institute of Child Health and Human Development and BNS-79-14118 from the National Science Foundation to the senior author. The chapter was written during the senior author's term as a Fellow at the Center for Advanced Study in the Behavioral Sciences, Stanford, California, and financial support for this fellowship from National Science Foundation Grant BNS-78-24671 and the Spencer Foundation is gratefully acknowledged. The present chapter draws, in part, upon previous treatments of this topic by the senior author (Lepper, 1981; Lepper & Greene, 1978b).

activity, the extent to which we are likely to enjoy it, and the likelihood that we will spontaneously choose to engage in that activity in the future. Reading *A Tale of Two Cities* either to satisfy one's own curiosity or because one's teacher has assigned it for a book report may have quite different consequences. Playing the piano may be a very different experience depending on whether one is being compelled to do so by one's parents or whether one has chosen to take up the instrument on one's own.

In short, the reasons we perceive as underlying our actions may have important effects on our perceptions of an activity as either work or play and may thus affect our later reactions to that activity. The attractiveness of various tasks and activities in the environment is not only a function of the objective characteristics of those activities, but also depends on what we make of those tasks and how we approach them in particular settings (Csikszentmihalyi, 1975). It is this fundamental thesis—that there are important cognitive, affective, and behavioral consequences to our perception of activities as either work or play, as either intrinsically or extrinsically motivated—and its implications for the study of motivational questions that have led to much of the research to be considered in this chapter.

The more specific context in which we shall encounter this thesis in the present paper lies in the recent research that suggests that the inappropriate use of salient, but functionally superfluous, tangible rewards with activities of high initial intrinsic interest may have detrimental effects on subsequent intrinsic interest and qualitative indices of task performance. This work indicates that systems of social control that serve to define an initially interesting activity as a "means" to some external "end" may adversely affect later interest and performance (Lepper & Greene, 1978b).

In the following sections, we will turn first to the evidence that superfluous social controls may indeed have detrimental effects on later behavior and to research illuminating the conditions under which such effects will be more or less likely to appear. We will then attempt to place this research in a broader context, by considering the multiple functions that rewards may serve, in terms of a conceptual model of the multiple processes by which the use of tangible rewards may affect task performance and subsequent behavior. In doing so, we hope to illustrate both the implications and the limitations of current experimental evidence on the potential adverse effects of inappropriately designed contingency systems. Finally, we will consider more specifically the relationship of these social-psychological investigations to traditional issues in developmental psychology and the study of the socialization process.

"Internalization" versus "compliance"

Let us begin with a consideration of the basic proposition that the use of superfluous extrinsic incentives to "reinforce" a child's engagement in an activity of initial intrinsic interest to that child may have detrimental effects—that is, the imposition of unnecessarily powerful or salient extrinsic constraints on behaviors that appear to be intrinsically motivated may undermine subsequent intrinsic interest or impair task performance. Immediately, this proposition raises an obvious question. Superficially, at least, this thesis seems inconsistent with the well-established finding that contingent reinforcement will increase the probability of the response it follows—the fundamental principle underlying the Law of Effect. Shouldn't we discard this hypothesis, at the outset, on the basis of previous research demonstrating the effectiveness of systematic reward programs on controlling human behavior?

The answer to this question depends, in part, on our recognition of an important distinction between two conceptually distinct responses to social control attempts—compliance and internalization. Within both social (cf. Kelman, 1958, 1961; Lewin, 1935) and developmental (cf. Aronfreed, 1968; Hoffman, 1970) psychology, there is a long history of attempts to distinguish between the processes that underlie immediate compliance (i.e., acquiescence with a social influence attempt in order to achieve some immediate instrumental gain) and those that underlie subsequent internalization (i.e., responses reflecting a personal acceptance of the principles or values underlying the social influence attempt).

The sources of this distinction are twofold. First, the distinction represents an attempt to partition responses to social influence in terms of their effects on subsequent behavior in different situations. Responses reflecting "mere" compliance are presumed to be reflected in later behavior only under conditions in which the individual continues to perceive that response as having further instrumental value; the individual's behavior is seen, in short, as extrinsically motivated. Responses reflecting internalization, by contrast, are presumed to affect subsequent behavior across a variety of situations; the individual's behavior is viewed as intrinsically motivated and does not depend on its instrumentality to the attainment of other goals.

Second, this distinction reflects a conviction that the factors that promote each of these processes may not be identical. That is, the social control techniques most likely to promote maximal compliance with a request will not necessarily be those most likely to promote internalization. In fact, the two may sometimes prove to be directly at variance with one another. Powerful and highly salient social control techniques will typically be most likely to ensure immediate compliance. However, when such powerful control strategies are employed in settings in which they are functionally superfluous, and when less salient and coercive social influence attempts would be sufficient to have produced compliance (Lepper, 1973, in press), such techniques may prove significantly less effective in promoting subsequent internalization.

Traditional research on the effectiveness of systematic reward programs in producing functional control over behavior (i.e., achieving compliance in the presence of the reward system) and the more recent research we will consider concerning the potential deleterious effects of superfluous extrinsic rewards on later intrinsic interest (i.e., internalized attitudes and preferences) are thus asking very different questions. That the two approaches may yield superficially opposite findings is less a function of their inherent incompatability than it is a function of differences in the goals of study and the questions raised by each approach (Lepper & Greene, 1978a). There is no inherent contradiction in the possibility that a reward program may have both a positive effect in producing increased engagement in the rewarded activity while the reward program is in effect and a negative effect on subsequent intrinsic interest in the activity, as reflected in later decreases in task engagement in settings in which the behavior is no longer instrumental in attaining further rewards. Let us turn, then, to the question of whether, and how, such effects might occur.

The "insufficient justification" paradigm: Enhancing internalization with minimally sufficient social control techniques

Although one may trace research concerned with this distinction as far back as Lewin's early research on group dynamics (e.g., Lewin, 1935; Lewin, Lippitt, & White, 1939), the systematic study of the proposition that later internalization or private attitude change following initial compliance will be greater the less the incentives provided to induce initial compliance appears first in research derived from Festinger's dissonance theory (Brehm & Cohen, 1962; Festinger, 1957; Wicklund & Brehm, 1976). The research most relevant to our present concerns involved an investigation of what came to be called the "insufficient justification" paradigm (Aronson, 1969).

This research was concerned with the use of relatively more or less powerful social control techniques to induce an individual to behave in a fashion contrary to his or her initial attitudes or inclinations and their effects on subsequent internalization (as indexed by the person's later private attitudes or behavior) of the values underlying the social control attempt. Dissonance theory suggested that engaging in counterattitudinal behavior should produce an aversive motivational state that creates pressure to change one's attitudes or behavior to minimize the dissonance created by this action. To the extent that it would be hard to revoke or take back one's public actions, the model suggested that people in such a situation would be motivated to change their attitudes toward congruence with their previous actions—that people would be motivated to shift their private beliefs so as to see their actions as rational and consistent with their attitudes.

However, the amount of dissonance experienced was hypothesized to depend on the power and salience of the incentives employed to induce the person to engage in the behavior initially. The more powerful and compelling the external pressures placed on the person to produce compliance, the less dissonance should result. The greater the external "justification" the person has to explain his or her otherwise counterattitudinal actions, the less the person should need to justify or rationalize those actions further. Hence, maximal attitude change is predicted to occur following compliance obtained with the minimal amount of pressure required—that is, in the face of objectively adequate, but psychologically "insufficient" justification.

Although there are a number of specific experimental paradigms to which this analysis may be applied (Lepper, in press; Wicklund & Brehm, 1976), let us consider one case that has particular relevance to developmental issues—the "forbidden toy" paradigm. In these studies, pioneered by Aronson and Carlsmith (1963), children are asked to resist the temptation to play with a highly attractive activity during a temptation period in which they are left alone with this forbidden activity and several other permissible alternatives. For some of the children, the prohibition of this activity is accompanied by a relatively mild threat of punishment for transgression; for others, it is

accompanied by a considerably more severe threat of punishment. In the former case, the external justification for not playing with this attractive toy is minimal, although it is objectively sufficient to prevent all children from transgressing. In the latter case, the external pressure applied is greater and, in this context, this added pressure is functionally superfluous for producing initial compliance with the adult's request. The effects of these two procedures are then observed on various indices presumed to be indicative of dissonance reduction—that is, the extent to which the child will subsequently devalue the previously forbidden activity and continue to avoid that activity in the later absence of any further prohibition, or the extent to which the child will resist temptation in other related situations.

Looking at a number of different studies and procedures, the results seem relatively clear: children who initially resist temptation in the face of relatively minimal external pressures are more likely to show internalization of the values underlying the initial prohibition than children who resist temptation in the face of more powerful and salient techniques of social control. Thus, children in the mild-threat conditions are more likely than children in the severe-threat conditions to show subsequent derogation of the previously forbidden toy (e.g., Aronson & Carlsmith, 1963; Lepper, 1973, in press). They are also more likely to avoid the previously prohibited activity when the activity is no longer forbidden, up to six weeks after the initial experimental sessions (Freedman, 1965; Pepitone, McCauley, & Hammond, 1967). Additional evidence indicates that other forms of superfluous external justification for the behavior (Freedman, 1965; Lepper, Zanna, & Abelson, 1970) will, like the use of unnecessarily powerful threats of punishment, also decrease subsequent internalization. Furthermore, the differential effects of mild versus severe threats may be enhanced by manipulations that draw the child's attention to the forbidden toy and the accompanying threat manipulation (Zanna, Lepper, & Abelson, 1973).

Perhaps more impressively, these procedures also appear to influence children's later willingness or ability to resist temptation in other, quite different situations that do not involve the specific forbidden activity prohibited initially. Lepper (1973) exposed children to a standard mild- or severe-threat procedure in a first session and then examined children's resistance to temptation in a very different setting several weeks later. In this second session, children were confronted by a different experimenter who introduced a bowling game that they were allowed to play by themselves. The object of the bowling game was to achieve a sufficiently high score to win a very attractive prize. The game, however, was designed to provide each child with a score that fell just short of that required to win a prize; hence, the child could win the prize only by falsely reporting to the experimenter a higher score than he or she had actually obtained.

The results in this second session suggested that children's prior resistance to temptation in the forbidden toy situation had important effects on their later resistance to temptation in this new setting. Relative to an appropriate control condition, children who had initially resisted the temptation to play with the forbidden activity under a mild threat of punishment proved more likely to resist temptation in this later situation as well; those who had resisted temptation initially in the face of a more severe threat of punishment tended to show less resistance to temptation in this subsequent situation. The former children, it seemed, had not only internalized the specific prohibition employed in the initial session, but had also internalized a more general principle that it was important or appropriate to comply with adult requests in a variety of situations.

Although these data were generated within the framework of cognitive dissonance theory and remain consistent with that model, they may also be conceptualized in somewhat broader terms from the perspective of attribution or self-perception theory (Bem, 1967, 1972; Kelley, 1967, 1973)—a model that focuses on the importance of the reasons we believe to underlie our actions and their effects on our later attitudes and behavior.

The attribution model suggests that an individual's personal attitudes and beliefs will depend, in part, on the person's perception of his or her own previous overt behavior and the conditions under which that behavior occurred. Just as we are likely to draw inferences about the attitudes, beliefs, or motivational state of another on the basis of these factors—assuming, in general, that the greater the obvious external pressures the person faces in a particular situation, the less his or her behavior will relfect internalized values or personal preferences rather than a response to those salient external pressures—we may also view our own actions in a different light as a function of the salience of external forces that may have constrained them. To the extent that the external constraints and contingencies controlling a person's actions are salient, unambiguous, and sufficient to explain those actions, the person will be likely to attribute his or her behavior to these evident external forces—to see himself or herself as extrinsically motivated. But, to the extent that such external contingencies are weak, unclear, or psychologically "insufficient" to explain an individual's actions, the person should be likely to attribute those actions to his or her own dispositions, interests, or attitudes—to view his or her behavior as intrinsically motivated. Under conditions of low justification, therefore, subjects will be likely to view their own previous behavior as reflective of their private preferences and values; under high justification conditions, by contrast, they will be more likely to see their previous actions as a response to, and as determined by, the extrinsic constraints and pressures inherent in the situation.

Both this attribution model and the earlier dissonance account provide an explanation of the "insufficient justification" effects described above. Indeed, in many contexts, it is difficult to distinguish between the two accounts, although more recent research provides suggestive evidence consistent with the motivational postulate of the dissonance account (e.g., Zanna & Cooper, 1976). However, the particular virtue of the attributional account was its suggestion that conceptually analogous effects of the imposition of functionally unnecessary external constraints on subsequent attitudes and behavior might be observed even in situations in which the behavior was not inherently aversive or counterattitudinal (e.g., Fazio, Zanna, & Cooper, 1977). This reinterpretation set the stage, in many respects, for the study of the effects of the imposition of functionally superfluous extrinsic rewards, contingent on one's engagement in an activity of initial inherent interest, on subsequent intrinsic interest in that activity when further external incentives or pressures were absent.

The "overjustification" paradigm: Undermining intrinsic interest with superfluous extrinsic rewards

Consider a child confronted with an activity of high initial intrinsic interest, an activity that he or she might spontaneously choose to engage in for the sake of the enjoyment that that activity might bring. Now suppose that this child were offered some salient, tangible reward for engaging in this activity—in other words, the child was induced to contract explicitly to engage in this activity in order to obtain this desirable extrinsic reward. How might this affect the child's later personal preferences or subsequent behavior in other situations in which there were no longer any tangible, or even social, rewards contingent on engagement in this activity?

The attributional model suggested that the imposition of such a functionally superfluous extrinsic contingency on the child's engagement in an activity of initial interest may lead the child to view his or her actions as extrinsically, rather than intrinsically, motivated. Under such conditions, the inappropriate use of tangible rewards may effectively undermine later intrinsic interest and define the activity as one that should be undertaken only when there is some extrinsic payoff for engaging in the activity. Hence, the child may show decreased interest in the target activity in later situations in which there are no longer any extrinsic rewards or constraints to promote task engagement.

Initial demonstrations

Like many ideas in the history of science, the notion that the inappropriate application of extrinsic rewards might reduce later intrinsic interest in the previously rewarded activity was a multiple discovery—an idea that occurred independently, and at roughly the same time, to a number of investigators in different parts of the world. As a result, even the earliest demonstrations of this phenomenon provide some evidence of the diversity of conditions under which it may occur.

In the earliest of these studies, Deci (1971) created an experimental setting in which college students were asked to spend several sessions playing with a geometric puzzle of high initial interest—the Soma cube—as part of a study presumably concerned with problem-solving techniques. After each of these sessions, the procedure was contrived to provide subjects with a "break" period, in which subjects were left alone between phases of the experiment. During this time, students could continue to play with the Soma cube, read magazines, or engage in other activities to pass the time until the experimenter returned. The experimental manipulation was introduced in the second of these sessions: Half the subjects during this session were paid for each puzzle they solved; half were offered no extrinsic incentive. The change in the amount of time subjects chose to spend playing with the activity during the free-choice periods—from the first, baseline period to the final, postexperimental period—in the absence of any further rewards constituted a measure of the effect of the reward manipulation on subjects' intrinsic interest in the activity. The results of this and succeeding (Deci, 1972a,

1972b) studies suggested that subjects who had been previously paid to work on the puzzles would show less subsequent intrinsic interest in this activity when extrinsic rewards were no longer available.

Pursuing the same issues from a related point of view, Kruglanski, Friedman, and Zeevi (1971) designed an experiment in which Israeli high school students were asked to engage in a number of psychological tests assessing memory, creativity, and the like. Half of these students were informed that, as a reward for taking these tests, they would be taken on a guided tour of research facilities at the nearby university; the remaining students were promised no such reward. Subsequently, measures of performance on these tests and several measures of subjects' enjoyment of these tests were compared for students in these two groups. Across a large number of measures, the results from this study also suggested that students who had been offered a superfluous extrinsic incentive showed less "intrinsic interest" in the activities. Subjects in the extrinsic incentive condition, for example, showed lower recall, less creativity, and less positive attitudes toward the activities.

In the third of these initial demonstrations, Lepper, Greene, and Nisbett (1973) approached this question from a somewhat different perspective. They suggested that detrimental effects of superfluous extrinsic incentives on subsequent intrinsic interest ought not to result from the mere association of an activity of initial interest with an extrinsic reward, but should occur only under conditions in which the receipt of reward would lead the person to think about his or her behavior as having been directed toward the attainment of that reward. From this perspective, negative effects on subsequent interest should be likely to occur when the reward is expected and the child is asked to engage in the activity in order to obtain the reward, but should be unlikely to occur if the child were to receive the same reward unexpectedly after having finished the activity.

To examine this more specific hypothesis,

Lepper, Greene, and Nisbett (1973) selected children high in initial interest in a target activity and exposed them to one of three experimental procedures. To assess the children's initial intrinsic interest in the activity, the children's spontaneous choice of the target activity was observed on several days, during free-play periods in the children's regular preschool classrooms—periods in which the children were free to choose among a wide variety of alternative activities in the absence of external pressures. Those children showing an initial interest in the activity were then exposed to this same activity in a quite different setting some time later.

In this experimental setting, children were exposed to the experimental manipulation. In the Expected Award condition, children were first shown an attractive reward—a Good Player certificate—and were told that they could win this award by drawing some pictures with the target materials. In the Unexpected Award condition, children were asked simply to draw some pictures with these materials, without the promise of any extrinsic reward. When they had finished their drawings, however, these children received exactly the same award and the same feedback as children in the Expected Award condition, but under conditions in which the children should not be likely to view this reward as their reason for having engaged in the activity. In a third, No Award, control condition, children were asked to draw pictures with the materials, but did not expect or receive any tangible reward for their efforts.

Several weeks later, children's postexperimental interest in this activity was again assessed through covert observations of their choices during free-play periods in their regular classrooms—in the absence of any further expectation of tangible or social rewards contingent on their choices. The results of this measure revealed the predicted detrimental effect of contracting to engage in this activity of initial intrinsic interest in order to obtain an extrinsic reward. Children in the Expected Award condition showed significantly less interest in the activity during these classroom observations than did children in either of the other two groups. Expected Award subjects also showed a significant decline in interest from baseline to postexperimental phases of the study; subjects in the Unexpected Award and No Award conditions did not show significant shifts in interest from baseline levels.

In each of these rather different studies, inducing people to engage in an activity of initial interest with the expectation of receiving some attractive extrinsic reward for doing so led to decreases in subsequent intrinsic interest in that activity. These comparable results were obtained, moreover, in the face of large variations in the nature of the rewards, the activities, and the subject populations studied. The important question these studies raise, then, is why the use of superfluous extrinsic rewards should have detrimental effects. To begin to answer this question, let us examine what further research in this area has indicated about the conditions under which such effects are likely to occur.

Further experimental research

Two broad classes of theoretical models have been proposed to account for these detrimental effects. Although there are a number of conceptually distinct variants within each class, these two general approaches may be characterized as follows. One set of models suggests that the adverse effects of superfluous extrinsic rewards on subsequent intrinsic interest occur only as a function of differences in a person's approach to, or performance of, the activity during the initial treatment period when the extrinsic rewards are available. According to this position, differences in performance during the treatment phase may result from a variety of mechanisms: The presence of a salient reward may distract subjects from the activity itself; waiting for the reward during the treatment phase may produce frustration; uncertainty about the receipt of the

reward may induce anxiety concerning the adequacy of one's performance; and so on. Such "competing responses" may adversely affect the manner in which subjects approach and engage in the task during the experimental phase in ways that decrease its attractiveness for the subjects. Hence, decreases in later intrinsic interest are seen as a function of these prior differences in performance induced by the reward manipulation.

By contrast, a second set of models, derived from a more cognitive perspective, suggests that the use of superfluous extrinsic rewards may have a more direct effect on subsequent intrinsic interest: an effect that is not mediated by differences in previous performance during the treatment phase, but may result from the perception or experience of one's actions as externally controlled or constrained. From this attributional viewpoint, engaging in an activity of initial interest in order to obtain some extrinsic reward may, by itself, lead subjects to reevaluate the perceived attractiveness of the activity—to come to see it as something less inherently interesting, as something worth engaging in only when that engagement will produce some further extrinsic payoff.

Of course, these two sets of models are not mutually exclusive. Both sets of processes may occur—either at the same time or under different conditions—and may lead to decreases in subsequent intrinsic interest. There are, however, several lines of research that may help us to understand the conditions under which both sets of processes may occur.

THE IMPORTANCE OF PERCEIVED CONSTRAINT. One possible distinction between these two sorts of models lies in their analyses of the types of reward manipulations that should be predicted to produce subsequent decreases in intrinsic interest and the role that perceptions of external constraint should play in this process. From the competing response position, for example, one might expect detrimental effects to occur as a function of the salience of the reward itself during the treatment phase, whether or not the reward is explicitly presented as contingent on one's engagement in the task. From the attributional perspective, on the other hand, detrimental effects resulting from a direct reevaluation process should occur only when the reward is perceived to be contingent on task engagement, as a function of the salience of external constraint rather than of the reward per se.

Considerable research has been directed to examining the role of perceptions of constraint in the production of negative effects on subsequent intrinsic interest. This research provides relatively strong evidence of the functional significance of perceptions of constraint in these settings. Recall that, in the study by Lepper et al. (1973), negative effects were observed only when the reward children obtained had been expected from the outset, but not when the same reward was administered, unexpectedly, after the fact. This difference has been replicated in a variety of studies with both children (Greene & Lepper, 1974; Lepper & Greene, 1975; Lepper, Sagotsky, & Greene, 1980a) and adults (Enzle & Look, 1980; Smith, 1976) and suggests the importance of an instrumental relationship between engagement in the activity and receipt of the reward.

Even more compelling evidence for the perceived constraint position comes from an intriguing study reported by Kruglanski, Alon, and Lewis (1972). In their study, Kruglanski et al. managed to demonstrate a detrimental effect of an unexpected-reward procedure on children's stated interest in a set of target activities— a finding that seems in conflict with the foregoing studies. Their procedure, however, was quite different: It involved an explicit attempt to lead the children to believe that they had, in fact, been promised the reward in advance. Under these conditions, a significant negative effect was obtained that could be accounted for almost entirely by the responses of children who (falsely) reported themselves to have undertaken the target activities in order to win the proffered reward. Furthermore, since the reward manipulation

did not, in fact, take place until all children had completed the activities, we can be certain in this study that children did not approach the task differently or perform in some different manner during the treatment phase. This reward manipulation, therefore, appears to have had some direct effect on the children's later evaluation of the activity that did not depend on prior performance differences across conditions.

A second line of research consistent with this general argument has involved a slightly different comparison between different sorts of expected rewards: rewards presented as contingent on task engagement and rewards presented as contingent on some other, irrelevant criterion. Ross, Karniol, and Rothstein (1976), for example, promised one group of children a reward for engaging in a target activity and other children a reward for simply waiting a specified amount of time during which they happened, incidentally, to be engaged in the same target activity. Relative to a nonrewarded control condition, children in the contingent-reward condition showed decreased subsequent interest; children in the noncontingent-reward condition showed no decrease in interest. Conceptually analogous results of a somewhat different version of this same comparison have also been reported by Swann and Pittman (1977).

Other experiments have investigated the effects of manipulations that directly vary the salience of the instrumentality of one's engagement in a target activity. Ross (1975) reports two studies of this sort with children. In the first, children in two conditions were promised an unspecified prize for engaging in an activity of initial interest. For some children, this prize was said to be under an opaque box in front of the child during the treatment phase; for others, no further reference was made to this prize. Again, relative to nonrewarded control subjects, children in the first, but not the second, case showed decrements in subsequent intrinsic interest in the previously rewarded activity. In the second of these studies, a more persuasive "cognitive" manipulation of salience of instrumentality was employed. Specifically, children in three groups were told that they could win an attractive reward of several marshmallows for engaging in a particular activity. Then, in two of these conditions, the children were instructed to think about the reward as they engaged in the task—either in instrumental terms (e.g., thinking about how good the marshmallows will taste) or in noninstrumental terms (e.g., thinking about how the marshmallows look like clouds). The results revealed a detrimental effect, relative to control subjects, for children in the no-instruction and instrumental-salience groups; however, the effect of making noninstrumental properties of the reward salient was to eliminate this negative effect. Along related lines, Reiss and Sushinsky (1975, Study 1) varied, orthogonally, the perceptual salience of a reward (and distractor) and the presentation of that reward as contingent on engagement in the target activity. Expectation of reward, but not the mere salience of the reward in the absence of a contingency, produced decrements in later interest in the target activity.

The results of these different studies, then, suggest the importance of perceptions of instrumentality in the production of detrimental effects on later interest through the use of unnecessary extrinsic rewards. Other research carries this proposition one step further, by suggesting that conceptually analogous effects may be obtained in the absence of explicit rewards through the application of other forms of salient social constraint. Lepper and Greene (1975), for example, crossed expectation of an extrinsic reward with the presence or absence of unnecessarily close adult surveillance of children's engagement in a puzzle-solving activity during the experimental treatment phase. Both expectation of reward and the presence of close adult surveillance produced decreases in subsequent interest in this activity in the later absence of further rewards or further adult surveillance. Comparable results have also been obtained in a quite different paradigm involving adult subjects (Pittman, Davey, Alafat, Wetherill, and Wirsul, 1980). Other studies investigating different sources of external constraint have produced similar findings. Amabile, DeJong, and Lepper (1976) found the imposition of functionally superfluous temporal deadlines on the performance of adult subjects produced decreases in later interest in the experimental activity, relative to appropriate control conditions. Similarly, Rosenhan (1969) has shown that forcing a child to display a previously modeled response will decrease the subsequent likelihood that the child will spontaneously display that response in the later absence of further adult pressure.

These various lines of research suggest a common conclusion. Decrements in subsequent intrinsic interest as a function of the presentation of superfluous external controls are most likely to occur under conditions that promote the perception or experience of one's engagement in the target activity as extrinsically constrained. Typically, extrinsic rewards appear to have adverse effects on subsequent interest only when the instrumentality of engagement in the target activity as a means to some external goal is made salient; unexpected, noncontingent, or unspecified reward procedures do not seem to produce negative effects. Moreover, the special cases in which these latter procedures do produce detrimental effects demonstrate that such detrimental effects can be obtained in the absence of any differences in response during the reward phase itself (e.g., Kruglanski et al., 1972). Finally, the appearance of conceptually analogous effects, following the application of other sorts of social control procedures that do not involve the use of rewards per se, suggests that these effects should be interpreted as a function of the salience of constraint in a more general sense.

IMMEDIATE AND SUBSEQUENT EFFECTS OF EXTRINSIC REWARDS. Such a conclusion, of course, does not mean that the adverse effects of extrinsic rewards on subsequent intrinsic interest will always be independent of the effects of these procedures on performance during the treatment phase in which the rewards are available. In fact, several of the preceding studies provide some direct evidence of negative effects on immediate performance measures that may have contributed to subsequent detrimental effects. In the Kruglanski et al. (1971) study with Israeli high school students, decreases in reported interest in the experimental activities were accompanied by a variety of performance decrements on measures of recall, creativity, and the like. Similarly, in the earliest studies by Lepper and his colleagues (Greene & Lepper, 1974; Lepper et al., 1973), the expected-reward procedure that produced significant decreases in subsequent intrinsic interest in the target activity in children's classrooms also produced performance differences during the experimental sessions: children in this condition tended to draw more pictures, but pictures of lesser quality, on the average, than did children in the other conditions.

As research has proceeded further in this area, evidence consistent with two basic propositions has accumulated. This research has documented, on the one hand, a variety of situations in which the inappropriate application of extrinsic rewards may impair task performance during the period when rewards are made available—effects that may contribute to later decreases in observed intrinsic interest. These potential detrimental effects of extrinsic rewards on task performance may appear at many stages in the sequence in which subjects approach, engage in, and complete a particular task. At the same time, this research also demonstrates that these negative effects on immediate performance are neither a necessary nor a sufficient condition for the production of later decreases in intrinsic interest, but appear to depend more specifically on the demands of the particular tasks employed and the precise nature of the contingency imposed on task performance. Let us examine both of these propositions in greater detail.

One class of adverse effects on task performance appears to result from the manner in which the imposition of an extrinsic contingency may alter one's goals in undertaking the activity. Given a sufficiently attractive incentive, a number of authors have suggested (Condry & Chambers, 1978; Kruglanski, 1978; Lepper, in press; Lepper & Greene, 1978c) that subjects may be led to adopt a strategy designed to ensure receipt of the proffered reward with a minimum of effort and investment. The precise level of minimal performance that remains necessary to produce the reward, of course, will depend on the nature of the contingency imposed on the subject. For example, if the receipt of a reward is contingent on the production of a correct answer alone, both adults (Condry & Chambers, 1978) and children (Holt, 1964) may be likely to circumvent the effort involved in problem solving by simply attempting to guess the answer. Or, if appropriate safeguards against the possibility have not been built into the program, subjects may be likely to search for ways of "cheating" the system (e.g., Kazdin & Bootzin, 1973; Silberman, 1970).

Similar effects can be observed when subjects are confronted with tasks that may be approached at different levels of difficulty in the face of varying contingencies. In a typical experimental situation, for instance, subjects may be confronted with some problem-solving activity and given a choice of attempting specific problems from a range of different levels of difficulty or challenge. In the absence of any external constraints, such a situation will usually lead subjects to select problems of an intermediate level of difficulty—problems that are sufficiently difficult to provide some challenge to the individual, but not so difficult as to prove impossible (e.g., Atkinson, 1957; Hunt, 1965; Weiner, 1974). The offer of an attractive reward for each correct problem solution, however, will radically alter this pattern of choices. Under these conditions, both adults (Condry & Chambers, 1978; Shapira, 1976) and children (Blackwell, 1974; Harter, 1978; Lepper, Gilovich, & Rest, in progress) show marked shifts in preference toward the exclusive selection of less difficult problems designed to ensure the attainment of the extrinsic reward. In short, children appear willing to sacrifice challenge—as indicated by decreased enjoyment of the task per se (cf. Harter, 1978)—for the certainty of reward attainment.

Once a task has been selected or presented, similar instrumental concerns may also govern the nature of one's engagement in the activity. More specifically, the imposition of an external contingency on one's engagement in an activity will necessarily serve to identify some aspects of performance as instrumentally relevant to the attainment of reward and others as irrelevant. As a result, subjects engaged in the task in order to obtain the reward will be likely to focus their efforts and attention on those parameters of performance that are instrumentally relevant (Condry & Chambers, 1978; Lepper & Greene, 1978c; McGraw, 1978; Simon, 1967). Such a process may involve conscious decisions concerning the allocation of limited attentional capacities and the like (Kruglanski, Stein, & Riter, 1977), or it may involve mechanisms that are less deliberate. Easterbrook (1959), for example, has argued that the availability of attractive incentives may produce a state of heightened arousal that will itself narrow the range of cues to which the individual will be likely to attend. In a similar fashion, Spence (1956) and others have suggested that such a heightened state of drive will enhance the organism's reliance on high-probability or well-practiced response patterns. Two consequences may be expected to follow.

First, one would expect the imposition of an external contingency to produce, typically, impairments in performance along parameters of task engagement that are seen as incidental to obtaining the reward. A considerable literature is available to document the adverse effects of extrinsic rewards on incidental learning (cf. McGraw, 1978), and comparable effects have been observed in recent studies of the effects of superfluous extrinsic rewards on subsequent intrinsic

interest (e.g., Harackiewicz, 1979; Kruglanski et al., 1971). Decreases along qualitative performance dimensions, in the face of contingencies that do not specify performance criteria as a prerequisite for reward attainment, also appear explicable in these terms (Greene & Lepper, 1974; Lepper et al., 1973).

At the same time, this line of reasoning also predicts that the offer of an extrinsic reward may either enhance or impair performance along "central" task dimensions (i.e., those relevant to obtaining the reward) as a function of the nature of the task at hand. For example, when the task is sufficiently simple so that its solution requires only the application of known algorithms, the presence of an extrinsic incentive may enhance central task performance. However, when the task becomes more complex and successful performance requires the use of more novel and heuristic approaches, the availability of external incentives may have detrimental effects even on central task performance (cf. McGraw, 1978). Examples of this latter, detrimental effect appear in a number of recent investigations. Both Kruglanski et al. (1971) and Amabile (1979) found decreases in creativity for subjects anticipating external evaluation of the creativity of their performance. Similarly, McGraw and McCullers (1979; McGraw, 1978) have shown that expectation of reward may impair central task performance on activities that require insight or the ability to break a prior mental set for successful solution.

More complex effects of this same general sort have also been reported by Garbarino (1975) and Condry and Chambers (1977, 1978). Garbarino (1975) engaged sixth-grade children to teach first-graders a novel game, offering half of his tutors an attractive reward if they were successful in tutoring the younger child. Instead of enhancing the tutor's performance at this complex task, the offer of an extrinsic reward produced a variety of negative effects. During the tutoring sessions, paid tutors became more harsh and critical toward their pupils, made less efficient use of their time, and, as a consequence, were less successful in achieving their primary goal of teaching the younger children. In the Condry and Chambers (1977, 1978) study, college students were presented with a complex concept attainment task, either with or without the expectation that successful performance would lead to a tangible reward. Subjects expecting a reward in this context proved more likely to try to guess the correct answer before sufficient evidence was available and made less efficient use of the materials and information available to them. Perhaps more impressively, when confronted with a similar task some weeks later, in the absence of further rewards and with strict instructions not to answer until they could be certain that they were correct, previously rewarded subjects continued to offer solutions before they could logically have verified their accuracy.

There is, then, considerable evidence that the use of inappropriately designed contingency systems may have adverse effects on task performance during the experimental phase in which the rewards are available. Such effects may provide one mechanism by which subsequent intrinsic interest in the activity is reduced. This same body of research, however, also provides evidence that such performance deficits are not necessary for subsequent decreases in interest to occur.

There is considerable evidence demonstrating that declines in subsequent interest can occur in the absence of detrimental effects of the reward procedure on task performance (Amabile et al., 1976; Boggiano & Ruble, 1979; Calder & Staw, 1975; Dollinger & Thelen, 1978; Enzle & Ross, 1978; Lepper & Greene, 1975; Lepper, Sagotsky, Dafoe, & Greene, 1980; Lepper, Sagotsky, & Greene, 1980a; Ross, 1975; Ross, et al, 1976; Smith & Pittman, 1978). Moreover, other factors that can be shown to produce performance decrements do not necessarily produce corresponding decreases in intrinsic interest (Ross, et al., 1976).

Similarly, it can be shown that manipulations that eliminate or reverse the detrimental effects of rewards on immediate task performance measures do not necessarily produce corresponding changes in subsequent interest. For example, Lepper, Gilovich, and Rest (in progress) examined the effects of different reward systems on children's choices of easy versus difficult problems. They found that one can reverse the tendency for rewarded subjects to choose less challenging problems by instituting a graduated reward system in which larger rewards are offered for the solution of more difficult problems and smaller rewards for the solution of less difficult problems. However, this success in leading subjects away from the easy problems and toward the more challenging problems did not produce corresponding increases in subsequent intrinsic interest. In a related context, Amabile (1979) demonstrated that creativity can be enhanced, as well as undermined, by extrinsic evaluation if the criteria by which creativity is to be assessed are presented in sufficient detail to transform the task from a heuristic to an algorithmic one. Again, however, procedures shown to enhance immediate task performance did not lead to corresponding increases in later intrinsic motivation.

In short, the effects of expected, and contingent, extrinsic rewards on task performance appear to be much more specifically dependent on the nature of the task under study and the precise contingency applied to performance than do the effects of such procedures on subsequent intrinsic interest. This difference makes theoretical sense because immediate performance measures are necessarily obtained in contexts in which both one's intrinsic interest in the activity and one's desire to obtain the reward should influence behavior; whereas measures of subsequent intrinsic interest are deliberately obtained in settings in which these latter, instrumental considerations are no longer relevant. Moreover, the partial independence of these two sorts of effects provides further support for the hypothesis that the use of superfluous extrinsic rewards may have both direct and indirect (i.e., performance-mediated) detrimental effects on subsequent intrinsic interest.

OVERCOMING OVERJUSTIFICATION EFFECTS. These two lines of research suggest that engagement in an activity of initial inherent interest in order to obtain some extrinsic reward or achieve some other extrinsic goal may undermine one's intrinsic interest in the activity itself. They also suggest that these results may be understood as a result of the subjects' perceptions or experience of their engagement in the activity as extrinsically controlled or constrained. Implicit in this argument, of course, is the assumption that expectation of an extrinsic reward and perceptions of constraint are not isomorphic—a proposition that has some important implications for ways of using rewards without undermining subsequent intrinsic interest.

A number of authors have noted (e.g., Deci, 1975; Lepper & Greene, 1976, 1978c; O'Leary, Poulos, & Devine, 1972) that rewards are used in many different contexts and for many different purposes. We speak of rewards as "bribes" or "bonuses," as "remuneration" or "incentives," and imply with these different terms distinct social contexts in which the offer of a reward may be perceived differently. One implication of these distinctions is that rewards may be presented in ways that may either maximize or minimize perceptions of constraint and control, or in ways that lead to quite different perceptions. If so, these differences may have an important influence on the effects that different procedures will have on later intrinsic interest.

Deci (1975), for example, has presented one approach, termed cognitive evaluation theory, that focuses on one such distinction—the use of rewards to control a person's behavior and the use of rewards to provide information to the person regarding his or her relative competence at a particular task. Reward procedures that emphasize the "controlling" aspect of rewards, he suggests, will be likely to have detrimental effects on intrinsic interest by enhancing perceptions of constraint; procedures that emphasize the "informational" aspect of rewards, by contrast, will be less likely to have negative effects and may even increase interest by enhancing perceptions of competence. Closely related accounts have been offered by others (Kruglanski, 1978; Lepper & Greene, 1976, 1978c).

Consistent with this argument are the results of a number of recent experiments comparing the effects of two types of reward procedures—"task-contingent" rewards (i.e., rewards contingent simply on engagement in the activity) versus "performance-contingent" rewards (i.e., rewards contingent on task performance that exceeds some specified standard of accomplishment). These investigations have yielded results that suggest that extrinsic rewards are less likely to have negative effects on intrinsic interest when they provide the individual with evidence of his or her superior competence at the experimental activity.

Karniol and Ross (1977) compared the responses of early elementary school children to task-contingent and performance-contingent reward procedures. They found, relative to the results of a nonrewarded control condition, a significant decrease in subsequent interest for task-contingent but not for performance-contingent subjects. Conceptually analogous effects, obtained in a very different paradigm with adult subjects, have been reported by Enzle and Ross (1978). Other data suggest an important developmental shift in children's responses to one class of performance-contingent rewards—those based on comparative performance standards, where one must perform better than one's peers to obtain the reward—between the preschool and elementary school years (Boggiano & Ruble, 1979). Specifically, performance-contingent rewards based on social comparisons of this type appear less likely to undermine subsequent interest in elementary school children than task-contingent rewards (Boggiano & Ruble, 1979; Karniol & Ross, 1977), but the two rewards seem equally likely to undermine interest with preschool children (Greene & Lepper, 1974; Boggiano & Ruble, 1979). Performance-contingent rewards based on an absolute, rather than a normative, performance criterion, however, seem less likely than task-contingent rewards to undermine later interest at both ages (Boggiano & Ruble, 1979).[1]

Other procedures that minimize the extent to which a proffered reward will provoke perceptions of external control and constraint should also be less likely to produce detrimental effects on later intrinsic interest. Presumably, if the availability of an extrinsic reward were seen as the product of some random process, or the consequence of some broader set of norms and expectations—independent of the particular activity being undertaken in that context—decreases in later interest should be less likely (cf. Staw, Calder, & Hess, 1978). Alternatively, if the criteria determining the receipt or magnitude of the reward are self-imposed, rather than externally imposed, detrimental effects may be less likely. In several studies comparing these two sorts of reward procedures, self-imposed contingencies have proved less likely to produce decreases in later interest (Brownell, Colletti, Ersner-Hershfield, Hershfield, & Wilson, 1977; Enzle & Look, 1980; Lepper, Sagotsky, & Greene, 1980b; Weiner & Dubanoski, 1975), though these findings are not universal (Dollinger & Thelen, 1978).

Perhaps it should be possible to affect more directly the likelihood of subsequent adverse effects through explicit manipulations designed to focus subjects' attention on either the activity or the reward as their reason for engaging in the activity. In one such demonstration, Pittman, Cooper, and Smith (1977) asked subjects to engage in an activity with the promise of an extrinsic reward for task engagement, but provided some subjects with false physiological feedback purportedly indicative of either their own interest in the activity itself or their desire to obtain the reward. The detrimental effect produced by this reward manipulation in the absence of false feedback was virtually eliminated when subjects were led to believe that the reason they had undertaken the task was its high interest value for them, but remained unchanged when subjects were "reinforced" in the belief that they had undertaken the activity in order to obtain

the attractive reward. Later results by Johnson, Greene, and Carroll (1980) make a similar point. In this study, subjects expecting a reward for task engagement were exposed, in the experimental conditions, to a procedure in which the experimenter explicitly labeled their agreement to engage in the task as a result of their interest in the task or of their desire to obtain the reward. Making salient "intrinsic interest" as the reason for subjects' task engagement served to eliminate the adverse effects of expected rewards that were apparent in both a no-instruction condition and the condition in which subjects' actions were labeled as extrinsically motivated.

Even the expectation of a contingent extrinsic reward, then, will not always undermine subsequent intrinsic interest. Instead, this analysis suggests that the likelihood that such effects will occur should depend on the manner and context in which rewards are offered—the extent to which they induce the individual to consider the offer of a reward as an attempt to control and manipulate his or her behavior, rather than an attempt to reward superior performance, to enhance one's enjoyment of the activity, or to fulfill normative expectations. However, before turning to a fuller consideration of the implications of the multiple roles that rewards may play one further set of questions concerning the conditions under which expected rewards will be observed to reduce later interest in the previously rewarded activity requires attention.

EXTENDED REWARD PROGRAMS. These final issues arise from research that has examined the effects of more extended, "multiple-trial" reward programs on subsequent task engagement and has suggested that more long-term programs, involving the systematic use of extrinsic rewards to increase task engagement, will not have detrimental effects on subsequent task engagment in the later absence of rewards. These considerations are of obvious importance to the questions of when and how rewards might be best employed to maintain or enhance interest.

Theoretically, there are a number of reasons for suggesting that more long-term reward programs should be less likely to produce decreases in later task engagement than short-term or single-trial reward programs of the type employed in most of the experimental research described above. On the one hand, it has been suggested that detrimental effects of rewards will only occur under conditions in which the "reward" used is not an objectively effective "reinforcer" (i.e., an event that will increase the probability of the response it follows) or that detrimental effects of the sort we have described are the result of transitory effects that would be expected to habituate or diminish over time during an extended application of rewards. On the other hand, it seems apparent that the use of more extended reward systems that do produce important increases in task engagement also introduce an additional set of variables that may influence subsequent responses to the rewarded activity. Increased task engagement, for example, may lead to increased proficiency or the acquisition of new task-relevant skills that may enhance the attractiveness of the activity for the person. It may also lead to greater liking through increased familiarity with, or "mere exposure" (Zajonc, 1968) to the task. Such effects may cancel, or overcome, the effects of rewards on perceptions of constraint or competence.[2]

Examining the consequences of long-term reward programs also makes questions concerning the assessment of intrinsic interest particularly salient. Throughout this chapter, and elsewhere (Lepper & Greene, 1976, 1978c), we have suggested that it is appropriate to regard subsequent task engagement as evidence of intrinsic interest only when that subsequent behavior is observed in a setting in which the individual no longer expects to receive further tangible or social rewards contingent on engagement in the target activity—in settings conceptually analogous to the free-play periods and conditions of covert observation employed in our earlier studies (Lepper et al., 1973). Yet one common effect of the use of contingent rewards, especially over a long period, should be to lead the child to expect that the previously rewarded behavior is particularly praiseworthy and likely to lead to continued tangible or social rewards later in the same or similar settings. Hence, children may continue to engage in the previously rewarded activity in settings of this sort in the hopes of further rewards rather than out of an interest in the activity itself.

There are, then, a number of theoretical reasons for expecting that long-term or multiple-trial reward programs may be less likely to produce decreases in later task engagement than short-term or single-trial reward manipulations. Certainly, the existing empirical literature provides general support for this contention, although the extreme form of this argument—that extended or multiple-trial reward programs will never produce detrimental effects—is probably inaccurate. Several studies (Brownell et al., 1977; Colvin, 1972; Greene, Sternberg, & Lepper, 1976; Lepper, Sagotsky, & Greene, 1980a; Sorenson & Maehr, 1976; Smith & Pittman, 1978), for example, have found detrimental effects on subsequent engagement in the previously rewarded activity following the removal of demonstrably effective multiple-trial reward programs. More commonly, by contrast, such long-term programs appear to have positive effects on the probability of subsequent engagement in the previously rewarded activity (Davidson & Bucher, 1978; Feingold & Mahoney, 1975; Reiss & Sushinsky, 1975, Study 2; Vasta, Andrews, McLaughlin, Stirpe, & Comfort, 1978; Vasta & Stirpe, 1979).

Yet the interpretation of these effects remains unclear. With few exceptions (Davidson & Bucher, 1978; Lepper, Sagotsky, & Greene, 1980a; Smith & Pittman, 1978), appropriate control conditions in which subjects are provided with an equal amount of exposure to, and practice at, the activity as subjects in the reward condition are lacking. Similarly, it is often difficult to know from these reports whether subjects expected that continued engagement in the activity, after the rewards were "withdrawn," would continue to lead to further social or tangible rewards. Lepper, Sagotsky, and Greene (1980a), for instance, performed a conceptual replication of one study in which a small-scale token reward program was used to provide differential reinforcement to children for engaging in one of a small set of target activities. Then, following the termination of this program, children's reactions to this target activity were observed in two very different settings. One replicated unobtrusive classroom observations employed in earlier studies using "single-trial" rewards; the other involved observation of the children's behavior when they were again confronted with the same small set of activities as in the prior token program, but in the presence of a different adult and in the absence of further tokens or tangible rewards. Independent evidence suggested that children would perceive the social demands of these two situations quite differently— that they believed that adults in the classroom situation would not care which activities they chose to engage in, but that the observer in the second experimental setting would prefer that they continue to play with the previously rewarded game. This difference was reflected in children's responses in the two situations. Relative to a number of control conditions, children who had been previously exposed to the multiple-trial reward procedure showed significantly less interest in the target activity when their behavior was covertly observed in their classrooms, but engaged in this same activity significantly more when returned to a setting in which they believed that this was the desired response.

Additional research is clearly needed to specify further the dynamics of multiple-trial reward procedures and their effects on subsequent task engagement and subsequent intrinsic interest. However, even this brief discussion should make clear that there are a number of conceptually distinct processes that may contribute to the general finding that such long-term procedures appear less likely to produce demonstrable negative effects. In combination with our earlier discussions, these considerations point to the complexity of effects that the use of extrinsic rewards may produce and illustrate the sorts of conceptual variables that will be needed in any comprehensive account of the effects of extrinsic rewards or constraints on task performance and subsequent motivation.

The multiple functions of reward

Although our foregoing remarks have been focused specifically on the issue of when the use of functionally superfluous extrinsic rewards may have detrimental effects on performance and subsequent intrinsic interest, implicit in this discussion is a more general model of the mechanisms by which the application of extrinsic incentives and constraints will affect subsequent behavior. Rewards, we have suggested, may simultaneously serve many functions. Their effects on later behavior will depend, in part, on the function they are perceived or presumed to serve by their recipients, which will depend on the manner and the context in which they are presented. Predictions concerning the effects of any given reward procedure, therefore, will require attention to each of several different processes. To make this clear, it may be helpful to consider more explicitly the range of factors implicated in our previous review.

For purposes of exposition, it is useful to think of three general functions that rewards may serve and their implications for performance and subsequent task engagement. These three primary functions, and their consequences, are presented schematically in Figure 1.1.

The most evident, and universal, function of the use of external rewards is an instrumental or incentive function, illustrated in the top half of Figure 1.1. Within this general category, however, there are several specific effects to be considered. First, the fact that rewards are delivered in a particular setting, contingent on engagement in a particular activity, will frequently imply that further engagement in that activity at later

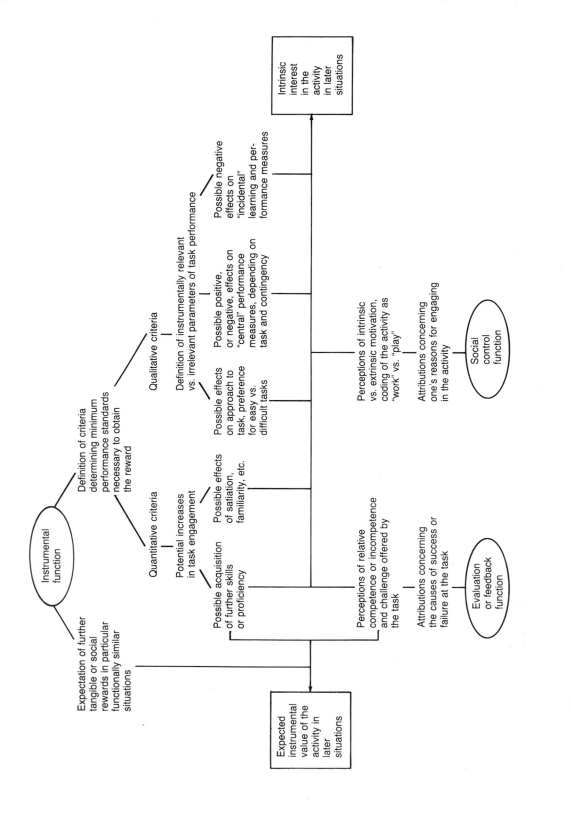

times in that same, or a similar, setting will also have some instrumental value. These expectations of continued instrumentality may include both the possibility that further tangible rewards may be achieved by continued engagement in the activity and the possibility that, even if such tangible rewards are no longer apparent, engagement in the activity may produce praise and social approval. To the extent that subsequent behavior is observed in contexts in which the activity is expected to have continued instrumental value of this sort, one would expect continued engagement in the task as long as these further extrinsic rewards retain their incentive value (cf. Bandura, 1977b; Estes, 1972; Lepper & Greene, 1978c; Lepper, Sagotsky, & Greene, 1980a; Mischel, 1973).

At the same time, the imposition of an external contingency that is not wholly superfluous may also have effects on immediate task performance, in the initial context in which rewards are available. As we have noted earlier, the precise form of these effects will depend on the specific nature of the contingency imposed, the nature of the task, and the subject's initial skills and interest in the task. In each case, however, we may think of the imposition of an external contingency as defining a set of criteria determining at least the minimum standards of performance that will be necessary to obtain the reward. These criteria may be quantitative, or qualitative, or both. Rewards may be presented as contingent on the subject's spending a greater amount of time at the task, on his or her performing the task at some particular level of competence (e.g., with some particular level of accuracy or success, or at some normatively superior level of performance), or on both (e.g., working on a larger series of problems but with some criteria of accuracy or performance). Contingencies of each type may have multiple effects on performance and subsequent behavior.

If, for example, the contingency imposed involves a quantitative component, so that increases in task engagement are produced during the initial treatment period, these increases may in themselves have important effects. Some of these effects may be relatively transitory: The individual may become satiated or bored with the activity. Others may have more important long-term consequences. If increased engagement in, and familiarity with, the activity should lead to increased proficiency or the acquisition of additional skills, the experience may profoundly change the individual's reaction to the activity, through changes in the individual's perceptions of competence in performing the activity or changes in the challenges the task affords the subject. Similarly, if the contingency imposed carried qualitative performance demands, the availability of an extrinsic reward may affect the manner in which the activity is approached, the quality of performance along both instrumentally "central" and "incidental" parameters, and the point at which the activity is terminated—effects that depend, as we have indicated earlier, on both the demands of the activity itself and the reward contingency employed. Performance differences of this sort may have effects on the subjects' enjoyment of the task and their perceptions of its inherent interest value that will also influence subsequent behavior (Lepper & Greene, 1978c; McGraw, 1978).

In addition to these instrumental functions that rewards may serve, extrinsic incentives may also frequently serve an evaluation or feedback function. In those cases, in particular, in which performance-contingent rewards are employed, the receipt of a reward may provide information concerning one's competence or incompetence at the activity—either relative to others or to one's own prior performance, or in absolute terms if the activity is one that contains some clear criterion of successful performance. Of course, the effects of information of this sort, conveyed by the receipt of rewards, will be mediated by the subjects' own interpretations of their relative level of success or failure at the activity and their attributions concerning the causes of their successes and failures—that is, the extent to which their performance is seen as a reflection of ability, effort, task difficulty, and the like (See Chapter 3 by Frieze; Bandura, 1977a; Bar-Tal, 1978; See Weiner, 1974, 1979). To the extent that the imposition of a particular reward procedure affects subjects' perception of their relative competence at the activity, and thus influences the degree to which the activity provides an appropriate challenge or the likelihood that further engagement will lead to greater success, these attributions will affect subjects' perceptions of whether the task will be of interest to them in the future. These factors are summarized briefly in the lower left corner of Figure 1.1.

Finally, we have suggested that rewards may also serve a social control or constraint function—that they may reflect or imply an attempt by the agent administering the reward to exercise control over the subject's actions. Emphasis on this function of rewards, illustrated in the lower right corner of Figure 1.1, may affect subjects' perceptions of their engagement in the activity as either intrinsically or extrinsically motivated and their conception of the activity as interesting in its own right or as something that is worth undertaking only in settings in which further extrinsic rewards or constraints are present. When the instrumental and evaluative functions are controlled experimentally—for example, when the rewards employed are functionally superfluous and do not produce differences in task performance, and when the rewards are contingent on task engagement but do not carry salient information concerning competence and ability at the task—the imposition of extrinsic constraints can be shown to produce decreases in subsequent intrinsic interest in activities that were of high initial intrinsic interest.

Clearly these latter processes, through which the offer of extrinsic incentives may influence perceptions of personal competence and social constraint, will be affected by differences among individuals in their initial interest in, their skills at, and their prior exposure to the target activity (Lepper & Dafoe, 1979). There is already considerable evidence to indicate that reward proce-

dures that will undermine interest in activities initially seen as intrinsically motivated, for example, may actually enhance later interest in activities initially perceived as uninteresting (Calder & Staw, 1975; Loveland & Olley, 1979; McLoyd, 1979; Upton, 1973). Related differences in the effects of extrinsic incentives as a function of prior differences in subjects' perceptions of competence in performing, or previous experience with, the activity might also be expected (cf. Condry & Chambers, 1978; Lepper & Dafoe, 1979). Any comprehensive analysis of the effects of extrinsic incentives, therefore, must eventually also consider these types of interactions between individual and situational factors (Mischel, 1977).

Of course, in many real-world contexts in which rewards are employed, these different factors are not easily isolated from each other. Thus, our expectations concerning the effects that a particular reward program will have on subsequent behavior will depend on the interaction of these different factors, which may individually produce counteracting tendencies. In addition, our predictions concerning the effects of a particular program must also depend on the context in which subsequent behavior is observed. If, on the one hand, we observe subsequent behavior in a setting in which the activity is expected to have some potential further instrumental value for the subjects, the most important factors may be the subjects' perceptions of the responses necessary to obtain further rewards and their own capabilities to perform the activity in the required fashion (Bandura, 1978). If, on the other hand, we observe subsequent behavior in a context in which it is clear to subjects that the activity will no longer produce further extrinsic rewards, then the factors that influence the subjects' own perceptions of the inherent interest value of the activity—perceptions of competence and constraint, or potential effects of previous differences in performance—will be the primary determinants of the subjects' responses to the activity.

Developmental issues

Having presented this broader context for examining the effects of the imposition of external contingencies on subsequent behavior, let us return to the central observation that sparked this interest—that the use of superfluous extrinsic rewards may have detrimental effects on subsequent intrinsic interest—and consider briefly the relationship of the literature reported here to traditional issues in developmental psychology.

Developmental differences

Perhaps the most obvious developmental issue—that of age-related changes in subjects' responses to extrinsic rewards—was adventitiously raised, and in part answered, by the earliest research done in this area. These early investigations appeared to demonstrate comparable detrimental effects of extrinsic rewards on intrinsic interest across the rather broad age range from preschool (Lepper et al., 1973) to high school (Kruglanski et al., 1971) and college (Deci, 1971) populations. At this general level, moreover, subsequent research has provided further evidence of comparable effects across this range. This apparent developmental invariance raises some important issues.

First, it raises some obvious questions, given the limited cognitive competencies of preschool children, concerning the cognitive processes that might be hypothesized to underlie such detrimental effects. We know, for example, that most adults in our society have a fairly clear understanding of the implicit assumptions underlying attempts at social control. If asked to infer the motives of another, who has been seen to engage in a particular activity either in the face of obvious external pressures or in the absence of such pressures, adults will typically infer less intrinsic motivation in the case in which external pressures are salient (e.g., Bem, 1972; Kelley, 1973). Young children, however, appear not to use such a "discounting" schema (See Chapter 8 by Kassin; Karniol & Ross, 1976; Shultz & Butkowsky, 1977;

Shultz, Butkowsky, Pearce, & Shanfield, 1975; Smith, 1975), at least when asked to make inferences from stories presented in a verbal format, about the motives of hypothetical others.

These data suggest that children may not have the same abstract appreciation of the implications of social control attempts as adults. This raises the question of whether young children sense any relationship between the presence of salient extrinsic constraints and the likely value of the activity for the individuals subject to those constraints. Although relevant empirical data are scarce, our tentative hypothesis is that children may learn at a relatively young age that, in their own lives, extrinsic rewards and punishments are applied typically to induce them to engage in activities they would not otherwise undertake. At first, however, this knowledge may be quite "episodic" and tied to particular recurring situations in which the child has been the subject of attempts to control his or her behavior; it is only some time afterward that this knowledge may become "hypothetical" and serve as a more sophisticated basis for understanding the implications of social control attempts in contexts outside the child's realm of immediate personal experience.[3]

Some evidence that this may be the case comes from recent work by Lepper, Sagotsky, Dafoe, and Greene (1980) examining the conditions under which preschool children do appear to employ a "discounting" principle. Starting with an informal analysis of the conditions under which young children are frequently exposed to external constraints, these investigators were led to consider one particularly prototypic setting that seemed familiar to their preschool subjects. The setting was the family dining table, and the "script" predictable—"You have to eat your X (e.g., carrots, meat, spinach) before you can have your Y (e.g., ice cream, cake)." A hypothetical version of this script, involving two nonexistent foods, one presented as a "means" of obtaining the other, was presented to children and revealed that all subjects understood the underlying implicit message that the food presented as a "means" was likely to be less appealing than the food presented as an "end." Children's obvious familiarity with this situation, moreover, suggested the possibility that similar effects might be observed if a comparable contingency were imposed on children's engagement in two activities, apart from the mealtime context. In two studies designed to investigate this more general effect, two activities of high initial and equivalent interest value were presented either in a means-end relationship to one another (e.g., if you do X, you will win the chance to do Y) or in a comparable temporal sequence without the imposition of any such nominal contingency. In one of these studies, the children served as actors, and the effect of a nominal contingency on their own later intrinsic interest in both tasks was assessed; in the second study, the children served as observers and were asked to make inferences about the preferences of another child shown in a short slide show undergoing these same two conditions. In both cases, presentation of one activity as a means led children to express less interest in that activity (in their own behavior, or in their inferences about the behavior of another). Presentation of the same activity as an end, however, produced nonsignificant increases in liking for the activity.

In addition to this social knowledge issue, the relative invariance of the general detrimental effect of extrinsic rewards also serves as a baseline against which more particular developmental questions may be framed. That is, are there specific contexts or procedures for presenting rewards that may have different consequences for children at different stages of development? We have pointed earlier to the one documented developmental change in this area—Boggiano and Ruble's (1979) finding that young children are not sensitive to social comparison information that may be conveyed through rewards and that is of critical importance to older children and adults. We suspect there may be other important developmental effects of this sort. For example, if one were to

take the simple hypothesis that young children's conceptions of the many contexts in which rewards may be used are likely to be less differentiated than adult conceptions, one would expect their responses to different reward procedures to show correspondingly less differentiation. Certainly, we might expect that children would be considerably less sensitive to information concerning normative standards or the equitability of remuneration that would affect an adult's interpretation of the motives of a social control agent. Furthermore, if issues of autonomy versus control are central in early childhood (e.g., See Chapter 5 by Brehm; Erikson, 1963), young children may prove particularly sensitive to the application of social control techniques to their behavior.

If significant developmental changes can be documented in children's interpretations of, and responses to, the imposition of extrinsic contingencies, they may be the consequence of two quite distinct processes. Such changes may occur, as indicated above, as a result of children's increasing cognitive capacities and their growing ability to comprehend and distinguish the different functions that rewards may serve in various contexts. However, they may also occur as a function of changes in the child's social environment. The child's initial entry into elementary school, as many writers have suggested (e.g., Holt, 1964; Jackson, 1968), may mark a significant point of transition. It is in the classroom, typically, that children are first exposed to a constant and systematic, if not always internally consistent, system of comparative rewards and punishments. It is here, one suspects, that children may truly learn to appreciate the meaning of comparative performance feedback or the relationships among effort, ability, and outcome.

In fact, it is these same considerations that suggest that the present analysis may have particular relevance for the lives of children even if the underlying processes were identical from early childhood to adulthood. In focusing on the potential detrimental effects of the use of functionally superfluous tangible rewards, we are dealing with social control techniques that are enormously more characteristic of interactions between adults and children than interactions among adults themselves. Excluding staff-inmate interactions in specialized custodial institutions, we suspect that adults are less likely to find themselves the targets of the sort of explicit and salient social control techniques that are routinely applied to children at home and in school. Rarely is the inherent differential in power between the agent and the target of social influence required for the use of such techniques as great between adults as between adult and child. For these reasons, it may be particularly important to consider the broader social context in which extrinsic incentive systems are rooted.

Implications for socialization

Beyond these basic questions of developmental changes in children's responses to the imposition of extrinsic constraints lies a second intersection of the research considered in this chapter with traditional concerns in developmental psychology—issues that arise from a consideration of the potential applications of the present research to the study of the socialization process. Although space does not permit a detailed analysis of these issues here (cf. Lepper, 1981, in press), it may be useful to sketch at least the basic argument.

Since the early days of the study of socialization, developmental psychologists have been concerned with the issue of how children develop internalized controls—attitudes, values, and patterns of behavior that lead children not only to comply with the rules and norms of society in the immediate presence of external sanctions and incentives designed to promote conformity, but also to accept most of those rules and standards as principles that should guide their conduct even in the absence of external surveillance or immediate extrinsic constraints (cf. Aronfreed, 1968; Hoffman, 1970; Sears, Maccoby, & Levin, 1957). Such a focus, it should be clear, is closely related to the issues raised in this chapter. Indeed, the reader may

recall that we began our discussion with a consideration of the effects of overly powerful social control techniques for inducing compliance in children's internalization of adult values. Hence, it may be useful to ask what implications this analysis has for understanding the types of social control techniques that parents might use to promote this long-term process of internalization.

If we think about both the earlier findings regarding the effects of psychologically "insufficient justification" and the more recent research on "overjustification" in combination, they suggest a common principle. In both these cases, the use of unnecessarily powerful or salient social control procedures will often have detrimental effects on subsequent internalization or intrinsic interest. Under conditions in which compliance could be obtained through the use of less coercive techniques, the addition of further, functionally superfluous, extrinsic pressures seems to have adverse effects. By contrast, when compliance is achieved through the application of minimal, but sufficient, external inducements, internalization may be enhanced or interest maintained. This "minimal sufficiency" principle of social control (Lepper, 1981, in press) suggests one general application of the present research to our understanding of socialization processes.[4]

This analysis provides a somewhat different perspective on the existing literature concerning the effects of different disciplinary and social control techniques on children's internalization of moral and social standards. Hoffman and his colleagues (1970, 1975b; Hoffman & Saltzstein, 1967), on the one hand, have gathered an impressive array of evidence concerning the effects of three types of parental disciplinary techniques on children's subsequent internalization of moral values. In brief, he finds the use of power-assertive social control techniques, involving primarily the use of physical punishment and the contingent withdrawal of tangible rewards and privileges, to be negatively correlated with subsequent indices of moral internalization. In contrast, the use of inductive disciplinary techniques, involving reasoning and a focus on the consequences of one's actions on others, is shown to be positively correlated with later internalization. (The use of a third, more conceptually ambiguous, class of love-withdrawal procedures appears generally uncorrelated with later internalization.) Similar conclusions may be gleaned from Baumrind's (1971, 1973) studies of parenting practices and their effect on children's social responsibility in different contexts. In her studies, children of "authoritarian" parents, who favor the use of rigid, forceful, and punitive measures to produce compliance from their children at home, appear less well socialized on a variety of measures than children of "authoritative" parents, who tend to employ less salient and more inductive techniques to produce obedience at home. In addition, children of "authoritative" parents also appear more socially responsible than children of "permissive" parents, who set fewer demands and employ social control techniques that frequently fail to produce compliance with parental demands. Other studies in the socialization literature also provide additional evidence consistent with these characterizations (cf. Dienstbier, Hillman, Lehnhoff, Hillman & Valkenaar, 1975).

The picture that emerges from these studies, it should be evident, is consistent with our minimal sufficiency analysis of social control techniques. Control techniques that are effective in producing initial compliance without resort to heavily coercive procedures appear more likely to promote subsequent internalization than either the use of effective, but overly powerful, social controls or the use of control procedures that often fail to produce initial compliance. These parallels suggest the utility of conceptualizing the effectiveness of different child-rearing practices as a function not only of their immediate success in producing obedience to parental demands, but also in terms of their effects on the child's perception of his or her compliance to those demands as intrinsically versus extrinsically motivated (See also Chapter 10 by Woody and Costanzo).

Of course, we do not mean to suggest that processes of this sort are the only, or even the most important, difference between naturally occurring patterns of parental control techniques. The apparent effectiveness of inductive techniques is not simply the consequence of the lack of overly coercive extrinsic pressures; inductive techniques also provide important opportunities for role-taking and empathy and present a comprehensible system of social values to guide children's actions. Conversely, there are many reasons why power-assertive techniques, especially the heavy use of physical punishment, might prove counterproductive. They are likely to promote anger and hostility, produce feelings of rejection, or provide the child with a model who solves social problems through aggression. Our argument is simply that the consequences of these different techniques for the child's feelings of competence and control may also be important.

At the same time, the implications of the present analysis extend beyond the reinterpretation of previous correlational findings. It suggests, for instance, the potential utility of a more direct approach to changing children's perceptions of their reasons for complying with adult requests. This strategy has been pursued, with success, in several recent studies examining the effects of manipulations that involve the direct labeling of a child's behavior as either intrinsically or extrinsically motivated. Dienstbier and his associates (Dienstbier et al., 1975), for instance, labeled children's reactions to a transgression in either internal or external terms and found that providing an internal label enhanced later resistance to temptation in a similar situation. Miller, Brickman, and Bolen (1975) obtained similar results that showed that labeling children as prosocial was more effective than exhorting them to behave prosocially, in terms of promoting later prosocial behavior in the absence of further explicit pressures (see Chapter 5 by Brehm for a more detailed discussion of this study). Similarly, Grusec and colleagues

(Grusec, in press; Grusec, Kuczynski, Rushton, & Simutis, 1978) found that labeling a child's altruistic behavior in internalized terms produced greater altruism in a subsequent test situation in which external pressures were absent.

In addition to such direct labeling procedures, the present analysis suggests that similar effects may be obtained through other, more indirect strategies of eliciting initial compliance while minimizing perceptions of external constraint. For example, Lepper and Gilovich (1980) examined the effects of "activity-oriented" requests—requests that involve presenting the task a child is asked to undertake in ways designed to enhance the attractiveness of the activity itself—on children's subsequent willingness to comply with other adult requests. Examples of this strategy are common in the home and the classroom. Thus, one might attempt to enhance interest in the task of doing long-division problems by presenting them in a context of greater intrinsic interest—computing, for instance, the batting averages of the school's baseball team. Or, one might attempt to increase interest in a household cleaning job by presenting it to children as part of a detective game or a race against the clock. To the extent that such techniques effectively focus children's attention on the activity itself, and not its instrumental value, the present analysis would predict enhanced compliance in subsequent situations for children previously exposed to such compliance techniques. This prediction was substantiated by Lepper and Gilovich (1980) across several different forms of activity-oriented requests. Children initially exposed to activity-oriented requests subsequently showed a greater willingness to comply with other adult requests than children in appropriate control conditions in which initial compliance was induced with comparable, but more direct, requests.

Other possible applications suggest themselves, but have not yet received empirical investigation. The last decade has witnessed, as one example, the development of a variety of techniques for teaching children to observe, evaluate, and reinforce their own actions through training in self-monitoring and self-management techniques (Bandura, 1976; Mahoney, 1974, 1977; Chapter 2 by Karniol and Miller). Although the data are not unambiguous, there is some suggestion in this literature that these self-administered contingency systems are more likely than comparable externally administered contingency systems to promote generalization of behavior to different settings (Brownell et al., 1977; Lepper, Sagotsky, & Mailer, 1975; Turkewitz, O'Leary, & Ironsmith, 1975; Weiner & Dubanoski, 1975). The present analysis suggests that one potentially important element in the apparent success of these programs may lie in the extent to which they effectively minimize perceptions of extrinsic constraints on one's actions. Similar considerations may also apply to procedures involving other cognitive behavior modification procedures (Mahoney, 1974; Meichenbaum, 1977). One question of obvious interest, then, would be whether the effectiveness of these techniques might be enhanced through the inclusion of procedures explicitly designed to enhance feelings of personal control and internalized motivation.

Summary

We began this chapter with some thoughts on the distinction between "work" and "play" and the general proposition that this distinction may depend, in part, on the social context in which activities are undertaken. These considerations led us to a review of experimental literature that suggested the potentially detrimental effects on internalization or intrinsic interest of superfluous and unnecessarily salient social control techniques. We have concluded with a speculative analysis of the possible implications of these experimental findings for broader developmental issues and the study of the socialization process. In closing, it seems worth emphasizing two points.

First, we should be quite clear about the complexity of the issues addressed in this chapter and the speculative character of our final remarks. Clearly, if one takes seriously the complexity of the multiple effects that rewards may have, as illustrated graphically in Figure 1.1, it is obvious that our speculations concerning the effects of different social control techniques in the socialization process must also include attention to these other factors as well. Although space does not permit a further analysis here, it is unfortunately the case that the complexity of the problem increases, rather than decreases, as one moves from the laboratory to the field (Lepper & Greene, 1978a).

Second, we should also make clear that there are many circumstances in which one may justifiably have little concern for issues of internalization or intrinsic motivation—situations in which compliance with a particular request is one's only goal. It is very likely impossible to convince children, or ourselves, that cleaning one's room, mowing the lawn, or doing the dishes are really inherently interesting, enjoyable, and exciting tasks, week in and week out. Nonetheless, we may find it valuable for children to take responsibility regularly for some of these tasks. In those other circumstances in which we do wish to attempt to foster intrinsic interest and internalization, however, the present findings suggest that we may benefit by avoiding the use of unnecessarily powerful and salient social control techniques that might, unwittingly, turn "play" into "work."

Notes

1. Two points warrant attention at this juncture. First, it should be clear that performance-contingent rewards—because they may simultaneously produce competing effects on perceptions of competence and perceptions of constraint—present an inherently more complex theoretical case than task-contingent rewards. This additional complexity seems particularly evident in the adult literature where, in contrast to the reasonably consistent effects obtained with children, even performance-contingent rewards may often produce significant decreases in subsequent intrinsic interest (cf. Deci, 1971; Harackiewicz, 1979; Weiner & Mander, 1978) relative to nonrewarded control conditions.

Second, we should note explicitly that our discussion and the studies we have reviewed deal specifically with tangible rewards of one sort or another. Other studies examining the effects of purely verbal rewards, for example, suggest that verbal praise will typically increase subsequent intrinsic interest (Anderson, Manoogian, & Reznick, 1976; Blanck, Reis, & Jackson, 1980; Deci, 1971; Dollinger & Thelen, 1978; Swann & Pittman, 1977; Weiner & Mander, 1978) in settings in which tangible rewards can be shown to produce decreases in later interest. At present, the interpretation of these positive effects remains unclear, because the verbal and tangible reward procedures in these studies typically differ along several dimensions. In terms of our previous discussion, the verbal reward procedures shown to enhance subsequent interest in these studies are perhaps inherently less salient than tangible rewards; at the same time, they are also unexpected and contain explicit comparative performance feedback, indicating to subjects their relative superior competence at the task. Further research is needed to examine the contribution of each of these factors to the enhancement of subsequent interest with verbal rewards (cf. Lepper & Greene, 1978c; Smith, 1976).

2. For the sake of completeness, it should also be pointed out that increases in task engagement can also lead to boredom or satiation effects that would produce decreases in later task engagement. In contrast to the potential long-term and lasting effects of the acquisition of new skills and knowledge about the activity, however, these potential negative effects of task engagement per se should affect subsequent behavior only during a relatively short period immediately following the treatment phase in which task engagement is increased.

3. Young children's seeming lack of sophistication in drawing inferences about the motives of others in this literature may, of course, stem partly from methodological difficulties inherent in assessing children's social knowledge with hypothetical verbal techniques (Lepper & Greene, 1978c). Were more vivid and concrete stimulus materials or nonverbal response measures employed, one might expect to find young children responding on a more advanced level (cf. Shultz & Butkowsky, 1977). But even under optimal conditions, however, it is not clear that one should

expect the development of self-perception processes to follow from the development of social-perception processes (cf. Lepper, Sagotsky, Dafoe, & Greene, 1980).

On a more general level, the considerations raised in this section may also bear on the broader issue of the mechanisms by which perceptions of constraint may influence subsequent intrinsic interest. Although there is substantial overlap among different theoretical accounts, some investigators have taken a primarily cognitive stand on this issue—focusing on the role of cognitive scripts or schemas that relate the presence of salient external pressures in the environment to a typical lack of intrinsic motivation in the subject. Others have taken a more affective stance—suggesting that the experience of one's actions as extrinsically controlled may be inherently aversive. We are suggesting here that these two processes may both occur and that they may reinforce one another. That is, the child may first begin to recognize the commonly inverse relationship between external pressures and intrinsic motives as a function of ' affectively negative experiences in which adults employ social control techniques to induce him or her to engage in activities that are not enjoyable or intrinsically motivating. Once the child has developed such a "script" for a particular situation, or some more general inferential principle, even relatively benign and less affect-arousing attempts at social control may trigger a set of inferences and associations that lead to the perception of the activity as less inherently interesting.

4. In drawing together these two related literatures to suggest a common theme, we are obviously ignoring a number of potentially significant differences between the two. These differences include the nature of the activity in question (e.g., whether it is of high or low initial interest), the contingency imposed (e.g., the relevance of performance-based criteria), the goal of the social influence attempt (e.g., whether inhibition of a particular response or production of a particular response), and so forth—distinctions that would have to be taken into account in examining the outcome of any specific social control encounter. A fuller discussion of these issues is beyond the scope of the present chapter, but may be found in other sources (Lepper, 1981, in press).

2

THE DEVELOPMENT OF SELF-CONTROL IN CHILDREN

RACHEL KARNIOL
TEL AVIV UNIVERSITY

DALE T. MILLER
UNIVERSITY OF BRITISH COLUMBIA

Enduring unpleasant or aversive events is part of life from its inception. We must learn to control our physical urges except under certain restricted conditions; go to school even though we cannot see its long-term benefits; suffer the pain a dentist inflicts on us because we are told that "it's for your own good"; and modify our eating, smoking, and drinking so that we do not eventually cause ourselves physical harm. In all these cases, aversive events must be endured in order to attain some long-term benefits, which are not always obvious or even demonstrable. The aversiveness may stem from ceasing a pleasurable activity (e.g., eating) or from commencing an intrinsically unpleasant one (e.g., studying). In some instances (e.g., incarceration or detention), there is simply nothing more pleasant to look forward to than the end of the unpleasantness.

Instances of behavioral maintenance under aversive circumstances fall into three general categories. In the first of these, delay of gratification, the aversiveness is produced by the temporal contingency associated with the reward; in the second, resistance to temptation, aversiveness is produced by the presence of rewards that must be foregone; and in the third, pain tolerance, aversiveness is produced by the discomfort and pain inherent in stimuli to be tolerated.

Despite the shared forcus of these various phenomena, theoretical advances and empirical enquiry have been fragmented and have failed to attempt, let alone produce, cogent integration of the research now available. In addition, the subject populations used in empirical investigations have not been comparable. Studies on delay of gratification have focused almost exclusively on children; those on resistance to temptation have focused on both children and clinical populations (e.g., alcoholics, obese persons); and pain tolerance research has focused almost exclusively on adults.

Portions of this chapter were written while the authors were summer participants at the Center for Advanced Study in the Behavioral Sciences in Stanford, California. The research reported in this chapter was supported by Social Science Research Council Grant 410-78-0583.

In this chapter, we concentrate primarily on delay of gratification, because this has been the principal focus of our own research program; but we also discuss the implications of our findings for the phenomena of resistance to temptation and pain tolerance. In all of our research, children were chosen as the appropriate subjects for our investigations. This choice does not imply that the phenomenon of gratification delay is unimportant in adults; it certainly is important. The choice of children as subjects was guided by three considerations—one practical and two theoretical. On the practical side, it is simply easier to create a situation for children in which the rewards involved constitute such compelling outcomes that their deferment engages self-control processes. Adults frequently put off an immediate reward for the sake of a future reward, but it is difficult to create an involving analog in the laboratory context.

A second reason for observing the process in children is the goal of tracing the development of the ability to delay gratification. It seems obvious that we do get better at this skill; yet it is not clear why this should be the case. By investigating children, one can attempt to chart the course of this development. Such an approach might also be expected to illuminate the constituent processes that operate in the behavior of adults. Finally, to understand children's social development is an important and theoretically meaningful enterprise in its own right, aside from any implications such investigations may have for the understanding of adults.

History of gratification delay research

The history of research on delay of gratification reflects a number of general changes in psychology. Early work in this area was characterized by two features. First, it dealt with the initial phase of the delay process—*the decision to wait* for a delayed outcome rather than accept some less desirable but immediately attainable reward or object. Second, early research concerned itself primarily with demographic or distal social variables, such as age, sex, ethnicity, social class, and so on, and how these variables related to the decision to postpone gratification (cf. Mischel, 1966b). This strategy emerged primarily because the prevalent theoretical orientation in the area was social learning theory, which at that time emphasized expectancy-value theory. Simply put, this theory holds that a person's decision to wait is a function of the value of the delayed reward over the immediate reward and the individual's expectancy that the delayed reward would in fact be forthcoming if he or she did forego the immediate gratification. From this perspective, trust in the social environment was assumed to be of critical importance, with the consequence that researchers examined delay-choice differences in individuals and groups that might reasonably be expected to differ in such trust. In a similar vein, experimental studies in this tradition focused on factors, such as exposure to delaying models (Bandura & Mischel, 1965), that were expected to influence the level of trust the observer held in the environment.

In the late sixties, Walter Mischel and his colleagues began to focus on the second phase of the phenomenon of gratification delay, that of delay maintenance. As we all know, one's initial commitment to defer gratification is not a guarantee that the commitment will actually be observed. Although it is the case that in some contexts we do not have the chance to revoke a decision (e.g., joining the army), we frequently *do* have such an opportunity and hence are continually faced with the temptation to terminate gratification delay. The early focus on variables that affect the individual's confidence in the social environment's commitment to deliver deferred gratification, therefore, shifted to a consideration of the factors that affect the individual's commitment to such deferment once initiated. Mischel's interest in the variables that affect the individual's ability to adhere to his or her decision was paralleled by increasing interest among clinical psychologists in factors that would aid clinical populations to maintain desired behaviors rather than lapse into habitual and undesirable behavior patterns. Mischel's research program also paralleled another general trend in psychology: the focus on the individual's phenomenology or cognitions in the situation rather than objective aspects of the situation. Hence, while Mischel's earliest investigations of delay maintenance involved the manipulation of situational variables such as reward salience during the delay period, he later turned to examine the way the individual viewed or thought about the rewards. He also explored the function of cognitive distractions during the delay period.

Our own research was undertaken with the hope of adding to Mischel's work in two ways. First, we have examined a third phase of the delay phenomenon, that of delay termination. As a consequence of the work of Mischel and others, a considerable amount is known about the decision to delay as well as the factors that affect how long one can maintain this commitment. We do not yet understand, however, the decision-making process that precipitates the cessation of gratification delay. In addressing this question, we sought to determine if children's evaluation of the rewards changes over the delay interval, and whether reward evaluation might be affected by the situational and cognitive factors Mischel and others have investigated.

A second direction in our research has been to investigate cognitive factors that underlie gratification delay in contexts in which the decision to delay gratification cannot, once it is made, be revoked. This situation, one we have called externally imposed delay (EID), also requires individuals to commit themselves to defer gratification. Once this initial commitment is made, however, the person has no choice but to wait for the deferred reward. In this paradigm, our research attempts were aimed at discovering whether the dynamics involved in the EID were similar to those involved in the self-imposed delay (SID) situation.

In this chapter, we first present research and theory concerning the delay of gratifica-

tion situation in which the decision to delay can be revoked (SID). We then discuss the situation in which the decision to delay gratification is irreversible once made; we contrast this situation with the self-imposed delay situation. In a final section, we discuss similarities between the phenomenon of gratification delay and the phenomena of resistance to temptation and pain tolerance.

The self-imposed delay paradigm

In their investigations of self-control, Mischel and his colleagues have relied extensively on the following procedure. A child, generally a preschooler, indicates his or her preference for one of two reward alternatives (e.g., marshmallows or pretzels). Subjects are then told that the food they did not select, the less preferred reward, can be obtained by them immediately. The second reward, the preferred reward, involves a contingency: Subjects must wait for the experimenter to return from doing some work in another room before they receive it. There is an "out clause," however. At any time during the delay, children who decide that they do not wish to fulfill the contingency requirements can "opt out" by employing a delay-terminating response (i.e., pressing a buzzer) which will summon the experimenter. However, by discontinuing the delay, the child forfeits his or her preferred reward and receives the less preferred reward instead.

With any experimental procedure two methodological questions can be asked. The first of these pertains to what Aronson and Carlsmith (1968) have called *mundane* realism, by which they refer to the extent to which the experimental situation is similar to situations experienced by the subject in the real world. The greater this similarity, the greater the mundane realism of the experimental setting. *Experimental* realism, according to Aronson and Carlsmith, refers to the extent to which the situation has a real impact on subjects and involves them, irrespective of whether it is similar to real-world situations. Aronson and Carlsmith contend that while both types of realism are important, it is more critical that an experiment have experimental rather than mundane realism.

In the present context, it may seem that there is no *precise* real-world counterpart to Mischel's procedure, but there are clearly a host of situations in the child's life, and in the adult's for that matter, that require him or her to wait before receiving a desired object or reward. As far as experimental realism is concerned, it is unlikely that any one who has ever watched a child in this situation would doubt that this type of realism exists to a high degree. Despite the apparent triviality of the rewards used (e.g., marshmallows, gum), children certainly appear highly involved in the situation and highly interested in the rewards.

Let us now take a closer look at the SID situation. There are two critical features of this situation. First, the child initially agrees to an arrangement that requires him or her to wait for a preferred reward. Second, children have continually available to them the option of escaping the situation by terminating the delay and obtaining the less preferred reward. The fact that the child has to wait to obtain the preferred reward produces the aversiveness of the situation. Within this context, there are two important questions one can ask about the child's behavior. First, why do some children choose to cease delaying? Second, what factors facilitate the child's coping with the delay period?

In our attempts (Karniol & Miller, 1980; Miller & Karniol, 1980) to understand the dynamics of waiting under SID, we focused on the process by which the child reaches the decision to terminate the delay and accept the originally less preferred reward. If we can comprehend this decision process, we may be able to infer what variables determine whether the decision is actually reached. Intuitively, it seems that such a decision must be precipitated by some changes in the child's perception of the situation. Even if we assume that the child simply decides "I don't want to wait any more," we must still account for why he or she decides to opt out at a particular point in time.

Let us try to analyze the situation from a child's point of view. To begin with, it seems reasonable to assume, since the SID situation pits two rewards against each other, that the perceived difference in reward value is an important factor in determining children's willingness to both initiate and maintain the delay. The larger this value differential, the more willing children should be to delay for the preferred reward and the less aversive they should find the delay situation. The reward value differential cannot be the only factor affecting the aversiveness of the situation, however, since this would presumably remain the same throughout the delay. It appears as though the passage of time itself increases the aversiveness of the delay situation.

Assuming that this analysis is valid, there are a number of possible explanations of what occurrences may precipitate the decision to terminate the delay (Kanfer, 1977). First, it is possible that with the mere passage of time, children's tolerance level for aversive situations will be reached, and at this point they will press the buzzer to terminate the delay. Second, it is possible that the delayed reward increases in attractiveness for children as they wait, thereby increasing the aversiveness of the situation until their tolerance level is reached. Both of these possibilities imply that the delay-terminating response serves to reduce the frustration children experience in the situation and that this response is the outcome of an aversive motivational state. Furthermore, the second of these alternatives suggests that reward value differential *increases* as the delay period continues.[1]

There are at least two more alternatives, both of which contend that delay-produced frustration activates cognitive processes that produce changes in the perceived attractiveness of the rewards. One possibility is that the preferred reward will become less attractive to children as they wait. An alternative possibility is that the immediately available reward will become more attractive to children. These explanations imply not only that reward value differential will *decrease* over time, but that delay frustration will be reduced as a consequence of this cognitive process. Moreover, as reward value convergence occurs, the child will find it easier to decide that it is no longer worthwhile to wait. In other words, a rational decision-making process will lead to the buzzer-pressing response.

Mischel (1974) has interpreted the dynamics of the SID situation in terms of the motivational explanations we presented first. In Mischel's words,

When the child attends to the immediate reward his motivation for it increases. . . . When the subject attends to the preferred but delayed outcome he becomes increasingly frustrated because he wants it more. (pp. 267–268)

A model of delay behavior

In watching children in the self-imposed delay situation, we found that while some children appear to press the delay-terminating buzzer impulsively, most seem to do so calmly and with few visible signs of distress. On the basis of this observation, we sided with the "cognitive" explanation—speculating that by the time children press the buzzer, thereby forfeiting the preferred reward, they no longer perceive the delayed reward as being more attractive than the immediately available reward. In other words, delay frustration initiates a process of reward reevaluation, and it is this cognitive process rather than frustration itself that initiates the buzzer-pressing response.

Let us attempt to explain how reevaluation of the preferred reward may occur given a contingency that requires the child to wait for some unspecified period of time before obtaining the preferred reward. To begin with, we propose that since the rewards are not both available at the same time, the relative value of the preferred reward must take two factors into account: (1) the child's subjective estimate of how long the delay will be and (2) how aversive the child thinks

the delay will be. One, or both, of these estimates can be exceeded during the delay interval. Once either of these estimates is exceeded (i.e., the delay is longer or more aversive than expected), the relative value of the preferred reward should begin to diminish. The more the estimated length and aversiveness of the delay are exceeded, the greater will be the reduction in the perceived relative attractiveness of the delayed reward. At some point, therefore, the attractiveness advantage of the delayed reward over the immediate reward will no longer be so great as to warrant waiting, and at this point the child should terminate the delay. Any situational manipulations that make the aversiveness of the delay exceed its anticipated aversiveness will therefore lead to shorter termination latencies.

We have been describing a model of delay of gratification that is based on two assumptions. First, when children start to wait, they have some subjective estimate of the delay's duration and aversiveness. These two factors combine in some fashion to influence the relative value of the preferred reward. The second assumption of our model is that the longer children wait in the situation, the greater the probability that their subjective estimate of the aversiveness of the delay will be exceeded. Hence, longer delay times should lower the relative value of the preferred reward until a point at which this value becomes functionally equivalent to the value of the immediately available but less preferred reward. Once this point is reached, the child should terminate the delay. Any factors that increase the perceived length or aversiveness of the delay will contribute to a reduction in the perceived reward value of the preferred reward and will therefore hasten the termination of the delay. According to this conceptualization, variations in children's delay times reflect differences in their initial aversiveness estimates and the speed with which cognitive processes are initiated once this estimate is exceeded.

A number of aspects of our model require further elaboration. To begin with, we must emphasize that we are not suggesting that during the delay the child sits engaging in mental calculations of reward value. We are simply saying that, for most children, the passage of time alters the relative value of the delayed reward so as to make it unworthwhile to wait for this reward any longer. This model predicts that, if we could measure how children evaluate the preferred reward while they are waiting, we would find that their evaluation of it decreases as they continue to wait. The model also predicts that any situational manipulations that change the anticipated aversiveness of the delay will hasten devaluation of the preferred reward and will therefore lead to shorter delay latencies. In sum, our model suggests that variations in delay times across experimental conditions reflect and are a function of differential rates of preferred reward devaluation in the different conditions.

Testing the model

In order to test the validity of our conceptualization of reward devaluation directly, we conducted a series of studies using variants of the paradigm we described earlier. Pretesting with third-grade children indicated that few children would press the buzzer to terminate the delay before 10 minutes had expired. To us, this implied that up to the 10-minute period, the point of functional equivalence in the value of the two rewards had not yet occurred for the majority of children.

On the basis of this pretest data, in our first study (Miller & Karniol, 1980, Study 1) we used a 10-minute delay period. For half the subjects, receipt of the preferred reward was made contingent on waiting for the experimenter to return; for the remaining (control) subjects, the rewards were not in any way linked with waiting. This was done to examine whether potential changes in reward value were simply a matter of time or were dependent on the temporal contingency involved in receiving the rewards. Subjects in the noncontingent conditions

were asked which of the two rewards they preferred. A similar preference statement was obtained in the contingent reward conditions before specifying the contingency associated with the preferred reward. For half the subjects, the rewards were left present during the delay; for the remaining subjects, the rewards were absent during the delay. The experimenter remained out of the room for 10 minutes. On returning, the experimenter told subjects they would have to continue waiting, but that she had forgotten to ask them some questions before leaving. The experimenter then explained that her "boss" not only wanted to know which of the treats they liked best, but also how much they liked them.

At this point, the subject was shown a board on which there were five squares of increasing size. With respect to each of the relevant rewards, the subject was asked, "Do you": (1) "hate them," (2) "don't like them very much," (3) "like them a little," (4) "like them quite a lot," or (5) "like them very, very much." One of these descriptions was printed below each of the squares on the board, and the subjects were asked to point to the square that described the way they felt about the reward. The larger the square they pointed to, the more they liked the reward and the higher the assigned value. The order of evaluation was counterbalanced. After collecting these judgments from the subject, the experimenter left the experimental room for one minute and then returned, allowing the child to consume his or her preferred reward.

Our predictions were two-fold. First, if our assumption is valid that reward devaluation occurs because of the temporal contingency associated with the rewards, then children for whom the preferred reward was contingent on waiting should assign lower preference ratings to it after 10 minutes of delay than those in the noncontingent conditions. Second, since reward presence increases the aversiveness of the delay, it was predicted that the relative value of the preferred reward should decrease faster in the reward-present condition than

Table 2.1. Attractiveness Ratings of Preferred Rewards as a Function of Reward Salience and Contingency

Reward	Reward Salience	
Relationship	Present	Absent
Contingent	2.76	3.61
Noncontingent	3.92	3.84

Note. The larger the number, the greater the attractiveness. (Adapted from Miller and Karniol, 1980, Study 1).

in reward-absent condition. No differential evaluation of the nonpreferred reward was anticipated since, from our perspective, it is only the relative value of the preferred reward that is involved in the decision to wait or to terminate the delay.

The results from the first study were generally consistent with our hypotheses. Subjects in the reward-contingent condition did evidence lowered evaluations of the preferred reward when the rewards were present during the 10-minute delay, but not when the rewards were absent (see Table 2.1). No differences in the ratings of the nonpreferred reward were found across conditions. The finding that reward devaluation did not occur in the reward-absent condition was unpredicted but is not particularly surprising. Presumably, devaluation was limited to reward-present conditions, because it was only in these conditions that aversiveness of the delay exceeded the child's estimate of how aversive the delay would be. When the reward was absent, the anticipated aversiveness of the delay was most likely not exceeded within the 10-minute period.

On the basis of our initial results, we began to consider what conditions besides reward presence might lead to reward devaluation. One of our speculations was that the more similar the preferred and less preferred reward are in value at the initial choice point, the less time it should take for devaluation of the preferred reward to result in convergence of the two rewards' values. This was thought to be the case because the

relative advantage of waiting for the preferred reward is lower to begin with when the rewards are similar in value (cf. Herzberger & Dweck, 1978).

In order to determine whether the discrepancy between the value of the two reward alternatives is a significant factor in determining the preferred reward's devaluation, we conducted another study (Miller & Karniol, 1980, Study 2). Our third-grade subjects were asked first to rank five food rewards. Receipt of the first ranked reward required their waiting for the experimenter's return, while they could receive either the second (reward-similar condition) or fifth ranked reward (reward-discrepant condition) whenever they terminated the delay. The experimenter interrupted the wait after 10 minutes to obtain the child's rating of the two reward alternatives that were left present in front of the child.

The results supported our hypotheses (see Table 2.2). When the rewards were present and similar in initial rating, the preferred reward was assigned a lower attractiveness rating than when the rewards were discrepant (means were 2.91 and 3.91 respectively). No differences emerged in the reward-absent condition. Again, no evaluation differences for the nonpreferred reward were found.

Since we found that reward similarity affected the reward evaluation process, we were interested in the possibility that this variable might also affect delay behavior. Accordingly, we predicted that delay times would be longer the greater the discrepancy

Table 2.2. Attractiveness Ratings of Preferred Rewards as a Function of Reward Salience and Initial Similarity

Reward	Reward Salience	
Similarity	Present	Absent
Similar	2.91	3.83
Discrepant	3.91	3.53

Note. The larger the number, the greater the attractiveness. (Adapted from Miller and Karniol, 1980, Study 2).

between the initial value of the preferred and nonpreferred rewards.

To test these predictions, we again varied reward discrepancy and allowed children to wait without interruption (Miller & Karniol, 1980, Study 3). The results strongly supported our prediction, with longer delay times occurring under reward-discrepant than under reward-similar conditions (means were 25.50 and 13.08 minutes, respectively).

These findings constitute further evidence that delay times are shortest in those conditions in which devaluation of the preferred reward has occurred most extensively. Specifically, it appears easier to wait for a preferred reward when it is clearly more attractive than the alternative reward. It becomes harder to wait when it is clear that one reward is really no better than the other. In the former case, reward value convergence occurs more slowly than it does in the latter. Taken as a whole, then, it would seem that the results of these three studies strongly support our model and suggest that reward devaluation is a critical factor in determining how long children will wait in SID situations before "opting out."

Estimation of delay duration

In presenting our model, we assumed that the relative value of the preferred reward is determined in part by a subjective estimate of delay duration as well as the estimate of the aversiveness of this delay. Devaluation of the preferred reward can be initiated by either exceeding the duration estimate, the aversiveness estimate, or both. In either case, our model suggests that conditions that lead to increased aversiveness of the delay should increase estimates of the delay's duration. In fact, research on the perception of time has indicated that the more aversive an interval of time, the longer it is judged as being (Filler & Meals, 1949; Irwin, 1961; Schonbach, 1959).

In one of our studies, we put this reasoning to the test and predicted that, if the rewards were contingent on waiting and were present during the delay, they should lead to longer delay time estimates than when the rewards were absent (Miller & Karniol, 1976a). Once again, third-grade children served as subjects. After subjects had delayed 4 minutes, the experimenter returned and asked them to indicate on a model clock how long they thought the experimenter had been out of the room. Consistent with our previous findings, reward salience emerged as an important variable. When rewards were present, we found overestimation, with delay time estimates for a 4-minute period being approximately 6 minutes. When rewards were absent, the delay estimates were almost accurate, with a mean of around 4½ minutes. It does appear, then, that the perceived duration of the delay differs depending on situational variations, with reward presence leading to overestimation of the delay's duration.

In summarizing this section, a number of points should be emphasized. First, we have seen that under contingencies that have an "out clause," a cost-benefit analysis appears to guide choice behavior. The value of the deferred reward is weighed against the more immediate one, and only to the extent that the former yields an advantage over the latter will the contingency requirements be met by the child. Meeting the contingency requirements can be made more difficult by increasing the aversiveness of the delay beyond its anticipated aversiveness (e.g., leaving the rewards present). Furthermore, it is easier to meet the contingency requirements if the child's choice is between clearly discrepant alternatives or similar alternatives that are not in his or her presence during the delay.

Delay of gratification—externally imposed delay

Up to now we have discussed delays that can be terminated at will. However, not all the unpleasant waiting or goal deferment we engage in can be terminated at our will. Often we not only must endure a period of deprivation before some desirable event occurs, but we also have no opportunity to terminate the delay interval. Once one enters a lecture, for example, one generally is committed to remain until the end. No matter how slowly one's holiday approaches, one cannot generally "opt out" of the delay interval. Any form of fixed-time incarceration or detention not only requires a person to endure a delay before a desirable outcome is available, but there is no opportunity for delay termination and hence no temptation to be combatted.

Freud's (1911) seminal discussion of gratification delay focused primarily on the externally imposed delay (EID) situation. Freud's prototypical case was that of the young infant who is deprived of its mother's breast. In order to cope with this delay that he or she cannot terminate, the child "binds the time" by generating hallucinatory wish-fulfilling images of the deferred reward (the mother's breast). Such mental activity is viewed by Freud as the precursor to rational thought processes and is utilized by the ego in its attempt to cope with gratification delay.

On the basis of Freud's speculation about ideation during the delay, we speculated that the relationship between reward-focused ideation and delay tolerance observed by Mischel and his colleagues in self-imposed delay situations may not exist in externally imposed delay situations. More precisely, we hypothesized that reward-focused ideation or attention may *facilitate* rather than inhibit delay tolerance under conditions of externally imposed delay.

To test this hypothesis, we conducted a simple experiment (Miller & Karniol, 1976b). Two delay situations were used: one that was virtually identical to the one used by Mischel and his colleagues (self-imposed delay) and one in which the child also had to wait until the experimenter returned to receive a preferred reward but in which there was no opportunity to terminate the delay (externally imposed delay). One-half of our third-grade subjects were assigned to each of the two types of situations. In

addition to manipulating the type of delay situation, we manipulated reward salience during the delay, so that half of our subjects were faced with the delayed reward during the delay and the other half had the reward removed from their sight. We used the subjects' estimation of a 4-minute delay interval to measure delay frustration in the two situations. As we noted earlier, previous research has indicated that the more frustrated individuals are in a situation the longer they estimate the duration of time spent in the situation.

The results from this experiment were clear. As reported earlier, subjects estimated a 4-minute self-imposed delay to be longer when the rewards were present than when they were absent (6.0 minutes versus 4.5 minutes). This is, of course, entirely consistent with the finding that reward salience increases delay frustration and reduces delay time in a self-imposed context. The results in the externally imposed delay context were completely opposite: Subjects estimated the 4-minute delay to be longer when the rewards were not present than when they were (5.4 minutes versus 4.2 minutes). It appears, then, that reward-focused ideation does reduce rather than intensify delay frustration under conditions of externally imposed delay.

Having shown that the presence of deferred rewards reduces delay frustration in the externally imposed delay context, we were interested in whether behavioral indices would reflect the differential aversiveness experienced when rewards were present under externally imposed rather than under self-imposed conditions. Consequently, we conducted an experiment (Miller & Karniol, 1976a) in which the subjects in both self-imposed and externally imposed conditions were provided with an activity (a pile of plastic blocks) that could serve as a distraction from the frustration of waiting. The data indicated that under reward salient conditions, subjects in the EID situation played with or attended to the blocks an average of 15.25 seconds out of their 5-minute delay. This time was contrasted to the 91.25 seconds during which subjects in the SID focused on the blocks. Our interpretation of this finding was that, because the presence of the delayed reward generated more frustration in the SID than EID conditions, subjects were more inclined in the former condition to distract themselves or "tune out."

Our confidence in interpreting the block-playing response as a distraction attempt was enhanced by the finding in another experiment (Miller & Karniol, 1976a) that increasing the time subjects *expected* to be in the delay situation increased the time subjects in both SID and EID contexts spent looking at or playing with the blocks. Actually the results were most dramatic. When third-grade subjects expected the delay period to last 10 minutes, they focused on the blocks an average of 135 seconds during a 4-minute delay. When the expected delay was only 5 minutes, this response was engaged in for an average of only 103 seconds. Regardless of anticipated duration of delay, subjects in the SID condition still played more with the blocks than EID subjects.

The general conclusion we can derive from our studies contrasting self-imposed and externally imposed delay situations is that the dynamics of each are quite different. In SID situations the individual is faced with the temptation to leave the situation. The more frustrated the individual is during the delay, the more likely the person is to succumb to this temptation and leave the situation. Frustration, however, does not appear to operate simply by making intolerable the wait for what is still considered a highly desired reward. Instead, frustration appears to produce a devaluation of the deferred rewards, thus reducing the justification for waiting and easing the decision to terminate the delay. In effect, the devaluation of the delayed reward makes it only *rational* to leave the situation. Individuals in SID situations can reduce the aversiveness of the delay and increase their chances of attaining the delayed reward by diverting their attention from the rewards.

Under EID conditions the situation is quite different. There is no temptation here. Frustration can and does exist in this type of situation, but it is not caused by temptation nor can it precipitate escape behavior. Salience of rewards, which increases delay frustration in the SID situation, appears to decrease delay frustration in the context of EID. Thus, the very same cognitive strategy, self-distraction, facilitates waiting under self-imposed delay and makes delay more difficult under externally imposed delay. To summarize, it appears that while the task of waiting for a preferred reward is common to both SID and EID the dynamics involved in each are quite different.

Developmental considerations

It is clear that children become better able to delay gratification as they get older. To begin with, children become better able to understand temporal concepts (e.g., Piaget, 1962). Second, and perhaps more important, children learn how to vary their attentional focus by engaging in self-distracting and self-instructional techniques.

A number of Soviet psychologists (Luria, 1961; Vygotsky, 1962) have focused on the use of self-guiding statements in the regulation of behavior. The most influential of these statements is Luria's, which proposes that there are three stages in the socialization of children. During the first stage, the speech of others controls the child's behavior. During the second stage, the child's own overt speech starts to regulate his or her behavior. In the third and final stage, the child's own overt speech "goes underground," and this inner or covert speech assumes a self-guiding function.

According to Luria, these three stages are evident in the acquisition of any voluntary act. Problems in voluntary behavior, then, can be conceptualized as reflecting either (1) the failure of overt or covert speech to serve a self-guiding function or (2) the failure of the person to use speech in a self-guiding manner. Although the problems evident in clinical populations are widely believed to reflect the former case (for a review, see

Meichenbaum, 1977), it is thought that developmental differences reflect the latter. For example, Meichenbaum and Goodman (1969) showed that younger children benefitted from self-guiding overt speech on a motor task while older ones were hindered by talking aloud during the performance of the same task. Presumably, the older children were already generating their own covert speech, and overt speech simply interfered with this process.

The findings described above suggest that the existence of differential abilities to generate or employ delay-facilitating strategies (like self-statements, attention, or ideation) may help explain why older children are better than younger ones at enduring delay situations. Unfortunately, direct data on this possibility are scarce, since researchers have seldom examined developmental differences in this particular context. Given that many of the variables examined (e.g., ideation, imagination, or self-statements) are thought to follow a developmental sequence (Inhelder & Piaget, 1958; Luria, 1961; Paivio, 1971), the failure to explore developmental differences in the delay of gratification paradigm is rather surprising.

In an attempt to examine whether the role of attentional focus in facilitating children's delay of gratification is related to a developmental stage, we conducted a study with kindergarten and third-grade children (Miller, Weinstein & Karniol, 1978). A SID situation was employed, with marshmallows and pretzels serving as the rewards. The experiment had four conditions. For all subjects, a red light flashed on every 15 seconds during the delay. Three of the groups were instructed to verbalize a particular statement when the light flashed, the other group was a control and was given no statements to verbalize. One of the verbalization groups was assigned an "instrumental" statement ("I'm waiting for the ———"). A second group was assigned a "consummatory" statement ("——— are yummy") and a third group an "irrelevant" statement (counting to three). A number of predictions were made for this experiment. The most straightforward pre-

diction was that in the no-verbalization condition, kindergarten children would find the delay more aversive than would third-grade children and would, therefore, delay for a shorter time. It was also predicted that, while number counting would aid kindergarten children by distracting them from the rewards, it would not facilitate the delay of third-grade children who were expected to be normally producing more sophisticated self-guiding statements. A final prediction was that consummatory verbalizations would interfere with delay behavior for both ages groups and that instrumental verbalizations would facilitate delay behavior.

The results yielded general support for the predictions (see Table 2.3). As predicted, younger subjects delayed for shorter periods than did older children. It was also the case that the irrelevant-verbalization condition aided younger but not older children. Furthermore, consummatory verbalizations reduced the delay times of older children, relative to controls, but not the delay times of younger children. It appears as if young children's natural thought or ideational processes are similar to, or at least no more effective than, those that are induced by the consummatory set. Finally, all children appeared to benefit from the instrumental verbalizations. On balance, these data suggest that young children have trouble thinking of ways in which to combat delay aversiveness once it is experienced. More specifically, verbalization strategies are not as available to young children as they are to the older ones, who apparently can reduce delay time aversiveness by employing particular strategies. Even older children can be made to terminate the delay sooner, however, if their verbalizations are consummatory and thereby facilitate rather than hinder *reward devaluation*.

Given that younger children do not appear to spontaneously employ either verbalizations or ideational strategies that are functional in reducing the aversiveness of the delay period, the question can be raised as to why this is the case. There is recent evidence that preschool children simply do

Table 2.3. Mean Delay Times (in seconds) According to School Grade and Verbalization Condition

Group	Experimental Conditions			
	No Verbalization	Irrelevant Verbalization	Reward-oriented Verbalization	Task-oriented Verbalization
Kindergarten subjects	385_a	722_b	363_a	744_{bcd}
Third-grade subjects	685_b	632_{bd}	409_a	933_c

Note. Cell means that do not share a common subscript differ ($p < .05$) as indicated by a Duncan range statistic. (Adapted from Miller, Weinstein, and Karniol, 1978).

not realize that specific attentional strategies might be beneficial in delay situations. Under self-imposed delay, for instance, preschoolers do not seem to know that by covering the rewards they facilitate delay maintenance, whereas older children (grades three and six) do seem to be aware of the benefits of such concealment (Mischel, Mischel, & Hood, 1978). Furthermore, preschoolers do not appear to know that by self-verbalizing instrumental (as opposed to consummatory) statements they facilitate delay maintenance, whereas older children seem to be aware of the efficacy of such self-statements as well as the virtue of cognitive transformations of the rewards (e.g., viewing marshmallows as puffy white clouds). Interestingly, in a recent study, Yates and Mischel (1979, Study 3) found that in an externally imposed delay situation preschool children did correctly indicate that looking at the delayed reward helped them wait the most. It is possible, therefore, that coping with externally imposed delay is simpler for the younger child since the attentional strategy that emerges first (i.e., focusing on the rewards) is most functional in that situation.

Cognitive transformations from self-imposed to externally imposed delay

One of the points we made earlier is that the strategy by which a decision to terminate the delay is reached under self-imposed delay contexts is antithetical to the strategy by which the maintenance of delay in such contexts is facilitated. Specifically, delay termination requires focusing on the rewards while delay maintenance requires self-distraction. Externally imposed delay, on the other hand, leaves the individual only a delay maintenance option; consequently, to focus on the rewards using self-persuasion as to their high relative value is the best coping strategy.

We have seen that young children in particular, but older ones as well, have trouble with maintaining self-imposed delays. A coping mechanism we have not discussed is one that may be of particular importance: cognitively transforming the self-imposed delay to an externally imposed one. Such a transformation would involve the child's elimination of the delay-terminating response as a response alternative. For instance, the child could say:

"Sure he left me the buzzer to press, but if I do so, he'll be angry. So I must not press the buzzer. I have to wait till he comes back."

The advantage of such a transformation is that the temptation to press the buzzer is removed. The child can then think about the reward, and this attentional focus will facilitate rather than hinder his or her coping.

Cognitive transformations of this kind are actually evident in the way we treat many choices—for instance, going to work. Every day we have a choice of either going or not going to work. The rewards for not going are immediate (e.g., sleeping late) while the rewards for going are delayed (monthly check). We tend to eliminate the daily choice since it would be frustrating and debilitating to have to decide every day "Am I or am I not going to work today?" Treating work as a forced choice rather than one of two alternatives is therefore quite adaptive.

There is a fascinating study with pigeons (Rachlin & Green, 1972) that relates to the issue of transformations. The basic assumption of Rachlin and Green's research was that the decision to delay is based on a ratio formula (Herrnstein, 1964) in which the relative value of each alternative reward is a function of its reward value multiplied by the delay time till the receipt of the other reward alternative [i.e., $V_1 / V_2 = (R_1 \times \text{Delay}_2)/(R_2 \times \text{Delay}_1)$]. Using this formula, we find that, if the choice is made when the immediately available reward is available (i.e., at point 0), the formula predicts that the immediate reward will be selected. As the choice point is moved to an earlier point in time, however, the relative advantage of choosing the delayed reward increases (e.g., if the choice is made 10 minutes before the immediate reward becomes available and the delayed reward is delayed a further 4 minutes).

Rachlin and Green hypothesized that if they gave pigeons the opportunity to choose between a delayed and immediate reward, before either reward became available, they would select the delayed reward. The pigeons in this study were given the option of choosing one of two keys to peck at point X. A peck on one key led them to another choice point, Y, at which they could either choose the immediately available small reward or the delayed larger reward. Pecking on the other key, however, led directly to the delayed larger reward's key, thus eliminating the second choice point. Rachlin and Green found that the greater the interval before either reward became available, the more inclined the pigeons were to peck the key that eliminated the second choice point and led directly to the delayed reward.

There are two conclusions to be drawn from this study. First, as immediate rewards become available, they become more attractive than delayed rewards that are more attractive in absolute value. Second, often it is possible to eliminate the temptation of the immediate reward by choosing to eliminate a choice point. This, in fact, means that the individual transforms a self-imposed delay to an externally imposed one. Setting the alarm clock at night can be viewed as the elimination of choice. The individual fears that if he or she does not set the clock he or she may choose not to get up in the morning. For this reason, many people place the alarm in a place removed from their beds so that they will in fact have to get up to turn the alarm off.

Individual differences in gratification delay

Individual differences have seldom been explored in the delay of gratification paradigm. In one rare effort, Mischel and Gilligan (1964) devised a delay of gratification scale that required subjects to choose between 14 small immediate rewards and larger delayed ones (e.g., small ball now, large one in one week). The scale was employed in the early work on delay choice, but Mischel and his colleagues have generally not reported correlations between this scale and delay maintenance behavior. Certainly no attempt has been made by researchers in this area to determine whether individual differences in delay tolerance are related to any of the strategies or cognitive processes that have been found to affect delay behavior.

One way of examining individual differences within this context is to consider the various factors or strategies that we found to be related to coping ability. Since processes such as cognitive distraction, self-verbalization, and transformations are related to coping skill, it seems reasonable to propose that some individuals are better at such activities than others. Moreover, we know that there are developmental differences in the use of such strategies, and there is also evidence to suggest that differences of this type may exist within individuals of the same developmental level.

Miller and Karniol (1976b) found, for instance, that children categorized as being low in the ability to delay gratification on the basis of the Mischel and Gilligan scale spent significantly more time attending to the rewards in a self-imposed delay situation than did children categorized as being high in this ability. Moreover, Mischel (1974) himself has reported that the manipulation of ideational content aids some children, presumably those not using it effectively, more than other children. Work with reflective and impulsive children similarly indicates that the difference between these two types of children in impulse control can be reduced if the impulsive children are instructed to verbalize particular self-statements (Meichenbaum & Goodman, 1971). Considering the results as a whole, it would appear that there are individual differences in coping effectiveness and that these differences may be related to cognitive processes that experimental work has identified as being important to coping generally (e.g., attention, ideation, self-verbalization, etc.).

Although it may be useful to talk of individual differences in terms of constituent coping processes, this leaves much of the picture still unclear. For instance, we do not know whether the fact that an individual uses one cognitive strategy effectively is predictive of whether he or she will use other strategies effectively. Furthermore, if we know that variations in coping strategies can differentiate good from poor copers, can we be confident that this is the only, or even the most important, difference between the two types of individuals? If coping strategies are simply symptoms of some more basic difference between the individuals, interventions designed to affect these skills may not be wholly effective in reducing these differences.

Moreover, since the effectiveness of strategies depends greatly on the situational context (e.g., self-imposed versus externally imposed delay), the question can be asked whether any one coping style would be effective across situations. As we have seen, distraction may help one cope in a self-imposed delay situation and yet may undermine coping in an externally imposed delay situation. Of course, what may characterize an effective coper, and thereby justify the designation of a general trait, is not the usage of particular strategies but the modification of a variety of strategies to meet the requirements of the particular situation. Unfortunately, there are not at present the necessary data to evaluate this possibility.

At least one of our studies (Miller, 1978), however, suggests that the search for one "coping" personality may be misguided. In this study, third-grade males and females estimated the duration of a 4-minute delay they had spent in either the context of a self-imposed or externally imposed delay. These subjects had previously completed the Nowicki-Strickland locus of control scale and had been categorized as either high external or high internal by their responses. An internally oriented child is one who feels that he or she can control events and outcomes in his or her environment, whereas an externally oriented child is one who feels events and outcomes are generally determined by external agents and are beyond his or her control. The results of this study indicated that, in the self-imposed delay conditions, the internals estimated the delay as being of *shorter* duration than did the externals. It appeared, then, that they found the delay less aversive and were less tempted in this situation. This finding is consistent with other research that has shown that internals actually do delay longer in self-imposed delay contexts than do externals (Higgins, 1975). In the externally imposed delay context, however, the opposite pattern emerged, with internals estimating the delay as being *longer* than did externals. Externals seemed less frustrated than internals in an EID situation. It appears, therefore, that the type of individual best suited to endure one type of delay situation is least suited to endure the other type of delay situation.

Applying the delay model to the resistance of temptation

Resistance to temptation differs from delay of gratification in one major aspect: It usually involves long-range negative consequences if the immediately desirable option is taken. Therefore, not enacting the immediately available response ordinarily has some positive consequences associated with it. Consider stealing as an example; the immediate reward is the attainment of goods, going to jail is the negative outcome, and being a good or a moral citizen is the positive outcome for not enacting the response. In the case of overeating, the immediate reward is the enjoyment of food, the long-range negative consequence is being obese or having a heart attack, and the positive consequence of not enacting the response may be the culturally valued outcome of staying slim or the knowledge that one is healthier.

The major problem the individual faces in resistance to temptation situations seems to be that the delayed aversive consequences do not exert the same degree of control over behavior that the immediate positive consequences do. The probability that a punished but enjoyable response will be enacted is a function of the delay time between the response and the punishment. The longer the interval of time until the punishment, the higher the probabilty that the forbidden response will be enacted by both children (Walters & Demkow, 1963) and adults (Banks & Vogel-Sprott, 1965). Evidence with clinical populations, such as alcoholics (Vogel-Sprott & Banks, 1965), suggests the interesting possibility that these populations are generally less deterred by future punishment than "normal" populations, and that this characteristic may be responsible for their lack of self-control. Treatment programs often endeavor to increase resistance to temptation by producing a negative reaction to the tempting response (e.g., aversion therapy).

Recall that the model of delay we have been developing suggests that the relative attractiveness of rewards changes over time. Recall also that Rachlin and Green (1972) illustrated that choices made at a time at which neither immediate nor delayed rewards were available tended to be choices for the delayed reward while choices at the point when the immediate reward became available tended to be choices for the immediate reward. To put it in concrete terms, when we are not hungry, dying for a cigarette, or for a drink we all choose to remain slim, unaddicted, and sober. As the craving increases, however, we tend to shift our choices to the immediate reward that will satisfy the craving. In short, when people go on diets or quit "cold turkey," they are unaware of how aversive the period of craving will be. This aversiveness so exceeds their estimation that they are unable to cope with it when it occurs. Only to the extent that they can deploy their attention from the craving or persuade themselves as to the value of not enacting the response will they resist temptation.

Thaler and Shefrin (1979) have suggested that people cope with these situations by "precommitment"—a phenomenon they discuss in their analysis of consumer choice behavior. Their model assumes that the consumer's current preferences are in conflict with his or her future preferences because the costs and benefits that accrue do not occur simultaneously. When either benefits precede later costs (e.g., addictions) or costs precede benefits (e.g., paying for education), the consumer is in conflict. The conflict can be resolved by eliminating choice through precommitment. Thaler and Shefrin give the example of a mandatory pension plan that precludes the continual temptation to spend the allotted sum of money.

Thus we see that, as in the case of changing self-imposed delay to externally imposed delay, people can choose to eliminate choices in temptation situations. Of course, such a possibility is only a tenable alternative for an individual who is aware of the fact that his or her preferences change over time. The onset of such awareness has not been studied and, hence, we do not know how relevant "precommitment" strategies are in children's self-control.

Plans to resist temptation

Much current research with children and with clinical populations has been aimed at teaching subjects the strategies or "plans" to resist temptation. In one experiment (Mischel & Patterson, 1978), 4- and 5-year-olds were offered a reward if they could fill all the holes in a pegboard during the experimenter's absence, without allowing themselves to be distracted by an attractive, talking-clown box. Some of the children were then provided with a set of plans to help them resist distraction. Three different plans were used: a temptation-inhibiting plan (suppressing attention to the temptation: "I'm not going to look at Mr. Clown Box"), a task-facilitating plan (directing attention to the task: "I'm going to look at my work"), and a reward-oriented plan (directing attention to the rewarding consequences of completing the task: "I want to play with the fun toys and Mr. Clown Box later"). The temptation-inhibiting and reward-oriented plans enhanced the children's ability to resist distraction, while the task-facilitating plan did not. These findings support our model since both the temptation-inhibiting and reward-oriented plans may have altered the relative value of the two outcomes (resisting and not resisting) while the task-facilitationg plan would not influence these relative values.

With clinical populations of obese and alcoholic subjects, Cautela (1971) has used a technique that is similar to teaching plans. Using a technique called *covert conditioning,* the therapist provides the client with explicit images of negative and positive consequences that will occur if the client does or does not resist temptation (e.g., resisting overeating—staying slim; not resisting—vomiting). Since these procedures also incorporate statements about what the clients should say to themselves in those situations that require resis-

tance to temptation, they too are plans to resist temptation. Cautela's technique seems to be effective, suggesting that clinical populations, like children, do not generate their own plans to resist temptation. Armed with these plans, however, individuals can produce changes in outcome evaluation and consequently actual resistance.

A procedure that is analogous to the type of self-distraction we have discussed under delay of gratification is one called *thought stopping* (Cautela, 1971, Cautela & Wisocki, 1977). In this procedure, when individuals experience the desire to enact responses that yield immediate positive consequences and long-range negative ones (e.g., overeating), they are to say "stop" to themselves and prevent themselves from thinking about the desire to enact the response. This procedure seems to be effective in reducing both overeating and smoking (see also Chapter 10 by Woody and Costanzo).

Two additional procedures appear to be variations on the transformation from self-imposed to externally imposed delay. One such transformation is a physical one—for example, the locking cigarette case (Azrin & Powell, 1968). Underlying this strategy is the assumption that the individual may be willing to eliminate the temptation at a later point in time if he or she can choose to do so directly after indulging in the undesirable immediate response, when craving is temporarily quiescent. The cigarette case Azrin and Powell designed, therefore, locked for a 2-hour period after a cigarette was taken; thus it prevented the individual from obtaining a cigarette for that duration. A similar procedure applied to drinking would involve locking the liquor cabinet and mailing oneself the key. While both of these procedures seem reasonable from a theoretical viewpoint, a practical problem with them is that one can often find others who are willing to provide the desired rewards during the externally imposed delay.

A second kind of transformation from self-imposed to externally imposed delay involves making contracts with others (Mayer, 1973). In this procedure, the individual contracts to call someone each time he or she wants to enact the reward-attaining response (e.g., overeat). The contacted individual asks the contractee to specify a delay period that he or she would be willing to endure (e.g., 2 hours) and offers suggestions as to how the contractee might spend them (e.g., go to a movie, read a mystery story). If after this 2-hour period the individual still wants to enact the response, he or she is free to do so. In other words, this procedure is based on the notion that, if we can distract people during the time they most want to enact the response in question, we can alter the desirability of making that response. A second concept underlying this type of procedure is that if individuals have a choice they will enact the response whereas if they "contract out" they will be freed of this choice and, consequently, resistance to temptation will be easier to enforce.

Let us now summarize this section on resistance to temptation. We have seen that in resistance to temptation, as in delay of gratification, individuals are faced with temptation because the reward values of different outcomes change over time. Those strategies that aid one in coping with this temptation are strategies that alter the relative values of the alternatives that produce the temptation. Specifically, distractions from the temptation-producing outcomes increase resistance to temptation. As in the case of delay of gratification, various procedures can be employed in which the individual who knows he or she will be tempted later gives up the option of yielding to the temptation.

Pain tolerance

Physical pain is perhaps the most difficult experience with which we ever have to cope. Pain occurs in many forms. It may come in the form of some deprivation of the body, such as hunger or thirst. It may also result from injury or something more fleeting like dental work or surgery. Pain differs from the other stimuli we have been describing (e.g., working for a delayed reward) in that it is

inherently aversive. To completely eliminate the experience of pain is extremely difficult, and likely maladaptive, but the aversiveness of pain appears to be greatly modifiable. Despite the fact that pain is considerably different from the other types of stimuli or events we have discussed, coping with pain shows a number of common features with other forms of coping. An initial correspondence is that pain can be experienced under both self-imposed and externally imposed conditions. Sometimes we can terminate the pain at will (e.g., physical exercise); other times we cannot (e.g., physician-administered injections). A second correspondence is that it is possible to describe the task of coping with pain by employing the same language we used earlier. Specifically, coping with pain generally involves a person enduring something unpleasant before he or she can experience something pleasant. The pleasantness following pain may take a number of forms. In the case of physical deprivation, such as hunger and thirst, it may refer to the enjoyment one receives in satisfying his or her drives. In the case of surgery or dental work, it may be the relief from preoperational pain or the knowledge that future pain has been averted. In addition, the tolerance of pain may be motivated by self-esteem concerns. How often have we observed the pride and self-satisfaction of someone who has lost great amounts of weight or someone who has observed a painful athletic regimen? In fact, our society seems to highly value the tolerance of pain for its own sake with the consequence that the failure to endure pain, especially for males, is often perceived as a sign of weakness.

However, even if desired future consequences are often expected to follow the experience of pain, this will not in and of itself go very far in reducing the aversiveness of pain. What can an individual, child, or adult do then to mute the experience of pain? We have already discussed a number of processes that appear to be adpative in other contexts and that may also be relevant here.

Understandably, research on pain does not typically employ children as subjects. It is surprising, however, how similar the adult-pain research is to the child-based delay of gratification research. Distraction, for example, has been shown time and time again to increase pain tolerance (Weisenberg, 1977). Distraction can occur by simply instructing subjects to ignore the pain or by providing them with more specific instructions, such as to think pleasant thoughts (Chaves & Barber, 1977). In one study (Ayer, 1973), needle-phobic children receiving injections were asked to imagine they were playing with their dogs who started to bark louder and louder. The clinician kept up a flow of talk, urging the child to make the dogs bark louder and louder. This procedure seemed to be effective, and all the children allowed the injections to be administered. Furthermore, research data indicate that, in both clinical and experimental settings, adults in pain tend to generate their own cognitive-coping strategies (e.g., Berger & Kanfer, 1975; McCaffery, 1972; Pliner, 1973a). McCaffery, for instance, found that hospital patients naturally employ self-distraction when they experience pain. In particular, McCaffery reports that many people talk to themselves, solve mathematical puzzles, hum, or count ceiling tiles. There is also evidence to suggest that many adults (McCaffery, 1972), obese people (Pliner, 1973a), and children (Eland & Anderson, 1977) who do not generate their own cognitive distractors for pain can do so when these are provided by others. McCaffery (1969) suggests that pain leads to a narrowing of one's attention to the pain-related cues and recommends that nursing personnel should make patients aware of self-distraction techniques in coping with pain. Supporting this suggestion are studies (e.g., Kanfer & Goldfoot, 1966) that have found that *focusing* on the pain experience by describing it reduces pain tolerance significantly.

Another cognitive strategy that appears to facilitate coping with pain involves attempts to reinterpret the painful stimulus (Lazarus, 1976). In the same way that reinterpreting delayed rewards in nonconsummatory terms (e.g., marshmallows as puffy white clouds) facilitates delay tolerance (Mischel & Baker, 1975), it appears that reinterpreting painful stimuli as something more benign facilitates pain tolerance. In one study, for instance, it was found that instructing children who were having their teeth cleaned to think of the experience as a "tickle" and laugh when it began greatly facilitated coping (Neiberger, 1978). This procedure was found to be particularly effective with 6- to 8-year-olds. In a similar vein, Blitz and Dinnerstein (1971) found that individuals were better able to tolerate their hand being in cold water if they were instructed to interpret the pain as being pleasant.

In addition to attempting to minimize the perception of pain, the strategy of enhancing the perceived value of pain endurance is also effective. Offering subjects points for doing well (Kanfer, Cox, Greiner, & Karoly, 1974) and instructing subjects to generate images that produce feelings of self-assertion and pride (Horan & Dillinger, 1974) have been found to significantly increase tolerance of cold pressor stimulation. Wolff and Horland (1967) have reported that subjects who were asked to imagine that they would receive $1000 if they would delay shouting "Stop," while receiving electrical pain stimulation, increased their pain tolerance compared with a group not so instructed. It appears, then, that the tolerance of pain is affected by many of the same strategies—distraction, transformation, outcome reevaluation—that operate in delay of gratification and resistance to temptation situations.

Summary

The phenomenon of self-control is multifaceted. It includes delaying the gratification of impulses till a later time, resisting actions or outcomes that may ultimately be harmful and enduring physical pain. The research and theory on these various aspects of self-control have generally proceeded independently of another, though there are many similarities in the variables and processes focused on in the different areas. Cognitive strategies, such as distraction, transformation, and self-verbalization, are examples of factors found to influence all of the various types of self-control phenomena.

Our own research has focused on delay of gratification behavior in children. We have found that situational factors—such as the salience of the delayed reward during the delay, the opportunity to terminate the delay, and the discrepancy in attractiveness between the delayed and immediate rewards—are all important determinants of delay frustration. There were also other factors we found to be important: the self-statements the child makes during the delay, the degree of distraction the child engages in, and the way in which the child perceives the situation and the relevant rewards. These various factors interact with one another in complex ways, but all appear to influence delay behavior by influencing the evaluation of the delayed rewards. The slower the devaluation of the delayed reward, the greater the delay tolerance.

Overall, our research, as well as the related data, suggests that self-control processes depend on how one evaluates the outcomes of action. These outcomes do not have a constant value but rather change with time. Self-control appears to depend on one's ability to cognitively manipulate the values of these outcomes in such a manner as to make them either less desirable (e.g., resistance to temptation) or more desirable (e.g., delay of gratification and pain endurance). Socialization must teach us not only that this type of self-control is desirable, but also what specific skills facilitate self-control processes.

In our research, we have attempted to understand and to clarify the processes by which younger children acquire these cognitive-coping skills. Many, but not all, of the factors affecting children appear to similarly affect the self-control behavior of adults. Our understanding of self-control behavior has already benefited greatly from pursuing a developmental perspective, both empirically and theoretically, and we will likely reap future benefits by maintaining this perspective.

Note

1. Notice that an explanation based on dissonance theory would also lead to the prediction that the two rewards will diverge in value, since such a divergence would be an effective means of self-persuading about the value of the delay. In this context, however, such self-persuasion would paradoxically be maladaptive to maintaining delay, because it would make the frustration level be reached sooner. Of course, it is still possible that dissonance will be reduced in other ways (e.g., enhancing the value of waiting, minimizing the aversiveness of the delay).

3

CHILDREN'S ATTRIBUTIONS FOR SUCCESS AND FAILURE

IRENE HANSON FRIEZE

LEARNING RESEARCH AND DEVELOPMENT CENTER
UNIVERSITY OF PITTSBURGH

Social and developmental psychologists have developed a number of theoretical frameworks to help them understand and predict the achievement behaviors of children. In the 1950s and 1960s a good deal of attention was devoted to discovering the antecedents of adult achievement motivation. Child-rearing strategies that stressed positive rewards for achievement and early independence and achievement training were found to produce children with higher achievement motivation levels (e.g., Crandall, 1963; Crandall, 1967; Feshbach, 1967; Winterbottom, 1958). However, there were problems with this research (Ruble, 1978). Results were often inconsistent from one study to another, with adults and as well as children, and the theory was not as strongly supported by data as researchers would have liked (Weiner, 1972).

In more recent years, social psychologists have attempted to understand achievement behavior through analyzing the cognitions individuals have about why success or failure occurs. This research has identified the types of causal attributions people make to explain academic successes and failures and how these attributions mediate changes in expectations for future success and affective reactions to successes or failures. More recent research with adults has suggested that this attribution model for achievement events is useful for understanding a variety of other life situations as well. Several of these applications are discussed in Frieze, Bar-Tal, and Carroll (1979).

Although much of the work to develop the attribution model for success and failure events was initially done with college students, increasing attention has been given to children's attributions for success and failure. It appears that quite young children are able to form meaningful causal attributions and that these attributions function in much the same ways as they do in adults. This chapter will review some of the basic principles of the attribution model for explaining achievement behavior. Then, we will turn to the question of how this model applies to children of various ages. Some possible

The author would like to thank Daniel Bar-Tal, Theodore A. Chandler, Saul Kassin, and Kathy Shomo for comments on an earlier version of this chapter. Much of the support for studies described here was provided by an institutional grant from the National Institute of Education to the Learning Research and Development Center, University of Pittsburgh.

directions for expanding the achievement attribution model for children will also be discussed in this chapter.

The attribution process for achievement events

In 1971, Weiner, Frieze, Kukla, Reed, Rest, and Rosenbaum proposed an attributional theory of motivation. This model proposed a framework for looking at one's affective and cognitive reactions to a success or failure on an achievement task as a function of the causal attributions that were used to explain why a particular outcome had occurred. For example, if the person attributed his or her failure to lack of effort, he or she would feel some shame about doing poorly, but would also be motivated to try harder in the future. If a young girl attributed her good performance on an arithmetic task to good luck, she would lack the pride of someone else who felt that they had succeeded because of high ability or trying hard. She would also have low expectancies for her performance on future tests of this type since people do not expect luck to continue. Other causal attributions were hypothesized to relate in systematic ways to these and other affective reactions and expectancies for the future. Affect and future expectancies were seen as important determinants of future achievement behavior.

The Weiner attribution model, then, conceptualizes the achievement process as a multistage process involving an achievement event that is first interpreted as a success or failure and then given an attribution or a causal explanation for why this success or failure occurred. This causal attribution has subsequent consequences for affect and for future expectancies which together determine future achievement orientation and behavior in a new situation. This model is diagrammed in Figure 3.1.

Causal attributions

Some of the central variables in the attribution process model are the causal attributions themselves. Attribution theorists assume that people are constantly forming causal explanations for why various events occur in their lives (Frieze & Bar-Tal, 1979; Weiner, 1979). Weiner (1979) suggests that these "why" questions are asked most for unpleasant events and for unexpected events. Attributions may be commonly made for other situations but they may be below a level of immediate awareness.

Following an achievement event, such as a test or examination, any of a number of causal explanations might be used to account for the exam's outcome. Success on the exam might be attributed to the person's ability in that subject, his or her trying hard, the exam's being easy, or good luck. Similarly, if the person failed, it might be attributed to lack of ability, lack of effort, the difficulty of the exam, or bad luck. An outcome might also be attributed to a variety of other factors including stable effort (a consistent pattern of diligence or laziness), other people (such as the teacher or other students who may aid or interfere with performance on a task), mood, fatigue or sickness, having a good or bad personality, and physical appearance (Elig & Frieze, 1975; Frieze, 1976a; Weiner, 1974).

The original Weiner et al. (1971) paper outlined ability, effort, luck, and task ease or difficulty as the four casual explanations most used in achievement situations. A good deal of evidence suggests that this list is too simplified. There are two strategies for deciding what set of attributions is being used in any given situation, and both of these have found subjects using more than these four causes. One strategy is to simply ask people why a particular success or failure occurred and then to code their unstructured responses into meaningful categories. Another is to give subjects a list of causes and to see which of them are used in systematic ways. Both techniques have been used.

In one of the first studies on this topic, Frieze (1976a) asked college students why someone might do well or poorly on a hypothetical exam. She found that effort, ability, the difficulty of the exam, and the

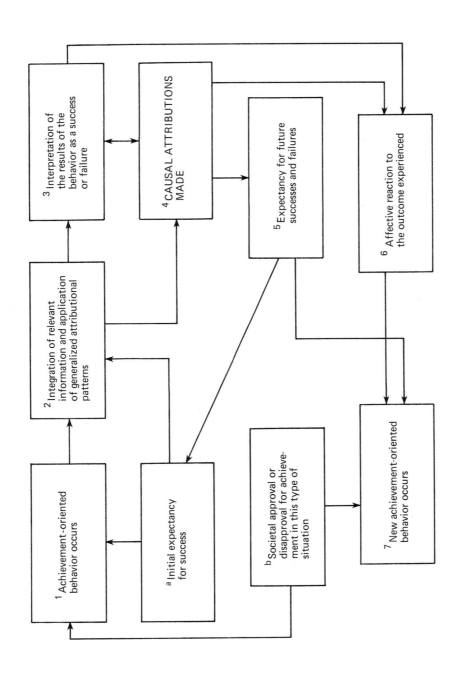

3 Interpretation of the results of the behavior as a success or failure

4 CAUSAL ATTRIBUTIONS MADE

5 Expectancy for future successes and failures

6 Affective reaction to the outcome experienced

2 Integration of relevant information and application of generalized attributional patterns

1 Achievement-oriented behavior occurs

a Initial expectancy for success

b Societal approval or disapproval for achievement in this type of situation

7 New achievement-oriented behavior occurs

teaching skill of the teacher were the most frequently cited causes. Luck, which was one of the four original causes, was only cited on one or two occasions. Mood was also occasionally mentioned as a cause of failure. Other studies report similar findings, although the labels used may vary (e.g., Bar-Tal, 1979b; Bar-Tal & Darom, 1979; Cooper & Burger, 1978; Frieze & Snyder, 1980). For example, Bar-Tal and Darom (1979) divide the category of "effort" into effort during the test and preparation at home before the test. Frieze (1976a) classified interest as part of the general category of "effort," but this is typically separated into its own category in more current research (e.g., Bar-Tal & Darom, 1979; Elig & Frieze, 1975; Frieze & Snyder, 1980). The general category of "ability" is also being broken down. Cooper and Burger (1978) separate "ability" into academic ability, physical and emotional ability, and previous experience. They also include ability-like factors such as habits, attitudes, and maturity. Frieze and Snyder (1980) include a category called ability x task interaction in their analysis of the attributions used by primary school children. This category is used for situations in which a child states that a particular subject area is hard for the person (i.e., she did well on the math test because math is easy for her). Such a statement seems to be a combination of a statement about the ability of the person and the difficulty of the task.

These differences in the labeling of similar causes present one of the difficulties with using free-response questions. Since the data are unstructured, they must be coded into a workable system of categories. Definitions of the categories vary among the different systems and across coders using any particular system. Furthermore, since the data are categorical rather than scaled, they present problems for complex statistical analysis. On the positive side, these free-response studies do appear to give us the best indications of the set of causes people actually do use in deciding why a particular success or failure occurred.

Studies have also been done in which the experimenter provides a list of causes that the subject is asked to rate for their applicability. These ratings can be done in a number of ways. Subjects can be asked to rate each cause independently. For example,

How much was each of these a factor in your success:

	Not a factor			Very much a factor	
Your ability	1	2	3	4	5
Your effort	1	2	3	4	5
Good luck	1	2	3	4	5
(and so on)					

Or, subjects may be asked to assign a percentage score to each of the causes listed, so that the total percentage adds up to 100%. Other methods have also been suggested, but these are the most commonly used. In a review and analysis of these structured methods of determining attributions for success and failure, Elig and Frieze (1979) showed that the independent scales had the greatest validity and reliability. The results generated from this or any of the other structured methods were not directly comparable to those given in an unstructured open-ended format, however; the two types of methods generate different rank orders of the most important causes as well as different overall frequencies. For example, luck is rarely cited in open-ended data as a cause of an academic success or failure, but it is systematically used by subjects when it is presented in a structured format. Effort is more used in open-ended data than it is in the structured systems (see Elig & Frieze, 1979, or Frieze & Snyder, 1980).

These findings raise questions about method variance in attribution research. Although this issue has not been adequately resolved, given the knowledge presently available, Elig and Frieze (1979) suggested that the format used for measuring attributions should depend on the goals of the study. If the researcher wishes to determine the set of relevant causes for a particular situation or sample, he or she should use an open-ended format to generate this list of causes. Other research has clearly shown that attributions vary greatly across situations (e.g., Frieze & Snyder, 1980) and across cultural groups (e.g., Barrett & Nicholls, 1978; Raviv, Bar-Tal, Raviv, & Bar-Tal, in press). Use of an open-ended format allows subjects to tell the researcher what they feel is relevant for the situation and that group of people without being cued by the causes listed on an experimental questionnaire. If the researcher wishes to see how attributions vary in different conditions or how they mediate other responses, it will be necessary for him or her to use a structured format. The list of attributions should be based on a list previously generated by an open-ended technique. When the structured scales are made up, independent scales are preferable to percentage measures.

One other source of variance generated by differences in the measurement of attributions is the exact wording of the attribution. Some studies rely on wording as in the example outlined a few paragraphs ago. Others do something like the following:

How high is your ability in this subject?
How much did you study before the exam?
How lucky were you?
(and so on)

These questions conceptually are quite different, although they have been used interchangably in attribution research. Research is needed to determine the effects of variations in the wording of attributions.

Causal dimensions

Many of the interesting predictions derived from attribution theory are related not to the specific causal categories themselves but to the underlying dimensions of the various causal categories. Causal categories can be analyzed in various ways (see Weiner, 1979). We have found that the most useful categorization system is based on three dimensions: *internality, stability,* and *intentionality.* Each of these dimensions is assumed to be independent, as shown in Table 3.1. Further-

more, although often conceptualized as dichotomies, each is more accurately described as a continuum. For example, the first dimension, internality, has to do with whether the cause of an event is associated with the primary actor in the situation, and is thus internal, or whether the cause is external to this person. Thus a person may succeed on an exam because of the *internal* causes of ability, trying hard, feeling good, or background. He or she may also succeed because of *external* factors: easy test, someone else's help, or a good teacher. These would represent the internal-external extremes. Other causes, such as doing well on an exam because of studying together with another student or getting a high grade on a group project because everyone tried hard would be intermediate between internal and external causes. These are labeled joint causes. Thus, when coding free-response data, it is often most useful to use a three-point scale rather than a dichotomy for internality and for other dimensions (Elig & Frieze, 1975).

Related to the internality dimension, and sometimes confused with it, is the third dimension of intentionality.[1] If the actor has control over the internal cause, it is intentional (see Elig & Frieze, 1975; Rosenbaum, 1972). Thus, effort is internal and intentional while ability and mood are unintentional, although still internal. External causes or joint causes are also intentional if the actors or persons responsible for the outcome had control over their behaviors and/or intended the effects that occurred. This distinction is important in determining our reactions to the actor. A teacher who is seen as purposively writing a very difficult test that causes nearly everyone to fail generates more anger and hostility than a teacher who prepares a test that turns out to be too difficult but which was not intended to be that hard (Baron, 1977). As we will see, emotional reactions are greater for intentional causes, regardless of whether they are internal, external, or jointly caused.

Like internality, intentionality can also be considered as a continuum or a three-point

Table 3.1. A Three-Dimensional Model for Classifying Causal Attributions for the Achievement Successes and Failures of a Student

	Stable	Unstable
	Internal	
Intentional	Stable effort of student (diligence or laziness)	Unstable effort of student (trying or not trying hard)
Mediate	Long-term interests of student Intrinsic motivation	Short-term interests of student
Unintentional	Ability of student Knowledge or background of student Personality of student	Fatigue of student Mood of student

	Stable	Unstable
	Joint	
Intentional	Peer-group pressure	Group effort
Mediate	Teacher and student don't get along	Teacher and student weren't getting along that day
Unintentional	Specific subject matter easy or hard for student	General subject matter easy or hard for student

	Stable	Unstable
	External	
Intentional	Others always help or interfere	Others help or interfere with this event
Unintentional	Task difficulty or ease Personality of others	Task difficulty or ease (task changes) Luck or unique circumstances Others accidentally help or interfere

scale. Elig and Frieze (1975) discuss several factors that cannot be readily classified as intentional or unintentional. Having an interest in a particular subject area is often cited as a cause of success. Being motivated to do well in school is a similar type of cause. Both of these are considered to be mediate causes. They are not under the direct control of the person, but they do function as mediators of effort. Psychologically, they seem to lie between intentional and unintentional causes.

Another dimension that is extremely important for classifying causal attributions is stability. Ability, background, and unchanging environmental factors are stable and change relatively little over time. Effort and mood are unstable; they are highly changeable. Stability involves a relatively unchanging cause during the time period and across

the situations one wishes to generalize to. Although the difficulty of the achievement task has typically been classified as stable, one would have to consider whether the *same* task would be repeated. If a future task would be similar but not the same, the task could not be seen as stable. Only in the former case is the task truly stable (Valle & Frieze, 1976; Weiner, Russell, & Lerman, 1978). If the situation is taking an exam in a class, the test difficulty would generally be considered unstable, since the next exam could well be harder or easier. One exception to this would occur if a particular teacher had a reputation for always giving easy or difficult exams. In this situation, exam difficulty would be a stable causal factor as long as the same teacher was involved. As well as stability over time, one must also consider if the attribution is stable over relevant situations (Elig & Frieze, 1975). If a boy gets a poor grade on a social studies test and attributes this to his low ability in this subject area, this low ability attribution would not be stable if he were considering how well he might do on his next arithmetic test. However, it would be stable if he wanted to generalize to another social studies class. Thus, stability must always be considered within the context one wishes to study.

A similar distinction has been proposed by Abramson, Seligman, and Teasdale (1978). They limit the concept of stability to stability for the same situation over time and use the concept of *globality* to define the generaliz-ability of the cause over other related situations. Abramson et al. suggest that attributing a negative situation to both stable and global causes leads to depression and feelings of helplessness. Stable causes pro-duce helpless feelings in regard to the particular situation. A negative outcome may not generalize to other situations if it is situational rather than global, and so there is less depression when the attribution is to a situational cause.

These dimensional analyses are based on a logical analysis of causes. Researchers have assumed that people believe that they can control their efforts, but that they have little control over their natural ability level or over their moods. Everyone may not share these assumptions. Chandler (1979) suggests that some people may see ability as unstable, especially the skill component of ability. Bar-Tal and Greenberg (1973) also found that college students saw ability as less stable than attribution researchers have defined it to be. Presumably, if one knew the assump-tions that were being made by subjects about the underlying dimensions of the causes they were using, the causal categories could be individually assigned in accordance with these assumptions. However, it is very diffi-cult to ask subjects of any age to assign causes along the three dimensions we have dis-cussed. Typically, the concepts are too com-plex for the typical subject to understand without extensive training. For this reason,

the causal categories used in any particular study are classified on the basis of the coder's understanding of the context in which they are used and on the logical definitions of the dimensions (see Elig & Frieze, 1975, for a discussion of how this is done).

Some empirical work has been done to justify these dimensions and the placement of the specific causal categories along them. Empirical studies based on a multidimen-sional scaling of a large number of causes have shown both an internality and an intentionality dimension (Passer, 1977; Weiner, 1979). Other studies using a factor analysis of the ratings, given the various categories of attribution, have also supported this dimensional analysis. For example, Bar-Tal and Darom (1979) found a stability dimension and an internality dimension.

Expectancies

The theoretical achievement attribution model makes certain predictions about the consequences of causal attribution for future expectancy. It has been proposed and sup-ported by several studies that changes in expectancy are related to the stability of the causal attribution made to explain the out-come (e.g., Fontaine, 1974; McMahan, 1973; Valle & Frieze, 1976; Weiner, Nieren-berg & Goldstein, 1976). Attributions to relatively stable causes, such as ability or the difficulty of an on-going task, produce ex-pectancies that outcomes will continue to be the same, while more unstable attributions (luck, effort, mood) produce expectancy shifts away from the outcome. For example, a student attributing failure on an exam to lack of ability (relatively stable) should continue to expect to do poorly on the next test, whereas if the failure were attributed to lack of effort in studying (unstable), the person may expect to get a good grade next time by trying harder. Unstable causes, by definition, suggest that there is more possi-bility for change in the future, while stable causes imply that the future will resemble the past. This stability effect is especially true for global attributions.

Expectancies are related in another way to the stability of the causal explanation. Along with the effect of the causal attribution on the expectancy for the future (the post-test expectancy discussed earlier), the initial or pre-test expectancy in turn helps to determine the causal attribution made. Outcomes that are consistent with the initial expectation are more attributed to stable causes. Unexpected outcomes are attributed more to unstable causes (Feather & Simon 1971a, 1971b; Valle & Frieze, 1976). Unexpectedly high or low outcomes are often attributed to luck. Expected outcomes (which tend to be consistent with what the person had experienced in the past) are typically attributed to ability (Frieze & Weiner, 1971).

Taken together, these two relationships imply that once an expectancy for success has been developed for a particular task, this expectancy is difficult to change. An expected outcome is attributed to stable factors (Simon & Feather, 1973; Valle & Frieze, 1976) which, in turn, lead to the expectancy for future outcomes to continue at the same level. If the outcome is unexpectedly high or low, an attribution will be made to unstable factors. Since unstable causes lead to the belief that this particular outcome was unusual and will not continue, there is little change in the future expectation from the initial pre-test expectancy (Valle & Frieze, 1976). This leads to a self-fulfilling prophecy whereby those who expect to do well will continue to have high expectations and those who have low expectations will maintain them regardless of how they actually perform. This effect seems to occur both for the individual and for someone else making attributions about the individual (such as a teacher having expectations for a particular student). Although this self-fulfilling prophecy model appears to have a number of important applications (see Chapter 12 by Gibbons), these have not been directly tested (Bar-Tal, 1977, 1979a, 1979b). Most tests of this model are laboratory studies with college students. We are not sure how this model works in actual settings. One major question is how long this effect lasts. Presumably, students who continually do poorly cannot keep attributing their low performance to unstable factors. At some point they would have to conclude that they had low ability or that some other stable factor was working. However, we still do not understand when, or how, this transition would take place. There may also be developmental differences in the effects of attributions on expectancies.

Affective reactions

Along with the formation of expectations for the future, the attribution model also predicts certain affective or emotional reactions to success or failure that are mediated by the type of causal attribution made for the outcome. It is common sensical and empirically documented that people feel good or happy when succeeding and bad or unhappy when failing, regardless of the causal attribution made (e.g., Nicholls, 1975; Ruble, Parsons, & Ross, 1976). Beyond this overall main effect, there is a general tendency for outcomes attributed to internal factors to produce stronger affective reactions than those attributed to external factors (e.g., Riemer, 1975; Weiner, 1974). Thus, successes attributed to ability or effort produce more pride than those attributerd to luck, the teacher, or the ease of the task. Similarly, failures attributed to internal factors produce more shame. Effort attributions (which are internal and intentional) tend to produce especially high rewards (Covington & Omelich, 1979; Nicholls, 1976; Weiner, Heckhausen, Meyer, & Cook, 1972; Weiner et al., 1978). Effort is also most strongly associated with self-reward (Weiner et al., 1972).

More recent research has further clarified the relationship between affective reactions and causal attributions. As implied by the earlier findings, not only internality, but intentionality as well, seems to be related to stronger affective reactions in general. External causes that are seen as intentional may also generate stronger feelings than those attributed to the external factors that are seen as unintentional. Angry and hostile reactions are mediated by the perceived intentionality of the person causing a negative outcome. Intentionality may, in fact, be a stronger predictor of affective reactions than internality, but this hypothesis has not received adequate empirical testing.

Weiner et al. (1978) have conducted a number of studies to show the specific affective reactions that are associated with various causal attributions. Happiness and pride are seen as common affective reactions to any type of success (although there is much less pride if the outcome is believed to be caused by other people or by luck). Attributing an event to one's abilities leads to feelings of competence and confidence, while attributions to effort produce feelings of relief and satisfaction. Feelings of gratefulness are especially strong when a good event is attributed to other people. Luck produces feelings of surprise, relief, and guilt. Attributions for failure were also associated with specific emotional reactions, along with the overriding negative feelings generated by the failure. Lack of ability attributions lead to feelings of incompetence and resignation; lack of effort is associated with guilt; bad luck again leads to surprise.

Summarizing these findings, Weiner (1979) suggests that there are three sources of affect that result from success or failure. First, there is the basic good or bad feeling depending on whether the outcome was positive or negative. Weiner further suggests that these basic emotions are the strongest ones and that they are directly related to the outcome experienced rather than mediated by the causal attribution made. Second, there are the specific reactions discussed earlier that are associated with the causal attribution. Finally, there is the mediation of the internality dimension on feelings associated with self-esteem. Thus, feelings of competence and pride or shame are greater when an internal attribution is made.

As mentioned earlier, the stability dimen-

sion also affects emotional reactions. Failures attributed to stable, global causes lead to depression and helpless resignation (Abramson et al., 1978). Arkin and Maruyama (1979) have also shown that attributing success to unstable causes leads to more anxiety and that attributing failure to stable causes leads to more fear, especially for less successful students.

Forming causal attributions

Research with college students has indicated that certain types of information are commonly and consistently used in forming causal attributions for success or failure. As mentioned earlier in reference to stability judgments, the initial expectancy for success is an important determinant of whether a stable or an unstable attribution is made. Outcomes consistent with what is expected are more attributed to stable causes. Another important determinant of the type of attribution that will be made is the outcome itself. Successful outcomes are more attributed to internal factors than failing outcomes (e.g., Arkin & Maruyama, 1979; Frieze & Weiner, 1971; Gilmore & Reid, 1979; Luginbuhl, Crowe, & Kahan, 1975; Miller, 1976). However, this effect is a relative one. Although people are more internal for success than failure, they are still internal to some degree for failure, especially for classroom activities. It is common to blame one's failure on an exam to lack of effort or lack of ability as well as task difficulty or bad luck (Frieze & Weiner, 1971; Luginbuhl et al., 1975; Miller & Ross, 1975).

In addition to outcome, people use a variety of other types of information to assess success or failure: the past history of the person, how well other people have done on the same task, the incentive the person had to do well, how the person was feeling during his or her performance, information about cheating by the person or others, and information about the teacher if the situation involves classroom performance (Frieze, 1976a, 1976b, 1980).

Defining the outcome as a success or failure

Box 3 in the model of the attribution process presented in Figure 3.1 deals with defining the outcome resulting from the achievement behavior of Box 1 as a success or failure. Until recently, it was implicitly assumed that this was a straightforward process that pre-ceeded the formation of the attribution (e.g., see Frieze, Fisher, Hanusa, McHugh, & Valle, 1978, for an example of previous conceptions of the achievement attribution process). In much attribution research, sub-jects are told how well they have done on a task and are then asked to state why they performed at this level. Typically, subjects have been told whether they should consider their performance a success or failure either by direct labeling (e.g., Riemer, 1975) or on the basis of (false) college student norms (e.g., Bar-Tal & Frieze, 1976). Even when such a procedure is used, however, subjects do not always accept the experimenter's evaluation (Elig & Frieze, 1979).

One of the difficulties with this type of approach is that defining an event as a success or failure appears to be a highly complex process and different people appear to use various criteria in making such a judgment. On an intuitive level, we all know that a "B+" grade on an exam might be responded to with joy and a clear feeling of success by one student while another will be quite disappointed and will feel that he or she has failed. Empirically, we now know that even when students are assigned to a "success" group and given feedback that indicates that their performance level is quite high in comparison to other students, some will accept this information while others will reject it and still feel that they have failed. Similarly in considering failure, when students are told that they did much worse than other students, some of them accept this as a failure for themselves while others still rate themselves as successful (e.g., Elig & Frieze, 1979). Thus, defining a performance as successful seems to involve as complex a process as that of determining why a particular success or failure occurred.

EMPIRICAL STUDIES OF SUBJECTIVE SUCCESS. In one of the few studies that have been done to investigate subjective success evaluations and their relationship to causal attributions, Frieze, Snyder, and Fontaine (1978) asked fifth graders to evaluate their performances on either a social studies or a mathematics exam. These ratings were compared to their actual scores. Other attributional measures were also taken before and after the exam. When correlations were done between the students' actual scores and their subjective ratings of how successful they were, the correlation between the two was .74. Al-though this is clearly significant, it also suggests that these subjective evaluations are influenced by a variety of other factors in addition to actual outcome.

In order to explore the relationship be-tween subjective and objective success more fully, a series of stepwise multiple regres-sions was done. Looking first at the variables impinging on subjects before they are told their exam scores, it was found that variables predicting subjective outcome and objective outcome (actual score) were quite different. Students who *actually* performed well were seen as trying hard by their teachers and themselves. Teachers also saw them as having high ability. This may indicate that teachers believe school success is dependent on both ability and effort. Students who *felt* they had done well (independent of their actual score) were seen by the teacher as trying hard. They felt that doing well was important for them and for their teacher and they felt that they were relatively bright. Aside from suggesting that subjective eval-uations of outcomes are indeed different psychologically from the actual performance levels, these data also demonstrate the importance of subjects' perceptions of others' expectations for them.

The correlates of the subjective success evaluations were further explored by using a stepwise multiple regression analysis that placed no prior restraints on the variables that might enter the regression equation. The most important predictors of the subjec-tive evaluations were the students' happiness

Table 3.2. Comparison of "Success" Ratings for Different Types of Success

	Mean (1–9 scale)[a]	Standard Deviation	Assumed Score[b]
High Success			
Doing better than everyone	8.5	1.1	93.7
Doing better than you've ever done	8.3	1.0	93.1
Doing better than everyone else thought you would	8.0	1.1	91.2
Doing better than you thought you would	8.0	1.1	91.0
Feeling you did a really good job	8.0	1.2	90.0
Moderate Success			
Did well in spite of being sick	7.6	1.4	85.6
Knowing everyone felt you did well	7.6	1.5	89.9
Better than most students	7.3	1.0	88.3
As well as you've ever done	7.2	1.5	88.6
Better than average student	6.0	1.7	83.2

[a]The lowest on the scale was 1: Not at all successful; the highest on the scale was 9: Extremely successful.
[b]Objective success levels assumed as a result of each type of success.

with their scores and their actual performance levels on the test. A similar analysis was done for the actual (objective) performance level. This analysis indicated that the best predictors of actual performance were the subjective performance evaluation, the teacher rating of the student's ability, and the students' ratings of happiness with their scores.

The above results suggest that subjective success relates more directly to affective reactions than objective success. They also indicate that for fifth graders the two types of success are related. In a similar study, college students showed a tendency for actual scores to be related to a pattern of general confidence while subjective success was more related to a kind of affective reaction and a feeling of having done well on a difficult task (Frieze, Snyder, & Fontaine, 1977).

Other researchers have suggested that a number of variables may be related to more positive affect about one's performance and, therefore, presumably to greater feelings of subjective success. House and Perney (1974) found that doing better than expected led to more positive affect in an achievement setting for college students. Crandall (1978b) suggested that the degree of improvement over one's minimal standards for performance is a major determinant of positive affect (also see Crandall, Katkovsky, & Preston, 1960). Other important factors may include how well other students do and doing better than one has in the past (e.g., Bar-Tal, Guttmann, Kvartz, & Naor, 1980; Festinger, 1954).

A recent study with college students showed that they saw all of these factors as important for subjective feelings of success (see Table 3.2). Doing better than everyone else in the class leads to the greatest feelings of success, while doing better than one had ever done in the past was the next highest in subjective success ratings. After this came success in terms of exceeding others' or one's own expectations. There was little deviation in the ratings, indicating that there was high agreement on the ordering and

Table 3.3. Comparison of "Success" Ratings for Attributionally Defined Success

	Success Ratings		
	Mean[a]	Standard Deviation	Assumed Score[b]
Tried your hardest	7.5	1.2	85.6
Good instructor	7.3	1.7	91.5
Easy test	6.5	1.9	91.7
Lucky	5.7	2.1	87.0
Cheating	3.4	2.6	83.5

[a,b]As in Table 3.2.

importance of these factors in determining subjective success.

As shown in Figure 3.1, it also appears that there is an interaction between the subjective success perceptions and the causal attribution. As mentioned earlier, much attribution research assumes a situation of success or failure and then asks for causal attributions. In more naturalistic situations, researchers have noted that the feelings of success may be dependent on the attribution for the performance. Several researchers have suggested that feeling a sense of control over the outcome is essential if one is even to apply the label of success or failure (e.g., Bialer, 1961; Maehr, 1974). As we have seen, attribution theorists have also noted that maximal feelings of pride in success and shame for failure are associated with outcomes attributed to ability and effort. Maehr and Nicholls (in press) have taken these ideas even further and have suggested that "Outcomes are most clearly experienced as success or failure when attributed to effort and ability and are less clearly perceived as success or failure when attributed to luck or difficulty" (p. 9). They go on to state that this association between internal attributions and perceptions of success and failure may not be culturally invariate but may depend instead on the specific value system of the culture.

We live in a culture that values effort (Weiner, 1972) and ability (Covington & Omelich, 1979; Nicholls, 1976). When these qualities are associated with an outcome, the outcome is considered successful in our culture. If we valued family loyalty, outcomes demonstrating this quality would be seen as the successful outcomes. Maehr and Nicholls (in press) go on to show that there are indeed different causal attributions associated with the concept of success in different cultures. Of course, this implies that for some people in our culture it may not be solely effort and ability that are associated with success. Instead, outcomes attributed to group efforts may be seen as more successful.

Some of these ideas were tested in the same study discussed earlier (p. 61); in this part, subjects were asked to rate how successful they would feel if success was associated with one of various attributions. They saw themselves as most successful if success were due to effort. Other success ratings, in order, were for success that resulted from having a good instructor, having an easy exam, being lucky, and cheating. Unfortunately, there was no ability condition. Only in the situation where success resulted from cheating did the rating fall below the midpoint on a success/failure scale. Success due to luck was seen as slightly more successful than the midpoint of the scale, as shown in Table 3.3. The objective success levels assumed for success as a result of each of these attributions followed a somewhat different order, with success due to an easy exam being seen as most objectively successful, followed by having a good instructor, and then luck. The variances were especially high for success due to being lucky or cheating, suggesting wide disagreement on how students viewed success due to these causes.

These data also indicate that success can be experienced even when the outcome is attributed to external factors, contrary to the theoretical writings of Maehr (1974) and others. However, there is somewhat less perceived success when attribution is external. Other work suggests that "success" is an additive function of the objective success score and the perceived internality of the cause for the outcome (Frieze, Shomo, & Francis, 1979). We are now further investigating the determinants of subjective success evaluations for adults and for children.

SUCCESS VALUES. Another variable used in deciding how successful one is is the value one attaches to doing well within a particular domain (see Frieze, Shomo, & Francis, 1979, for more discussion of this issue). One example of this is that failure in a task defined as appropriate for one's sex to do well in creates more negative affect than failure in an area typically associated with the other sex (Kipnis & Kidder, 1978). Parsons and Goff (1978) discuss how the incentive value for successful performance may vary as a function of one's motives. In general, women are seen as having more social motives and goals whereas men are perceived as being more motivated by competition (Parsons & Goff, 1978). Astin (1978) cites evidence for this distinction in a study of career aspirations of college students. Women choose jobs that relate to their basic interests and give them an opportunity to contribute to society, to work with ideas and people, to be helpful to others, and to express their identity. Men, on the other hand, want jobs with an opportunity for high salaries, high prestige, rapid advancement, and a stable future. This means that men and women probably define job success very differently. Other research shows that college women are most likely to define general success in terms of personal life satisfaction (being happy) and interpersonal relationships (Jenkins, 1979). Achieve-ment-motivated men would attach more importance to career success and to acquiring money and status (e.g., Atkinson, 1964).

Success values in children have not yet been studied systematically. Research is needed to more fully comprehend how boys and girls view success in various subject areas and to learn when the sex differences found in college students begin to occur in younger people. There may well be race differences in success values as well as class and other ethnic differences. All these differences may be an important key in helping us to better understand differences in the achievement patterns of various types of students.

Factors influencing the attribution process

As we have seen, the attribution process for achievement events has been well defined theoretically. Empirical support for the theory is good. As with any theory, however, the data are not always as supportive of the theory as one would ideally like it to be. One reason for this may be that in any situation, there are many variables that impinge on the attribution process, affecting the types of attributions made as well as the ways in which information is perceived and processed. There may also be differences in the ways in which an outcome is evaluated as a success or failure. In addition to these general influences, we also suspect that children do not always form attributions in the same way as adults do, and the attribution process may function somewhat differently depending on the age of the child. Along with the age of the perceiver, there are three other major types of variables that affect the attribution process. There are (1) demographic factors such as the sex, race, class, and level of achievement motivation of the person; (2) other people, both as a source of information and as a source of influence on the attributions made by others; and (3) variables relating to the specific task about which the attributions are made. Each of these factors will be briefly reviewed in the following pages.

The attribution process for children

Originally, achievement attribution research was concerned with the causal attributions of college students performing some laboratory task defined by the experimenter as relevant for their achievement concerns (see Weiner et al., 1971). Many of the tasks they were asked to do involved describing a hypothetical achievement situation and asking subjects to imagine how they would feel in that situation. Others were artificial laboratory situations in which success and failure were manipulated. Over the last 10 years, as more and more researchers have been working within this theoretical framework, the range of subject populations and situations used to elicit attributions has been greatly expanded. Studies have been done with children from preschool age through college age; and research has looked at attributions for laboratory tasks as well as for actual school achievement and other real situations. All of this empirical work has indicated that people of all ages make causal attributions for success and failure.

MEASURING THE ATTRIBUTIONS OF YOUNG CHILDREN. For children in the fourth or fifth grades and older children, the same types of techniques can be used to measure their causal attributions as are used for adults. Both rating scale and open-ended techniques have been successfully used (e.g., Frieze & Bar-Tal, 1980; Frieze & Snyder, 1980). However, most researchers who want to study the causal attributions of very young children use open-ended response techniques. With these techniques, children are simply asked to explain why they did well or poorly or why another child did well or poorly on some task.

In one study with young children, we asked first, third, and fifth graders about why a hypothetical child got a high or low grade on a test in school (Frieze & Snyder, 1980). The children were also asked about why another child did a good or poor job on an art project, why a child's team won or lost a football game, and why a child did or did not catch a lot of frogs. These stories were selected to sample different types of achievement activities that a child might encounter during a school day. Children were individually tested and were shown a picture of the child being described in each situation. After being told a brief story, they were asked to finish the story by explaining why the event had happened. The children were told "Because you know a lot about kids, I would like you to help me make the stories as true as possible." Using this procedure, children as young as the first grade had no trouble giving causal attributions that were codeable into the categories used by adults. Categories of attributions used included ability, effort, stable effort, interest, personality, mood, the difficulty of the task, ability x task interactions, other people's personalities and efforts, outside conflicting activities, and luck. There were few differences that were a function of age or sex of the children, although there were large differences in the attributions made in the four situations. Of course, there may have been more age and sex variation if children had been asked to give attributions for themselves rather than for another child.

In another unpublished study, we asked 39 first-, second-, and third- grade children why they do well or poorly in reading, math, and art. Results of this study are shown in Table 3.4. Here again, there were differences across subject matter areas but few sex or age differences, even though here the children were asked about their own successes and failures. There was a higher percentage of uncodeable responses with this very young group, but the majority of them were able to answer the direct attribution questions they were asked.

Other researchers using open-ended procedures have reported similar data (e.g., Bar-Tal, 1979b; Stipek & Hoffman, 1979). Children as young as the first grade use familiar attributional categories. Age differences in the use of specific attributional categories tend to be relatively minor, but there is much situational variation in the causes children use.

Table 3.4. Attributions of Primary School Students

Attribution	Subject Area					
	Reading		Math		Art	
	Success	*Failure*	*Success*	*Failure*	*Success*	*Failure*
Ability	7	1	5	4	9	3
Effort	13	9	9	5	10	6
Mood	0	2	0	3	1	2
Intrinsic motivation	7	0	4	2	11	5
Ability-task interaction	1	0	3	4	2	4
Task ease/difficulty	1	5	0	2	0	0
Extrinsic motivation	1	0	5	0	0	0
Environmental factors	1	0	0	0	1	0
Other people help/hurt	0	1	1	0	0	0
Uncodeable	8	21	12	19	5	19
Total	39	39	39	39	39	39

DEVELOPMENTAL CHANGES IN THE USE OF ATTRIBUTIONAL DIMENSIONS. Looking at the attributional dimensions being used at different ages, Frieze and Snyder (1980) found that the use of unstable causes and interpersonal causes increased with age from the first to fifth grade. Ruble (1978) also reports that children show an increasing sense of personal responsibility for their outcomes as they get older, although the exact ages involved in this change and the process by which it occurs are not well understood. In a similar study with third, sixth, ninth, and twelfth graders, Bar-Tal (1979b) found less use of internal causes in the older children and more use of stable causes. Unintentional causes were increasingly common until the ninth grade, after which they decreased. Bar-Tal also noted that the children used more causal categories as they got older. However, the Bar-Tal study differed from the Frieze and Snyder study on a number of dimensions, so that it is hard to compare them directly. Frieze and Snyder asked relatively young children about others in four different settings. In contrast, Bar-Tal assessed self-attributions for doing well or poorly on a test. Bar-Tal's subjects were Israeli students whereas Frieze and Snyder's were American parochial school children. Clearly more research is needed in this area in order to better understand how children's attributional conceptions change with age.

USE OF INFORMATION TO FORMULATE ATTRIBUTIONS. Developmental factors interact with various phases of the attribution model. As Ruble (1978) points out, developmental influences can be seen in children's concepts of the various constructs important for achievement and in the ways in which these constructs are processed or integrated. For example, along with developmental differences in the types of attributions used by children of different ages, there are also developmental effects in the types of information used by children of different ages to form causal attributions and in the ways in which this information is processed (see Chapter 8 by Kassin). For adults, we know that stable attributions such as ability are more common when the person's performance is higher or lower than those of other people engaging in the same type of task. Events that are inconsistent with the past are attributed to unstable causes, and outcomes shared with other people are attributed to the task or to some other aspect of the situation (see Frieze, 1976b, 1980).

Several studies have been designed to investigate how children of various ages form causal attributions for success and failure situations involving themselves and involving other children. The general finding is that children as young as 4 years of age will generally make the same attributions as adults would for the same situation, if the situation is described in simple terms (e.g., Shaklee, 1976). As children get older, however, they become more systematic in their judgments and they make finer discriminations (Frieze & Bar-Tal, 1980; Nicholls, 1979; Ruble, 1978; Shaklee, 1976; Weiner, Kun, & Benesh-Weiner, 1980).

Along with these general differences, there is also evidence that children respond differentially to certain types of information at different ages. Ruble (1978), in a review of the literature, concludes that children do not begin to systematically use information about the performances of other children in evaluating their own performances until the second grade. Nicholls (1979) has found that children as young as 5 years of age can use information about the difficulty of the task (which is dependent on normative data) if it is presented in simple enough form. The form in which the information is presented does appear to make a big difference in how easily the children can utilize the information. Of course, the same could be said of adults (Carroll, Payne, Frieze, & Girard, 1976).

There are some other developmental differences in the ways in which information is used in making attributions. Nicholls (1978) has shown that a developmental process is involved in children's understanding that more difficult tasks require more ability for successful completion. Several studies have also demonstrated changes as children mature in their inferences about relative levels of ability and effort as they relate to task performance (e.g., Kun, 1977; Kun, Parsons, & Ruble, 1974; Nicholls, 1978). At very young ages, children tend to see ability and effort as positively correlated. If a child is seen as trying hard, he or she is also seen as being smart. As children get older, they come to see ability and effort as negatively correlated. If one is seen as trying hard, the inference is made that the person does not have as much ability as one who does not try as hard to achieve the same outcome. Older children also realize that for a very hard task both ability and effort may be needed, but for an easier task either one is sufficient in order to do well.

Meyer et al. (Meyer, Bachmann, Biermann, Hempelmann, Ploger, & Spiller, 1979) also report that children infer ability from the feedback they are given after performing a task, but that these inferences depend on the age of the child. Older children and adults feel that praise after success (especially on an easy task) implies that the person being praised is seen as having low ability. Criticism for failure implies that the person is seen as having higher ability. However, children in elementary grades see praise as being given to those seen as having high ability. These age differences may relate to the experiences of the children in the classroom, but further research is needed to investigate the relationship between praise and attributions in children.

Children also differ from adults in their reactions to success and failure. A number of studies have shown that in the first and second grades children tend to be optimistic after success and to feel that they will do well if they try the task again. They also feel more positive about themselves after experiencing success on a task (e.g., Nicholls, 1978, 1979; Parsons & Ruble, 1972; Ruble & Underkoffler, 1976). Starting in the second grade, they begin to show an attributional mediation in their affective responses. As they get older, the degree of positive feeling after success and the degree of negative feeling after failure are highly dependent on the internality of the attribution made to explain the outcome. This is similar to the adult response. Weiner et al. (1980) further report that the specific emotional responses to success and failure become increasingly more like those of adults as children get older. One of the last adult emotional reponses to develop is the linkage of surprise to luck attributions.

Concepts of success and failure also change with age. Veroff (1969) feels that children evolve from defining success in terms of one's own past history to definitions based on social comparison. The latter basis is seen as occurring after the child enters school (see Ruble, 1978, for a review of this literature).

SEX DIFFERENCES. A good deal of research has shown that males and females of all ages tend to make somewhat different causal attributions for success and failure and to have different expectancies for future success. The most consistently reported effect of sex is that females of all ages tend to have lower initial expectancies for success than males (e.g., Crandall, 1969; Calsyn & Kenny, 1977; Cole, King, & Newcomb, 1977; Frieze, et al., 1978; Gjesme, 1973; Sumner & Johnson, 1949). Beginning at preschool ages, when girls are asked to estimate how well they will do on an unfamiliar task, they will tend to underestimate the performance level they will later achieve. Boys, on the other hand, are more likely to overestimate their eventual performance. This pattern occurs for intellectual tasks as well as for artistic tasks and for tasks involving physical skills (Crandall, 1978a). These findings replicate for all ages of students—girls and young women consistently demonstrate lower expectations for success than boys and young men. Even male college students give higher estimates for the grades they will receive than women, although for college students both sexes overestimate their actual performance levels to some degree. College men's estimates are very high while women's are only slightly higher than what they will actually receive (Cole, King, & Newcomb, 1977). College women also underestimate performance on other tasks (Gjesme, 1973).

As discussed earlier, having low expectations can be debilitating in a number of ways. One may be less likely to attempt difficult tasks if one continually underestimates how well one will do (Crandall, 1978b; Frieze et al., 1978). The fact that adolescent girls continue to have lower educational aspirations than boys (Marini & Greenberger, 1978) may be an example of

this phenomenon. Low initial expectations also create a self-fulfilling prophecy since they lead to perpetuating causal attributions (Jackaway, 1974). Indirect evidence for this is seen in the fact that boys tend to be more optimistic after failure than girls (Dweck & Gilliard, 1975). More directly relevant data indicate that females of all ages are more likely than males to attribute their successes to unstable and external factors such as luck and task ease. Females are less likely to see their successes as caused by ability, but they make more attributions to lack of ability and bad luck for failure (e.g., Bar-Tal & Frieze, 1977; Dweck & Repucci, 1973; McMahan, 1973; Nicholls, 1975; Simon & Feather, 1973; Wiegers & Frieze, 1977).

Commonly held stereotypes about the personalities of men and women include the idea that men are basically more competent than women in handling a variety of achievement tasks (e.g., Broverman, Vogel, Broverman, Clarkson, & Rosenkrantz, 1972). Other more specific research further indicates that, for a number of different types of achievement tasks, males are expected by others to outperform females, even on tasks commonly defined as female-related (see reviews by Frieze et al., 1978; O'Leary & Hansen, 1979). Given these general beliefs, it is not too surprising that girls and women have lower achievement expectations for themselves than males. Success may be seen as unfeminine, especially in fields such as mathematics that are seen as especially strong male domains. Girls who are successful may see themselves as tomboys or in ways that make them different from other girls. Many girls still consider it a compliment to be told, "Gee, you did that just as good as a boy." Other, equally competent girls may simply direct their skills to areas outside the traditionally defined academic setting, especially as they reach adolescence.

RACE AND CLASS DIFFERENCES. Just as our stereotypes tend to reflect a perception that females are less competent than males, racial stereotypes include the idea that blacks are less intelligent and less motivated to do well in school than whites (Feldman, 1972; Karlins, Coffman, & Walters, 1969). It would be reasonable to assume that blacks also have lower expectations for themselves than whites. However, in one of the few studies that has compared black and white achievement expectancies, Entwisle (1979) found that blacks had higher performance expectancies despite their achieving at lower levels, and that these expectancies remained after a number of low performances. Middle-class children also had high initial expectancies but, over time, the expectancies of middle-class white children became increasingly realistic and similar to their actual performances. The high expectancies of the blacks may be maintained by their use of unstable causal attributions for failure.

Looking directly at causal attributions, a good deal of research suggests that blacks in general make more external attributions for success and failure than whites. Blacks are especially likely to attribute their outcomes to good or bad luck (e.g., Friend & Neale, 1972; Lefcourt, 1970; Murray & Mednick, 1975). In a study of college students, Murray and Mednick (1975) further found that black females with high achievement motivation made attributions similar to whites with high achievement motivation. Overall, however, black females used luck attributions more, and made greater use of ability and effort as causal explanations. In this same study, black males with high and low achievement motivation made similar types of attributions. This makes a rather confusing picture, but it does suggest that both class and race affect patterns of attributions.

Israeli and Hawaiian studies further support the idea that there may be a different pattern of attributions in lower-class or disadvantaged groups. Falbo (1973) reports that middle-class children in Hawaii were more likely to choose "try hard" as an explanation for an outcome than were welfare children. Raviv, Bar-Tal, Raviv, and Bar-Tal (in press) found that sixth graders from disadvantaged backgrounds in Israel were more likely to attribute their failures to stable factors. Such an attributional pattern would lead them to form low expectancies for the future and should decrease motivation. These implications, however, were not directly tested.

The influence of other people on the attribution process

The theoretical attribution model presented thus far has been primarily concerned with internal attribution processes—how the individual forms a causal attribution to explain a particular achievement event and the consequences of that attribution for the person. Other people have been peripheral to this process. However, there are a number of ways in which others do influence this process. On a simple level, one can attribute his or her outcomes to other people. The teacher is mentioned as a cause of success or failure by some students when asked why they succeeded or failed on an exam (e.g., Frieze, 1976a). The interference of other students (who cheated or otherwise obstructed one's performance) is also a spontaneously mentioned attribution, although neither cheating nor the teacher is especially common for academic achievement settings (e.g., Frieze, 1976b; Frieze & Snyder, 1980). As discussed earlier, another person can be perceived as intentionally influencing one's outcomes or as inadvertently or accidentally doing so. Attributions can also be made to stable features in the other person (she is a naturally good teacher) or to a particular behavior (he tried hard to make the test very fair). In all these cases, the outside person is seen as a central factor in determining one's performance.

Other people also enter into the attribution process by providing standards with which one can compare oneself. If a student does well, but everyone else does too, the attribution is made to task ease, whereas discrepant outcomes are more attributed to internal factors. The use of information about other people has been extensively studied as a general phenomenon known as *social comparison*. Although this has not been directly tied to the achievement attribution processes to the degree to which it could potentially be, a brief examination of this literature is clearly relevant.

COMPARING ONESELF WITH OTHERS. Popular knowledge suggests that students are well aware of how well other students in their classes are doing. In college, the comparison process is made explicit through the instructor making the grade distribution for various exams publicly available. In lower grades, students also make it a point to find out how well their classmates are doing, even in settings that are designed to minimize ability comparisons and grade competition (Levine, 1979). Levine and Snyder (1978) found that first and second graders were able to give reasonably accurate evaluations of the reading and math ability of their fellow students. In fact, these students were in an individualized instruction setting where each child worked independently and was not in competition with any other student.

The question then arises as to why students are so anxious to compare themselves with others even when discouraged from doing so by the classroom environment. Festinger (1954) suggested that there is a basic drive in humans to compare themselves with others in order to gain an accurate assessment of their abilities. Others have continued to view the social comparison process as a basic human response and have clarified some of the variables affecting this behavior (see Suls, 1977). Although there are a number of variables that may affect the choice of persons used for comparison (e.g., Gruder, 1977; Miller & Suls, 1977), it appears that the individual is most interested in comparing himself or herself with others who are belived to be similar in attributes that are predictive of performance levels for the ability in question (Goethals & Darley, 1977). For the child in school, relevant variables would usually include age, grade level, sex, and, possibly, race. In one test of this idea, Suls, Gastorf, and Lawhon (1978) found that, after giving high school students possible comparison persons of the same sex or a different sex and of the same age, older, or younger for evaluating performance on an "Unusual uses test," students chose a same-age-same-sex person with whom to compare their score. As a second choice, someone of the same age but of the other sex was chosen. These results indicated that subjects choose the most similar person they could for comparison purposes. It is hypothesized that such a choice gives people the maximum amount of information about their own ability levels.

The use of social comparison information affects the attribution process in various ways. As already noted, this information determines whether an ability attribution or a task ease (or difficulty) attribution is made for a particular success or failure. Even primary school children have been shown to use such information in making causal attributions (Frieze & Bar-Tal, 1980). Knowledge about how well others with similar characteristics to oneself have done on a particular task will also determine one's own expectations for success on the task. This influence is especially salient for unfamiliar tasks and for tasks where others' performances are attributed to their abilities (Fontaine, 1974).

ACHIEVEMENT EXPECTATIONS OF OTHER PEOPLE. Other people can affect the attribution process in yet another way. In most real-life achievement situations, there are other people who know about an individual's performance and who have prior expectations of how the individual will do. These expectations may be based on knowledge about how well the person has done in the past or on other prior experiences, or they may result from generalizations based on stereotypes about the group to which the individual belongs. In either case, the actor is often aware of these expectations, and they may well influence performance. Having others rooting for you and expecting you to do well is often cited as a factor in sports success (e.g., Frieze, McHugh, & Duquin, 1976). Data also indicate the children who are high in achievement motivation have parents who are supportive of their accomplishments and who expect them to do well in achievement tasks (e.g., Hoffman, 1972). Teacher expectations have also been shown to influence student performance (Cooper, 1977, 1979; Rosenthal & Jacobson, 1968).

Along with these influences of others' expectations on performance, the expectations and attributions others make for the performance of a particular student can have very direct effects on the experiences of that student. Teachers, counselors, and parents make many decisions about the types of classes and special training programs the student will be exposed to. There is a wider range of these for the students seen as having high abilities and who are seen as doing well because of their efforts and abilities. Rewards given by these significant others will also depend on the attributions made for performance (which are, in turn, at least partially determined by the initial expectations for success of the individual).

The negative effects of stereotypes on attributions and performance can be seen in girls and blacks, as reviewed earlier. They can also be devastating for the mentally retarded (see Chapter 12 by Gibbons). The unreasonably low expectations held for retarded students may result in these students having very low views of their own abilities and a resulting inability to approach even quite simple tasks. Attributional retraining of these students and their teachers can have surprising results for their performance (Gold & Ryan, 1979).

The effects of task variations

As we have already seen, different types of causal attributions are made for different tasks. The same person will make one attribution in one situation and a completely different attribution for another situation (Frieze & Snyder, 1980; Teglasi, 1977). There are also individual differences in attributional tendencies. For example, females are more likely to make external attributions than males. However, these individual differences in attributional patterns tend to be small; the situation carries the major variance in causal attributions made. For example, nearly everyone will make different attributions for success compared to failure. Success is typically attributed to internal factors while failure is attributed less to internal causes (e.g., Arkin & Maruyama, 1979; Frieze & Weiner, 1971; Gilmore & Reid, 1979; Miller, 1976). There are also consistent attributions made after certain patterns of past successes in comparison to the present performance (see Frieze, 1980). People may also spend more time making a careful and complex attribution in a situation in which they feel that it is important that they do so than they would in the typical laboratory study (Kassin & Hochreich, 1977).

An area in which task variables have been extensively investigated is that of tasks defined as appropriate or inappropriate for one sex. Making bread well is defined as a sex-appropriate task for women and as an inappropriate task for men. Conversely, fixing a car would be sex-appropriate for men and inappropriate for women. Research has shown that people tend to expect a better performance on tasks defined as appropriate for their own sex (Rosenfield & Stephan, 1978; Stein, Pohly, & Mueller, 1971). However, college students of both sexes have also been found to set higher goals for themselves for tasks they were told that men do especially well on (Stake, 1976).

Along with these expectancy effects, there are also effects of the sex-linkage of the task on the causal attributions made for success or failure on that task. Generally, men and women tend to designate more internal attributions for success on sex-appropriate tasks and fewer internal attributions for success on the inappropriate tasks (Rosenfield & Stephan, 1978). Green, Green, and Festa (1979) also showed that women will tend to make more ability attributions for success at making bread and at solving anagrams (a sex-neutral task), whereas failure on the bread making is more attributed to bad luck. For women, succeeding at fixing cars was attributed to good luck and failure to lack of ability. However, men tended to attribute their successes at all of these tasks to their ability and their failures to bad luck. These differential findings are probably a function of the specific task used as an example of the sex-appropriate or inappropriate task. Since task attributions are so variable, great caution must be used in assuming that any two tasks will carry the same patterns of causal attributions.

Needs for future research

As this chapter has shown, the attribution model developed to explain the beliefs of college students for why they succeeded or failed on an achievement task has proven to be applicable to people of all ages doing all types of tasks. We can measure the attributions of preschool and elementary school children using open-ended techniques, and these attributions appear to be sensible. Older children appear to use the underlying dimensions of the attributions they make in much the same ways as adults. Younger children are different in ways we don't fully understand. For example, affective responses to success and failure are more related to internality after the second grade than they are in younger children. By the early elementary school years, children also begin to use information in much the same ways as adults in making causal attributions. There are some differences, however, which need to be looked at more carefully.

This review suggests that the basic attributional model for assessing achievement events can be meaningfully applied to children shortly after they enter school, but that there will have to be some modifications in the basic model as we apply it to young children. Affective responses and expectancy judgments do not appear to be mediated by attributions until the second grade or later. We need to better understand what factors do determine these responses. We also need research to help us understand how children of various ages define the tasks they confront. And there are other questions that we need to know more about. How do children think about success and failure? How do they decide which is the more appropriate label for their performance? Since the attribution model has shown promise in the work that has already been done, these questions are worth pursuing, especially by researchers knowledgeable in developmental psychology.

Note

1. Weiner (1979) now calls this a controllability dimension, since people presumably do not intend to fail but may fail because of not doing something they had control over (such as studying).

4

THE DEVELOPMENT OF PROSOCIAL BEHAVIOR

BERT MOORE
THE UNIVERSITY OF TEXAS AT DALLAS

BILL UNDERWOOD
THE UNIVERSITY OF TEXAS AT AUSTIN

Are human beings intrinsically good or evil? Thomas Hobbes felt that we were born as evil, aggressive creatures and that only society's controls prevented our rapacious qualities from leading to destruction. Rousseau held the opposite view of children and society. He felt that we were born "naturally good," caring and concerned about our fellow human beings, and that it was society that corrupted us. Our goal in this chapter is not to try to resolve this age-old conundrum; indeed, most psychologists would believe that we are not "born" one way or another, but that we all have the capacity for both antisocial and prosocial behaviors within us. Our focus will be on what factors influence the development of our prosocial capacities.

First, we need to give some attention to the question of exactly what we mean by prosocial behavior or altruism. Social psychologists have wrestled with the issue of how we define these terms, and there is not complete agreement. Acts that may be considered prosocial include a wide range of behaviors—from saving a person who is drowning to helping someone carry their packages, from donating a kidney to donat-

ing a penny, from the heroic to the merely thoughtful. The common denominator of these acts is their apparent selflessness, the voluntary doing of "good" for another person where the motivation does not appear to be self gain.

Dennis Krebs (1970) has identified three aspects by which conventional wisdom defines prosocial acts: A prosocial act is performed voluntarily by an actor; the actor intends for the act to benefit another person or group of persons; and the act is performed as an end in itself and not as a means of fulfilling an ulterior personal motive of the actor. Obviously, this way of describing prosocial behavior highlights people's *motivations* for performing acts of goodwill. Ervin Staub (1978) believes that a person's motivations are important in distinguishing between behavior that is prosocial and behavior that is *altruistic*. He states that ". . . prosocial behavior refers to behavior benefitting others. A prosocial act may be judged altruistic if it appears to have been intended to benefit others rather than to gain either material or social rewards" (p. 10). Staub goes on to say that, doubtlessly, there may be internal rewards associated with the performance of prosocial acts, such as a sense of self-satisfaction or virtuousness. Although we can never fully know the motives of another person's behavior, we will focus in this chapter on behaviors that are done with the apparent intent of benefitting another more than oneself.

The current significance of prosocial behavior

Prosocial behavior is interesting to social psychologists as a social problem as well as a scientific puzzle. The complexity of our technological society makes us more vulnerable and more dependent on each other. At the same time, because of depersonalization and increased mobility, we rely less on traditional sources of aid such as family and long-term friends. This leaves a vacuum that might be filled by increased helpfulness and generosity between slight acquaintances and even total strangers. We wish to understand what factors are important in the development of these altruistic behaviors so that concern for others might be promoted.

There are theoretical reasons also for interest in the development of prosocial behavior. Most developmental theory—whether based on analytic, cognitive, or learning theory—has tended to see children as coming into the world as egoistic and essentially self-oriented. How then can we explain the development of behavior that is done for the apparent benefit of another? What are the mechanisms that could occur in a child to produce such change? This chapter will be concerned with trying to establish how it is that prosocial behavior develops. Before addressing this issue, however, we need to see what evidence exists that shows us that it *does* develop, that there are age changes in prosocial behavior.

In the present review we are going to restrict our attention to forms of prosocial behavior, such as sharing or helping, that do not involve emergency situations or an exchange. While behaviors such as a bystander's intervention or an exchange-

based cooperation are clearly important instances of prosocial action, they may involve different processes than sharing and helping and will not be considered here. (Indeed, a bystander's intervention has been shown to follow a different age-course, whereas cooperation is usually clearly self-beneficial and therefore not an instance of altruism.)

The focus of our effort then will be on examples of sharing and helping and those processes that might be important in underlying their development. We will examine the evidence for age-related changes in these forms of prosocial behavior. Then mechanisms that have been proposed as possible mediators for age-changes in these behaviors will be discussed. We will focus our attention on a set of conceptually related processes: perceptual role-taking, cognitive role-taking, and affective role-taking (empathy). The evidence relating to the interrelationships among these mechanisms will be evaluated and suggestions for ways of conceptualizing apparent inconsistencies will be made. Finally, we will suggest possible directions for future research on the development of altruism.

Age changes in prosocial behavior

One of the most replicable findings in developmental social psychology is that older children seem to show "more" prosocial behavior. They are more likely to engage in a given act of helpfulness or sharing than are younger children and they show a greater variety of prosocial behaviors.

Rudimentary forms of concern for others can be found in very young children. Sagi and Hoffman (1976) found that infants who were 34 hours old would cry more intensely when exposed to the cries of another child than when exposed to a noise of equal intensity or a synthetic cry. While this is not prosocial behavior, it may be an example of some form of primitive empathy that is a precursor for the development of prosocial behavior. Rheingold, Hay, and West (1976) found in children as young as 15 months that there were examples of behaviors that could be labeled as sharing: showing or giving objects to others and partner play (i.e., giving someone an object and then playing with it while the other person has possession of it). Other studies also find examples of prosocial behavior in quite young children. Taken as a whole, however, the behavioral repertoire of children up to around two years of age is characterized more by self-interested activity than prosocial behavior. Taking toys from another child is more likely than sharing them. Curiosity is more apt to be the response to the injury of another child than is consoling.

What is generally found is that as the child gets older there is increasing evidence of prosocial concern. The Rheingold et al. (1976) study found that even in a fairly restricted age range, 15 to 24 months, there was an increase with age in sharing and partner play. Green and Schneider (1974) used subjects varying in age from 5 to 14 years. They found an increase with age in the number of candy bars their subjects donated to other students in the school and the number of children who picked up pencils knocked over by an experimenter, although the latter behavior reached an asymptote and did not differentiate among the older children. On one measure, the amount of time that children volunteered to make books for poor children, Green and Schneider found no differences with age. In general, children of all ages expressed good intentions. A number of other studies (Elliot & Vasta, 1970; Midlarsky & Bryan, 1967; Rushton, 1975; Rushton & Wiener, 1975) also have found more or less linear increases with age in children's willingness to donate material goods to children who are absent but who are described as needy.

Developmentally relevant situational determinants of altruism

In talking about possible mechanisms that underlie changes in prosocial behavior over age, we must distinguish among the variety of determinants of prosocial action, such as presence or absence of observers, effects of models and being exposed to environmental stressors that have been the traditional domain of social psychologists, and those developmental determinants that are the focus of this chapter. Here we are trying to understand how differences among persons develop. The situational variables that social psychologists have investigated can, however, often offer helpful insights as to possible developmental mechanisms in that they interact with age (Staub, 1978) and thus suggest changes that may be occurring with age.

SOCIAL NORMS. One factor that is seen as covarying with age and that may be important in explaining the development of prosocial behavior is the increasing impact that social norms have on children. Societal rules and norms are seen as becoming increasingly evident with age, so that older children may simply be more knowledgeable about socially prescribed behaviors. Furthermore, children may become increasingly sensitive and responsive to social cues and social norms as they get older (a phenomenon that is most evident in the great sensitivity of adolescents to social pressures). Finally, it may be that norms are increasingly internalized with age, with the result that the relationship between children's knowledge of such norms and their overt behavior in relevant situations becomes increasingly stronger.

Schwartz (1968, 1977) has proposed a model for altruism in adults that focuses on norms and on the conditions under which altruistic behavior will be consistent with personal norms. Schwartz suggests that altruism will be determined by norms only when potential altruists are aware of the consequences of their action or when they feel a sense of personal responsibility for taking care of the situation. Although norms are often either unrelated or only mildly related to altruism, Schwartz (1968) has demonstrated that the correlation between prosocial norms and prosocial behavior can be as high as .47 (Schwartz, 1968) among people who are aware of the consequences in a situation where altruism is appropriate and who feel a personal responsibility for correcting the situation. While this approach has not yet been applied directly to the development of altruism in children, it would obviously be possible to do so. Schwartz' approach may serve to indicate, at least, the sorts of norms that are important determinants of altruism and that could be responsible for changes in prosocial behavior during the childhood years.

SOCIALIZATION PRACTICES. A somewhat related factor is the influence of socialization practices on altruism. This factor focuses on the treatment of children by people in their immediate environment rather than on more abstract prescriptive norms. Parents would, of course, play a major role here, since their modeling of prosocial behavior and positive responses to children's prosocial actions could be expected to have a cumulative effect that would progressively strengthen children's tendencies toward altruism. Parents, however, are not the only socializing agents, and the impact of other adults and other children could also be expected to influence the development of altruistic behavior.

There have been numerous studies confirming the efficacy of altruistic models in promoting children's altruism, studies of both adult models (e.g., Rushton, 1975) and child models (e.g., Hartup & Coates, 1967). Rushton's (1975) study revealed the significant effects of modeling, both in an immediate test and in a retest eight weeks later. It has also been suggested that children are particularly responsive to models who have had a nurturant relationship with them (Yarrow, Scott, & Waxler, 1973). These findings are consistent with studies of the family background of altruists, people chosen because they had demonstrated altruistic behavior ranging from sharing candy with friends (Rutherford & Mussen, 1968) to major life activities such as full commitment to civil rights activities (Rosenhan, 1970) and rescuing Jews from the Nazis during World War II (London, 1970). Such studies

have found that people who behave altruistically tend to have had a close relationship with a nurturant parent (or parents) who modeled prosocial concern and behavior. These studies present striking documentation of the power of socialization practices on prosocial behavior in adulthood. The cumulative effects of such practices might very well be wholly or partly responsible for the increase in altruism during the childhood years.

Cognitive determinants of altruistic behavior

MORAL JUDGMENT. Another area that has been investigated in terms of the development of prosocial behavior is the quality of children's moral reasoning. According to Piaget (1932) and Kohlberg (1976), moral reasoning is intimately involved with cognitive growth and the development of role-taking ability. As Staub (1979) has pointed out, however, role-taking as defined by Kohlberg is an integral part of moral judgment; yet Kohlberg's concept of role-taking refers to a much more broadly defined type of role-taking than has been tapped by the usual measures of cognitive and perceptual role-taking. Later in the chapter we will examine data on the relationship between these measures of role-taking and prosocial behavior. Here we will briefly discuss research relating the quality of children's moral judgment and altruism.

The relationship that one might expect between moral reasoning and prosocial action is not immediately clear. What is assessed in studies of moral judgment is reasoning about moral dilemmas; yet by definition altruism goes beyond what is required by moral norms. We might speculate that such reasoning about roles, social obligations, and moral obligations would be related to altruistic behavior, but this relationship may be rather complex and certainly requires empirical verification.

Rubin and Schneider (1973) used Kohlberg's scheme and studied moral judgment and altruism. Seven-year-olds were given opportunities to donate candy to poor children and to help a younger child complete a task. They found that level of moral judgment was positively correlated with both measures of altruism, and this relationship was maintained even after IQ was partialed out. Similarly, Emler and Rushton (1974) studied children who were between ages 7 and 13 and assessed their level of moral judgment and willingness to share resources with needy children. When the effects of age were partialed out, moral maturity was significantly correlated with sharing.

Eisenberg-Berg and Hand (1979) assessed moral reasoning with their own experimental instrument. They presented nursery school children with four moral reasoning stories and rated the responses in several categories (e.g., "hedonism," "authority and punishment reasoning"). They found that sharing was negatively related to "hedonism" in moral reasoning and positively related to "needs oriented reasoning," whereas helping appeared to show no relation to moral reasoning.

These studies appear to indicate that, apart from age, the moral maturity of the child bears a relationship to the child's tendency to engage in at least some forms of altruistic behavior. What cannot be concluded from these data is whether the effect results from moral reasoning per se or perhaps some more basic mechanism. This question will be addressed later in this chapter.

COGNITIVE MATURATION AND EMPATHY. Piaget's theory, of course, is the most prominent position describing qualitative changes in children's thought that may be related to prosocial behavior. Taken to the social domain, theorists such as Kohlberg (1976) and Rushton (1976) have emphasized the development of the capacity to role-take as being central to the development of prosocial behavior. The ability to take the perspective of someone in distress is seen as being a necessary component in the performance of acts to alleviate that distress. The development of this ability is seen as both relying on more basic cognitive developmental processes (movement from cognitive egocentrism) and as having special characteristics having to do with reasoning and moral/ethical issues.

A mechanism closely related to cognitive development is empathic responding. The distinction usually made between empathy and role-taking is that role-taking may be seen as a purely cognitive process whereby the child can predict the responses of others, whereas emphatic responding has to do with the extent to which children vicariously experience the suffering of another. Empathy has had a difficult history as a construct, but many theorists (e.g., Hoffman, 1976; Krebs, 1975) have pointed to its importance in understanding why an individual would voluntarily self-sacrifice for another. Since this is an area of much current activity, both empirical and theoretical, we will focus our attention for the remainder of the chapter on the role of these cognitive and affective mechanisms in the development of altruism.

Cognitive/affective mediators of altruism: Perspective-taking

There are, of course, many levels on which one person may take the perspective of another. There is the purely physical level, in which a child may or may not recognize that people who see the same scene from different locations will have seen something slightly different. This might be considered the most basic or primitive sort of perspective-taking, since it involves perspective on external events rather than on internal states. A somewhat more advanced type of perspective-taking might be called social role-taking, in which children are aware that other people's thoughts, motives, and reactions to events may be different from their own. This might be thought of as an extension of perspective-taking from the sensory into the cognitive realm. Although the ability to anticipate the cognitions of another may be a more complex cognitive feat than the ability to recognize different visual perspectives, they are usually assumed to generate from a common basis. For example, in writing of the adolescent's cognitive egocentrism, Piaget has said, "Although it differs from the child's egocentrism . . . it results, nevertheless, from the same mechanism" (Inhelder & Piaget, 1958). Thus, the differing forms of egocentrism (or its opposite, perspective-taking) are held to represent different manifestations of a common, continuing process.

Finally, there is affective perspective-taking, which may itself take several different forms. Children may simply realize that other people's feelings and emotions are different from their own, or they may be able to judge accurately what the other people's feelings and emotions actually are. Empathy might be considered a still more advanced form of affective perspective-taking, although it is important to realize that workers in this field do not always agree on what the definition of empathy should be. Some insist that an affective reaction in one person must produce the same affect in another before empathy has occurred (Feshbach & Roe, 1968), while others are willing to accept a nonmatching affective response to another person's affective state as indicative of empathy (Stotland, 1969). Here we examine several of these forms of perspective-taking and their relationship to prosocial action.

Since the various forms of egocentrism are held to result from a common mechanism, it may be that this common mechanism is what is linked to altruism. Certainly, the most stringent test of such a hypothesis would involve the examination of a potential relationship between altruism and perceptual perspective-taking, since perceptual mechanisms would not ordinarily be expected to relate to altruism, except through some mechanism common to all forms of perspective-taking.

As we examine the research literature, there are several notions that we need to keep in mind. One is that we are looking, at the most basic level, for evidence of a relationship between perspective-taking and altruism; otherwise perspective-taking cannot qualify as a mediator of the development of altruism. We would normally expect to find this evidence in the form of a significant Pearson coefficient of correlation between a measure of altruism and a measure of perspective-taking.

A second focus of our inquiry is just how much of the age-related change in altruism can be accounted for by perspective-taking. Toward this end, we examine the evidence for a significant relationship between age and altruism; this is also usually in the form of a Pearson correlation coefficient. In addition, however, we will try to assess whether the relationship between age and altruism can be completely explained by differences in perspective-taking. For this purpose, we examine the partial correlation between age and altruism, with perspective-taking partialed out. If this sort of statistical control of the influence of perspective-taking reduces the relationship between age and altruism to nonsignificance (i.e., partial correlation not statistically significant), then we can maintain that perspective-taking could potentially be responsible for all of the age-related change in altruism. Of course, such a finding would not mean that perspective-taking is definitely the sole causal factor in age changes in altruism or even that it is a causal factor at all. It would merely indicate the possibility that perspective-taking could be the sole causal factor, while a significant partial correlation would indicate that perspective-taking could not possibly be the sole causal factor. In that case, other factors, either instead of or in addition to perspective-taking, would have to be invoked to explain why there are such large age differences in altruism.

A somewhat less central focus will be to examine whether the relationship between altruism and perspective-taking might be an artifact resulting from the fact that both measures tend to increase with age. Since older children will generally score higher than younger ones on both measures, any sample of children across a broad age range will likely produce a positive correlation between the two for reason of age differences alone. We therefore examine the partial correlation between perspective-taking and altruism with the effect of age partialed out. A significant partial correlation will inform us that the relationship between altruism and perspective-taking is not an artifact of their joint relationship to age. A nonsignificant partial correlation will be somewhat less informative: It could mean that the relationship between altruism and perspective-taking is artifactual (as one might find an artifactual relationship between height and altruism in children), but it might also occur in a case where perspective-taking is a primary causal factor in the age differences in altruism. A significant partial correlation would therefore allow a definitive conclusion, but a nonsignificant partial would not.

Since we will be examining a variety of correlation coefficients, some partial correlations and others not, we will need some way to distinguish the partial correlations from the ordinary Pearson correlations. The usual distinction is to refer to correlation coefficients that have not had any factors partialed out as "zero-order correlation coefficients," and we adopt that convention for the remainder of this chapter. In addition, the correlational data to be reviewed are summarized in Table 4.1.

Perceptual perspective-taking

A recent study (Underwood, Froming, & Guarijuata, 1980) examined the relationship between perceptual perspective-taking and altruism, using a Piagetian measure of perspective-taking called the three-mountain task (Piaget & Inhelder, 1967). In this task, a child is placed before a model of a mountain scene and is asked to imagine what would be seen if the child were placed at some other position. The child is asked to choose which of several photographs accurately represent the view from the alternative position. The perspective-taking measure is simply the number of correct responses to a number of such requests. The first- to fifth-grade children in this study were given 25 pennies when they entered the experimental room, ostensibly for helping

the experimenters with their work. Following completion of the three-mountain task, the children were given an opportunity to donate some of their pennies anonymously to a fund for children who wouldn't get a chance to earn pennies. Perspective-taking scores were significantly correlated with the number of pennies donated ($r = .25$). Grade level was correlated with both perspective-taking ($r = .50$) and generosity ($r = .25$). When the effect of grade level was partialed out, the correlation between perspective-taking and generosity was no longer significant ($r = .15$). This nonsignificant partial does not necessarily mean, as we have pointed out, that perspective-taking is not the causal factor involved in the age change in altruism. When perspective-taking is partialed out, the previously significant relationship between grade and generosity becomes nonsignificant ($r = .15$), so that differences in perspective-taking could account for the age differences in altruism in this study.

There are several other studies of perceptual perspective-taking and altruism, and the results of those studies are, for the most part, consistent with the results of the Underwood, Froming, and Guarijuata (1980) study. One study, however, that was rather inconsistent with these results was reported by Zahn-Waxler, Radke-Yarrow, and Brady-Smith (1977). In this study, a battery of 10 perspective-taking tasks was given to children ranging in age from 3 to 6 years. Four of these tasks involved perceptual perspective-taking. The children were also given two opportunities to share with another person, two opportunities to help clean up minor messes, and two opportunities to comfort an obviously distressed adult. The perceptual perspective-taking measures were not correlated with sharing, helping, or comforting, either over all ages or within any one age.

There are several reasons why this study might have produced results different from those reported earlier. One is that there might have been too small a sample to detect a relationship existing in the population.

Table 4.1. Studies of Perspective-Taking and Altruism[a]

Study	Age of subjects	Type of perspective-taking	Measure of altruism	Zero-order Correlations			Partial Correlations	
				Altruism with perspective-taking	Age with perspective-taking	Age with altruism	Altruism with perspective-taking, controlling for age	Altruism with age, controlling for perspective-taking
Buckley, Siegel, & Ness (1979)	3 to 8 years	Perceptual and affective	Helping a peer clean up a mess or sharing a cookie with a peer	$r_p = .43^b$	$r_p = .65$ r_a not reported	n.s.^{c}	$r_p = .46$ r_a not reported	Not reported
Coke, Batson, & McDavis (1978)	College students	Empathy	Volunteering to help peer	$r = .59^d$	Not reported	Not reported	Not reported	Not reported
Eisenberg-Berg & Mussen (1978)	9th to 12th grades	Empathy	Helping experimenter on a task	$r_{bis} = .40$ (boys) r_{bis} n.s. (girls)	n.s.	Not reported	Not reported	Not reported
Emler & Rushton (1974)	7 to 13 years	Social	Generosity toward a charity	Not reported	Mean $r = .26$	$r = .22$	n.s.	Not reported
Iannotti (1978)	6 and 9 years	Social and empathy	Sharing candy with anonymous peer	r_{6s} = n.s. r_{9s} = .48 r_e not reported	Mean $r_s = .59^e$ $r_e = -.46$	$r = .58$	$r_s = .43^e$ r_e not reported	Not reported

Table 4.1. (continued)

Study	Age of subjects	Type of perspective-taking	Measure of altruism	Zero-order Correlations			Partial Correlations	
				Altruism with perspective-taking	Age with perspective-taking	Age with altruism	Altruism with perspective-taking, controlling for age	Altruism with age, controlling for perspective-taking
Krebs & Sturrup (1974)	7 to 9 years	Social	Composite rating	$r = .46$	Not reported	Not reported	Not reported	Not reported
Mehrabian & Epstein (1972)	College students	Empathy	Helping a peer	$r = .31$	Not reported	Not reported	Not reported	Not reported
Peraino (1977)	11th and 12th grades	Empathy	Altruistic choice in Prisoner's Dilemma Game with a peer	n.s.	Not reported	Not reported	Not reported	Not reported
Rubin & Schneider (1973)	7 years	Social	Sharing candy with a peer; helping a peer	$r_s = .31$ $r_h = .44$	Not reported	Not reported	$r_s = .29^f$ $r_h = .64^f$	Not reported
Rushton & Wiener (1975)	7 and 11 years	Perceptual and social	Generosity toward a friend; generosity toward a charity	Not reported	$r_p = .65$ Mean $r_s = .32$	$r_f = .68$ $r_c = .47$	n.s.	Not reported

Sawin, Underwood, Mostyn, & Weaver (1980)	1st and 3rd grades	Empathy	Sharing marbles with anonymous peers	n.s.	r = 23	r = .25	n.s.	r = .24
Underwood, Froming, & Guarijuata (1980)	1st to 5th grades	Perceptual	Generosity toward anonymous peers	r = .25	r = .50	r = .25	n.s.	n.s.
Zahn-Waxler, Radke-Yarrow, & Brady-Smith (1977)	3 to 6 years	Perceptual and social	Helping, sharing with, and comforting an adult	n.s.	Not reported	n.s., except $r_c = -.26$[g]	Not reported	Not reported

[a]Studies by Aronfreed & Paskal (1965), Midlarsky & Bryan (1967), Brehm, Powell, & Coke (1980), and Krebs (1975) were omitted from this table because their experimental formats did not lend themselves readily to the format used in the table.
[b]The data for affective perspective-taking were analyzed by a nonparametric statistic that could not be converted to a correlation coefficient.
[c]Nonsignificant correlation inferred from nonsignificant chi-square analysis.
[d]Correlation computed for combined experimental and control conditions.
[e]Converted from F-value.
[f]What was controlled for in this partial was not age but a measure of mental age derived from the Peabody Picture Vocabulary Test.
[g]Reported in Yarrow & Waxler (1976).

Since the sample included just over 100 children, however, we can justifiably ignore this possibility. Another possible reason is that the altruism measures were scored on a dichotomous scale (shared–didn't share, helped–didn't help, comforted–didn't comfort). Such a small range of possible scores makes it more difficult to find significant relationships. Put another way, perspective-taking may be more important in predicting the extent of a child's altruism than it is in predicting whether the child will show any altruism at all. Still a third possible explanation for the lack of significant results in this study is the fact that a very young sample was studied, much younger than the elementary-school-age children in the Underwood, Froming, and Guarijuata study. It may be that the relationship between perspective-taking and altruism is itself something that develops over time, perhaps only after children are old enough to have reached a certain level of facility at perspective-taking.

Finally, the differing results may have occurred because the Zahn-Waxler et al. study involved altruism by a child toward an adult while the Underwood et al. study involved altruism toward another child. It may be that children's interactions with adults follow a different set of rules than do their peer interactions. For example, it could be that children view adults as not needing help (or at least very much help), or it could be that situations in which a child has an opportunity to help an adult are sufficiently novel to counteract some of the usual influences on children's altruism.

Another study focusing on perspective-taking and prosocial behavior was conducted by Rushton and Wiener (1975), employing a measure of perceptual perspective-taking with 7- and 11-year old subjects and three different measures of prosocial behavior, of which two could be considered to be truly altruistic: generosity toward a friend and generosity toward a charity. These investigators report only partial correlation coefficients, controlling for age and IQ; the partial correlations of the two altruism measures with perceptual perspec-

tive-taking are all nonsignificant, as was the partial correlation in the Underwood, Froming, and Guarijuata study. Unfortunately, there is no report of zero-order correlations in the study, but we might assume that there were significant zero-order correlations since there were significant age differences on all three measures. It is not possible from inspection of these data to see if differences in perspective-taking could account for all of the significant age differences in prosocial behavior, but the data that are reported show the same pattern as the analogous data in the Underwood et al. study (1980).

A partial replication of previously obtained results was reported in a recent study (Buckley, Siegel, & Ness, 1979) in which researchers obtained a measure of visual perspective-taking in children from 3 to 8 years old. There were also two measures of altruism, helping another child clean up a mess and sharing a cookie with another child. These investigators coded altruism into a dichotomous scale (was altruistic or wasn't altruistic), based apparently on whether the children showed any altruistic behavior in either of the two situations, and obtained a significant correlation between perspective-taking and altruism ($r = .43$), as had Underwood, Froming, and Guarijuata. There was no significant correlation between age and altruism in this study, and because of this nonsignificant correlation, the partial correlation between perspective-taking and altruism (controlling for age) was significant, unlike the results of previous studies (Rushton & Wiener, 1975; Underwood, Froming & Guarijuata, 1980).

The Buckley et al. study, with its finding of a significant correlation between perspective-taking and altruism, allows some further reflection on possible explanations for the failure to obtain a significant correlation between perspective-taking and altruism in the Zahn-Waxler et al. study. Since Buckley et al. found a significant relationship using a dichotomous measure, there is the suggestion that it was not simply the use of a dichotomous measure that caused the absence of a significant relationship between perspective-taking and altruism in the Zahn-Waxler et al. data. Moreover, because the Buckley et al. sample was somewhat older and involved altruism toward a child rather than an adult, the potential moderating influences of age of the altruist and age of the beneficiary remain possible explanations for the lack of significance in the Zahn-Waxler et al. data.

To summarize, then, there is ususally a significant correlation between perceptual perspective-taking and measures of altruism, but this correlation usually becomes nonsignificant when the influence of age is controlled in the study. In the only research that allowed a direct assessment of the possibility (Underwood, Fróming, & Guarijuata, 1980),the relationship between perspective-taking and generosity was strong enough to account for the relationship between age and generosity. A failure (Zahn-Waxler et al., 1977) to replicate the usually significant relationship between perspective-taking and altruism led to the suggestion that perspective-taking may be related to altruism only for older (at least elementary-school-age) children or only for acts of altruism directed toward other children rather than toward adults.

Given that we have found one form of the supposedly unitary construct of perspective-taking to be related to prosocial behavior, we might think that it is not necessary to look at cognitive and affective role-taking and altruism. A review by Shantz (1975), however, questions the extent to which these constructs tap the same process. On reviewing several studies that included several measures of role-taking, she concludes "that there is, at best, only a moderate relationship among the various role-taking skills" (p. 300). Whether this results from differences in measurement techniques or differences in underlying mechanisms is unclear. It does suggest that the different constructs as currently operationalized may hold different relationships to prosocial action.

Social perspective-taking

Having examined the data for perceptual perspective-taking, we now turn to social perspective-taking. There has been more altruism research in this area of perspective-taking, perhaps because of the obviously social nature of altruistic actions. There are a variety of different measures that might be included in a review of social perspective-taking, ranging from the ability to predict other people's thoughts and actions to the ability to communicate with another person in a nonegocentric fashion. The measures used in the research to be reviewed reflect this diversity. It is uncommon for different studies to have used the same measure of perspective-taking (although their different measures often generate from a common idea), so that differing results may be attributable to the differing ways of operationalizing social perspective-taking. With this caveat in mind, let us proceed to examine the research findings.

An early study (Rubin & Schneider, 1973) examined the relationship between a measure of communicative egocentrism and two measures of altruism, sharing candy with "poor children" and helping a younger child complete a task. The data from Rubin and Schneider's 7-year-old subjects revealed that the less egocentric children (those more adept at perspective-taking) were more likely to share their candy ($r = .31$) and to help the younger child ($r = .44$). Since the data came from only one age group, these correlations are very nearly analogous to partial correlations controlling for the influence of age. Moreover, Rubin and Schneider did have a measure of mental age derived from the Peabody Picture Vocabulary Test (Dunn, 1959). In controlling for this mental age score by means of partial correlations, there remained a significant relationship between perspective-taking and both sharing ($r = .29$) and helpfulness ($r = .64$).

Another study involving social role-taking was reported by Krebs and Sturrup (1974). In this study, 24 second- and third-grade children were observed at school over a period of several weeks. Observers rated the children's behavior both in class and on the playground, and a measure of altruism was derived from the ratings. Social role-taking scores were derived from two rather standard measures. One measure came from a game in which the child was supposed to outwit an oponent. Questions revealed the child's ability to take the perspective of the opponent in plotting strategy. The other measure was based on the child's ability to tell a story from the perspective of another child. Social role-taking proved to be significantly correlated with altruism ($r = .46$) and was also correlated with teacher ratings of the child's altruism. An important contribution of this study is the ecological validity of the measure of altruism employed by Krebs and Sturrup. Their findings increase our confidence that social role-taking is an important determinant of altruism as it occurs in settings other than the laboratory.

The study by Rushton and Wiener (1975), described in the prior section on perceptual perspective-taking, also included two measures of communicative egocentrism. As with the perceptual measure, Rushton and Wiener found no significant correlation between these social perspective-taking scores and either of their measures of altruistic behavior, once the relationship with age had been partialed out. Again, while the zero-order correlations between perspective-taking and altruism were not reported, it is possible that they would be significant because of the common relationship with age.

Emler and Rushton (1974) performed an experiment involving two measures of social perspective-taking as well as a manipulation designed to induce varying degrees of sympathy for the beneficiaries of a donation. Perspective-taking was scored on a dichotomous scale so that the influence of perspective-taking and the sympathy manipulation on the generoisty of the 7- to 13-year-old children could be examined by an analysis of covariance. The covariate whose effects were controlled statistically was age. Analysis of these data revealed no significant ef-

fects (although there was a near-significant interaction between perspective-taking and the sympathy manipulation). This finding is precisely analogous to the finding of no significant partial correlations in the Rushton and Wiener (1975) study, and—as in that study—it is not possible to tell whether there were significant effects before the influence of age was removed.

Six of the ten measures of perspective-taking in the Zahn-Waxler, Radke-Yarrow, and Brady-Smith (1977) study were more social than perceptual. As with the perceptual measures, there was no significant relationship between social perspective-taking and any of the measures of altruism. The authors did report that, when all ten measures were combined into a single perspective-taking score, there were some near-significant correlations with some altruism measures, but even this held true only for 3-year-olds. It is perhaps most reasonable to conclude that there is no evidence in this study for a relationship between altruism and either perceptual or social perspective-taking, even given the marginal findings with 3-year-olds. This stands as the one study that has failed to provide any evidence for such relationships (excepting the Rushton studies in which the data were not reported in a form that allowed a definite conclusion). As with perceptual perspective-taking, the explanation for the lack of significant findings could be the fact that altruism was directed toward an adult rather than toward another child, the very youthful age of this sample of children, or some other, as yet undetected, factor.

Iannotti (1978) has reported a study that involved not only measures of social perspective-taking, but also experimental procedures to train 6- and 9-year-old children in perspective-taking. The children were read a series of stories, and children in a control condition were asked questions about the stories' content. Children in a perspective-taking condition, however, were asked to imagine themselves in the position of a particular character in the story and were asked questions about that character's reactions. Children in a perspective-switching condition were asked to imagine the perspective of more than one character in the story (on consecutive readings, not simultaneously) and were asked questions about the different characters' reactions. The one measure in this study that could be considered clearly altruistic was sharing candy with an anonymous other. Iannotti found a significant correlation between perspective-taking and amount shared ($r = .48$), but only for the 9-year-olds. Since Iannotti's younger subjects were about the same age as the oldest children in the Zahn-Waxler et al. study (1977), this finding would be consistent with the contention that the lack of results in the Zahn-Waxler et al. study was due to the fact that their subjects were too young to have developed the relationship that one would expect to find in older children.

The perspective-taking training conditions influenced both social perspective-taking and the altruism measure. Both the perspective-taking and perspective-switching training conditions produced higher social perspective-taking scores than did the control condition, but there was no significant difference between the two training conditions. For the 6-year-olds, there was significantly more sharing in the perspective-switching than in the perspective-taking condition and significantly more sharing in the perspective-taking condition than in the control condition. There was no significant effect of the training condition on sharing among the 9-year-olds. These findings are consistent with the idea that a relationship between perspective-taking and altruism develops only after the children are old enough to have achieved a minimal facility at perspective-taking. The training conditions increased perspective-taking scores at both ages, but increased sharing only among the younger children who were perhaps still sufficiently poor at perspective-taking that an increase in it could be expected to produce an increase in sharing. The older children, perhaps sufficiently capable at perspective-taking to have already derived its beneficial effect on altruism, increased still further at perspective-

taking as a result of the training but showed no concomitant increase in sharing.

One possible problem for this explanation of the findings is that, if training in perspective-taking leads to increased perspective-taking ability, which leads to increased sharing for the younger children, we should expect to find a positive correlation between perspective-taking and sharing in this age group. It could be that such a correlation existed for the younger children in the experimental conditions but that the absence of a relationship in the control condition diluted this positive relationship to such an extent that it could not be detected. Or, perhaps, it could be that perspective-taking is not causally related to altruism, although this explanation would make it difficult to understand why the training conditions would produce increased sharing in the younger children.

In summary, then, the evidence on social role-taking generally supports the notion that it is related to children's altruism, although perhaps only for older children or for altruism toward another child. While perceptual perspective-taking and social role-taking may represent distinct response systems (Shantz, 1975), they both seem to be positively related to altruism toward another child by elementary-school-age children.

Cognitive/affective mediators of altruism: Empathy

Although most developmental psychologists would agree that the development of role-taking capacity is central for the development of prosocial behavior, most would also agree that role-taking ability alone is not sufficient to promote prosocial action. Instead, the additional component of *affect* seems important. The distinction is one of being able to predict the actions or experience of another (role-taking) or the vicarious emotional experiencing of another's situation (empathic affect). Empathic responding has been the cornerstone of several theories of prosocial behavior (Hoffman, 1975a; Krebs, 1975). These positions see affective responding as the mediator of prosocial intervention. Hoffman (1975a) has been the most explicit writer in explaining how empathy develops and becomes linked to prosocial behavior. He says:

The central idea of the theory . . . is that since a fully developed empathic reaction is an internal response to cues about the affective states of someone else, the empathic reaction must depend heavily on the actor's cognitive sense of the other as distinct from himself which undergoes dramatic changes developmentally. The development of a sense of the other . . . interacts with the individual's early empathic responses to lay the basis for altruistic motivation. (p. 610)

Hoffman believes that origins of empathic response may be biological, but this contention is not central to his theory. Whether through built-in human tendencies or early classical conditioning, Hoffman believes that infants can come to experience the distress of another. Because in the infant the boundaries between self and other are not distinct, the child's witnessing the suffering of another evokes previous suffering of her or his own. Hoffman gives the example of a child who cuts himself or herself, feels the pain, and cries. Later, on seeing another child cut himself or herself, the sight of blood, the sound of the cry, or any other distress cue or aspect of the situation having elements in common with the child's own prior pain experience can now elicit the unpleasant affect initially associated with that experience.

As children mature, of course, they become able to distinguish their own distress from the distress of another, but Hoffman feels that children retain a component of "empathic distress" that serves to mediate and motivate prosocial intervention. The changes that children go through in the process of maturing are thought to be primarily cognitive ones, so that, for example, at about the age of 1, infants acquire a sense of themselves as distinct from others. However, according to Hoffman, while children are aware of others as distinct individuals after about age 1, they still see things only from their own perspective and so

assume that others think and feel as they do. Hoffman gives the example of a 13-month-old who brought his own mother to comfort a crying friend even though the friend's mother was present also. Another child, on seeing an adult who looked sad, offered his own favorite doll in an apparent attempt to cheer up the adult.

At about the age of 2, the child begins to be able to recognize that others have their own feelings, thoughts, and emotions. Hoffman feels that from this age until about 7 or 8 the child is evolving the capacity for role-taking. The child becomes better and better able to recognize subtle distinctions in the affective experience of others and respond in ways that may relieve the other's distress.

At about 7 or 8, the child begins to be able to respond to conditions other than immediate situational instances of distress. With greater cognitive maturity, children may begin to respond to more generalized conditions such as illness or poverty. One often finds children of this age extremely upset over the plight of animals, or they may begin to make the connection between the Kentucky Fried Chicken they had for dinner and the chick that they received for Easter.

While Hoffman sees the changes in children's prosocial concern as being mediated by the cognitive changes that the child goes through, those cognitive changes have effects on the affective experience of the child as well. It is the affective response that creates the desire to alleviate the suffering of another, and that affective response is the transformed empathic distress that was first seen in the infant.

Hoffman's theory is provocative because it traces the developmental course of empathy and links it to broader cognitive changes taking place in the child. It raises several important questions that, to varying degrees, have begun to generate empirical investigation. The first of these is what is the general influence of affect or mood on prosocial behavior? Second, what evidence exists that another's distress produces affective responding in observers? Finally, what relation exists between one's affective responding to the distress of another (empathic distress) and prosocial intervention?

Affect and prosocial behavior

Moore, Underwood, and Rosenhan (1973) attempted a direct examination of the effects of affective state on children's prosocial behavior. They asked second- and third-grade children to recall events from their lives that had made them particularly happy or particularly sad. Children assigned to a control condition spent the same amount of time doing nothing or counting slowly while the experimenter listened. After the mood manipulation, subjects were given an opportunity to donate some of the 25 pennies that they had received for participating in the experiment to other children who would not have an opportunity to participate. The experimenter emphasized to the children that donating was entirely voluntary. The child was then left alone and allowed to make a donation.

The child's affective state had a potent effect on the child's tendency to donate some of his or her resources. Children who had focused on happy thoughts gave significantly more than did control or "sad" subjects. Children who had recalled unhappy events contributed significantly less than control subjects. Moore et al. (1973) concluded that even the transitory affective states tapped in this experiment may influence the child's orientation toward others' needs. Positive affect may generate a general expansiveness to the external world—a feeling of more than adequate resources. Negative affect may generate the opposite sense—a turning inward emotionally and perhaps even perceptually. A subsequent unpublished study by the same authors extended these findings by demonstrating the same relationship with a measure of helpfulness toward an anonymous other child.

Underwood, Froming and Moore (1977) tested the idea that what might be happening under conditions of negative affect is that

subjects are less attentive to external cues and thus less aware of the needs of others. These investigators used an experimental situation almost identical to that of Moore et al., except they included in the room a bulletin board containing a number of pictures. Underwood et al. hypothesized that, if negative affect produced decreased attention to external information, the negative-affect subjects should be less able to report what was on the bulletin board. They found, however, while they replicated the previously obtained difference in donation between positive- and negative-affect subjects, there was no difference in terms of subjects' ability to recall the items on the bulletin board. So it appears it is not mere attentional deficit that produces the reduced sharing under negative affect.

Cialdini and Kenrick (1976) have raised a number of questions regarding the effects of negative mood on altruism. They contend that as the child matures, he or she increasingly internalizes social norms regarding the desirability of exhibiting prosocial behavior. Because prosocial action is valued by society, we are able to feel good about ourselves when we help others. Thus one would expect that people in a negative mood should be *more* helpful to others than people in a neutral mood, since the people in a negative mood should want to improve their mood by doing something as socially desirable and reinforcing as altruism. Cialdini and Kenrick, therefore, contend that, although negative mood may inhibit prosocial action in young children prior to the internalization of norms regarding such behavior, in older subjects the relationship should reverse.

To test their explanation, Cialdini and Kenrick replicated the procedures used by Moore and his colleagues, but with children at three different age levels in order to see if negative affect had different consequences for altruistic behavior at different ages. They found that younger children tended to donate less money after reminiscing about sad experiences; however, with tenth and twelfth grade subjects, negative affect led to increased rates of donation as compared to neutral controls. The authors interpreted these results as supporting their ideas regarding the acquired reinforcing value of prosocial action.

Unfortunately, for the sake of theoretical parsimony, two studies using adult subjects (McMillen, Sanders, & Solomon, 1977; Underwood, Berenson, Berenson, Cheng, Wilson, Kulik, Moore, & Wenzel, 1977) point out the need for further clarification of this issue. Underwood et al., using movies prerated for affective content, and McMillen et al. using negative personality feedback, found lower donation rates and helping, respectively, under conditions of negative affect. So while the general results are fairly consistent regarding the facilitative effects of positive moods on prosocial behavior, the role of negative affect is less certain and may involve counteracting tendencies.

This confusion may be partially reconciled by looking at recent work that shows that negative mood can result in increased helping when the costs of helping are low and the potential benefits are high (Kenrick, Bauman, & Cialdini, 1979; Weyant, 1978). This suggests that, when we are sad or depressed, helping someone else may be *one* way to terminate those negative feelings. It also suggests, however, that we must not perceive the costs of helping as too great if we are to help and that we need to expect to derive some benefits in terms of recognition and feeling good about ourselves.

The results of studies using direct inductions of negative affect thus present a complicated picture. The picture seems even more murky when we go back to Hoffman's theory, since it is the negative "empathic distress" that has served as the motivation for prosocial behavior in his and other (Krebs, 1975; Piliavin, Piliavin, & Rodin, 1975) theories of prosocial intervention. On one hand, then, negative affect is seen as inhibiting prosocial behavior (Moore et al., 1973; Underwood et al., 1977) and, on the other hand, as inducing prosocial action (Cialdini & Kenrick, 1976; Hoffman, 1975a).

A study that offers potential clarification

of this dilemma has been recently reported by Barnett, King, and Howard (1979). They proposed that the focus of the negative affect is likely to have a pronounced effect on what sort of behavior is produced. Barnett et al. had children focus on happy, neutral, or sad events that had been experienced either by themselves or by another child. Following the affect induction, the children were given the opportunity to share their experimental earnings with some less fortunate children. It was found that when children focused on their own sad events they were less likely to share their earnings than were neutral subjects but, when they focused on the sad events of others, it promoted sharing. This, of course, is consistent with Hoffman's ideas regarding empathy and emphasizes the necessity of explicitness when discussing the role of "negative affect" as a mediator of prosocial action. That is, it is not some generalized negative affect that promotes altruism but rather a fairly specific subvariety of negative affect.

Empathic distress

The second question we raised earlier concerning the role of empathy was whether empathic distress actually resulted from viewing another person's negative experiences. There have been several studies demonstrating that adults show physiological arousal when viewing other people's difficulties. Lazarus, Speisman, Mordkoff, and Davidson (1962) monitored the physiological responding of subjects who watched a film about particularly gruesome aspects of puberty rites in a primitive Australian tribe. This film depicted an operation on the genitals of an adolescent male performed with crude stone tools. There was evidence of abundant physiological arousal—presumably reflecting an emotional response— among the observers of the film, much more arousal than was shown by observers of a control film. This basic result has been found many times by other investigators (e.g., Bandura & Rosenthal, 1966; Geer & Jarmecky, 1973) using other means of inducing the vicarious arousal, but we need to demonstrate that similar "empathic distress" occurs in children if we wish to use it as an explanation for the development of children's prosocial actions.

Feshbach and Roe (1968) have shown that verbal reports of children often indicate distress when they are exposed to slide presentations of other children in various affect-arousing situations. For example, children may report that they "feel sad" when they see a narrated slide scene of a child who has lost a dog. Although such reports may be affected by factors such as similarity of the observer and the subject of the slide scene, and although there are obvious problems with verbal reports of affect, this research has been important in establishing an empirical basis for the existence of emotional arousal in children who witness the distress of others.

Empathic responding has also been found in a study of aggression (Thomas, Horton, Lippincott, & Drabman, 1977) that included a measure of physiological arousal (galvanic skin response) as subjects watched a violent segment from a television series or an exciting volleyball match, as well as while they watched a subsequent videotape of a supposedly "live" aggressive interaction between two kindergarten children. These researchers found evidence of physiological arousal during all these viewing times for their 8- to 10-year-old subjects. While it would be difficult to imagine arousal while watching volleyball as reflecting empathic distress, this study does provide evidence of physiological (and presumably emotional) responding to others' experiences and supplements previous findings with verbal self-reports (Feshbach & Roe, 1968).

Empathy and altruism

In spite of the extensive theoretical attention to empathy as a potential mediator of altruistic action, there has been relatively little work in this area. We will first consider studies that attempt to relate measured empathy to altruism—studies whose basic methodology is analogous to that of most of the work on social and perceptual perspective-taking. Following that, we turn to a series of studies that have attempted to induce empathy by experimental treatments and we examine the effect of this experimentally induced empathy on altruism.

The Buckley, Siegel, and Ness (1979) study, which was mentioned in the section on perceptual perspective-taking, also included a measure of empathy. This empathy measure involved telling the children a story and then questioning them about which affect was felt by the main character in the story. The empathy score was simply the number of stories in which the child was able to choose the appropriate affect. Buckely et al. found that the children who were altruistic had significantly higher empathy scores than those who were not altruistic ($p < .01$). While there was a significant relationship found in this study, some people would undoubtedly question whether such "empathy" scores truly measure empathy. That is, the scores do not reflect the child's own affective reaction to another person's distress, but merely the child's accuracy in understanding the other person's affective reaction. This is the sort of response that has been described by Feshbach and Roe (1968) as a kind of cognitive empathy, which they believe to be a precursor of the more complex mechanism of affective empathy. It could even be argued that such a measure has more in common with social perspective-taking than it does with empathy as an affective process.

Feshbach and Roe (1968) have devised a measure that focuses on the more traditional definition of empathy. In this assessment procedure, children are told a series of brief stories, and each story is accompanied by three slides that illustrate the story. There are two different stories for each of four different affects (happiness, sadness, anger, and fear), for a total of eight stories. Following each story, the child is asked how he or she feels, and the child's response can be scored in two different ways. For the more liberal scoring criterion, full credit is given only if the child's self-reported affect matches precisely the affect depicted in the story. Half-credit is given if the child reports an affect that matches the general tone of the affect in the story but is not identical to it (e.g., "feels good" for happiness, "feels bad" for the other three affects). A more stringent scoring criterion gives full credit for a matching response and no credit for any other. We might think of these scoring systems as reflecting the two major definitions of empathy. The stringent scoring system seems to measure empathy as an affective match, while the liberal score seems to be a measure of empathy as an appropriate (though not necessarily identical) affective response to another person's affect.

A recent study (Sawin, Underwood, Mostyn, & Weaver, 1980) examined the relationship between Feshbach and Roe's empathy scale and the generosity of first-grade and third-grade children. They tested more than 100 children in three different church-supported elementary schools. Children in this study were brought individually to a research trailer for the empathy measure. The children played with an attractive game in between hearing the stories that depicted the four different affects in an attempt to avoid contamination of later empathic reactions by earlier ones. At another experimental session, either one week earlier or one week later than the session in which the empathy measure was taken, the children were given a sack containing 25 marbles for helping the researcher. They had a subsequent opportunity to make an anonymous donation of some of their marbles to a collection for children who wouldn't have a chance to earn any marbles of their own, and the measure of generosity was the number of marbles donated.

Sawin et al. found no significant relationship between the Feshbach and Roe empathy measure and generosity, using either the stringent ($r = .01$) or liberal ($r = .06$) scoring system for empathy. It might be thought that the reason no significant relationship emerged was the age of the subjects. One might argue that a reliable relationship between empathy and generosity existed among the third-graders but that the absence of a relationship for the first-graders obscured the pattern for the older children. Or, perhaps it might be argued that there is no relationship for girls, that they give the marbles indiscriminately because marbles have little value for girls. These explanations are not supported by an examination of the nonsignificant empathy-generosity correlations for boys and girls within each grade level ($p > .10$ for each such test).

Sawin et al. did find a smattering of significant empathy-generosity correlations when they separated the empathy measure into the four components representing the four different affects. They also noted some significant correlations between generosity and their experimenters' subjective ratings of the children's empathy on the Feshbach and Roe task. From these findings and an analysis of the psychometric properties of their empathy measures, they suggested that empathy may not be a unitary construct. That is, empathy with another's happiness may not result from the same mechanism as empathy with the other's sadness. Furthermore, the relationship between empathy and altruism may be restricted to empathy for a few particular affects, perhaps certain types of negative affect in others. This could be one focus of future research on empathy and altruism, but it leaves us with a sense of uncertainty as to the conclusions that should be drawn from research in this area.

There have been two studies (Eisenberg-Berg & Mussen, 1978; Peraino, 1977) that have examined the relationship between empathy and altruism in adolescence, with both studies using the affective empathy questionnaire devised by Mehrabian and Epstein (1972). Eisenberg-Berg and Mussen related this empathy measure to high school students' willingness to volunteer for a dull task in order to help the experimenter and found a significant positive relationship for their 35 male subjects (biserial $r = .40$, $p <$

.05) but not for their 37 female subjects (biserial $r = -.02$, n.s.). There was no report of a correlation between age and volunteering, but the relationship between age and the empathy measure was found to be nonsignificant for both boys ($r = .09$) and girls ($r = .08$).

Peraino (1977) used a modified Prisoner's Dilemma Game in which there was a clearly altruistic choice. His subjects were 27 males in the eleventh and twelfth grades of a parochial high school. There was no significant relationship between the empathy measure and the number of times the prosocial alternative was chosen in a series of trials on the game. The findings in these two studies of adolescents, then, reveal only a rather inconsistent pattern of empathy-altruism relationship.

Mehrabian and Epstein's (1972) original report of their affective empathy questionnaire included a validation study that employed a measure of altruism in 78 female college students. These women were given an opportunity to volunteer some of their time to assist a fellow student (actually an experimental confederate). Mehrabian and Epstein reported a significant positive relationship between their empathy measure and the amount of time volunteered ($\beta = .31$ with both variables normalized, $p < .05$), but it is not clear whether this represents a zero-order correlation or a partial correlation controlling for some of the other factors in the study (liking for or perceived similarity to the confederate, etc.).

There are at least two possible ways to summarize these studies relating measured empathy to altruism. One is to note that there are occasional significant findings and occasional nonsignificant findings, point out the lack of clarity in the implications of these studies, and simply await the often-invoked "further research in the area" before arriving at definite conclusions. A second, and more speculative, summary would involve noting that significant results were found in the only study with adults (Mehrabian & Epstein, 1972), that significant results in one subsample of one study with adolescents (Eisenberg-Berg & Mussen, 1978) were apparently contradicted in the other study with adolescents (Peraino, 1977), and that the only study of truly affective empathy in children (Sawin et al. 1980) found nonsignificant overall results. This might be interpreted as indicating that there is a relationship between empathy and altruism and that it develops over time, so that it is not present during childhood, is present only partially or unstably during adolescence, and emerges as a stable relationship only during adulthood. We feel somewhat uneasy about this second way of summarizing the findings, since it is based on only one or two studies within each age grouping, but it certainly must be considered as a possible explanation for the divergent findings.

There have been several studies in which experimenters have attempted either to induce empathy or provide an experimental analogue to the acquisition of empathy. Aronfreed and Paskal (1965) examined the role of an experimenter's affective expression and the social reinforcement of the experimenter in affecting the child's altruism. The 6- to 8-year-old girls in this study played a game which included pressing a lever on a machine. One lever would dispense a piece of candy that the child could keep, while the other would turn on a red light. When the child pressed the lever that turned on the the light, the experimenter would provide either social reinforcement (smiling and hugging the child) or an expression of positive affect (exclaiming joyfully at the appearance of the light) or both. Following this training period, the experimenter would exclaim joyfully whenever the child pressed the lever that turned on the red light. The measure of altruism was the number of trials on which the child pressed the lever that pleased the experimenter rather than the lever that provided candy for the child. The children who had received both the social reinforcement and an expression of positive affect scored higher on altruism than those who had received only the social reinforcement or only an expression of positive affect.

The implication of these findings is that the child's positive affect (produced by the social reinforcement) had become associated with the experimenter's expression of positive affect through a conditioning process. The experimenter's positive affect would then be a conditioned stimulus that leads to positive affect in the child, producing the sort of affective match required by one definition of empathy. The altruistic action would be mediated, according to this analysis, by the child's empathy with the positive affect produced in the experimenter by the child's altruistic act. Midlarsky and Bryan (1967) replicated these results and also showed that children who received the combined reinforcement-plus-positive-affect training were more generous in anonymous donations of candy to "poor children." The latter finding demonstrates that the training effect was not due solely to a desire to appear nice to the experimenter, since the experimenter would have no way to know about the anonymous donation.

Even so, these findings do not automatically establish the role of empathy in altruism. We might argue that the experimenter's positive affect served as an exhortation to behave altruistically and that the results indicate only that combining exhortation with reinforcement is more effective than either treatment in isolation. We might note that there is no direct evidence that empathy was even produced by these treatments, since empathy was not actually measured in either study. And even if we conceded that empathy was the crucial factor in producing these experimental findings, we might maintain that empathy is not involved in naturally occurring altruistic acts, where there is no special empathy training.

A recent study by Brehm, Powell, and Coke (1980) investigated the effect of an attentional empathy manipulation on children's generosity. First-grade children (35 girls and 32 boys) were given 10 pennies for allowing their answers to questions about their summer vacations to be tape-recorded. They were then asked to listen to a conversation between a boy or girl named Chris and an adult female. Subjects in the empathy condition were asked to focus on Chris' feelings and to pretend that what happened to Chris had happened to them. Subjects in the control condition were asked to listen carefully to see what Chris said and did. Thus the conditions differed in the focus of attention they promoted—the control condition emphasizing overt behavior and the empathy condition emphasizing feelings. The children then heard Chris tell how he/she would be unable to have a birthday party because his/her family didn't have enough money to buy candy and cake for the party. Finally, the children were given an opportunity to donate anonymously to a fund for Chris' party. Analysis of variance revealed a marginally significant interation ($p < .06$) between subject sex and type of instruction. Males donated significantly more in the empathy condition [$F(1,59) = 4.75, p < .05$] while there was no significant difference for females.

This study represents a methodological step forward, since the manipulation is much more directly and unambiguously linked to the concept of empathy than was the case in the earlier (Aronfreed & Paskal, 1965; Midlarsky & Bryan, 1967) studies. However, there are still problems, including the fact that the finding was only marginally significant. Moreover, empathy instructions did not affect children's self-reports of their own emotional state while hearing about Chris' needy situation and, thus, there is no direct evidence that empathy instructions increased empathic response. We should also point out, however, that the responsiveness of males but not females to the manipulation in this study may parallel Eisenberg-Berg and Mussen's (1978) finding of a relationship between measured empathy and altruism for male but not female adolescents. Both studies may be illuminating a consistent pattern in which the empathy-altruism relationship develops earlier for males than for females, although this obviously must remain a tentative conclusion until more evidence has been collected.

There are two studies of manipulated

empathy and altruism in adults, including one by Krebs (1975), who investigated the impact of certain situational factors on both empathy and altruism. Adult male subjects watched another person perform a game in which he could win or lose on each trial. Subjects in the high-empathy condition were told that the performer would be rewarded (with money) for wins and punished (with electric shocks) for losses, whereas those in the low-empathy condition were not given such expectations. Within each empathy condition, the performer was portrayed as either highly similar or highly dissimilar to the subjects. Krebs measured subjects' affective reactions to a series of trials by means of a physiograph. Finally, subjects were given the opportunity to divide the amount of reward for a win and punishment for a loss between themselves and the performer. Assigning more money to the performer or more shock to oneself was scored as a more altruistic action. Krebs found that subjects in the high-empathy, high-similarity condition displayed both the most intense affect on physiological measures (and thus, presumably, the most empathy) and the greatest amount of altruism.

This is a somewhat more convincing study than the ones previously discussed, since it does demonstrate that the condition that produced the most altruistic action also produced the most affective reaction. However, if it is true that the affect reflects empathy and that it is this empathy that produces the altruism, it is necessary that the affect measure and the altruism measure be positively correlated in the high-empathy, high-similarity condition (Underwood, 1975). Otherwise, these results may reflect only parallel—but unrelated—effects of the independent variables on the two dependent measures. Unfortunately, Krebs does not report this within-condition correlation, so we are still left without a definite conclusion regarding the relationship of empathy to altruism.

Perhaps the most convincing single source of evidence for a relationship between empathy and altruism is a pair of studies by Coke, Batson, and McDavis (1978). These investigators attempted to induce empathy by manipulating the inferences their subjects (college students) made about their own arousal states. In the initial study, both males and females were given a capsule whose described side effects included a state of either relaxation or arousal. The subjects then listened to a tape-recorded "newscast" about a recently orphaned undergraduate student who was struggling to finish her degree while supporting her younger brother and sister; an observational set that highlighted either the broadcasting techniques or the feelings of the student depicted in the recording was also used. It was anticipated that subjects who focused on the student's feelings would feel arousal, which the relaxation-state subjects would attribute to their empathic reaction and the arousal-state subjects would misattribute to the pill they had taken. It was anticipated that subjects in the imagined-feelings relaxation-state condition would experience more empathic distress and would therefore volunteer more time to help the student depicted in the recording when given an opportunity to do so. Analysis of the data on amount of time volunteered to help the student confirmed this expectation, but—as we have seen in other studies—there was no direct measure of empathic distress.

Coke et al. set out to rectify this omission in a second study with female students as subjects. In this study, all subjects listened to a taped appeal for help from a graduate student under an instructional set similar to that in the imagined-feelings condition of the initial study. Perceived arousal was manipulated by false feedback about galvanic skin response (GSR) activity. The feedback indicated either that the subject was in the normal range of arousal or was highly (and increasingly) aroused during the taped presentation. Following the presentation, subjects filled out an adjective checklist that included five items to make up an empathic concern index: empathic, concerned, warm, softhearted, and compassionate. Subjects then filled out other questionnaires and responded to a written request for help from the student in the taped presentation. The helping response was coded according to the amount of time that was volunteered to help the student. Subjects in the high-arousal condition volunteered significantly more time than those in the normal-arousal condition, $F(1, 31) = 9.73, p < .005$. Furthermore, the index of empathic concern was significantly related to the helping measure, $r(31) = .59, p < .001$. There was a further suggestion, from a stepwise regression analysis, that this result was not due simply to generalized arousal but was due instead to the specific mechanism of empathic concern.

Alas, even this study has some aspects that are less than ideal, although the inclusion of a measure of empathic concern represents another important step forward in establishing definitely the role of empathy in altruism. One difficulty with the study is that the empathy-helping correlation was apparently computed for the two groups combined, but a stepwise regression analysis implies that the correlation would still have been significant (though perhaps not of the same magnitude) if it had been computed for the two groups separately. Moreover, there seems to be an obvious possibility that demand characteristics could have produced the results obtained in the second study, though it is difficult to imagine that the similar results of the first study could have been due to experimental demand.

Our evaluation of the evidence in this section inclines us toward the belief that empathy is related to altruism, at least among adults. This is not, however, a conclusion that we hold to with as much conviction as we do our conclusions about the relationship of perceptual and social perspective-taking to altruism. Much of the empirical support for this conclusion is too indirect to inspire great feelings of confidence, and the existence of several instances of negative results may erode confidence still further. Yet, in view of the present evidence, we cling uneasily to the belief that empathy and altruism are related.

Summary

We have seen that there is a sound basis for concluding that both perceptual and social perspective-taking are positively related to altruism (see Table 4.1). What we cannot evaluate as yet is whether this relationship involves a causal influence of perspective-taking ability (see Figure 4.1a) or is merely an artifactual relationship produced by the increase in both variables with increasing age (see Figure 4.1b). It is even possible that altruism plays the causal role in this relationship (see Figure 4.1c). It could be that altruism is increased by other mechanisms (increasing salience of norms, cumulating socialization pressures, etc.) and that this increased responsiveness to others promotes increased attention to the potentially different perspectives and feelings of others. Perhaps the most important focus of future research on perspective-taking and altruism is the clarification of the causal pathways involved in the relationship, using both experimental treatments and advanced correlational methodologies, such as path analysis.

The situation is very different in the area of empathy, for the very existence of an empathy-altruism relationship can be questioned. Here the research should focus on solidifying the basis for inferring that such a relationship exists. One method for doing this would be a cross-sectional study using the same measures of empathy and altruism at different ages to show whether an empathy-altruism relationship does or does not exist and does or does not develop with age. Prior research would seem to indicate that the most fruitful age range for such research would be the years between late childhood and early adulthood. A further contribution in the area would be a conceptual replication of studies on the experimental induction of empathy, without the attendant drawbacks of current efforts. This would include using a measure of empathy not only to validate the manipulation, but to confirm that individual differences in altruism are correlated with individual differ-

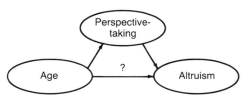

(a) Age has a causal influence on perspective-taking (and perhaps on altruism) and perspective-taking has a causal influence on altruism.

ences in empathy within the condition that promotes both empathy and altruism. It would also include avoiding the possibility of experimental demand as an alternative explanation, as least insofar as possible. Only once the existence of a relationship between empathy and altruism has been firmly established can we reasonably move on to the more interesting research issues of the causal pathways involved and the types of situations in which empathy assumes greater or lesser importance as a determinant of altruistic action.

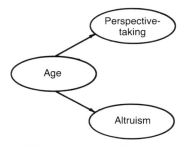

(b) Age has a causal influence on both altruism and perspective-taking, but those two variables have no causal influence on each other.

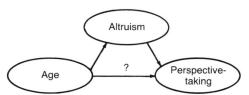

(c) Age has a causal influence on altruism (and perhaps on perspective-taking), and altruism has a causal influence on perspective-taking.

5

OPPOSITIONAL BEHAVIOR IN CHILDREN:
A REACTANCE THEORY APPROACH

SHARON S. BREHM

UNIVERSITY OF KANSAS

Every parent and every teacher at one time or another has had experience with oppositional behavior in children. The "terrible two's" are legendary, and the teenage years sometimes seem like an elaborate chess game in which the goal for the adolescent is to do the exact opposite of whatever an adult has requested. The apparent pervasiveness of oppositional behavior by children in the "real" world is matched by the ubiquitous appearance of this behavior as a topic of psychological inquiry. Early references to oppositional behavior are found in the writings of Baldwin (1900), R. MacDougall (1911–1912), and F. Allport (1924). The 1920s and 1930s marked a period of especially intensive research on what was then called "resistant" or "negativistic" behavior in children, with a number of investigators seeking to delineate the determinants and correlates of this behavior (e.g., Caille, 1933; Goodenough, 1929; Levy & Tulchin, 1923, 1925; Mayers, 1935; Nelson, 1931; Reynolds, 1928; Rust, 1931; Thom, 1924; Wooley, 1924).

More recently, interest in children's oppositional behavior has continued to flourish. Numerous research efforts have examined both compliant and oppositional behavior in both normal populations of children and with children having a history of chronic oppositionalism. Complete coverage of all this literature would vastly exceed the scope of this chapter (and, perhaps, the endurance of the reader as well). Instead, the present discussion will approach oppositional behavior in children from the perspective provided by a specific theoretical framework—that of J. Brehm's theory of psychological reactance.

The application of reactance theory to oppositional behavior in children would seem to be distinctly advantageous. Reactance theory was formulated as a way to account for and predict oppositional and resistant behavior. The only leap of faith involved in the present discussion will be a developmental one: from a theory based on adult behavior to an application of this theory to the behavior of developing organisms. The relevant research literature to be reviewed in this chapter suggests, I believe,

Portions of this chapter also appear in S. S. Brehm and J. W. Brehm. *Psychological reactance: A theory of freedom and control.* New York: Academic Press, in press. Preparation of this chapter was supported, in part, by a grant from the General Research Fund of the University of Kansas. Special thanks to Jack W. Brehm for his suggestions and comments.

that such a developmental shift has considerable empirical support and will involve only a modicum of faith.

This chapter will first present an overview of the basic theoretical framework, and then two categories of literature will be reviewed. The initial category is a summary of reactance research that has been conducted with children. These investigations, while not designed with this purpose in mind, do seem to indicate that the theory "works" with children as well as with adults. The second category of literature to be discussed is more diverse. Three topic areas involving different aspects of oppositional behavior in children have been selected for more extensive examination. Some of the research on these topics has been conducted within the rubric of reactance theory; most, however, stems from other theoretical perspectives. In the present consideration of these topics, reactance theory will be used in an attempt to provide an integrative approach to these various research findings.

Theoretical overview

The empirical support for reactance theory that has been garnered from adult populations has been reviewed in J. Brehm's original presentation of the theory (Brehm, 1966), in R. A. Wicklund's subsequent volume (Wicklund, 1974), and is discussed in considerable detail in a forthcoming book (Brehm & Brehm, in press). In the following pages, I will not attempt to cover this rather well-trodden ground. The theoretical overview to be provided will be purely theoretical, without reference to the empirical details. The interested reader who wishes to examine the empirical support for these theoretical propositions is referred to the above sources.

Behavioral freedoms

Reactance theory assumes that every individual possesses a finite number of specific behavioral freedoms. A behavior is free if the individual is currently engaging in it and/or expects to be able to engage in the behavior in the future. "Behavior" here is used in its broadest sense. It refers to subjective states such as emotions, attitudes, and beliefs as well as overt behaviors. As long as the person perceives the freedom to do "it," "it" is a specific behavioral freedom.

Two attributes of the behavior are necessary if the behavior is to be considered a freedom. First, the person must be aware that the behavior exists (at least potentially) and that he or she is free to engage in it. This characteristic indicates the *subjective* framework of reactance theory's concept of freedom. It is irrelevant to the theory whether other people regard a person as having a freedom or not. What is solely relevant is the person's own perspective. If Johnny Jones believes he has the freedom to go to bed when he pleases, then, for the theory, this constitutes a free behavior for Johnny even if Johnny's parents don't view the bedtime situation in quite this way.

The second necessary behavioral attribute is that the person believe that he or she is competent to exercise the freedom. I may believe that I have the freedom to win an Olympic gold medal for the 100-meter dash, but since I know perfectly well that I am not competent to do this, the freedom exists in only a trivial sense. Again, however, it is important to emphasize that it is *perceived* competence that is the issue. If I believed that I were competent to win this gold medal, no matter how foolish and ill-founded my belief, this would be sufficient to establish this freedom as a meaningful one.

One other aspect of behavioral freedoms should be noted. Reactance theory does not address the general notion of freedom. Instead, it focuses on specific behavioral freedom*s*. Moreover, the theory has nothing to say about people's need or desire for freedom. All the theory posits is that people view themselves as having certain behavioral freedoms. How they came to have this view, or what psychological functions are served by such perceptions, are interesting questions, but ones that lie outside the purview of the theory.

Threats and eliminations

Since, according to the theory, freedoms exist, their existence can be threatened with elimination or, indeed, be eliminated. Such threats to or eliminations of freedoms produce psychological reactance, a motivational state directed toward the reestablishment of a specific behavioral freedom. If a person believes that an existing free behavior is threatened with elimination, then reactance should be aroused. Actual eliminations of freedom pose a more difficult theoretical issue. Presuming a person expects to be free to do X, the elimination of his or her freedom to do X should arouse reactance. At some point, however, eliminations can be irrevocable, and the person should no longer perceive the freedom to exist. After this point, reactance arousal should no longer take place in regard to this specific behavior. The distinction between what kinds of eliminations will arouse reactance and what kinds will not is still not entirely clear. We might suppose, however, that repeated eliminations of freedom are likely to result in giving up the freedom and that some eliminations, though occurring only once, would be perceived by the person as irrevocable and that the freedom would be given up almost immediately.

Determinants of the magnitude of reactance arousal

Reactance is posited to be a motivational state that can vary in its strength. The magnitude of reactance that is aroused will, in general, be determined by characteristics of the freedom that is threatened and by characteristics of the threat. One determinant of the magnitude of reactance aroused is the importance of the freedom that is threatened. Freedom importance is deemed to be an interactive function of the unique instrumental value that a specific behavior has for satisfying a specific need *and* of the

magnitude of the need state. If behavior X and behavior Y can both satisfy need A *equally well,* then a threat to eliminate behavior X should not arouse reactance. Behavior Y still exists, and the need can still be satisfied. The "equally well" provision in this theoretical statement is, however, crucial and severely restricts the instances where behavioral freedoms will not have unique instrumental value. Indeed, since "equally well" is hard to obtain once behaviors are at all different—even though they satisfy the same need—we could, for practical purposes, rephrase this proposition to apply only to identical behaviors. In general, then, importance of the freedom will depend on the magnitude of the need that would be satisfied by engaging in the free behavior, *unless* there are multiple *identical* free behaviors available and only one is threatened. In this case, no reactance should be aroused regardless of the strength of the need.

Since all this gets a bit abstract, let us consider an example in which magnitude of need and unique instrumental value are varied. Suppose that I walk up to a soft drink vending machine, believing that I have the freedoms to press any one of the levers displayed there for orange soda, grape soda, and cola. While I am contemplating my choice, a friend of mine comes along and presses the cola lever. My friend's rather clumsy attempt to control my soft drink consumption should clearly threaten my freedoms to choose orange or grape soda, and reactance should be aroused. How much reactance will be aroused will depend on the strength of my thirst for the eliminated types of soft drinks. Now let us change the situation a bit. Suppose that the vending machine again has three levers, but this time each lever is for the same kind of cola. If my friend presses one of the cola levers, reactance should not be aroused by this action. The colas dispensed by each lever are identical, and thus none of the levers has unique instrumental value to satisfy my thirst for cola.[1]

Another characteristic of the freedom that determines magnitude of reactance aroused is the proportion of freedoms that are threatened. In general, the greater the proposition threatened, the more reactance will be aroused. Suppose, for example, that Cindy goes to the library and finds four books she would like to read. If her freedom to read any one of these books is threatened (perhaps, by an intrusive librarian who tells her the book is too hard for her), her reactance arousal in this situation will be greater than if she had found ten books to read. In the first instance, 25% of her total available freedoms in that situation have been threatened; in the latter case, only 10% would have been threatened.

The number of freedoms threatened can also determine the magnitude of reactance aroused. This notion becomes particularly important when we consider that threats to a specific freedom at one time can have implications for future freedoms. If, in the example above, Cindy had taken the librarian's interference with her reading habits to imply that the librarian might well interfere on future occasions, more reactance should be aroused than if Cindy perceived the librarian's behavior to be restricted to this one book. When threats are seen as having implications for future freedoms, a greater number of one's freedoms are threatened and more reactance should be aroused.

Having considered the determinants of the magnitude of reactance that are related to characteristics of the *freedom,* we can now turn to those characteristics of the *threat* that determine the magnitude of reactance aroused. The general principle is quite simple: the greater the magnitude of the threat, the greater the magnitude of reactance aroused by that threat. In practice, however, magnitude of threat can be influenced by a number of factors. Sometimes threats will be greater in force because they are issued in such a way that they exert more pressure on the person to comply. "Do this" is a greater threat to freedom than "Would you consider doing this?" The force of the threat also depends on characteristics of the agent. If someone who has authority over me tells me to do something, the threat to

my freedom *not* to do this is much greater than if someone without authority makes the same statement.

Force of threat can also be increased by perceived intent to persuade. If a disinterested party gives us some information that would tend to lead us to choose X instead of Y, very little threat to freedom may be perceived. When, however, someone that we perceive as wanting us to do X gives us this information, the knowledge that the person desires a certain behavior from us can increase the perceived threat to freedom. Finally, magnitude of threat can vary according to the number of threats received. Telling Billy over and over again to clean up his room poses a greater threat to his freedom *not* to clean it up than just telling him once. In all these instances—the more forcefully worded the influence attempt, the greater the power of the influence agent to punish noncompliance, the greater the perceived intent to persuade of the influence agent, and the greater the number of threats posed to a freedom—the magnitude of threat is increased, and so should be the magnitude of reactance aroused.

It is important to note that two factors limit the amount of reactance that can be aroused relative to the magnitude of threat. First, the importance of the freedom places limits on the amount of reactance that potentially can be aroused; the more important the freedom, the greater the amount of potential reactance. Thus, for a relatively unimportant freedom, the maximum possible reactance arousal is less than for a relatively important freedom. Once the maximum amount of potential reactance is reached, further increments in magnitude of threat will not increase the amount of reactance aroused. A second factor limiting the amount of reactance that can be aroused occurs when a freedom is unequivocally eliminated. Once the freedom has been given up, the magnitude of threat involved is irrelevant. Without an established freedom, reactance will not be aroused.

Effects of reactance arousal

Reactance arousal constitutes a state in which the individual is motivated to restore the behavioral freedom that has been threatened or eliminated. The most direct effect of reactance arousal, then, would be engagement in the threatened free behavior. To go back to some of the previous examples, I could restore my freedom by inserting some more money in the vending machine and pressing the lever for grape soda; Cindy could insist on her right to read the threatened book and read it as soon as she possibly can; and Billy could continue not to clean his room and, even, restore his freedom more forcefully by making sure it gets messier than ever.

Two counterforces will reduce the amount of direct restorative behavior that is likely to take place. First, all of the factors that increase the magnitude of threat to freedom, and thus increase reactance, are also factors that increase the likelihood of compliance. Thus, we have the apparent paradox that the harder an offer becomes to refuse, the more we will be motivated to refuse it. This relationship between compliance forces and reactance forces is mediated by the importance of the specific behavioral freedom involved. When the importance of the freedom is low, threats to freedom should reduce compliance to the extent that reactance is aroused (i.e., proportional to the magnitude of reactance aroused), but oppositional behavior is unlikely to occur. Overall, the forces toward compliance will always outweigh the reactance forces, because only a relatively small amount of reactance is maximally possible for a relatively unimportant freedom. When the freedom is of moderate importance, reactance arousal will result in oppositional behavior, but oppositional behavior will only increase up to that point where the maximum amount of reactance has been aroused. Past that point, the amount of reactance aroused cannot increase while the forces toward compliance can. Thus, past the point of maximum reactance, oppositional behavior should be reduced and, at some point where strong pressures toward compliance are used, compliance rather than opposition should occur. Finally, consider the case of an extremely important freedom. In this instance, the potential amount of reactance that can be aroused is for all practical purposes limitless. With such a freedom, opposition to influence will increase as a direct function of the magnitude of threat.

The above comparisons would apply, however, only to those situations where the costs for either reduced compliance or actual opposition are relatively low. There are times, and these times may be especially frequent for children in relation to adults, that the power of the influencing agent to punish noncompliance is such that direct restoration of freedom is not feasible. It is important to distinguish this kind of situation from an irrevocable elimination of freedom. When, for example, a social agent eliminates a freedom in such an irrevocable fashion that the freedom no longer exists for the target individual, reactance arousal should be brief. On the other hand, a social agent may be powerful enough to prohibit expression of reactance arousal, but still not irrevocably eliminate the freedom. In this instance, reactance would still be aroused, but no direct restorative action would occur. Viewed externally, the target individual would appear to comply.

From an internal point of view, however, the reactance that has been aroused may have significant psychological consequences. The person is still motivated to engage in the behavior that has become unavailable, and the behavior should be seen as attractive and desirable. Thus, if a future opportunity should arise where the person could engage in that behavior (without risking punishment for it), one would expect him or her to do so. Moreover, even if another opportunity for direct restorative behavior does not occur, the person may seek to indirectly restore his or her freedom. Methods of indirect restoration could include getting someone else (who runs less risk of punishment or, at least, is less concerned about being punished) to engage in the forbidden behavior, engaging in a similar but unforbidden behavior, or opposing the social agent whenever opposition does not risk prohibitive amounts of punishment.

A final internal consequence of reactance arousal may be especially important for future interpersonal relationships between a social agent who arouses reactance and the target individual. Although reactance arousal is not invariably accompanied by hostility toward the agent, hostility is certainly a possible response. One would suppose that the probability of hostility being generated would be higher in those situations where direct restorative action was effectively prohibited by the power of the agent to punish noncompliance. Thus, when compliance is obtained through strong social influence attempts that also arouse reactance, the likelihood of future amiable interactions may well be significantly impaired.

Reactance research with children

Reactance theory addresses itself to basic motivational processes that are assumed to be widespread and universal. The content of these processes—that is, the exact freedoms that an individual perceives himself or herself to possess and the exact nature of threats to or eliminations of those freedoms—would be expected to vary widely among different individuals and different cultural milieus, but the processes themselves should remain constant. Constancy of motivational process has also been assumed in regard to age and developmental status of the organism. Indeed, many reactance researchers appear to have viewed children as interchangeable with adults when it came to serving as subjects in experimental investigations. Most of the reactance research that has been conducted with children was not designed to demonstrate the applicability of the theory to younger organisms, but, instead, was simply taking advantage of a convenient subject population for investigating theoretical propositions. Taken as a whole, however, this research does provide empirical

support for using the theory to help us understand the oppositional behavior of children as well as adults.

Importance of freedom

A study by Worchel (1972) demonstrated that reactance arousal could be increased for children when the importance of the freedom that was threatened was increased. Subjects in this study were boys and girls between the ages of 6 and 12 who were attending summer camp. Subjects were either shown a movie or not. For those who were shown a movie, one-half of them saw an aggressive movie about boxing, and the other half a nonaggressive movie about boats and ships. All subjects were led to believe that they would choose to engage in one of two activites: having a pie fight or riding one-person rubber rafts. When a second experimenter entered to get their choices, this experimenter (same sex as subjects) either verbally pressured subjects to choose the pie fight, to choose the raft, or did not pressure them to choose either of the two alternate activities. The major dependent measure was subjects' choice of their subsequent activity.

Worchel had reasoned that viewing a movie would make the freedom to engage in activities similar to those depicted in the movie more salient and more important. Reactance arousal was, therefore, expected to be greatest for subjects who saw a movie and were then pressured to choose the activity that was *different* from that depicted in the film. These subjects should restore freedom by choosing the activity that was similar to that shown in the movie.

The results from this study are displayed in Table 5.1. First, let us examine subjects' choices when they either saw a movie *or* were pressured to choose a subsequent activity. Although these differences were not statistically reliable, it can be seen that subjects who saw a movie but did not receive any verbal pressure tended to choose a subsequent activity that was similar to the one in the movie, while subjects who had not

Table 5.1. Percentage of Subjects Who Chose the Film-Related Activity[a]

Movie Seen	Verbal Pressure		
	To Choose the Pie Fight	To Choose the Raft	None
Aggressive movie	56%	88%	67%
Boat movie	100	67	78
No movie			
chose pie fight	67	25	33
chose raft	33	75	67

Note. Adapted from "The effects of films on the importance of behavioral freedom" by S. Worchel, *Journal of Personality,* 1972, *40,* 417–435. Copyright © 1972 by the Duke University Press. Reprinted by permission.
[a]There were nine subjects in every condition, except the No Movie–Verbal Pressure to Choose Raft, in which there were eight subjects.

seen a movie tended to choose in line with the verbal pressure they received. Second, when we consider only those subjects who both saw a movie *and* were verbally pressured, significantly more subjects chose the film-related activity when the verbal pressure was to choose the dissimilar activity (94%) than when the verbal pressure was to choose the similar activity (61%). Pressuring children *not* to choose a film-related activity thus led to more choices of this type of activity than when they were pressured to choose a film-related activity.

Proportion of freedoms

Reactance arousal in adolescents has been shown to be a function of the proportion of freedoms that is eliminated. In a study by Brehm, McQuown, and Shaban (reported in Brehm, 1966), eighth-grade students read a brief description of each of six movies and rated and ranked these movies according to how much they would like to see each one. In a later session, groups of subjects were told either that they could choose one of the movies to see from a list provided by the experimenter or that they would be assigned one of the movies. Subjects were then provided with lists of either all six movies or of each individual's three top-ranked movies. Following inspection of the list, subjects in the No Elimination condition were asked to re-rate all six movies. For all

other subjects, before they could begin to fill out the rating questionnaire again, an assistant entered the room and whispered something to the experimenter. After this, the experimenter announced that one of the movies did not arrive with the others and, therefore, could not be seen.

The experimenter and assistant then went to each subject individually and marked off his or her second-ranked movie. Subjects were instructed, however, to go ahead and re-rate all of the six original movies. The data from this study confirmed the theoretical predictions that had been made. Subjects who expected to choose a movie and who had a high proportion of their freedoms eliminated (one movie from the list of three) became more favorable to the eliminated movie than did subjects in the Choice-Low Proportion condition (one movie eliminated from the list of six), the No Choice-High Proportion condition, or the No Elimination control group (although this last difference was only marginal, $p = .10$). Reactance arousal was thus maximized when the freedom to have any one of the choice alternatives had been established and when the elimination of one of these freedoms eliminated a large proportion of the subjects' available freedoms.

Threat to freedom

A study by Weiner (reported by Brehm, 1966) examined children's responses to a peer's threat to their decisional freedom. Subjects in this study were first-grade students who were seen individually and told that they would get to choose a gift toy for themselves as a reward for helping out the experimenter. All subjects rank-ordered seven toys. About a week later, these children were asked to rank the toys again, and this second ranking was described as constituting the child's final choice of a gift. Half of the subjects re-ranked the toys without further comment from the experimenter. To the other half, the experimenter remarked, "Oh, by the way you remember the day when all the boys (girls) came to look at the toys for the first time? Well, one of them said something to me about you. Let's see, (s)he said, '(*Name of the subject*) *has* to choose the (*name of subject's preferred toy*). (S)he can't *choose* anything else.' So I asked him/her why (s)he said that, and (s)he said (s)he didn't know, just that '(*Name of the subject*) has to choose it, that's all.' " These subjects then re-ranked the toys. As had been predicted, children who had been told that a peer was pressuring them to choose their initially most preferred toy reduced the ranking of that toy ($M = -1.38$) significantly more than children who were not informed of any peer pressure ($M = -.43$).

Elimination of freedom

Two studies by Hammock and Brehm (1966) investigated children's responses to an elimination of freedom. Subjects in their first study were male and female black children ranging in age from 7 to 11. Each child was seen individually in the experiment. When subjects arrived at the first experimental room, they were randomly assigned to either a Choice or No Choice condition. Subjects in the Choice condition were told that, as a reward for telling the experimenter how much they liked each of nine candy bars, they would be allowed to choose one of the two candy bars that were in another room. No Choice subjects were given the same information, except that they were told they

would be *given* one of the two candy bars in the other room.

All subjects then ranked the nine candy bars (by a process of eliminating the one the subject liked best from each set of diminishing number). On the pretext of obtaining a form, the experimenter left the room and informed the second experimenter in the other room of the subject's third- and fourth-ranked candy bars. The experimenter then returned to the subject and escorted him or her to the other room. For Choice subjects, the experimenter told the second experimenter that they could choose whichever candy bar they wanted. For No Choice subjects, the experimenter stated that the subject should be given a candy bar. After the first experimenter left the room, the second experimenter displayed the child's third- and fourth-ranked candy bars and gave the child his or her third-ranked candy; no child was given any opportunity to express a preference. The child was then returned to the first room and the first experimenter, claiming that he had made a mistake in recording the subject's preferences, asked all subjects to re-rank all the candy bars.

Hammock and Brehm had predicted that, relative to the rankings by subjects in the No Choice conditions, children in the Choice condition should increase their rankings of the candy they had been denied (initially fourth-ranked) and decrease their rankings of the candy they had been given (initially third-ranked). Their results provided partial support of these hypotheses. Although a total reactance score (combining changes from both items) was significantly different between the two groups, the separate components of this total score were not particularly robust. For the candy they had not received, Choice subjects tended to rate ($p = .08$) this candy bar as more attractive than subjects in the No Choice condition (see Table 5.2). For the candy they were given, No Choice subjects did not differ significantly from Choice subjects. Thus, while the general pattern of results supported the experimental hypotheses, the effects were somewhat weak.

Table 5.2. Mean Ranking Changes

Study	No Choice Conditions		Choice Conditions	
	Eliminated Fourth[a]	Given Third	Eliminated Fourth	Given Third
Hammock & Brehm, 1966, First Study	−.43	.00	+.23	−1.23
Brehm, in press				
Males	−.97	−.66	−.08	−1.50
Females	+.13	−.97	−.82	−1.00
	Eliminated Third[a]	Given Fourth	Eliminated Third	Given Fourth
Hammock & Brehm, 1966, Second Study	−.94	.00	−.11	−.86

Note. Adapted from "The attractiveness of choice alternatives when freedom to choose is eliminated by a social agent" by T. Hammock and J. W. Brehm, *Journal of Personality*, 1966, *34*, 546–554. Copyright © 1966 by the Duke University Press. Reprinted by permission. Adapted also from "Psychological reactance and the attractiveness of unobtainable objects: Sex differences in children's responses to an elimination of freedom" by S. S. Brehm, *Sex Roles*, in press. Copyright pending by Plenum Publishing Co. Reprinted by permission.
[a]Initial ranks

In their second study, Hammock and Brehm used a similar procedure with some modifications. Subjects were white, all male, and ranged in age from 8 to 12. Instead of nine candy bars, ten toys each costing $1 were used as stimulus materials. It was made explicit to all subjects that the two toys (that, as in the first study, either they could choose between or one of which would be given to them) would be two of the ten they ranked, although possibly not the two they liked best. One further modification in this study was especially important: All subjects were given their fourth-ranked toy and denied their third-ranked one.

This latter change in procedure creates some interpretive ambiguity. The procedure used in the first study (giving subjects the more preferred of the two toys) clearly rules out frustration as an alternative explanation for the obtained results. In the second study (where the subjects were given their less preferred toy), the elimination of frustration is

not so clear. Neither of the toys was the subjects' favorite, or even their next most favored toy, and yet it could be argued that subjects would be frustrated by being denied that toy (of the two available) that they found most attractive. Moreover, frustration might be increased for subjects who had expected to choose and who had, presumably, intended to choose the toy they liked best. In any case, the results continued to be somewhat weak statistically. Again, the total reactance score was significantly different between the two experimental conditions, but the component comparisons were only marginal. For the toy they were denied, Choice subjects tended ($p = .09$) to rank this toy as more attractive than No Choice subjects; whereas for the toy they were given, Choice subjects tended ($p < .08$) to rank this toy as less attractive (see Table 5.2).

The Hammock and Brehm studies have recently been replicated by S. Brehm (in press). Following essentially the same procedures used in their second experiment, Brehm was particularly interested in possible differences between the sexes and different ages. While Hammock and Brehm had included both boys and girls in their first study, the number of members of each sex was quite small and precluded obtaining any sex differences unless these differences were quite strong. A similar problem existed in regard to age. It is important to note that Brehm attempted to eliminate frustration by following Hammock and Brehm's initial procedure of giving the child his or her more attractive (third-ranked) alternative and denying the child the less attractive (fourth-ranked) one.

Subjects for this experiment were 140 first- and sixth-grade children from two public elementary schools. An overall analysis of the ranking changes of the eliminated toy revealed a significant interaction between experimental condition and sex of subjects, and separate analyses by sex were performed. Although such an interaction was not obtained for the ranking changes of the given toy, separate analyses by sex were also conducted on these data in order to parallel the analyses done on the eliminated object. For males, a clear confirmation of the reactance theory prediction was obtained (see Table 5.2). Relative to males in the No Choice condition, males in the Choice condition were significantly more favorable to the eliminated alternative and significantly less favorable to the given alternative. For females, theoretical predictions were not confirmed. Females in the No Choice condition were more favorable to the eliminated object than those in the Choice condition, and females in the two conditions did not differ in regard to the given alternative. Grade did not interact with either experimental condition or sex on the rankings of either toy.

The behavior of female subjects in this study was not predicted and is not easy to explain. One possibility is that female subjects anticipated being able to influence what toy they were given and that, for them, the interpersonal situation of being given a toy constituted a more important freedom than the situation of making one's own choice between two, not very attractive toys. The preemptory behavior of the second experimenter may have constituted a threat to the freedom of being given what they wanted, thereby enhancing the attractiveness of the eliminated toy in that condition. While this interpretation is entirely speculative, it is interesting to note that the only evidence of an absolute increase in attractiveness (initial rank = 4; final mean rank = 3.87) for either toy occurred when female subjects in the No Choice condition re-ranked the eliminated object.

The studies described thus far offer fairly good support for the general applicability of reactance theory to children's motivation and behavior. Children, ranging in age from the early elementary school years to middle-level junior high school students, have displayed reactance in response to threats to, and elimination of, freedom. Reactance arousal has been increased by increasing the proportion of freedoms eliminated and the importance of the freedom threatened. Children in these studies have opposed a choice forced on them by an adult as well as one supposedly advocated by a peer. Items eliminated by circumstance as well as by a social agent have become more attractive. Except for the study by Brehm (in press), however, these studies were not designed with any specifically developmental issues in mind, but there are a number of topics that have received considerable attention by developmental psychologists and that are clearly relevant to reactance theory. In the following sections, three such topics will be discussed. The relationship between reactance theory and research conducted on these topics will be described, and an effort will be made to sketch out the implications of reactance theory for a variety of developmental processes.

Barriers

Oppositional behavior can occur in response to physical obstructions as well as in response to directives or prohibitions by social agents. Since physical barriers do not involve the myriad of interactive factors that often complicate interpersonal relationships, responses to barriers offer a particularly suitable paradigm for studying children's oppositional behavior.

Barriers and object attractiveness

A number of studies have investigated the relationship between physical barriers and children's perceptions of object attractiveness. For example, in their classic study of frustration and regression in young children, Barker, Dembo, and Lewin (1941) presented children age 28 to 61 months old with a variety of attractive toys behind a transparent but insurmountable barrier. While the toys differed in attractiveness, the procedures of this study (in which many toys of many different attractiveness levels were used) make it difficult to determine what effects the barrier had on toy attractiveness.

A series of studies by Wright (1934, 1943) provided a more detailed examination of barriers and object attractiveness. Working with children 4 to 8 years of age, Wright obtained evidence of a general preference for barricaded objects when these objects were *not* identical to the nonbarricaded choice alternatives. Subsequent studies by Child and Adelsheim (1944) and Child (1946) failed to replicate Wright's work and did not obtain evidence that children preferred barricaded over nonbarricaded objects. Unfortunately, it is highly questionable whether these latter two studies constituted an acceptable test of Wright's hypothesis; both studies utilized choice alternatives that were either identical or only minimally different.

Furthermore, there are a number of methodological problems with the studies conducted by both Wright and Child. Both investigators allowed an experimenter to remain in the room while the child approached the choice alternatives; in Wright's work it is clear that this experimenter was aware of the experimental hypothesis. Wright's studies and Child's (1946) investi-gation may also have been affected by communication among subjects. Moreover, the ages of the children participating in these various experiments covered a wide range, and only Child (1946), who conducted the only study that did *not* include preschool children, provided an analysis of differences between age groups. Neither Wright nor Child mention possible sex differences in children's responses to barriers.

The hypothesis that object attractiveness should be increased by barriers is consistent with reactance theory as well as the Lewinian notions that stimulated much of the previous work. Brehm (1966) discussed this relationship and reported a study by himself and Hammock that examined this hypothesis. Subjects for this study were boys and girls from the first, fourth, and fifth grades of a public elementary school. The experimenter took each individual child to an experimental room where there was a table. Subjects in the Choice condition were told they could choose between two different pieces of candy and have whichever one they thought was best. Subjects in the No choice condition were told they could have a piece of candy and were asked to tell the experimenter which of the two *other* pieces was the best. For all subjects, the experimenter then placed one piece of candy 3 inches from the near edge of the table and another piece 33 inches from the same edge. Candies were pink and yellow after-dinner mints, and the colors were rotated between the two different placements. No Choice subjects were told they would receive a green mint, which the experimenter held up to them while giving them their instructions.

Brehm and Hammock expected that giving subjects choice would establish the two freedoms of having the yellow mint and having the pink mint. Since the candy that was furthest removed from the subject should be more difficult to obtain, distance was expected to act as a barrier and, therefore, as a threat to the child's freedom to have the further candy. Subjects in the No Choice condition had not had the freedoms to have either candy on the table established. It was predicted that the reactance aroused by the distance barrier should lead more children in the Choice condition than in the No Choice condition to designate the further candy as "the best one." There was a trend for this expected difference, but it did not reach acceptable levels of statistical reliability. Forty-seven percent of the subjects in the No Choice condition said that the far candy was best, while 65% of the subjects in the Choice condition said the far one was best. This difference is significant only at the 12% level.

There are a number of methodological problems with this study. Again, the experimenter was present during the child's choice and, indeed, Brehm refers to the seemingly large effect that experimenter behavior had on children's choices. Very similar items were used as choice alternatives, and possible intersubject communication cannot be ruled out. Moreover, Brehm and Hammock report no analyses for sex or age differences.

Sex differences in barrier response

As it happens, there is a fair amount of evidence that would suggest that sex and age differences may be important in determining children's responses to barricaded items. Goldberg and Lewis (1969) reported that 13-month-old children behaved differently in reaction to barriers as a function of sex. Males in their study spent more time at the ends of an insurmountable barrier than females, while females spent more time at the center of the barrier and cried more. These behaviors can be interpreted as indicating more effort on the part of males to get around the barrier and obtain the barricaded object. In their extensive longitudinal study of newborns and preschoolers, Bell, Weller, and Waldrop (1971) also obtained sex differences in young children's (27 to 33 months of age) responses to contrived barriers.

Males showed a cluster of behaviors involving variations in goal directedness and vigorous, sustained response to two different levels of contrived barriers. In females, a cluster of barrier behavior featuring variations in speed and persis-

tence was organized around only one contrived barrier in which cognitive aspects appeared important, and in which an assertive response to the barrier was modeled by teachers. (p. 80)

On the other hand, Jacklin, Maccoby, and Dick (1973) obtained findings that directly contradict those reported by Goldberg and Lewis. For 13- and 14-month-old children, these investigators found no evidence of males' making more purposive efforts to surmount the barrier and found that girls cried more than boys only in a moderate stress condition (and not in a high stress condition also included in their study).

Data obtained by Van Lieshout (1975) suggest that age as well as sex differences may play a role in determining young children's responses to barriers. Van Lieshout had Dutch children at 17 to 19 months and then again at 23 to 25 months of age interact with their mothers through a series of experimental procedures. At one point, the mother placed a toy inside a plexiglass box that the child could not open. Although the sex of the child did not affect behavior directed at the box, negative emotional responses (e.g., crying, anger) to the mother who placed the toy in the box differed as a function of the child's sex and age. While males and females did not differ in negative emotional response at the younger age period (17 to 19 months), males displayed more negative emotional response than females at the older age period (23 to 24 months). Examining this interaction from a different perspective, negative reactions for females significantly decreased between 18 and 24 months, while negative reactions for males tended ($p < .10$) to increase across this age span.

These studies suggest, then, that sex differences in responses to barriers are more likely to occur around the age of 2 than before. Of the three studies in which children before the age of 2 participated, only Goldberg and Lewis obtained sex differences. Jacklin et al. did not, nor did Van Lieshout find sex differences when the children in his study were under 2 years of age. On the other hand, both Bell et al. and Van Lieshout obtained sex differences with children around the age of 2, although it should be noted that Bell et al. found differences in manipulative behavior while Van Lieshout obtained sex differences only in emotional response.

Physical barriers and psychological reactance

Consideration of the literature described above suggested a number of elements that would need to be taken into account in order to generate an adequate examination of children's responses to barriers. First, the age of 2 is suggested by empirical evidence as well as anecdotal report ("the terrible two's") as being of distinctive interest. Second, males and females need to be included in a study of barrier behavior to see if sex differences might appear. Third, a variety of methodological cautions are necessary: The experimenter should not be in the room when the child interacts with the barrier; intersubject communication should be minimized; and while objects (both barricaded and not) should be equally attractive, they should be clearly different.

The need for this latter design characteristic is theoretical as well as methodological. As has been noted previously, if a person is choosing between two items and one is threatened with elimination, reactance arousal should result only if the two are not identical. Identical items do not provide unique instrumental value for satisfying needs, and an object or behavior must be of unique instrumental value in order for it to constitute a sufficiently important free behavior. Finally, it would also be important to show that preference for a barricaded object would increase as the barrier becomes more difficult to overcome. The barrier, according to reactance theory, acts as a threat to freedom, and with increasing threat, motivation to reestablish the freedom should increase.

With these theoretical and methodological points in mind, the following study was conducted to examine the relationship between physical barriers and reactance arousal. S. Brehm and Weinraub (1977) obtained

volunteer parents and children from the local community. Two-year-old children (range: 21 to 27 months) were brought individually by their mothers to a university laboratory, the age of the subjects and the experimental setting thus eliminating intersubject communication about the experimental procedures. After the experimental procedures were explained to the mother, she and her child were brought to the door of the experimental playroom where the experimenter was standing in the middle of the room in clear sight of the mother and child. The experimenter proceeded to hold up and name each of two toys, placed each toy at an equal distance from the child, and informed the child that he or she could play with whatever toy he or she wanted. The mother then was seated unobtrusively in a corner of the room, and the experimenter left the room.

The toys used in the experiment were a Fisher Price Ring Stack and a Fisher Price Color Stack; in a pilot study with other children this age, both toys were shown to be equally attractive. These toys are similar in color and size, but clearly different in shape. For each child, a toy was placed either behind the barrier or beside it. The barrier was always located to the right of the child and consisted of a blue-tinted, transparent Plexiglass sheet inserted into a wooden base.

Three experimental conditions were run in this study. In two conditions, both toys were used (and counterbalanced between being behind the barrier or being beside it), but the barrier was either small (0.33 m high) or large (0.66 m high). In the third condition, only the large barrier was used, but the toys were identical (and counterbalanced between the Ring Stack and the Color Stack). Children's behavior toward the toys and the barrier was videotaped from behind a one-way mirror. The major dependent measure was the child's latency to touch each toy.

Brehm and Weinraub predicted that maximum reactance arousal, and thus maximum initial preference for the barricaded toy, should occur when the barrier was large and the toys were different. For males, this pre-

Table 5.3. Latency to Touch (in seconds) for 2-Year-Old Males

	Large Barrier Identical Toys	Large Barrier Different Toys	Small Barrier Different Toys
Barricaded toy	56.00	22.30	45.22
Free-standing toy	37.33	70.10	47.33

Note. From "Physical barriers and psychological reactance: Two-year-olds' responses to threats to freedom" by S. S. Brehm and M. Weinraub, *Journal of Personality and Social Psychology,* 1977, *35,* 830–836. Copyright © 1977 by the American Psychological Association. Reprinted by permission.

diction was confirmed (see Table 5.3). When the two toys were identical, boys touched the free-standing toy somewhat more quickly than the barricaded toy, although this difference is not statistically significant. When the toys were different and the barrier was small, latency to touch was essentially equivalent for both toys. When, however, the toys were different and the barrier was large, 2-year-old males touched the barricaded toy significantly sooner than they touched the free-standing toy. The behavior of female subjects did not conform to the reactance theory prediction. Female 2-year-olds touched the free-standing toy more quickly (M = 30.19 sec) than the barricaded one (M = 57.65 sec), regardles of the size of the barrier or the difference between the toys.

These findings are essentially consistent with those of previous investigations of 2-year-olds' responses to barriers. Two-year-old males do seem to oppose the barrier (or the social agent who has implemented it), and the conditions under which this opposition occurs can be predicted from reactance theory. Two-year-old females, however, appear not to oppose physical barriers. This latter finding is perhaps best regarded in light of Van Lieshout's research. His data suggest that at an early age, males and females behave similarly in response to a barricaded object, but that as development proceeds the sexes begin to differ. Male children appear to become more negative in their responses toward barriers than earlier in their lives, while female children appear to become less negative. Taken together, the Van Lieshout and Brehm and Weinraub

studies raise the possibility that, for male children, the freedom to oppose physical obstructions is affirmed, while for females either the freedom itself becomes irrevocably eliminated *or* the cost of engaging in direct restorative action becomes prohibitive. As has been noted previously, there are important psychological differences between irrevocably eliminating a freedom versus suppressing freedom restorative behavior, and it would seem important that future research on young children's responses to barriers try to determine which of these processes is affected during the socialization of young girls.

Compliance with adult social influence

When an adult tries to influence the behavior of a child, the pressures on the child to conform will be considerable. Many adults control resources that are essential for the child's survival or, at least, for his or her psychological well-being. Most adults are capable of physically enforcing their demands on the child by brute force; even if this force is not likely to actually be used, the very fact that it could occur may be sufficient to enforce compliance by the child. Furthermore, even if a specific adult does not control resources valuable to the child and does not have potential physical power over the child, most children are quite aware that relatively nonpowerful adults can frequently enforce compliance by communicating with the more powerful adults in their lives. Adults, then, are extremely powerful social influence agents in relation to children (see also Chapter 1 by Lepper and Gilovich).

This power can have a variety of effects on the possibilities for reactance arousal. Because of their power, adults have extensive control over defining the child's behavioral freedoms. This would be especially true for young children who typically spend more time with adults than do older children and for whom other sources of information, such as peers and TV, have less impact. For example, the young child who has never been allowed to snack after dinner time probably does not see himself or herself as free to do this. Continued enforcement of such a regulation by adults, then, would not be expected to arouse reactance.

Children do, however, come to perceive themselves as having certain freedoms. Sometimes these freedoms are established by the parents, sometimes by other sources of information. Whatever the source, once the child perceives engaging (or not engaging) in a certain behavior as a specific behavioral freedom, then the possibility for reactance arousal is created; if this freedom is threatened or eliminated by an adult, reactance arousal should occur. These conditions are not, however, sufficient to generate freedom restorative behavior. For children, the cost of noncompliance may often be too high and, if so, opposition to the adult's influence will be suppressed.

This analysis suggests that, at least for preadolescent children, compliance with adult requests will be more likely to occur than opposition. In order to obtain actual behavioral opposition, it will be necessary to ensure that (1) a freedom of sufficient importance is established for the child, (2) a threat of sufficient magnitude occurs, and (3) the cost of noncompliance is not so high that opposition is suppressed. These prerequisites appear to have been met in the previously described studies by Hammock and Brehm (1966), S. Brehm (in press), and Worchel (1972).

When we examine the research on children's compliance with adult requests that has been generated from other theoretical perspectives, we find, as might be expected, a very mixed picture. Clearly, children often

do comply and factors such as contingent reinforcement (e.g., Goetz, Holmberg, & LeBlanc, 1975) and verbal reprimands for noncompliance (e.g., Forehand, Roberts, Doleys, Hobbs, & Resick, 1976) can increase compliance.

Children do not, however, *always* comply, and some of the variables that have been found to reduce compliance are consistent with a reactance theory analysis. For example, Forehand and Scarboro (1975) found that, as mothers increased the number of commands to their children (in an observed interaction in the laboratory), compliance decreased. The procedure in this study involved mothers' instructing their children to play with each of six toys, one at a time, and giving each instruction twice. Each single freedom was, therefore, threatened twice and, over time, the number of freedoms threatened increased.

A study by Patterson, Littman, and Brown (1968) found that *implied* influence by an adult model can also increase oppositional behavior. In this study, male first-graders were first asked to designate their preferred picture in each of 68 pairs of pictures of objects. The pictures were presented in drawings contained in a booklet. Approximately two weeks later, subjects were exposed to these picture pairs projected on a screen and again asked to indicate the one in each pair that they preferred. The first 28 slides presented were used to measure variability in picture preferences by comparing children's preferences when slides were shown with those expressed earlier in response to the drawings in the booklet. During the next 40 slides, a female adult who was seated beside the child indicated her preferences prior to the child's response. On 31 of the 40 slides, the adult's preference disagreed with the child's initial preference; on 9 of the slides, the adult's preference agreed. The number of times the preferences expressed by the child disagreed with those of the model constituted the major dependent measure.

The data obtained in this study indicated a considerable amount of oppositional behavior. The mean variability for picture prefer-ence (established during the baseline) was 37%. When the model disagreed with the child's initial preferences, variability was significantly lowered to 18%; children op-posed the model by staying with their previous initial preferences. When, how-ever, the model's preferences agreed with the child's initial preferences, variability was significantly increased to 71%; children op-posed the model by reversing their own initial preferences. In a second study re-ported by Patterson et al., only "negative set" variability (i.e., children's opposition to an agreeing model) was reported. Male children between the age of 6 and 10 participated, and it was found that the younger children (6 to 7) had significantly higher negative set scores than the older children (8 to 10).

The influence in Patterson's et al. study was implicit rather than direct. The adult model did not tell the child which picture to prefer; she simply stated the one that she preferred. While this may have constituted a threat of low magnitude, this kind of influ-ence may also have implied to the child that the costs of noncompliance were not poten-tially high, allowing the reactance that was created to be expressed in direct restorative behavior.

Theoretically, this kind of trade-off is problematic; it is difficult to predict whether the sort of implicit influence that will reduce the perceived costs of noncompliance might also reduce the magnitude of threat to such a degree that little reactance would be aroused. It is possible, however, to reduce the perceived costs of noncompliance with-out simultaneously reducing the magnitude of threat. One way to do this would be to have the adult not be present when the child has the opportunity to restore freedom by opposing the adult's influence. Although the evidence is somewhat mixed (see, for ex-ample, Redd, 1974; Winston & Redd, 1976), there are some studies that have found that having the adult who has given instructions to a child leave the room decreases the child's compliance with these instructions

(Peterson & Whitehurst, 1971; Redd & Wheeler, 1973).

Another way in which an adult's social influence power over a child can be reduced was suggested in a study by S. Brehm (1977). Subjects in this study were male and female first- and fifth-graders who participated in a modified version of the paradigm used ear-lier by Worchel and Brehm (1971). Each individual child was taken by Experimenter 1 (E1) to the experimental room and, there, introduced to Experimenter 2 (E2). The children were told that both experimenters were trying to find out what children like and dislike about toys. All subjects were informed that they would look at some toys, tell another person (Experimenter 3, E3) how much they liked the toys, and then get to choose a toy and play with it.

In the No Influence condition, children simply looked at two toys displayed on a table; two different sets of toys were used for the two grades to ensure sufficient toy attractiveness. In the Influence condition, subjects' inspection of the two toys was interrupted by E1's saying, "Of course, I think you should choose this one. There's no question about it." As she made this state-ment, E1 touched one of the displayed toys. Subjects in the Restoration condition re-ceived the same influence attempt by E1, but immediately after this statement, E2 (who had been quietly working at a desk) looked up and said, "Wait a minute, I think you should choose whichever one you want." For all subjects, E1 and E2 left the room, and E3 then entered the room to assess subjects' ratings of each of the two toys. Children were asked whether they liked or disliked a given toy and, if they said they liked it, were asked to point to one of a set of five blocks of increasing size (dis-played on a poster board) that were verbally labeled for the child as indicating increasing amounts of liking. Which toy the child was urged to choose or (in the No Influence condition) rate first was counterbalanced. After ratings were obtained, all subjects chose the toy they wished to play with.

Brehm had predicted that children's re-

Table 5.4. Mean Compliance Ratings[a]

	No Influence	Influence	Restoration
First-graders	.42	1.6	−.75
Fifth-graders	−.17	1.9	1.00

Note. Adapted from "The effect of adult influence on children's preferences: Compliance vs. opposition" by S. S. Brehm, *Journal of Abnormal Child Psychology,* 1977, 5, 31–41. Copyright © 1977 by Plenum Publishing Co. Reprinted by permission.
[a]Ratings of the toy-not-urged (or the toy rated second) subtracted from the rating of the toy-urged (or the toy rated first). In the Influence and Restoration conditions, therefore, negative scores would indicate opposition to the advocated choice alternative.

sponses to these experimental procedures would be similar to those obtained by Worchel and Brehm with college-age adults. That is, liking for the advocated toy was expected to decrease in the Influence condition and increase once freedom was restored in the Restoration condition. The rating data obtained did not confirm these predictions (see Table 5.4). Instead, children complied with the adult influence in the Influence condition, although the difference between the Influence and No Influence condition was significant only for fifth-graders. First-graders displayed significantly less compliance with the advocated choice in the Restoration condition than in the Influence condition. For fifth-graders, there was only a nonsignificant trend for compliance to be reduced in the Restoration condition, relative to the Influence situation. In general, children's choices were consistent with their rating preferences, only 13% of them choosing their less favorably rated toy.

Although these findings failed to confirm Brehm's initial predictions, they are congruent with the analysis offered in this chapter. While the children in this study had their freedoms to choose and evaluate the toys according to their own preferences clearly established, there is no reason to believe that these freedoms were of any great importance. The adults who interacted with the child were strangers and had no direct power over the child's behavior, but they appeared in the child's classroom with permission from the child's teacher. Thus, in the Influence condition, a reasonably powerful adult threatened a relatively unim-

portant freedom. Furthermore, E1's advocacy of a particular toy was received in silence by E2; this lack of response on E2's part may have suggested to the child that she agreed with E1's advocacy. While the child's ratings of and choice between the toys was obtained by a third individual and neither E1 nor E2 remained in the room, children may have presumed that the other experimenters would learn of their behavior. Given this context, one can (admittedly, after the fact) understand the high levels of compliance that were obtained in the Influence condition.

This type of analysis can also suggest an explanation of why there was some tendency for first-grade children in the Restoration condition to oppose the experimenter's influence attempt. It does not appear that this opposition to E1 was generated by compliance with E2. E2 never directly expressed a preference and, indeed, one-third of the first-grade subjects did *not* see E2's preferences as differing from those of E1. Furthermore, the same proportion of children in both grades (one-third) perceived their choice as agreeing with E2's preference and disagreeing with E1's preference. Thus, the majority of children in both grades did not see themselves as agreeing with E2 and opposing E1, and the level of this perception was constant across grade and did not parallel the greater oppositional tendencies on the part of first-graders.

Instead of complying with E2, then, it seems possible that the children in this study perceived E2's statement as undercutting the power of the influencing agent, E1. By supporting the child's freedom to choose, E2 may have implicitly opposed the first adult's control over the child's behavior. This reduction in power may have signaled to children that E1 would have reduced ability to punish noncompliance and, thus, may have made it permissible to oppose her influence. To push these speculations one step further, it would also seem possible that fifth-graders have a more long-range view of the power of adults and that E2's statement supporting the child's freedom to choose was less effective in reducing E1's power for them than for the more socially naive first-graders.

Given our previous references to possible sex differences in children's responses to adult influence, it should be noted that the above effects obtained by Brehm were not modified by the sex of the child. It should be emphasized, however, that very few subjects of each sex were available in each of the relevant experimental conditions and that only very strong sex differences could have shown up on the statistical analyses that were conducted.[2]

Compliance in naturalistic settings

All of the above studies examined children's responses to adult influence in experimental settings. It would also seem interesting and worthwhile to provide a brief review of some of the findings that have been obtained in naturalistic settings (i.e., in the family's home). None of the studies described below were conducted with reactance theory in mind, and the reader is cautioned that all of the following interpretative statements are sheer, if perhaps intriguing, speculation.

In a study of the interactions between mothers and year-old infants, Stayton, Hogan, and Ainsworth (1971) reported that compliance to mothers' commands was not a function of either frequency of verbal commands or frequency of physical interventions. Instead, maternal sensitivity, acceptance, and cooperation were found to be "the primary correlates of an infant's compliance to commands" (p. 1065). Stayton et al. concluded that a "disposition toward

obedience" will emerge in a supportive social environment and that calculated attempts to shape the emergence of compliant behavior are not necessary.

A similar picture of the predominance of compliance with maternal directives was reported by Minton, Kagan, and Levine (1971). Even with the supposedly "terrible" 2-year-olds who served along with their mothers as subjects, these investigators observed little disobedience. It was noted, however, that "disobedience among boys . . . was positively associated with frequent physical punishment and maternal failure to explain prohibition" (p. 1889).

Lytton and his associates have published a number of studies describing the interaction between parents and their 25-to-35-month-old male children (both twins and single children being included in the sample). Lytton and Zwirner (1975) concluded that maternal consistency, play with the child, use of psychological rewards, and reasoning facilitated compliance. However, maternal use of psychological punishment and material reward, as well as paternal use of physical punishment, was negatively associated with compliance. Similar findings were reported in Lytton's 1977 paper with the additional observation that maternal use of physical punishment was a negative predictor of compliance. In a more recent presentation of the findings from this research project, Lytton (1979) found that physical control when combined with verbal commands detracted from compliance, while the combination of positive action (e.g., smiling, expression of love or approval, hugging) and commands increased compliance.

These findings would appear to be quite consistent with the general analysis offered earlier in this chapter. Among these very young children, compliance appears to be overwhelmingly more frequent than disobedience. Considering both the physical power (i.e., physical control and control of resources) and the informational power (i.e., defining the child's behavioral freedoms) that parents have over young children, this is presumably what any of us would expect. With children beyond the infancy stage, however, compliance is not all pervasive. Disobedience appears linked to the use of strong control techniques (such as physical punishment and control, and—at least, for mothers—use of psychological punishment and material rewards). An additional factor promoting noncompliance appears to consist of the way in which information is presented to the child. Maternal failure to explain prohibition was cited by Minton et al. (1971) as related to disobedience among male 2-year-olds, while Lytton has pointed to consistent enforcement of rules by the mother and reasoning as facilitating compliance.

All of these factors are easily encompassed within a reactance theory framework. The use of strong control techniques can be seen as increasing reactance arousal by increasing the magnitude of threat to the child's freedom. Failure to explain prohibition or to use reasoning may also increase reactance arousal by increasing implications for future threats to future freedoms. When a prohibition is clearly explained, the child knows the limits of the threat to, or elimination of, freedom. In the absence of a clear explanation, other free behaviors may be threatened by implication.

Lytton's emphasis on the importance of consistency in rule enforcement also would appear related to a central tenet of reactance theory. The inconsistent parent may, in effect, "mislead" the child into thinking that he or she has a freedom that the parent does not regard as a freedom. Consequently, when the parent does attempt to enforce the rule, the child perceives this as a threat to, or elimination of, a freedom, and psychological reactance should be aroused. If, however, rule enforcement is consistent, then parental control is more likely to be exercised over those behavioral acts that the child has never regarded as free. In this case, reactance should not be aroused, and neither the motivation to oppose the parent nor actual behavioral opposition would be produced.

As a final point, we might note that enforcement of rules is often a two-person endeavor. Based on both Lytton's findings and the experiment by S. Brehm (1977), we would expect that disobedience from a child should be increased by conflict between the parents about rules as well as inconsistent rule enforcement by a single parent. When parents disagree, and the child knows about this disagreement, the child may perceive a specific behavioral freedom to be established that will not be seen as a free behavior for the child by at least one parent, and the social power of both parents may well be reduced by the conflict between them.

Modifying noncompliant behavior

So far in this chapter, we have considered what might be termed "normal" oppositional behavior. In the case of children, this normal oppositional behavior may be unpleasant for the adult recipients of it (usually parents or teachers), but such opposition is certainly typical and, in general, would be seen as a positive developmental event indicating the child's increasing autonomy.

Beyond these normal levels of failure to comply, many clinicians have encountered what might be called "deviant" oppositional behavior. This type of oppositional behavior is considered deviant presumably because it occurs more frequently, more intensely, and/or over a longer period of time than the "normal" type. Some children are brought to mental health professionals specifically because of problems with oppositional behavior. Indeed, the recently proposed DSM-III (*Diagnostic and Statistical Manual of Mental Disorder,* American Psychiatric Association, 1980) includes a specific category called Oppositional Disorder for diagnostic use with children and adolescents.

Other children are brought to mental health professionals or to governmental agencies, such as the police or the court system, because they have violated more formalized societal norms. Cohen (1955) has emphasized that much of delinquent behavior consists of direct opposition to more general norms.

The delinquent's conduct is right, by the standards of his subculture, precisely because it is wrong by the norms of the larger culture. (p. 28)

Furthermore, children whose problems are severe and of psychotic proportion may also display deviant oppositional behavior (see, for example, Cowan, Hoddinott, & Wright, 1965). DesLauriers and Carlson (1969) have noted this feature among some autistic children and have described a procedure that uses this problem behavior to benefit the child's treatment.

The most general strategy used here is neither uncommon, nor is it unknown to most mothers confronted with the *No, No* phase of their young child. It consists, essentially, either of demanding of the child the exact opposite of what one might actually want him to do, or of pretending convincingly that one doesn't really care one way or the other whether the child does what he is asked. (p. 156)

There have been three major theoretical approaches to the treatment of deviant oppositional behavior. In this section, each will be briefly described and then some possible treatment strategies that could be derived from reactance theory will be discussed.

Psychoanalytic approaches (based on Freud's writings and the work of later neo-Freudians such as Erikson) have been remarkably nonspecific in their treatment of deviant oppositional behavior. For example, in Anthony and Gilpin's (1976) consideration of oppositional behavior, psychotherapy with oppositional children is described as focusing on the therapist-child relationship, with the therapist calling attention to the oppositional behavior and attempting to elevate the child's self-esteem. Very little of this would seem specific to oppositional behavior; yet, it should be noted that such an approach would presumably minimize direct therapist control over the child's behavior and, thereby, oppositional behavior by the child might be reduced at least within the confines of the therapeutic relationship. Whether any such reductions will generalize to other aspects of the child's life is debatable. Gilpin and Worland (in An-

thony & Gilpin, 1976) report successful interventions in 4 out of 15 completed cases of deviant/excessive oppositional behavior. In the absence of any kind of placebo or waiting-list controls, however, it is impossible to evaluate this rate of success.

A more clearly effective therapeutic intervention has been generated by behavior therapists. The general approach is to combine modified parental attention (i.e., attention and praise for desirable/compliant behavior) with the use of time-out (i.e., placing the child briefly in a nonreinforcing environment) in response to undesirable/oppositional behavior. Describing this approach, Wahler (1969) noted that, in his study, (1) parental reinforcement value was initially low and increased as a function of the treatment program and (2) oppositional behavior was reduced. The theoretical questions raised by these findings are summarized by Wahler.

First, if parental reinforcement value was intially quite low, why should the timeout procedure be effective? . . . Secondly, if parental reinforcement value was initially quite low, what was maintaining the children's oppositional behavior during baseline? (p. 170)

Wahler proposed that a "plausible answer" to the second question would be that the oppositional child suffers not from an excess of oppositional behavior, but rather from a deficit of cooperative behavior. Low parental reinforcement value would, then, be consistent with such a deficit, condition.

This explanation would appear to run into difficulty on two fronts. First, as we have seen, compliant behavior seems to develop quite easily and spontaneously among most children, without specific parental strategies to induce it. One would wonder why the children in Wahler's study appeared to need something above and beyond typical parental behavior to induce compliance. Second, Wahler's explanation would still seem to leave unanswered the questions of why time-out was effective and why parental reinforcement value increased during treatment. While numerous other investigators (e.g.,

Baer, Rowbury, & Baer, 1973; Forehand, Cheney, & Yoder, 1974; Forehand & King, 1974; Scarboro & Forehand, 1975; Walter & Gilmore, 1973) have confirmed the effectiveness of combined modified attention and time-out in reducing oppositional behavior, the theoretical issues raised by Wahler still appear to be largely unresolved.

A reactance theory approach to Wahler's findings would be substantially different. First, reactance theory would not find it peculiar that certain kinds of parent-child interactions could lead to both low positive effects on behavior (i.e., low reinforcement value) and high negative effects (i.e., high levels of opposition). Instead, this theoretical perspective would hypothesize that the parents are not serving as effective control agents over the child: freedoms have been established for the child that the parents do not regard as free behaviors, social influence attempts are of sufficient magnitude to arouse reactance and of insufficient magnitude to irrevocably eliminate freedom, and the costs of noncompliance are not sufficiently high to suppress direct opposition.

Second, the effectiveness of time-out may, from a reactance theory point of view, reflect parental reassertion of control in a dramatic and unmistakable way. Time-out may redefine free behaviors for the child such that what was perceived as a freedom no longer is, or it may increase the costs of noncompliance such that direct restorative behavior is suppressed. If time-out operates through either (or both) of these theoretical pathways, there may be undesirable psychological costs associated with its use. If too many freedoms are eliminated (or eliminated in such a way that elimination of a large number of freedoms is implied), the child may become not only nonoppositional, but helpless and unmotivated to engage in desirable as well as undesirable behaviors. (Typical treatment programs try to counter such a possibility by including positive reinforcement for desirable behaviors.) On the other hand, if restorative behavior is merely suppressed, rather than reactance arousal being eliminated, the reduction in opposi-

tional behavior may not generalize to other settings with other social agents.

Furthermore, it should be noted that using time-out as a treatment procedure has become highly controversial (Anderson & King, 1974; White, Nielson, & Johnson, 1972) and has been banned with some populations (*Wyatt* v. *Stickney*, 1973). As Forehand et al. (1976) have noted, such concerns over severe restrictions of children's behaviors have highlighted the need to develop alternative methods of reducing oppositional behavior.

The third major approach to the treatment of excessively oppositional children is a combination of systems analysis and behavior therapy. This approach is largely associated with the work of Patterson (e.g., Patterson, 1974, 1976a). Although there has been some dispute about generalization and persistance of the reduction in oppositional behavior attained by this treatment method (see Kent, 1976; Reid & Patterson, 1976), Patterson's treatment approach appears to be reasonably successful in reducing oppositional behavior in the immediate environments of concern (i.e., home and school).

Patterson (1976a) describes the theoretical context that has formed the basis for his treatment of conduct-disorder boys. First, he hypothesizes that the parents of conduct-disordered children will often use both punishment and reinforcement inconsistently. Undesirable behaviors will be rewarded (at least by parental attention), while desirable behaviors will often go unnoticed. Thus, a major element of Patterson's treatment program is to generate more consistent use of reinforcement and punishment. Parents and teachers are taught to reward desirable behaviors consistently and to respond to undesirable behaviors by withdrawing reinforcers (including the use of time-out, as described in Patterson, 1975 and 1976b). This treatment approach is, then, essentially equivalent to that employed by Wahler and the other investigators cited previously. The theoretical rationale, however, is quite different. Patterson does not maintain Wahler's position that the problem lies in a deficiency of compliant behaviors brought about because parents are not sufficiently reinforcing to induce compliance. Instead, he proposes that the inconsistent use of punishment and reinforcement by parents decreases parental control over the child's behavior and allows oppositional behavior to flourish.

Patterson's second major concern is with the coercive system that he sees as developing within the family of a conduct-disordered child. He contends that when one person uses "pain control techniques" over another, the second person will learn to use these same techniques.

Presumably, as one member of a system applies pain control techniques, the victims will eventually learn, via modeling . . . and/or reinforcing contingencies . . . , to *initiate* coercive interactions. (p. 269)

This interactive learning can, according to Patterson, lead to "extended interchanges in which *both* members of the dyad apply aversive stimuli" (p. 269). Moreover, increases in the intensity of the aversive stimuli will tend to be reinforced whenever an increment in intensity results in the most coercive person's "winning" the immediate battle and the other person's ceasing his or her attack.

Both of Patterson's hypotheses about the kind of family environment that is most likely to produce an excessively oppositional child are congruent with a reactance theory analysis. As described earlier, inconsistency can (unwittingly) establish freedoms. Moreover, being aggressed against by another can also establish a freedom—the freedom to counteraggress (Nezlek & Brehm, 1975)—and watching other people interact aggressively can serve to increase the importance of acting aggressively oneself (Worchel, 1972).

Unfortunately, the data reported by Patterson (1976a) are somewhat at odds with these hypotheses about the etiology of excessive oppositionalism. First, it is not clear that consistency of parental reinforcement schedules is as important as either Patterson

initially believed or, indeed, as one would expect in terms of reactance theory.

Several reviewers, including the present writer . . . , have suggested that training parents to reduce positive consequences for coercive behaviors would be followed by reductions in rates for these behaviors. Analysis by Taplin (1974) showed that the hypothesis may not be tenable. The analysis showed a nonsignificant correlation between children's baseline Total Deviant behavior scores and the parents' schedules of positive consequences for these behaviors. A cross-lag correlational analysis also showed no support for the hypothesis. Finally, his data showed significant *reductions* for mean rates of the child's Total Deviant behavior during the initial phases of treatment at which point parental mean rates of positive consequences for these behaviors were *increasing!* (Patterson, 1976a, p. 304)

These findings led Patterson to believe that the modeling provided by coercive disciplinary acts may be more important than parental schedules of punishment and reinforcement. This hypothesis received only partial support.

It was hypothesized that as the behavior of the problem child was brought under control, the coercive behaviors of all other family members would display commensurate reductions. . . . In keeping with the hypothesis, the data at termination showed reductions in Total Deviant scores for all family members. However, only the changes for siblings were significant. (pp. 304–305)

Although Patterson's specific hypotheses regarding the role of reinforcement consistency and modeling of coercive behaviors in the generation and maintenance of excessive oppositional behavior have not been fully supported, there is evidence that, at a general level, disciplinary inconsistency and punitiveness are both associated with undesirable behavior in children. For example, Rosenthal, Finkelstein, Ni, and Robertson (1959) found that maternal inconsistency and punitiveness were related to the problem behavior of children seen at the Illinois Institute of Juvenile Research; paternal punitiveness and authoritarian control were also associated with problem behavior in these children (Rosenthal, Ni, Finkelstein,

& Berkwits, 1962). Inconsistency *between* parents has been found to be related to undesirable behavior in young children (Baruch & Wilcox, 1944; Read, 1945), delinquency (Glueck & Glueck, 1950; McCord, McCord, & Zola, 1959), and excessive aggressiveness (Bandura & Walters, 1959).

These findings are strikingly similar to the data on noncompliance in normal children that have been described previously in this chapter and suggest that, rather than focusing on inconsistent (or inappropriate) reinforcement schedules per se, an alternative approach would be to investigate parental formulation of rules that define desirable and undesirable behaviors. Such an approach would be highly consistent with reactance theory's emphasis on the need for a freedom to exist in order for a threat to that behavior to evoke opposition.

Reactance theory approaches

In the preceding sections, various treatments of and conceptual approaches to excessive oppositional behavior in children have been interpreted in terms of reactance theory. All of this has been, of course, strictly post hoc, and it would be valuable to have a more direct application of the theory to the problem behavior of interest. One such application is described by Ayllon, Allison, and Kandel (1979). These investigators made use of a treatment for oppositional behavior based on Varela's (1971) "persuasion by successive approximation using reactance." The initial component of this technique is the formulation of a hierarchy of statements relevant to the desired behavior, which range from the most likely to be accepted by the client to the least likely. The therapist then tries to persuade the client of the opposite of each statement, attempting, thereby, to create reactance and motivate the client to publicly commit himself/herself to the desired statement. The therapist progresses up through the hierarchy until the client has committed himself/herself to all the desired statements. Typically, the last

statement(s) concerns a behavioral intention on the part of the client that, if carried through, would ameliorate the problem behavior.

Ayllon et al. report two interventions with normal children who were classified by their teacher as the most disruptive in the class. All were male, from 11 to 13, and all were performing poorly in their academic subjects as well as being disruptive. The teacher considered all four boys as capable of at least average work, and repeated efforts by the teacher to discourage the disruptive behavior as well as conferences with the parents had failed to improve the children's classroom behavior.

After a baseline of the children's disruptive behavior and academic performance had been established, each of the four children was counseled successively by one of two therapists. The therapist (presumably in consultation with the teacher and the parents) drew up the hierarchy of statements that the therapist wished each child to agree with. A condensed version of that hierarchy is displayed in Table 5.5 along with a few excerpts from the dialogue between one of the students and his therapist.

For three of the children in this study, the successive persuasion technique was quite successful. Disruptive behavior was reduced from a mean of 47% to a mean of 19%; academic performance in math increased from 22% correct to 83% correct. Ayllon et al. report that these children's desirable behavior increased dramatically on the first day after "behavioral persuasion," and that the desired changes were maintained for the rest of the study (an average of 12 days for each child).

For the fourth child, success was only temporarily achieved. Although there was impressive improvement in both disruption and math performance on the first day after the intervention, these improvements vanished the following day. Ayllon et al. decided to repeat the behavioral persuasion session with this child, but this time with the school principal, the teacher, and the child's father in attendance. After this session, this

Table 5.5. Persuasion by Successive Approximation Using Reactance

Condensed Hierarchy

1. What I will say will be the truth.
2. I am not working too hard in school right now.
3. I care about school.
4. When I'm disruptive, it is on my own volition.
5. I can change on my own volition.
6. I can do academic work on my own volition.
7. I will commit myself to doing my school work.

Transcript Excerpts

Therapist:	Before we even start talking, I must admit I'm not sure whether we should even bother. I have found that a lot of students don't even tell the truth and can't keep their word. You probably won't tell the truth, either.
Student:	I'll tell the truth to you.
Therapist:	Well, that's good to hear; we won't be wasting our time talking, then. I guess you must really be working hard in school these days.
Student:	Myself, I'm not. I'm really just kind of loafin' around. The other kids are workin' hard. You know, the ones who get good grades.

 . . .

Therapist:	I guess it's hopeless, then. You wouldn't even consider trying it the other way around—work first, play later.
Student:	No. Well, I could try. *I* know what you're trying to do—you're trying to get me to do my work in school, aren't you?
Therapist:	I'm not trying to get you to do anything—I can't make you do anything you don't want to do.
Student:	But you and Mrs. Q would like me to do my work, right?
Therapist:	I would like it if you would like it. But I know you aren't willing to even give it a try.
Student:	I would give it a try.

 . . .

Therapist:	Would you write something for me?
Student:	Like what?
Therapist:	Like what you have told me you are going to do.
Student:	You write it. I don't like to write. You write it and I'll sign it.
Therapist:	You dictate it to me, OK? I, *(student's name)*. . . .
Student:	I, *(student's name),* give my word that I will get my seat work done and handed in by Mrs. Q's deadline. I will do this until the end of school. (Student then signs the statement immediately.)
Therapist:	*(Student's name)*, are you sure you want to do this until the end of school? We could make it for just a couple of days instead.
Student:	No, I'll work until the end of school.

Note. From "Behavioral persuasion: A technique to eliminate chronic discipline problems" by T. Ayllon, M. G. Allison, and H. J. Kandel, unpublished paper, Georgia State University, 1979. Adapted by permission of the senior author.

child's disruptive behavior decreased from a mean of 50% to a mean of 30% and his math performance increased from 11% correct to 73%; the improvement figures are averages of the six days after the second treatment session during which this student's behavior was monitored.

It would be inappropriate to generalize too much from these findings. A very small sample of subjects was used and, while all of the subjects in this study exhibited problem behavior in school, the level of their problem behavior was far less than that exhibited by, for example, the children in Patterson's project (who are typically referred by community agencies including the Juvenile Court, schools, and community mental health clinics). Nevertheless, the findings of the Ayllon et al. study are extremely interesting. They suggest the possibility that the reactance techniques developed by Varela and used by him with adults can be effectively applied to children. They also point out that one cannot assume that the immediate improvement that may be obtained through such a technique will be maintained. For the fourth student, a booster session that involved a stronger public commitment (and, thus, presumably came closer to actually eliminating his freedom *not* to carry out the behaviors to which he had committed himself) was necessary. Moreover, Ayllon et al. point out the need to integrate the new behaviors into the child's social environment by taking "steps to assure that new behavior patterns come under reinforcing environmental contingencies."

Another possibly effective intervention technique to enhance student compliance has been described by Miller, Brickman, and Bolen (1975). In their first study, fifth-grade students were exposed to eight days of either Attribution or Persuasion treatments that addressed the topic of littering. The Attribution treatment consisted of a variety of ways of telling students in one class that they were neat and tidy: The principal, the teacher, and the janitor were all involved in telling the class how neat and tidy it was. In the Persuasion treatment, the same school personnel delivered a variety of messages informing another class that it should be neat and that students should not litter. A third class served as a no-treatment control, and no messages about neatness were delivered to it. On both an immediate (two days after the treatment) and a delayed (two weeks after the treatment) post-test, the classroom that had received the Attribution treatment was more conscientious about discarding litter than either of the other two classrooms.

In their second study, Miller et al. focused on second-graders' math-related self-esteem and math skills. All experimental conditions were presented individually to children in each of four classrooms. Children in the Attribution Ability condition were told they were doing very well in arithmetic; children in the Attribution Motivation condition were told they were working hard in arithmetic; children in the Persuasion Ability condition were told they should do well in arithmetic; children in the Persuasion Motivation condition were told they should be working harder at arithmetic; children in the Reinforcement condition were praised for their progress in arithmetic; and children in the Control condition received no treatment whatsoever. The various treatment conditions lasted eight days and involved a number of variations on the treatment theme. On math self-esteem, only the two Attribution groups were significantly different from the control group in their increase in self-esteem from pre- to post-test (which took place the day after treatment ended). A similar pattern of results was obtained on both immediate and delayed post-tests of math skills.

Miller et al. suggest two advantages for their approach to inducing behavioral compliance and attitudinal acceptance. First, attribution techniques appear to be more effective than either persuasion or straight reinforcement (at least, the social reinforcement used in their study). Relative to persuasion, Miller et al. suggest that attribution may be more effective "because it is less easily recognized as persuasion, and hence less likely to arouse resistance, counterarguing, or reactance" (p. 438). Second, Miller et al. note that attributional techniques may have longer lasting effects than behavior change induced by reinforcement. Attributional techniques such as those used by Miller at al. do have clear reinforcing properties; however, they also presumably serve to induce intrinsic motivation (see Chapter 1 by Lepper and Gilovich) to perform the desired behavior that will not be dependent on receiving extrinsic reinforcement. As they put it, "Thus to some extent a reinforcement procedure that produces enduring change may require elements of attribution, while successful attribution treatment may involve elements of reinforcement" (p. 439).

It is important to remember that, while the Miller et al. studies involved an intervention technique designed to increase compliance, the targets of this intervention were normal children who, on the whole at least, had not displayed excessive oppositional behavior. It remains to be seen whether such a technique would be successful with chronically disobedient children, but the Miller et al. findings coupled with other investigators' observations (e.g., Ayllon & Roberts, 1974) that "indirect" methods may be more effective than direct ones certainly support the need for future research on such reactance-minimizing techniques.

Conclusion

This chapter may well have raised more questions than it has answered. We still do not know what accounts for the apparent change in young girls from opposition to a barrier to acceptance of its restrictions, nor do we understand a great deal about the factors that lead a child to oppose an adult, nor can we clearly explain why some children become excessively oppositional. The major goal of this writing, however, was not to answer all possible questions about oppositional behavior in children—such an undertaking would be impossible given our present data base. Instead, this chapter has attempted to demonstrate that all of the above questions, as well as the other developmental issues that have been considered here, can be addressed within the framework of reactance theory, and that this theory offers a cogent and powerful perspective on oppositional behavior at all levels of development. It is hoped that reactance theory will assist us in formulating good questions for future research on this pervasive and crucial aspect of social development.

Notes

1. Interpersonal interactions being the complex behaviors that they are, reactance arousal could take place in this situation if the person receiving the threat to freedom interpreted the other person's behavior as indicating that he or she is likely to threaten future freedoms. This implied threat could arouse reactance, even though no reactance should be aroused by the direct threat itself.

2. Although a thorough consideration of the issue of possible sex differences in reactance arousal is not feasible within the confines of the present chapter, such a review is provided by Brehm and Brehm (in press). Two major conclusions can be derived from that review. First, since reactance studies have been conducted with both male and female *adult* subjects, and since predictions from the theory have been confirmed with subjects of both genders, there is no reason to believe that the theory holds only for one sex. Second, there is, however, the suggestion from a number of studies that gender may interact with specific theoretical variables such that arousal of reactance in specific situations is differentially affected. Furthermore, the reactance studies conducted with children that are described in this chapter suggest that developmental level may be an additional factor modifying such gender-situation interactions.

two

INTERPERSONAL PERCEPTION

Psychologists have long recognized that an individual's beliefs and perceptions of other people can have a profound impact on his or her interpersonal behavior. As Asch (1952) put it, "to act in the social field requires a knowledge of social facts— of persons and groups. To take our place with others we must perceive each other's existence and reach a measure of comprehension of one another's needs, emotions and thoughts" (p. 139).[1] A good deal of attention has therefore been directed toward examining how people form and change impressions about others in their environment.

Historically, social and developmental psychologists interested in various aspects of person perception had acted as though a barrier separated the two disciplines. Flavell (1974) lamented this segregation when he noted that "there tends to be less than adequate interchange and mutual stimulation between the social psychologists who study the various forms of adult social cognition and the developmental psychologists who investigate the growth of the same or similar forms during adulthood and adolescence" (p. 67).[2] Indeed, developmentalists have assumed that all meaningful variation in person perception unfolds from within the organism, while social psychologists have focused on dimensions of the stimulus field that convey meaning to adults. Fortunately, the two traditions have begun to merge. Today an increasing number of researchers are testing our cherished person perception phenomena from the complementary perspectives of both traditions.

Getting to know another person is a multistaged process. As interpersonal perceivers, we obtain information about the enduring characteristics of another person from a variety of sources, such as his or her physical appearance, facial expression, overt behavior, and heresay, to name only a few. Based on these direct and indirect observations, we determine whether our data reflect something about the makeup of that perceived individual by making judgments of ability, intentionality, and causality. Finally, having concluded that the actor has a particular trait, we must integrate this new information with our preconceptions to form an overall impression. In line with the theme of our book, we will see that developmental and social factors may interact at each stage in this process. As such, organismic variables like age, level of cognitive development, and social learning experience are considered alongside situational factors such as informational complexity, the importance of the task to the perceiver, and familiarity with the stimulus person. Some of this new and exciting work is reviewed in this section that we have entitled "Interpersonal Perception."

This section opens with Buck's discussion of the evolutionary significance of emotion expression and communication. One of the richest sources of information that we typically have about another person is his or her nonverbal behavior. Eye contact, physical distance, bodily orientation, and paralinguistic cues in speech all serve as raw data through which we come to understand temporary states such as moods and feelings and, hence, people's "inner selves." Perhaps the most informative and revealing nonverbal cue that guides us, and the focus of Buck's chapter, is *facial expression*. Buck reviews a fascinating series of studies conducted with adults and young children in which he assesses the process of and ability to send and receive nonverbal messages. Based on this research, Buck proposes a model to account for sex and personality differences in the development of emotion expression and communication. He also presents an innovative technology for measuring the sending ability of infants and the receiving ability of preschoolers.

Whereas facial and gestural expression conveys information about in individual's current state of mind, a variety of physical appearance cues arouse stereotypic expectancies that contribute to more stable impressions of others. People hold all sorts of beliefs about the behavior and personality of those of us who are tall, short, fat, thin, muscular, long-haired, short-haired, blonde, and near sighted. Moreover, these beliefs often direct our first encounters with others. In a compelling chapter partially entitled "Beauty and the Beast," Langlois and Stephan discuss one of the most powerful dimensions of appearance—physical attractiveness. Apparently, person perceivers of all ages disregard the "you shouldn't judge a book by its cover" proverb. Langlois and Stephan review a literature that shows that the "beautiful is good" stereotype is present even in the eyes of preschool-age children who respond to peers partly on the basis of attractiveness. Accordingly, the authors present a developmental model in which children's expectations represent only a starting point. They go on to suggest that these beliefs influence the perceivers' behavior toward the perceived which, in turn, ultimately affects the behavior of the perceived. The implications of these findings for the regulation of parent-child and teacher-student interactions are addressed, and issues for future research are outlined.

The mere observation of an individual's actions and appearance is tantamount to collecting raw data without analyzing it. Perceivers' conclusions about an actor are instead largely based on the *meaning* they attach to their observations and their answers to questions such as "What caused the individual to act and look this way?" The third chapter in this section is Kassin's critical review of the vast empirical literature on developmental *causal attribution.* Specifically, this chapter looks at attributional rules of thumb and principles of varying complexity (e.g., temporal contiguity and covariation) that children of various ages employ either tacitly or explicitly. Kassin's review is structured around his conceptualization of attribution in an experimental setting as a three-stage event—subjects must extract information from the environment, make a causal judgment, and finally express that attribution in some way. Accordingly, it is shown that age differences may arise from differences in any of the above stages. Strategies for simplifying informational displays and response measures for research with young children are discussed, and future research directions are suggested.

The final chapter of this section, Feldman and Ruble's look at the development of *person perception,* represents the natural culmination of the previous three chapters. Once an actor's behavior and appearance is observed and causally understood, the impression formation process begins; traits are ascribed to the actor and then are implicitly combined somehow into a unified impression. Moreover, Feldman and Ruble's work represents an excellent theoretical and empirical blend of the cognitive-developmental and social approaches to the problem. The authors first review the well-established finding that, at about the ages of 7 to 8, children shift from describing others in superficial, concrete terms and inaccurately predicting behavior to spontaneously making more abstract, dispositional inferences and more accurate predictions of others' behavior. Then, Feldman and Ruble discuss some of their own research that shows that this transition is affected by both cognitive skills and situational factors surrounding children's interactions. In short, this final chapter illustrates quite convincingly the advantages of our developmental-social theme and its implications for the area of interpersonal perception.

Notes

1. Asch, S.E. *Social psychology.* Englewood Cliffs, N.J.: Prentice-Hall, 1952.
2. Flavell, J.H. The development of inferences about others. In T. Mischel (Ed.), *Understanding other persons.* Oxford: Blackwell, Basil, Mott, 1974.

6

THE EVOLUTION AND DEVELOPMENT OF EMOTION EXPRESSION AND COMMUNICATION

ROSS BUCK
UNIVERSITY OF CONNECTICUT

The phenomenon of emotion is being rediscovered by social and developmental psychology after a long period of relative cognitive domination. This renaissance has been influenced by a series of interrelated developments over the past 20 years, particularly in the analyses of brain functioning, animal behavior, and human emotion expression. These developments include the continuing revolution in the understanding of psychopharmacological mechanisms, in which biochemical processes intimately related to human consciousness are now being studied literally at a molecular level, and the study of cerebral lateralization, with its new appreciation of the functions of the right hemisphere which had previously been viewed as "silent" and subservient to the verbal "major hemisphere." The developments in animal behavior involve the increased appreciation of the complexity of animal social development and behavior that was realized when animals began to be observed in their natural environment rather than in experimental apparatus. The developments in human emotion expression involve particularly the study of nonverbal

communication, which will be discussed in some detail in this chapter. These developments are related to one another in that they all represent new ways of approaching the elusive phenomenon of emotion, and they are mutually reinforcing, with new findings in one area often being directly or indirectly related to the others.

This resurgence of interest in emotion is viewed by many social and developmental psychologists from the primarily cognitive and social learning theory point of view that has been dominant in these fields. The result is an opportunity for an empirical and theoretical synthesis that can represent an important step in our overall understanding of the nature of human beings. This chapter will begin with a general consideration of the nature of emotion and the evolution of emotion expression. It will then outline some of the major findings relevant to the development of emotion expression, including both human and animal studies. It will then consider the development of the nonverbal communication of emotion, both nonverbal sending accuracy and nonverbal receiving or decoding ability. Finally, this

The research reported in this chapter was supported in part by NIMH grant #MH20286 and by funds from the University of Connecticut Research Foundation.

chapter will consider new directions for research, particularly the promise of adapting segmentation techniques to the analysis of the development of nonverbal emotional expression and perception.

The evolution of emotion expression

A definition of emotion

EMOTION EXPRESSION AS "READOUT." Traditionally, emotion has been associated with the process of homeostasis and bodily adaptation, has involved subjective feelings, and has involved external expressions. Here we will consider emotion as a process by which central nervous system mechanisms concerned with homeostasis and adaptation signal or "read out" their condition, both internally to the consciousness of the respondent and externally to others via expressive behaviors. We will consider the subjective experience of emotion to be involved in the internal readout and the nonverbal communication of emotion to be involved in the external behavioral readout.

The argument for this point of view is derived from Darwin's (1872) analysis of the adaptive value of emotion expression. Darwin suggested that facial expressions and other means of external emotion expression have evolved in given species because those kinds of emotion communication were useful for survival. It can be argued that, for analogous reasons, the subjective experience of emotion has evolved in part as an "internal readout" of the emotion state. It should be useful for an animal, particularly a creature with important cognitive capacities, to be aware of the state of its own tendencies toward fight, flight, attachment, interest, and so on, as well as its needs for food, drink, oxygen, and so forth.

In other words, the "emotion state" involves the state of central nervous system mechanisms concerned with bodily homeostasis and adaptation.[1] Subjective experience and expressive behavior have evolved as readout devices that carry information about the state of these mechanisms internally to the individual and externally to others. Thus, we are defining two conceptually independent sorts of emotion "expression": an internal subjective readout and an external behavioral readout.

THE FACIAL FEEDBACK HYPOTHESIS. Many contemporary theorists do not regard the subjective experience of emotion to be independent of external expressive behaviors and, in fact, regard these to be closely associated with one another. The "facial feedback hypothesis" holds that the experience of expressive behavior, particularly facial expressions, *is* the subjective experience of emotion to at least some extent. This point of view is derived from the classic James-Lange theory of emotion (James, 1968), which suggested that emotion experience is a joint function of the physiological response to the arousing event mediated by the autonomic nervous system and the overt behavioral response to the arousing event mediated by the skeletal muscles (including the facial musculature). This theory was criticized by Cannon (1932), who argued in part that autonomic responses are too slow-acting and undifferentiated to account for human emotion experience. The facial feedback hypothesis counters by emphasizing the importance of the feedback functions of the facial musculature: "The face might . . . fill the informational gap left by a solely visceral theory of emotion, distinguishing one emotion from another, changing rapidly and providing feedback about what is occurring to the person" (Ekman, Friesen, & Ellsworth, 1971, p. 173).

The facial feedback hypothesis is consistent with Darwin's (1872) contention that the free expression of the external signs of an emotion intensifies it, while the repression of these signs "softens" the emotion state; it is also an important aspect of Tomkins' (1962, 1963) and Izard's (1977) highly influential theories of emotion. Izard, for example, argues that in naturally occurring emotion distinctly different emotion experiences are generated by sensory input from differentiated patterns of proprioceptive and cutaneous impulses associated with expressive behavior (Personal communication, 1979b). On the other hand, the evidence supporting the facial feedback hypothesis is scanty and susceptible to alternative interpretation (see Buck, 1980), and recent studies have not been supportive (Notarius & Levenson, 1979; Tourangeau & Ellsworth, 1979). It may therefore be useful to consider as an alternative the present view that the external and internal "expression" of emotion have been subject to different evolutionary histories and may therefore be relatively independent of one another.

Our reasoning concerning the evolution of internal emotional expression, or subjective emotion experience, is derived from the analysis of the evolution of external emotion expression. We will therefore outline this evolution before considering the process of internal expression.

The evolution of emotion communication

THE PROCESS OF EVOLUTION. The essence of Darwin's theory of evolution is that there are individual differences among members of a given species in attributes that are relevant to survival, and that those individuals who are better adapted will have a slightly better chance to survive and reproduce. Therefore, attributes that are adaptive to the survival of the species will naturally tend to increase, or be selected, over the generations. For example, Glickman and Schiff (1967) have noted how each species has evolved behavioral patterns that are adaptive to that species. Curiosity behavior, for example, tends to be high in species that must search for their food and that are not threatened by predators, while species that have an easily obtained food supply who are threatened by predators do not tend to be so curious. Curiosity is more likely to kill a mouse than a cat. Similarly, an aggressive rabbit would not stand up long to a wolf.

Clearly, there are general similarities among species in the central nervous system mechanisms associated with emotion. For example, certain temporal lobe mechanisms appear to be associated with aggression and fearful behaviors in many species of mammals, whereas septal mechanisms are commonly associated with sociability and sexual behaviors (MacLean, 1968, 1969, 1970). It is also clear, however, that these mechanisms must differ in detail from species to species in ways that are compatible with their survival.

THE EVOLUTION OF SOCIAL STRUCTURES. It is difficult at first glance to imagine how social structures can be determined by evolution— after all, social structure is a property of groups, whereas evolution would seem to affect only the properties of individuals. However, some social structures clearly evolve, such as those of insects (e.g., bees, ants). The resolution of this apparent paradox lies in the fact that social structures may be based on communication systems that may have evolved within the individual. Such communication systems involve both *sending accuracy,* that is, the encoding of relevant information in a form that can be accurately decoded by others, and *receiving ability,* that is, the ability to accurately decode this information.

This evolution of social structures via communication systems can be seen most clearly in the insects. Von Frisch (1968), for example, has described the "language" by which bees communicate the location of food to their fellows. Such communication may be reflexive and nonpropositional, in that the sender does rot *intend* to communicate the information. But the information must activate the sender's behavior in an appropriate way—one dictated by evolution—that can influence the behavior of the receiver.[2] That such communication can go wildly astray is illustrated by the observation that ants normally give off an odorous substance when dead, which allows their fellow ants to detect them and typically carry them to a "graveyard" within the colony. If a live ant is dabbed with this substance, it is carried kicking and struggling to the graveyard and unceremoniously dumped. It then may jump up and try to escape, only to be captured and dumped again. This process may continue until the substance finally wears off.

There is growing evidence that analogous kinds of communication systems support the more complex social structures of vertebrates, including human and nonhuman primates. As we will see, however, "higher" animals must increasingly *learn how to use* these communication systems as their social structures increase in complexity. The next question to which we will turn is how these communication systems evolve.

RITUALIZATION. According to ethologists, behaviors that serve as signals in these communication systems are termed *displays,* and they evolve in a process termed *ritualization* (Blest, 1961; Tinbergen, 1952). The source or precursor of a display is some behavior of the sender that must be (a) potentially informative about the referent message, and (b) available or "visible" to the receiver via sensory cues.

If the "message" involves the sender's emotion state, the display most likely evolves from some behavior associated with the emotion state that is "visible" to others. For example, Eibl-Eibesfeldt (1972) has noted that the state associated with visual attention to some unusual or unexpected circumstance is naturally associated in primates with a widening of the eyes, which increases visual acuity. This widening is accompanied naturally by a raising of the skin above the eyes, which is visible to others. Thus eyebrow-raising appears to be a proper candidate for ritualization, and Eibl-Eibesfeldt argues that indeed it has been ritualized into a display associated with surprise or interest. In humans, he notes that eyebrow-raising has acquired different meanings in different cultures, indicating that social learning must play a role in determining the communicative role of the display.

The ritualization of displays is often accompanied by the evolution of associated physical characteristics that amplify or emphasize the display—for example, the eyebrow in humans, which emphasizes the

eyebrow-raise; the colorful tail feathers of the male peacock, used in courtship displays; and the tympanum of the grasshopper, used to produce acoustical signals (cf. Eibl-Eibesfeldt, 1970; Wilson, 1975). It has been suggested that the complex facial musculature of primates, and particularly humans, has evolved in part to serve communicative functions. Communicative demands in the life of highly social species presumably create selection pressures favoring individuals with a greater range of facial expression and, thus, a more complex facial musculature. For example, Andrew (1965) has noted that the displays of the highly social plains-dwelling baboon are more complex than those of the related mandrill or drill baboon, which lives a more solitary existence in the forest.

HUMAN FACIAL EXPRESSION OF EMOTION. The evolution of emotion expression has major implications for the analysis of human facial expression. The debate over whether human facial expressions of emotion are innate and universal to the human species or learned and culturally variable has been long and, at times, heated. Darwin delineated the former position in 1872 in *The Expression of the Emotions in Man and Animals.* Like other explanations of human behavior that rested on innate mechanisms, Darwin's position was challenged by those who argued that human behavior is based on learning. This latter view has been challenged, in turn, by more recent and more sophisticated studies of the biological bases of behavior that take both innate mechanisms and learning into account (cf. Ekman, Friesen, & Ellsworth, 1971).

Sylvan Tomkins' *Affect, Cognition, and Personality* (1962, 1963) was a landmark study using this new approach. In this book, Tomkins argued that there are eight *primary affects:* happiness, sadness, anger, fear, surprise, interest, disgust/contempt, and shame. He felt that each primary affect was innately based on a physiological "program" and associated with a specific and universal facial display. Tomkins' theory heavily influenced the work of both Paul Ekman and Carroll Izard, who found support for it using photographs of posed facial expressions (cf. Ekman, Friesen, & Ellsworth, 1971; Izard, 1971, 1977). For example, Ekman and his colleagues found that the posed expressions of certain primary affects by Westerners could be accurately decoded even by persons from preliterate tribes who had had little or no contact with Western culture (Ekman & Friesen, 1971; Ekman, Sorenson, & Friesen, 1969).

Ekman and Friesen (1975) discussed in detail the kinds of facial configurations associated with some primary affects. They also stressed, however, that the facial expression is not a simple and automatic function of an emotion state. Each person learns a variety of "facial management techniques" based on *display rules,* which are learned but largely unwritten rules about what facial displays are appropriate under what circumstances. For example, a person might *qualify* the display by adding a further expression as a "comment" on the felt expression, as when one smiles following a display of a negative emotion (fear, sadness, anger) in order to instruct another that "I'll go through with it anyway," or "I can take it," or "I won't go too far." Similarly, one can *modulate* the expression of emotion, increasing or decreasing its intensity relative to what one actually feels. Finally, there are a number of ways in which one can falsify emotion: *simulating* an unfelt emotion or *masking* what one actually feels.

THE EVOLUTION OF RECEIVING ABILITY. The evolution of emotion displays may be summarized as follows: Given that emotion communication of a certain sort is adaptive to a species, individuals who show evidence of this emotion state more clearly in their external behavior will tend to be favored, so that over the generations these behaviors will become ritualized into displays. In addition, we would expect that individuals who respond appropriately to these displays would also be favored, so that the perceptual systems of species members may be-

come "preattuned" to the pickup of these displays.

The evolution of emotion-receiving ability has received less study than the evolution of emotion displays, but it is consistent with Gibson's (1966, 1977) theory of perception, which emphasizes how perception must be determined by the nature of the ecological niche in which a species evolves (cf. Baron, 1980; Baron & Buck, 1979). It has also received at least indirect support in several studies. For example, Sackett (1966) showed that infant rhesus monkeys raised in isolation from other monkeys since birth react with appropriate fear to a photograph of a large male making a threat display. Also, Ohman and Dimberg (1978) and Orr and Lanzetta (1980) have demonstrated that human facial expressions of anger or fear are more readily associated with aversive events in a classical conditioning experiment than are happy or neutral expressions.

The evolution of emotion experience

One could argue that the processes underlying the evolution of subjective emotion experience may be analogous to those underlying the evolution of emotion communication. Just as the communication of emotion-related information is useful to the coordination of social behavior, awareness of one's own emotion state must be useful in the coordination of one's own behavior. This could be the impetus for the evolution of "readout" mechanisms that provide emotion information directly to the cognitive system.

It seems clear that some aspects of emotion experience involve feedback from peripheral autonomic and endocrine responses associated with bodily homeostasis and adaptation (Buck, 1976a, 1980). Patients report deficits in emotion experience following spinal cord injury (Hohmann, 1966) and unilateral sympathectomy (removal of one side of the sympathetic branch of the autonomic nervous system; Delgado, 1969). It is also clear, however, that such peripheral physiological responses are not capable of supporting *all* kinds of emotion experience.

Cannon (1932) presented strong evidence against such a claim. In particular, such responses are too slow-acting and insufficiently differentiated; peripheral visceral structures are not liberally endowed with "interoceptive" sensory fibers. Thus, for example, we cannot be aware of the position of our food during the digestive process to the same extent that we may be aware of our right foot from proprioceptive cues.

It is, therefore, unlikely that autonomic and endocrine responses can underlie all emotional experience, and we have seen that current evidence regarding the facial feedback hypothesis makes it seem unlikely that skeletal muscle feedback plays a major role in such experience. As an alternative, it may be suggested that the central nervous system mechanisms underlying emotion states may provide a direct experiential readout, without the need for feedback via peripheral structures. This experiential readout may have evolved through a process analogous to the ritualization of external emotional displays: Aspects of the activity of the emotion mechanisms were potentially informative; these aspects were "ritualized" in species in which such a subjective readout was useful; experiential receiving or decoding mechanisms evolved hand in hand with this process.

The development of emotion communication

This consideration of the evolution of emotion and emotion expression in a species provides a useful background for the analysis of the development of emotion and emotion expression in the individual, because it suggests the basic nature of the systems that are acted on by the processes of social learning and cognitive development during the individual's growth. We will now consider the development of emotion communication, which involves the maturation of the central nervous system mechanisms underlying emotion states and the provision of appropriate social experiences. We will also look at the nature of the social learning process when applied to emotional responses.

Maturation of the emotion systems

Any extensive consideration of the nature of the central nervous system mechanisms or "substrates" underlying emotion states is beyond the scope of this chapter (cf. Buck, 1976a, Chapter 3). Suffice it to say that whereas some kinds of emotion-related behaviors are present at birth, others appear later, and that this may well be based in part on the maturation of the neural substrates underlying these behaviors. There is evidence that this maturational sequence is related to the kind of social learning environment in which the infant is likely to develop. This evidence largely comes from studies conducted by H.F. Harlow and his colleagues on the social and emotional development of rhesus monkeys.

EMOTION MATURATION IN RHESUS MONKEYS. Harlow's famous series of studies of cloth and wire "surrogate mothers" demonstrated convincingly that isolation from conspecifics during the first year of life has devastating and lasting effects on social behavior in rhesus monkeys (Harlow, 1962, 1971). It is noteworthy from our point of view that, although the isolated animals had no opportunity to learn fearful or aggressive behaviors from other monkeys, their level of fearful and aggressive behaviors toward other monkeys was much greater than normal.

The above research was followed by careful observational studies of normal monkey infants and their mothers and peers. These studies suggested that, given contact comfort, affectionate behaviors are present in the infant monkey virtually at birth, but there is little evidence of fear or aggression in the very young infant. The infant shows curiosity about everything and fear of nothing, so that the presence of a protective adult is essential for survival. After a few weeks, fearful responses begin to appear, and by 6 months of age they are well established. Harlow suggests that the neural mechanisms underlying fear have matured by 6 months of age. However, aggression has not yet fully appeared. The 6-month-old monkey shows some aspects of aggressive behavior during play, such as biting, grimacing, and gesturing threat and submission, but play does not really become violent and abusive until the end of the first year. It is at this point that the neural circuits associated with aggressive behavior are presumably mature. A dominance ordering gradually emerges from these bouts, and open fighting generally declines and is replaced by gestures of threat and submission. Deets and Harlow (1971) reported a series of deprivation studies that were generally consistent with this model.

In other words, the neural substrates underlying fearful and aggressive behavior may fully mature in rhesus monkeys only after they have normally had much experience in social relationships with other monkeys. The infants, however, are born capable of experiencing affection, and their initial social experiences allow them to become familiar with, learn to trust, and form strong affectional bonds with other monkeys in their group. The infant becomes capable of experiencing fear only after such affectionate social ties have had time to become established, and the experience of aggressive feelings is even later to emerge. However, if the infant is isolated from other monkeys while the neural substrates underlying fear and aggression mature, its relationships with others may be forever colored by these negative emotions.

EMOTION MATURATION IN HUMANS. Deets and Harlow (1971) suggested that human infants also show an absence of fearful and aggressive responses during the first months of life, while affectionate behavior such as smiling, laughing, and clinging are clearly present. A "fear of strangers" often emerges during the second half of the first year of life, and the "terrible two's" are well known to parents for revealing impressive aggressive capacities of their offspring.

A number of investigators have attempted to trace the development of emotion-related behavior in human infants (e.g., Bridges, 1932) but have been hampered by problems of controlling the elicitation of emotion and specifying the infant's emotional responses by precise criteria. The possibilities of experimentally inducing emotion in children are clearly restricted by ethical restraints, and even with controlled emotional stimuli it is difficult to assess the emotion state of the infant and the very young child because subjective reports and judgments of the intentionality of their behavior are suspect.

It is possible, however, to develop criteria for emotion response in very young children based on their facial expressions and other nonverbal displays, and this fact has opened new possibilities for the study of emotion maturation and development in humans. Izard (1979a), for example, has embarked on an important, ambitious, and extremely well-designed naturalistic and longitudinal study of the facial expressions of infants and young children in response to a series of immunization injections and medical tests that begin at 2 weeks of age and continue until 2 years of age (see Izard, Huebner, Risser, McGinnes, & Dougherty, 1980). As the child's facial response is videotaped, the following events occur: (a) a nurse takes the child, (b) the nurse plays with the child and then returns the child to its mother, (c) an acutely painful injection or medical test is performed on the child, (d) the child is comforted, and (e) the nurse again plays with the child. Initial results indicated that "classical" facial expressions of fear or anger do not appear in their entirety following the painful stimulus in infants younger than 6 months of age. Instead, the typical initial facial response to pain is similar to the adult anger expression, with the eyebrows down and together at the midline and the mouth open and squared, but the eyes squeezed tightly shut (see Figure 6.1a). This expression is associated with a scream of protest that Izard suggests may have the evolutionary function of alerting the caregiver. It is often followed by components of the classical sad expression that is regarded by adults as cute and lovable (see Figure 6.1b). Izard suggests that this latter expression may function to increase cuddling and soothing behaviors and thus facilitate the bond be-

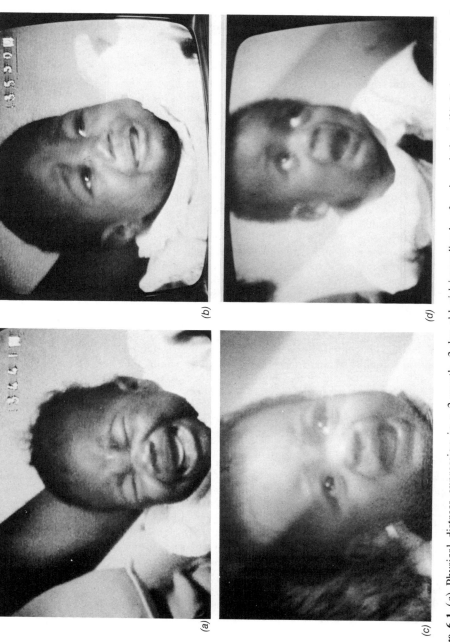

Figure 6.1 (*a*) Physical distress expression in a 2-month, 2-day-old girl immediately after inoculation. (*b*) Sad expression about 11 seconds after inoculation. (*c*) Anger expression directed toward nurse in an 8-month, 28-day-old boy after inoculation. (*d*) Fear expression as nurse approaches after inoculation. (Photographs courtesy C. Izard)

tween the caregiver (summoned by the scream) and the injured infant. It is only later that classical expressions of fear and anger appear (see Figures 6.1*c* and 6.1*d*). Thus, Izard's data to date appear to be quite consistent with Harlow's regarding the maturation of emotion systems.

Social experience and emotion communication

SOCIAL EXPERIENCE AND EMOTION COMMUNICATION IN MONKEYS. By observing the interactions of young rhesus monkeys and their mothers, siblings, and peers, Harlow and his colleagues were able to characterize in general terms the kinds of social experiences that tend to occur normally as the monkey grows. From this, they speculated about the possible role that these experiences play in social and emotional development. The general outlines that emerged have been consistent with the findings of observational studies carried out with other species of monkeys and apes, such as Jane Goodall's (1971, 1979) as well as recent analyses of early human development (Sroufe, 1979).

The *maternal affectional system* characterizes the first year in the life of the infant rhesus monkey. It begins with a *stage of contact,* a period of relatively unrestricted contact with the mother. After the end of the second or third month, however, the mother begins to discourage unrestricted contact, beginning with gentle punishment and gradually increasing it in frequency and intensity as the infant grows. As a result of this *stage of rejection,* the infant is obliged to go off on his or her own to an increasing extent, which is consistent with the infant's high level of curiosity and rapidly developing locomotor skills. As the infant learns to be more independent, the incidence of material punishment peaks at about 5 months and then gradually declines, beginning the *stage of relative separation* vis à vis the mother. Often this separation is increased by the birth of a new sibling that dominates the mother's time, an event that may be quite traumatic to the older infant. Normally, this

"cutting of the apronstrings" results in increased interaction of the infant with similar-aged peers, which appears to be essential for normal social development. Harlow (1971) suggested that contact with peers may be more important than contact with the mother in the development of normal social behavior, and Goodall (1979) has described the develpment of a young chimpanzee, Flint, who remained dependent on his elderly mother and died at a young age shortly following her death.

With the relative decrease in contact with the mother, the *peer affectional system* begins. The maternal experience lays the emotional groundwork in that it establishes a basic sense of trust in other monkeys that persists in the face of the fearful and aggressive emotions that mature during the second half of the first year of life. The peer affectional system is characterized by much "rough and tumble" play, during which elements of adult social behavior can often be discerned. For example, there is much immature sexual gesturing and playing at aggression with immature threat and submissive gestures. These are the kinds of experiences that are sorely missed by the infants who are raised in isolation. They culminate in the development of the *heterosexual affectional system,* which is characterized by normal monkey sexual behavior, a dominance order that is largely maintained by signals rather than fights, and various greeting and grooming behaviors that together transform these irascible creatures into social animals (Harlow, 1971).

One of the major lessons that may be learned by the infant in this process is how to begin to use the system of emotion communication that has evolved in the species. We have seen that systems of emotion communication, involving both external readout mechanisms and presumably decoding mechanisms, have evolved in social species. However, as Mason (1961) has noted, the behavior of the isolated animals suggests that, at least in rhesus monkeys, these are rather elementary forms of communication that require learning in order to function effectively. This kind of learning is normally provided to the developing monkey during the course of the affectional systems, but the isolated animals have no opportunity to acquire these social skills.

This concept of a communication system based on innate mechanisms but requiring experience to function effectively was illustrated in an ingenious study by Robert E. Miller and his colleagues at the University of Pittsburgh Medical School. Miller developed the "cooperative conditioning" technique to measure emotion communication in rhesus monkeys. He first taught two monkeys to press a bar when a signal light came on in order to avoid a painful electric shock. After the animals had learned this task, they were paired in different rooms so that one animal, the "sender," could see the light but could not press the bar, while the second animal, the "receiver," could press the bar but could not see the light. The receiver was provided with the televised image of the head and facial region of the sender. It was reasoned that, if the sender made an emotion-related facial expression when the light went on, and if the receiver perceived and correctly interpreted that facial expression, then and only then could the receiver press the bar at the right time, a response that would avoid the shock for both of them. Miller found, in several experiments, that normal rhesus monkeys could solve this task with little difficulty, thereby proving their ability to communicate via facial expression (Miller, Banks, & Kuwahara, 1966; Miller, Banks, & Ogawa, 1962, 1963; Miller, Murphy, & Mirsky, 1959). Animals from the Harlow laboratory who had been isolated for the first year of life, however, could neither send nor receive accurately in the Miller paradigm, even though they had been able to learn the initial avoidance task. Apparently, they could not accurately communicate with other animals using the systems of emotion communication employed by normal rhesus monkeys. "It was strikingly apparent . . . that the monkeys deprived of social relationships during the first year of life do not utilize social information as do normals even

after 3–4 years of social opportunities following the isolation period" (Miller, Caul, & Mirsky, 1967, p. 239).

SOCIAL EXPERIENCE AND EMOTION COMMUNICATION IN HUMANS. It can be argued that, in broad terms, the relationships between the developing child and its caregivers and peers provide social experiences that serve functions similar to those served by analogous relationships in monkeys and apes (see Sroufe, 1979). These functions include creating an emotional basis for later social behavior and learning how to use the human version of the emotion communication system. In addition, experiences during this time may well lay the groundwork for the learning of language.

It is clear that early interactions between human infants and their caregivers, like the maternal affectional system in monkeys, help to form the emotional and communicative basis for later social behavior. Much of the traditional work in infant development has been concerned with identifying how parental caregiving affects the infant. Thus the traditional approach of social learning theory regards the caregiver as the model who is imitated. More recently, studies have been directed toward examining the influence of the infant on the caregiver (e.g., Lewis & Rosenbloom, 1974). As Thoman (1975) has noted, the caregiver's behavior is in large part a function of the child's characteristics—both the nature of the child's precipitating behavior and the child's response to the caregiver's response.

This kind of mutual influence process has been emphasized in recent analyses of language learning and processing (Bruner, 1979). Condon and his colleagues identified the phenomenon of interactional synchrony, in which both speaker and listener "move in precise synchrony with the articulatory structure of the speaker's speech" (Condon, 1979, p. 161). Condon suggested that the listener's body movements are peripheral reflections of the central neurological processing of speech. When the listener is really listening, his or her body movements are in rhythm with the speaker's articulation; when the listener's "mind wanders," it is reflected in a decrease in synchrony. The result is, in effect, an external "readout" of the listener's state of involvement in the speaker's articulation, which may play an important role in the establishment and maintenance of the interactional relationship.

Condon (1979) argued that interactional synchrony plays an important role in language acquisition and reports that marked synchronization of body movement with speech sounds has been observed in the movements of 1- to 4-day-old infants responding to both live and tape-recorded human voices (Condon & Sander, 1974). He also reports that the analysis of films of dysfunctional children (autistic, aphasic, dyslexic, etc.) reveals distorted forms of synchrony.

Fraiberg (1974) has contributed a compelling example of a possibly analogous kind of distortion in her observation of responses to blind infants. In the course of her studies, Fraiberg noted that she did not *talk* to blind infants as she did to sighted infants and concluded that this occurred because talking does not evoke the responses (eye responses, smiles, etc.) in blind infants that it evokes in sighted children. She suggested that, in general, there is a "sense of something vital missing in the social exchange" with blind infants. Fraiberg noted that this is often reflected in the faces of observers as they watch films of children: "With sighted children it is always interesting to see the resonance of response on the viewer's face. We smile when the baby on the film smiles; we are sober when he is distressed. . . . But the blind baby on the screen does not elicit these spontaneous moods. . . . There is a large vocabulary of expressive behavior that one does not see in a blind baby at all. The absence of differentiated facial signs on the baby's face is mirrored on the face of the observer" (Fraiberg, 1974, p. 217).

TEMPERAMENT AND SOCIAL EXPERIENCE. The mutual influence of infant and caregiver increases the potential importance of the role of temperament in the process of social and emotional development. Temperament refers to general emotional-behavioral dispositions that may be based in part on individual differences in the physiological mechanisms underlying emotion (Buck, 1976a, p. 242). Thomas, Chess, and Burch (1970) have demonstrated in a longitudinal study, lasting from birth to teenage years, that many (although not all) children show a basic constancy of behavioral disposition over this span of time. They point out that the effects of the environment in general, and of the behavior of caregivers and other socialization agents in particular, depend in part on the temperament of the individual child. An approach to child rearing or education that works well for one child may fail miserably for another if it is incompatible with his or her temperament.

Social learning and emotion responding

We saw above that the "visibility" of a response—the extent to which it is available via sensory cues—determines whether that response is a candidate for the ritualization process. Such a "visibility dimension" also has important implications for a social learning analysis of the development of emotion responding. Some responses, particularly overt behavioral ones, are easily available to both the responder and others. Other responses, particularly the responder's subjective emotion experiences, are available only to the responder. Still other responses, particularly physiological ones, are normally not apparent without special equipment.

Social learning theory emphasizes the role of imitation and social reinforcement in the development of response patterns (Bandura & Walters, 1963). This approach implies that responses with different degrees of visibility must be associated with different patterns of social learning. Highly visible, overt behavioral events (i.e., facial expressions) can be easily seen by both the responder in other persons and others in the responder, and they therefore can undergo thorough training through imitation and social reinforcement. A child can see and learn directly from the overt emotional behaviors of others, and others can "shape" the overt behaviors of the child via social reinforcement. Thus, in the development of his or her overt behavioral responding, a child can learn to make many discriminations about how a given emotion may be expressed appropriately, which emotions may be expressed and which may not, and so on. These overt responses should increasingly reflect the child's learning about what kinds of emotional responding others expect.

The kind of fine discrimination learning described above can occur only with relatively "visible" manifestations of emotion; it cannot apply to subjective feelings. A child can learn to model the overt behavior of others quite directly, but he or she has no direct access to the subjective emotion experiences of others, and others have no direct access to his or hers. Learning about subjective events must therefore take place indirectly, via the verbal reports and descriptions of subjective experience that the child gains from others and the reports that he or she gives to others.

Several theorists, including Skinner (1953) and Schachter (1964), have discussed the process by which learning about subjective events is achieved.[3] Through the process of associating one's private experiences with interpretations provided by others, one develops a set of "labels" by which to identify and categorize subjective experience. For example, a child might learn to correctly identify and label feelings of anger by repeated direct or vicarious experience with situations that arouse such feelings and then label them appropriately. When the child is overtly expressing anger, a parent might say, "I see that you are angry," or the child may see others overtly angry and hear them describe their feelings as anger. On the other hand, this labeling of subjective experience may be erroneous. A child who is fed whenever he or she overtly expresses hostility could conceivably learn to label the subjective experience associated with anger as "hunger."

Physiological responses must be generally associated with still a different kind of social learning experience. Most physiological events take place outside conscious awareness, so that a child would not ordinarily learn to identify or label them.[4] However, it appears that physiological responses can be modified by learning experiences. Both Russian studies of interoceptive conditioning and American experiments indicate that subtle physiological responses are quite readily conditionable and that such conditioning may occur under everyday circumstances (Brozek, 1964; Miller, Barber, DiCara, Kamiya, Shapiro, & Stoyva, 1974; Razran, 1961). Other investigators have demonstrated that such conditioning can be vicarious as well as direct (Berger, 1962).

These findings suggest that conditioning that involves physiological responses must be a constantly occurring process, and that a given person's physiological response in a given situation may be determined largely by his or her conditioning history in similar kinds of situations (cf. Buck, 1976a, Chapter 4). For example, the more stimuli that have been conditioned to cause physiological arousal in a given situation, the higher the arousal will be. If a child has intense and physiologically arousing experiences in situations involving anger, it is likely that he or she will show arousal in situations involving anger as an adult. In contrast, another child may have relatively mild arousing experiences associated with anger and may manifest relatively little arousal in such situations.

We have outlined a general point of view regarding the nature of emotion and emotion communication that considers both the evolution of emotion within the species and its development within the individual. We will now consider in some detail a series of studies on emotion communication in preschool children, which will be discussed in terms of this point of view.

Studies of emotion communication: Nonverbal sending accuracy

The slide-viewing paradigm

The series of studies that we consider uses a measure of emotion communication accuracy derived from Miller's cooperative conditioning precedure described earlier. Essentially, the procedure involves having a sender view and describe his or her reactions to a series of emotionally loaded color slides while his or her facial/gestural responses are unobtrusively televised (see Buck, 1978). The images of the sender's responses are viewed (without audio) by one or more receivers who attempt to judge what kind of slide the sender viewed on that trial, and how pleasant or unpleasant the sender's emotional response was to that slide. The former judgments are then compared to the actual type of slide viewed by the sender in order to obtain the percentage of slides correctly identified; this constitutes the "percent correct" measure of communication accuracy. The latter judgments are correlated with the sender's own rating of the pleasantness or unpleasantness of his or her emotion experience; this constitutes the "pleasantness" measure of communication accuracy. Both of these constitute objective criteria of communication accuracy whose significance relative to chance may be evaluated statistically (Buck, Savin, Miller, & Caul, 1969, 1972).

The types of slides presented in the slide-viewing paradigm with adult senders have included Sexual slides, showing nude and seminude males with females; Scenic slides, showing pleasant landscapes; Pleasant People slides, showing happy-looking children and adults; Unpleasant slides, depicting severe facial injuries and burns; and Unusual slides, showing strange photographic effects. For preschool-aged children, the types of slides included Familiar People slides, showing the child him/herself and the child's friends at the preschool; Unfamiliar People slides, showing persons unknown to the child; Unpleasant slides, depicting mildly unpleasant scenes (i.e., a woman crying, an infant crying, etc.), and Unusual slides. It should be noted that these slide categories were chosen to represent a range of different kinds of emotions that could reliably be produced within ethical limitations in a laboratory using color slides; there was no intent to suggest

any particular "theory of emotion" from this choice of categories, and some emotions, notably anger, are not tapped by this procedure.

It should be noted that the percent correct and the pleasantness measures resulting from the slide-viewing paradigm are *communication* measures in that they reflect both "sending accuracy"—the tendency of the sender to display or "encode" expressions that accurately reflect the emotion state produced by the slides—and "receiving ability"—the ability of the receiver to accurately read or "decode" the correct emotion state from the sender's behavior.[5] For accurate communication to occur, both sending accuracy and receiving ability must be present to some extent. If accurate communication does not occur, it could be due to a lack of sending accuracy, a lack of receiving ability, or both. To investigate sending accuracy, one shows the displays of different senders to the same group of receivers. Any variation in communication accuracy scores would then be attributable to differences in sending accuracy. Conversely, if one shows the same sender's display or set of displays to a number of receivers, any variation in accuracy scores would be attributable to individual differences in receiving ability. The slide-viewing paradigm may thus be used to investigate both sending accuracy and receiving ability. We will review the studies of sending accuracy in the remainder of this section.

Studies with adults

BASIC RESULTS. the first studies using the slide-viewing paradigm were conducted with college-age persons as senders and receivers (Buck et al., 1969, 1972; Buck, Miller, & Caul, 1974). The results may be summarized as follows: (1) Females were higher than males in sending accuracy, (2) there was no significant gender difference in receiving ability, (3) sending accuracy was related to a number of personality measures that are consistent with a free expression of emotion, including extraversion, self-esteem, and a "personal" description of one's subjective emotional response to the slides, and (4) the pleasantness measure of sending accuracy was negatively related to the sender's physiological response to the slides, both the skin conductance response to the slide presentation and the heart rate acceleration to the sender's discussion of his or her feelings.

THE EXTERNALIZING-INTERNALIZING DISTINCTION. The latter finding, that senders who accurately communicated the nature of their emotion state to others showed a *smaller* physiological response to the slides than did less expressive senders, has aroused considerable interest (cf. Buck, 1979). It is consistent with a distinction proposed by H. E. Jones in the mid-1930s between an externalizing mode of response to emotion, characterized by a large overt behavioral response but a small electrodermal (skin conductance) response, and an internalizing mode of response, in which the overt response to the emotion is absent but there is a large electrodermal response. Jones (1950) suggested that the internalizing mode of response develops as the child encounters social disapproval for overt and visible displays of emotion. The "internal avenues of affect discharge" are not inhibited by such social learning experiences, and Jones suggested that (but did not fully explain why) their activity increases as the external expression of emotion is inhibited.

In the course of their studies of the externalizing-internalizing phenomenon, Jones and other investigators (e.g., Block, 1957) described a number of personality attributes that seem to distinguish between high and low electrodermal reactors. For example, low reactors seem to be open, sociable, talkative, active, and extraverted, but also somewhat impulsive, aggressive, and dominating. High reactors, on the other hand, were found to be good-natured and cooperative, but also somewhat quiet, shy, reserved, withdrawn, introverted, isolated from others, and inhibited.

The studies using the slide-viewing para-

digm suggest that the gender difference in sending accuracy is related to this externalizing-internalizing distinction. Males tended in these studies to show an internalizing mode of response to the slides, with lower sending accuracy but higher skin conductance responding, relative to the females. Females, in contrast, seemed to show an externalizing mode of response (Buck et al., 1974). Also, a review of the literature on skin conductance responding (i.e., Prokasy & Raskin, 1973) revealed that adult males seem to have larger physiological responses than do females in a wide variety of situations (see Buck, 1979). In contrast, there is no gender difference in electrodermal responding in young children.

These findings suggested that studies of sending accuracy and physiological responding in young children would prove very interesting. First, they could show whether the gender difference in sending accuracy is present in young children, in which case it might be based on gender-related temperamental factors, or whether, like the difference in electrodermal responding, it appears as the child grows, in which case it would suggest that (barring some maturational process linked to gender) the gender difference in adult expressiveness is based on sex-role-related learning experiences. Second, such research could investigate the development of the relationship between sending accuracy and electrodermal responding. If Jones' (1950) theory is correct, this relationship requires social learning in order to develop; if the child has not yet learned to inhibit the overt response to emotion, there would be no increase in electrodermal responding and, hence, no significant relationship between these variables. Third, such studies could investigate the range of facial/gestural expressiveness shown in young children and test whether the personality descriptions found by Jones and other early investigators to distinguish externalizing and internalizing modes of emotion response are related to facial/gestural sending accuracy and electrodermal responding in children.

Studies with children

THE PARADIGM. The slide-viewing paradigm was adapted to the study of children as follows. First, slide categories were chosen that would reliably evoke emotion in children yet would not be upsetting. After watching the responses of my own children to pictures of themselves and their friends, we decided to use these "familiar people" slides in the study. This proved quite successful, evoking strong but pleasant emotion in young children and making the whole experience a positive one for most. Second, the child's mother brought the child to the laboratory and, viewing the televised image of the child from a different room, also served as the primary receiver. The mother's presence was reassuring to the child and also ensured informed consent throughout the study. Third, an undergraduate who was friendly and at ease with young children stayed with the child while the slides were shown. The undergraduate received careful instructions about how to keep the child's attention on the slides and how to avoid encouraging or inhibiting the child as much as possible (see Buck, 1978).

The procedure went as follows. The child and undergraduate set together facing a back-lighted screen (Figure 6.2*a*), while the mother viewed the child from another room (Figure 6.2*b*). The television image appeared just before the slide was presented, so that the mother saw the initial response of the child to the slide. Figures 6.2*c*, 6.2*d*, and 6.2*e* illustrate common responses to familiar, unpleasant, and unusual slides. If the child made no spontaneous verbal or motor response to the slide, the undergraduate waited for five seconds and then said "Who's that?" or "What's that?" The undergraduate did not initiate interaction with the child in any other way, but responded in a friendly fashion to any interaction initiated by the child. After 12 seconds, the slide was removed, the television was turned off, and the undergraduate asked the child to rate the slide by pointing to one of a series of five faces that went from "very happy" to "very

unhappy" (Figure 6.2*f*). At this point, the mother made her judgments about what kind of slide the child had seen and how pleasant or how unpleasant the child's emotional response to it had been. Later, if image quality permitted, the videotapes of the children's expressions were similarly judged by groups of undergraduates who did not know the child.

GENDER DIFFERENCES. Results indicated that there was no significant gender difference in sending accuracy when the mother was observing the child (Buck, 1975, 1977). When the undergraduates were observing, however, the 1975 study found that girls were superior senders, a result that has been replicated in a recent unpublished study (Alper, Buck, & Dreyer, 1978). Also, the 1977 study showed that sending accuracy was negatively correlated with age for boys but not girls. This pattern of results tentatively suggests that there is no large gender difference in sending accuracy among preschool children, but that during this period (3½ to 6), boys are learning to inhibit and mask their spontaneous facial/gestural responses to emotion and that this emerging gender difference is revealed when the child's expressions are judged by strangers.

PERSONALITY DIFFERENCES. Although the gender differences in sending accuracy revealed in these studies were not large, there were considerable individual differences in sending accuracy that were not linked to gender. Some of the children responded openly and appropriately, whereas others showed virtually no overt response to the slides.

To explore whether these individual differences in sending accuracy as measured in the laboratory were related to behavior in the preschool, and also to explore whether the attributes listed by Jones and Block were related to sending accuracy, the *Affect Expression Rating Scale* (AERS) consisting of these attributes was given to the preschool teachers who had no knowledge of the child's performance in the laboratory. This

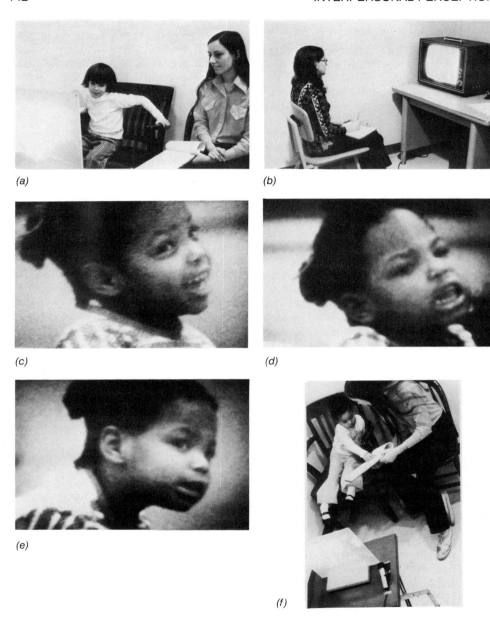

Figure 6.2 (*a*) Child and experimenter view slide on back-lighted screen. (*b*) Mother views the televised expressions of the child in another room. (*c*) Typical facial response to a familiar-person slide. (*d*) Typical facial response to an unpleasant slide. (*e*) Typical facial response to an unusual slide. (*f*) Child rates emotional response by pointing to one of a series of facial drawings.

procedure was very successful; the teachers' ratings on many of these attributes were significantly and meaningfully related to the children's sending accuracy. For example, sending accuracy was positively related with being rated as active, expressive, friendly, and "extraverted," but was also related to being aggressive, bossy, and dominating. Sending accuracy was negatively related to being rated as quiet, reserved, and cooperative, but was also related to being shy, isolated, inhibited, and "introverted" (Buck, 1975).

PHYSIOLOGICAL RESPONDING. To assess whether these personality attributes and sending accuracy are related to skin conductance responding, as the externalizing-internalizing distinction would predict, a replication of the 1975 study that employed skin conductance measurement was carried out (Buck, 1977). The results indicated a marginally significant negative relationship between skin conductance responding and sending accuracy ($r = -.42, p < .06$). Factor analyses of the AERS scale, using both teachers' ratings of children and college students' self-ratings, revealed three orthogonal factors that were named Expressive-Inhibited, Antagonistic-Cooperative, and Independent-Dependent. The Expressiveness factor scores of male children were positively related to sending accuracy and negatively related to skin conductance responding. For the female children, it was the Antagonism factor that was positively related to sending accuracy and negatively related to skin conductance responding. The meaning of this somewhat complex set of results has been tentatively suggested. First, sending accuracy, as measured in the laboratory, is clearly linked to the attributes previously associated with externalizing-internalizing distinction as assessed in the preschool setting. This relationship supports the construct validity of both the sending accuracy measures and the externalizing-internalizing attributes. Second, it appears that these attributes are present and related to sending accuracy even in preschool children. This latter finding tends to shed doubt on Jones' contention that the externalizing-internalizing modes of response are a result of social learning, as it seems doubtful that very early learning experiences could account for such large and consistent individual differences. Instead, it may be that the externalizing-internalizing distinction reflects temperamental factors.[6] Third, the fact that sending accuracy and skin conductance responding are related to "expressiveness" in boys but "antagonism" in girls suggests the possibility that similar behavior in boys and girls might be labeled differently by teachers; the same behavior that suggests that a boy is "active," "expressive," and "talkative" may suggest that a girl is "dominating" and "bossy."

The development of sending accuracy: A model

Taken together, the studies employing adult and preschool-age senders suggest a model in which sending accuracy is related to a personality dimension involving attributes similar to those suggested over 40 years ago by H. E. Jones. In contrast to Jones' view, however, it appears that this personality dimension may be based on temperamental factors rather than on social learning experiences associated with the inhibition of overt expression. At the same time, it appears that the gender difference in sending accuracy may well be based on such social learning exeriences; boys appear to learn to inhibit and mask their expressive responses to the kinds of emotion stimuli employed in these studies, whereas girls do not.

Considering these results, and the general point of view of the nature of the evolution and development of emotion expression, it appears that sending accuracy may be based on a mechanism that is both innate and modifiable by experience. We suggested above that emotion is based in neurochemical systems whose activation leads to tendencies toward external expression in certain species. It is possible that such neurochemical systems underlie externalizing and internalizing modes of emotion response and that they could account for the personality difference in sending accuracy. There are neurochemical systems that seem particularly concerned with the excitation and inhibition of behavior, including subcortical "reward-punishment" systems whose properties were first explored by Olds (1958) and are the subject of much investigation today. Also, there are suggestions that right versus left cerebral hemisphere processing may be involved in emotion expression and inhibition (Buck & Duffy, in press). Regardless of the specific systems that are involved, however, neurochemical systems underlying the excitation and inhibition of emotion expression can account for the data we have considered if one assumes: first, that there are individual differences in the levels of activity in these systems early in life; second, that learning experiences can result in situationally specific changes in these levels of activity; and third, that a predominance of activity in inhibitory systems relative to excitatory systems is directly or indirectly related to increases in skin conductance responding and other kinds of autonomic nervous system arousal (see Buck, 1979). For example, a male who early in life has a preponderance of activity in excitatory systems relative to inhibitory systems should generally show the active, aggressive, and sociable temperament that is associated with an externalizing mode of response as well as relatively low electrodermal responding. However, if such overt responding leads to social disapproval in certain situations (as he learns, for example, that "big boys don't cry," etc.), the pattern of dominance between excitatory and inhibitory systems may be altered in similar situations in the future, resulting in the inhibition of overt expression, increased skin conductance responding, and thus an internalizing mode of response in that situation. It should be noted that overt responding may not be punished in other emotional situations. The same male child may be rewarded and encouraged in aggressive situations and continue to show an externalizing mode of response in such situations in the future. It might be imagined that the social experiences of a little girl with a similar initial temperament would tend to encourage the opposite pattern of responses in these situations.

Studies of emotion communication: Nonverbal receiving ability

Measuring nonverbal receiving ability via the slide-viewing paradigm

THE CARAT INSTRUMENT. It was pointed out above that the communication accuracy score derived from the slide-viewing paradigm may be used to assess receiving ability as well as sending accuracy. To this end, the *Communication of Affect Receiving Ability Test,* or CARAT, was contructed by assembling videotaped sequences taken in past studies. Each sequence shows the response of a given adult sender to a given slide, and the sequences were selected using conventional item-analysis techniques (cf. Buck, 1976b). The finished instrument involves 32 items, each depicting a male or female sender responding to a Sexual, Scenic, Unpleasant, or Unusual slide. A total of 23 different senders is included in the instrument. The receiver is instructed to watch the sender's reactions to the slide carefully and to guess the type of slide viewed on each trial and the pleasantness of the sender's emotional response.

The test-retest reliability of the CARAT instrument is satisfactory ($r = .79$), but internal consistency as measured by coefficient alpha is only .56, a figure that was not improved during the process of item analysis. The evidence for construct validity is mixed at best. Science majors were found to be inferior to business and fine arts majors on CARAT, and some weak relationships with gender and personality have been found (Buck, 1976b). Correlations between CARAT and another measure of nonverbal receiving ability, the Profile of Nonverbal Sensitivity (PONS) by Rosenthal and his colleagues (Rosenthal, Archer, Koivumaki, DiMatteo, & Rogers, 1974; Hall, Rosenthal, Archer, DiMatteo, & Rogers, 1978), have proved disappointing. Buck and Carroll (1974) found a nonsignificant correlation between CARAT and the full PONS (r = .04), and Klaiman (1979) has found the face score of the PONS short form to be correlated with CARAT among females (r = +.24, p < .01) but not males (r = +.09).

Although it is clear that CARAT cannot be considered a definitive test of nonverbal receiving ability, it is also clear that there are problems with other measuring instruments as well. There is a considerable literature, for example, on the relationship between nonverbal sending accuracy and receiving ability that is notable for the range of its results; some investigators have found no evidence of significant relationships, others have found substantial positive relationships, while still others have found significant negative relationships between these variables (cf. Harper, Wiens, & Matarazzo, 1979; Zuckerman, Hall, DeFrank, & Rosenthal, 1976; Zuckerman, Lipets, Koivumaki, & Rosenthal, 1975).

NONVERBAL RECEIVING ABILITY IN PRESCHOOL CHILDREN. To investigate nonverbal receiving ability in preschool children using the slide-viewing technique, and its relationship with sending accuracy, Alper (1977) constructed a child's version of CARAT, termed CARAT-C, from videotapes taken in the Buck (1975) study. CARAT-C was designed to be shorter and easier than CARAT in that only 18 items were employed and the most expressive sequences available were chosen. The instrument includes segments showing boys or girls viewing Familiar People, Unpleasant, or Unusual slides. Thirty-two children viewed the videotape with an investigator who asked them, after each sequence, to point to a picture similar to the one the sender had viewed. The choices included a picture of a laughing little boy (Familiar people), a crying infant (Unpleasant), and an ambiguous time exposure (Unusual). Children's ability to decode posed expressions was also measured. They were read sentences describing emotion-provoking situations, then shown three photographs of posed expressions taken from Ekman and Friesen (1975), and asked to point to the photograph that matched the feeling in the sentence. Later in the year, 16 of these children served as senders in the slide-viewing paradigm, so that their ability to receive via spontaneous and posed expressions could be related to their sending accuracy (Alper et al., 1978).

Results indicated that the children showed significant receiving ability both on CARAT-C and the posed photographs. These two measures of receiving ability, however, were not significantly related to one another (average r = .16), and they had very different patterns of relationship to sending accuracy. Sending accuracy was negatively related to receiving ability as measured by CARAT-C (r = −.60, p < .025), but tended to be positively related to receiving ability as measured by the posed photographs (r = +.43, p < .10). An explanation for the latter finding is not readily apparent.

Problems in the study of nonverbal receiving ability

The lack of significant correlations between different measures of nonverbal receiving ability, the finding of both positive and negative relationships between receiving ability and sending accuracy, and the inability to improve coefficient alpha through the successive item analysis of CARAT sequences reflect similar experiences throughout the history of the study of what has been variously called "empathy," "social sensitivity," "accuracy in person perception," and so on (see Cline, 1964; Frijda, 1969). Despite decades of study, measures of these phenomena with proven reliability and validity have not emerged.

It may well be that nonverbal receiving ability as presently conceived is not a single ability but, instead, reflects a number of abilities and tendencies, some related to one another and others quite independent. For example, Rosenthal et al. (1974) have demonstrated that the ability to decode paralinguistic cues is different from the ability to decode facial or bodily cues. Buck and Lerman (1979) have suggested that the ability to decode the expressions of known persons with whom one has a specific relationship (specific receiving ability) may differ from the ability to decode the expressions of strangers (general receiving ability). Also, it may be that any measure of nonverbal receiving that presents the filmed behavior of a sender and asks the receiver to attend to it begs the question of whether that receiver would spontaneously attend to those cues during real social interaction. The point of view outlined above—that the ability to decode nonverbal cues in others may be based in part on innate factors—would suggest that one need only attend to nonverbal cues in many cases. Possibly the individual variation in nonverbal sensitivity in real social situations is largely a function of attention to nonverbal cues rather than the ability to read them when one attends. The measurement situation that forces attention to nonverbal cues may thus ensure that any individual differences that remain are trivial.

There are at least four conceptually independent factors that might help to account for an individual's nonverbal receiving ability in a given situation. (1) Experience and skill in decoding nonverbal displays in general, (2) experience and skill in decoding the particular nonverbal displays of a specific individual known to the receiver, (3) attention to the nonverbal behaviors of others, and (4) the nonverbal expressiveness of the receiver. Most past studies have dealt with (1)—they have assessed the ability of a person to decode the nonverbal displays of strangers with attention specifically directed to that display. Relatively few studies have been done involving specific receiving ability—the ability to decode the expressions of a person whom one knows (see Sabatelli, Buck, & Dreyer, 1980). The study of the role of the focus of attention in nonverbal receiving ability is promising, and we will consider a possible way of measuring it in the concluding section of this chapter.

The role of nonverbal expressiveness in receiving ability was suggested by the results of studies of the relationship between cognitive style and communication accuracy. Many studies have suggested that field-dependent people are more oriented toward social cues than are field-independent persons; for this reason Sabatelli, Dreyer, and Buck (1979) predicted that field-dependent people would be better receivers of nonverbal cues. Field-dependence was, however, unrelated to either general nonverbal receiving ability (CARAT score) or specific nonverbal receiving ability (ability to decode the expressions of an intimate dating partner). Instead, field-dependence was positively related to nonverbal sending accuracy among both males and females. This finding suggests the possibility that field-dependent persons may extract information from the social environment by providing information to that environment; by being nonverbally expressive themselves, they encourage others to be more expressive in return (Sabatelli et al., 1979). Studies of this phenomenon would appear to require the measurement of nonverbal receiving ability in an interactional setting, where the nonverbal expressiveness of the interactants over time is assessed.

Studies of emotion communication: Segmentation studies

The segmentation technique

The studies of nonverbal sending accuracy and receiving ability that we have considered have measured emotion communication in the form of overall communication accuracy scores, but have not analysed the *process* of emotion communication—that is, the specific behaviors in the sender and the attentional/perceptual processes in the receiver that underlie accurate (or inaccurate) communication. There is evidence that behavior segmentation techniques introduced by Barker and Wright (1955) and developed recently by Newtson (1976) may prove uniquely useful in the analysis of this process.

The segmentation technique is deceptively simple. Subjects are exposed to a videotape or film of the behavior in question and asked to press a button when, in their judgment, a "meaningful event" occurs. The definition of a "meaningful event" is largely left to the subject. When the subject presses the button, the response is recorded on an event recorder that shows where on the videotape the event was thought to occur. Based on a number of studies, Newtson has presented evidence that subjects tend to agree on the location of these "meaningful" points in the behavior stream, and that these "consensual breakpoints" contain more information about the videotaped action sequence than do non-breakpoints (Newtson, Engquist, & Bois, 1977).

The segmentation technique provides a new way to examine emotion communication by which both the nature of the sender's behavior and the attentional/perceptual process in the receiver may be approached. The data on how a number of receivers segment a dynamic emotion display can consensually define high-information points in the spontaneous flow of behavior that may be "cues" related to sending accuracy as defined above. Also, the data on how different receivers segment a given display will allow the investigation of different patterns of attention and perceptual organization and suggest how these patterns may be related to nonverbal receiving ability. In other words, using the segmentation data of a number of receivers, one can characterize exactly what events in the stimulus display the receivers are responding to, thereby allowing the objective specification of the stimulus properties of the display. The same data will allow the study of differences in the segmentation patterns of different receivers, allowing the objective specification of the perceptual/attentional organization of each. These analyses may then be related to sending accuracy and receiving ability as defined above.

The results of two studies applying the segmentation technique to the videotaped sequences taken during the slide-viewing paradigm have been very promising (Buck, Baron, & Barrette, 1979; Buck, Baron, Goodman, & Shapiro, 1980). Both studies involved in part the segmentation of the CARAT instrument, and there was a high degree of reliability in the number of button presses to the individual CARAT sequences in the two studies (average $r = +.79$, $p < .001$), Given the complexity of the behavior being segmented and the substantial differences in procedure between the two studies, this level of reliability is encouraging.

These studies found strikingly different segmentation patterns for female and male senders that relate to the gender differences in sending accuracy previously reported. For example, Buck et al. (1979) found that female senders were segmented more finely, with a greater degree of consensus among receivers, and with more consensually defined "high-information points" than male senders; also, these high-information points were more likely to involve facial expressions among female senders than male senders. These points in male senders may have been based on gestures or body movements rather than on facial expressions. These results were interpreted as indicating that females show more overall emotion-related expressive behavior, show more emotional behavior that observers agree is "meaningful," and that the latter is more likely to involve facial expressions among females than males. Also, Buck et al. (1980) found that the sex of sender x type of slide interactions was significant in both the segmentation and accuracy data: Males' expressions to sexual slides tended to be more finely segmented and were more accurately decoded than those of females; while the expressions of females to unpleasant slides were much more finely segmented and more accurately decoded than the expressions of males. Finally, both of these studies found strong positive relationships between fineness of segmentation and sending accuracy for female senders (average $r = +.69$, $p < .001$) but not male senders (average $r = +.15$, NS). These data suggest some of the specific kinds of behaviors that underlie the gender difference in sending accuracy in adults found in past studies, and it may be that the investigation of childrens' behavior using the segmentation technique will yield clues about how these behavioral differences develop.

The segmentation of infants' and children's expressions

The Buck et al. (1980) study showed the CARAT-C film of the facial/gestural expressions of preschool children as well as the CARAT film showing adults. In contrast with the data on adults, there was no significant main effect in the fineness with which boys' and girls' expressions were segmented. Also, whereas adult males showed the least expression to the unpleasant slides, the expressions of preschool boys to unpleasant slides were segmented more finely than those of girls. These data seem consistent with the notion that the gender difference in nonverbal sending accuracy is based on sex-role-related learning experiences (Buck, 1979). Also, the children's expressions were segemented more finely than were the adults' expressions: an average of .24 button presses per second for the children compared to .11 presses per second for the adults.

The data on the relationship between the sending accuracy of the children's expressions and the fineness with which these expressions were segmented revealed a pattern similar to that shown by the adults: The sending accuracy of girls' but not boys' expressions was positively related to the fineness of segmentation ($r = +.54, p < .10$ and $r = -.09$, respectively). Perhaps sending accuracy in females is more closely related to processes that are tapped by the segmentation procedure; that is, females' sending accuracy may involve perception-based processing in the receiver, while sending accuracy in males may require cognitive processing that is less closely related to the segmentation pattern (Baron, 1980; Buck et al., 1980).

Figure 6.3 illustrates the results of the segmentation of a 6-month-old infant's behavior during a "peek-a-boo" game. As shown, the points where the infant's caregiver said "peek" are clearly reflected in the infant's behavior which, in turn, is reflected in the segmentation data. It is also interesting that the infant's behavior was segmented quite finely: an average of .18 button presses per second during the 63-second sequence.

Segmentation and receiving ability

Both of the studies of segmentation have investigated the relationships between the receivers' segmentation patterns and receiving ability, or the accuracy with which the receiver identifies the category of slide viewed by the sender. When viewing the expressions of adults on CARAT, both studies revealed that receiving ability was negatively correlated with the number of button presses for female receivers (average $r = -.31, p < .01$) but not male receivers (average $r = -.01$). Thus when viewing adults, accurate female receivers tended to segment less finely than did less accurate female receivers, while male receiving ability was not related significantly to fineness of segmentation. On the other hand, when viewing the expressions of children on CARAT-C, the Buck et al. (1980) study found that accurate male and female receivers tended to segment *more* finely ($r = +.23, p < .05$).

The Buck et al. (1979) study assessed the quality of segmentation by determining (a) the number of times a given receiver pressed the button during the same second that a consensual high-information point occurred (number of "hits"), and (b) the number of times a given receiver pressed the button more than 1 second away from a consensual high-information point (number of "misses"). These measures proved to be significantly related to receiving ability only among female receivers, with hits being positively correlated (average $r = +.47, p < .05$) and misses negatively correlated (average $r = -.59, p < .005$) with receiving ability. The comparable fig-

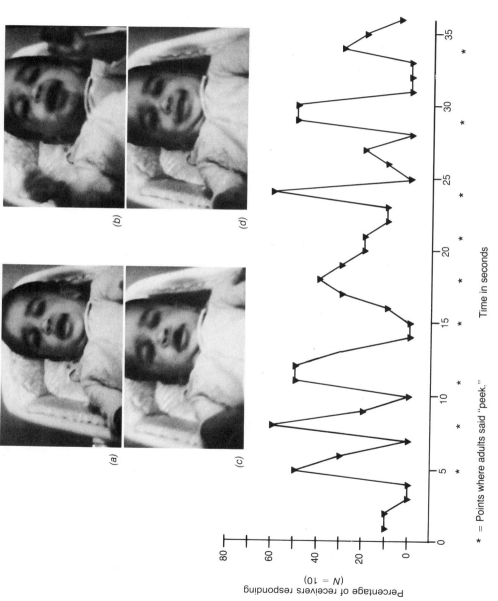

* = Points where adults said "peek."

* = Points where consensually "meaningful" points (b and d) and points where no receiver indicated that meaningful behavior occurred (a and c).

Figure 6.3. Segmentation analysis of the responses of a 6-month-old boy during a "peek-a-boo" game. Photographs were taken at consensually "meaningful" points (b and d) and points where no receiver indicated that meaningful behavior occurred (a and c).

ures among male receivers were +.22 and −.13 (not significant).

These findings suggest that, as with sending accuracy, receiving ability is more closely related to segmentation variables in females than in males. Perhaps receiving ability, too, is related to direct perceptual processing in females and a more mediated cognitive processing in males (Baron, 1980). In any case, the process of nonverbal communication appears to be qualitatively different in females and males, and further developmental research will be crucial to the eventual understanding of this difference.

Features of the segmentation approach to emotion communication

The segmentation approach to emotion communication has features that are different from, but complementary to, other approaches. For example, one of the most sophisticated attempts to specify the facial behaviors associated with different affects is the Facial Affect Scoring Technique (FAST) developed by Ekman, Friesen, and Tomkins (1971). This procedure, which related facial expressions to the primary affects, defined the expressions from a *perspective external to the observer;* that is, the primary affects and expressions associated with them were defined in a manner external to the affective situation per se. The segmentation approach, on the other hand, focuses on the information that is personally relevant to the receiver. In effect, this technique employs the *naive receiver's perspective* in order to define the important elements of the emotion display. Clearly, neither approach is right or wrong; both are useful, and it may be that a combination of the two approaches will prove uniquely powerful.

Summary

This chapter defined emotion as a state associated with activity in neurochemical mechanisms within the central nervous system that are concerned with bodily adaptation and the maintenance of homeostasis. It suggested that both subjective emotion experience and external emotion expression evolved as "readouts" of this central emotion state. We then considered the process of the evolution of emotion communication in some detail and found that emotion experience may have evolved for analogous reasons and via analogous mechanisms.

We then moved to the development of emotion communication, taking into account the interaction between the maturation of the physiological systems underlying emotion and social experience. The importance of social experience in learning how to use the emotion communication system that has evolved in the species was stressed. Also, the interaction between social experience and temperament was noted, as well as the fact that social experience will have different effects on different types of emotional response because of the differential "visibility" of those responses.

We then looked at a series of studies on nonverbal sending accuracy and receiving ability, summarizing the results in terms of the view of emotion and emotion communication presented above. In particular, it was suggested that personality differences in nonverbal sending accuracy may be based in part on temperamental factors, with nonverbal expressiveness being related to general "externalizing" and "internalizing" modes of response even in young children. Gender differences in sending accuracy, on the other hand, may be based largely on sex-role-related learning experiences. A model for the development of nonverbal sending accuracy was suggested based on these observations.

Nonverbal receiving ability was briefly discussed, and we found that present measures of receiving ability do not adequately address all aspects of the phenomenon. In particular, present measures beg the question of whether an individual actually attends to nonverbal cues during normal interaction.

Finally, we discussed the utility of segmentation techniques for analyzing the process of emotion communication—both sending accuracy and receiving ability. It is clear that the study of emotion expression and communication will provide a new perspective for understanding the emotion systems that are so basic to the nature of human beings; the segmentation technique appears to provide an efficient and rigorous approach to this analysis.

Notes

1. The nature of these mechanisms cannot be considered in detail here, but they involve neurochemical systems found in the brainstem and subcortical and limbic structures of the brain (see Buck, 1976a, Chapters 2 and 3). They may include mechanisms traditionally labeled "motivational" as well as "emotional."

2. In G. H. Mead's (1934) terms, this is a "conversation of gesture" that takes place via signs as opposed to symbols. He gives as an example a dogfight, in which each antagonist responds to the signs of attack and flight implicit in the behavior of the other. Mead did not term this "communication," but we are defining communication as occurring whenever the behavior of one individual influences the behavior of another.

3. We suggested above that subjective emotion experience evolved as an internal readout of neurochemical systems underlying emotion, and this would imply that such experience must be "self-explanatory" to some extent. For example, if the neurochemical system underlying anger becomes spontaneously active because of disease, the person may react with felt rage and aggressive behavior regardless of social learning (Mark & Ervin, 1970).

4. The biofeedback paradigm makes normally "invisible" physiological responses visible through the feedback.

5. The term "sending accuracy" is used rather than "sending ability" because the sender does not know that the camera is present and is thus not intentionally sending any facial/gestural messages. The receiver, however, is intentionally attempting to decode the facial/gestural message, hence the term "receiving ability."

6. Field and Walden (in preparation) have recently reported that facially expressive infants show less cardiac responsivity and higher thresholds to auditory stimuli, suggesting that individual differences in facial expressiveness and physiological responding—possibly analogous to externalizing and internalizing response modes—are present from birth.

7

BEAUTY AND THE BEAST: THE ROLE OF PHYSICAL ATTRACTIVENESS IN THE DEVELOPMENT OF PEER RELATIONS AND SOCIAL BEHAVIOR

JUDITH H. LANGLOIS
THE UNIVERSITY OF TEXAS AT AUSTIN

COOKIE WHITE STEPHAN
NEW MEXICO STATE UNIVERSITY

The ability of children to make friends and be liked by others is considered by most parents, teachers, and child development specialists to be a major developmental milestone (see, for example, Spock's *Baby and Child Care,* 1973). Being disliked and not having friends can cause parents or teachers to refer children to mental health professionals (Hartup, 1978). Indeed, social acceptance and liking by others in young children predicts later adult social competence and positive mental health (Roff, 1961, 1963; Roff, Sells, & Golden, 1972; Sullivan, 1953). Despite these known relationships between peer relations and positive social adjustment, little research has been conducted on the development of interpersonal attraction and behavior (Adams, 1977; Lickona, 1974). The purpose of this review is: (1) to demonstrate that physical attractiveness is an important component in the development of children's peer relationships and social behavior;[1] (2) to call attention to research that should be undertaken to understand the influence of physical appearance on children's peer relations and social development; and (3) to present a conceptual framework for the role of physical attractiveness in development of peer preferences, differential socialization and treatment, and the genesis of behavioral differences in children.

The discussion that follows is structured around the three most central components of the developmental model to be presented later. First, it is proposed that differential expectations for the behavior of others are elicited by varying levels of physical attractiveness in adults and in children. Second, these differential expectations lead to differential treatment of attractive and unattractive children by adults and peers. Third, this differential treatment leads to behavioral differences between attractive and unattractive children.

We thank Catherine R. Cooper, Robert G. Cooper, A. Chris Downs, Van Pancake, Douglas B. Sawin, and Walter G. Stephan for their suggestions and critical reading of the manuscript.

Differential expectations and the physical attractiveness stereotype

Although it is commonly said (e.g., Ann Landers) that "inner beauty" is what is really important in life, there are now considerable empirical and anecdotal data indicating the existence of widely held identification rules, or stereotypes, that relate outward appearance to "inner" behaviors and personality characteristics. Many of us, for example, have heard mothers from the southern part of the United States admonish their children not to "act ugly."

The idea of the exterior as a mirror of inner qualities of a person is much older than our contemporary culture. Through fairy tales children have learned for many generations that Cinderella, who is sought by Prince Charming, is very beautiful as well as good and kind. Her stepsisters, however, are unpopular, ugly, selfish, and cruel. The ugly duckling is rejected by his "peers" and can find happiness and friends only when he grows up to become a beautiful swan.

The viewpoint that pestilence, resulting in a scarred or marked appearance, is a punishment for sin and "bad" behavior is prominent in Greek and Hebrew literature (Crawfurd, 1914). In witchcraft, we see another example of how appearance is a reflection of inner beauty. With witches, we immediately associate their ugliness with evil. Scot (as cited in Hueffer, 1973) provides a representative description of witches; "Witches be commonly old, lame, bleare-eied, pale, fowle, and full of wrinkles . . . . They are leane and deformed." A notable witch from the 1700s, variously known as Jinney, Mother Damnable, Mother Redcap, and the Shrew of Kantish Town, has been described as having a "large broad nose, heavy shaggy eyebrows, sunken eyes, and lank and lethern cheeks; her forehead wrinkled, her mouth wide, and her look sullen and unmoved"(Hueffer, 1973).

Fairy tales, plagues and pestilence as punishment for sin and undesirable behaviors, and the evil deeds of ugly witches all point out the long-held association between physical appearance and inner qualities and characteristics. Moreover, recent evidence suggests that even very young children stereotype others on the basis of physical attractiveness. Indeed, physical attractiveness appears to be a significant determinant of social attraction as early as age 3. A major portion of this developmental research has employed an impression formation paradigm in which expectations are elicited concerning two areas of childhood functioning: academic performance and interpersonal behavior.

Academic performance

Clifford and Walster (1973) asked fifth-grade teachers to rate unfamiliar children on the basis of identical report cards, to which a small photograph was attached. The teachers believed attractive children to be more intelligent, more popular with their peers, likely to achieve more education, and to have parents more interested in their education. These data were replicated in a later study (Clifford, 1975), and similar data for elementary school-age children have been reported by Adams (1978), Adams and Cohen (1976), Rich (1975), and Ross and Salvia (1975).

One study suggests that adults even have differential expectations for the academic potential of neonates who differ in physical attractiveness. Corter, Trehub, Bonkydis, Ford, Celhoffer, and Minde (1975) collected attractiveness ratings and developmental prognoses from nurses attending a small sample of premature infants. Consistent with the findings for older children, infant attractiveness and intellectual prognosis were highly related ($r_s = .90$).

Thus, a consistent finding emerges: When the children are not known to the adults, attractive children are expected to be more intelligent, get better grades, and score higher on achievement tests than unattractive children. In a later section, we will discuss whether these differential expectations affect the actual IQ and achievement scores of attractive and unattractive children.

Interpersonal behaviors

Attractiveness also plays a role in adults' expectations for children's interpersonal behaviors. Dion (1972) gave undergraduate women photos of attractive and unattractive children along with a description of a transgression each child had allegedly committed. The women evaluated a transgression more negatively when it was committed by an unattractive than by an attractive child. In addition, a severe transgression was perceived to be a reflection of an enduring, negative personality characteristic when committed by an unattractive child. Thus, unattractive children were generally perceived as more dishonest and unpleasant than attractive children.

Children also hold behavioral expectations for unknown agemates that are based on appearance. Langlois and Stephan (1977) showed 6- and 10-year-old black, white, and Mexican-American children photographs of attractive and unattractive children from each of the three ethnic groups. Attractive children from all three ethnic groups were liked better, were rated as smarter and more prosocial, and were rated as less antisocial than were unattractive children. In fact, physical attractiveness was a more powerful predictor of the children's evaluations than was ethnicity. Similarly, Dion (1973) found that, compared with attractive children, unfamiliar unattractive children were rated by preschoolers as hitting without good reason, scaring the child raters, and likely to hurt the child raters. Attractive children were viewed as children who did not hit, even if someone else hit first, who did not like to fight or shout, and who were friendly to other children. In addition, attractive children were significantly preferred as friends to unattractive children.

Taken together, the results from these studies indicate that physical attractiveness is an important determinant of expected liking and expected behavior for unacquainted child and adult raters. However, caution must be exercised in making inferences from these laboratory-based studies of

expectations based on appearance to interactions in real-world settings. Although it is important to determine how physical attractiveness cues are utilized by children in formulating first impressions of unfamiliar children, it seems premature to infer that the relationship between appearance and behavior among acquainted children is the same as that for unacquainted children. Indeed, such stereotypes may have only transient effects. In the discussion that follows, we examine this issue by considering the impact of familiarity on differential expectations.

Mediating variables

FAMILIARITY. We have suggested the commonsense notion that the importance of physical attractiveness may change subsequent to social interaction and the accumulation of information about personality factors. There are also more formal theoretical considerations that would imply that the beauty-is-good stereotype is not necessarily valid for acquainted individuals. Interaction theorists such as Gottman and Parkhurst (1980), Levinger (1974), and Murstein (1971, 1974) argue that, in examining interpersonal attraction, actual relationships should be studied since influential variables may have differential effects at various stages in the relationship. Duck (1973) has proposed a filtering theory of interpersonal attraction in which there are different stages of attraction. According to this theory, different types of cues are salient at various stages, and certain cues lose their influence as the acquaintance develops. Duck suggests that attractiveness plays an important role in initial interactions and evaluations by presenting cues on which selections can be based in the acquaintance process. Thus, physical attractiveness operates as a filter or "gatekeeper" for social interactions and interpersonal attraction, but may then become less important as more information about the person is acquired.

Only a few studies are available that assess the physical attractiveness stereotype in children who are familiar with one another. Dion and Berscheid (1974) report that acquainted preschoolers exhibited behavioral stereotypes similar to those found in unacquainted children (Dion, 1973). Similarly, Lerner and Lerner (1977) found that fourth- and sixth-grade children viewed attractive classmates more positively than unattractive ones. Low to moderate correlations have also been reported between physical attractiveness and popularity by Cavior and Dokecki (1973), Kleck, Richardson, and Ronald (1974), and Salvia, Sheare, and Algozzine (1975) in samples of acquainted children.

Other data, however, suggest that physical attractiveness does not always have the same influence on behavioral evaluations and liking in acquainted as compared with unacquainted raters. Langlois and Styczynski (1979) found that for both preschool and elementary school children, attractive boys were perceived by their classmates as being more disliked, more antisocial, and more incompetent than unattractive boys and all girls. In another study, the behavioral attributions of acquainted and unacquainted preschoolers were directly compared to assess this question (Styczynski & Langlois, 1977). The unacquainted children did expect attractive agemates to behave prosocially and unattractive children to exhibit negative behaviors. In contrast, the acquainted children did not consistently view their attractive peers more positively. Instead, consistent with the Langlois and Styczynski (1979) data, acquainted children, particularly boys, rated attractive boys as more incompetent, antisocial, and disliked than unattractive boys.

Methodological factors may account for the differences among studies assessing the beauty-is-good stereotype in acquainted children, particularly the type of photographic stimuli and length of acquaintance. Cavior and Dokecki (1973), Dion and Berscheid (1974), and Lerner and Lerner (1977) used photographs that presented body build cues. Since body build also elicits distinct positive and negative preferences and evaluations (e.g., Lerner & Korn, 1972; Staffieri, 1972), the physical attractiveness ratings

in these studies may have been based on, or have been confounded with, preferences for body build. Moreover, while the children in the Langlois and Styczynski studies were rated for attractiveness by both their familiar classmates and by unacquainted, same-age children, children in the Dion and Berscheid, Kleck et al., Lerner and Lerner, and Salvia et al. studies were not rated for physical attractiveness by acquainted peers. Thus, it is not known whether the children evaluated as attractive and unattractive by the unacquainted raters in these studies would have been similarly evaluated by their peers who made the behavioral expectation ratings.

Furthermore, the children in the Dion and Berscheid (1974), Kleck et al. (1974), Lerner and Lerner (1977), and Salvia et al. (1975) studies may not[2] have been well acquainted relative to the children in the Langlois and Styczynski (1979; Styczynski & Langlois, 1977) studies who had been classmates for over 8 months. Indeed, researchers in this area have conceptualized familiarity as a single summary variable representing the amount of information available to the perceiver about the target. Hence, familiarity has been treated as a dichotomous variable (known versus unknown) that represents either no knowledge about the target's personality and behavior or some unspecified amount of knowledge. However, the degree of familiarity should be examined more closely. It is the amount and type of available information about a child that sets the context from which stimulus information is selected and processed by the perceiver. Consequently, the actual *amount* of familiarity is an essential component in determining the extent to which appearance elicits differential expectations and treatment from the perceiver.

COGNITIVE DEVELOPMENT. Although it might appear from the results of previous studies that physical attractiveness exerts a significant effect on social cognitions and peer relations throughout development, research investigations typically have been limited to single developmental periods: nursery school children (e.g., Dion, 1973; Dion & Berscheid, 1974; Langlois & Downs, 1979; Styczynski & Langlois, 1977), elementary school children (e.g., Langlois & Stephan, 1977; Lerner & Lerner, 1977), or adults (e.g., Berscheid, Dion, Walster, & Walster, 1971; Efran, 1974). Nursery school and adult subjects have received rather extensive research attention, whereas elementary school children and adolescents are underrepresented in this work.

The literatures on the development of social cognitions and on the development of peer relationships (e.g., Hartup, 1978; Shantz, 1975) suggest competing predictions regarding the influence of age on the impact of physical attractiveness on behavioral expectations and peer preferences. Peer responses to physical characteristics might be expected to have a greater impact on children in elementary school than on nursery school children, since peer relationships seem to be more significant for the grade school child (Hartup, 1978; Wright, 1967). Social learning theory would predict that as exposure to societal stereotypes regarding attractiveness increases, positive and negative stereotypes associated with physical attractiveness would be strengthened with age. Thus, the peer relations literature and social learning theory suggest that appearance should become more important for peer preferences and perceptions among older children.

In contrast, according to cognitive-developmental theory and the social cognition literature (Shantz, 1975), as children mature and their cognitive abilities increase, the importance of physical attractiveness on peer liking and evaluations should decline. The increased role-taking and decentering skills associated with the transition from preoperational to concrete operational logic (Piaget, 1970; Selman & Byrne, 1974) should allow the older child to discount physical attractiveness as a primary determinant in responding to peers. According to Piaget (1970), young children center or focus their attention on visible, concrete, physical characteristics of objects or persons. In fact, when describing liked and disliked peers, young children do emphasize physical characteristics such as attractiveness (e.g., Austin & Thompson, 1948; Flapan, 1968; Hartup, 1978; Livesley & Bromley, 1973). Other determinants of interpersonal attraction that are known to be influential in adult liking preferences, such as attitude similarity (Bryne, 1971), do not seem to play an important role at earlier stages of the life cycle. Instead, similarity of physical characteristics such as age, sex, and appearance are more important than attitude or behavioral similarity in the expression of social behaviors (Jacklin & Maccoby, 1978; Langlois & Downs, 1979; Langlois, Gottfried, Barnes, & Hendricks, 1978; Langlois, Gottfried, & Seay, 1973) and in friendship selection in children (Hartup, 1978).

The research findings of Livesley and Bromley (1973) provide a compelling example of the importance of appearance on the social cognitions of children (see also Chapter 9 by Feldman & Ruble). Despite the fact that subjects (ages 7 to 15) were given specific instructions *not* to use information about appearance in describing their friends, younger children used appearance as their primary descriptor of friends. Statements about appearance were used by subjects from *all* age groups in their descriptions, although the frequency of statements about appearance did decrease with age. Brierley (1966), Little (1968), Watts (1944), and Yarrow and Campbell (1963) also report that physical appearance is an important component of the perception of peers in children ranging in age from 7 to 18.

It thus seems that, consistent with general cognitive-developmental theory, the frequency of use of appearance variables does decrease with age, but also that the perception of others is still influenced by appearance long after children enter the stage of concrete operations. Indeed, during adolescence, physical attractiveness becomes even more potent as a determinant of social attraction (Cavior & Dokecki, 1973; Duck, 1975; Little, 1968). This increased influence during adolescence is consistent with the nature of adolescent thought as described by Elkind (1967). Elkind proposed that, because of physiological changes that take place during this period, adolescents are primarily concerned with themselves and, in particular, with their appearance. Since adolescents tend not to distinguish between what others are thinking about and their own self-preoccupation, they assume that their peers are as obsessed with their behavior and appearance as they are. Similarly, Havighurst (1972) proposed that a major developmental task of adolescence is accepting one's body and appearance. Adolescents should thus become extremely conscious of their appearance, and appearance should assume a central role in their evaluation of and liking of others.

Simmons, Rosenberg, and Rosenberg (1973) report significant increases in self-consciousness during adolescence, supporting both Havighurst's (1972) and Elkind's (1967) positions. Physical attractiveness has been found to be an important component of self-concept in elementary school age children as well as in adolescents (Kuhlen & Lee, 1943; Lerner & Karabenick, 1974; Montemayor & Eisen, 1977). Moreover, both Duck (1975) and Little (1968) have found that the primary basis of friendships and person perception during adolescence is outward appearance.

We know of only one study that has examined the effects of physical attractiveness on children's social cognitions of peers across more than one developmental period. Langlois and Styczynski (1979) assessed peer liking and behavioral evaluations in 160 children, ages 3, 5, 8, and 10. These children were asked to select classmates who were most likely to exhibit particular prosocial, antisocial, and competence behaviors. Peer attractiveness was equally or more important in the evaluations of the two older compared with the two younger groups of children, although the linear relationships between physical attractiveness and positive peer evaluations predicted by a learning theory model were not obtained.[3] Further-

more, consistent with previous work (Brierley, 1966; Flapan, 1968; Livesley & Bromley, 1973; Peevers & Secord, 1973; Scarlett, Press, & Crockett, 1971) and cognitive-developmental theory (Piaget, 1970), a shift in peer perception typically occurred between the ages of 5 and 8. At or about age 8, children's perceptions changed such that, either attractive children were evaluated more positively than unattractive children when the converse had been the case at earlier ages, or substantial increases or decreases occurred in the evaluation of positive attributes. Thus, both the cognitive-developmental and socialization positions receive some support from the available data, and both perspectives should be considered in accounting for age-related changes in peer perceptions and evaluations.

SEX DIFFERENCES IN THE BEAUTY-IS-GOOD STEREOTYPE. Although there is a large body of data showing that, for both males and females, beauty is thought to be associated with a variety of positive qualities, other data suggest that there are sex differences associated with this stereotype. Langlois and Styczynski (1979) and Styczynski and Langlois (1977) found that, for acquainted children, attractive boys were rated as more incompetent, antisocial, and disliked than unattractive boys. Other data on behavioral expectations for attractive males are consistent with these findings. Two studies of teachers' expectations for unacquainted children—Kehle, Bramble, and Mason (1974) and Kehle, Ware, and Guidubaldi (1976)—found that attractive boys were rated as more uncontrolled, impulsive, and unpredictable, relative to unattractive boys. However, the data for girls were consistent with the beauty-is-good stereotype.

One study has shown sex differences in behaviors exhibited by attractive and unattractive boys and girls that are consistent with the above findings for behavioral expectations. In a situation involving peer pressure, Dion and Stein (1978) found that attractive fifth- and sixth-grade girls were more successful than unattractive girls of the same age in influencing opposite-sex peers. Yet, unattractive boys were more effective than attractive boys at same-sex persuasion.

Finally, one study has found sex differences in behaviors directed toward attractive and unattractive boys and girls. Dion (1974) has demonstrated that when adult females monitor a child's performance on a picture-matching task and then administer penalities to the child for incorrect responses, they behave more leniently toward attractive boys than toward attractive girls or unattractive children of both sexes. This laboratory-based finding closely parallels findings from correlational studies of teachers' behavior toward their students.

The above data on sex differences in behavioral expectations for attractive and unattractive children and the data on adults' behavior directed toward such children suggest that physical attractiveness provides social advantages in peer relationships for girls but that, for boys, familiarity and beauty may bread contempt. One additional finding may be relevant here: Relative to unattractive children, attractive children have been shown to be less active and to prefer feminine sex-stereotyped toys (Langlois & Downs, 1979). It may be that the "prettier" and less active boys are perceived negatively and as undesirable by their peers who expect boys to prefer the toys and active games more characteristic of young boys.

On the other hand, it may be that physical attractiveness and passivity are seen as positive attributes by female adults. If so, there is no inconsistency between the negative peer ratings of attractive boys and their positive treatment by female adults. We need more physical attractiveness data employing both male and female subjects to examine potential sex differences in behavioral expectations for children, behaviors directed toward these children, and, finally, the children's actual behaviors.

SIMILARITY OF LEVEL OF ATTRACTIVENESS. Research with children has made little attempt to examine the influence of the subject's physical attractiveness level on his or her evaluations of target children. The adult literature, however, suggests that the subject's level of attractiveness may well influence both behavioral expectations and liking of others. Two effects due to the subject's physical attractiveness have been distinguished; the first is matching on the basis of similarity (e.g., Berscheid et al., 1971; Huston, 1973; Stroebe, Insko, Thompson, & Layton, 1971). Much of the available evidence suggests that heterosexual attraction is governed, in part, by similarity in level of physical attractiveness. For example, both Murstein (1972) and Silverman (1971) found highly similar levels of attractiveness among dating partners. Cash and Derlega (1978) have also reported similar findings for adult same-sex friendships.

Two studies suggest the existence of a second effect: jealousy. Dermer and Thiel (1975) state " . . . physically unattractive women may, for a number of reasons, most likely carry well-honed hatchets for attractive female targets" (p. 1169). These authors found that, while both average and attractive women rated attractive female targets as having more socially desirable personalities than unattractive targets, unattractive women did not. Indicating that hatchets are not confined to the female sex, Tennis and Dabbs (1975) reported that less attractive males assigned lower attractiveness ratings to targets than did more attractive males.

The scant evidence that is available suggests that similarity of the subject's and target's level of physical attractiveness is an influential determinant of interpersonal behaviors for very young children. Langlois and Downs (1979) examined behaviors displayed by and toward attractive and unattractive same-sex preschoolers and found that the level of attractiveness of both children in the dyad was important in the expression of behavior. Both attractive and unattractive children exhibited higher levels of positive social behavior when paired with peers who were similar in levels of attractiveness than when paired with peers dissimilar in level of attractiveness.

The adult data (e.g., Berscheid et al.,

1971; Cash & Derlega, 1978; Dermer & Thiel, 1975; Tennis & Dabbs, 1975) and the Langlois and Downs (1979) preschool data indicate that subjects' level of physical attractiveness may influence their physical attractiveness ratings and behavioral expectations of target persons, as well as their behaviors toward attractive and unattractive targets. Examining the rater's level of physical attractiveness and the target's physical attractiveness seems worthy of further examination, since it has important implications for interactions occurring in a real-world setting. For example, a very beautiful mother may hold different attitudes about the importance of attractiveness than a less attractive mother. Consequently, the unattractive child of a beautiful mother may be treated differently than an equally unattractive child of an unattractive mother. Similarly, the highly attractive younger sibling of a less attractive first-born may receive treatment from the sibling consistent with the "jealousy" hypothesis proposed by Dermer and Thiel (1975), whereas a less attractive younger sibling may not. A developmental approach to this issue seems particularly useful, since there are developmental differences in role-taking abilities and thus children's comprehension of similarity (Shantz, 1975). We might expect, then, that similarity of attractiveness may have a differential impact on evaluations of others at different stages of development.

Summary

The existence of the physical attractiveness stereotype is well documented for both adults and for children as young as age 3 who evaluate unfamiliar children. Physical attractiveness is clearly important in the initial stages of peer interaction and in the formation of liking and behavioral expectations. Although both interaction theory and common sense suggest that appearance declines in importance in adults and children who are well acquainted, the data generally do not support this conclusion. In several studies, familiar and unfamiliar attractive girls were evaluated more positively than unattractive girls. Such consistent data do not exist for boys. The data for boys, however, still indicate that appearance is an important component of peer evaluation and liking. What is at issue is the nature of the influence of physical attractiveness for boys. Some studies suggest that adults and peers evaluate familiar attractive boys most positively (e.g., Dion & Berscheid, 1974), while others suggest that such attractive boys are viewed most negatively by their peers (e.g., Styczynski & Langlois, 1977).

Differential treatment and socialization

Compared with the rather extensive literature on differential expectations associated with physical attractiveness, there are few data relevant to the issue of differential treatment of attractive and unattractive children. To put in perspective the limited data on differential treatment of children, representative research examining differential treatment of adults by other adults will be discussed briefly. We will also suggest two additional mediating variables—stability and level of attractiveness—that may serve to limit the impact of physical attractiveness on differential treatment.

Several studies have shown that adults display differential behaviors toward attractive and unattractive adults and children. For example, attractive individuals benefit from more positive outcomes in simulated jury cases. Efran (1974) found that attractive defendants were given milder punishments than unattractive defendants and that subjects were less certain of the guilt of attractive than of unattractive defendants. Stephan and Tully (1977) report that attractive plaintiffs (both children and adults) were more often awarded judgments in personal injury cases and were awarded more money than were unattractive plaintiffs.

Sroufe, Chaikin, Cook, and Freeman (1977) found that adult subjects were more likely to return lost money to an attractive than to an unattractive confederate. Similarly, Benson, Karabenick, and Lerner

(1976) demonstrated that adults were more likely to help an attractive than an unattractive person by mailing a "lost" graduate school application with a photograph attached to it. Moss and Page (1972) report that helping behavior increased after interaction with an attractive female confederate, particularly if the interaction was positive.

Several studies suggest that adults also display differential behaviors toward attractive and unattractive children. Berkowitz and Frodi (1979) demonstrated that adult females punished unattractive children more severely than attractive children in a role-playing situation in which the women were to behave as if they were the child's parent. These results are consistent with those of Dion (1974). Lerner and Lerner (1977) report low but significant correlations between attractiveness and grades given by teachers to elementary school children. Adams and Cohen (1974) found that teachers interacted more with attractive than unattractive seventh-graders, although a similar effect was not found for younger children. Barocas and Black (1974) report that attractive third-graders were more frequently referred by their teachers for psychological, speech, reading, and learning disability assessments than were unattractive third-graders. Since these referrals were for remedial help rather than for control of behavior problems, Barocas and Black infer that these teachers were more willing to help attractive than unattractive children.

Other research has indicated that even young infants are treated differently as a function of their level of attractiveness. Hildebrandt and Fitzgerald (1978) presented photographs of infants to adults and found that attractive infants were looked at significantly longer than infants ranked as less attractive—a finding that replicates one obtained by Dion (1977), who used preschool-age children as subjects. Since looking behavior is related to the maintenance of parent-infant interaction (Robson, 1967), Hildebrandt and Fitzgerald propose that infant attractiveness plays an important role in the regulation of parent-infant social interactions. Data supporting this notion come from several studies of actual parent-infant interaction.

Parke and Sawin (1975) informally assessed infant attractiveness and noted that mothers maintained more eye contact and more ventral holding contact and also more frequently kissed attractive infants compared with the mothers of less attractive infants. Differential behavior as a function of infant attractiveness was also observed in fathers; they stimulated attactive infants more than less attractive infants by touching, kissing, and moving them. In a second study (Parke, Hymel, Power & Tinsley, 1980), the effects on paternal attitudes and behaviors of an intervention consisting of a film presentation were examined immediately following the birth of the infant and again at three weeks and at three months. Photographs and attractiveness ratings of a subset of the sample of infants were collected before the infant left the hospital. Parke et al. report that the film intervention was more successful in increasing fathers' involvement with their infants when the infants were rated as attractive rather than unattractive.

Fathers' expected degree of responsibility for infant caregiving was also assessed during the postpartum period by Parke et al. It was found that infant attractiveness and expectations for responsibility were significantly related: The greater the infants' attractiveness, the higher were fathers' expectations for involvement. Three months later, the attractiveness ratings of the neonates were significantly positively correlated with fathers' actual participation and caregiving behaviors with their infants.

In a recent study, Adams and Crane (1980) have shown that both mothers and fathers expect their own preschool-age children to prefer attractive over unattractive target stimuli and to attribute positive personality characteristics to more attractive individuals. Although these data do not provide a direct assessment of parental socialization, they demonstrate the existence of differential expectations of parents for the behavior of their own children. Such parental expectations are necessary prerequisites to the differential treatment and socialization of children. Thus, Adams' data provide a link between the differential expectation literature and Parke's data on parental treatment.

While the studies reviewed suggest that attractive and unattractive infants and children are treated differently by parents (e.g., Parke & Sawin, 1975), teachers (e.g., Adams & Cohen, 1974), and adults who are not directly acquainted with them (e.g., Dion, 1972, 1974: Hildebrandt & Fitzgerald, 1978), additional data on the role of physical attractiveness in the socialization process are needed. Longitudinal data would be particularly useful, since the child's level of physical attractiveness and parental attitudes and expectations may change over the course of development. Information on the stability of attractiveness is needed, because substantial changes in appearance would also affect the type of feedback and treatment received, rendering attractiveness an inconsistent influence on social development (Berscheid & Walster, 1974).

Unfortunately, there are few data on the stability of attractiveness. Adams (1977) collected school photographs of children when they were in elementary school, when they were adolescents (16 to 20 years), young adults (30 to 35), and older adults (45 to 50). The photographs were rated for attractiveness by college students, and the ratings were compared across the various life stages. Moderate to high correlation coefficients between attractiveness ratings were obtained from adolescence to young adulthood ($r = .87$ for women, $r = .63$ for men) and from adolescence to middle-age ($r = .79$ for women, $r = .59$ for men). Similarly, stability in facial attractiveness was found for children, with adjacent years showing stronger relationships than intervals of two or more years. In our own work, 35 infants were photographed when they were 3 and 6 months of age. The correlation of attractiveness ratings between 3 and 6 months was $r = .68$. Thus, facial attractiveness does evidence considerable stability across a range of

developmental periods. For most individuals, then, appearance can exert a consistent unitary effect on development. A longitudinal study of those individuals who do change in level of attractiveness would provide researchers with a natural experiment in which the antecedent and consequent effects of changes in attractiveness could be examined.

Another factor to consider in evaluating the role of attractiveness in the differential treatment of, as well as expectations for, children is level of attractiveness. Most children are neither beauty nor the beast. Nevertheless, previous research has typically employed only two categories of physical attractiveness, high and low. The assumption is made that the relationship between physical attractiveness and interpersonal behaviors, expectations, and liking is a positive linear function. The supposition of a linear relationship, however, is not supported by the few studies that have employed more than two levels of attractiveness. Moreover, the available studies have examined only differential expectations, and then only with adults. Hence, even though level of attractiveness seems particularly relevant to differential treatment, we must turn to the literature on behavioral expectations for an assessment of the role this factor may play in influencing behavior.

Dermer and Thiel (1975) report significant differences between expectations made about high- and low-attractive female targets but no significant differences between medium- and high-attractive targets. In contrast, Dion, Berscheid, and Walster (1972) found that medium- and low-attractive targets did not recieve significantly different expectations but that both such targets received significantly lower ratings than did high-attractive targets. Thus it is not clear whether a moderate level of attractiveness is sufficient to elicit the positive stereotypic expectations associated with high levels of attractiveness or if a moderate level of attractiveness is equivalent to unattractiveness.

Dermer and Thiel (1975) also found that high levels of physical attractiveness were associated with some negative interpersonal judgments. While viewed more positively overall than low-attractive targets, high-attractive female targets were perceived as being more vain, egotistical, likely to have marital difficulties (requesting a divorce, having an extramarital affair), and as more likely to be materialistic and snobbish. Thus, for a small constellation of traits, the correlation between attractiveness and expected behaviors may actually be negative.

Cavior and Dokecki (1973) inferred, from ratings made by and about fifth- and eleventh-graders, that the role played by physical attractiveness in interpersonal attraction and in the development of social behaviors differs depending on level of physical attractiveness. The behavior and personality characteristics of the person average in attractiveness may mitigate or even override the impact of physical attractiveness on liking and person perception. However, for persons who are at either of the extremes of the attractiveness continuum, expectations, behavior, and liking may be determined primarily by physical attractiveness.

Summary

Modest empirical support exists for differential treatment as a function of appearance. The support is modest only in its quantity, not in its strength or consistency. Adults behave more positively toward attractive adults, children, and infants than toward their unattractive counterparts. The bulk of such research consists of laboratory studies involving unfamiliar individuals, but the findings from these studies are highly consistent with those from less numerous studies of familiar persons in natural contexts. Teachers and even parents do appear to behave differently toward their attractive and unattractive students and infants.

The impact of such differential treatment seems likely to be mediated by the factors already discussed for expectations of behavior (i.e., age and cognitive development, sex, similarity of level of attractiveness, and familiarity). In addition, the stability and level of physical attractiveness may be important interacting or limiting factors on the influence of appearance on differential treatment. That most children are neither extremely attractive nor unattractive further underscores the need to examine medium levels of attractiveness in the expression of differential treatment.

Behavioral differences as a function of appearance

There is ample evidence documenting the existence of differential expectations for the behavior of others based on their appearance. Moreover, a body of data shows that attractive and unattractive children are treated differently by socialization agents. We will now ask whether attractive and unattractive individuals actually behave differently. Since little behavioral data are available for attractive and unattractive children, one illustrative experimental study employing adults as subjects will be examined.

Kurtzberg, Safar, and Cavior (1968) tested the hypothesis that social deviance and appearance are related by studying the effects of cosmetic surgery on subsequent behavior. Inmates with facial or body disfigurements from the New York City jail system were assigned to one of four major groups: experimental groups receiving either cosmetic surgery only or cosmetic surgery plus rehabilitative social services, groups receiving no surgery but other rehabilitative services, or groups receiving no treatment. Kurtzberg et al. collected data one year following the inmates' release from prison to assess recidivism, job success, psychological adjustment, and social relations. With the exception of inmates who had been heroin addicts, the authors found that individuals who had undergone cosmetic surgery had significantly lower recidivism rates and better psychological and social adjustment than the other groups. The group receiving social services plus surgery did not have more positive outcomes than the group receiving surgery only. Surgery was more effective for individuals with facial disfigurements than for those with bodily disfigurements. Lansdown and Polak (1975) found results consistent with these for children with facial disfigurements. Similarly, Cavior and Howard (1973) report that facial photos of delinquents were rated as significantly less attractive than photos of matched, nondelinquent high school students. These three studies suggest that there is indeed a relationship between appearance and actual behavior.

Two studies have examined the association between children's performance on standardized achievement and intelligence tests and their attractiveness. Clifford (1975) found no significant relationship between attractiveness and measures of achievement or IQ in second-, fourth-, or sixth-graders. Likewise, Styczynski (1976) found no relationship between attractiveness and IQ in fourth-graders; however, there was a significant relationship between attractiveness and achievement test scores. Using the second-grade achievement test scores of these fourth-graders, Styczynski also found a trend in the achievement test scores of attractive and unattractive children that became more divergent with age. The scores of attractive children tended to increase with age while the scores of unattractive children decreased.

There are two observational studies of the behaviors of attractive and unattractive preschool children. Trnavsky and Bakeman (1976) assessed behavioral differences by observing preschoolers during free play. Types of play such as solitary, onlooker, and interactive play (e.g., Parten, 1932) were recorded. The play behaviors were further categorized as negative if such behaviors as hitting or verbal disagreements were observed. Full-length photos were taken of all the children and were rated for attractiveness by unacquainted adult judges. The authors found no differences between attractive and unattractive children in the number of social contacts or in the number of negative behaviors. However, one difference emerged: attractive children spent less time engaged in solitary play than average and unattractive children.

In a naturalistic play setting, Langlois and Downs (1979) found that acquainted attractive and unattractive preschoolers exhibited several behavioral differences. Three- and 5-year-old boys and girls were formed into same-age and same-sex, attractive, unattractive, and mixed attractiveness (one attractive, one unattractive) dyads. An inference-free categorical observational system was employed by observers naive to the purposes of the study. Positive social behaviors, aggressive behaviors, activity, and object-directed behaviors, including play with sex-stereotyped toys, were recorded. Unattractive children were found to be more active and to prefer masculine toys; attractive children were found to be less active and to play more often with feminine toys. Furthermore, a developmental trend was observed for aggressive behaviors: No differences were found for 3-year-olds, but 5-year-old unattractive children hit peers more than 5-year-old-attractive children.

Methodological differences seem to account for the discrepancy between the Langlois and Downs (1979) and Trnavsky and Bakeman (1976) findings. Perhaps most importantly, the behaviors coded in the studies were dissimilar; Trnavsky and Bakeman used molar play categories while Langlois and Downs employed a molecular, inference-free category system. Recording specific behaviors appears to be a more sensitive technique, allowing for the detection of behavioral differences that may go unnoticed when only broad behavioral categories are coded.

Summary

Considered together, the studies of actual behavioral differences between attractive and unattractive children suggest that some behavioral differences do exist. Attractive children scored higher on standardized achievement tests, although not on intelligence tests. When paired with same-sex peers, attractive children were less assertive, aggressive, and active than their unattractive peers. Moreover, as noted in the behavioral expectation literature, attractiveness seemed to exert a consistent, positive effect on the behavior of girls but not on that of boys.

The genesis of differential behaviors as a function of appearance: A developmental model

Our literature review suggests that appearance is an influential factor in three developmental processes. First, for both children and adults, differential expectations for the behavior of others are elicited by varying levels of attractiveness. Second, attractive and unattractive children receive differential treatment by adults as well as other children. And third, positive behaviors and characteristics are more frequently exhibited by attractive children and adults than by unattractive individuals. The ontogenetic model presented here suggests a multidirectional causal chain in the development of such differential behaviors and specifies the links between appearance and differential expectations, treatment, and behavior. The proposed conceptual framework takes a view of development similar to that of an organismic (e.g., Bell & Harper, 1977; Lerner, 1976) or transactional (e.g., Sameroff, 1975) model of development. Figure 7. 1 shows a schematic representation of the genesis of behavioral differences as a function of appearance.[4]

The model specifies that organismic characteristics of the child, such as appearance, influence development; appearance can determine, in part, the reactions of others to the child which, in turn, affect the child's behaviors. Thus, a fundamental assumption underlying this approach is that development must be viewed as a function of reciprocal interchanges and multidirectional causality in which both children and their interactants are recognized as agents affecting each other (Sameroff, 1975).

The model assumes that attractiveness serves as a sign stimulus that releases differential expectations for the behavior of infants and children. The releasing mechanism is thought to operate in a similar manner to releasers in nonhuman species. Ethologists

have demonstrated that physical characteristics of infants of many nonhuman species can elicit and then maintain maternal behavior (e.g., Rosenblatt, 1970). Such maternal behavior, in turn, alters the behavior of the infant. Thus, in humans, it is proposed that the appearance of the infant releases differential expectations in the parent. Such an hypothesis has received preliminary support by the work of Corter et al. (1975), Hildebrant and Fitzgerald (1978), Parke et al. (1980), and Parke and Sawin (1975).

The released differential expectations are derived from a process involving two types of information: immediate stimulus information and stored information. The immediate stimulus information (Box A) includes factors such as the level of attractiveness perceived in the target, the degree of familiarity with the target, and the specific social situation in which the interaction occurs. Stored information (Box B) includes the physical attractiveness stereotype extant in the society and memory of previous interactions with attractive and unattractive persons. Behaviors associated with an attractive or unattractive appearance are acquired through processes such as observational learning (Mischel, 1966b). Such an association is communicated to even very young children through television, movies, and children's books.

The input selector (Box C) is the mechanism by which information about the target that is used to form expectancies is screened or selected from the immediately available stimulus information and the stored information (e.g., Treisman, 1969; Warr & Knapper, 1968). Not all immediate stimulus information and stored information is processed; information is selectively perceived, remembered and, hence, processed. Information about attractiveness is very likely to be selected, however, due to the high salience of attractiveness, the strength of the stereotype, and the tendency of young children to focus on overt physical stimuli.

Characteristics of the perceiver (Box D) interact with the information filtered by the input-selector mechanism. Important per-

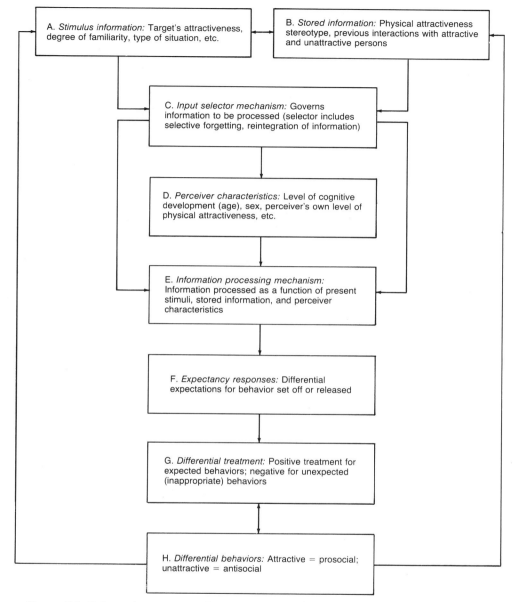

Figure 7.1. Schematic representation of mechanisms leading to behavioral differences.

ceiver characteristics include factors such as level of cognitive development, level of attractiveness, and the sex of the perceiver. Sameroff (1975) provides an example of how one such perceiver characteristic—cognitive development—can influence expectancy re-

sponses. Sameroff maintains that mothers may cognize their infants at a variety of levels. In one mode of thinking described by Sameroff, mothers differentiate characteristics of the child into domains of attributes related to the child's appearance, personality, and intelligence. This differentiation contributes to a static view of the child's characteristics. "The child is seen as maintaining the same position on these dimensions throughout life and is given a value according to prevalent social norms. The ugly, ignorant, and obnoxious child is seen as remaining so for the rest of its years. Conversely, the beautiful, intelligent, personable child is viewed as remaining equally wonderful throughout life" (Sameroff, 1975, p.70)

In the next step (Box E) in which a specific expectancy is formulated, information is processed (e.g., Treisman, 1969; Warr & Knapper, 1968) as a function of the filtered, stored, and immediate stimulus information and of the perceiver's own characteristics. These filtered and selected perceptions of the target and the characteristics of the perceiver interact to determine a particular expectancy (Box F). The expectancy is thus a function of the interaction of target and perceiver characteristics as perceived and selected by the individual adult or child. We assume that much of the cognitive activity involved in the input selector and the processing of information is not available to direct introspection. Instead, the processing is largely automatic (Neisser, 1967) and judgements are made primarily on the basis of a priori, implicit, causal theories (Nisbett & Wilson, 1977) or unconscious, primitive beliefs (Bem, 1970).

Once physical appearance has released differential expectations, these expectations lead to differential treatment (Box G). Adults and peers will behave in a manner largely consistent with their expectations for attractive and unattractive children (e.g., Adams & Crane, 1980). Attractive children should therefore receive positive reinforcement for exhibiting prosocial behaviors. However, the same behavior in unattractive children may be ignored (extinguished) or even punished. Such an hypothesis receives empirical support from the work of Adams and Cohen (1974), Barocas and Black (1974), Dion (1972), Hildebrant and Fitzgerald (1978), Langlois and Downs (1979),

Parke et al. (1980), and Parke and Sawin (1975), all of whom found that attractive and unattractive infants and children receive differential treatment from adults or peers.

Because of this differential treatment (Box H), it is also proposed that children learn to emit those behaviors that are consistent with the behaviors expected of them. When these expected behaviors are exhibited, their presence will, in turn, lead to further reinforcement of "correct" (i.e., expected) behavior (thus the arrow from Box H to Box G).

Finally, behaviors emitted by attractive and unattractive children will influence both stimulus information (Box A) and stored information (Box B). For example, the social learning history of an individual will mediate reactions toward attractive and unattractive persons, since from previous interactions, children learn not only the behavior expected of them, but also the behavior to expect from others. A self-fulfilling process is begun whereby attractive children, who are more successsful in social interactions with others, will elicit more and more positive reactions from others. Therefore, more positive reactions and behaviors will be elicited from these attractive children.

Sameroff (1975) describes this self-fulfilling process in the labeling behavior of parents: "The mother who comes to label her infant as 'difficult' may come to treat the child as difficult irrespective of his actual behavior. The transaction then moves back toward the child. As the child advances into cognitive stages where he can recognize the value the world places on himself, he will come to accept 'difficulty' as one of the central elements in his self-image; thereby, indeed becoming the 'difficult' child for all time" (p. 73).

Adams (1977) has also discussed a similar model, arguing that there is an influential interdependence between outer appearance and inner behavioral processes. Consistent with the present model, Adams believes that physical attractiveness serves as a releasing stimulus for a variety of social actions and evaluations that are similar in many social situations. As a consequence of receiving relatively consistent reactions from others, important developmental outcomes result. Thus attractive and unattractive individuals are thought to internalize differing social-images, self-expectations, and interpersonal behaviors.

Similarly, Snyder and Swann (1978) propose a process of behavioral confirmation that is consistent with the perspective presented here. According to Snyder and Swann, a perceiver's belief about a target person can lead the perceiver to channel subsequent interaction with the target in ways that cause the target's behavior to confirm these beliefs. Furthermore, if the behaviors exhibited by the target are in any way close to the target's self-image, such behaviors may become internalized. Thus, what began in the mind of the perceiver becomes a reality in both the behavior and the mind of the target. Snyder and Swann (1978) documented such a process of behavioral confirmation in successive interactions between one target and two perceivers. Targets who first interacted with perceivers who anticipated them to behave hostilely displayed greater hostility than targets whose partners expected nonhostile behavior. When targets then interacted with a second perceiver who had no information about the behavior or personality of the target, the targets behaved in a similar, aggressive manner toward the naive perceivers. The correlation between the hostile behavior exhibited in the two interaction situations was .90 for targets who also believed that their new behavior was representative of their disposition.

Although the developmental nature of the proposed links among differential expectations, treatment, and behavior as a function of appearance has not yet received direct empirical validation, Snyder, Tanke, and Berscheid (1977) have demonstrated contemporaneous links among these components of the model. In their study, male and female adults held a telephone conversation in which the males were led to believe that the females were physically attractive or unattractive. In reality, females were as-

signed randomly to the attractive and unattractive conditions. Tape recordings of each participant's conversations were analyzed by naive judges for evidence of behavioral confirmation of the expectancies elicited in the males. Snyder et al. found that the men who had interacted with women they believed to by physically attractive were rated by the judges as more sociable, interesting, outgoing, humorous, and socially adept then their counterparts who thought they were interacting with unattractive women. Moreover, the "attractive" females behaved in a friendly, likeable, and sociable manner compared with those whom the males thought to be unattractive. Such differential interactions seem likely to foster the perseverance of the physical attractiveness stereotype, since they place limits on opportunities to learn more about behavioral similarities between attractive and unattractive persons.

Data for children (Langlois & Downs, 1979) are also suggestive of the process of development proposed here. As mentioned earlier, an age trend was found for aggressive behaviors; no differences were observed in attractive and unattractive 3-year-olds, but 5-year-old unattractive children hit peers more often than their attractive counterparts. This finding suggests that differential behavioral expectations for attractive and unattractive children and a self-fulfilling prophecy work together: Unattractive children may be labeled as such and learn the stereotypes and behaviors associated with unattractiveness. Consequently, they may then exhibit aggressive behaviors consistent with this label and actually behave in accordance with others' expectations of them.

Summary

The literature thus far reveals considerable support for some parts of the proposed model. There are abundant data to indicate the existence of differential expectations as a function of appearance. More modest empirical support exists to show that attractive and unattractive children are treated differently and that they may actually behave différently. Other data point out that the degree of familiarity with the target, the level of attractiveness of both the target and the perceiver, and perceiver characteristics such as level of cognitive development are important mediating variables in the expression of differential expectations and treatment.

Based on our review, several directions for future research seem clear. First, the socialization practices of parents, teachers, and peers should be examined to determine the nature and consistency of differential treatment as a function of attractiveness. Parent-child interactions would be particularly fruitful to explore. Certainly in other areas, such as the development of self-esteem, the importance of interaction with positive treatment by the parent is well documented (e.g., Rosenberg, 1967). This research would necessitate assessing the stability of physical attractiveness, since significant changes in appearance imply that the type of treatment received would also change. Thus, longitudinal investigations would provide data linking differential teatment with the development of differential behaviors and would be especially valuable.

Additional data are also warranted to further explicate the impact of the peer group on the development of behavioral

differences as a function of attractiveness. Longitudinal research in which children are observed from the onset of the formation of the group when the children are unacquainted, through the course of the acquaintanceship process, would be particularly enlightening. The emergence of differential patterns of peer interaction and behavior could thus be examined. Furthermore, by including assessments of the behavioral expectations of children, data regarding the relationships between social cognition and social behavior could be obtained.

The social implications of the differential treatment of children as a function of attractiveness and the behavioral consequences of such treatment are great. If the stereotype of the attractive or unattractive person is powerful enough to influence and modify behaviors through the mechanisms we have discussed, then we are all prey to a nonconscious form of discrimination that has enormous consequences for the physically unattractive. The fact that many of the targets of such differential treatment are children, who do not have the cognitive and intellectual capacites to compensate and overcome the negative impact set into motion by the stereotype, makes the issue even more crucial.

Notes

1. In this review, we will deal primarily with research relevant to the effect of physical attractiveness on children. For a review of adult effects, see Berscheid and Walster (1974).

2. The length of acquaintance is typically not reported.

3. Recall also that the antisocial and dislike scores for attractive boys were in the reverse direction from the beauty-is-good stereotype.

4. The schematic representation includes only the variables and their direction of influence that we view as most central to the developmental process. Thus, we do not note all possible directional influences. For example, differential expectations will have an effect on information processing. Such an effect is shown here only indirectly by the arrows from Box E through Box H, to Boxes A and B, and ultimately back to Box E.

8

FROM LAYCHILD TO "LAYMAN": DEVELOPMENTAL CAUSAL ATTRIBUTION

SAUL M. KASSIN
PURDUE UNIVERSITY

> The child's basic orientation towards causal explanation
> intrudes throughout the length and breadth of his cogni-
> tive life.
>
> J. H. Flavell
> *The Developmental Psychology of Jean Piaget*

In a world where many physical, natural, and behavioral events are multidetermined, we are constantly faced with the attributional dilemma inherent in the question "Why?" Our incessant quest for causal explanations, once referred to as a "causal drive" (Oppenheimer, 1922), is so pervasive that it often goes unnoticed. People implicitly and spontaneously make attributions for all sorts of phenomena, ranging from achievements and failures in their own lives to more remote and far-reaching events in the arena of international politics. More importantly, people's explanations often mediate their own everyday behavior. From a *developmental* perspective, empirical interest in how children explain various phenomena can be traced to Piaget's early landmark work on causality (1928, 1930), which was subsequently (Inhelder & Piaget, 1958) rooted in his theory of cognitive development. From the standpoint of *social* psychology, Heider's *The Psychology of Interpersonal Relations*

(1958) has stimulated a remarkable growth in the science of lay epistemology and, particularly, in the study of how the "man in the street" satisfies his or her causal drive in the realm of person perception. Taken together, it comes as little surprise that an increasing amount of attention is currently being directed toward the intersection of developmental and social aspects of causal inference.

This chapter will be devoted to describing the attributional processes of and strategies invoked by the "child in the street." In essence, it will explore whether children of different ages analyze cause-effect relations systematically and, if so, how the principles they use differ, quantitatively or qualitatively, from those employed by adult observers. In so doing, it is necessary to narrow the scope of the chapter, first, by concentrating solely on the determinants rather than the consequences of causal inferences. Indeed, some of the behavioral implications of attribution are reported elsewhere in this book (see Chapter 1 by Lepper & Gilovich, and Chapter 3 by Frieze). A second distinction is that between attributional structure and content. Most Piagetian research on causality tests the content of children's beliefs. Subjects are asked questions about natural events such as "What makes the wind blow?" or mechanical events such as "What makes a clock tick?" Their responses thus often reflect experience and familiarity with the target phenomenon (see Berzonsky, 1971). In contrast, attribution theory emphasizes the stimulus parameters that give rise to the perception or inference of a causal relationship between *any* two events. Within this latter framework, this chapter will focus on the logical structure of children's attributions and on the kinds of information they employ.

The developmental attribution experiment

Causal attribution in an experimental setting can be viewed as a three-stage process. First, the attributor must extract causally relevant information from the environment or stimulus display. Factors affecting attention, selection, encoding, and retrieval thus become important ingredients of this rudimentary phase. Second, the subject who has processed the information contained in an event must then draw the appropriate inferences. At this stage, the perceiver's naive theories and his or her level of causal sophistication will influence the attributions he or she makes. Finally, the subject must somehow express an attribution in response to the experimenter's specific inquiry. This latter stage is perhaps what most distinguishes attribution in the laboratory from attribution in the real world; that is, subjects are forced to verbalize and sometimes justify the outcome of an analysis that might otherwise remain implicit.

This three-stage conceptualization is introduced here because it will prove useful for outlining the bases on which developmental differences in attribution might appear. When a psychologist observes age-related differences in the kinds of information children employ, he or she hopes that these differences reflect genuine changes in children's modes of attributional logic (Stage 2). Unfortunately, one must exercise extreme caution when drawing such a conclusion because developmental differences could stem from two sources that are unrelated to the ways in which a perceiver thinks about cause and effect. First, age-related differences might simply reflect the differences in children's capacity to process an experimenter's stimulus presentation (Stage 1). The danger here is that young children might appear less competent than they really are, solely because they were unable to comprehend or recall the causally relevant information, and that when these problems are solved, more adultlike inferences would follow (for an excellent discussion about how preschoolers' cognitive capacities have been underestimated, see Gelman, 1978). Second, a developmental difference could follow directly from young children's primitive linguistic skills and their relative inability to verbalize their attributions. As such, alternative (i.e., nonverbal) response modes need to be considered, and the controversy over what constitutes an acceptable response criterion will be discussed.

Stimulus (input) factors

Michael Ross has commented that "there are hazards facing the social psychologist who has only conducted experiments with adults and suddenly decides to perform research on children. Children are simply not college sophomores and cannot be treated as such" (1976, pp.123–124). Needless to say, children are not adultlike in their information-processing capacities. With this limitation in mind, and the fact that the accomplishment of Stage 1 is a precondition for "appropriate" causal inferences, factors associated with presenting information to a child take on added importance.

In current research with adults, the most extensively employed method is the questionnaire in which subjects make attributions from an experimenter's written or oral description of a behavior. Indeed, a number of developmental investigators have applied this technique in its pure form, whereby children are confronted with live or audiotaped *verbal descriptions* of either a behavioral or a physical event. These descriptions often consist of a single sentence to which the causally relevant information is appended, or they may consist of more embellished vignettes in which the causal data are embedded. Although this method has a number of advantages when used with adults (McArthur, 1972), young children have difficulty with this type of material which is, after all, abstract (Piaget, 1932), hypothetical (Damen, 1977), and relatively difficult to process (Kail & Siegel, 1977). Also, the use of verbal descriptions may actually encourage subjects to adopt an inferential response set that could prove bothersome to young children (Baron, 1980). Many social and developmental psychologists have therefore devised a variety of "simplification strategies."[1]

In order to facilitate information recall, some experimenters supplement their verbal descriptions with illustrations of the characters or with "live" models (e.g., Kun, 1977, provided her subjects with the puzzle on which a hypothetical actor had worked). Since young children make better use of pictorial than verbal information (Osler, Draxl, & Madden, 1977), the use of pictures in this context represents an important advance. Others have concretized their stimulus "packages" by allowing their subjects to perceive the causal events directly.[2] These dynamic visual displays may take on a variety of forms, having been conveyed through videotapes, animated films, and live presentations depicting an event or chain of events.[3] In any case, it will be clear when we survey the literature that disparate findings may often be explained by differences in the simplicity-complexity of the stimulus task.

Response (output) criteria

Having "observed" an event, subjects must express their causal beliefs within the constraints of a particular response system. At this stage of the process, factors such as the wording, format, and timing of an attribution question can conceivably have significant and unpredictable effects on a child's judgment. Perhaps the single most crucial issue, however, concerns how we interpret a subject's response. Put simply, what must a child do in order to convince a psychologist that he or she possesses a causal scheme or understands the principle being tested? In general, three broad classes of response can be measured: (1) *overt behaviors* that are presumed to be manifestations of an underlying causal attribution, (2) *judgments* that involve a choice among alternatives (e.g., attributing an effect to one of two possible causes, x or y), and (3) *explanations* that demand that subjects articulate the reasons for their judgments (e.g., "How do you know X (Y) caused the effect?"). Some theorists maintain that a child can be said to possess an underlying structure only when he or she can logically explain the attributional basis for a judgmental or behavioral response. Proponents of this stringent criterion (Bingham-Newman & Hooper, 1975; Reese & Schack, 1974; Smedslund, 1969) caution us about overestimating children's cognitive capacities in cases where they rely on irrelevant hunches that permit them to make correct judgments but not correct explanations (i.e., when they make the right choice for the wrong reason). Other theorists (Braine, 1964; Brainerd, 1973, 1977) defend a weaker form of evidence—a judgments-only standard of proof. Brainerd argues, first, that irrelevant hypotheses are infrequent and readily correctable through refinements in stimulus presentation and, second, that the explanation criterion forces the subject into a linguistic mode, thereby making it unnecessarily difficult for younger children to demonstrate their competencies (for a review of the critique of the verbal response mode, see Miller, 1976). Finally, investigators sometimes rely on weaker, more indirect evidence in the form of overt behavior rather than self-report. When a reaction that is presumed to be mediated by causal attribution is observed, the underlying cognitive link is inferred to be present (e.g., Ross, 1976). These distinctions will enable us to compare different studies along the behavior-judgment-explanation dimension and to examine the different rates of causal development implied by these criteria.

Structural principles of attribution

One of the cornerstone assumptions of attribution theory is that the inference process is systematic and rule-governed, and that people follow a relatively small number of general principles or causal "schemata." When and how, in the course of a lifetime, do these schemata develop? In order to answer this question, attributional principles will be organized roughly according to the amount and complexity of information that an observer must encode in order to make an attribution.

First-order principles

Suppose you are sitting in a subway that is hot, stuffy, noisy, and overcrowded with suspicious-looking characters. Suddenly, you hear a commotion, the train screeches to a halt, the lights flicker, and you see a fellow passenger collapse and fall to the ground. To what do you attribute this incident? You quickly attempt to reconstruct the event in order to discover to which of various possible causes the incident might be attributed. This scenario illustrates a rather ordinary human problem—to attribute an effect to one of many independent factors based on whatever limited information can be derived from *a single observation*. This task is illustrated in Table 8.1 [where $C_{(1-n)}$ represent factors that are potentially causal, as indicated by the broken-line arrows, in relation to an effect (E)].

What basic, first-order rules guide people's causal ascriptions in this ambiguous, low-information situation? First, adults intuitively follow the rather obvious unidirectionality rule which states that causes precede effects. In the above ex-

ample, only events that occurred before the target person's fall would qualify as causal candidates. Second, observers perceive as causal those events that are temporally contiguous with an effect. Thus, if the victim had accidentally been pushed, that incident might be perceived as causal if it preceded the collapse by a fraction of a second but not if it had occurred minutes earlier. Third, people are likely to search for causes among those factors that are spatially proximal to the effect. In our example, the presence of a knife-wielding teenager might be linked to the event if he is within striking distance of the target but not if he stood 50 feet from the fallen victim. What follows is a review of the stimulus parameters that compel an observer's attribution in this type of situation. Experiments will be described in which subjects are confronted with an event that occurs in the presence of two or more independent forces that differ along some relevant dimension. A picture of what principles children use and the age at which they develop should emerge.

TEMPORAL AND SPATIAL CONTIGUITY. Perhaps the most fundamental rule guiding a perceiver's attribution is that causes and effects coincide in time. Thus, according to Duncker (1945), when a gust of wind blows a door shut and at the same time an electric light happens to go on at the other end of a corridor, the impression of causality is immediately "forced upon" us. Employing the classical case of one object striking another, Michotte (1963) was able to demonstrate the importance of a temporal and spatial relationship between two events for adults' attributions. In a series of studies, he had subjects watch sequences in which one object moves toward a second object and stops when it has reached it; the second object then moves away from the first at the same or slower speed (the launching effect) or with an increase in velocity (the triggering effect). Subjects were then asked to describe the sequence, explaining what caused the second object's movement. In this and in more recent research (e.g., Bassili, 1976),

Table 8.1. Classification of Causal Principles

Types of Principle	Diagram

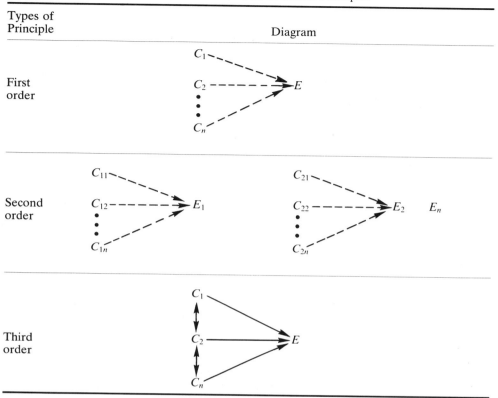

First order

Second order

Third order

the most consistent finding to emerge is that timing is crucial and that the presence of even a short delay between events 1 and 2 can erase the causal impression.

It seems reasonable to expect that very young children make attributions partly on the basis of temporal contiguity. Some indirect behavioral evidence for this contention can be gleaned from the instrumental conditioning literature, which suggests that learning among preschool children is superior when reward follows a response immediately than when it is delayed (e.g., Terrell & Ware, 1961). From a cognitive perspective, Piaget (1930) believed that young, preoperational children base their attributions *exclusively* on the contiguity between an effect and its possible causes. In fact, Piaget suggested that young children are hypersensitive to this variable, often linking events that happen to co-occur only by chance.

Despite the behavioral evidence cited above, and despite Piaget's observations about the preoperational child, some investigators have reported that preschoolers and early elementary-age children do not perceive a causal link between two contiguous and proximal events. Olum (1956) conducted the first developmental study involving Michotte's (1963) well-known paradigm.[4] Subjects observed repeatedly a sequence in which one object *(A)* approached another *(B)* which, almost immediately on contact, moved away from or was "displaced" by the first object. Subjects described what the two objects seemed to be doing, and their descriptions were coded for whether the first object was perceived to have set the second one in motion. Results showed quite clearly that adults were far more likely than second-graders to perceive a causal link between the contiguous actions of *A* and *B*. In a similar study, Lesser (1977) "trained" first- and fourth-graders by having them push one magnet toward another, enabling them to observe how the first magnet could repel the second one without actual contact. As before, children did not spontaneously describe the event in causal terms; moreover, although the training procedure increased the number of causal inferences among fourth-graders, it proved unsuccessful in the younger group.

In contrast to the aforementioned research, some studies have shown that children are indeed receptive to the causal implications of temporal contiguity. Siegler and Liebert (1974) devised an ingenious mechanical event consisting of an effect and two plausible causes—one that was temporally contiguous with the effect and one that was not. Specifically, subjects were shown two metalic boxes—a "computer" equipped with various sounds and continually flashing lights (Cause 1) and a "card programmer" containing a slot for IBM program cards (Cause 2)—both attached by wires to a large electric light bulb (effect). A card was inserted and a light went on either immediately or after a 5-second delay, and subjects chose whether the programmer or computer had produced the illumination. As it turned out, kindergarteners as well as third-graders were strongly influenced by the contiguity factor, choosing the card programmer more often in the immediate than in the delayed condition. This finding has proven to be replicable and extremely robust. Others have found that preschoolers attribute an effect to a temporally contiguous event even when the two are inconsistently associated, that is, paired on only half of the trials (Mendelson & Shultz, 1976, Siegler & Liebert, 1974). Moreover, this perceived link persists even when the antecedent event is not intuitively related to the effect (Ausubel & Schiff, 1954).

At first glance, it appears that the various research attempts have yielded mixed results. A closer inspection of the various experiments and their respective response criteria, however, suggests that the data are not necessarily inconsistent. When subjects' attributions are extracted from their open-ended and often spontaneous descriptions of a "scene" (Lesser, 1977; Olum, 1956), they appear to be uninfluenced by temporal factors. Unlike older children, preschoolers do not naturally describe contiguous events in causal terms. On the other hand, when more sensitive (or less stringent) response criteria are adopted, that is, when attributions are assessed nonverbally through some kind of judgment (Mendelson & Shultz, 1976; Siegler & Liebert, 1974) or through behavior (e.g., Terrell & Ware, 1961), very young children do indeed appear to make a causal connection between contiguous and proximal events. In fact, we will see later that children mature, not by becoming increasingly sensitive to this factor, but in their ability to distinguish temporally contiguous events that are causally related from those that are not. With age, children's inferences are mediated by the consistency of an association, the plausibility of the antecedent event, and so on.

CAUSAL DIRECTION. When two events co-occur, we naturally assume that the first event is the *cause,* while the second is its *effect.* Immanual Kant emphasized the overriding importance of this intuitive principle when he stated that "the idea of one thing following another in time is the schema of causality" (1781/1961). In the realm of interpersonal perception, Heider and Simmel (1944) also underscored the importance of ordinal relation, noting that "the unit which moves first is . . . more likely to be seen as the origin" (p. 256). The developmental question is, then, at what age do children begin to adopt this unidirectionality-of-cause assumption?

As before, the conditioning literature provides us with some indirect behavioral evidence. Specifically, infants and young children can be classically conditioned through traditional procedures [i.e., where the conditioned stimulus (CS) precedes the unconditioned stimulus (US)] but not through the procedure of backward conditioning (Reese & Lipsitt, 1970). Subjects in the latter situation thus behave *as if* they did not attribute the presence of the antecedent US to the CS. When we turn to cognitive tests of the unidirectionality principle, those that rely primarily on self-report measures, quite a different picture emerges: "The traditional view of the young child is of a child who cannot keep straight the order of events let alone be able to order more than two events in temporal succession . . . he seems perfectly satisfied with the idea that causes and effects can take place in such a way as to allow a reversal of their order" (Gelman, 1978, p. 308).

The somewhat pessimistic view of the preschooler's abilities can be traced directly to Piaget's early work on children's beliefs about time and causality (1926, 1928, 1930). He observed that preoperational children's thinking is diffuse and that they often juxtapose and confuse the order of events that occur close together in time. Piaget (1928) demonstrated his point with sentence-completion tasks by showing that young children frequently construct statements like "The man fell off the bicycle because he broke his arm." More recently, Piaget's views have received further empirical support. In one study, Kuhn and Phelps (1976) presented subjects of kindergarten through second-grade age with drawings of events that could be described in the form "*A because B*." One drawing, for example, protrayed a glass tipped over on a table with water spilling out onto an adjacent chair. Accompanying the sketches were two sentences from which subjects chose the one that "goes best with the picture." In the above example, children could thus describe the scene as either "the chair gets wet because the water spills" or "the water spills because the chair gets wet." Their results indicated that while the older subjects had no trouble identifying the correctly worded description, the youngest children re-

sponded randomly, without apparent concern for causal order. Shultz and Mendelson (1975) reported parallel findings using a very different method. In their study, children watched mechanical sequences in which a marble was dropped into one side of a box, a hidden bell rang, and another marble was deposited into the other side of the box. Although 7-year-old children consistently attributed the bell to the covariate that preceded the effect, 3- and 4-year-olds did not. In fact, many of the younger children showed the reverse tendency to attribute an effect to the consequent event.

Taken together, the above studies appear to corroborate Piaget's observation. A closer look at these experiments, however, reveals that the tasks employed demanded cognitive skills that strain young children's information-processing and linguistic capacities. In Piaget's research paradigm, subjects were able to demonstrate their knowledge only through verbalization. Kuhn and Phelps (1976) improved on this conservative method by collecting judgmental data, but their verbal presentations still required that subjects understand the syntactic implications of the word "because" (See Corrigan, 1975). Shultz and Mendelson (1975) avoided the pitfalls of a verbal stimulus presentation, but attributions in their experiment depended on subjects' ability to recall three elements in the chain of events, a task not easily accomplished by preschoolers (Bryant & Trabasso, 1971).

When stimulus presentation and response mode are simplified, quite a different view of the preschooler emerges. For example, Kun (1978a) provided a pictorial, nonverbal test of unidirectionality. She presented children with causal chains such as: "Scott pulled the dog's tail" (*A*): "the dog bit Scott" (*B*); "Scott cried" (*C*). With pictures of the three events in view, subjects were asked why *B* happened and responded by pointing to either *A* or *C*. Having thus concretized the task, Kun found that children as young as 3 years old mastered the causal order problems. In another study, Bullock and Gelman (1979) had subjects make attributions for a mechanical effect (similar to the one devised by Shultz and Mendelson, 1975), but they gave their subjects demonstration trials that presumably facilitated recall of the otherwise unfamiliar event. They too found that 3-year-old children understood the concept of unidirectional causation. In fact, subjects continued to respond correctly even when the antecedent event was spatially removed from the effect while the consequent event was spatially proximal. The only developmental difference among age levels appeared in subjects' ability to explain the principle that guided their choices.

SIMILARITY OF CAUSE AND EFFECT. Several theorists, among them John Stuart Mill (1843/1974), have suggested that in the absence of logically compelling evidence, people search for causes that are similar along some dimension to the effect. Duncker (1945) illustrated this bias with examples of physical similarity: "the wetness of the rain resembles the wetness of the street, and the color of the light becomes the color of the illumination . . . heavy things make 'heavy' noise, dainty things move daintily, etc." (p. 68). Others have discussed more subtle forms of similarity—instances where people believe that great events should have great causes, complex events shoule have complex causes, and emotionally relevant events should have emotionally relevant causes (Rothbart & Fulero, 1978). In the realm of person perception, Heider (1944) also discussed the importance of affective similarity, which leads to the assumption that bad people produce bad outcomes.

Adults' attributions are often biased by similarity factors. Nisbett and Ross (1980), for example, noted how many ancient medicines resembled properties of the disease (e.g., the belief that epilepsy is cured by a drug made from a monkey whose movements appear epileptic). At what age are children influenced by similarity considerations? Michotte (1963) implied that this belief is innate. In contrast, Kelley (1973)

suggested that it develops out of a perceiver's experience with instances in which causes and effects are indeed similar. In the only test of the developmental question, Shultz and Ravinsky (1977) had kindergarten through sixth-grade children watch an effect that was preceded simultaneously by two possible causes, one that was similar and the other dissimilar to the effect (problem 2 of the experiment). The investigators operationalized similarity in four ways.

1. A *sound* apparatus consisted of a box with a heavy (cause X) and a delicate (cause Y) lever that could emit the sound of either a loud (effect x) or soft (effect y) bell.

2. A *number* apparatus consisted of a single light and a row of three lights mounted on top of a box, a single switch mounted on one side, and three switches on the other.

3. A *color* apparatus consisted of pink and blue dropper bottles and a jar of clear liquid that turned either pink or blue.

4. A videotaped *aggression* scenario showed a bully provoke one of two children either verbally of physically, with the victim retaliating either verbally or physically.

For each event, subjects attributed the effect to one of its two possible causes. As it turned out, children of *all* ages were influenced by the similarity factor. That is, they all attributed the loud sound to the heavy lever, the single light to the single switch, the pink change to the pink dropper, and, to some extent, physical retaliation to physical provocation. Duncker (1945) had suggested that people fall back on their similarity assumptions when other, logically appropriate information is unavailable. A question arises, however, about what effect similarity has on children when it conflicts with very basic cues about temporal contiguity. Shultz and Ravinsky (1977) addressed this question with a study where either the similar or dissimilar cause immediately preceded the effect while the other preceded it by 5 seconds. In instances of conflict, subjects tended to attribute the effect to cues that were temporally contiguous but physically dissimilar. Apparently, contiguity is the more fundamental rule on which even pre-schoolers' attributions are based.

Second-order principle: Covariation

Thus far, we have discussed cases in which attributions are based on the limited observation of a single event or "cause-effect sequence." A somewhat more complex task confronts the observer who has access to more extensive information that is based on *multiple observations* of cause-effect relationships. This problem is illustrated in Table 8.1 in which the effect occurs on a number of occasions in the presence/absence of one or more possible causes. In these instances, people's attributions are said to be affected by the regularity or consistency with which events co-occur (Duncker, 1945; Heider, 1958; Hume, 1960). In the subway example, suppose you had ridden on the train every day for a week, during which you witnessed three people suddenly collapse. Of course, the specific circumstances of each situation were different, except that on each occasion of a collapse, a certain shady-looking character stood at the victim's side. Moreover, this individual was not present on those days when nobody fell to the ground. Equipped with this temporally extended information, adults who observe and recall the details of each event will probably infer a causal connection between the presence of the individual and the recurring incident.

Adult observers have attributed events to covariant factors in various studies. For example, Valins (1966) conducted a self-perception experiment in which male undergraduates viewed a series of slides of nude women. Subjects, supposedly hearing their own heartbeats throughout the presentation, heard it increase or decrease consistently in response to some of the slides. The nudes that were associated with perceived changes in heart rate were subsequently rated as more attractive, suggesting that the effect was attributed to those factors with which it covaried.[5]

In 1967, Harold Kelley formalized the *principle of covariation* which states that "an

effect is attributed to the one of its possible causes with which, over time, it covaries" (p. 64) and proposed a model to describe people's attributions for *behavioral* events. Specifically, Kelley described three types of information that observers of person-stimulus interactions employ: (1) *distinctiveness*, pertaining to whether or not a target person behaves similarly toward other stimuli (covariation of person across stimuli); (2) *consensus*, pertaining to whether or not other persons behave similarly toward a target stimulus (covariation of stimulus across persons); and (3) *consistency*, pertaining to whether or not a target person behaves similarly toward a target stimulus on other occasions (covariation of person and stimulus across time). Empirical tests of this model have essentially supported Kelley's predictions (e.g. Frieze & Weiner, 1971; McArthur, 1972). Events that are high in consensus, dinstinctiveness, or consistency are attributed to the target *stimulus;* those that are low in consensus and distinctiveness and are high in consistency are attributed to the target *person.* Events that are inconsistent across time tend to be ascribed to transient *circumstances* rather than to stable qualities of the person or stimulus. Thus, for example, the event "Susan hits a home run off the pitcher" will be attributed to the pitcher if other players hit home runs off the pitcher, if Susan does not hit home runs off other pitchers, and/or if Susan often hits home runs against that pitcher. In contrast, Susan will be seen as causal if others do not hit home runs off the pitcher, if Susan hits home runs off many other pitchers, and/or if Susan often hits home runs against this pitcher. Finally, the effect will be attributed to circumstantial factors (e.g., maybe the current game was played in a particularly small stadium) if Susan had never previously hit a home run against this pitcher.

Although Kelley's model has received its share of empirical support, two unexpected findings have emerged. First, consensus appears to be the least effective of the three types of information (McArthur, 1976) and is sometimes even "ignored" by adult attributors (Nisbett & Borgida, 1975). This finding is theoretically puzzling. An inspection of the literature, however, reveals that observers often have access to two types of normative data—implicit consensus, which is an individual's expectation about how actors would behave if present (assumed covariation, as in Jones & Davis', 1965, theory), and explicit consensus, which is covariation information about how actors in a sample actually behave (Lowe & Kassin, 1977). With this distinction in mind, it appears that people's attributions are influenced by explicit consensus only under certain conditions—when potentially interfering expectancies are held in abeyance or when the sample-based information is strengthened in a variety of ways (Kassin, 1979).

A second "bias" that is characteristic of adult observers is their tendency to perceive actors as causal (McArthur, 1972), while, at the same time, underemphasizing the role of situational factors (e.g., Snyder & Jones, 1974). One reason for this bias is that, compared to the background situation, an actor's behavior "engulfs" the visual field (Heider, 1958) and is perceptually salient to an outside observer (Arkin & Duval, 1975; Jones & Nisbett, 1971). A second possible explanation is that observers rarely know about an actor's behavioral history and inconsistency across a variety of settings (Eisen, 1979; Mischel, 1968).

PHYSICAL CAUSES AND EFFECTS. At what age do children attributors employ the covariation principle? Some compelling, though indirect, behavioral indicants are again provided by developmental learning psychologists. Infants who are less than a week old can be classically conditioned better to a neutral stimulus that *consistently* precedes an US than to one that is unpaired with the latter event (Kaye, 1967; Lipsitt & Kaye, 1964). Although the conditions under which subjects respond to this covariation among stimuli are highly controlled and specific, this phenomenon does suggest that, at some level, infants "understand" the underlying

principle. On the other hand, Inhelder and Piaget (1958) contend that preoperational children (i.e., below the ages of 7 to 8) have difficulty integrating information that they obtain from multiple events that are extended in time.

In order to examine young children's use of simple covariation (when only one of two causes co-occurs with an effect), Siegler and Liebert (1974) employed a task described in the section on temporal contiguity. Kindergarten and third-grade children attributed the ringing of a bell to either a "computer" with its continuously flashing lights and sounds or to the insertion of a card into a "card programmer." For subjects in a 100% regularity condition, the effect followed the insertion of a card into the programmer on all 6 consecutive trials. In a 50% regularity condition, the effect followed the card insertion on 6 of 12 trials. Subjects made trial-specific attributions as well as a global judgment at the end of the session. Whereas third-graders' causal impressions were influenced in the later trials by the consistency of this cause-effect relationship, kindergarteners' attributions were not. Instead, these younger subjects based their judgments solely on the contiguity cues (see also Mendelson & Shultz, 1976).

Can one conclude that kindergarteners do not understand the principle that causes and effects covary? To answer this question, Siegler (1975) entertained a series of hypotheses to account for why young children in his earlier study failed to make the logical inferences. First, Siegler (1975) reasoned that, because subjects made attributions after each trial, the preschoolers might have committed themselves to a causal response in the early stages of the experiment before the regularity manipulation had time to unfold. He tested this possibility (Experiment 1) by having subjects make only a single attribution at the conclusion of all trials, but found that kindergarteners were still not influenced by regularity. Second, Siegler suggested that maybe young children were simply *slower* to detect the consistency of the relationship (Experiment 2). A group of children were thus presented with 12 rather than 6 trials but again failed to respond "correctly." Next, Siegler simplified the attributional task by rewording the verbal question (Experiment 4) and by assessing judgments nonverbally (Experiment 3), again without a net change in results. Finally (Experiment 5), Siegler tested the hypothesis that young subjects might have been distracted by the flashing lights and sounds of the computer. He removed the distractors and found that kindergarteners did reliably attribute the effect to the antecedent with which it covaried. In short, it appears that preschoolers understand the covariation principle, but that developmental changes take place in their attentional skills and the ability to detect the regulairty amidst perceptually salient but irrelevant stimuli. Indeed, even 3-year-old children attribute mechanical events to covariate causes in the absence of distracting influences (Shultz & Mendelson, 1975).

BEHAVIORAL EVENTS. Despite the fact that Kelley's (1967) attribution theory has had a large impact on social psychology, surprisingly little empirical attention has been directed toward children's use of consensus, distinctiveness, and consistency information. In an insightful discussion of the issue, DiVitto and McArthur (1978) proposed that the extent to which each type of information influences a particular attribution depends on the number of cognitive steps that a child must make. For example, high consensus provides covariation information about the target stimulus (i.e., it identifies how different actors behave toward a single stimulus), whereas low distinctiveness provides person-relevant covariation information (i.e., it identifies how a single actor behaves toward a variety of stimuli). In contrast, the task of inferring stimulus qualities from distinctiveness or person qualities based on consensus requires that an individual first eliminate the causal factor that does not covary with the effect and then infer that the other factor must have been present. Thus, high-consen-

sus behaviors like "Susan (and many other players) hits a home run off the pitcher" immediately identify the pitcher as a causal agent. For low-consensus actions (e.g., "Susan is the only player to hit a home run off the pitcher"), the causal role of the pitcher is first eliminated via covariation. Having concluded that the target stimulus did not covary across actors, observers must then apply the discounting principle (to be discussed later) and infer that the target actor must have been a potent force since the effect occured in the absence of stimulus-based causes.

Research with adults clearly supports the above analysis—person inferences are influenced most by distinctiveness information, and stimulus inferences are most influenced by consensus (Garland, Hardy, & Stephenson, 1975; Kassin & Lowe, 1979a; Orvis, Cunningham, & Kelley, 1975). In the only extensive developmental study, DiVitto and McArthur (1978) presented subjects in grades one, three, six, and college with illustrated story pairs that described positive (e.g., sharing), negative (e.g., aggression), and neutral (e.g., running) acts. For each pair, subjects were shown two identical events varying in their levels of consensus, distinctiveness, and consistency. For example, "John is giving Bob a cupcake" was accompanied by "almost everyone else gives Bob a cupcake" (high consensus), while its counterpart act, "Paul is giving Doug a cupcake," was accompanied by "hardly anyone else gives Doug a cupcake" (low consensus). Consistency and distinctiveness information were similarly manipulated. After each presentation, subjects compared the two persons or actors (i.e., John and Paul) and the two stimuli or targets (i.e., Bob and Doug) in terms of who is nicer in the positive stories or meaner in the negative stories (for stories about neutral events, the comparative questions fit the content). Overall, first-graders applied the covariation principle in their attributions; more specifically, first-graders used distinctiveness and consistency information to make causal inferences about the person, while third-graders reliably used consensus and consistency to make stimulus attributions.[6] In contrast, subjects were less likely to draw the more complex inferences that demanded the dual applications of covariation and discounting. Only sixth-graders and adults employed consensus information for making personal attributions, while only adults used distinctiveness information for stimulus attributions. Further support for the finding that young children use the covariation principle has also been obtained in a study on consensus and attribution among preschoolers (Karlovac, Feldman, Higgins, & Ruble, 1976).

Third-order principles

Thus far, we have reviewed the development of principles that influence how people attribute something to one of two *independent* possible causes. As such, only inferences that are based on a child's consideration of cause-effect relations have been discussed. This section is devoted to the development of higher order theories that guide inferences about how various *nonorthogonal* causes combine to produce an effect. For this more complex situation, observers must coordinate not only cause-effect relations, but the direction and magnitude of the cause-cause relationship as well. In short, attributions may be based on a single observation of an event that is preceded by two or more interacting causes (see Table 8.1, where the solid arrows represent a causal influence). To illustrate one of the tasks that follows from this situation, let us return to the victim-in-the-subway example. If the fallen passenger was a frail and elderly gentleman, his age would constitute one plausible cause for the incident. If this victim had been shoved before collapsing, that event would constitute a second plausible cause. Clearly, these two factors are not independent—collapsing after having been pushed is a more likely outcome among weak than strong persons. Attributors in this ambiguous situation must therefore fall back on their pre-event information or "causal theories" in order to assess the magnitude of

the effect and the relative contribution of each factor.

Research on how children and adults draw causal inferences from multidetermined events has been stimulated primarily by Harold Kelley's comceptualization of the "causal schema":

[It] is a conception of the manner in which two or more causal factors interact in relation to a [given] effect. A schema is derived from experience in observing cause and effect relationships, from experiments in which deliberate control has been exercised over causal factors, and from implicit and explicit teachings about the causal structure of the world. . . . The mature individual . . . has a repertoire of [such] abstract ideas about the operation and interaction of causal factors. These conceptions [enable him to make] economical and fast attributional analysis, by providing a framework within which bits and pieces of relevant information can be fitted in order to draw reasonably good causal inferences. (Kelley, 1973, p. 115)

Some important attributional principles and their implications have been derived from this framework and developmental tests have been conducted.

THE MULTIPLE SUFFICIENT CAUSE (MSC) SCHEMA. Kelley (1972) suggested that perhaps the most common experience people have with causation is when two or more causes are sufficient to produce an effect. For example, a lamp may be turned off either by turning off the switch or by pulling the plug. Each act is sufficient by itself, and only one is necessary to achieve the outcome. Observers who have knowledge about an effect and one of its sufficient causes can thus make inferences concerning the status of the other cause. Actually, two causal patterns are distinguished since any cause may stand in either positive or negative relation to the effect. A causal force may *facilitate* an effect (e.g., an offer of reward increases behavior pótential) so that its presence predicts the presence of the effect. Others may inhibit an effect (e.g., a threat of punishment may decrease behavior potential) so that the presence of the cause predicts the absence of the effect. This distinction between facilitative and inhibitory causes is especially important; when an individual knows that an effect occurred in the presence of one cause, the valence of that factor will determine his or her inferences concerning the status of a second factor. At this point, two extensions (though not completely justified ones, see Kun, Murray, & Sredl, 1980) of the MSC schema are reviewed.

The discounting principle. We very often encounter events whose occurrence may have been facilitated by more than one factor. Consider, for example, the causal ambiguity that arises when you see a student tell his professor that he is the best thing that ever happened to the university. If we accept the flattery at face value, we would conclude that the professor's teaching excellence prompted the remark. Another obvious possibility, however, is that the student is ingratiating himself and that his remark was motivated by the desire to get a good grade. To what, then, do we attribute the compliment? In the absence of any more information about the student, the professor, or the circumstances, we are likely to throw our hands up in uncertainty about why this causally ambiguous behavior occurred. In situations such as this (i.e., when E and C_1 are given and the presence of C_2 is to be inferred), Kelley proposed the operation of a discounting principle which states that "The role of a given cause in producing a given effect is discounted if other plausible causes are also present" (1971, p. 8).

Common sense suggests that adults implicity use this princple all the time. Indeed, the results of many social perception studies support this observation (Karniol & Ross, 1976; Kruglanski, Schwartz, Maides, & Hamel, 1978). For example, Thibaut and Riecken (1955) had subjects request help on a task from two confederates, one believed to be a person of high status and the other of low status. Both complied, after which subjects were asked whether each had done so because he wanted to or because he had been pressured. As it turned out, more subjects attributed the high- than low-status person's compliance to internal factors, presumably because external pressure was perceived as sufficient only for eliciting the compliance of the lower status individual. Put another way, subjects discounted the internal causes of compliance when a reasonable external cause was present.

At what age do children discount? Research directed at this question has yielded interesting, though inconsistent, results. For example, intrinsic and extrinsic motivation studies show that preschoolers behave as if they employ the discounting principle. Young children who are rewarded for engaging in an enjoyable activity subsequently show a decrease in their intrinsic interest in that activity (e.g., Lepper, Greene, & Nisbett, 1973; Ross, 1975). Apparently, children discount their own interest when their behavior takes place in the presence of reward (or any salient extrinsic cause). This cognitive mechanism provides a reasonable interpretation of the phenomenon. At the same time, investigators have only *presumed* the operation of a discounting principle from changes in children's overt behavior. We turn now to research aimed at assessing children's attributions more directly.

The operation of a discounting principle is typically tested by having subjects attribute a hypothetical behavior to either an actor's intrinsic motivation or to an extrinsic cause present in the environment. In one study, Smith (1975) presented subjects with pairs of illustrated stories about two children who chose to play with a particular toy—one in the presence of situational constraint (i.e., reward, command, or obligation) and the other without any type of inducement. Consider the following sample story.

1.   Tom was at the playground and he saw two toys there: A hammer and a shovel. And he said that he wanted to play with the shovel.
2.   Joe was at the playground, and he saw the two toys: The hammer and the shovel. Joe's mother was there, and she said that Joe could have some ice cream if he played with the shovel. And Joe said that he wanted to play with the shovel. (Smith, 1975, p. 740)

Subjects then chose the actor who they thought wanted to play with the toy. Overall, fourth-graders and adults responded in the schema-consistent manner (i.e., they ascribed greater "want" to the actor who played with the toy in the absence of an external cause), whereas kindergarteners did not. Second-graders fell between these two extremes. This general finding, that children do not begin to discount reliably until the second or fourth grade, is supported in other research conducted along similar lines (e.g., Baldwin & Baldwin, 1970). In fact, Karniol and Ross (1976) and others (Cohen, Gelfand, & Hartmann, 1979; Costanzo, Grumet, & Brehm, 1974; Karniol & Ross, 1979; Kun, 1977, 1978b) discovered that although young children do not discount, they do not respond randomly, either. Instead, they employ an *additive* logic, inferring more "want" in the *presence* of an extrinsic cause. Apparently, younger children view the command or reward offer as an added incentive that actually increases one's intrinsic motivation, a logic that undergoes a qualitative shift with age.

What accounts for the disparity between the intrinsic-extrinsic motivation phenomenon and the attributional data? One possibility is that the former rests on nonattributional mechanisms. Thus far, however, alternative explanations for the effect have received little empirical support (e.g., Ross, Karniol, & Rothstein, 1976). A second possibility is that children are simply more sophisticated in a self-perception context than when making judgments about other people's behavior (Piaget, 1930). Unfortunately, this hypothesis has never been directly tested. A third possibility is that preschoolers are capable of discounting, but do so only under certain, easily violated task conditions. The question thus arises, do children's failures to discount reflect the genuine absence of a MSC schema or do they instead reflect young subjects' inability within the constraints of the experimental paradigm?

One could argue that preschoolers' powers of reasoning are underestimated in the discounting research. After all, the story-pair

method, because it entails a linguistic mode of stimulus presentation, is abstract and difficult for young children to process. Also, this method confronts the subject with target behaviors that elicit strong behavioral expectations that could interfere with an "objective" use of causal information (e.g., subjects might not discount the intrinsic motivation of any actor who chooses to play with an attractive toy). Perhaps the most important limitation of previous efforts is that the concept of facilitative cause is nearly always operationalized as an interpersonal event whose inducement value may not be appreciated by young children. Karniol and Ross (1979), for example, found that subjects who employ an additive principle are relatively insensitive to the constraint or "facilitation" implied by a reward contingency. Specifically, they do not interpret the reward as a bribe offered by a manipulative agent and, hence, do not infer that the target activity must have been less enjoyable. This latter finding highlights the need for taking children's causal theories into account when choosing an operational definition of concepts like facilitative cause (to be discussed later).

Experiments designed to improve on one or more of the above factors have met with some success. Recently, we (Kassin & Gibbons, in press; Kassin, Lowe, & Gibbons, 1980) created a perceptual analog of the standard story pair by illustrating the information through the animated movements of geometrical objects. Subjects of various age levels watched a 9-second cartoon in which two triangles, one red and the other blue, moved along a linear horizontal path toward a house. These two "actors" approached the house simultaneously, with equal velocity, and from opposite directions. One triangle was carried to its destination by a black square, and the other moved without external assistance. While the film was still in progress, subjects indicated either which triangle wanted to go to the house more (Kassin et al., 1980) or which triangle was trying harder (Kassin & Gibbons, in press) and then explained the basis for their choice. As it turned out, second-graders made the discounting-consistent choice at above chance probability, and kindergarteners tended to do the same. Age differences emerged only in the ability to verbalize the principle—adults more often cited the presence of the external facilitator (e.g., "since the blue was on its own, it had to work harder") than did fourth-graders and younger children. In short, all subjects demonstrated use of the discounting principle in their causal judgments, but only sixth-graders and adults were able to explain their resonses.

Other investigators (e.g., Shultz & Butkowsky, 1977) have also reported that preschoolers can use the discounting principle under certain conditions. Recall Karniol and Ross' (1979) discovery that children who did not discount in their research also did not infer that the reward agent was trying to influence the target actor's behavior. Accordingly, they conducted a provocative study with a sample of "additive" kindergarteners (i.e., those who had previously ascribed greater intrinsic motivation to the rewarded actor). One group heard a woman attribute manipulative intent to the reward agent in the story, while a second group heard the same woman attribute nonmanipulative intent. Subjects then participated in the experiment, and the results showed that kindergarteners who were in the manipulative-intent group were more likely to discount than the others. Taken together, more recent research suggests that preschool children can discount when they understand the inducement value of interpersonally based causes (Karniol & Ross, 1979; also, Lepper, Sagotsky, Dafoe, & Greene, 1980, reported that preschoolers are intimately familiar with the causal implications of the "dinner table debate" in which dessert is contingent on the completion of the meal) or when they are presented with physical types of cause that do not require the ascription of ulterior motives (Kassin et al., 1980; Kassin & Gibbons, in press).

The augmentation principle. As formalized by Kelley (1972), the augmentation principle states that "If, for a given effect, both a plausible *inhibitory* cause and a plausible *facilitative* cause are present, the role of the facilitative cause in producing the effect will be judged greater than if it alone were present" (p. 120). The reasoning here is that a facilitator must have been potent if the event occurred despite an opposing force. Adults' use of the augmentation principle is well documented (Enzle, Hansen, & Lowe, 1975; Kruglanski et al., 1978) and can explain a variety of social perception phenomena (see Kelley, 1972), such as people's sympathetic attitudes toward handicapped persons (Scheier, Carver, Schultz, Glass, & Katz, 1978).

At present, only two published studies have examined the development of the augmentation principle.[7] As with research on discounting, the general strategy is to have subjects compare two identical effects, one of which occurs in the presence of an inhibitor, and to assess their inferences about the presence or strength of a facilitative cause. In one such study, Shultz, Butkowsky, Pearce, Shanfield (1975) presented children with verbal descriptions of behaviors that occurred in either the presence or absence of inhibitory causes. Subjects were then tested for their inferences concerning the status of plausible facilitative causes. For example, "Johnny is afraid of the dog" was accompanied by either "Johnny is alone" or Johnny is with his father," the latter statement representing an external factor that should suppress the effect (i.e., the presence of Johnny's father should inhibit his fear of the dog.) Subjects were then asked whether they thought an internal facilitative cause was present or absent: "Is Johnny usually afraid of dogs or is Johnny almost never afraid of dogs?" Whereas eighth-graders understood the augmentation principle (i.e., they inferred the facilitative cause more when the inhibitor was present than when absent), kindergarteners and fourth-graders did not.

In view of some of the shortcomings associated with the verbal description method, Kassin and Lowe (1979b) "perceptualized" the augmentation principle through the animated-film technique described earlier. Subjects watched a brief film of two triangles moving toward a house simultaneously and from opposite directions. One actor overcame an obstacle en route toward the goal (a black square that, when contacted, fell with little apparent resistance), while the other triangle proceeded without external interference. As in the discounting study, subjects chose which triangle they thought wanted to go to the house more, explained their judgments, and then indicated the extent to which each triangle wanted to go to the house on 4-point scales. In sharp contrast to the findings of Shultz et al. (1975), children of all ages, including kindergarteners, made the augmentation-consistent choice. Age differences appeared only in the extent to which subjects cited the presence of an obstacle in their explanations. In fact, a second experiment showed that second- and fourth-graders even understand a more advanced, quantitative implication of the principle— that differences in the *magnitude* of inhibitory cause imply correspondent differences in the degree of facilitative cause. This latter finding was tested by showing subjects a sequence in which the two "actors" were inhibited by obstacles of different sizes.

Summary: The MSC schema. Having reviewed the literature on the MSC schema, what is the relationship between the discounting and augmentation principles, and which one develops first? Anna Kun (1977) recently classified both as examples of a general *compensation schema* "which leads to the inference that, if an effect remained invariant, a change in the magnitude of one cause was accompanied by a change in the magnitude of a second cause" (p. 863). Augmentation thus represents an instance of *direct compensation*—where the strengths of two opposing forces, one facilitative and the other inhibitory, change in the *same* direction so that increased inhibition must be counteracted by a simultaneous increase in facilitation without a net change in outcome.

In contrast, discounting involves the process of *inverse compensation*—where the strengths of two like forces, both facilitative in nature, change in *opposite* directions so that an increase in one cause must be matched by a decrease in the other in order to maintain a constant effect. Citing the fact that adults have more trouble learning negative relations then they do learning positive ones (Slovic, 1974), Kun predicted and found that the direct compensation schema develops prior to the inverse schema.

Additional support for this proposed sequence is mixed. Shultz et al. (1975) presented children of different ages with descriptions of behavior that occurred in the presence/absence of either a facilitative or inhibitory cause and then assessed their inferences about the status of a second cause. They found that, although fourth-graders employed the discounting principle, only eighth-graders understood the concept of augmentation. In contrast, our own research with the animated-film technique supports Kun's (1977) prediction. Kassin and Lowe (1979b) found that kindergarteners overwhelmingly made augmentation-consistent judgments and that most second-graders were even able to explain their choices. Kassin et al. (1980), however, found only a nonsignificant tendency for kindergarteners to discount; also, most subjects were unable to explain their judgments until the sixth grade. Taken together, these latter studies thus suggest that augmentation developmentally precedes discounting.

The discrepancy among these studies is puzzling. Finding that children generally make less sophisticated attributions when responding to verbal material than visual stimuli makes intuitive sense. Why presentational differences should produce a reversal of the sequence with which two rules emerge, however, is not at all clear. Further work is therefore needed in which children are presented with both visual and verbal events along with manipulations of facilitative and inhibitory causes that are empirically equivalent in both their strength and functional relatedness to the effect.

THE MULTIPLE NECESSARY CAUSE (MNC) SCHEMA. The MSC schema described in the previous section reflects the operation of what John Stuart Mill called "the prejudice that a phenomenon cannot have more than one cause" (1843/1974), p. 763). Although people often do behave as if there exists a single sufficient cause for events (e.g., the intrinsic-extrinsic motivation phenomenon), there are times when attributors do perceive events to have been multidetermined. To account for these latter instances, Kelley (1972) formalized the notion of a MNC schema which, in its simplest form, implies that both of two facilitative causes must be present for an effect to occur. For example, knowing that a lamp is illuminated enables an individual to infer that its wire is plugged into an electrical outlet *and* that its switch is turned on. By way of implication, knowing that one of these two causal preconditions is not met enables one to infer the absence of the effect. What determines whether we adopt a multiple necessary rather than a sufficiency schema? Kelley (1972) proposed the more extreme or uncommon a target event, the more likely we are to assume that it entails more than one cause. This hypothesis has been supported in research with adults (Cunningham & Kelley, 1975). Kun and Weiner (1973), for example, found that subjects infer that success at an easy task can be achieved with high effort *or* high ability, but that success at a difficult task requires both effort *and* ability.

In the context of interpersonal perception, Heider (1958) suggested that bipolar attributions (i.e., those made to both personal and environmental factors) are more complex and sophisticated than those made to a single pole. The most fundamental developmental question concerns the age at which children begin to recognize that events-in-general may be determined by more than one factor. Erwin and Kuhn (1979) told children from kindergarten, fourth, eighth, and twelfth grades stories about a hypothetical individual who, in the presence of two possible motives, performed a particular act. Subjects were then asked to explain the actor's behavior. Not until early adolescence did children understand that behavior may be determined by more than one motive. Moreover, development progressed gradually through the following stages: Denying multiple causation, admitting the possibility of two sequential causes, admitting the possibility of two simultaneous causes, spontaneously attributing behavior to two causes (see also Kuhn & Ho, 1977).

If indeed children do not recognize the possibility of multiple causation until early adolescence, then at what age do they invoke a MNC schema to explain events of *extreme* magnitude? Shultz et al. (1975) conducted a developmental test of Kelley's (1972) extremity hypothesis. Subjects were presented with descriptions of mild and extreme behaviors (e.g., "Johnny is afraid of the dog" and "Johnny is so afraid of the dog that he starts to cry," respectively), told about the presence of one possible cause (e.g., "the dog is very large"), and asked to infer whether a second possible cause was present or absent (e.g., "Is Johnny usually or almost never afraid of dogs?"). Overall, eighth-graders responded in the predicted manner, inferring the second cause more for extreme than mild effects, whereas kindergarteners and fourth-graders did not.

For a variety of reasons, some of which were discussed earlier, the findings of Shultz et al. (1975) may seriously underestimate children's use of the MNC schema. Kun (1977), for example, tested the effectiveness of their magnitude-of-behaviors manipulation in children and found that the mild and extreme effects employed were not differentially perceived by them (e.g., a group of third-graders did not distinguish between the badness of "George fights with a kid" and "George fights with a kid so hard that the kid has to go to the hospital"). In fact, Kun (1977) found that preschoolers understand the related principle that extreme effects (e.g., high levels of task success) require strong causes (e.g., high levels of ability or effort). In summary, although it currently appears that the MSC schema developmentally precedes the schema for multiple necessary causes, further research on the developmental vicissitudes of the MNC schema is still needed.

Causal theories

A good deal of the research reviewed thus far was aimed at determining how children's attributions are affected by their observation of "new" data. It has been found that preschoolers attributed events to temporally contiguous antecedents, that children in lower elementary grades take into account the covariation between potential causes and effects, and so on. The present literature review, however, has ignored one very important consideration—the perceived plausibility or reasonableness of prospective causal candidates. The importance of "causal theories," defined as expectancies concerning the relationships among events, or "assumed covariation" (e.g., the belief that rewards increase the frequency of behavior), has been amply demonstrated in adults (Tversky & Kahneman, 1978). Ajzen (1977), for example, had subjects predict fictitious students' grade point averages from two cues—one that was intuitively plausible (e.g., IQ) and one that was not (e.g., income). In addition, subjects were told that each cue had demonstrated either a strong or weak empirical relationship to the effect. Overall, cues that were intuitively plausible but empirically weak had a greater impact on subjects' judgments than cues that were implausible but empirically valid (e.g., even when IQ was a weak predictor and income was strong, IQ carried more weight in subjects' decisions). The effect of a priori theories is also well established in the consensus information literature which shows that people's attributions are often influenced by their normative expectancies rather than by actual, sample-based information (Kassin, 1979).

From the standpoint of causal "accuracy," the utility of a priori theories is open to question. On one hand, cues such as temporal contiguity or covariation are often insufficient grounds for causal attribution, since many events may precede an effect closely in time. Plausibility considerations may thus serve as a useful mediator, enabling the mature observer to distinguish betwen contiguous or correlated antecedents that are causally related to the effect and those that are only coincidentally related. On the other hand, the Chapmans' well-known work on "illusory correlations" (Chapman & Chapman, 1969) shows that people can be overly biased by their a priori theories and that these theories can distort the "objective" perception of an association between events. Leaving aside this important but difficult issue of accuracy, let us now look at the developmental literature on how causal theories affect children's inferences.

DEVELOPMENTAL LITERATURE. How do children learn that an event possesses causal force? Wells (1980) distinguishes between two sources of such knowledge. First, causal theories follow from socialized processing—simply, that parents communicate cause-effect relationships to their children. Second, by means of original processing, children directly observe the repeated co-occurrence of events. In either case, we can assume that, as children get older and their knowledge about the world expands, they become increasingly sophisticated at judging the reasonableness or what might be called "causability" of various factors. Accordingly, causal theories should, with age, play a greater role in attributional processes.

A number of investigators have examined developmentally the extent to which the plausibility of an antecedent mediates the relationship between temporal contiguity and causal inference. In one experiment, Bullock and Gelman (reported in Gelman, 1978) showed children a box on which one handle started a ball rolling down an incline, while another switched on flashing lights that created the impression of a single light moving down an incline. Subjects watched the light (an intuitively irrelevant antecedent) and ball (an intuitively relevant antecedent) simultaneously traverse a path, disappearing into a second box, after which a jack-in-the-box was released. Children were questioned about the event and given the opportunity to "make jack jump." Results showed that even preschoolers were more likely to perceive the reasonable event as causally related to the effect (see also Mendelson & Shultz, 1976). In contrast, Ausubel and Schiff (1954) showed children a teeter-totter that worked on either a relevant principle (the longest side fell when supporting pins were removed) or an irrelevant principle (the side containing a red block, as opposed to a green one, fell when the supports were removed). They found that, whereas older children had trouble learning an irrelevant contingency, kindergarteners willingly accepted the correlated but irrelevant factor as causal.[8] Although seemingly inconsistent, the above findings do form a coherent pattern. In ambiguous situations where two or more factors are contiguous with an effect, children of preschool age infer that the more intuitively relevant event is causal (Bullock & Gelman, 1978). However, when irrelevant events are coincidentally predictive of an effect, preschoolers are more likely than older children and adults to accept that relationship at face value (Ausubel & Schiff, 1954). Apparently, for better or for worse, children's a priori theories become increasingly important determinants of attribution as they grow into adulthood.

Finally, although it is not strictly within the scope of this chapter, an important question that has been posed is—How do children's theories about human behavior influence the *content* of their attributions in an interpersonal context? It was noted earlier that adult observers generally tend to perceive behavior as caused by enduring personal characteristics of actors. Some psychologists have recently investigated this causal locus bias from a developmental perspective. Interestingly, this research has shown that, with age, children shift from situational to personal explanations of others' actions (Chapter 9 by Feldman & Ruble; Ross, Turiel, Josephson, & Lepper,

1978: Swann & Collins, 1978). Whether this content bias affects the structure of children's attributions and the kinds of information they employ, however, remains to be seen.

Summary and conclusions

The current review of the literature suggests that, although some conclusions about attributional development may be drawn, they must be tentative and task-specific. One pattern that does stand out reliably is that children's reliance on first-order principles overwhelms and precedes their use of the second- and third-order rules that are often employed by adults. Perhaps the relatively late development of the more complex principles stems from the fact that they require the integration of at least two relationships (see Table 8.1), a task not easily accomplished by preoperational children.

To summarize briefly, preschoolers as young as 3 and 4 years of age who observe a single cause-effect sequence perceive as causal those factors that are temporally contiguous, spatially proximal, physically similar, and antecedent to the effect. Kindergarteners and first-graders who "observe" extended sequences that contain more than one cause-effect instance can, when external distractions are eliminated or when the information is presented in simple summary form, make limited use of the covariation principle. At the same time, kindergarteners and first-graders who observe multidetermined events sometimes, again under "optimal" conditions, invoke the principles derived from a multiple sufficient cause schema, while the concept of multiple necessary causes does not appear until later in childhood. Finally, subjects' use of all principles is mediated by their a priori causal theories which, of course, develop through socialization and direct experience.

Perhaps the strongest conclusion that can be derived from the literature is that our interpretation of data must be qualified on methodological grounds. On the stimulus-presentation side, we consistently saw that young children are better able to utilize causally relevant information when it is concretized through the use of pictures, dynamic displays, and live events than when presented through verbal descriptions that make excessive linguistic, memorial, and conceptual demands on the perceiver. Related to these considerations, Kassin and Gibbons (1980) demonstrated that mentally retarded people employ the augmentation principle when it is illustrated in animated films but show no understanding of the same concept when the films are described verbally.

On the response side, another consistent pattern emerges. At the most primitive level, children behave as if they comprehend various principles before they can make the appropriate judgments using self-report techniques. (This pattern is reminiscent of Piaget's (1932) observation that active moral behavior precedes verbal moral judgments.) For example, the fact that infants are conditionable suggests that they are, at some level, perceiving the causal link between the associated stimuli or between the co-occurrence of their own behavior and a reinforcement. Yet, research in the cognitive tradition shows that preschoolers have extreme difficulty using the covariation principle. At the next level, children make schema-consistent causal judgments long before they are able to explain the attributional logic underlying these responses. For example, research on the MSC schema has demonstrated unequivocally that although kindergarteners can discount and augment, the ability to articulate the principle does not appear until the middle elementary-school years. In short, there appear to exist three levels of causal comprehension: (1) tacit, behavioral (the "as if" level) comprehension, (2) self-report, judgmental comprehension, and (3) symbolic, explanatory comprehension. This levels-of-understanding continuum helps to clarify why investigators who rely on different response criteria might arrive at seemingly incompatible views of development.

Future research directions

In order to delineate two directions of research that ought to be followed concurrently, it is instructive to introduce the distinction between *competence* and *performance* (e.g., Flavell & Wohlhill, 1969). In the context of attribution, these concepts may be translated into two questions: What causal principles does the child understand (competence) and what causal principles does the child actually use (performance)? With this distinction in mind, two somewhat divergent, though complementary, directions might fruitfully be pursued.

First, it is clear that all the material reviewed in this chapter, including my own research, has been aimed at exploring various manifestations of the competence question (e.g., What schemata does the child possess? What principles does the child know?). Subjects are thus brought into the laboratory and exposed to a very specific, finely controlled "event" and asked to make an attribution. Underlying this strategy is the goal of uncovering the child's "capacity" as an attributor. Certainly, few scholars would disagree that this goal is valuable and worthy of pursuit. Toward that end, an important direction for future research, one that has already been alluded to in previous discussions about methodology, is to strive to create the "ideal" operational conditions for testing subjects. We have seen that many conflicting findings arise because some investigators simplify the experimental task for their subjects more than others do. A good deal of attention should therefore be directed toward using attention-getting stimuli, concretizing information through the use of film, pictures, or live models, minimizing linguistic and memorial constraints, heightening subjects' level of involvement (see Chapter 9 by Feldman & Ruble), and so on. Moreover, attempts should be made to devise behavioral response modes that would provide reliable and sensitive indices of attribution in children under 3 years old. Infants' causal beliefs could, for example, be inferred from their efforts to reproduce interesting effects (Piaget, 1954) or from their nonverbal reactions of "surprise" to cause-effect sequences (Keil, 1979). In short, only when a task is presented in its simplest form and attribution is measured in its simplest mode can we make conclusive statements about competence or knowledge.

Having established what children of various ages *can* do in the artificial confines of the laboratory, a second approach should be to determine what children *actually do* in more natural, ecologically valid settings. In other words, how and when does the individual's competence translate into real-world performance? It is interesting to note the shift in emphasis of social perception research with adults. Most of the early work was oriented toward discovering the kinds of theoretically meaningful data observers can employ under informationally impoverished conditions. Consequently, the lay attributor was portrayed as a scientist. In contrast, recent research conducted in the area of social judgment has explored the attribution process in less than ideal settings, focusing on judgmental heuristics or "shortcuts" that people often invoke to reduce the cognitive load that is demanded by a full-blown causal analysis. This latter approach has proved useful for identifying some of observers' inferential shortcomings (Nisbett & Ross, 1980).

The utility of investigating the performance question in developmental research cannot be overstated. Siegler's (1975) study of the covariation principle is a case in point. His experiments showed that preschoolers can attribute an effect to covarying antecedents, but only when external distractions are removed from the environment. Siegler thus concluded that preschoolers do indeed understand the covariation principle. Psychologists who are concerned with performance, however, will inevitably wonder if preschoolers can really be relied on to detect and employ covariation information. After all, in the course of everyday life, we rarely perceive the relationship between two variables unfolding in a vacuum. In short, another potentially useful avenue for research would be to parallel some of the social judgment work currently being conducted with adults in order to define boundary conditions for the child's competencies and identify the development of judgmental heuristics (see Ross, in press).

Notes

1. For an interesting debate about the merits of simplification strategies, see Larsen (1977) and Surber (1979).

2. The term "direct perception" refers here to instances in which a person observes an event firsthand, that is, without the aid of an experimenter's *description*. This phrase should not be confused with a definition that stresses the presence or absence of an intervening communication medium (e.g., Warr & Knapper, 1968). Thus, although watching an event unfold on videotape is defined by Warr and Knapper as an instance of indirect perception, it is here treated as an example of direct perception.

3. For a more extensive discussion of the advantages of the animated-film technique, see Kassin (1980).

4. Specific details of Michotte's disk method are presented in his book, *The Perception of Causality* (1963); critiques of the method may be found in Boyle (1960) and Joynson (1971).

5. We should mention here that in more natural settings where the perceiver must detect a relationship between two events amidst a complex stimulus array and retain that information, people appear to make relatively inefficient use of the covariation principle (Cordray & Shaw, 1978).

6. No firm conclusions about the relative efficacy of consensus and distinctiveness can be drawn from the fact that the distinctiveness-personal attribution relationship preceded the link between consensus and stimulus attribution. The reason for this uncertainty is that the stimulus attribution question always came second, creating the potential for an order effect (DiVitto & McArthur, 1978).

7. Kun (1977) tested a variant of this rule in the context of performance attributions. However,

Kun operationalized the degree of inhibitory cause as a difficult versus easy task, thereby testing something stronger than the augmentation principle per se. That is, although a difficult task may be viewed as an inhibitory cause (i.e., success despite task difficulty), an easy task is not simply a case of lessened inhibition, but one of increased facilitation (i.e., success thanks to an easy task).

8. Related to the text discussion, young children's attributions for another person's behavior are influenced by their perceptions of that behavior's social desirability (Dix, Herzberger, & Erlebacher, 1978).

9

THE DEVELOPMENT OF PERSON PERCEPTION: COGNITIVE AND SOCIAL FACTORS

NINA S. FELDMAN
EDUCATIONAL TESTING SERVICE

DIANE N. RUBLE
UNIVERSITY OF TORONTO

The need both to understand and to act effectively in one's environment has been posited as a general human motivation (e.g., Heider, 1958; Kelley, 1972; White, 1959). Forming impressions of others is one mode through which persons seek to structure their interactions with others and thus organize their world. One indication of the importance of the person perception process is its omnipresence at all levels of social interaction. Writers of biography and fiction seek to explain the motivations of their characters to the reading public; news commentators provide insights and reasons for the behaviors of our major political figures; co-workers conjecture on the idiosyncrasies of their boss; and children seek to understand the foibles of their peers and parents.

Person perception refers to the processes of forming impressions and gaining understanding of other individuals. Researchers in this area have investigated various types of human attributes, ranging from overt behaviors and physical attributes to covert intentions, psychological traits, or attitudes. One particularly interesting aspect of the person perception process is that a conclusion drawn about an individual, regardless of the attributes on which it is based, has more far-reaching consequences than simply satisfying short-term curiosity about the individual. Such conclusions may lead to a set of expectations about the other which, in turn, is capable of influencing the perceiver's future behavior.

The purpose of this chapter is to explore the developmental process of children's understanding of others from a social psychological viewpoint. Taking a developmental approach to the study of person perception allows one to study not only the process itself, but also the evolution of the process as the interpersonal experiences and cognitive skills of the individuals increase. Unfortu-

This chapter was written while the first author, now at the University of Maryland, was supported by a National Research Service Postdoctoral Fellowship award administered by the Educational Testing Service. Portions of the research and writing were supported by grant no. APR77-16278 from the National Science Foundation to the second author.

nately, this combination of approaches has not been widely used. Social psychological and cognitive developmental investigators have examined some of the same issues, yet often have framed their questions very differently (e.g., Guttentag & Longfellow, 1977).

Our discussion of person perception is based on a framework that demarcates four distinct areas of inquiry: causality, process, content, and impact (see Figure 9.1). These aspects will serve as a means of differentiating the approaches taken by social and developmental researchers and will be described in greater depth as we discuss the two perspectives. The first, causality, refers to a concern over how person perception is initiated. Why does one seek to form impressions of others? A second question, regarding process, follows logically: How are impressions formed once person perception has begun? The issue of content next arises: Once the process of person perception is completed, what information has become available to the perceiver? And, finally, one may ask: How are these impressions used? What impact does the impression have? This framework traces an impression formation event from its inception (causality) though formation (process) and resolution (content, impact). In doing so, it attempts to provide a clearly defined structure, taking into consideration the varying emphases of the social and developmental approaches in this area of research.

An underlying theme of this chapter is that a number of advantages accrue through a merger of the two perspectives—social and developmental—in the study of person perception. Accordingly, in the first section, we will briefly describe and contrast the ways in which social and developmental psychologists have conceptualized and investigated the problem of person perception.

The second section will consist of a selected review of studies examining developmental changes in impression formation. We conclude this section by noting the consistencies in the nature of the developmental shifts observed and by suggesting possible

Social psychological concerns	Issues	Developmental concerns
Attributional framework (e.g., motivation factors)	Causality ↓	Realizing the existence of the target's traits
Averaging versus additive	Process ↓	Perspective-taking
Prototypicality	Content ↓	Developmental shift from concrete to abstract
Self-fulfilling prophecy	Impact	Vertical decalage

cognitive developmental and social psychological explanations for this shift. Finally, we will describe some of the conceptual issues that may be raised by a merger of the social and developmental approaches and will present some of our own studies to illustrate these points.

Overview of social and developmental perspectives

The social psychological approach

Two basic social psychological questions posed in impression formation research are those of *process* and *causality*—that is, *what* happens in everyday life when persons observe each other, and *why* does the impression formation process occur? We will discuss briefly some of the ways social psychologists have addressed these questions in order to provide an orientation to person perception that can later be contrasted with a developmental perspective.

Early research was concerned with issues mainly related to *process*. For example, Asch's early work (1946) established a paradigm to study the process of forming impressions, and this paradigm has dominated the literature for many years. Subjects were given lists of traits (e.g., intelligent, skillful, industrious, etc.) and were asked to form impressions of hypothetical target individuals. From this initial work, controversies have arisen over the manner of impression formation: Is the process better described by an additive or averaging model of trait integration (e.g., Anderson, 1965)? Is there a change in the connotative meaning of the traits when the terms are combined (e.g., Zanna & Hamilton, 1977)? How do primacy or recency effects influence the impression (e.g., Jones & Goethals, 1971; Luchins, (1957)? More currently, Higgins and Rholes (1976) have used pencil-and-paper measures to show that the fit between a target individual and a social role (e.g., "casual surgeon") is an important aspect in the process of impression formation. Also, distortions of the process have become increasingly interesting to researchers who seek to understand the errors and biases that occur in person perception (cf. Jones, Kanouse, Kelley, Nisbett, Valins, & Weiner, 1972).

Recent social psychological research on person perception has focused on issues of *causality* and *impact,* two major concerns listed in Figure 9.1. The question of causality has been approached primarily within the framework of attribution theory (e.g., Jones et al., 1972). Impression formation tasks in everyday life can be seen to involve more than one level of interpersonal assessment. The observer must first perceive and describe the target's behavior, then decide whether the behavior is dispositionally or situationally caused, and finally, when necessary, arrive at trait terms that are seen as representative of the disposition of the other. The process through which dispositional attributions are made has been described elsewhere in detail (e.g., Heider, 1958; Jones & Davis, 1965; Kelley, 1972).

Generally speaking, the formation of dispositional attributions is presumed to make the person perception event more *predictively* meaningful. That is, perceiving a person as friendly or aggressive is likely to influence an observer's expectations regarding future behaviors or related personality characteristics. The motivation usually ascribed to this attributional process is the observer's need for control, that is, the desire to explain and predict the behaviors of others. The importance of this idea has been shown in several recent studies. For example, Berscheid, Graziano, Monson, and Dermer (1976) manipulated the observer's need to understand a target person and found that college students felt they had learned more about their target when watching someone they expected to date than from watching a non-date target. Similarly, Miller, Norman, and Wright (1978) had college students overhear a series of moves in a prisoner's dilemma game. Subjects who expected to interact with one of the players believed they had been able to infer a greater amount about the target's personality after hearing the moves than did subjects who were simply asked to listen to the game. Since subjects were only asked to indicate how well they thought they could describe the target, we do not have available a direct measure of the effect of need for control on inference. However, a second study (Miller et al., 1978) revealed that subjects who showed a high need for effective control believed they would be able to form more personality inferences about an unknown player than did subjects scoring low on need for effective control. Thus, within an attributional framework, the purpose of forming an impression is presumably to gain usable knowledge regarding the probable future behavior of others.

As shown in Figure 9.1, this conclusion regarding *causality* will eventually lead to the question of the *impact* of forming an impression. A number of psychologists have investigated the issue of impact in terms of whether or not behaviors are congruent with inferences. For example, research on the self-fulfilling prophecy effect (e.g., Jones & Panitch, 1971; Kelley, 1950; Snyder & Swann, 1978) indicates that forming inferences about a person can promote differential styles of interaction toward the other based on the expectations one has established. Typically, in these studies, the subject is led to form an inference about an unknown other, and then the two are asked to interact. Behavioral patterns consistent with the expectations formed can be seen to occur, linking the inference to a subsequent action and indicating the external validity of the impression formation process.

In the social psychology literature, relatively little attention has been paid to the actual *content* of an impression. One early possible exception was the concern with the issue of accuracy in impression formation. A number of early researchers sought to discover the characteristics of good interpersonal judges (cf. Hastorf, Schneider, & Polefka, 1970; Tagiuri, 1969). In order to pursue this goal, the content of the impression was evaluated. However, this concern with content was of subordinate interest to the emphasis on individual differences in accuracy, that characterized this research. Although the methodology of presenting impression targets varied, including the use of films of behaviors or actual interactions, the criteria used to assess accuracy was criticized (e.g., Cronbach, 1955). Response biases such as stereotype-based (all *x's* have trait *y*) and similarity-based (*x* is similar to me and I have trait *y*) accuracy, which elevated the level of correct responses, were acknowledged as methodological problems, while the semantic content was generally overlooked.

Finally, pencil-and-paper measures are currently used to investigate the effects of social knowledge on the content of person perception. For example, Cantor and Mischel (1979) discuss studies illustrating the phenomenon of prototypicality—that is, the effect on social judgments of labeling a target as a member of a particular category (e.g., introvert, extrovert). The impact that social categories have on subjects' memories for the content of an impression is also the subject of current research (e.g., Snyder & Uranowitz, 1978).

The developmental approach

Developmental researchers have approached the issue of how children come to understand others primarily within the framework of cognitive developmental theory (e.g., Piaget, 1926; Werner, 1948). These theories bring an interest in role-taking and information-processing skills to the task of person perception (e.g., Selman & Byrne, 1974). Changes in social skills are often related to changes in cognitive-developmental level, such as a shift away from egocentrism towards perspective-taking. Shantz (1975), in her excellent review of the development of social cognition, discusses many aspects of social inference (i.e., what is the other: seeing, feeling, thinking, intending) within this developmental framework.

The issue of the *content* of the person perception event has concerned developmental much more than social psychologists. As Figure 9.1 indicates, research in the development of impression formation content has generally been based on children's unstructured verbal responses regarding others and has attempted to describe the changes in constructs, depth, and organization of impressions as they occur with age (e.g., Flapan, 1968; Gollin, 1958; Livesley & Bromley, 1973; Scarlett, Press, & Crockett, 1971). Developmental researchers have been largely concerned with categorizing the various types of information that become available to the subject through impression formation. This concern stands in clear contrast to social psychologists' interest in motivational factors underlying impressions. The developmentalists' use of free description as the *content*-oriented dependent measure also stands in contrast to much of the *process*-oriented social psychological work with adults in which both stimulus and response measures have consisted of artificially constrained sets of information. As Tagiuri (1969) points out regarding many previous social psychology studies, subjects may have been forced to use insufficient information to form a general impression and unwanted categories to describe their responses.

The advantages of a free description methodology are worth noting. In this format, subjects are simply asked to describe a target person. This open-endedness allows children to provide information in a more natural manner than is possible when a list of traits is given as a stimulus and a forced-choice response format is provided. Analyses of the subject's own emphasis and approach to understanding another, the depth and complexity of the impression, the types of descriptors used, and the order in which they occur, all become accessible to investigation.

However, the problem of a linguistic bias emerges in this response measure, as verbal skills may not have a congruent relationship with judgmental skills. Parents and teachers of young children will attest to the fact that class "bullys" are avoided very early on. Descriptions of playmates will often generate glee (she's good at games) or outrage (he never shares anything). Almost invariably, these clear-cut uses of inference appear within the context of a situation in which the actor is meaningful to the young child's personal world or welfare. Thus, the de-emphasis of social factors (e.g., level of involvement, need for control, social context) in developmental research on person perception may have contributed to an inadequate assessment of children's interpersonal understanding.

Referring again to Figure 9.1 regarding the *process* of impression formation, we find that the developmental approach has emphasized the impact of cognitive developmental levels on the use of information-processing skills. Stage theorists have described the development of perspective-taking as an integral part of the person perception process (e.g., Flavell, 1974; Oppenheimer, 1978). In contrast to social psychological approaches, research interest has often been expressed using a competence-versus-performance distinction of whether or not the child's emerging cognitive capacities are sufficient for the required information-processing. That is, questions may revolve more around the limits of the subjects' abilities, as indicated in the developmental concerns listed for causality and process in Figure 9.1, than around the motivational component or behavioral applications of the inference process. The concern with why impression formation is begun (*causality*) and the translation of inference into social behaviors (*impact*) are steps that have been relatively neglected by developmental psychologists.

The question of *impact* has been discussed in other areas of social inference. Empirical work (e.g., Borke, 1971; DeVries, 1970) suggests that children may be able to show their use of social inference on nonverbal measures before verbal measures. Indeed, this aspect of vertical decalage has been mentioned by Piaget (1932) in reference to the discrepancy between young children's moral judgments and moral behaviors. Both developmental and social psychological researchers, though coming from different directions, have been sensitive to the need for behavioral measures in person perception research (see Chapter 8 by Kassin).

Summary

The social psychological and developmental literatures have remained quite distinct in their orientations toward the topic of person perception. With some exceptions, social psychologists have tended historically to use a hypothesis-testing approach with a predominant focus on (1) the process of forming impressions (e.g., information integration) and (2) the implications of such impressions for behavior. One problem with this approach is that it presupposes and therefore possibly constrains the categories used in forming impressions. A second, related problem is that it may not fully represent the richness of impressions people hold about others, since the studies are rarely concerned with real individuals who are meaningful to the subjects; instead, they consist largely of more artificial stimuli, such as trait adjectives.

In contrast, the developmental approach has remained at a more basic empirical level, with a focus on: (1) determining what categories of impressions emerge and (2) describing the sequence of developmental changes in such categories. This approach may provide a richer understanding of the nature of impressions, though the relative lack of theoretical guidance may have limited the scope of questions being addressed.

In the next section, we will describe in some detail the research findings concerning the development of impression formation. Then, in the context of the social and cognitive developmental approaches just described, we will suggest possible ways to interpret and explain these findings.

The development of impression formation skills

Research on the development of impression formation has produced a consistent pattern of results. Young children (under approximately 7 to 8 years of age) do not appear to form inferences about other people (e.g., Flapan, 1968; Gollin, 1958; Livesley & Bromley, 1973; Peevers & Secord, 1973; Scarlett et al., 1971; Wood, 1978) in the same manner as older children. That is, when young children are asked to describe their impressions of others, they generally tend to center on concrete aspects of the target individual such as physical appearance (he is tall and has blue eyes) or specific actions (she hit me). Older children have generally been found to use more abstract concepts in their descriptions of the target individual. These concepts extend the inferences drawn from the concrete facts to allow a predictive use of traits. Older children's descriptions of others often include reference to stable dispositions (he is selfish) and explanatory concepts (she doesn't talk because she is shy). Thus, for example, a young child might view an actor's behavior and say, "He wears glasses. He has a lot of toys. The other boy doesn't have any." An older child might watch the same sequence and decide, "He doesn't give things to other people. He's probably mean." It is this pattern of results that has led to the description of young children as relatively lacking in the ability to form abstract impressions, or inferences.

Review of studies

The shift in impression formation at 7 to 8 years of age is intriguing, partly because it is so dramatic (Livesley & Bromley, 1973; Shantz, 1975), and partly because it is apparently so pervasive. Below we detail a few representative studies in order to provide a better feeling for the methods employed and the nature of the developmental shifts. These studies are grouped into two types: (1) descriptions of others who are known to the subjects and (2) descriptions of unknown others who are presented by means of videotapes, stories, or lists of traits.

DESCRIBING KNOWN OTHERS. Scarlett et al. (1971) interviewed boys in the first, third, and fifth grades and recorded descriptions of liked and disliked male and female peers. Responses were categorized based on egocentrism (as present, e.g., "we play together," or as absent) and level of concreteness (concrete or abstract). The findings revealed a developmental shift in the content of the constructs used to describe peers. Younger children's statements tended to fall within the egocentric and concrete categories, whereas the responses of older children showed an increased use of nonegocentric and abstract statements. Length of descriptions increased with age and was also affected by characteristics of the target person such as sex and valence.

Using a similar methodology, Peevers and Secord (1973) performed a study using naturalistic descriptions of known others to investigate the systematic development of concepts used in person perception. Subjects at five age levels, ranging from kindergarten to college, were asked to name one disliked and three liked acquaintances and to describe each of them. Their responses were coded based on the four dimensions of: descriptiveness, personal involvement, evaluative consistency, and depth. Of these factors, the dimensions of descriptiveness and depth are most relevant to an analysis of the extent to which a person is seen and understood as a "unique individual" with a discriminable and consistent set of traits.

Results indicated that descriptions of both liked and disliked peers generally showed an increase in dispositional terms with age, a pattern more clearly seen for liked than disliked other. Kindergarteners used the fewest dispositional items of any age group and were the most likely of any age to use concrete characteristics such as possessions in defining a peer. A pattern of increasing depth of perception with age was also clearly visible; older subjects made more attempts to explain the targets rather than providing only superficial judgments.

Livesley and Bromley (1973) had English children write descriptions of eight acquaintances in a systematic study of stimulus person variables. Eight groups of boys and girls, ranging in age from 7 to 15, described males and females at two age levels (child or adult) who were liked or disliked. Responses were analyzed for both the quantity and quality of statements. Peripheral statements were those referring to the external qualities of a person, including such aspects as appearance, possessions, surroundings, and actual behavioral incidents. Central statements were more abstract and referred to inner, psychological facets of the targets, such as personality traits, habits, and motivations.

Consistent with the studies previously described, Livesley and Bromley found that the number of statements produced increased with age and that the proportion of central statements also increased significantly with age. However, when the pattern of developmental change was viewed more closely, it became apparent that the largest increase in proportion of central statements occurred in children between 7 and 8 years of age. In fact, the 8-year-olds were not significantly different from the 13-, 14-, or 15-year-olds in their proportion of central statements. The authors went on to suggest that the span from 7 to 8 years of age may be an important milestone in the development of person perception, marking the transition from dependence on concrete, perceptually salient impressions to the use of an abstract, inferential understanding of others.

DESCRIBING UNKNOWN OTHERS. The studies described thus far have tapped children's impressions of targets, chosen by themselves, with whom they are actually familiar.

Another approach in this area has been to assess impressions of unknown stimulus persons. While this methodological change loses some of the richness found in the naturalistic settings, where subjects know their targets, it has several experimental advantages. It provides all subjects with an identical stimulus that the experimenter is able to control. In addition, it allows exposure to the target stimulus immediately preceding the recording of a response. This minimizes the problem of developmental differences in recall for target person observations; the extent of memory for the target persons may also be directly assessed and related back to the impression, if desired. A number of researchers have investigated the development of impression formation regarding an unknown other.

A study done by Hendrick, Franz, and Hoving (1975) provides an example of developmental research with a social psychological format. The authors presented subjects in kindergarten, second, fourth, and sixth grades with simple ratings of single traits and trait pairs. Subjects used a face scale, choosing a smile or a frown to indicate their like or dislike of the person described. Results showed that children's responses to trait pairs were best described by an averaging model combining the positive and negative valences (e.g., friendly, mean). This study illuminates the process through which children may arrive at impressions; however, the dependent measure is quite limited.

Snodgrass (1976) read stories about unknown peers to children from kindergarten through sixth grade who were then asked to "tell about the target." Subjects in a spontaneous inference condition simply gave their impressions, whereas those in a suggested inference condition were asked specific questions regarding their assumptions about the presence of traits not portrayed in the target story. The findings indicated that by first grade most of the subjects were able to respond correctly in assessing suggested inferences, although spontaneous inference lagged behind this level of competence. On the spontaneous measure, kindergarteners and first-graders differed from the other groups' levels. Differences in young subjects' competence, along with their performance levels, are suggested by this pattern of results. That the assessment of different dependent measure typologies yielded qualitatively different results emphasizes the need for multiple response measures in expanding our knowledge of developmental changes. The pattern of the change does remain the same, however, in its shift from a concrete to an abstract description of others, although the age range expands slightly.

A study using segments of filmed social interactions involving adults and children (two episodes taken from a movie) also indicates that these changes in impression formation style take place between the ages of 6 and 9 (Flapan, 1968). Girls at ages 6, 9, and 12 watched one of the movie episodes and then were asked to tell what happened. The findings revealed the expected developmental shift. Six-year-olds' descriptions were largely in concrete situational terms, often with direct recounting of dialogue, and offered few interpretations or inferences about the actors. In contrast, the older children were significantly more likely to make inferences and to use psychological terms in their explanations of the actors' behaviors.

Flapan also asked her subjects specific questions regarding the actors' intentions. She found that, although the youngest subjects often replied "I don't know" to these questions, children were frequently able to expand on their spontaneous initial descriptions. Again, the fact that children's verbalizations do not necessarily reflect the full extent of their knowledge emerges as an important consideration. This issue will be discussed in greater depth later on.

Finally, the effect of meeting and interacting with the target was investigated in a study that analyzed the social context in which an impression is formed. In a study by Rosenbach, Crockett, and Wapner (1973), personal contact with a previously unknown peer was actually manipulated prior to the dependent measure. Boys, ages 6 to 7, 12 to 13, and 18 to 19, played a game with a same-age confederate who either helped, hindered, or was uninvolved with the subject's winning a prize. After the game, all subjects watched a silent movie of the target performing both positive (e.g., helping) and negative (e.g., cheating) actions. Degree of contact with the target was manipulated by having half the subjects view the confederate acting as the target of the movie and half view an unknown peer.

Subjects answered a series of questions that included free responses ("describe . . . the kind of person he is," p. 124) and direct evaluations of the actor. Free responses were scored for their measure of differentiation, that is, the number of different personality constructs ascribed to the target. A developmental trend on this response revealed that, consistent with the typical pattern, the number of constructs used increased significantly with age. Older subjects were found to use a greater proportion of abstract, dispositional constructs in their impressions, whereas those used by the youngest subjects were more concrete. Interestingly, subjects who were directly involved with the actor gave more positive (helped win) and negative (hindered win) evaluations of the actor's personality than uninvolved subjects who, after viewing the movie, responded with more neutral evaluations of the identical content.

Other recent studies have found developmental changes in related areas of person perception. Bigner (1974) has found developmental changes in children's descriptions of their siblings. Montemayor and Eisen (1977) have found trends in self-description that are congruent with the concrete to abstract shift described previously. Emmerich and Goldman (in press; Emmerich, 1974) have found that the values children place on single traits (e.g., sociableness, forcefulness) differ developmentally from the fourth to the eleventh grade, suggesting that the evaluative dimension may be changing along with the process of impression formation.

Summary

Three related issues are central to an examination of the developmental shift from concrete to abstract impressions in person perception. The first concerns the descriptive component of analysis. What type of developmental changes are occurring in the impression formation process? Are the age differences in inference usage consistent across varying measures of response? The studies described in this section reveal a consistent pattern of developmental shift from concrete to increasingly abstract free-response statements. These findings occurred across studies that varied in subjects' age range, degree of familiarity with the target, liking for the target, sex and age of the target, and method of recording response. Evidence supporting the existence of this pattern appears to be quite straightforward and thus allows us to raise our next issue.

Evaluating the developmental shift

Our next concern is with the reasons behind the developmental changes observed. Why are these differences emerging? How might current psychological theory explain this pattern? This section will discuss the ways in which cognitive developmental and social psychological theories might approach this task.

A final issue of interest related to the developmental shift centers on the significance of young children's inability to produce spontaneous inferences, as seen in the developmental literature. What are the implications of this shift for the way in which one views the world at different ages? Does this shift provide a valid portrayal of children's changing phenomenology?

If this developmental shift from concrete to abstract person perception is a generally accurate reflection of children's abilities and orientations, then its implications may be stated in terms of the young child's world view and behavior. Do young children view the world as a place where traits are meaningless,—that is, where an actor's present behavior has no predictive value for future behavior? Do children form merely concrete, descriptive impressions of others in their first year at school? Do young children lack a stable, predictive base for their interpersonal actions? Intuitively, this static description does not seem plausible. Some current research will be used to illustrate this issue in a further section of this chapter.

Why might this developmental shift occur?

The developmental shift from concrete to abstract has primarily been explained in cognitive developmental terms, based largely on the work of two theorists. Werner's (1957) organismic theory of development states that, "Whenever development occurs, it proceeds from a state of relative globality and lack of differentiation, articulation and hierarchic integration" (p. 126). Several psychologists have used this principle to explain why the number and complexity of constructs found in impressions increase with age (e.g., Rosenbach et al., 1973; Scarlett et al., 1971). That is, as the individual matures, his or her thoughts regarding the world and the people in it should become more differentiated and facilitate a shift from dependence on concrete percepts to abstract representation of others.

Within a Piagetian framework (e.g., Piaget, 1970), this change in children's impressions with age has been construed as reflecting the differential cognitive skills that are present at the stages of preoperational (before approximately ages 7 to 8) and concrete operational (approximately ages 8 to 11) intellectual development. Preoperational children are described as being unable to understand the concept of transformations—that is, reversible changes in objects—and as unable to integrate events occurring over time. Their information-processing is therefore termed static; in other words, it is bound to concrete perceptual evidence (e.g., Ginsberg & Opper, 1969). Children who have reached the stage of concrete operations, however, lose their egocentric orientation and are able to decenter their thinking (focus on more than one aspect of an object or person at a time) and integrate pieces of information that are separated over time. This shift in cognitive capacities, at approximately 7 to 8 years of age, coincides with the empirical evidence of changes in the use of inference in person perception. The increased ability to work with information is presumed to mediate inferential ability; thus, the older child is able to seek out underlying consistencies in other persons' behaviors to formulate inferences and to use this information predictively. In using the emergence of cognitive skills to explain age-related changes in person perception, developmental research has tended to emphasize factors within the individual that have led to this particular pattern of results.

In contrast, the social psychological orientation has tended to emphasize the importance of factors outside the individual in its approach to the study of person perception. Variations in the social stimulus or in the situational context of the impression formation event have received attention, while changes within the individual have been somewhat neglected. For example, the need for effective control over one's environment, as discussed by attribution theorists (e.g., Heider, Kelley), is seen as an important contributing factor in the impression formation event. Thus, from a social psychological perspective, motivational factors such as the need for control may be relevant in explaining developmental shifts in impression formation. Unfortunately, such social psychological factors have, to date, generally been ignored in attempts to understand the development of person perception.

The social developmental approach seeks to integrate more fully these two variants on perspective. Rather than assuming that most of the variation will be found either within the individual or within the social stimulus, it seeks to explore the interaction of these aspects. Interest in motivational and social factors as they affect children's interpretations of a situation and subsequent responses

are important to this approach. The following section describes some of our current empirical work as it fits into a social developmental view of person perception.

Merging the two traditions: Examples from our own research

Taking a social developmental view of person perception has led us to ask several questions to which neither tradition alone could fully respond. These concerns have already been mentioned earlier in our discussion: Why are developmental differences emerging, and do these patterns accurately represent the child's changing world view? We will describe three studies that address different steps of the framework presented in Figure 9. 1.

The first study focuses on understanding developmental differences in the *content* of children's impressions. It also investigates the *impact* of an impression by analyzing the link between impression content and subsequent behavior (Feldman, 1979). In so doing, it provides an example of the way in which combining social psychological and developmental approaches leads to a reassessment of the effect of motivational factors on young children's interpersonal cognitions.

The second study is relevant to the issue of *causality* (Ruble, Feldman, Higgins, & Karlovac, 1979). Presumably, one important reason for forming impressions is based on the need to control and predict future interactions. If there are developmental differences in the attribution process, however, such that younger children are less likely to believe that persons are causal agents, then this type of motivation to form an impression is less likely to operate for young children. Thus, in this study, we examined developmental changes in perceived locus of causality for an event.

The third study represents a social developmental approach to the question of *process* (Higgins, Feldman, & Ruble, in press). It was concerned with the question of what strategies people use in forming impressions of other persons' attitudes or preferences. In this study, an integration of the developmental research on perspective-taking with the social psychological literature on accuracy of person perception led to the suggestion that the two traditions have been addressing similar issues in very different vocabularies.

STUDY 1. Based on a social developmental approach, the situational context, the cognitive capacity, and the previous social history of the child are all presumed to interact in affecting the child's performance during an impression formation event. Because young children have less experience with the predictive usefulness of forming impressions about others, their perceptions of how and why one formulates an impression might differ from those of older children. Indeed, the idea of a personal need for control based on an in-depth understanding of the other might not be salient to a young child. In addition, divergent interpretations of the situational requirements by the younger and older children (such as perceiving implicit demands for inference or the need for a "correct" answer) might occur. Thus, as the possibilities noted above indicate, causes for the developmental trends, other than differences in inferential abilities per se, are possible.

This conceptualization suggests a developmental process of impression formation in which the motivation (or perceived need) to form an inference about another is a critical factor that interacts with cognitive skills to produce inferential activity. When cognitive skills are insufficient for performing inferences, motivational factors will have no facilitating effect on inferential activity. When cognitive skills are sufficient, but insufficient motivation toward inference is present, subjects may not spontaneously call these skills into use. In summary, when presented with a videotape and asked "What is the actor like?" a young child might be motivated only to construct a simple goal, use a passive information-processing strategy, and thus produce the most readily available answer—a superficial description of the actor and his or her actions.

By explicitly varying motivation toward inferential activity, we can begin to identify the relative importance of motivational and information-processing factors that underlie the developmental changes observed.

In two studies (Feldman, 1979), children viewed videotapes of unknown peers who had been filmed so that dispositional inferences were clearly available. Study 1 evaluated the effect of a general motivation toward inferential activity (the expectation of future interaction with the target individuals) on the *content* of the impressions of children at two different ages. Study 2 investigated the *impact* of inferences on subsequent behavior by providing an opportunity for young subjects to act on their impressions of the actors.

A set of videotapes was composed with four child actors protraying different dispositional traits (generosity, stinginess, coordination, uncoordination). Two instances of each type of behavior were presented in order to enhance the likelihood of an inference. An uncoordinated actor, for example, was seen missing the targets on both an easy ball toss and an easy Frisbee game.

Participants in the study were children ages 5 to 6 and 9 to 10 who were all asked to watch movies of children they did not know. Half the subjects in each age group were told that they would be playing games with these children later on. They expected to have to choose partners from among the actors after watching the movies (future interaction expected). The rest of the subjects were told that they would be asked to answer some questions so that the experimenter could find out what they thought about the children in the movies (no future interaction expected). All subjects believed that the movies had been made while the target actors were working with a different experimenter and that the actions represented unconstrained behaviors.

After each movie, subjects were asked to give their impressions of the target person. Their statements were tape-recorded, transcribed, and coded. All actor-relevant statements were categorized as either peripheral (i.e., concrete statements of a reportorial nature, such as features, clothing, possessions of target) or central (i.e., abstract statements of an inferential nature, such as personality traits, motives, general habits). A test of interrater reliability performed on a sample of statements by two independent judges found agreement to be 98%.

The data were examined in terms of the following line of reasoning. If the difference in types of statements generally found between younger and older subjects represents a developmental change in inferential abilities, then the motivational manipulation would not be expected to have a significant impact on the younger subjects. Alternatively, if part of the difference is due to some aspect of a social factor, then providing a situation to enhance the motivation toward inference would be expected to increase the level of young subjects' abstract responses.

The pattern of results indicates that the future interaction manipulation had a significant impact on subjects' responses. The total number of statements made reflected the standard developmental pattern in that older children consistently produced more central statements. However, the quality of both younger and older children's responses was affected by the manipulation. The proportion of central statements increased significantly when future interaction was expected, as shown in Figure 9. 2. Subjects expecting interaction were also found to use a wider variety of traits in their impressions, providing a more differentiated and enriched description. For example, the following are the impressions of two young female subjects regarding the coordinated actor.

No future interaction:
"She was throwing balls into the bucket. She was throwing Frisbees at the target. She has dark hair. She went into another room."

Future interaction expected:
"She is good at games and she's probably nice. She tries very hard. I think she likes to play games."

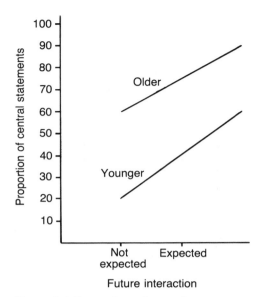

Figure 9.2 Proportion of central statements as a function of age of subject and expectation of interaction. (From Feldman, 1979)

Subjects were also asked to indicate *why* they thought the actor's behavior (i.e., performing well or poorly on a game, sharing or not sharing a snack) had occurred. Their responses to these causal questions were a forced choice between an internal (e.g., high game score due to actor's talents) and an external (e.g., high score due to an easy game) attribution. The relationship between number of internal attributions and enrichment of impression was found to be positively correlated for the younger subjects; that s, increased attributions to internal causes paralleled increased enrichment of trait responses.

One may speculate about subjects' reactions to the experimental manipulation. A possible mediating factor is the realization that locus of causality may be internal. If one does not see others as responsible for behaviors, then one is unlikely to see the utility of spontaneously predicting and generalizing about a behavior. When primed, however, as in the future interaction condition, young subjects may have been able to see the need for effective control and begin to think in terms that would aid in a predictive understanding of the actors. Thus, the social factor of motivational involvement emerged as an important facilitator of younger and older children's impressions. The conceptual and methodological issues raised by this finding will be discussed in a later section.

A second study performed with a single-age group (5- and 6-year-olds) that viewed two actors with multiple traits (generous-uncoordinated, coordinated-stingy) replicated the effect of personal involvement in increasing the proportion of abstract responses (Feldman, 1979). In addition, the results indicated that this effect was not simply due to heightened attention paid to the actor. A group of subjects who were asked to pay careful attention to understanding a quality of the actors' did not elaborate as many central statements as those who expected future interaction.

This study also asked participants to allocate toys to the two actors. Subjects decided how many out of six small, wrapped toys to leave for each actor to play with, keeping the remainder to entertain themselves. Subjects generally left fewer toys for the stingy ($\bar{x} = 2.5$) than the generous ($\bar{x} = 3.9$) actor, and those expecting future interaction were found to differentiate most clearly between actors in number of toys allocated. A regression analysis found that the variable that best predicted the number of toys left for the stingy actor was the number of inferential statements made regarding the actor's traits. As the inferences regarding stinginess increased, the number of toys allocated decreased.

This set of results suggests that young children's behavior toward an unknown peer can be influenced by the inferences formed in a first impresison. Furthermore, social factors—such as interpersonal context and characteristics of the other—exerted a strong impact on subjects' impressions and subsequent reactions toward others. However, cognitive factors—such as perceived locus of causality and the basic ability to form inferences—also appeared to be implicated in determining the content and impact of an impression formation event.

STUDY 2. Another aspect of person perception that has become a focus of research is children's understanding of why people act the way they do (e.g., Costanzo, Grumet, & Brehm, 1974; Karniol & Ross, 1976; Shultz & Butkowsky, 1977; Smith, 1975), and this focus has been set within an attributional framework (see Chapter 8 by Kassin). We have applied a social developmental approach to this area by examining developmental changes in perceptions of locus of causality—that is, whether subjects viewed an event's occurrence as being due to an internal (e.g., disposition of the person) or external (e.g., characteristic of the entity) cause (Ruble et al., 1979). A major premise of this research is that children may differ with age in their assumptions regarding causality; in other words, young children may tend to see the causes of events as primarily external. Such assumptions may affect children's tendencies to search for internal or dispositonal causes of behavior which, in turn, affects their depth of understanding and ability to predict future behavior.

Subjects at three age levels (4 to 5 years, 8 to 9 years, and college) were shown a videotape of a target actor selecting an item from an unseen array.[1] Subjects were then asked to decide *why* the actor liked the item, that is, to make a person or entity attribution. In this study, we sought to determine whether use of this information was age-related and whether patterns of causal attributions would shift in a manner that would be predicted from other developmental shifts (e.g., Piaget, 1932; Shantz, 1975). In keeping with documented shifts in orientation from external to internal information (e.g., moral judgment, impression formation), we expected to find a similar change in judgments of causality, moving from entity-oriented to person-oriented responses.

The results indicated that this developmental shift did occur. Figure 9.3 reveals that the youngest subjects were most likely to make entity attributions while the oldest participants tended to make person attributions. The middle age group made attributions that showed no clear bias in either

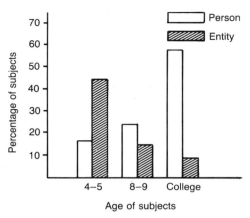

Figure 9.3. Percentage of subjects making primarily person or entity attributions at each age level. (Ruble et al., 1979, Study 1)

direction. A second study investigated subjects' responses to an attributional question concerning their own choice from an array of items. Consistent with the first study, an entity to person shift was again found. Young children tended to describe a chosen item as being inherently nice, while older subjects explained the same choice as being due to the person's own set of preferences.

As noted previously, this shift appears to be congruent with the developmental changes found in children's impressions of other persons. Indeed, as stated above, Feldman (1979) found that the number of internal attributions of causality positively correlated with the number of trait inferences. These findings lead to the intriguing speculation that age-related beliefs about the causes of events may be related to the ability or need to form predictive inferences. Young children who view others' acts as externally caused would be less likely to think in terms of trait inferences than would young children who understand that actions are likely to be due to an internal aspect of the individual. Thus, it is possible that beliefs about the extent to which individuals control events may be an important basis for certain developmental shifts of person perception. In this study, by applying a question that arose within an attributional framework

to a developmental problem we were led to investigate a relatively under-researched aspect of the development of person perception—*causality*. The issues that emerge suggest that additional research along these lines may facilitate our understanding of when and why children seek to form impressions of others.

STUDY 3. In two studies, Higgins, Feldman, and Ruble (in press) investigated issues related to developmental changes in the *process* of person perception. Understanding of others was examined by asking subjects (4 to 5 years, 8 to 9 years, and undergraduates) to predict the preferences of target groups on several arrays of items. Eight pictures were presented in each array (e.g., snacks, activities). Participants first rank-ordered their own preferences and then responded with the preferences both of peers (e.g., most people your own age) and nonpeers (e.g., most 2-year-olds).

This approach allowed us to examine, within the same format, issues in person perception that have interested both social and developmental researchers in previous work. Social psychologists have been concerned with "assumed similarity" as a strategy employed in the judgments of adults (e.g., Cronbach, 1955; Ross, Greene, & House, 1977; Tagiuri, 1969). Developmentalists have discussed egocentrism as a process affecting changes in children's understanding of others (e.g., Borke, 1971; Chandler & Greenspan, 1972; Zahn-Waxler, Radke-Yarrow, & Brady-Smith, 1977). Subjects' responses to the arrays were thus used to explore whether assumed similarity influenced responses (own preferences matching predictions for others), and whether assumed similarity was used strategically or indiscriminately (egocentrically) for similar and dissimilar others at the three developmental stages involved.

The results showed that subjects at all ages differentiated similar (peer) from dissimilar (nonpeer) others in preference predictions. Although assumed similarity was not widely used by any age, in the sense that self and other preference were identical, all age groups thought peers' preferences would be closer to their own than nonpeers' preferences. This pattern of results indicates that even the youngest children were able to formulate and use an impression that differentiated similar from dissimilar others.

There was, however, a developmental increase in judgmental accuracy. The 4- and 5-year-olds were relatively inaccurate about predicting the preferences of nonpeers. As mentioned above, their inaccuracy could not be explained in terms of an "egocentric" selection of preferences identical to their own for others because the selection of a personal preference for nonpeers was extremely rare. Instead, other types of processes such as "social reference" or "social category knowledge" (see Higgins, in press), which are largely based on social experience, seem better able to explain the impressions of others' preferences.

Thus, the social developmental approach used in this study provided insights about the strategies *(process)* used in person perception by children and adults. By asking the same question—How is an impression formed?—of both younger and older persons, backed by the traditions of the social and developmental approaches, we can acknowledge and explore a continuum of similarities where age differences are generally presumed to exist.

Implications for future research

A major theme underlying the studies and ideas presented in this chapter is that a developmental approach to social psychological research (or a social approach to developmental research) may cross-pollinate and energize both traditions. As already mentioned, developmental research in impression formation has tended to center on *process* and *content* issues, while the social psychological approach has been oriented more toward issues of *causality* and *impact* (see Figure 9.1). In this final section, we will discuss some issues that are relevant to

further integration of these two traditions in the study of person perception.

As discussed by Aronson and Carlsmith (1969) in the *Handbook of Social Psychology,* questions of internal/external validity and experimental/mundane realism are critically important in experimental research: Is the experimental variable having the intended effect on the subject (internal validity)? Is the situation realistic and involving for the subject (experimental realism)? And, how likely is it that the experimental event would occur in the real world (mundane realism)?

Issues such as these provoke additional questions about specific aspects of research regarding the development of person perception. For example, in the Feldman (1979) study, a social variable (expectation of future interaction) was found to have an impact on subjects' depth of inference. One might then be led to reconsider the level of involvement of subjects in the "uninvolved" conditions. However, is a lack of experimental realism in any way contributing to the pattern of results? In designing future developmental research in impression formation, it may be necessary to reconsider motivational factors explicitly.

We should also ask, Can the mode of presentation influence responses? Recent studies (e.g., Chandler, Greenspan, & Barenboim, 1973; Shultz & Butkowsky, 1977) found that children respond more differentially to social judgment situations presented on videotape than to stories. This varying impact of the manipulation (internal validity) reminds us that media cannot be treated casually in person perception research. This caveat touches on the issue of mundane realism and may be stated more generally: How often are persons in everyday life presented with a list of traits or a brief paragraph and asked to form impressions of an unknown target? Admittedly, a trade-off is involved between experimental control (defining an answerable issue) and realism, and the solution is neither clear-cut nor static. It seems important, however, that developmental and social psychological investigators continue to attempt to find a balance and, in doing so, develop new types of dependent measures.

In summary, research taking a developmental social approach to the area of person perception gives the experimenter a twofold advantage. The cognitive developmental tradition may serve to sensitize the researcher to certain issues that have emerged in the study of children (e.g., Are there concurrent intellectual changes that are influencing subjects' responses? How is the question being interpreted by subjects? How is the task environment perceived?). The background of social psychology will suggest new vantage points in formulating questions (e.g., What is the effect of motivational factors? In what direction would an attributional framework take us?) Historically, the subject's age has generally defined the approach of the research. It would be profitable, at this point, to discard that arbitrary distinction and to recognize that a new look at a content area may benefit from the joining of two long-standing, often separate, approaches.

Note

1. The effect of an additional factor—consensus information—is not relevant to the present discussion. See Ruble et al. (1979) for a description of this part of the study.

three

APPLICATIONS TO INDIVIDUAL AND SOCIAL PROBLEMS

This third and last section deals with the application of developmental-social psychology to various kinds of individual and social problems. As in the previous two sections, a wide variety of topics is covered by researchers and theorists with very diverse interests. In some of the chapters the reader will find that the authors have attempted to present a new perspective on an old and familiar social issue or social problem (such as racial integration); in others, topics are discussed, such as mental retardation, which up until now had been considered to be outside the domain of traditional social or developmental psychology. Four of the chapters deal with attitudes and behavior toward children who, for one reason or another, are different from their peers. Thus, we will be looking at children with proclivities toward obesity and coronary-prone behavior as well as children who have been "stigmatized" by virtue of a particular label, such as those with mental retardation or members of a minority group. The fifth chapter concerns the development of attitudes toward the social institutions of government, law, and justice.

As the reader might expect, given the heterogeneity of research interests being presented in this section, there is no common theme to be gleaned from these contributions. All of the authors, however, do share a common belief and a common perspective that is evident in their writing: that the development of children's attitudes and behavior clearly reflects the kinds of social relationships in which they are involved and, as Emler and Hogan put it, their emotional reactions to these relationships. As these relationships change, so do children's attitudes and behaviors. Therefore, the integration of social and developmental psychology is most evident in this section in the emphasis that the authors have placed on the influence that social relations have on the development of various kinds of cognitive and social behaviors.

In the first chapter, Woody and Costanzo discuss the developmental course of obesity. They review the current theories in this area (such as "externality" and "set point" theories), which they feel are very much physiologically oriented, and they suggest that it is time for psychologists to bring the study of this kind of behavior back within the realm of social science. Their own approach to obesity emphasizes the socialization that obese children receive from their parents, and they feel that the onset of overweight can be traced back to the child-rearing habits of parents. In particular, they suggest that these parents are particularly sensitive to the social sanctions that exist against being fat. They react to these sanctions by attempting to control—overcontrol, in fact—the eating behavior of their children. Because of this, the child fails to develop sufficient self-mediated controls over his or her eating behavior and, eventually, over his or her behavior in general. The result is that the child begins to develop a sense of "externality," or overdependence on external rather than internal cues in determining behavior. This type of externality has been shown in previous research to characterize overweight adults. Thus, according to the view advocated by Woody and Costanzo, externality is the *result* of an inability to control eating behavior rather than a *cause* of it; and both externality and obesity have their roots in social as well as biological or physiological factors.

Matthews' chapter also deals with a social/health problem that is prevalent in our society—coronary heart disease. She cites previous research conducted with adults that has demonstrated convincingly that people who exhibit a certain kind of behavior pattern, called "Type A," are twice as likely to suffer from coronary heart disease as are those who do not. This behavioral pattern is characterized by competitiveness, a sense of time urgency, and agressiveness. As an epidemiologist and a social psychologist, Matthews feels that this type of behavior is, to a large extent, socially controlled, and that it is important, therefore, that psychologists begin to examine its etiology. According to her model of development of Type A behavior, the normal tendency to socially compare is stronger in Type A children than it is in others. Moreover, the parents of these children tend to encourage this kind of behavior by constantly pushing the child and urging him or her to try harder and to improve. Very quickly these children find themselves caught up in a difficult behavioral cycle in which they are striving to do well, which leads to more pushing from the parent, which, in turn, results in even greater effort by the child. Eventually the child will internalize the cycle until he or she becomes a hard-driving competitive type who runs an increased risk of having some form of heart disease.

Gibbons' chapter deals with a different kind of social problem: The effect of the mental retardation (MR) label on both retarded and nonretarded children. He believes that the behavior of retarded children, possibly even more so than that of obese or Type A children, is affected by their relationships with others, and that these relationships are significantly affected by the MR label. In a series of studies, he has examined the question of whether the MR label acts as a self-fulfilling prophecy for retarded children. His research indicates that two of the three steps associated with this process do, in fact exist: (1) the label is associated with very low behavioral expectations and (2) mentally retarded children *themselves* are aware of the expectations and maintain them for other retarded children as well.

Moreover, the fact that these children have internalized an expectation of failure is evidenced in the pessimistic expectations that they have for their *own* future social behaviors, such as getting married or having a family. For this reason, Gibbons feels that one of the major problems that those who are involved with the supervision and socialization of retarded children have to deal with is a "group concept" problem—that is, their attitudes toward each other, as well as the attitudes and behaviors of others toward them.

The effect of a label and the expectations associated with it is also the focus of the next chapter by Rosenfield and Stephan. In this case the label is physical rather than mental, and the chapter concerns the interethnic relations of white and minority children. The research that they discuss was prompted by the onset in our schools of various programs of racial integration, which they consider to be "one of America's most important social experiments." They discuss the effects that a sudden increase in contact between white and minority (black and Mexican-American) children has on their perceptions of each other and of themselves. Like mentally retarded children, minority children are not expected to do well academically and in other behaviors; and, like retarded children, they typically do not do well when they are integrated (or "mainstreamed" as is the case with retarded children) in classrooms along with academically advantaged white students. Again, there is some evidence of a self-fulfilling prophecy in Rosenfield and Stephan's research in the form of a behavioral cycle that is not unlike that found with obese and mentally retarded children: Minority children are not expected to do well in schools; because of a disadvantaged academic background, they typically do not do well; this, in turn, reinforces the stereotype that white children have of them and, therefore, promotes prejudiced behavior. Racial integration, like mainstreaming, is a very risky proposition in which the desire to improve social relations is pitted against a need for special kinds of educational opportunities and facilities. Of course, there are no easy solutions to these problems. Rosenfield and Stephan feel that a system in which minority and white children can be encouraged to work and cooperate together in their schoolwork may provide the environment that will promote racial harmony. The system they describe is not unlike that discussed by Gibbons with regard to the integration of retarded and nonretarded children.

The final chapter by Emler and Hogan offers a proposition that is central to this entire section. These authors articulate the ways in which children's attitudes and behaviors, in this case toward the institutions of law and justice, reflect the social relationships in which they are involved. They suggest that young children tend to have very authoritarian views of government and society because their primary relationships at the time—those with their parents—are authoritarian in nature. As they get older, the types of relationships that they have with others tend to change and, consequently, so do their attitudes toward law and justice. For example, the research cited by Emler and Hogan indicates that older children's opinions of justice and law tend to reflect the more egalitarian relationships in which they are involved. However, this process appears to be a two-way street: Children's relationships with others affect their attitudes toward social laws, which in turn affect how they interact with others, and so on.

In summary, these five chapters deal with topics that should be of considerable interest to psychologists, educators, and sociologists as well as people in the fields of law, special education, and health. The breadth of this research and its potential relevance make this final section particularly provocative and illustrate most dramatically the fruitfulness of attempting to integrate social and developmental approaches to important real-world issues.

10

THE SOCIALIZATION OF OBESITY-PRONE BEHAVIOR

ERIK Z. WOODY
PHILIP R. COSTANZO
DUKE UNIVERSITY

Obesity and overweight are enduring national preoccupations. A casual perusal of a wide range of popular magazines and Sunday newspaper supplements reveals the staggering extent of "weight-loss capitalism." The print marketplace extols the magical weight reduction qualities of polyethylene jogging suits, rubber waist belts, appetite suppressant capsules, dietetic food replacements made of tasty candies or creamy liquids, and best-selling books detailing arcane systems of diet regulation. This surfeit of marketing fervor is apparently occasioned by the preoccupations of the consumer. While obesity can result in a wide variety of health-related difficulties, it seems unlikely that consumer preoccupation is the result of concern about the biological difficulties brought about by overweight. Instead, being overweight is most alarming because it is an obvious marker variable for social deviance. If one is considerably overweight, he or she is viewed as physically unattractive, is prone to experience social rejection, and is likely to be trait-typed as weak, lacking in self-control, slovenly, and so on. In short, consumer demand for easy weight reduction agents is a reflection of obesity's status as a culturally deviant adaptation.

If one takes the above perspective, it is surprising to find that the research and theoretical literature of social psychology has typically ignored the significance of obesity as a form of social deviance. Behavioral characteristics that have been found to differentiate obese from normal subjects have typically been explained by reference to either maladaptive biological processes (e.g., cellular anomalies or midbrain lesions) or to long-standing, almost congenital, personality styles or traits of ambiguous origin (e.g., obese externality). A consequence of this relative neglect of the socially determined aspects of the behavior of the obese has been a concomitant lack of research and theory probing the socialization of obesity-prone behaviors. While theorists such as Schachter and Nisbett have expressed views concerning the etiology of obese behaviors, these views have typically suggested general historical antecedents rather than specific developmental processes. This absence of an explicitly developmental focus is particularly surprising since the major source of subjects in recent adult obesity studies in social psychology has been the young adult population. It is likely that this population of subjects is characterized by juvenile onset of overweight.

One rather important and intriguing question that we will concern ourselves with in this chapter is whether the juvenile onset of obesity is accompanied by the juvenile onset of the behavioral and stylistic characteristics that have been found to be descriptive of obese young adults. Furthermore, we will explore the relative developmental priority of obese behavioral characteristics and physiological obesity. In other words, do the distinctive behavioral tendencies of the obese result in obesity, or does being obese in a culture that negatively values such an adaptation lead to the development of an obese behavioral style? The predominant supposition in the current literature is that the obese behavioral style precedes and disposes the individual to an anomalous orientation to food cues and thus to obesity. Because of our conceptual bias toward focusing on obesity as a socially regarded deviance, we will end this chapter by proposing the opposite sequence; that is, we will conjecture that obese behavioral characteristics are the consequences of socialization practices employed with obese or obesity-prone children. Our primary point is that parental awareness of the cultural norms governing appropriate weight leads to social control strategies that simultaneously sensitize an already obese child's reactivity to food cues and undermine specific eating controls.

The kind of conceptual framework implied by our perspective is certainly not a novel one in either social or developmental psychology. A wide variety of obvious and important cultural maladaptations has been tracked to the process by which the observed deviance of the individual on a particular dimension is followed by the application of strong external control strategies by socializers (e.g., parents), which serve the twofold role of undermining internal control over the behavioral domain and sensitizing (positively or negatively) stimuli within that domain for the "deviant." The data of Lepper (Lepper & Greene, 1975; see also Chapter 1 by Lepper & Gilovich on internal and external constraints on behavior) and Dweck (Dweck & Goetz, 1978) on achievement behavior, Hoffman (1970) and Aron-

freed's (1964) research on the acquisition of moral and social behavior, and general models detailing the consequences of various child-rearing strategems (e.g., Baumrind, 1971; Becker, 1964), all propose compatible perspectives on the socialization origins of one or another form of external control adjustment.

The failure of adult-oriented social psychologists and most developmental psychologists to conjoin their observations and theories concerning the ubiquitous construct of external control (or for any other relevant process, for that matter) has resulted in an undesirable gap in the conceptual and empirical base probing general socialization paradigms that might commonly lead to the phenomena associated with externality (see Chapter 2 by Karniol & Miller on the development of self-control). We would maintain that obese externality is one instance of a process in which strong socialization constraints undermine the self-control of the socialized. This proposal is intriguing not because such socialization constraint *causes* deviant or maladaptive behaviors, but because, despite the best intentions of socializing agents, it induces a style that paradoxically serves to *maintain* the deviant adjustment once it has occurred. While we are specifically interested in understanding the socialization of obesity-prone behaviors, we are also generally hopeful that such an understanding will contribute to a general perspective on the socialization of maladaptive response dispositions.

The subsequent chapter will be structured so that the proposal we offer can be considered within the context of a range of both theory and data concerning obesity. The reader will find that while we have not in any sense confirmed our proposal we at least will have presented it as a strong and plausible suggestion. The remaining portions of this chapter will include the following discussions.

1. A review of the primary perspectives and representative data base from studies of adult obesity in social, personality, and clinical-behavioral psychology. While this is

a departure from the central issue of this chapter (i.e., the socialization of obesity-prone behavior) it forms a central and necessary background for understanding developmental issues.

2. Some previous perspectives, suppositions, and data on childhood obesity and the development of obesity will be presented.

3. Our preliminary research with populations of "middle-aged" (7 to 12 year old) children will be detailed for the purpose of hypothesis generation.

4. Finally, we will offer a summary and prospective section in which we conjoin the implications of past perspectives on obesity with the inferences we draw from our own limited data base to expand the general perspective on the socialization of obesity-prone behavior as presented in this chapter.

Review of models to explain obesity-prone behavior in adults

Response dispositions to internal and external cues: Schachter's externality theory of obesity

The work of Schachter and his colleagues has both strongly influenced thinking about obesity and contributed a new methodology to the field. Not only has this research shifted psychological views of obesity strongly toward the consideration of perceptual and cognitive dispositions to stimuli, but it has also illustrated the power of laboratory experiments on psychological influences to uncover and verify factors that discriminate the obese from the nonobese.

Schachter's theory consists of two fairly independent hypotheses. The first is that the eating behavior of obese persons is much less influenced than that of normals by internal, physiological cues such as gastric motility and blood sugar level. The second is that the eating habits of obese persons are much more influenced than those of normals by salient external cues such as the sight of food, its taste quality, and the time of day. An impressive range of experimental support for each of these hypotheses is brought together in the book, *Obese Humans and Rats* (Schachter & Rodin, 1974). In sum-

mary, Schachter's evidence consistently suggests that obese eating is undercontrolled by internal cues and overcontrolled by potent external cues.

Schachter and his colleagues have worked to extend the basic theory in two ways. For one thing, they have attempted to demonstrate that the hypersensitivity to external cues in the obese is a general response disposition that applies to a range of non-food-related cues and behaviors. Schachter (1971) has advanced the broad hypothesis that "any stimulus, above a certain intensity level, is more likely to evoke an appropriate response from an obese than from a normal subject" (pp. 137–138). A range of experimental data supports this broader hypothesis. Obese subjects appear to show faster disjunctive reaction times, better short-term recall, and lower tachistoscopic recognition thresholds (Rodin, Herman, & Schachter, 1974), indicating a greater tendency for a salient stimulus to trigger a response in the obese. In addition, in studies involving time estimation (Pliner, 1973a) and distraction (Rodin, 1974b), obese subjects appear to be more responsive to highly salient external cues, but less responsive to cues of low salience, than are normal subjects. Finally, there have been demonstrations that the thinking of obese subjects is more strongly affected by external cues than the thinking of normal-weight subjects. As Pliner (1973a) has noted, "For the obese, it seems indeed to be the case that out of sight is truly out of mind" (p.238). Thus, even the obese person's cognitions appear to be strongly under the control of external cues.

Another way Schachter and his colleagues have extended the basic theory is by drawing exhaustive behavioral parallels between obese people and rats that have become obese as the result of hypothalamic lesions. Schachter and Rodin (1974) compare obese humans to VMH-lesioned rats and find them similarly emotional, finicky about taste, distractible, and otherwise different from normal humans and rats. While this comparative strategy has led to some interesting findings about obese people, Schachter's

(1971) speculation that the eating behavior of obese humans may be due to brain lesions of some kind is regarded by most medical researchers as a very unlikely explanation in the great majority of cases of obesity (Greenwood & Johnson, 1975; Silverstone, 1974). However, a proper evaluation of the tenability of this idea would depend on a more detailed analysis of hypothalamic function in humans than is presently available.

Failures and successs in replicating differential response dispositions

Careful investigation by other researchers has not always replicated the phenomena reported by Schachter and his colleagues. In particular, the hypothesis that internal physiological cues exert significantly less control over the eating of obese than normal-weight individuals appears to have been seriously vitiated. In an experiment that provided key evidence for the view held by Schachter and his colleagues, Pliner (1973b) tested the regulation of eating by obese and normal-weight subjects after liquid or solid preloads of 200 or 600 calories. Normals regulated their subsequent eating in accordance with the caloric preload on both the liquid and solid diets; while the obese regulated their eating on the liquid diet but not on the solid one. However, other research definitely casts doubt on these findings insofar as they suggest differences in caloric regulation. Wooley, Wooley, and Dunham (1972) found that neither obese nor normal subjects were able to tell high-calorie from low-calorie drinks and that long-term regulation to compensate for caloric variability tended to be slow and incomplete in both groups. Moreover, Wooley (1972) criticized the caloric-regulation experiments of Schachter and his colleagues on the basis that in all cases subjects had complete knowledge of what they were eating. Hence, subsequent regulation of intake may have been primarily cognitive—perhaps a feeling of satiety based on the belief that one has eaten enough. Wooley performed an experiment very similar to Pliner's, studying the effect of

200 and 600 calorie preloads on subsequent eating, but was very careful to dissociate the physiological effects of food intake from the psychological consequences of knowledge about intake. Not only did the number of calories consumed in the preload have no effect on the amount of food eaten at the test meal for either obese or nonobese subjects, but, in addition, cognitive cues had a significant effect on regulation for both groups. Both groups ate significantly less and reported feeling fuller when the preload was perceived to be high calorie. Since obese and normal-weight subjects did not differ on these measures, this experiment obviously casts doubt on the differential abilities of normal and obese subjects to detect internal cues, as postulated by Schachter and his colleagues. A similar conclusion has been reached in research on gastric motility (Stunkard & Fox, 1971). Gastric motility appears to have only a weak and inconstant effect on hunger, and deficiencies in its perception do not account for poor control of eating by the obese. In summary, it would appear that eating for both the obese and nonobese is very largely controlled by external cues as compared to internal ones; thus, Schachter's theory must stand or fall on the basis of its hypothesis of differential reactivity to external cues.

In contrast to the evidence relevant to the internal-cues hypothesis, independent replications of the external-cues hypothesis seem to have borne it out fairly well. A highly impressive demonstration of the externality theory was provided by McArthur and Burstein (1975). They showed that both the food-related and nonfood-related behavior of obese subjects was more influenced by external cues than was that of normal-weight subjects. In addition, they found a highly significant correlation between dependence on external cues in eating behavior and dependence on contextual cues in a nonfood-related, perceptual task. In this task, the rod-and-frame test, the subject makes judgments of verticality on the basis of conflicting internal (gravitational) and external (contextual) cues, and the type of cue that is more relied on is thought to reflect an enduring stylistic orientation to the environment (Witkin, Dyk, Faterson, Goodenough, & Karp, 1962). The demonstration of a relationship between this measure of response disposition and a measure of food-related behavior strongly supports Schachter's hypothesis of an enhanced general sensitivity to external cues in the obese.

A recent study (Elman, Schroeder, & Schwartz, 1977), however, has shown that it is difficult to apply the externality hypothesis to more complex stimuli and behaviors, such as are involved in social interactions. It was predicted from the externality hypothesis that overweight persons would be more reactive than normal-weight persons to salient social stimuli "such as persuasive messages or requests for help" (p.408). Experimental results did not support this prediction. Furthermore, the investigators argued that it is difficult to make clear predictions about social influence situations from the externality hypothesis, in that it "apparently contains a number of indeterminant parameters, including the specification of the degree of salience of a particular stimulus and the exact nature of direction of the expected response to a certain stimulus" (p. 413). While this study does not really controvert the contention that externality is a generalized trait, it does suggest that it may be premature to view the externality hypothesis as an explanation of a range of real-world behaviors in obese individuals, such as interpersonal style, rather than simply as an etiological explanation of overeating.

Methodological difficulties with the externality theory

It is difficult to generalize from the results of Schachter and his colleagues, with a limited range of subjects in a limited range of laboratory settings, to different subgroups of the obese population and to diverse settings in the natural environment. For example, Schachter has been criticized for attempting to explain all obesity on the basis of his studies of a highly selected population—namely, upper-middle and upper class, college-age students. Both medically oriented (Silverstone, 1974) and psychologically oriented (Milich, 1975) reviewers have noted that generalizing from such a select group to the whole spectrum of obesity is unwarranted. They point out that some medically oriented research has indicated that there may be important distinctions between obesity that develops in childhood and obesity that develops in adulthood (Knittle, 1971, 1972; Salans, 1974). There appear to be differences in adipose cellularity and differences in physiological and psychological reactions to short-term deprivation (Glucksman & Hirsch, 1969; Glucksman, Hirsch, McCully, Barron, & Knittle, 1968; Grinker, 1973; Grinker, Glucksman, Hirsch, & Viseltear, 1973; Grinker, Hirsch, & Levin, 1973). Surveys indicate that 70% of all obese adults are characterized by adult onset of overweight (Mullins, 1958; Silverstone, 1974). Hence, it would appear that Schachter and his associates have mainly been studying juvenile-onset obesity, and their results may not generalize well to two-thirds of the population of obese adults.

Even if we limit externality theory to juvenile-onset obesity, it is not at all clear when the external style develops and what relationship it bears to the development of obesity. For example, externality may only emerge during the obese person's adolescence, as a result of being obese. Similarly it may not equally characterize infant-onset, childhood-onset, and adolescent-onset obesities. It would be interesting in this regard to know if the phenomena of externality differentiate obese from normal-weight children. Rather surprisingly, there has been almost no attempt to investigate this question (Stimbert & Coffey, 1972). It would seem essential to investigate which segment of the obese population the phenomena of externality actually characterize and to find out when they begin to characterize these individuals developmentally.

Unfortunately, there is also evidence to suggest that the externality theory may not generalize across socioeconomic subgroups of the obese population. In their experiments, Schachter and his colleagues have predominantly drawn samples from expensive, prestigious, private universities; therefore, the majority of their subjects were probably from the middle and upper classes. Since it appears that socioeconomic factors play a strong role in obesity, some reviewers (Milich, 1975; Silverstone, 1974) have expressed doubts that externality theory generalizes to obese individuals from lower socioeconomic status levels. (There is a provocative literature on the relationship between socioeconomic status and obesity. The interested reader is referred to Goldblatt, Moore, and Stunkard (1965); Stunkard, d'Aquili, Fox, and Filion (1972); and Garn, Clark, and Guire (1975).) Moreover, there appear to be considerable cultural variations in the degree of concern with being overweight, in the prevalence of dieting (Dwyer, Feldman, & Mayer, 1967), and in the proportion of body fat that is considered to be optimal and appealing (Goldblatt, Moore, & Stunkard, 1965).

Clearly the kinds of sociocultural physiological factors related to obesity that we have only briefly reviewed are potential confounders of experimental results. It is evident that obesity is a complex phenomenon and that any one theory that attempts to account for the behavior of all obese persons invites criticism. As Milich (1975) points out, researchers in this field must take care to "define explicitly" the segment of the obese population that they study.

Problems of ecological validity

It is not clear that the externality view does a good job of explaining how obese people became overweight or why they remain overweight. According to Schachter's data, obese people eat somewhat less often than normal-weight people, but they eat somewhat more at a sitting (Schachter & Rodin, 1974). Hence, somewhat paradoxically it would seem, a world full of salient food cues does not at all increase the frequency of eating by those who are postulated to be

hyperreactive to such cues. The critical aspect in explaining overeating appears to be differences in the mechanism whereby eating behavior is terminated. The only contribution that externality theory makes concerning this is that the obese should not be able to terminate eating until all the food is consumed or removed. However, neither obese rats nor humans appear to eat continuously, or more often, in the presence of food (Singh, 1973).

It may also be remarked that very few studies have been conducted to test the externality theory in the natural environment. Two such studies—one involving supermarket-shopping behavior (Nisbett & Kanouse, 1969) and another involving whether or not people attempt to eat with chopsticks at an oriental restaurant (Schachter, Friedman, & Handler, 1974)—are clever, but they are indirect and correlational. Neither measures the impact of external cues on amount eaten (which is, after all, what we are most interested in finding out), and it is difficult to know exactly which of many factors are responsible for the results. In brief, successes in verifying the theory have nonetheless carried researchers somewhat away from the initial concern of explaining why and under what conditions some people overeat.

An important limitation that is a consequence of failing to evaluate the theory in the natural environment is that variables that are operative there, but not in the relevant laboratory experiments, may invalidate generalizations from experimental results. It is hard to disagree with Milich (1975) when he makes the following claim:

Obesity and eating behavior are complex phenomena and they cannot be isolated from the environment in which they exist without distorting one's understanding of them. It may well be that naturalistic factors limit the importance of those factors which have been explored in the laboratory by Schachter and others. (p.587)

While this criticism might appear a bit dog-eared, it has in fact been demonstrated (apparently unknown to Milich) in a series of ingenious experiments by Singh (1973) that if we manipulate just one additional variable—one which is about as ubiquitous in the natural environment as any could be— we can mediate whether obese individuals show "external" characteristics or not. In particular, we must take account of preexisting response tendencies.

The role of stimulus-compatible and stimulus-incompatible response habits

Singh (1973) proposed that obese people exhibit a deficit in response inhibition—that is, they fail to suppress potent response tendencies when faced with altered situational demands. He hypothesized that "external" behavior would not be evident in obese individuals when external cues were incompatible with preexisting response tendencies. In an experiment to test this view, he found that obese subjects, unlike normal-weight subjects, ate significantly less when the response required was incompatible with experimentally induced response tendencies. Furthermore, Singh found that the obese showed greater negative transfer of training on a non-food-related task and greater rigidity in breaking out of a cognitive set than normal-weight subjects. In each experiment, habit strength was based on very few trials. This indicates that the behavior of the obese is more strongly affected by the nature of existing response tendencies than that of normal-weight individuals.

On the basis of the deficit-in-response-inhibition theory, overeating in obese individuals can be explained as a deficit in terminating the response of eating. Since the initiation of eating is not affected, the obese would be expected to maintain a meal frequency just like that of normal-weight individuals. Nonetheless, since obese individuals would continue the eating response longer in the face of cues for satiation (which are probably largely cognitive) than would normal-weight subjects, they should have larger meals. These predictions fit what is known about the naturalistic eating habits of the obese; they consume more food at a meal but no more meals than normal-weight persons.

In addition, Singh's theory makes some very interesting predictions about some of the experiments of Schachter and his colleagues. For example, Nisbett (1968) found that obese subjects eat only whatever is present and do not go to the refrigerator to obtain more food. According to Singh's theory, this result was to be expected, since in the laboratory situation subjects have no existing response tendency to go to the refrigerator. However, if the experiment were to be repeated in the obese person's home, the results would be expected to be very different. Similarly, Singh (1973) has found that cashews wrapped in foil differently decrease eating in the obese, fitting Schachter's hypothesis about the effect of cue salience; however, a similar wrapping on chocolates has no effects on eating in the obese. Singh explains this peculiarity by noting that everyone is used to unwrapping chocolates, whereas no one is used to unwrapping a cashew before eating it. Such existing response tendencies have a differentially greater effect on the behavior of the obese.

These experiments suggest that the externality hypothesis generally applies only in rather well-controlled and artificial situations. In any generalization to real-world settings, the role of response tendencies is clearly of great importance.

Biological "set point" and the concept of "normal" obesity

In a theoretical review, Nisbett (1972) has attempted to integrate a wide range of psychological and physiological data concerning hunger, obesity, and surgically induced hypothalamic hyperphagia. He comes to the conclusion that the major indices that have been shown to differentiate obese from normal-weight humans exactly parallel the indices affected by semistarvation or "hunger." The obese behave as though they were actually in a state of chronic energy deficit and were thus genuinely and inflexibly hungry. The greater quantity and rapidity of their eating, their high taste responsiveness, and their insensitivity to short-term changes in deprivation are hypothesized to be results of their chronically maintaining their weight at a level below its biological "set point." In Nisbett's view, this biological set point is a reflection of the number of fat cells in the body and the tendency of hypothalamic centers to defend the fat content of the body's adipose tissue. Since the hypothalamic centers may be defending different set points in different individuals, obesity may represent a "normal" or optimal body composition for some individuals. When social constraints prevent such a person from reaching his or her biological set point, a situation that presumably occurs mainly in the obese, the person is physiologically hungry—as reflected by an inflexibly high, free fatty acid level—and hence shows the behavioral characterisitcs that Schachter and others point out as characterizing the obese.

The theoretical dissociation between set point and obesity leads to rather surprising predictions concerning the eating habits of extremely overweight and extremely underweight subjects. Extremely overweight subjects should show a "normal" pattern of eating, since presumably they have cast off social pressures and achieved their set points. On the other hand, extremely underweight subjects should show an "obese" pattern of eating, since presumably they are below their set points. What little evidence there is supports these predictions (Nisbett, 1972; Rodin, 1975). In addition, this aspect of the set point hypothesis makes sense of the other puzzling fact that replications of Schachter's eating experiments have tended to be much more convincing with slightly overweight subjects (McArthur & Burstein, 1975) than with grossly overweight ones (Price & Grinker, 1973).

The notion of a hypothalamically defended set point is very appealing theoretically, especially since it accounts for why most people find it relatively easy not to become obese. The regulation of caloric intake, at least over the long run, has to be unerringly precise. A daily excess of a handful of peanuts would be enough to add 10 pounds of fat tissue per year (Hervey, 1969). Hypothalamic centers appear to be responsible for the fact that most people unthinkingly regulate their weight within a very fine tolerance.

Unfortunately, "set point" as a variable is difficult to measure even indirectly. Since the relevant factor in behavioral studies is the individual's distance from set point, Nisbett (1972) simply used degree of overweight or underweight as the index of nearness to or distance from set point. However, this procedure has been criticized by Rodin (1975), since there does not appear to be any a priori reason to think that 40% overweight subjects are necessarily closer to their set points than 20% overweight subjects, assuming that adipose tissue mass is continuously and normally distributed in the population. Some 40% overweight subjects may even be over their set points. Thus degree of overweight seems to be a very problematic index of deviations from set point.

Rodin proposed that set point could be inferred from long-term weight stability. Subjects were defined as below set point if their weights had varied more than 7% in the last two years and they reported dietary restrictions. Subjects whose weights had varied not more than 3% and who did not restrict their eating were defined as close to set point. However, Rodin found no important effects for the variable so defined.

Probably the most defensible way of evaluating the set point theory is to look for changes in "obese" psychological variables when weight is lost. Nisbett (1973), for example, has shown that rats that lose weight due to exercise become more taste responsive. In comparing the predominantly psychogenic view of obesity proposed by Schachter with Nisbett's more biogenic view, it would be interesting to look at noneating externality in obese people during a successful weight-reducing diet. If the more psychogenic view is correct, then successful dieting should shift the degree of external behavior little or not at all; if the more biogenic view holds, the successful dieting will exaggerate the difference between the weight and the set point, increasing physiological hunger and thus exaggerating externality.

Two types of eater: The restrained and the unrestrained

Herman has proposed a clever corollary to Nisbett's theory, and this corollary effectively brings "obese" behavioral characteristics back into the psychogenic sphere. Herman and Polivy (1975) point out that an implication of Nisbett's theory is that "normal weight persons who are constantly dieting and concerned with not gaining weight, and who presumably would gain substantial weight if they were to 'let themselves go,' ought to resemble the obese behaviorally" (p. 667). In a series of experiments (Herman & Mack, 1975; Herman & Polivy, 1975; Hibscher & Herman, 1977), Herman and his colleagues have demonstrated that normal-weight individuals who are self-rated as chronic dieters on a "restraint" scale show the behaviors previously thought to characterize the obese. Indeed, the study by Hibscher and Herman (1977) statistically dissociated dieting from degree of overweight and showed that dieting, and not overweight, was the key factor. It also supported Nisbett's suggestion that extremely obese people, who presumably have given up the attempt to diet, would show a "normal" or nonobese pattern of behavior. In summary, the restrained eater, whether overweight or not, appears to be relatively insensitive to short-term deprivation manipulations, more emotionally reactive, and more distractible than the unrestrained eater. In addition, the restrained eater shows higher free fatty acid levels in the blood, indicative of physiological stress due to deprivation. From this evidence it would appear that restraint is "an important behavioral mechanism affecting the expression of physiologically based hunger" (Herman & Mack, 1975, p. 647).

In Herman's view, the problem facing the obese person is one of maintaining or breaking restraint. In fact, high-restraint subjects respond to forced preloading in a very peculiar manner. In a study by Herman and Mack (1975), low-restraint subjects ate in inverse proportion to preload size, as indeed one would expect due to caloric compensation. However, the food intake of high-restraint subjects varied directly with preload size, indicating that they responded to the forced preloading as if it warranted abandoning all caloric restraints. That it is the psychological aspects of the preloading which mediate this behavior was demonstrated by Polivy (1976), who looked at the relationship between perception of calories and regulation of intake. Restrained eaters repond to their perception of the caloric values of food rather than the actual caloric value. They overeat only after they think they have consumed a high-calorie preload. Thus eating behavior in the restrained subject appears to be an all or nothing affair, depending on the perceived extent to which caloric restraint has been broken.

Herman's theory poses a parsimonious explanation of emotion-induced eating (Herman & Polivy, 1975). Polivy and Herman (1976) found that clinically depressed patients who were restrained eaters tended to gain weight during their depression, whereas patients who were unrestrained eaters tended to lose weight. For the unrestrained eater self-control is not an important determination of eating behavior, and his or her emotional experience tends to inhibit appetite physiologically. However, strong emotions may disrupt the chronic self-control of the restrained eater, releasing deprivation-motivated eating behavior.

Also, it is worth noting that Herman's theory is the only one that explicitly confines itself to juvenile-onset obesity (Herman, 1975). In addition, it is clearly consistent with the data concerning sociocultural influences on obesity. With regard to these influences, it is evident that if restraint, or degree of chronic dieting, is the factor that keeps actual weight below set point, it would be predicted that, as restraint varied across social groups, so would the incidence and degree of overweight.

Recently, it has been found that social cues moderate the consumption patterns of restrained eaters. Herman, Polivy, and Silver (1979) found that restrained females failed to compensate for a prior preload when unobserved, but compensated strongly when observed. A study by Polivy, Herman, Younger, & Erskine, (1979) indicated that the presence of an observer generally suppresses food intake for restrained females. Hence it would appear that solitude is an essential mediator of counterregulatory eating in restrained females.

Social cues may not have the same effects for males as for females. A study of the effect of social context on eating behaviors (Conger, Conger, Costanzo, Wright, & Matter, 1980) suggested that obese females may eat less than normal weight females when another person is present, but more when no one is present. Such an effect was not found to discriminate obese and normal-weight males. Taken together, the results of this study and those of restrained females suggests two things: (1) As we learn more about obesity, we may require somewhat different models for males and females, with the restraint orientation perhaps being more typical of females than males; and (2) for obesity-prone females the presence of others seems to become a discriminative stimulus for not eating, a phenomenon which suggests relatively low intrinsic self-control and relatively high dependence on agents of external control, as embodied both in social cues and sensory cues (e.g., the presence of a nutshell).

Behavioral and naturalistic perspectives

What the theories of obesity reviewed above have in common is the conception of the obese person as overcontrolled by potent external cues. If there has been a consistent bias in the behavioristic approach to psychology, it has been to regard the individual as overcontrolled by external cues. One of the most interesting observations that has been made about the externality hypothesis is Stunkard's (1973) suggestion that it may help explain why behavior modification strategies have tended to be more successful in reducing weight than routine medical management and traditional psychotherapy. Behavior modification focuses attention on the environmental influences to which the obese person is so reactive, whereas other therapies tend to disregard them as relatively peripheral.

A valuable upshot of the application of behavior modification techniques to the control of obesity has been an interest in finding out more about the eating habits of the obese in natural settings and how these differ from those of normal-weight individuals. Some studies have looked in detail at the motor responses involved in eating and how they distinguish obese from nonobese eaters. It has been found that adult, nonobese eaters show a lower frequency of bites, smaller mouthfuls, and more extraneous responses such as hesitation and putting down utensils than do obese eaters (Gaul, Craighead, & Mahoney, 1975). Similarly, nonobese children eat slower (fewer bites and more chews per bite), leave more food on their plates, hesitate between bites, toy with food, put utensils or food down between bites, and drink more often between bites (instead of during them) than obese children (Marston, London, & Cooper, 1976). Hence obese children are already showing the eating pattern of obese adults. Marston, London, and Cooper speculate that "the parent who chastizes [the] child for toying with his food or urges him to clean his plate would appear to be contributing toward the development of an eating pattern associated with obesity" (1976, p. 3). While the causality is not clear from these studies, there does not seem to be any reason to assume that obese children would be more deprived physiologically than nonobese children. It would be interesting to look at parental feeding practices and attitudes toward children's eating habits to see if they discriminate obese from normal-weight children.

Self-report surveys tend to support the hypothesis that emotional states evoke eating in the obese. For example, Leon and Chamberlain (1973a, 1973b) surveyed overweight persons successful or unsuccessful in maintaining weight loss and control subjects. They found that regainers reported eating in response to a variety of states of emotional arousal; maintainers reported that eating was more specific to loneliness and boredom; while controls reported that food consumption was primarily in response to hunger. Thus, decreasing self-control of eating would appear to be associated with greater vulnerability to emotional states as discriminative stimuli for food intake.

Developmental implications

We have reviewed a range of response dispositions that appear to distinguish obese from normal-weight adults. A matter of great potential interest and importance is how such response dispositions develop and what relationships they bear developmentally to the onset and maintenance of the obese state. Yet there is a wide gap between the relatively profuse experimental and theoretical work on obese adults and the relatively scanty comparable work on obese children. This disparity is particularly surprising, since all of the views on obese adults reviewed here contain implicit, strong etiological assumptions. These views are interesting because they suggest causes of overeating in the obese person's life span, not just during the span of an experiment. Nonetheless, there has been little attempt to clarify developmental implications of the views and test these implications, either cross-sectionally or longitudinally. The rare experimental study that has involved children, such as that conducted by Rodin and Slochower (1976), has used them as equivalent to adult subjects and sought little or no developmental implication. In summary, then, the adult perspectives on obesity presume a history; but that history has not been investigated.

Some important aspects of childhood obesity

Although psychologically oriented researchers have given little attention to the condition of childhood obesity, it has been the subject of much medically oriented research, some of which is of relevance here. In looking at obese children to illuminate some aspects of obesity across the age spectrum, we imply that obesity in childhood bears a strong relationship to obesity at adolescence and, in turn, to obesity in adulthood. A number of studies have indicated that those who are obese in infancy, childhood, or adolescence tend to remain obese into adulthood (Heald & Hollander, 1965; Knittle, 1972; Mullins, 1958; Rimm & Rim, 1976; Rose & Mayer, 1968). In an adult follow-up study of earlier public health examinations (Abraham, Collins, & Nordsieck, 1971; Abraham & Nordsieck, 1970), it was found that 86% of overweight boys and 80% of overweight girls became overweight adults, as compared to 42% of average-weight boys and 18% of average-weight girls. An extremely poor prognosis for juvenile-onset obesity was given by Stunkard and Burt (1967), who estimated that the more than 4 to 1 odds against an obese child's becoming a normal-weight adult rise to 28 to 1 if weight has not been reduced by the end of adolescence. It should be remembered, however, that among obese adults only about 30% are characterized by juvenile-onset obesity (Mullins, 1958).

Obesity appears to be strongly familial (Garn & Clark, 1976). Mayer (1975) found that for adolescents graduating from high school, 7% of those with two normal-weight parents, 40% with one obese parent, and 80% with two obese parents were themselves obese. Mayer (1975) and Withers (1964) have produced data that indicate that the strong correlation between the weight of children and the weight of their biological parents disappears between children and their adoptive parents. However, Garn, Cole, and Bailey (1976) have recently produced data that do show that the familial relationship holds for adopted as well as biological children. From such data, Garn (1976) has inferred that the origins of obesity may be in patterns of behavior learned and maintained in the family setting early in life.

Finally, a number of studies have tried to estimate caloric intake and energy expenditure in obese children and adolescents. Coates and Thoresen (1978) have reviewed these studies and seriously questioned the validity of some of them. Nonetheless, it would appear to be important to consider psychological factors that lead to decreased activity in obese children, since low activity levels may contribute to the development of obesity (Bullen, Reed, & Mayer, 1964; Durnin, Lonergan, Good, & Ewan, 1974).

The limitations of developmental views based primarily on underlying physiological causation

Perhaps the most coherent developmental theory of juvenile-onset obesity available is that based on the hypothesis that overnutrition up to the age of about 20 years has profound and lasting consequences on the number of fat cells laid down in the body (Brook, 1974; Salans, 1974; Winick, 1975), leading to relatively intractible obesity. In light of this, it is not surprising to see the medical and nutritional literature concentrating on the impact of infantile overfeeding (Dwyer & Mayer, 1973). But there are important limitations inherent in the attempt to locate the causes of "external" behavioral dispositions in an underlying biological state, as Nisbett (1972) has done. The extent to which this type of view has permeated psychological thinking on obesity may be gauged from Herman's (1975) suggestion, following Grinker (1973) and Court and Dunlop (1975), that losing weight may simply be biologically inappropriate for juvenile-onset obese adults and that the physiological and psychological liabilities of a body weight below set point may not be worth it.

Although it is not appropriate to try to review all of the evidence bearing on the hypercellularity theory, it does seem important to focus on a few relevant points. First,

much of the evidence for this theory comes from studies of laboratory animals. Even among laboratory animals, there is evidence that infantile overnutrition does not necessarily lead to a tendency to overeat later in life. For example, Bruch and Voss (Bruch, 1973) found that baboons who had been fat as infants did not outgain their controls when exposed to an unlimited food supply at 2 ½ years of age. Also, it should be kept in mind that the feeding habits and weights of even laboratory animals are quite susceptible to psychosocial influences. For example, a normal mouse sharing a cage with a hypothalamically lesioned obese mouse will gain more weight than its littermates not exposed to a fat model (Liebelt, 1963). In human beings, compared to such laboratory animals, it is reasonable to expect more variance due to psychological influences and less due to physiological determinism.

Second, in studies that attempt to relate underlying physiological conditions to behavioral tendencies in humans, the hypothesized physiological causes are hopelessly confounded with the range of experience that may contribute to possible psychological causes. The point here is not that physiology is unimportant, but that it is unreasonable to ignore psychological influences in the development of the organism, particularly when one is acknowledging the importance of behavioral tendencies in the maintenance of the obese state. Juvenile-onset obese individuals differ from their adult-obese counterparts not only in the structure of their fat tissue, but also in their developmental history as it encompasses a wide gamut of psychosocial influences on eating and physical appearance.

Although the above argument is a digression from our major concerns here, it is necessitated by the remarkable propensity of the social psychologists who have studied response dispositions in the obese to embed them in theories of physiological causation—for example, Schachter's (1971) VMH lesion proposal and Nisbett's (1972) "set point" mechanism. These theories sandwich psychological mediators between an inferred physiological cause and an observed physiological result (obesity). Unfortunately, this type of theorizing tends to define the key issues in obesity research as lying outside the expertise of psychologists. It is possible that some breakthrough in physiological research would support such inferences; meanwhile, however, Schachter's lesion proposal has been criticized by medical researchers as improbable (Greenwood & Johnson, 1975; Silverstone, 1974), and Nisbett's "set point" proposal appears to be inaccurate in its physiological assumptions (Faust, Johnson, Stern, & Hirsch, 1978).

Perhaps a more productive direction to take, and one which falls clearly in the bailiwick of psychologists, is the exploration of the developmental psychology that may underlie the response dispositions found in young adults. Generally speaking, however, social psychologists have not attempted to link their findings in adult subjects with compatible developmental frameworks. Perhaps it is symptomatic of this that research in the psychology of obesity has become somewhat sidetracked in physiological speculations rather than pursuing psychological antecedents in the development of response dispositions.

Questions of developmental priority

If we take the developmental psychology of obese response dispositions seriously, we immediately encounter important issues of developmental priority. For example, Rodin and Slochower (1976) neatly describe three tenable hypotheses linking food-related externality with general external responsiveness in obese samples: (1) Obesity itself may induce an external orientation to the environment; (2) obesity and generalized externality may be correlated but both caused by a third heretofore unknown underlying mechanism; and (3) externality in general style may lead to overeating which, in turn, leads to obesity. This set of hypotheses highlights how difficult it is to assess the nature of the relationship of externality, and other response dispositions as well, to obesity without first disentangling the related developmental issues.

The response disposition theories that we have reviewed pertain much more clearly to juvenile-onset obesity than to adult-onset obesity; and much juvenile-onset obesity appears to date from early childhood. Hence, looking at response dispositions in obese young adults, as Schachter and others have done, is essentially looking at a developmentally late state of affairs, when questions of causal priority and developmental significance are likely to be unresolvable. What the researcher observes in young adults may be the product of any of a range of possible developmental sequences with very different implications. It would appear that, until we have some data to help resolve the developmental issues, the significance of response dispositions to the state of obesity will remain unclear. More generally, we might comment that phrasing questions about the psychology of obesity in developmental terms is not just a detour into past history, but a potent and perhaps essential way of understanding what is seen in the "developed" organism.

The time span of development and the role of socialization

On the basis of observations of obese patients in psychoanalytic treatment, Bruch (1973) has presented a model of child development that purports to account for the psychogenesis of juvenile-onset obesity. This model places great emphasis on the infant-mother interaction in early feeding experiences and focuses on whether the mother's responses to cues from the infant indicating hunger or satiety are appropriate or inappropriate. Bruch hypothesizes that, when the mother's responses to the infant's expressions of biological need are inappropriate, the infant does not learn to recognize internal cues of hunger or satiation, or to discriminate need for food from other feelings arising internally. Bruch cites evidence from Schachter and others (reviewed earlier) that suggests that the obese are hyposensitive to internal cues. She also attempts to integrate her model with some developmental data on mother-infant interaction (e.g., Ainsworth & Bell, 1969). Perhaps the central component of her model is the view that "seemingly innate functions, especially hunger, require early learning experiences in order to become organized into distinct and useful behavior patterns" (Bruch, 1973, p. 54).

The attempt at a developmental perspective, which underlies Bruch's model, is notable; but the model itself is rather weak for several reasons. One is that it emphasizes as an end point the idea of a hyposensitivity to internal cues that has been seriously vitiated by more recent research, as we have already seen. Normal-weight individuals appear to be no more aware of internally mediated hunger cues than are the obese (Wooley, 1972). Another problem is that it makes little or no contact with data that would indicate any differential relationship of parenting patterns to the development of obesity as opposed to other disorders. In fact, in discussing family influences Bruch makes little distinction between the etiologies of developmental obesity and schizophrenia. A good model of the development of obesity has to tell us something important about specific differences between circumstances in which obesity arises and ones in which it does not. Finally, Bruch's model focuses mainly on very early parent-child interactions as a "pacesetter" for later developments, but does not really tell us much about what actually happens later and what its significance might be. In this sense, the model is somewhat nondevelopmental, since it postulates that parents simply continue to prevent the obese child from ever learning to perceive internal sensations accurately and adpatively—a self-regulatory function that normal children supposedly learn as infants. Bruch's case studies suggest that parents must be very pathogenic to manage this, suppressing not only appetitive cues in their children but general individuality as well.

We concur with Bruch's claim that the child must learn self-regulation of eating and that this learning is crucially affected and mediated by the responses of parents. In other behavioral areas, however, such as moral behavior (Hoffman, 1970), the child's development of self-control is a gradual achievement that extends throughout childhood and over which parents exert an extended and evolving influence. If the development of self-control of eating is viewed in this way, then it is clear that we know very little about the process and about how parents function as socializers of the self-regulation of eating. Yet, parents are more clearly the prime socializers of food intake than of most other areas of behavior, since there is less involvement and control by peers and other adults than in many other domains. Also, if the response dispositions found in obese young adults are in fact strongly associated with the effectiveness of self-control of eating, then they may reflect important differences in parental socialization practices.

Some psychological data on obesity in children

Although we have stressed the potential importance of exploring the developmental implications of obese response dispositions, there is a paucity of direct psychological evidence comparing obese and normal-weight children that would serve as a basis for such implications. The following studies were designed to provide such data, which could be drawn on in constructing plausible developmental models. One goal was to determine whether some of the response dispositions that seem to characterize obese young adults could differentiate obese from normal-weight children. Information of this sort is essential in order to suggest a developmental course for such dispositions. Another goal was to collect some pilot data eliciting comprehensive parental views of obese and normal-weight children. Such information was expected to offer clues about parenting parameters that may have an important effect on the development of obesity-prone behavioral and attitudinal adjustments, as well as to provide nonexperimental, observational data about possible differences along theory-relevant dimensions between obese and normal-weight children.

The presence and pervasiveness of externality as a discriminator of weight status in children

A multifaceted experiment recently conducted by us (Costanzo & Woody, 1979) focused on the main tenets of the externality view of obesity—that external cues exert a greater influence on obese than on normal-weight individuals' eating, and that this difference is a manifestation of a generalized sensitivity to external cues in obese individuals. A replication of the major results of a study conducted by McArthur and Burstein (1975) with university students was attempted in our experiment with children ages 7 to 13. The importance of such a replication with children is in assessing the developmental significance of the externality phenomenon—whether it is simply an epiphenomenon in adults or an enduring trait of possible significance in the development of obesity. The main predictions in this experiment were those verified in the McArthur-Burstein experiment: (1) The tendency to consume more nuts without shells than with shells would be greater for obese than for normal-weight children; (2) obese children would be more influenced than normal-weight children by external visual cues from a tilted luminous frame when setting a tilted luminous rod in the dark to gravitational vertical; and (3) greater inhibition of eating due to the presence of the shells would be related to greater deviation from gravitational vertical in setting the rod due to the presence of the frame. McArthur and Burstein interpreted the first prediction as testing the hypothesis that external cues have a greater influence on the eating of the obese than normal-weight individuals, the second prediction as testing the hypothesis that the obese show greater field dependence than the nonobese, and the third prediction as testing the hypothesis that the greater responsiveness of the obese to external food cues is a manifestation of a generalized sensitivity to external cues.

In addition, our study with children used boring and interesting films as filler tasks to enable an assessment of the effects of boredom on both incidental eating and time estimation. Although boredom is often cited by obese individuals as a cause of overeating (Leon & Chamberlain, 1973a, 1973b; Winick, 1975), there has been little attempt to verify this claim. Furthermore, time estimation has been investigated under the rubric of externality theory (Pliner, 1973c; Rodin, 1974b)—the hypothesis being that the obese individual's sense of time will be more affected by external cues than the normal-weight person's. On this basis, it would be expected that the difference in time estimation between boring and interesting films would be greater for obese than for normal-weight subjects.

The results of this experiment concerning externality theory strongly support its hypotheses about food-related behavior, but fail to support the hypothesis that externality is a generalized trait. Figure 10.1 presents a graphic comparison of the eating-behavior dimensions of the McArthur-Burstein experiment with university students and the attempted replication with children. It is evident that the overall magnitude and pattern of the original results are closely matched in the replication. In both cases, the eating of obese subjects is more effected by external cues than is the eating of normal-weight subjects. In the replication with children, this pattern of results generalized across the boring and interesting conditions, with no main effect for this variable.

However, the respective results for the field-dependence dimension of the experiments are far less congruent. In the McArthur-Burstein experiment, there was a strong relationship between degree of overweight and field dependence for obese females ($r = .60$) and normal females ($r = .41$), but no such relationship for male subjects. By contrast, in our replication with children, there was a strong relationship between

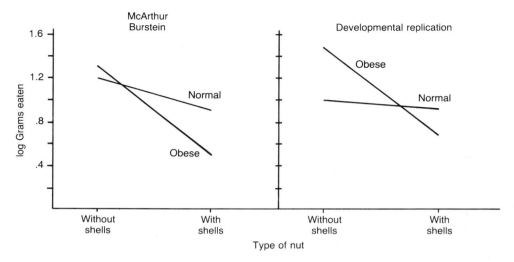

Note. From "Externality as a function of obesity in children: Pervasive style or eating-specific attribute?" by P. R. Costanzo and E. Z. Woody, *Journal of Personality and Social Psychology,* 1979, *37,* 2286–96. Copyright © American Psychological Association. Reprinted by permission.

Figure 10.1

weight and field dependence for obese females ($r = .45$) and obese males ($r = .57$), but no such relationship for normal-weight subjects. Furthermore, the strong relationship between field-dependent eating and field-dependent perception ($r = -.58$; that is, less consumption of nuts with shells was associated with greater field dependence) found in the original experiment was totally lacking in the replication ($r = .08$). These contrary results in the attempted replication cast serious doubts on the hypothesis advanced by Schachter that externality is a long-standing, generalized trait of which overeating is just one manifestation.

Two additional aspects of our experiment with children definitely support the above findings that externality in obese children is a potent response disposition, but one restricted to food-related cues. First, the results of the time-estimation phase of the experiment were also clearly incompatible with the generalized trait formulation. In a recent review (Leon & Roth, 1977) of externality theory and the evidence supporting it, it has been claimed that the studies on time estimation constitute the "greatest sup-

port for the external control theory" (p. 129) among non-food-related behaviors. While these studies are somewhat contradictory methodologically, they do consistently report that the time estimation of the obese is more manipulable by external cues than is the time estimation of normals. However, in the present study, the time estimation of obese children was somewhat *less* affected by the boring-interesting distinction than was the time estimation of normal children. This evidence, along with the field-dependence evidence, suggests that externality in response to food cues precedes other manifestations of externality in the obese. This developmental sequence is clearly incompatible with the hypothesis of food-related externality as merely one manifestation of a long-standing personality trait.

Second, in contrast to the obese children's relatively low responsiveness to interest cues in the time-estimated task, these children exhibited a remarkable and unanticipated responsiveness to food cues in their interest ratings of the boring film. They rated it as significantly more interesting when it was viewed in the presence of nuts without shells than when it was viewed in the presence of nuts with shells. There was no such difference for normal subjects. While it may be contended that this difference in ratings for the obese children might be due to a difference in nut consumption between the groups, the correlations between nut consumption and film ratings do not support this view (for shells-off group, $r = .30$; for shells-on group, $r = .61$; and for the two groups combined, $r = .08$). This result suggests that rather small variations in incidental food cues may have a considerable effect on how the obese child experiences an unrelated, fairly neutral stimulus. While externality in obese children may be confined mainly to food cues, these cues may affect the obese child's experience and behavior in ways not closely related to eating.

To summarize, all of the evidence from this study indicates that obese children by about 10 years of age already show externality in response to salient food cues, but this response style has not yet generalized to nonfood cues. It may be that as obese children approach young adulthood their externally induced eating style is a countervailing force that interferes with socially mediated attempts to control their eating. Obese persons may then perceive themselves as unable to resist eating in the face of potent food cues and unable to ignore potent and negative social cues. This real and apparent responsiveness to external cues may generalize cognitively, leading to a more generally "external" view of the world.

Although this experiment was not designed to test the deficit-in-response-inhibition theory (Singh, 1973) or the set point theory (Nisbett, 1972), it is interesting to consider how the eating results bear on them. It may be remembered that these views provide alternative explanations for some of Schachter's results, but also make somewhat different predictions about the behavior of the obese. There are aspects of the procedure and the sample that make the results incompatible with either view. From the viewpoint of the deficit-in-response-inhibition hypothesis, it would have been ex-

pected that the substitution of peanuts in shells in the replication for almonds in shells that were used in the low-salience condition in the original experiment would seriously decrease its replicability. This is because naive consideration suggests that shelling peanuts is a much more common response than shelling almonds. Thus, the generality of the results with the two kinds of nuts does not sit well with the hypothesis of deficit-in-response inhibition.

It is also implausible to explain the experimental results with children as a manifestation of differences in "physiological hunger," as we would from the viewpoint of the set point hypothesis. First, ancillary information from parent interviews indicates that obese children of this age group are not yet engaged in physiologically meaningful dieting. Second, although it could be argued that parents, having chronically overfed the child at some earlier stage, are now the agents of restraint of caloric intake, children who become obese are almost invariably still obese when they reach adolescence (Heald & Hollander, 1965; Mullins, 1958), and there is no evidence suggesting a regression toward normal weight, at least up until puberty. Hence, although parentally mediated restraint may have psychological impact, it does not have the physiological impact necessary to support the construct of "physiological hunger."

Parental views of obese and normal-weight children

A second, preliminary study we have done (Costanzo & Woody, 1980) involved extensive interviews with parents of obese and nonobese children. Parents were asked to reflect on their own experiences with their children and give their perception of their children's behavior. The structured interview inquired about the children's eating habits and behaviors, their dispositions and the effects of various moods on eating, their social inclinations and behavior, and their food preferences and activity level. Also, some relevant parent behaviors were surveyed. The interview took about one hour to administer and encompassed both 6-point rating scales and free-response items. The principal aim in this pilot study with 40 parents was to see how well parents' descriptions along theory-relevant dimensions would discriminate obese from normal-weight children.

While it is not possible to present all of the results of this study here, Table 10.1 gives a summary of the most interesting findings. The table presents selected questionnaire items grouped into nine post-hoc, conceptually based indexes, and the correlations of the items and indexes (formed by summing the items) with percent overweight for boys and girls. Although the table does not show mean differences, these will be alluded to occasionally to clarify the nature of the relationship represented by a significant correlation.

Although there is very little in the obesity literature that would lead to a theory-based expectation of sex differences in factors relating to obesity, these results strongly suggest that parents view the concomitants of obesity in boys and girls very differently. In most cases, a significant relationship of an item to overweight in one sex corresponds to little or no relationship in the other sex or, in some cases, to the opposite relationship. To summarize the pattern of correlations, greater overweight in boys is associated with less exercise, less emotional excitability, less peer involvement, greater compliance, and a peculiar pattern of tastes emphasizing a desire for meat. No part of this pattern appears to characterize obesity in girls very much. Greater overweight in girls is associated with greater influence of moods—both good and bad—on eating, more parental restraint of eating, more emotionality and displeasure with self, and greater peer abuse. No aspect of this pattern seems to characterize obesity in boys very much; furthermore, emotionality and eating in response to positive moods may actually be uncharacteristic of obese boys.

An important point is that these relationships with percent overweight are mostly markedly linear. That is, overweight is related to the questionnaire items quantitatively throughout the range of weight deviations, rather than simply qualitatively to the overweight versus normal-weight distinction. Hence, the correlations reflect differences between very obese and slightly obese individuals at least as much as differences between slightly obese and normal-weight individuals. In some cases—particularly with the mood-induced eating items for girls—it is possible that the correlation is largely due to extreme parental attributions about the most obese children. For example, the correlation of percent overweight in girls with the item "eats more when lonely" is .72. The mean for girls from −13 to 4% overweight is 3.1; for girls from 14 to 50% overweight, 3.5; and for girls from 54.5 to 124% overweight, 5.0. The small number of subjects for each sex makes it difficult to determine whether this trend represents a truly linear function or just extreme attributions about the most extreme subjects. However, while the sex-difference results require replication, they certainly suggest a range of differences that would be difficult to anticipate on the basis of the obesity literature.

In obese boys, the often posited imbalance between energy intake and expenditure seems to be one whose nature may be very difficult for parents to detect. The obese boy appears to get too little exercise; however, parents of obese boys are unlikely to recognize this. On exercise items, the obese boys are rated with a mean of about "average" on the scale, as are obese and normal-weight girls. It is the normal-weight boys who deviate from the other groups; they are rated as extremely active. Similarly, on emotionality items obese boys are rated about "average," while normal-weight boys are rated as highly emotional and more so than girls. Thus, parents may see normal-weight boys as somewhat hyperactive and excitable, but obese boys as "average" and easier to cope with. The characterization of the juvenile-onset obese as placid and inactive (Mayer, 1975) may be especially applicable to males. Although peer rejection may lead to low activity levels for obese boys, it

Table 10.1. Post-hoc Indexes, Selected Parental Questionnaire Items, and Correlations with Percent Overweight for Boys and Girls

Indexes and Their Items[a]	Correlations with Overweight	
	Boys ($n = 16$)	Girls ($n = 26$)
Eating Induced by Positive Affect	−.49*	.51*
Eats more when cheerful	−.42	.44*
Eats more when proud	−.48	.48*
Eats more when confident	−.46	.49*
Eating Induced by Negative Affect	−.03	.72*
Eats more when lonely	.23	.72*
Eats more when nervous	.44	.62*
Eats more when angry	−.04	.56*
Eats more when rejected	.14	.47*
Eats more when teased	.11	.67*
Eats more when frustrated	.00	.50*
Eats more when scolded	−.18	.42*
Eats more after failure	−.46	.52*
Parental Restraint of Food Intake	.39	.66*
Would eat more without parental restraint	.10	.51*
No food left out around house	.08	.55*
Only permitted to eat at meal times	.49*	.33
Not free to eat whenever hungry	.19	.53*
Amount of Exercise	−.72*	−.21
Active in sports	−.59*	−.29
Likes to play outdoors	−.78*	−.09
Emotionality	−.63*	.51*
High-strung or emotional	−.49*	.24
Distractible	−.47	.49*
Overreacts	−.54*	.32
Often excited	−.55*	.19
Sociability	−.65*	.01
A joiner	−.67*	−.07
Has lots of friends	−.49*	.10
Peer Rejection	−.27	.65*
Easily hurt when left out	−.38	.44*
Picked on by peers	.26	.72*
Compliance	.64*	.08
More obedient than other children	.53*	−.05
Infrequently stands up for rights	.58*	.11
Food Preferences	.82*	.07
Likes meat	.59*	.23
Dislikes vegetables	−.65*	−.18
Dislikes fish	−.68*	.23
Other Items of Interest		
Tends to be pleased with self	.29	−.43*
Eats when sees food	.03	.47*

[a]Overall index terms and correlations are underlined and are followed by the component items making up the index and their correlations.
*$p < .05$.

would appear likely that obese boys tend to be asocial because they do not care for the higher activity levels of their normal-weight, male peers. If obese boys are indeed less active than other boys, it appears important to teach parents that obese boys might naturally need less food than other boys to maintain a normal weight.

In addition, the obese boy's strongly pronounced pattern of food preferences may tend to mask his relatively high caloric intake. Obese boys in this sample strongly dislike vegetables and fish; whereas normal-weight boys and obese and normal-weight girls tend to like them fairly well. Hence, the obese boy may tend to decline or be disinterested in a fair amount of mealtime food; and his parent may see no harm in giving him extra portions of meat and perhaps other "nutritious" foods he likes. In addition, the obese boy appears to be highly compliant, and he may make few demands on the parents that are as strong as those associated with his food likes and dislikes.

It might also be conjectured that the obese boy's obedience and lack of self-interest have positive consequences for the parent, and hence obscure any connection between the boy's disposition and his weight problem. In particular, parents of obese boys may be unlikely to "blame" the child's weight problem on his behavior, because his behavior seems especially satisfactory. Behavioral intervention with obese boys may be difficult because their parents cannot readily attribute the weight problem to problematic behavior in the child. The obese boy may not appear to "deserve" a re-engineering of his behavior or seemingly harsh restrictions by the parent.

For obese girls, we find a very different pattern. Parents of obese girls appear to be more actively involved in attempting to restrain their child's food intake than are parents of obese boys. They see the obese girl as liable to eat in response to both negative and positive moods. Thus, it would appear that any affective arousal could induce undesirable eating; and it may be that parents feel it is necessary to intervene and restrain this eating pattern. The parent of the obese girl appears more inclined to see the child's obesity in terms of problematic eating behavior and more inclined to take an active role in restraining that behavior than the parent of the obese boy. It may be conjectured that parents of obese girls are likely to "blame" the child's weight problem on a range of eating habits that seem to reflect lack of self-control and therefore try to instill such self-control by applying parental restrictions on eating. By influencing the standards that the child internalizes, these parental concerns and behaviors may be the origins of the "restraint" orientation discussed earlier.

The high correlation between peer rejection and degree of overweight in girls suggests that obese girls may have a low rate of positive social reinforcement (probably due to their deviant status). A lack of social reinforcers may make the reinforcement available in eating especially salient to the obese girl. Parental restriction of eating may also enhance the reinforcement value of food. In summary, internalization of the value of restraint in eating may be accompanied by the emergence of food as an especially prominent reinforcer for the obese girl.

The results strongly suggest that "restraint" as a psychological mechanism may characterize juvenile-onset obese females far more than their male counterparts. In fact, we have found that obese women of college age tend to rate high on Herman's restraint scale, whereas obese males do not. Restraint appears to be an important aspect of the obese girl's socialization, much more so than for obese boys. In general, parental influence and training after the onset of obesity may make the female's eating behavior more complex than the male's. One example of such a sex difference is provided by the results of the following experiment.

Children's eating as a function of sex, weight, and the presence of another person

An experiment that we recently conducted (Woody & Costanzo, 1980), again with obese and normal-weight children ages 7 to 13, was designed to test the psychosomatic hypothesis of obesity (e.g., Kaplan & Kaplan, 1957)—that some individuals, especially the obese, eat in response to negative feelings such as anxiety and poor self-esteem. The results of this experiment are difficult to interpret unambiguously with regard to the psychosomatic hypothesis, largely because of the lack of a neutral affect condition. They are, however, very interestingly congruent with experimental results with adults, showing greater dependence on social cues in the eating behavior of female restrainers (Herman, Polivy, & Silver, 1979) and of obese females (Conger, Conger, Costanzo, Wright, & Matter, 1980).

In the experiment, each child was given a structured interview in which he or she was asked to recall and tell about social experiences and his or her feelings about them. The interview served as a mood manipulator—half the children were asked about experiences of rejection by peers and the other half about positive experiences with peers. At the end of the interview, the interviewer told the child, "Let me collect my thoughts and make a few notes. Meanwhile please think about what you've told me. I'll want to ask you a few more questions in a while." For one 5-minute period the interviewer was present, while for another 5-minute period he was absent. Incidental eating of peanuts was recorded for both these conditions.

An analysis of variance was performed on the log of the nut consumption of obese and normal-weight, male and female children. For all types of children, those who recounted positive experiences with peers consumed significantly (and considerably) more than those who recounted negative experiences. However, there were no significant interactions of the affect conditions with any of the other variables. The only other significant sources of variance were the main effect of the presence of another person and the three-way interaction of sex, weight, and the presence of another person. Table 10.2 gives antilogs of the mean logged grams of

Table 10.2. Antilogs of the Mean Log Grams Consumed as a Function of Sex, Weight Group, and the Presence of Another Person

	Males		Females	
	Normal	Obese	Normal	Obese
Together	9.62	10.94	6.95	5.85
Alone	16.63	13.24	8.22	17.46

peanuts eaten for the experimental groups, collapsed across affect conditions. It may be seen that, while all subjects tended to eat more when alone than when together with the interviewer, obese girls ate the least of any group when together with the interviewer, but the most of any group when alone. The difference between log grams consumed when together versus alone was very significant for obese females ($F = 10.26$; $df = 1,34$; $p < .01$), but insignificant for each of the other groups. These results suggest that, already in childhood, obese girls are beginning to show the enhanced dependence of eating on social cues that has been found to characterize young-adult obese women (in particular, in a successful replication by us of the results of this experiment with college undergraduates) and female restrainers.

Summary, conclusions, and prospective issues

This chapter began with a general perspective and a rather novel proposition. We had proposed that the behavioral characteristics associated with an obese physiological adaptation in adulthood arise from the manner in which middle-class parents and socializers attempt to "save" the child from the negative social consequences of being fat. More specifically, it was argued that phenomena, such as obese externality, result from parental attempts to constrain and control the overweight child's exposure to and intake of food. From the perspective of this speculative model, the child's external response set to food and eating-related cues generalizes to a variety of nonfood-related circumstances, because the socialized eating constraints of parents undermine the child's control over an important, socially meaningful domain. In short, generalized externality in the obese was proposed to be a consequence of their juvenile experiences with parental control over an important set of stimuli—food.

The review of the adult obesity literature reveals that the primary rationales offered for the etiology of obesity are *not* sociogenic in nature. Instead, the seminal works of Schachter, Nisbett, Rodin, and their colleagues provide accounts of obese-normal differences that are predicated on the effects that particular biogenic and personologic determinants have on *both* body composition *and* psychological response tendencies. As the reader can note through our review of the adult literature, little evidence exists to confirm that the *specific* biogenic determinants of obesity bear an empirical association to the behavioral characteristics of young adult obese individuals. Furthermore, the notion that general externality is an early appearing, predisposing antecedent of specific food-related externalities is an embattled proposition at best. What does seem reasonably well confirmed in the main-line research on obesity is that both general external responsiveness and food-related externality are simultaneous characteristics of the *adult* obese. The developmental priority of the personal style over the food-related propensities for obese individuals had existed primarily as an untested presumption. Moreover, the literature on the social psychology of obesity contains little in the way of "prioritization" studies, and neither children nor developmental progression have been frequently examined in obesity-determinant research.

Our own characterization of the sociogenic determinants of obese externality grew out of, rather than preceded, the preliminary research reported on earlier in this chapter. Our initial intent in performing the described research was to examine prevailing views on obesity as they applied to a childhood sample, so that some of the typical assumptions that the adult literature made concerning obesity determinants could be directly examined. What was found in these initial inquiries is in no way a solid confirmation of the social-control-based model for the development of obese behavioral characteristics. Instead, given our failure to obtain confirmation for the more traditional notions, and the intriguing pattern of results obtained, we find that the social-control-based model is plausible and worthy of direct examination. In addition, given the compelling parallels that can be drawn between the personal development of obese externality and other kinds of extrinsic control adjustments examined in the literature of social development, we feel it appropriate for social science researchers to bring the phenomenon of obese externality into the domain of control-based adaptations that have been invoked to characterize the development of a wide range of social and achievement behaviors.

An alternative model of obese externality

What should be clear is that neither our conceptual analysis nor the current studies are offered in order to gainsay the important role of externality in response style for the *maintenance* of an overweight adjustment. Obviously, it is a characteristic of both overweight children and adults with respect to food cues and for obese adults with respect to a variety of stimuli. What the above data render as less plausible is the argument that generalized stylistic externality is a functional antecedent of chronic overeating which is, in turn, an antecedent condition for obesity. If children who are already obese show no evidence of greater stylistic externality than their normal-weight counterparts, then it seems logically implausible to argue that generalized externality in style *results* in obesity. In light of the adult data and some of the results of our childhood studies, we propose that it is obesity which induces an external orientation.

One underlying, implicit assumption of the externality→obesity formulation is that an individual's eating behavior is comprised of free-operant responses to environmental or internal stimuli. In the case of young children, however, the access to and availability of food, as well as the timing and quantity of eating is largely determined by parents and socializers. Thus children who may be generally external may not overeat in response to salient food cues because parents may control access to such cues. Correspondingly, children who are not distinctly external might overeat in response to parental encouragement and overfeeding. Hence, in children one would expect a somewhat inconsistent relationship between externality and obesity. The naturalistic logic of the externality-to-obesity link so elegantly laid down by Schachter is undermined by the fact that the early instances of eating in children are largely mediated by parents and socializers. While parents may not directly overfeed their children, they purchase household foods, stock their cupboards and refrigerators, dispense meals, and control the accessibility and prominence of edibles in the household. This control function is a bi-directional one in that parents can both oversupply and undersupply caloric food stimuli. For children with biologic-genetic propensities toward obesity, oversupply results in obesity. Once obesity is achieved however, parents may come to adopt undersupply strategies that directly and indirectly constrain the child's eating behavior. We would propose that the intensity of parental undersupply strategies would vary directly with parental concern about the deviant status of obesity or about the potentially negative social outcome that might accrue to the child because of his or her obesity.

A major prediction of the above-described parental constraint model is that high eating constraints *overjustify* the obese child's noneating such that the child should fail to experience and develop intrinsic and self-mediated controls over the eating process. In the absence of either social or environmental obstacles to eating, the typically constrained obese child will over-ingest food when it is attractive, salient, and accessible. However, when either social constraints (e.g. parental sanctions) or environmental obstacles (e.g. nutshells) are in evidence, the typically constrained child complies with the external control. This beginning formulation can be viewed as a derivative of the overjustification model (cf. Lepper & Greene, 1975 and Chapter 1 by Lepper & Gilovich) which proposes that external rewards or punishments undermine a child's perception and enactment of intrinsic controls over the constrained behavioral domain. An implication of this general model is that the developmental acquisition of a general external style should follow from the low self-attribution of agency in a specific but important behavioral domain. This movement from specific food-related externality to generalized-stylistic externality is compatible with the cross-sectional inferences that might be drawn from the comparison of the findings of the current studies using childhood samples with the findings of similar adult inquiries.

Although it is clear that we draw some of our major propositions in this skeletal model from the nut-eating study described earlier, the studies of parental views on obesity and the studies on the effect of social presence on the eating behavior of obese and normal children are also reasonably compatible with the proposed framework. Specifically, we propose the following two points.

1. Parents tend to view obesity differently in their male and female children. They tend to see their female obese children as psychologically difficult, emotional, and in need of restraint in eating. Male obese children, on the other hand, are viewed as especially "adjusted" and less in need of food-related restrictions. We would argue that the social deviance associated with an obese adult adjustment is much earlier perceived by parents in the case of female than male children because of prevailing sex-role norms concerning attractiveness. As a consequence, the application of constraints and the initiation of developmental overjustification processes occur earlier in girls than in

boys. We would propose either that parental attitudes and practices toward their *adolescent* boys would resemble their attitudes toward their preadolescent girls *or* that the model of the antecedents of obese externality proposed above is more pertinent and descriptive of females than males. Some of Herman's research concerning the consequences of restrained eating orientations specific to females would suggest the latter conclusion. We would propose the former conclusion. Research examining the food orientations of adolescents as they relate to the rearing strategies of their parents would help settle this issue.

2. The social inhibition of the eating behavior of obese female children when affectively aroused is compatible with the parental view data and may impose the same kind of sex-based limitation on our model. The reader will recall that in our study testing the psychosomatic hypothesis obese female children exhibited significantly less *ad lib* eating in the presence of the experimenter than in the experimenter's absence (see Table 10.2). Obese males and normal-weight children of both sexes did not show significantly depressed food consumption in the presence of another. One might conjecture that this distinctive pattern of socially inhibited eating is a manifestation of self-conscious complicity to implied social constraint in eating for young females. Clearly further inquiry into the distinctive determinants of obese behavioral characteristics in males and females is warranted by both the parental view and social inhibition data cited earlier.

In short, our data indicate that the social-constraint-based origin of obese behaviors appears highly plausible for females and not so plausible for males. This gender distinction may provide a crucial direction in subsequent research on the socialization of obesity. As noted in our model, it is the socially deviant nature of obesity that arouses parental concern and mediates the parental constraint-oriented strategies toward already obese children. While the gender of the child may be pivotal in arousing such parental concern, a number of other status variables may also function to differentially trigger socialized overjustification processes. For example, the differential findings on the characteristics of overweight individuals from different social classes cited earlier could well be linked to the differential alarm occasioned by overweight in the different socioeconomic groups. It may well be that the primary boundary conditions on a social constraint model of the development of obese externality inhere in status variables that reflect normative orientations toward overweight adjustment. Further research along these lines, along with direct tests of the applicability of the social constraint model, would appear warranted at this time. It is our hope that this chapter will provoke such inquiries.

11

"AT A RELATIVELY EARLY AGE . . . THE HABIT OF WORKING THE MACHINE TO ITS MAXIMUM CAPACITY": ANTECEDENTS OF THE TYPE A CORONARY-PRONE BEHAVIOR PATTERN

KAREN A. MATTHEWS

UNIVERSITY OF PITTSBURGH

> In the worry and strain of modern life, arterial degeneration is not only very common, but develops often at a relatively early age. For this reason I believe that the high pressure at which men live and the habit of working the machine to its maximum capacity are responsible, rather than any excesses in eating or drinking. . . .
>
> W. Osler
> *Lectures on Angina Pectoris and Allied States*

Osler's proposition that ". . . the habit of working the machine to its maximum" leads to premature atherosclerosis has evoked an indulgent smile from twentieth-century cardiologists. However, more recently, serious consideration has been given to the role of similarly described behavior known as Pattern A in the etiology of atherosclerosis and subsequent coronary heart disease. This is because both retrospective and prospective studies reveal that Pattern A is associated with at least twice the occurrence of coronary heart disease as is an opposing Pattern B, which is defined as the absence of Pattern A (Jenkins, Rosenman, & Zyzanski, 1974; Rosenman, Brand, Jenkins, Friedman, Straus, & Worm, 1975). This relationship remains when statistical controls are introduced to partial out the effects of traditional risk factors for coronary heart disease, such as serum cholesterol level and systolic blood pressure. Moreover, Pattern A is associated with the degree of atherosclerosis in the coronary arteries (e.g., Blumenthal, Williams, Kong, Schanberg, & Thompson, 1978; Frank, Heller, Kornfeld, Sporn, & Weiss,

The author thanks Margaret Clark and Michael Scheier for their helpful comments on an earlier version of this chapter.

1978; cf. Dimsdale, Hackett, Hutter, Block, & Catanzano, 1978).

The Type A behavior pattern is defined as ". . . a characteristic action-emotion complex which is exhibited by those individuals who are engaged in a relatively chronic struggle to obtain an unlimited number of poorly defined things from their environment in the shortest period of time possible, and, if necessary, against the opposing efforts of other things or persons in this same environment" (Friedman, 1969, p. 84). The major behavioral manifestations of this struggle are competitive achievement-striving, a sense of time urgency, aggressiveness, and hostility (Rosenman, 1978). Individuals who display these behaviors are called Type As, whereas those who do not are called Type Bs.

Pattern A is thought to be encouraged by contemporary Western society because it appears to offer special rewards and opportunities to those who can think, perform, and even play more rapidly and aggressively than their peers. Although Type A behavior may indeed be more prevalent in a society like the United States than in an Eastern society, it is unclear why within the United States, which presumably rewards fast and aggressive behavior uniformly, some individuals become Type As and some become Type Bs.

The overall objective of this chapter is to review the progress in identifying factors that contribute to the development of the Type A coronary-prone behavior pattern. The chapter is divided into major sections as follows. First, I will look at why the study of the antecedents of Pattern A is important. Second, I will describe why I chose to focus my efforts on children. The third section presents the techniques for assessment of Pattern A in children and adolescents. Fourth, I will review the known familial influences on Pattern A. The final substantive section of the chapter offers one set of environmental factors that may contribute to the development of Pattern A. Throughout this review, I will specify the assumptions underlying the present approach and review the Type A adult literature as is necessary for understanding why certain procedures were followed.

Why study the antecedents of Pattern A?

There are three reasons why the gradual establishment of Pattern A deserves systematic investigation. First, understanding how any pattern of behavior develops aids in understanding how the pattern functions in its mature form (Kagan, 1971). This is true although factors that maintain the behavior are often different from the factors that explain the etiology of the behavior. For example, even though the factors that maintain human sexual inadequacy are not the same as the factors that describe how the inadequacy developed (Masters & Johnson, 1966), an understanding of the current sexual problems of an individual is facilitated if one knows, for example, that the person had a traumatic first sexual experience and has been sexually inactive thereafter.

Similarly, an understanding of Pattern A in adulthood is facilitated by an understanding of the developmental antecedents of Pattern A. For example, we gain insight into the current behavior pattern of a Type A man if we know that his mother responded to his childhood successes by telling him to try harder (cf. Glass, 1977). Moreover, knowledge about the development of Pattern A may be particularly useful because at present we lack a precise, rigorous conceptualization of Type A behavior. We do know that Type A men describe themselves as ambitious and rising to meet the competition, while, at the same time, they suffer from a sense of insufficient time to do what is necessary. Indeed, they behave as they report they do (Glass, 1977). However, beyond these descriptive details, our present understanding is limited. Knowledge of the antecedents of Pattern A should lead to a refinement in the concept of Pattern A and clearer descriptions of the essence of Pattern A behavior.

A second reason for inquiring into the development of Pattern A is the practical need to be able to predict the adult behavior pattern. In this way, those who are at risk for coronary disease can be identified at an early age. Prediction of adult behavior is also relevant for prevention (Kagan, 1971). Most of the psychobiological ills that plague individuals and, in turn, society as a whole are difficult to modify in the adult. Schizophrenia, drug addiction, criminality, and alcoholism are each thought to be the result of a long history of specific experiences interacting with a biological predisposition (Kagan, 1971). In the absence of data suggesting that Pattern A is easier to alter than the above disorders, it seems reasonable to assume that Pattern A would be modified most successfully early in its etiology.

Third, atherosclerosis is a life-long process that apparently begins in the first or second decade of life (Enos, Holmes, & Beyer, 1953; McNamara, Molot, Stremple, & Cutting, 1971). Type A behavior is associated with progression of coronary artery disease over time in a group of men 35 years of age and older (Krantz, Sanmarco, Selvester, & Matthews, 1979). Thus, it is reasonable to suggest that Pattern A begins to exert its pathogenic influence prior to the mid-thirties. Research on the origins of Pattern A will eventually allow (when technology permits) examination of the progression of atherosclerosis in relation to Type A behavior and its antecedents.

Why study children?

In order to investigate the antecedents of Pattern A, we must first identify the age range during which Pattern A first emerges and begins to stabilize across time. Then individuals within that age group can be studied in order to ascertain the etiological factors that contribute to the development of Pattern A. (On the other hand, a study of factors that maintain Pattern A requires an age group in which Pattern A has been stable for a substantial period of time.)

Does the existing literature provide any clues to when Pattern A might first emerge and stabilize? Yes, several longitudinal studies of children from birth or early childhood to adulthood have revealed that individual differences in the major behavioral manifestations of Pattern A stabilize in late childhood. For example, the level of achievement-striving by elementary-school-age children relative to others their age is similar to their relative level in adulthood (Block, 1971; Kagan & Moss, 1962). For males, there is continuity over time from childhood to adulthood in competitiveness, anger arousal, and aggressiveness (Block, 1971; Kagan & Moss, 1962; Olweus, 1979). For both sexes, impulsivity, which is related to Pattern A probably via its association with impatience, maintains an unusually high persistence across time (Block, 1971). Therefore, in order to understand the origins of Pattern A and the etiological factors contributing to its development, it seems reasonable to study children.

Two additional reasons should lead us to focus our efforts on children. Investigators have gathered data on the physical risk factors for heart disease in adulthood among 15,000 children in three major centers in the United States (U.S. Department of Health, Education, and Welfare, 1978). Particular attention has been paid to the prevalence of the risk factors and how stable they are over time among children. The only major risk factor not included in these efforts is Pattern A behavior. Thus, it is important to begin collecting such basic data on Pattern A among children.

The final reason is related to efforts to determine the pathophysiological mechanisms accounting for the association between Pattern A and coronary risk. At present, it is unknown precisely why or at what age Pattern A begins to exert its pathogenic influence. (It is known, however, that its major influence is not exerted through the standard risk factors because statistical controls for other risk factors do not substantially reduce the coronary risk associated with Pattern A.) However, among the suspected mechanisms are elevated systolic blood pressure, heart rate, and catecholamines exhibited by Type A adults,

18 years of age and older, in response to stressful circumstances (e.g., Dembroski, MacDougall, & Lushene, 1979; Dembroski, MacDougall, & Shields, 1977; Glass, Krakoff, Contrada, Hilton, Kehoe, Mannucci, Collins, Snow, and Elting, 1980; Manuck & Garland, 1979; Simpson, Olewine, Jenkins, Ramsey, Zyzanski, Thomas, & Hames, 1974). It is thought that episodic elevations in blood pressure and heart rate might damage the inner layer of the coronary arteries, thereby increasing the likelihood of atherosclerosis and subsequent coronary heart disease. Also, elevations in catecholamines are thought to heighten coronary risk by accelerating the rate of arterial damage, inducing myocardial lesions and facilitating the occurrence of fatal cardiac arrhythmias (e.g. Eliot, 1979; Haft, 1974; Raab, Chaplin, & Bajusz, 1969).

Two recent studies suggest that the above biobehavioral relationships might emerge in childhood or adolescence. For example, while executing challenging games, Type A sixth grade girls (as measured by the MYTH to be described later) show elevations in systolic blood pressure and heart rate (Lawler, Allen, Critchner, & Standard, in press). Also, in one epidemiological study, adolescents who report that they do things quickly and that they feel a sense of time urgency show elevated serum cholesterol level and mean arterial blood pressure, respectively, which are two risk factors for coronary disease (Hunter, Wolf, Sklov & Berenson, 1980). Given these intriguing findings and the desirability of ascertaining how and at what age Type A behavior becomes coronary-prone behavior, it is worthwhile to further investigate the relationships between Type A behaviors by children and adolescents and the pathophysiological processes implicated in coronary artery and heart disease.

Measurement of children's Type A behavior

The first step in investigating the antecedents of Pattern A is to develop an adequate technique for identifying children who char-

acteristically exhibit Type A or Type B behaviors. In this section, we will look at the available techniques. Prior to doing so, however, we will consider six properties that should characterize the techniques and provide a rationale for each of the properties. Some of these properties are derived from research findings on the two primary tools to assess Pattern A in adulthood, the structured interview (Rosenman, 1978) and the Jenkins Activity Survey or JAS (Jenkins, Zyzanski, & Rosenman, 1971); others are derived from general criteria for scale development (APA, 1974). These properties are presented to facilitate the discussion of the adequacy of the current measures of Type A behavior by children and adolescents. The properties are as follows.

1. A measure of Type A behaviors by children should include an adequate sampling of items, rating the three major behavioral components of Pattern A. These are competitive achievement-striving, a sense of time urgency and impatience, and aggressiveness-hostility (Glass, 1977; Rosenman, 1978).

This property presumes that measurement in children of behaviors that are phenotypically similar to those displayed by Type A adults are also genotypically similar. For example, it is assumed that both children and adults who play games to win rather than to have fun are competitive.

2. It should permit scoring of individual Type A behaviors.

This property is desirable for measures of Pattern A in adulthood because only a subset of Type A behaviors may be coronary-prone. Support for this view comes from a factor analysis of the structured Type A interview responses of 186 men enrolled in the Western Collaborative Group Study or WCGS (Matthews, Glass, Rosenman, & Bortner, 1977). (The WCGS is a major prospective study of the physical and behavioral risk factors for coronary heart disease.) Although five primary factors were revealed, only two—competitive drive and impatience—were associated with the later onset of clinical coronary heart disease. Scores for individual Type A behaviors allow further identification of coronary-prone Type A behaviors in adulthood.

Scores for individual Type A behaviors in children are necessary, not merely desirable, because the antecedents of the component behaviors may emerge at different times, become stable across time at different ages, and only covary in late childhood.

3. The ratings should be completed by an external observer.

There are two reasons for this property. First, the interview assessment of Pattern A, which is based on an external observer's assessment, is a better predictor of coronary disease than is self-assessment (Brand, Rosenman, Jenkins, Sholtz, & Zyzanski, 1978). Second, young children tend to be unreliable in making self-assessments (Matthews & Angulo, 1978).

4. The scale should be reliable or dependable (APA, 1974).

5. The scale should be valid in the sense that it accurately classifies children who exhibit Type A behaviors (APA, 1974). We are not concerned, however, that the scale be a valid measure of coronary-proneness (cf. Matthews, 1978). As noted earlier, at present, we do not know the age when Pattern A becomes associated with processes inimical to cardiovascular health.

6. A measure should be as convenient as is suitable for the task.

These six criteria are listed in the left-hand column of Table 11.1. At present, there are four instruments designed to measure Pattern A in children and adolescents. These are also identified and their properties summarized in Table 11.1.

The first instrument is the Bortner battery of performance tests (Bortner & Rosenman, 1967). Bortner and his associates selected a series of tests that were thought to measure the components of Pattern A. For example, time urgency is assessed by the Writing

Speed task. Individuals are asked to write the words, United States of America, at their regular writing speed, very rapidly, slowly, and very slowly. Because Type As have difficulty slowing down, three scores can be computed to reflect speed and impatience: (1) slow minus regular writing speed; (2) regular minus fast; and (3) very slow divided by regular. Unfortunately, in contrast to the above test that is clearly related to Pattern A, other Bortner tests are not, for example, the Flicker Fusion test. Nor is it clear that the Bortner battery adequately measures the aggressiveness-hostility aspect of Pattern A. On the other hand, a strength of the Bortner battery is that a test score is derived from the experimenter's observations of Type A behaviors that are similar to the behaviors exhibited by a Type A adult during the structured interview.

The scores from the Bortner tests are weighted according to the regression weights that maximized the prediction of the adult interview classification in a small sample of middle-aged men. The Bortner battery score and the structured interview classification were similar in 72% of the cases (Bortner & Rosenman, 1967). The Bortner battery has been used with children as young as 9 years old. It takes approximately an hour to complete and must be administered by trained experimenters; thus, it is an expensive procedure.

The second assessment method is the Butensky-Waldron interview (Butensky, Faralli, Heebner, & Waldron, 1976). This short 10-minute interview was adapted from the structured interview of adults and from the JAS. Examples of the questions concerning time urgency and competitiveness, respectively, are: "When you agree to meet a friend, do you get there on time? When you play games with little kids, do you purposely let them win?" The answers to the interview questions are coded on a scale from zero (extreme Type B) to 1 (extreme Type A) and summed to yield an overall score that can range from zero to 11. Normative data on adolescents living in rural, suburban, and urban settings have been gathered.

Table 11.1. Assessment of Pattern A in Children and Adolescents

Scale:	Bortner test battery	Butensky-Waldron interview	Hunter-Wolf A-B rating scale	MYTH
Age group:	Adolescents, possibly children	Adolescents	Adolescents, possibly children	Children
Property				
1. Does it measure the 3 major behavioral indicators of Pattern A?	Unknown	Yes	Presently it excludes aggressiveness-hostility; items to be added in the future	Yes
2. Does it permit scoring of individual characteristics?	No	Yes	Yes	Yes
3. Is it completed by an external observer?	Yes	No	No	Yes
4. Is it reliable?				
Interrater	Unknown	Unknown	Not applicable	Unknown
Test-retest	Unknown	Unknown	$r(83) = .53$ (across 6 weeks)	$r(428) = .83$ (across 3 months)
Internal consistency	Unknown	Unknown	Unknown	$\alpha = .90$
5. Is it valid?	Yes in 1 test	Unknown	Unknown	Yes in 4 tests; unclear in 1 test
6. Is it convenient?	No	Yes	Yes	Yes

The third method is the Hunter-Wolf A-B rating scale developed by Hunter, Wolf, and their associates (Wolf, Hunter, & Webber, 1979). This self-report questionnaire contains 17 items rated on a 7-point scale. The items were derived from the Bortner A-B rating scale, which assesses Pattern A in adulthood (Bortner, 1969). Sample items (reflecting time urgency) are: "I feel time passes quickly, I think about many things at the same time." Excluded from the present A-B rating scale are items measuring hostility and aggressiveness, although these items are to be included in future research (Hunter & Wolf, personal communication, December 1979).

Hunter and Wolf are in the process of ascertaining the reliability and validity of their A-B rating scale. In one sample of 85 eighth-grade children, test-retest reliability

of the Hunter-Wolf A-B rating scale across six weeks was .53. While there were no gender differences in this sample, there was a racial difference such that Caucasians scored higher on the A-B scale than did blacks. Also, children who scored high on the scale had a lower self-concept than did children who scored low on the scale, in contrast to Type A college students who have higher self-esteem (Glass, 1977). In another sample, adolescents, 14 years old and older, scored higher than did those 13 years old and younger. It should be noted that Hunter et al. (1980) also are examining the association of their A-B rating scale and cardiovascular risk factors in a sample of 400 adolescents.

The final scale is the Matthews Youth Test for Health, or MYTH (Matthews & Angulo, 1980). This scale contains 17 statements that describe competitive achievement-striving, aggressiveness-hostility, and a sense of time urgency in children. A sample item is, "When working or playing, she/he tried to do better than other children." Another illustration is, "This child is patient when working with children slower than she/he is." Each statement is rated by an external rater—the children's classroom teacher—on a scale of 1 (extremely uncharacteristic) to 5 (extremely characteristic). After three items are reverse coded (because they describe Pattern B), the scores are summed to yield an overall score that can range from 17 to 85.

Two subscale scores are also available in the MYTH. One is the sum of all the items describing children's competitiveness and achievement behavior. The second is the sum of all items describing children's aggressiveness, hostility, and a sense of time urgency. These two subscales were developed because repeated factor analyses of the MYTH items in various samples consistently yielded the above two dimensions.

Normative, reliability, and validity data were gathered in a sample of approximately 500 elementary-school-age children residing in a small midwestern university town (see Matthews & Angulo, 1980, for a full report). The children were enrolled in grades kindergarten, 2, 4, and 6 and were predominantly Caucasian and from middle socioeconomic class families. Children in the study represented 95% of the potential participants. All participants were evaluated on the MYTH scale three times by their classroom teacher.

The results revealed that, while the total MYTH scores did not vary by grade, boys did have higher MYTH scores at all grades than did girls in this sample. This gender difference in rated Type A behavior is consistent with gender differences in adult Pattern A (Waldron, 1978) and in childen's aggressive and competitive behavior (Maccoby & Jacklin, 1974), two components of Pattern A. Thus, it appears likely that the gender differences in Pattern A in adulthood have their beginning in childhood.

The validity of the MYTH has been tested by several laboratory studies. In general, the results have been supportive. For example,

to assess whether the MYTH is a valid measure of children's impatience, second- and sixth-grade children were asked to trace the outline of a star four times with their preferred hand (Matthews & Angulo, 1980). On the fifth time, they were no longer allowed to look directly at their hand during the task. Instead, they were required to use their hand's mirror image to guide their efforts. This task was frustrating to the children and elicited considerable impatience. Impatient behaviors were coded by an observer present in the room, who was blind to the children's MYTH score.

Analyses revealed that MYTH Type A children were significantly more impatient in this setting than were Type B children. For example, MYTH Type As sighed, were restless, and interrupted the experimenter; similar behaviors are diagnostic criteria of Pattern A in the adult interview (Scherwitz, Berton, & Leventhal, 1977; Schucker & Jacobs, 1977).

Further evidence of MYTH's validity is provided in a study by Matthews, Barnett, & Howard (1979) in which the association of Type A behaviors (excluding aggressiveness) and suppressed empathy was tested. It has been suggested that any factor that distracts an individual from the feelings and needs of others should suppress empathy (e.g., Feshbach & Feshbach, 1969; Hoffman, 1976). Competitive, impatient, hostile feelings should distract from a concern about another's welfare. To the extent that Type A children experience these feelings during social interactions, they should be less empathic than Type B children.

To test this notion, Type A and Type B first-graders, identified by a subset of MYTH items (excluding aggressiveness items), were told that they would play a new etch-a-sketch game either in a competitive, cooperative, or neutral situation. Then they viewed a videotape of same-age and same-sex children playing the game in the same situation in which they anticipated playing. Prior to playing the game themselves, the children were administered the Feshbach-Roe (1968) measure of empathy, which assesses the emotional empathy of children in response to stories of children presented by slides.

While anticipating to compete, to cooperate, or to be neutral had no effect on children's empathy, Type A behavior did. Type A behavior was significantly correlated with suppressed empathy in boys, $r(40) = .66$, $p < .001$, but not in girls, $r(40) = .05$, $p > .30$. This pattern of findings parallels a previous pattern reported by Feshbach and Feshbach (1969). In their study, one Type A behavior, aggressiveness, was related to suppressed empathy in first-grade boys, but not in girls. Although the reason for the lack of association of girls' Type A behaviors and suppressed empathy is unknown, nevertheless, the consistency of the findings of the present study and those of Feshbach and Feshbach (1969) lends support to the validity of the MYTH.

Let us return at this point to Table 11.1. It appears that each assessment technique may be useful in certain settings. For example, the Hunter-Wolf A-B rating scale may measure adolescents' Type A behaviors and perhaps children's when teachers are unavailable to rate them. The MYTH appears to be a useful measure of children's Type A behavior. It is also clear from this table that at this time all the techniques lack some of the suggested six properties. To the degree that the six properties are reasonable, the table suggests appropriate directions for future research and for modification of existing measures. However, it is safe to say now that several techniques do show promise as satisfactory measures of children's and adolescents' Type A behaviors. With continued psychometric research, it is likely that Pattern A can be adequately assessed via its three major behavioral components. In addition, in the process of validating any of the instruments, a more precise, rigorous conceptualization of Pattern A than is currently available may be developed.

Conceptualization of Pattern A behavior

To illustrate this last point, we can look at the experimental work by Glass (1977) and his colleagues. They have reported experimental evidence showing that Type A college students work hard to succeed, suppress subjective states such as fatigue that might interfere with their task performance, conduct their activities at a rapid pace, and express hostility after being frustrated or harassed in their efforts at task completion. It has been argued that a commonality underlies these behaviors. At their core may be an attempt by the Type A person to maintain and assert control over environmental demands and challenges. Stated differently, Type As may engage in a continual struggle to control and, as a consequence, appear aggressive, impatient, and competitive.

To test this notion, Glass (1977) and his associates conducted a series of experiments in which Type As and Type Bs were exposed to uncontrollable events. By and large, the data support the conceptualization of Pattern A as a specific style for coping with uncontrollable stress, although a number of issues remain to be resolved (see Glass, 1977, chapter 12).

Returning to the present interest in Type A behavior of children, it seems reasonable to suggest that underlying children's aggressiveness, competitiveness, and impatience is also a response style aimed at maintaining and asserting environmental control. This is most likely to be true for older children who presumably have behaved in a Type A fashion for a number of years. To test this possibility, we conducted an experiment (Matthews, 1979) that essentially replicated a previous study in which control of a task was manipulated (Glass, 1977, chapter 9). Male Type As and Type Bs were asked to earn nickels by pressing a button located on a response box in front of them. Thirty-one nickels were awarded to them through a coin dispenser either on every seventh button press (FR/7) or on an average of every seventh button press (VR/7). It was assumed that the VR/7 schedule would be perceived as more uncontrollable than the FR/7 schedule because the VR/7 schedule contains no immediately discernible contingency between responding and reinforcement. The measure of effort to control was the response rate.

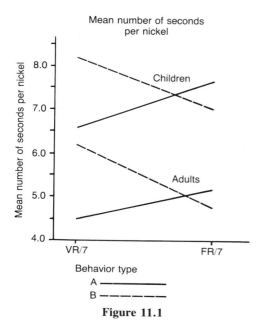

Mean number of seconds per nickel

Figure 11.1

The subjects in the study were of two age groups: fourth- and fifth-graders and college undergraduates. The children were classified as exhibiting Type A or Type B behaviors by an early version of the MYTH; the adults were classified by the Jenkins Activity Survey for Health Prediction (Jenkins et al., 1971), adapted for students by Glass (Glass, 1977).

If previous findings by Glass were to be replicated, Type A adults and children should respond at a higher rate than Bs when initially threatened by a loss of control. There should be no difference in the rate of performance of As and Bs when not threatened by a loss of control. The relevant data are presented in Figure 11.1. As this figure reveals, the predictions were confirmed. Both Type A adults and children made more effort to control their environment than did Type Bs when initially threatened by a loss of control. However, when no threat existed, there were no differences between the Types.

The striking parallels between the behavior of Type A children and adults in this circumstance suggest the worthiness of fur-

ther research on the efforts of Type A children to control and to master environmental demands and stressors. Furthermore, they suggest that, like adults', children's Type A behaviors may represent a distinctive style of coping with potentially uncontrollable events. These parallels gain significance because of speculations that persistent efforts to control stressors by adults are accompanied by pathophysiological processes inimical to cardiovascular functioning, for example, by elevations in catecholamines (Glass, 1977). To the extent that Type A children's efforts to control are accompanied by similar pathophysiological processes, biobehavioral studies can also shed light on the age range when Type A behaviors might become coronary-prone behaviors.

Familial influences on Pattern A

Should biobehavioral studies reveal that Type As' efforts to control are associated with pathophysiological processes in young children, then early familial influences on children become of great interest. In this section, we will look at three major ways that families might exert a significant influence on the development of Pattern A. These are familial transmission of genetic factors in Pattern A, modeling of parental Type A behavior, and child-rearing practices.

Several studies using the twin method have addressed the possibility of genetic influences on Pattern A behavior. The twin method is based on the fact that monozygotic or identical twins share 100% of their genes in common, whereas dizygotic or fraternal twins share 50% on the average. If the degree of similarity on an attribute between monozygotic twins is greater than the degree of similarity between dizygotic twins, then it is assumed that there is a genetic component to the attribute in question. Of course, this conclusion rests on the assumption that the environment of the monozygotic twins is no more similar than the environment of the dizygotic twins.

Twin studies to date concur in reporting little evidence for a genetic component to

Pattern A as assessed by the structured interview (Rahe, Hervig, & Rosenman, 1978). On the other hand, there does appear to be a genetic contribution to the JAS (the self-report measure) assessment of Pattern A (Rahe et al., 1978; cf. Matthews & Krantz, 1976). This conflicting state of affairs is somewhat clarified by subsidiary analyses of the JAS items. These analyses revealed that the heritable aspect of the JAS appears to be psychomotor activity (Rahe et al., 1978), which is not measured by the interview (Matthews et al., 1977).

I suggest, however, that a more accurate picture of the role of genetic factors in Pattern A must await further psychometric research. Pattern A assessment in adulthood is based on exhibiting a simple preponderance of Type A behaviors. Thus, individuals can be classified as Type A for different reasons. One Type A individual could be very impatient, but not at all concerned about excelling at work. Another could be very patient and careful, but at the same time aggressive in his approach. As a result, the global Type A classification is an imprecise measure of specific behaviors and may mask genetic contributions to a subset of Type A behaviors. Therefore, in order to elucidate the heritability of Pattern A, we are examining at present the heritability of individual Type A behaviors. Only then can we possibly describe the heritable and environmental contributions to the development of Pattern A.

Parental effects

Children tend to imitate the behavior of same-sex models who are reinforced for their behavior (Cohen, 1976). Given the general belief that our society reinforces Type A behavior, it seems likely that children might model their same-sex parents' Type A behavior. Data from one of the twin studies are available to test this hypothesis (Matthews & Krantz, 1976). This twin sample was drawn from a roster of twins who had enrolled at the University of Texas at Austin. They had an average age of 21.2 years and an average educational level of 15.5 years. Their parents had an average age of 52.4 years and an average educational level of 14.7 years. Both the parents and twins completed the JAS. Then the association of the average twin JAS score and the parents' JAS scores was computed. Results revealed that the male twins were somewhat more similar to their fathers, $r(22) = .33, p < .06$, than to their mothers, $r(22) = .09, p > .20$, whereas female twins were somewhat more similar to their mothers, $r(22) = .45, p < .05$, than to their fathers, $r(22) = .19, p > .20$. These findings provide support, albeit weak, for the notion that children tend to model their same-sex parents' Type A behavior.

The data from another study are relevant here (Bortner, Rosenman, & Friedman, 1970). Male adolescents ages 11 and older and their fathers were assessed on the Bortner test battery. The correlation between the father's and son's test score was .16. Another way to examine the relationship of fathers and their sons is to examine the similarity of their A-B classifications. A significant contingency coefficient of .31 was yielded from this approach. In summary, Bortner et al. (1970) found, like Matthews and Krantz, weak but positive evidence for father-son similarity in Pattern A.

Although the Bortner et al. and Matthews and Krantz findings are instructive, they also probably underestimate the magnitude of the parental modeling effect on children. It is unlikely that children imitate all of their parents' Type A behaviors. Instead, they probably imitate a subset of them. Thus, the weak association between children's and parents' global Type A scores is likely to mask stronger associations between parents and children in individual Type A behaviors. Hence, a fruitful approach in future research would be to examine parent-child similarity of individual Type A behaviors.

Whether or not parental modeling of specific Type A behaviors contributes strongly to the development of Pattern A, parents may substantially affect their children in other ways. One way is through the nature of the parents' child-rearing practices. As a first step in examining this possibility, we observed the child-rearing practices used with Type A and Type B children (Glass, 1977, p. 154). Mothers interacted with their sons, who had been nominated by their teachers as exhibiting Type A or Type B behaviors on an early version of the MYTH called the Children's Activity Survey (Glass, 1977). The boys were required to complete three tasks: stack a set of odd shaped blocks with one hand while blindfolded; copy a pictorial representation of a geometric figure with a set of cubes; and throw bean bags into a basket. The mothers were allowed to assist their sons in any way they wished, with the exception of completing the tasks for the children. An observer present in the testing room coded the behaviors of the mothers and children. After completion of the testing period, the mothers were administered the structured interview, in order to assess their behavior type. In this way, we were able to examine the child-rearing practices used by Type A and Type B mothers with their Type A and Type B sons.

The results revealed that Type A boys were treated differently from Type B boys. Specifically, Type A and Type B mothers gave fewer positive evaluations of task performance to Type A boys than to Type B boys, and Type A boys were pushed to try harder than were Type B boys, particularly by Type B mothers. An example of the latter is, "You're doing fine, but next time, let's try for 5."

Because of the correlational nature of the study, we could not conclude that the differences in child-rearing practices associated with the Type A and Type B boys caused the children's behavior pattern. In fact, children have such an impressive range of effects on caregivers (e.g. Harper, 1975) that the differences in maternal behavior may have been elicited by the children's characteristic behavior.

To test this possibility, the above study was repeated with two modifications (Matthews, 1977). First, the boys in this study were confederates who were actual As or Bs and who were instructed to exhibit Type A or Type B behavior, respectively, according to a prearranged script. They did this during the performance of the bean bag toss task while a female stranger (a mother of another same-age boy) observed. In this way, the women had an opportunity to form an initial impression of the children's behavior pattern. The second modification was that, following the bean bag performance, the children interacted with the women on the other two tasks. The boys did not follow a script during this portion of the experiment. We expected that if the female strangers responded to Type A and Type B boys in a manner similar to the mothers in the previous study, then it is likely that the Type A children in the previous study were causing their own mothers to behave as they did. However, if the female strangers responded to the Type A and Type B boys in a manner different from the boys' own mothers, then it is likely that the maternal child-rearing practices in the previous study were not caused by the children and may have, in fact, contributed to the children's Type A behavior.

Analyses of the coded interactions of the children and women revealed that, in contrast to the previous findings, Type A boys received more positive evaluations of their task performance than did Type B boys from female strangers. Similar to the previous findings, Type A boys were pushed to accelerate their efforts more often than were Type B boys. However, only the Type B women consistently showed the above pattern of responding.

Taking the results of the two studies together, it seems probable that Type A boys do not cause their own mothers to give them few positive evaluations because they do not elicit such from female strangers. Instead, a low intrafamilial frequency of positive evaluation of task performance and a high extrafamilial frequency may play a causal role in the development of Pattern A. On the other hand, it does appear that Type A behavior by boys elicits comments from Type B mothers and strangers designed to improve the children's performance. Thus, a curious phenomenon results: Type A boys elicit precisely that behavior from Type B women that may encourage them to continue striving to achieve ever-escalating goals.

It is worthwhile to speculate here on other possible consequences of the behaviors that Type A children elicit from their environment. Assume that the caregivers' remarks designed to improve task performance are perceived as a potential threat to the children's sense of control. For example, the comment to try harder on the next trial may be interpreted to mean that the children's previous efforts were less than satisfactory and that a better performance is required to gain a sense of control. Recall also that Type A boys respond to a threat to their sense of control by making vigorous efforts to reassert control (Matthews, 1979). Taking these findings together, it is reasonable to suggest that Type A children may respond to comments to improve their performance by vigorously attempting to reassert control. Women, particularly Type Bs, apparently respond to Type A behavior by children (persistent efforts to excel) by again attempting to accelerate the children's efforts to do well. Thus, this adult-Type A child interaction is likely to be a self-perpetuating dynamic, which also should maintain the Type A child's continual struggle to control into adulthood.

A theory of development of Pattern A

Up to this point, I have suggested that Type A behaviors are likely to be a self-perpetuating set of behaviors, and, thus, somewhat resistant to change. We have seen a number of behavioral parallels between children and adults who exhibit Type A behaviors. Other than familial influences on children's Type A behaviors, however, we have not looked at specific etiological factors that might encourage children to initially display such behaviors, which later would become self-maintaining. In this section, I propose and make a case for one set of environmental factors that may be critical to the etiology of Type A

behavior—namely, a combination of a strong value in productivity and ambiguous standards for evaluation of that productivity.

Two distinctly different theories converge on the importance of these factors. Ornstein's theory of time perception provides the notion that ambiguous standards of excellence contribute to a sense of time urgency. Ornstein (1969) argues that perceived time duration lengthens as the size of the storage space for information occurring in a given time interval increases. The size of storage space, in turn, depends on the amount of information or number of occurrences in the interval that reach awareness and the way that information is coded and stored. Time duration is perceived to be greater, that is, more time passed relative to objective (clock) time, when there is an increase in amount of information coded, an increase in the complexity of the material, or a decrease in efficiency of the processor. The complexity of encoding material should increase with the degree of ambiguity for evaluating task performance. Hence, ambiguous standards should elicit a sense that time is passing quite rapidly. And, to the extent that productivity is valued, ambiguous standards for evaluating accomplishments should lead to a sense that time is insufficient to accomplish all that one wants to get done.

Situations that do not yield clear standards for evaluating performance may also elicit chronic achievement-striving. Festinger (1954) suggests that individuals have a basic drive to evaluate their abilities. Thus, people engage in a number of information-seeking behaviors that are designed to determine how good they are at a given activity. Initially, objective physical bases for evaluation are sought. If such criteria are ambiguous or unavailable, people look to others for subjective standards of ability levels. Generally speaking, they choose to compare their performance to someone who is similar, but slightly better than they are, on a given dimension (cf. Suls & Miller, 1977). As a result, they should believe that they have just "missed the mark." Provided that they value productivity, they should struggle harder next time, which is, of course, yet another ambiguous standard. Thus, this pattern of behaviors, in the absence of developing clear internal or external standards, is likely to be a self-perpetuating one. Moreover, these individuals may also be likely to perceive their performance as incomplete or a failure. Such perceptions are difficult to encode; consequently, the sense that time is passing rapidly may also intensify.

I do not mean to suggest, however, that the above processes are true of children at all ages who are in ambiguous achievement situations. In fact, it appears quite likely that the above processes do not apply to young children. This is because the few relevant studies with children have revealed that only after the age of 7 are children able to use information about how other children performed on the same task in making self-evaluations (Ruble, Parsons, & Ross, 1976) or do they spontaneously compare their performance with that of a partner (Ruble, Feldman, & Boggiano, 1976). Consequently, it is likely that ambiguous information about one's performance does not elicit Type A behaviors from the average child until she or he is in the second or third grade. Nonetheless, at this age, it would seem that children who become Type As are confronted more frequently with ambiguous standards to evaluate their performance by their parents or by others than are children who become Type Bs. As a consequence, developing As should seek to compare their own performance with peers more than Type Bs do. They may be particularly likely to compare with a superior other, who should make them feel slightly inferior, resulting in a sense that they must struggle harder. Because of the difficulty encoding such information, they should sense time passing quickly.

Are there extant data consistent with this formulation? Minimal, but direct evidence is available, indicating that Type A adults frequently compare their performance with others, because they lack clear, internal standards for evaluating their performance. For example, Type A college students report that they evaluate their performance by comparing it to others more often than do Type Bs (Pennebaker & Burnam, 1974). While waiting for an impending stressful situation to occur, Type As prefer more often to wait with others than alone, presumably because they want information about how others are viewing the situation, to guide their own behavior (Dembroski & MacDougall, 1978). In a pilot study by Angulo and Matthews (1978), Type As compared their performance on an ambiguous ability test more often than did Type Bs. More importantly, Type As chose to compare with a superior other more often than did Bs.

The available evidence is indirect for children. Recall that Type A boys are told to try harder next time by their own mothers as well as by strangers (particularly Type B women; Glass, 1977; Matthews, 1977). In other words, Type A children are given an ambiguous standard for evaluating the next performance—doing better than previously. They are not told precisely how much better is desirable.

A cross-cultural study of boys in five different societies is also relevant here (Toda, Shinotsuka, McClintock, & Stech, 1978). Supplying boys with information about how well they performed relative to a partner on a game that had no clear performance criteria (Prisoner's Dilemma game) led to enhanced competitiveness. Presumably achievement situations that lack clear standards yield a search for information similar to that provided the boys in the Toda et al. (1978) study. If so, it seems reasonable to suggest that ambiguous standards for evaluation of performance would lead to competitiveness by children.

Although the present theorizing has dwelled on the role of ambiguous performance standards in the early development of Type A behaviors, there is no reason why such standards might not also play a role in later fluctuations of Type A behaviors. Let's assume that an adult is hired to do a job in which there are no clear standards for evaluating peformance. We would expect that the individual would exhibit more Type A behaviors until a clear standard is set or some external clear reward is given that signifies previous behavior was adequate (unless, of course, internal standards are imposed by the individual).

It is worthwhile reiterating here that a combination of a value in productivity and ambiguous standards for evaluating productivity is only one set of etiological factors that might produce Pattern A. There are undoubtedly others, including perhaps genetic factors. Nonetheless, as future research specifies the role of ambiguous performance criteria as well as other environmental factors in the etiology of Pattern A, we can more adequately understand the struggle of the Type A from childhood to adulthood. In consequence, refinements in the definition of Pattern A may be forthcoming.

Summary

I have suggested that the study of the antecedents of Pattern A is important because it will aid in understanding the adult behavior pattern, in predicting the adult behavior pattern, and in studying the behavioral risk factors associated with coronary artery disease, which apparently begins in the first or second decade of life. We have seen why childhood is an appropriate age to investigate the antecedents of Pattern A. We have looked at six criteria that should characterize techniques for assessment of Pattern A in children and adolescents as well as evaluated the available techniques in light of those criteria. Familial influences on Pattern A have also been reviewed. One specific set of environmental factors—value in productivity and ambiguous standards for evaluating productivity—has been suggested as critical to the etiology of Pattern A. Although at present it is unknown precisely why or at what age Pattern A begins to exert its pathogenic influence, we noted that episodic heart rate and systolic blood pressure arteries, thereby increasing the likelihood of atherosclerosis and subsequent coronary heart disease. These hemodynamic changes also characterized the cardiovascular responses of Type A sixth-grade girls in a recent study (Lawler, et al., in press). Given these intriguing findings, it seems worthwhile to investigate further the relationships between Type A behaviors by children and adolescents in theoretically relevant situations and the pathophysiological processes implicated in the etiology of coronary artery and heart disease. In consequence, we can more fully explore Osler's proposition that the habit of working the machine to its maximum leads to arterial degeneration at a relatively early age.

12

THE SOCIAL PSYCHOLOGY OF MENTAL RETARDATION: WHAT'S IN A LABEL?

FREDERICK X. GIBBONS
IOWA STATE UNIVERSITY

It may come as somewhat of a surprise to the reader to find a chapter on mental retardation in a volume that concerns developmental social psychology. For the most part, social psychologists have been reluctant to include so-called abnormal populations in their research. They have chosen, instead, to leave the study of these people to clinical psychologists and to sociologists who have been interested for years in the topics of "stigma"[1] labels and their effects on labeled persons (e.g., Goffman, 1963). Thus, social psychologists have studied how others respond to stigmatized and to stereotyped persons, because these are interesting social psychological issues. However, stigmatized persons themselves have seldom been included in this research, perhaps because it is thought that their behavior does not adhere to the social psychological principles that have been developed through observations of "normal" persons. Of course, since we do not study stigmatized people, we have no way of determining whether this is true or not. Consequently, although we know quite a bit about the attitudes and opinions of others toward this group, we know very little about their attitudes and opinions toward others and toward themselves.

This chapter represents an attempt to promote a social psychology of stigmatized groups. In doing this, we will be looking at research that has attempted to apply social psychological theories, such as social comparison and attribution theory, to the behavior of a group of stigmatized persons that up to this point has been almost completely ignored by social psychologists: mentally retarded children and adolescents. The primary focus of this chapter will be reactions to the mental retardation (MR) label. Unlike previous stigma or label research, many of the studies to be discussed have been conducted with stigmatized persons as *subjects,* rather than as attitude *targets.* In fact, one of the major questions to be examined concerns how mentally retarded children themselves respond to the MR label and to others who are so labeled. Since retarded persons' self- and group-concepts are influenced by the reactions of others, we will also look at some research that concerns nonretarded children's and adolescents' attitudes toward their retarded peers.

Rosenthal and Jacobson's (1968) classic and pioneering work on self-fulfilling prophecies provides a basis and an outline for the chapter. Although their research has received a good deal of theoretical and empirical criticism (e.g., Jose & Cody, 1971), it still stands as one of the most informative and provocative treatises on labeling effects that has ever been published. In fact, few books have stimulated as much controversy and as much research as their 1968 volume *Pygmalion in the Classroom*. One of the central themes of the chapter, then, will be the question of whether the mental retardation label does act as a self-fulfilling prophecy. In order to present this information in context, however, we will first look at some brief background information on what mental retardation is.

The traditional definition of mental retardation, and perhaps the one most familiar to psychologists, is simply an IQ score that is more than two standard deviations below the mean; for the WAIS test that cutoff score is 69. However, this definition has been replaced several times by the American Association on Mental Deficiency (AAMD). The newer definitions reflect an increasing emphasis on "adaptive behavior," which is the ability to function adequately in a social environment. According to AAMD,

Mental retardation refers to significantly subaverage general intellectual functioning existing concurrently with deficits in adaptive behavior, and manifested during the developmental period. (Grossman, 1977, p. 5)

A recent estimate by H. Carl Haywood (1979), former president of AAMD, put the number of mentally retarded persons in this country at about 7 million, of which by far the largest group (about 92%) is categorized as mildly retarded (generally having IQ scores between 50 and 70). Since these are the people who are most likely to be living in the community or to be candidates for community placement and, therefore, most often come in contact with nonretarded persons, we will be restricting our discussion to them.

Approximately 85% of retarded persons live in the community, either in their own homes or in some type of residential program (e.g., "supervised apartments"). Although the number of retarded persons living in the community has not increased dramatically in the last decade, their visibility definitely has. For the most part, this is attributable to recent federal legislation (and related litigation) that was intended to promote the rights and welfare of persons with various kinds of handicaps. This legislation was fostered by the policy of "normalization" which advocates "making available to the mentally retarded patterns and conditions of everyday life which are as close as possible to the norms and patterns of the mainstream of society" (Nirje, 1969, p. 181). As a result of the passage of these laws, mentally retarded persons and other handicapped persons now have much greater access to community services and facilities, which heretofore they were unwilling or unable to take advantage of.

A prime example of this legislation is the Education for All Handicapped Children Act (PL 94–142), passed in 1975, which mandated that educational opportunities be provided to handicapped children in an environment that could be considered "least restrictive" for them. This law has been interpreted to mean that mentally retarded children should have the same access to all educational facilities as do nonretarded children. It has, therefore, been used as the legal precedent for many of the current "mainstreaming" programs in our school systems, in which handicapped children are integrated into classes along with their nonretarded peers. This policy has tended to replace the previous one in which retarded children received special education in classes where they were segregated from their peers.

In summary, the result of recent legislation and litigation (and of a more general shift in policy toward handicapped persons) has been a tremendous increase in the amount of contact that is taking place between retarded and nonretarded children and among retarded children in noninstitutionalized settings. This increase in contact is what prompted most of the research to be discussed in this chapter.

A self-fulfilling prophecy

The publication of Rosenthal and Jacobson's *Pygmalion in the Classroom* (1968) had a significant impact on both educators and researchers working with handicapped and learning-disabled children. The results of their work indicated that labels, even when bogus, can have a strong impact on children, primarily because of the behavioral expectations associated with them. In their research, a group of elementary school children was given an intelligence test. About 20% of the group was then chosen to receive the label of "late bloomers" or "spurters." Although these labels were supposedly based on the results of the test, the selection of the "gifted" group was actually done randomly, and there was no connection between test scores and the label. When the intelligence tests were given again at the end of the year, however, there was a strong relationship between the label and children's performances. Those who had been classified as bright actually gained significantly more IQ points than the others; in fact, 47% of the "bright" group gained 20 or more total IQ points over the course of the year. Although subsequent analyses of teachers' behavior revealed no obvious differences in their reactions toward the "gifted" and the control groups, the implication was still clear. Somehow the labeled children were receiving the message that they were expected to do well, and they did.

Of course, those in special education were particularly interested in Rosenthal and Jacobson's research. If teachers could convey expectations of success to children arbitrarily labeled as bright, then it stands to reason that the opposite message could be communicated to children who were legitimately labeled as learning disabled or educationally handicapped. This would be particularly problematic for the segregated retarded child who, by virtue of his or her special class placement, is clearly labeled as a slow learner. Not surprisingly, the question of whether the diagnostic labels of educationally handicapped or even mentally retarded could act as self-fulfilling prophecies for labeled children quickly became an important research topic.

The self-fulfilling prophecy that Rosenthal and Jacobson described appears to work in three distinct steps. The first involves the expectations that are associated with the label. With Rosenthal and Jacobson's "late bloomers," the expectation was that they would begin to show intellectual growth at some point in the semester; with retarded or educationally handicapped children, presumably the expectation is that they will not do well intellectually or academically. The second step is that these expectations are somehow communicated to the children so that they become aware of what is expected of them. This latter step is a crucial one in the process. If the prophecy is going to become self-fulfilling, that is, if children are actually going to demonstrate the expected behavior on their own, then at some level they must be aware of what is expected of them. The third step involves internalization of the expectations so that the child begins to expect the (expected) behavior of himself or herself and eventually demonstrates it.

The research I conducted has examined each of the three steps of the self-fulfilling prophecy with regard to the MR label. That research and other similar studies will be discussed in three sections of this chapter. The first section deals with popular attitudes toward retarded children and adolescents. In this section, the question is raised as to what kinds of behavior are expected from retarded children—not just for cognitive tasks, but also for social behaviors such as getting married and raising a family. A second question to be examined in this section is how do nonretarded adults and children respond to the behavior of retarded children, especially when those behaviors disconfirm strong expectancies that they might maintain. In the second section, we will look at mentally retarded children's and adolescents' awareness of their own label, including the label that is associated with placement in an institution. The third section deals with retarded persons' expectations of other retarded persons.

Step I: Attitudes toward retarded children

What kinds of behavior are expected from educationally handicapped or mentally retarded children? A recent study by Gottlieb (1975) provides some interesting data on this question. Subjects were third-grade students who had had some contact with mentally retarded children through the special classes in their school. Gottlieb presented them with a videotape of a boy who was either labeled as mentally retarded or not labeled and who either did or did not act in a very aggressive manner. He then asked subjects to evaluate the boy on a number of adjective and social distance questions. Although there was a strong tendency to derogate the aggressive child, there was only a slight tendency to give the retarded child less favorable evaluations. Of particular interest, however, was a label x aggressiveness interaction: The aggressive child received the most negative evaluations when he was labeled as mentally retarded.

Special dispensation

Very different results were reported three years earlier by Goodman, Gottlieb, and Harrison (1972) in a study that concerned the effects of mainstreaming on sociometric reactions to retarded children. They found that educable mentally retarded (EMR) children who had been mainstreamed into a regular classroom, and thus were not labeled, were not accepted socially by their peers any more than were EMR children who had been labeled by virtue of their special class placement. In fact, the integrated children in the study were actually *rejected* more often than were segregated children. In discussing their results, Goodman et al. suggested that the retardation label may have affected the expectations that the nonretarded children maintained for the EMR children. In particular, they stated that nonretarded individuals "may accept more readily, deviant behaviors when the behaviors are manifested by children who are clearly labeled as deviant. . . . The same behaviors, which lead to rejection when exhibited by nonretarded children may not result in sociometric rejection when manifested by children who are classified as

retarded" (p. 417). Thus, the label provides the retarded child with "special dispensation" for his or her behavioral inadequacies (see also Guskin, Bartel, & MacMillan, 1975). Apparently this applies only to academically deviant behavior rather than socially deviant acts such as aggression, however (cf. Gottlieb, 1975).

The results of this study did not provide support for the mainstreaming movement; and there were other previous studies that had led to similar conclusions. Gottlieb and Davis (1973) found that when nonretarded children were asked to choose a partner for a ring-toss game, they did not choose integrated EMR children any more than they did segregated (labeled) EMR children; and Gottlieb, Cohen, and Goldstein (1974) found that contact with EMR children actually led to more negative attitudes from nonretarded children. Although it would not be fair to conclude from this research that integration or *mainstreaming*, per se, was causing problems (socially) for retarded children, at the same time, there was really no evidence to suggest that the MR label was causing problems for them either (cf. Gottlieb, 1974).

At the very least, this research put the MR label in a new light. It appeared that those who had been afraid that diagnostic labeling, together with placement in special classes, might lead to lower academic performance and lower social status for handicapped and retarded children were mistaken. In a review of this labeling literature, MacMillan, Jones, and Aloia (1974) came to the conclusion that there was no conclusive evidence indicating that the MR label, by itself, produced *any* negative consequences for retarded children. Furthermore, they suggested that, if MR children do get into trouble of some kind, it is usually because of the behavior they demonstrate (e.g., aggressiveness) rather than the label.

"Privileges and punishments."

Subsequent research took the conclusion of MacMillan et al. (1974) one step further, by suggesting that MR children may actually *benefit* from their label. For example, Farina, Thaw, Felner, and Hust (1976) had a group of college students administer a shock to children via a learning/shocking machine, ostensibly in order to help them learn a list of nonsense syllables. As might be expected, children received significantly less severe shocks when they failed at the task if they were labeled as mentally retarded. In a similar study, Budoff and Siperstein (1978) had nonretarded children view a videotape of a child of their own sex who was either labeled as MR or not labeled and who either did well or poorly at a cognitive task (spelling words). When the child failed, he or she received more *favorable* evaluations from the nonretarded children if he or she was labeled than if not. Finally, Foley (1979) found that nonretarded children evaluated a target child who was behaving poorly—both academically *and* socially—more favorably if he or she was thought to be mentally retarded. In short, the results of these studies seem to corroborate the hypothesis of Guskin (1963), which states that for retarded persons the label may produce

certain privileges as well as punishments, including the absence of demands for self-support and protection and the acceptance of certain unusual behaviors contrary to norms for nondefective individuals. (p. 322)

Although the results of these studies seem intuitive, nevertheless, there are some inconsistencies in the literature. For example, Gottlieb's (1975) study indicated that MR children are blamed more when they act up, whereas Foley's (1979) study suggested they are not. Also, Seitz and Geske (1976) presented some data that suggested that the *long-term* social effects of the MR label may not be as beneficial as people had thought. They had mothers of retarded children and graduate trainees in social welfare view a videotape of a child who was either retarded *or* nonretarded and who was also either labeled as retarded or not. In many respects, their results paralleled those obtained in the academic competence/label studies discuss-

ed earlier with regard to the label. That is, the retarded child who was labeled correctly was liked as much as the nonretarded nonlabeled child and more than the retarded child who was not so labeled; and the retarded child was thought to be more happy and appealing when labeled than when not labeled. However, the noticeable increase in reported liking of the retarded child as a function of the retardation label was not accompanied by a corresponding increase in ratings of competence, or by a decrease in social distance. In fact, when the children were evaluated as to their "adoptability," the nonretarded child always came out on top, followed by the nonlabeled retarded child, and then the labeled retarded child. In other words, on questions reflecting close social distance, rather than detached evaluation, the retardation label had unfavorable effects for the MR children.

The social distance data of Seitz and Geske (1976) raised some questions about much of the earlier labeling research and, specifically, about the conclusion drawn from these studies—that the MR label does not have any negative consequences for retarded children (e.g., MacMillan et al., 1974). Nevertheless, the results in one area of this research appear to be quite consistent; that is, MR children are not blamed as much as nonretarded children when they fail at an academic or cognitive task. That finding, together with the general lack of evidence of negative labeling effects, suggested that the initial fear that the MR label acts as a self-fulfilling prophecy may have been unwarranted. We will examine more recent data before drawing a final conclusion, however.

In order to understand why retarded children tend to receive more favorable evaluations when they fail, it is helpful to examine the results of previous studies that were concerned with reactions to persons with other kinds of handicaps. As might be expected, perceived ability (or lack of ability) plays a very important role in determining how people respond to handicapped persons. If the handicapped person's performance, whether successful or unsuccessful, is thought to have been influenced primarily by a lack of ability, then he or she is likely to receive more "credit" both in the form of higher estimates of effort expenditure and more favorable evaluations. For example, success by a physically handicapped person is typically thought to be the result of greater effort by that person and he or she is liked more because of this (Weiner & Kukla, 1970). By the same token, a handicapped person's failure is usually attributed to low ability (cf. Severance & Gasstrom, 1977), and seldom does the person receive unfavorable evaluations for this reason. In contrast, failure by a person of average ability is more likely to be considered an indication of a lack of motivation or effort, and this does result in less liking (Jones & deCharms, 1957).

Sympathy and stigma

Further evidence that persons with various kinds of stigmas are not blamed when they fail is provided by Carver and his colleagues (Carver, Gibbons, Stephan, Glass, & Katz, 1979; Carver, Glass & Katz, 1978). The paradigm used in the Carver research is fairly straightforward and it is similar to that used in much of the research by the author and others that is discussed in this chapter (e.g., Budoff & Siperstein, 1978). Briefly; subjects read a bogus transcript of an interview supposedly conducted with a person in his or her teens; the target is either labeled (e.g., handicapped) or not and is either doing quite well or quite poorly in life.

The results in each of these stigma studies were similar: The target persons received more favorable evaluations if they were labeled—regardless of how well they were doing in life. This tendency toward positive prejudice in favor of the stigmatized person was termed a "sympathy" effect.

WHY SYMPATHY? In discussing their results Carver et al. (1978) suggest that the augmentation principle (Kelley, 1972) may be relevant. The augmentation principle states that when an actor succeeds in the presence of an inhibiting factor, observers are more likely to infer the presence of another facilitating factor, such as ability or effort. In the case of a handicapped person, of course, that inferred facilitative factor is likely to be seen as enhanced effort. Thus, a handicapped person who is doing well in college in spite of his or her handicap, as was the case in the Carver et al. (1978) study, is thought to be more highly motivated than a similarly described student who is not handicapped. In turn, he or she is also liked more and is thought to be more successful. Based on this reasoning, one might assume that a mentally retarded child who is performing well in his or her life would also receive augmented attributions and more favorable evaluations. In short, the augmentation principle appears to be particularly appropriate for explaining how people perceive the behavior of handicapped persons, including those with mental retardation.

As it turns out, this speculation is wrong—people do not respond the same way to mentally retarded persons as they do to those with other kinds of stigmas. Mentally retarded persons do tend to receive low ability attributions, as do other handicapped persons. Unlike physically handicapped people or members of minority groups, however, these attributions also tend to influence the perceptions of other characteristics of retarded persons, including behaviors that are not specifically related to their handicap. Asch (1946) used the term "central trait" when referring to an important trait that can influence all of the impressions formed of a person by others. As we will see, when the trait involves intelligence, the stereotypes or expectations associated with it are very strong and very resistant to change, even when considerable conflicting information is available.

Behavioral expectations

Several investigators (e.g., Goodman et al., 1972; Guskin et al., 1975) have suggested that children with mental retardation tend to receive "special dispensation" for their behavioral inadequacies. A fundamental assumption of this work is that incompetent or deviant behavior is actually expected from MR children and that, presumably, is why it is tolerated. This basic assumption was validated recently in two studies.

In one study, Severance and Gasstrom (1977) asked college students to respond to the successful or unsuccessful outcome of a young girl who was working on a jigsaw puzzle. Subjects reacted quite differently to her behavior when she was labeled as mentally retarded than when she was not labeled. Lack of ability and increased effort were seen as more influential factors for the retarded child in the failure and success condition, respectively. In addition, the labeled girl was thought to be less likely to succeed on the cognitive task in the future, regardless of her past outcome.

More recently, Gibbons, Sawin, and Gibbons (1979) assessed college students' reactions to the general life performance of an adolescent who was or was not labeled as retarded. A modification of the method developed by Carver et al. (1978) was used in this study in which subjects read a transcript of an interview supposedly conducted with a 17-year-old girl. The girl attended a school and, in the successful condition, she had a job as a kitchen helper, was a good cook, had lots of friends, and was doing very well in life; in the unsuccessful condition, she had lost her job, was not a good cook, and did not have many friends. The information about the job and school were presented in order (1) to counteract the image usually connoted by the MR label of a severely retarded person with multiple handicaps (cf. Hollinger & Jones, 1970) and (2) to make it clear that the target being evaluated in the labeled condition was an *educable* mentally retarded person. After reading the transcript, subjects were asked to evaluate the person on several trait dimensions (e.g., hard-working) and social distance questions, and then make attributions for her previous behavior as well as predictions for her future *social* behaviors (getting a job, getting married, and raising a family).

In contrast to the Carver et al. research, there was evidence of a sympathy effect *only* in the unsuccessful condition. On the adjective and social distance items, the retarded person received more favorable evaluations then the nonretarded person in the unsuccessful condition and somewhat *less* favorable evaluations in the success condition. This same interaction occurred on the questions pertaining to expectations of social success: The unsuccessful retarded person received more optimistic (sympathetic) predictions, while the successful retarded person received significantly more *pessimistic* predictions. Moreover, when subjects were asked if the girl was likely to do better in life if she put more effort into what she was doing, the retarded girl again received much less optimistic predictions. (These means are presented in Table 12.1.)

The attribution items also revealed an interesting pattern of responding that was different than that seen in the "sympathy" research. As in the Severance and Gasstrom (1977) study, lack of ability was thought to be a more important factor for the retarded than the nonretarded girl. In addition, apparently as a result of this internal attribution, she was also thought to be much more susceptible to exogenous factors and, in general, to "factors beyond her control." Luck, for example, was thought to have a much greater influence over what happened to her, especially in the unsuccessful condition.

Patronization

Gibbons et al. (1979) called this attributional pattern a "patronization" effect. Specifically, the term refers to the tendency not to hold retarded persons responsible for their behavior—any behavior, regardless of outcome—because they are seen as having very low ability. Consequently, they receive less blame when they fail; and, more importantly, they receive *less* credit when they succeed, even though they are clearly seen as handicapped. This latter aspect of the pattern distinguishes it from the "sympathy"

Table 12.1. College Students' Evaluations and Attributions

		Target Description			
		Positive Transcript		Negative Transcript	
Question[a]	Label:	Retarded n = 20	Nonlabeled n = 19	Retarded n = 20	Nonlabeled n = 18
How successful is this person?		4.30	4.26	1.89	1.65
What is the reason? (other things/their doing)		2.95	5.00	2.39	5.60
Do better with more effort?		3.40	5.32	4.44	5.70
Social success[b]		15.10	17.74	10.72	8.50

Note. Adapted from "Evaluations of mentally retarded persons: 'Sympathy' or patronization?" by F. X. Gibbons, L. S. Sawin, and B. N. Gibbons. *American Journal of Mental Deficiency,* 1979, *84,* 124–131. Copyright © by the American Association on Mental Deficiency. Reprinted by permission.
[a]A high number represents a more favorable evaluation or a dispositional attribution. Scale = 1 to 7.
[b]This represents the sum of the three social success questions (get a job, get married, and raise a family). Scale = 3 to 21.

effect (Carver et al., 1978, 1979). Whereas persons with other kinds of stigma tend to be liked more and to receive extra "credit" when they succeed (augmentation), mentally retarded persons do not. Success is seen as being atypical and unlikely to recur even if the retarded person were to exert more effort at what he or she is doing. Moreover, this attitude applies to noncognitive behaviors that are presumably not related to mental retardation, as well as to cognitive behaviors such as puzzle performance. Heider (1958) calls this tendency—of one important attribute to influence the perception of other seemingly nonrelated traits—a "halo" or "spread" effect.

What effect does patronization have on mentally retarded children? Dweck and Goetz (1978) state that giving children feedback that suggests their failures are due to stable and uncontrollable factors, especially lack of ability, can promote a state of learned helplessness in them (see also Chapter 3 by Frieze on children's attributions for success and failure). Similarly, Weisz (1979) stated recently that "feedback from the teacher, the unguarded comments of nonretarded children and the institutional feedback inherent in assignment to a 'special class' or a 'resource room' may suggest to retarded children that their failures generally are attributable to deficient ability" (p. 312). Moreover, he suggests that many years of experience with this kind of stable internal attribution can lead to a sense of learned helplessness in these people.

As we will see, there is not much evidence to suggest that retarded children experience chronic learned helplessness, at least not until they get much older. Nonetheless, the major concern here is that, if retarded children are aware of the patronizing attitude and believe that they are not totally responsible for their behavior, regardless of what they do, then it is very likely that their motivation to improve or increase their effort will remain low.

The results of Gibbons et al. (1979) verify the assumption of earlier studies (e.g., Farina et al., 1976; Foley, 1979; Gottlieb, 1974, 1975) that incompetent behavior is expected from retarded children. It should be mentioned, however, that the label in this study included reference to a state school for retarded persons, in addition to the term "educable mentally retarded." Although a pilot study had indicated that when both labels are used subjects respond primarily to the EMR term, nonetheless, the fact that the retarded girl was institutionalized was important because it could have influenced subjects' expectations of her social behavior. It should also be pointed out that the subjects in this experiment had all completed high school before the passage of the Education for All Handicapped Children Act (PL 94-142, 1975). Therefore, it is entirely possible that many of them had not had much contact with mentally retarded persons. In fact, this information was volunteered by many subjects, even though it was not asked for. Consequently, a second study (Gibbons & Kassin, 1980, Experiment I) was run in which students at a junior high school that included mainstreamed retarded children participated as subjects.

Male and female subjects (ages 12 to 15) read a story about a boy named John who was said to be a student at a nearby junior high school. In the labeled condition he was also described as being mentally retarded and a member of a special class at the school. In the story, John was about to work on a jigsaw puzzle, and subjects were asked to predict his success at this task. They then received information about his outcome (successful or unsuccessful), made attributions (to effort, ability, and luck) for his behavior, and predicted his future social success (again, marriage, employment, and raising a family).

RESULTS. Both the male and female subjects thought that the retarded target was less smart than the nonretarded person. They also thought he was less likely to succeed on the puzzle than was the nonretarded target (even if he had put more effort into it), and less likely to succeed than they themselves were (all $p < .005$). In the failure condition, subjects were asked to attribute blame for the outcome, and there was again evidence of patronization. As in the Gibbons et al. (1979) research, less blame was attributed internally (to John) when he was mentally retarded ($p < .01$). On the attribution items, the results were different from those in Gibbons et al. (1979), since neither luck nor

ability was thought to be a more important factor for the retarded than for the nonretarded person. Instead, there was a significant label x outcome interaction on the *effort* question. This factor was thought to be more important in explaining the success and less important in explaining the failure of the retarded than the nonretarded person. Finally, on the social success items, the retarded girl was thought to be less likely to get a good job, but the label effect was *not* significant on either the family or the marriage questions.

In summary, the data provided by these "mainstreamed" children were somewhat more encouraging than those obtained in earlier research with college students (e.g., Gibbons et al., 1979). Although there was some indication of patronization in their responses (the retarded girl was not blamed when she failed), the evidence was weak. These younger subjects did not show sympathetic or overly positive reactions toward the retarded girl, nor did they attribute her behavior to luck or make an overriding attribution to a lack of ability for her. Instead, they relied on what appeared to be a very reasonable effort attribution when explaining her behavior; they saw her success as a result of increased effort while her failure was thought to be the result of insufficient effort. Clearly, this type of response does allow room for improvement by the retarded person.

It may be somewhat premature to suggest that these mildly encouraging results are attributable to the increased contact between handicapped and nonhandicapped children that comes with mainstreaming. If knowledge about mental retardation can be considered a factor contributing to their relatively "enlightened" attitudes, however, then there is reason to be optimistic. These children appeared to be surprisingly well-versed on the subject. When asked to define what mental retardation is, 87% responded, and by far the largest group (more than two-thirds) referred to learning and/or intellectual problems in their answers (e.g., "a slow learner").

Patronization and the law

Recent studies with nonretarded persons (Gibbons et al., 1979; Gibbons & Kassin, 1980, Experiment I) have indicated that mentally retarded children are usually not expected to succeed on various cognitive tasks nor are they blamed when they fail at them. These studies also indicated that retarded children are thought to be fairly inept socially. One relevant question that remains to be answered is whether retarded children are also not blamed for their failure or incompetence at noncognitive behaviors. In the Gottlieb (1975) study, retarded children were derogated more than were nonretarded children when they acted aggressively. This reaction is generally contradictory to the patronization pattern, however. Consequently, another study was conducted to determine if retarded adolescents are patronized (not held responsible for their actions) when they evidence anti-social behavior. Specifically, are mentally retarded offenders punished more severely when they commit a crime, as the Gottlieb (1975) research would suggest, or are they "let off the hook?"

College students in this study (Gibbons, Gibbons, & Kassin, 1980) read a vignette of an incident in which one of two types of crimes had taken place, either vandalism of a store or burglary of a store and assault of the store owner. These crimes were chosen because previous research conducted with lawyers, judges, and police (Schilit, 1979) and pilot research with college students (by the authors) indicated that vandalism is thought to be the type of crime that is most frequently committed by mentally retarded offenders, whereas assault and burglary are not thought to be committed by this group very often. In the narrative of the crime, an eyewitness identified a young man named Toby as the person he thought he saw running away from the scene. Toby was 21 and, according to the condition, was either labeled as retarded or not labeled. Subjects indicated how likely they thought Toby was to have committed the crime, *before* he

confessed and then again *after* he had confessed to it.

An interaction on the intitial likelihood-of-commission question replicated the results of the Schilit (1979) study, as the percentage was very low in the labeled, unlikely crime (assault and burglary) condition (these data are presented in Table 12.2). There was a strong main effect for the label on the second commission question, as the retarded person was thought to have been much less likely to have committed either crime after the confession than was the nonretarded target (the confession increased the likelihood of commission by only 18% for the labeled target, compared with 45% for the nonlabeled target). One reason for this was that subjects thought it was much more likely that mentally retarded Toby was coerced into confessing.

Finally, subjects made causal attributions, suggested an appropriate sentence, and indicated if they thought Toby was likely to commit the crime again. There were significant label effects on all three questions. When the target was mentally retarded, he received a smaller percentage of the blame (internal attributions) for the crime (41% versus 73%) and a lighter sentence, and he was thought to be less likely to commit the crime again, whether or not he was punished for it now.

These results provide an illustration of the patronization pattern "at work." They also indicate how this type of attitude can sometimes be beneficial for retarded persons (cf. Farina et al. 1976). In this case, even when subjects were told that the young man had committed the crime, they still let him off much easier if he was mentally retarded—because they did not consider him to be totally responsible for his actions. These results are different from those of Gottlieb (1975) who found that a retarded child received more blame when he acted aggressively. Of course in that study, the "victim" of the target's aggressiveness was another child, whereas in the present study the retarded boy was confronting first an adult and later the court system. Perhaps the

Table 12.2. College Students' Reactions to a Crime

Question	Label:	Vandalism		Assault and Burglary	
		Retarded n = 18	Nonlabeled n = 19	Retarded n = 16	Nonlabeled n = 19
Likelihood of commission:	Preconfession	40.28	29.79	30.69	44.74
	Postconfession	63.94	80.05	42.00	83.53
Coerced		4.83	4.11	5.00	3.32
Sentence		3.67	5.21	3.44	6.16
Toby's fault (%)		42.61	74.21	40.06	72.63
Likelihood of recidivism (if punished) (%)		24.17	40.37	26.19	37.63

[a]A high number reflects a higher estimate of likelihood or a harsher sentence. Scales for "Coerced" = 1 to 7 and for "Sentence" = 1 ("no sentence") to 10 ("15 or more years in jail").

relative power of his opponent made a difference in how much blame and responsibility was attributed internally to him.

Step II: Awareness of the expectations

Despite the numerous inconsistencies in the labeling research, one reliable finding emerges clearly; that is, the MR label does elicit very pessimistic behavioral expectations. As was stated earlier, however, expectations alone do not create a *self*-fulfilling prophecy; the question of what effect the label actually has on labeled children is really what is at the core of this issue. The following research is concerned with the second step of the prophecy: Are retarded persons aware of the expectations created by their label?

Shortly after the publication of *Pygmalion in the Classroom,* Anderson and Rosenthal (1968) attempted to replicate the pygmalion expectancy effect using institutionalized mentally retarded persons as subjects. Some people were initially administered an IQ test and then the names of a group of arbitrarily chosen "late-bloomers" were given to their day-camp counselors. After a period of two months, IQ scores were again assessed. The results of the study proved inconclusive, however, since there was no evidence at all of a self-fulfilling prophecy. In fact, the "late-bloomers" actually tended to show a

decrease in IQ scores over the course of the experiment!

In discussing these rather surprising results, or absence of results, Jones (1977) suggested that the lack of an expectancy effect may have been due to the fact that the retarded subjects were not "capable of picking up emitted cues in order for [those] expectations to be successfully communicated and, hence, fulfilled" (p. 110). As Jones indicates, this is a very important question. If the "objects of interpersonal communications" cannot understand the message—and therefore are not aware of the expectations—it is not likely that they will ever demonstrate the expected behavior *on their own.* Although this may be less true in the classroom where teachers can exert a significant influence over a student's academic performance, regardless of the student's self-expectations, it is nonetheless, clear that if a general behavioral expectation is to become *self*-fulfilling the child must have some idea of what it is that is expected of him or her.

Self-concept

Until recently, retarded children's awareness of what their label means had never really been directly examined. One reason for this, of course, is that this kind of research was thought to be difficult, if not impossible, to conduct with retarded persons. Consequently, most of the earlier work that can be loosely classified as being in this area concentrated on the more basic question of self-concept among retarded persons.

Given the pessimistic nature of the results in the expectation research, it might be expected that this would be reflected in negative self-impressions among retarded persons. Actually, there is very little evidence to suggest that this is the case. For example, Fine and Caldwell (1967) assessed the self-concepts of EMR children and found that they rated themselves at least as good if not better than others of their own age—including nonretarded children. The authors concluded that these children's self-concepts were "inaccurate, inflated and unrealistic." Similar results are reported by Willy and McCandless (1973).

Although Fine and Caldwell did not elaborate on the characteristics of their sample, one possible explanation of their results is that the retarded children in their study were of a relatively low intelligence level. It seems to be the case, in fact, that *higher* level retarded persons tend to have *lower* self-concepts. This pattern was reported by McAfee and Cleland (1965), who suggested that higher level persons are more likely both to use nonretarded persons as a reference group and to be aware of their own shortcomings relative to a societal ideal.

Certainly nonretarded children are aware of retarded persons' shortcomings, but are retarded persons themselves aware? Put more simply, do they realize what a terrible stigma it is in our society to be mentally retarded? Gallagher (1976) thinks they do. He says that students in special classes and mildly retarded adolescents and adults in state institutions experience "humiliation" because they realize the "inferior status of their placement" and the "social inferiority" of their group (see also Jones, 1972, 1973). His conclusion seems reasonable enough; however, what little data there is on this point is far from consistent.

In two separate studies, Gozali (1972) and

Warner, Thrapp, and Walsh (1973) asked special-class students what their impressions were of their placements. They obtained very different results. Gozali found that 85% of the special-class graduates that she interviewed classified their placements as "degrading and useless." In contrast, Warner et al. interviewed students (ages 8 to 17) who were currently enrolled in special classes and found evidence of mildly positive results. Sixty-one percent of those questioned said they liked being in the class, and 41% said they had no desire to be elsewhere. When asked why they were in the special class, 53% of the grammar school children gave academic or remedial reasons ("to learn," "to read," or "to catch up"); however, that figure dropped to only 18% for the high-school-age students. Nonetheless, Warner et al. concluded that the special class provided a "stimulating" and "comfortable" placement for children who had difficulty adjusting elsewhere.

One of the most interesting findings of the Warner et al. research is that less than 10% of the special-class students surveyed characterized themselves as mentally retarded. This tendency to dissociate oneself from the MR label is also the major theme of Edgerton's classic study of 48 mentally retarded persons who had been released from a state hospital in California (*The Cloak of Competence*, 1967). The case histories of these people, as presented in the book, indicate that all of them were obsessed with the desire to deny their retardation, or to "pass," as Edgerton calls it. He believes that the stigma of having been adjudged mentally retarded is totally unacceptable for most former institution residents because it prevents them from living a normal life outside the institution. He presents this opinion very clearly in the conclusion of his book:

The label of mental retardation not only serves as a humiliating, frustrating, and discrediting stigma in the conduct of one's life in the community, but it also serves to lower one's self-esteem to such a nadir of worthlessness that the life of a person so labeled is scarcely worth living. (p. 145)

Knowledge of mental retardation

In an attempt to ascertain mentally retarded persons' objective knowledge of their condition, Gan, Tymchuk, and Nisihara (1977) asked a group of persons from a sheltered workshop what mental retardation is and what mentally retarded persons can and cannot (or shouldn't) do. Not surprisingly, this group exhibited very favorable attitudes toward retarded persons. Seventy-five percent agreed with basic rights questions, such as mentally retarded persons should have the right to marry, vote, and have children (61% agreed with this latter specific question). Two-thirds answered favorably on questions pertaining to job skills, and 97% felt that a retarded person could hold down a job. Although the tone of the responses in this study was quite positive, some caution is warranted in interpreting the results for two reasons. One reason is that only 66% of the sample surveyed actually responded to the questions; the other reason is that the sample consisted of persons who were being trained to improve their job (and social) skills, and thus they may have been somewhat more optimistic or favorable than, say, an institutionalized sample.

AN INSIDER'S VIEW. One final anecdote deserves mention before the experimental research is described. That is an interview conducted by Bogdan and Taylor (1976) with a mentally retarded person whom they called "Ed Murphy" (not his real name). Essentially, Ed was asked what it was like being mentally retarded and living in a state institution. As might be expected, he did not find either situation very enjoyable; however, the most striking aspect of the interview was the insight and understanding that Ed seemed to have with regard to his status in the community and that of others like him. Talking about the reactions of others (i.e., friends, parents, etc.) he said, "Sometimes I think the pain of being handicapped is that people give you so much love that it becomes a weight on you and a weight on them" (p. 48). On the institution he says,

"Being in a state school, or having been in a state school isn't fashionable and never will be. Deep down you want to avoid the institution" (p. 49). Provocative and informative as Ed Murphy's statements are, it is surprising that Bogdan and Taylor's article represents one of the few attempts in the literature to "go to the source" to find out what retarded persons (or any group of stigmatized persons) think about their label and their place in society. As was the case in their study, when such an effort is made, the results are often quite different from what the investigators expect. As Bogdan and Taylor suggest,

People who are labeled retarded have their own understanding about themselves, their situations and their experiences. These understandings are often different from the professionals'. (p. 51)

Group concept

The first step in determining retarded persons' reactions to the label is to examine their perceptions of other labeled persons—their peers. Based on previous research in social psychology, it would appear that there are two very different reactions that might be expected from retarded persons who are evaluating others like themselves. On the one hand, social comparison theory (Festinger, 1954), Byrne's (1971) work on similarity and attraction, and Festinger, Schachter, and Back's (1950) proximity research would suggest that if institutionalized persons are like other people (and if the institution is like other environments) then they should like their retarded peers, possibly even more than they do nonretarded persons. One reason for this, as Festinger et al. (1950) demonstrated, is that people tend to like most those persons who live closest to them, and it is certainly the case that one cannot live any closer to his or her neighbor than in the dormitory of a state institution. Similarly, the reference group of institutionalized retarded persons is likely to consist almost exclusively of other retarded persons, and so they are the ones who are most likely to provide social validation in terms of beliefs, attitudes and abilities (cf. Festinger, 1954).

Social comparison theory is particularly appropriate for explaining the social behaviors of higher level retarded persons living in an institution. It would predict that they might enjoy their status in the institution, because they are most likely to benefit from social comparison with other, lower level residents. This is consistent with the reasoning of Edgerton (1967), who has suggested that higher level retarded persons have a need to deny their retardation and that the hospital or institutional environment allows them to do this, since it provides an opportunity for "self-aggrandizement" through comparison with lower level persons. In short, higher level persons may like the institution because it helps them maintain a feeling of superiority relative to others inside it.

On the other hand, the results of McAfee and Cleland (1965) suggest that higher level EMR persons are aware of the stigma associated with their label. Because of this they tend to have very negative self-concepts and, presumably, negative perceptions of each other. This would be even more true for mainstreamed EMR students who are likely to have primarily nonretarded children in their reference group and, therefore, should be more aware of what the label implies and what their own shortcomings are. Perhaps the ideal situation would be to expose handicapped children to *two* reference groups— handicapped peers as well as nonhandicapped children. This is exactly what Strang, Smith, and Rogers (1978) found. They suggest that having two reference groups results in higher self-concepts for these children because it allows them to socially compare favorably with their handicapped peers (on abilities, for example), while at the same time they are able to feel they "belong" with the nonretarded children.

It would appear that the fundamental question here is whether EMR children are, in fact, aware of the stigma that is associated with their label. If not, then it may be expected that they would respond favorably toward their retarded peers because of the positive affect associated with social comparison, familiarity, propinquity, and so on. But if they are aware of the stigma, this should be manifested in their relatively poor evaluations of persons who are labeled and in a desire to dissociate themselves from the label. This question was recently examined (Gibbons & Gibbons, 1980).

Fifty-nine male and female EMR persons (mean age = 24, mean IQ = 56) who were residents in a state school were interviewed individually in the study. A version of the Gibbons et al. (1979) procedure was used which was modified for a retarded population.[2] Subjects were read a story about a 17-year-old boy who was either doing well or poorly in life and who was either labeled as living in a state school for retarded persons, or not labeled. After evaluating the person on a series of adjectives (e.g., "friendly") and social distance items (e.g., "have as a friend"), they were read a second story about a person whose label was the opposite of the first person's and they were asked to compare the two targets on adjective and social distance items.

THE RESULTS. The negatively described target received much less favorable ratings on all of the adjective evaluations, but there were no differences that resulted from the label on any of these questions. There was a large label effect on the social distance questions and comparisons, however: The *nonlabeled* person was consistently preferred on such items as "have as a friend" and "live near." In short, these subjects did not display negative attitudes toward the retarded person; they just did not want to be associated with him or her. In addition, one of the sample characteristics was significantly related to the subject's choices: The longer they had been in the institution, the more likely they were to prefer the nonlabeled (noninstitutionalized) target.

These results indicate that mentally retarded persons are aware of the stigma connected with the institutional label and prefer not to be associated with institutionalized persons. It is difficult to draw any conclusions, however, about how they perceive mentally retarded persons *in general.* In fact, the lack of an effect on the trait evaluations may indicate that they do not perceive retarded and nonretarded persons any differently, but rather they just do not like institutions (an opinion that was volunteered by several subjects during the debriefing session). Yet it can be concluded from a recent study (Budoff & Siperstein, 1980) that mentally retarded persons do have negative reactions to the MR label. These authors extended the findings of the Gibbons and Gibbons study to include non-institutionalized EMR children attending special education classes. Subjects viewed a videotape of a child who was behaving competently or incompetently (i.e., misspelling words) and who was either identified as being retarded or not. The incompetent child received less favorable ratings from these retarded children on an adjective checklist and on an "Activity Preference List" that measured behavioral intentions toward the target (e.g., desire to play with). The *retarded* child also received less favorable ratings on the adjective checklist.

Expectations and the label

Having determined that mentally retarded persons are aware of the label and that it does have an effect on their evaluations of others, we then attempted to determine what are their behavioral *expectations* of their peers and of themselves. In this experiment (Gibbons & Kassin, 1980, Experiment II) institutionalized mentally retarded adolescents were asked to make predictions and attributions for the behavior of a retarded or a nonretarded target.

THE METHOD. Each subject was shown a picture of a boy and a jigsaw puzzle of about 30 pieces. They were asked to indicate how smart and friendly they thought the boy was and how well he would do on the puzzle that he was about to work on. After receiving information about his outcome (success or

failure), subjects made attributions for his performance and then predicted his success later in life in social activities (again, getting a job, getting married, and raising a family).

THE RESULTS. There were no differences on the ratings of friendliness, but the retarded target was thought to be much less *smart* than the nonretarded target ($p < .001$), and somewhat less likely to succeed on the puzzle ($p < .12$). This latter difference was again stronger for people who had been in the institution longer (these data are presented in Table 12.3). Predictions on the social success questions were quite pessimistic: The retarded target was thought to be much less likely to get a job and to be able to raise a family and slightly less likely to get married. (The combined social index is presented in Table 12.3). Moreover, there was a near-significant label x outcome interaction ($p = .07$) as the retarded, unsuccessful target received the most pessimistic evaluations (this cell was significantly different from all others at the $p < .005$ level). Finally, the female subjects tended to be more harsh on the retarded (male) target on all of the questions than were the males.

When asked to predict their *own* success at the social behaviors, subjects thought they were more likely to succeed than was the unsuccessful target and less likely to succeed than the successful target. In addition, a comparison of their *average* self-rating with their other ratings (see Table 12.3) indicated that they considered themselves to be about equal to the retarded person in likelihood of success and much less likely to succeed than the nonretarded person ($p < .01$).

ATTRIBUTIONS. There was no evidence of augmentation, since the label did not affect the attribution responses of the subjects in this study. There were significant main effects for puzzle outcome on each of the three factors (effort, ability, and task difficulty), however, as each one was thought to have been more important in explaining the behavior of the successful than the unsuccessful target. The lack of label effect on the

Table 12.3. Retarded Adolescents' Evaluations and Behavioral Predictions

Question[a]	Target: Retarded n = 22		Nonretarded n = 23	
Friendly	3.64		3.70	
Smart	2.77		3.87	
Expected outcome	3.45		3.74	
	Retarded		Nonretarded	
Puzzle Outcome:	Successful	Unsuccessful	Successful	Unsuccessful
Social success				
Other[b]	8.20	6.58	8.59	8.18
Self–other[c]	−.62	1.00	−1.01	−.60

[a]These questions were asked *before* the outcome information was provided, scale = 1 to 4. A higher number represents a more favorable assessment.
[b]These numbers are the sum of the three social success questions (job, marriage, and family); scale = 3 to 9.
[c]This represents the *mean* self-rating (for all subjects, $m = 7.58$) minus the other-rating.

ability question was particularly surprising and disturbing for us. For one thing, it is discrepant with the results of previous research with college students (Gibbons et al., 1979; Severance & Gasstrom, 1977). More importantly, if retarded persons are not capable of understanding the role that ability (or lack of ability) plays in determining the outcome of other retarded persons and those with different kinds of handicaps, then it may not be possible to measure their expectations of labeled persons. Still, the clear pattern of results on the smart rating and the puzzle prediction items indicates that retarded people are aware of what the label means. Perhaps the attribution questions were just too difficult for them to understand.

Augmentation—Do mentally retarded persons understand it?

As was mentioned earlier, Carver and his colleagues (Carver et al., 1978) have suggested that the augmentation principle may be one reason why physically handicapped or stigmatized persons receive more sympathetic evaluations than do nonstigmatized persons. This principle, which states that people are more likely to infer the presence of a facilitating factor (such as enhanced effort) when an actor succeeds in spite of an

inhibiting factor, appears to be fundamental to a complete understanding of the behavior of persons with various types of handicaps. Consequently, another study was conducted to assess mentally retarded adolescents' understanding of augmentation.

Recent work by Kassin (see Chapter 8 on the development of attributional principles) has indicated that the augmentation principle is used by children at a much younger age than was first thought, when it is presented by means of a "perceptual technique," involving the use of an animated cartoon (cf. Kassin, Lowe & Gibbons, 1980). This technique was recently presented to a group of institutionalized mentally retarded adolescents (Kassin & Gibbons, 1980). The results were encouraging: 76% of the subjects made the accurate choice (this percentage is significantly above chance), indicating that they do understand the principle when it is presented visually, although they were not able to explain it verbally. These results together with those in the Gibbons and Kassin (1980) study, indicate that mentally retarded persons do use the augmentation principle and, in particular, that they do infer enhanced motivation when a behavior is performed in spite of an inhibiting factor. They *cannot* understand the principle when it is presented to them orally, however (as in Gibbons & Kassin, 1980), nor can they explicate it accurately.

Special dispensation?

Attribution items aside, the results with retarded persons in Gibbons and Gibbons (1980) were similar to those with college students in the Gibbons et al. (1979) and Severance and Gasstrom (1977) studies in the successful, but *not* in the unsuccessful, conditions. In other words, the most noticeable distinction between college students' and mentally retarded persons' evaluations of retarded persons occurs after a failure experience of some kind. Under these circumstances, college students tend to display sympathy toward retarded persons, attributing their failure to a lack of ability and, as a consequence, liking them more than unsuccessful, nonretarded persons. In contrast, retarded persons do not show sympathy toward their retarded peers. In fact, the unsuccessful retarded target tended to receive the most *negative* evaluations from the retarded sample. Surprisingly, this occurs even though retarded persons are apparently well aware of the handicap associated with mental retardation and the problems that the handicap creates. It would appear, then, that mentally retarded children do not provide "special dispensation" to their retarded peers who fail but, instead, they are more critical of them than are nonretarded children and college students.

Step III: Internalization

It would be safe to say at this point that the first two of the three steps of the self-fulfilling prophecy do exist. The remaining question to be answered is whether retarded children internalize the pessimistic expectations that were evident in the previous research.

A motivational-developmental theory

Zigler (1969, 1971) argues that mentally retarded children do have a much greater internalized expectancy of failure than do nonretarded children. This is the basis of his motivational-developmental theory of mental retardation, which will be elaborated on here. Zigler's theory is "stage-developmental," in the tradition of Piaget and Kohlberg, in that he contends that all persons, regardless of their level of intelligence, tend to progress through the same stages of cognitive development in precisely the same order. The only distinction between retarded and nonretarded persons is that, by definition, the former tend to proceed through these stages much more slowly and, of course, there is an upper limit to their development. Theoretically, therefore, the cognitive behavior of children of the same mental age should be roughly equivalent. Obviously it is not, and the discrepancy, he claims, is attributable to differences in their levels of motivation.

Zigler believes that parents and, to some extent, others interacting with children initially tend to base their behavioral expectations on the child's chronological age (CA), regardless of his or her mental age (MA). Since mentally retarded children are less likely to be able to live up to these expectations, they are more likely to experience failure. Consistent exposure to failure has two detrimental effects on retarded children. One is that they tend to become excessively dependent on their parents for outcome information (i.e., how well they are currently doing), an orientation that Zigler labels "outer-directedness." As might be expected, this tendency is exacerbated by institutional placement. Institutionalized retarded children are quite likely to develop an exceptionally strong need for social reinforcement from adults in the institution (Zigler calls this a "positive reaction tendency"). Because of this, they become increasingly dependent on the reactions of others, and it is easy to see why the expectations of nonretarded persons would have a strong effect on their behavior.

A second consequence of mentally retarded children's repeated exposure to failure, according to Zigler, is that they develop both very low expectations of success and a willingness to accept or be satisfied with low levels of accomplishment. At the same time, their motivation is directed more toward avoiding failure than to achieving success, so that they tend to set achievement goals that are well below their capabilities.

Zigler's theorizing has led to a considerable number of research efforts aimed at determining whether or not retarded children do anticipate failing and how they react to failure experiences. Two of the earlier such attempts (MacMillan, 1969; MacMillan & Keough, 1971) offered support for Zigler's contentions. In those studies, retarded and nonretarded children were asked to work on a task and then they were arbitrarily interrupted by the experimenter. The retarded children were much more likely to interpret the interruption as evidence of their own failure. In addition, Hayes and Prinz (1976) found that, while retarded and nonretarded children reacted similarly to successful outcomes, the retarded children appeared jaded in their reaction to failure since it seemed to have little or no affect on them. Apparently, this situation becomes worse as retarded children get older. Weisz (1979) found evidence of "learned helplessness" among older retarded children. He suggests that the reduction in motivation that is characteristic of the learned helplessness state is the result of a "cumulative deficit" acquired after years of experience with failure feedback, *especially* when that failure is attributed to low ability.

As with the labeling issue, however, researchers were quick to question the pessimistic results of the early work on expectancy of failure. For example, in a more recent study, MacMillan (1975) measured the chronic and situational expectancies of a group of EMR children and two groups of nonretarded children—one matched with the retarded group on CA, the other matched on MA. He found no differences between the groups in chronic failure expectancies, or in reactions to manipulated success and failure. Similar results are reported by Schuster and Gruen (1971).

Several investigators have looked at the important question of how mentally retarded persons compare with nonretarded persons in the type of attributions they make for their own behaviors. In one of those studies (Horai & Guarnaccia, 1975), the retarded subjects tended to attribute their successful behavior to ability and failure to a lack of effort—hardly the type of response that is typical of persons who constantly expect to fail. In fact, this kind of attributional pattern most resembles that adopted by *high* (rather than low) achievement-motivated persons.

Effect of attributional feedback

Weiner (1974) has suggested that certain kinds of attributional feedback have a facilitative effect on a child's motivation, whereas others tend to be debilitating. For example, attributing successful outcomes to the internal factors of effort and ability suggests to the child that success is likely in the future if he or she will again try hard. By the same token, attributing failure to a lack of effort also suggests to the child that future success is possible if effort is increased (see also Chapter 3 by Frieze).

Hoffman and Weiner (1978) tested these principles with retarded children. Specifically, they were interested in the amount of effort expended on a second task as a function of the type of attribution received for performance on the first task. Their results indicated that these children tend to react in the same way as do nonretarded children to the attributional feedback they receive. Of particular interest were their reactions to ability attributions: When their successful outcomes were attributed to ability, they subsequently tried harder than when the same attribution was made for their failure. Similarly, when failure was attributed to a lack of effort rather than ability, they again increased their effort. These data point out the beneficial effect that effort rather than ability attributions can have on retarded children.

Two conclusions can be drawn from these expectancy studies. One is that institutionalized retarded children have internalized an expectancy for failure on a variety of *social* behaviors. The second conclusion is that mentally retarded children will respond favorably to certain kinds of attributional feedback—in the same way that nonretarded children do. Specifically, they will exert more effort at what they are doing if debilitating low-ability attributions are avoided and effort attributions are stressed when explaining their successful and unsuccessful behaviors. Finally, it may be recalled that this is the type of attributional pattern that the "mainstreamed" nonretarded children adopted in the Gibbons and Kassin (1980, Experiment I) study, when explaining the behavior of a retarded child.

Conclusions

There are some encouraging and some mildly discouraging findings in the multitude of studies reported here. On the negative side is the fact that all of the studies conducted with mentally retarded persons indicated that they are very much aware of what the MR label means and what the negative connotations of the label are. In particular, they reject association with the institutional label and with persons so labeled. This tendency is strongest for retarded peers (targets) who are unsuccessful, indicating that retarded persons do not provide "special dispensation" to others who behave incompetently, just because they also are mentally retarded. In addition, and perhaps of most importance, is the fact that the retarded subjects maintained low expectations of the retarded targets; moreover, this tendency appeared to become stronger the longer the subjects had lived in the institution.

Implications for mainstreaming.

One of the basic presumptions of the mainstreaming movement is that increased contact between handicapped and nonhandicapped children will be "psychologically healthy" for both groups; in other words, their attitudes toward each other should improve as a consequence of their interactions. The results of the Gibbons and Kassin (1980, Experiment I) study with students from a mainstreamed school suggest that this may be true, although it is too early to draw any definitive conclusions. Ironically, it appears that the primary attitudinal problem actually exists among retarded children—toward each other, especially members of the opposite sex—possibly even more than among the nonretarded children. As long as retarded children maintain low opinions and very low expectations of their peers, then it is unlikely that they will ever learn to expect success of themselves. In other words, if their group concept is negative, it stands to reason that their self-concept will also be unfavorable.

This is particularly true for institutionalized retarded persons who are candidates for community placement. A negative "group concept" can only interfere with the process of deinstitutionalization and with the socialization processes that occur in the community among formerly institutionalized persons. In community settings, as they exist now, formerly institutionalized retarded persons are typically placed together with other retarded persons as roommates. It is also possible that this will exacerbate the group concept problem that we have detected. The more contact they have with peers who do not expect them to succeed, the more likely they are to internalize those expectations and the smaller are the chances that they will actually achieve success.

This group concept problem is related to, and possibly responsible for, the pessimistic expectations that institutionalized mentally retarded children have for their own future social behaviors. If they have low opinions of their peers—particularly those of the opposite sex—then, of course, they would not be very optimistic about their chances for a successful marriage or their prospects of being able to raise a family. Our data suggest that this may be one of the areas of greatest concern for people involved with community placement of formerly institutionalized retarded children.

In summary, it would appear that the MR

label can act in an inhibitory manner for retarded children, primarily because of the negative or pessimistic expectations associated with it. One goal of the deinstitutionalization and normalization movements, therefore, should be a reduction of the behavioral restrictions that are produced by these expectations and an improvement of the attitudes that retarded children and young adults maintain toward each other. One way to do this is to allow retarded children the opportunity to see others like themselves attempting and succeeding at behaviors that are unfamiliar to them; exposure to other retarded persons, possibly graduates of special classes or sheltered workshops, may provide them with much-needed examples of retarded persons who have been successful. In many respects, retarded persons themselves may be the best equipped to conduct the attitude change program that is necessary for the continued success of the various normalization programs.

A self-fulfilling prophecy?

There are some encouraging findings in the data reported here as well. On the positive side is the fact that, with the exception of social success items (e.g., Gibbons & Kassin, 1980, Experiment II), there is generally no conclusive evidence that mentally retarded children and adolescents have internalized a strong failure expectancy on learning tasks. Therefore, it appears that, at least for these children, the prophecy associated with their label has not become self-fulfilling and presumably does not become so at least until they are much older (Weisz, 1979). Perhaps the most encouraging finding is that retarded and nonretarded children react in a very similar manner to different kinds of attributional feedback (Hoffman & Weiner, 1978; Horai & Guarnaccia, 1975).

The type of attributional feedback that retarded children receive has a very strong effect on their future performance—perhaps even more of an effect than it has on nonretarded children. The reason being that

they are more dependent on others both for information as to how they are doing and for positive reinforcement in general (cf. Zigler, 1969). In this regard, Weisz's (1979) data indicate that years of experience with stable/internal (low ability) attributions can lead to a sense of learned helplessness in retarded persons. On the other hand, out of a desire to avoid this obviously inhibiting attributional response, people frequently go to the other extreme—patronization—when dealing with retarded persons. We suggest that isolating retarded persons from the instructional feedback that comes with both success and failure (which is essentially what patronization is) can easily lead to the same severe motivational problems that Weisz talks about. What approach should be adopted then? A recent article by Perske (1972) is relevant to this question.

Dignity of risk

Perske observed the service delivery systems for retarded persons in Scandinavia. He noted that in Sweden and Denmark retarded persons are allowed or even encouraged to enter the community and attempt a variety of "normal" behaviors—just as nonretarded persons do—even though they may run a great "risk" of failure. Perske feels that, in this country, we sometimes try to shelter retarded persons from the dangers of the real world and, in so doing, deny them basic human dignity. He states,

We cannot continue the type of over-protection we usually give the mentally retarded in our country. . . . To deny any retarded person his fair share of such experiences is to further cripple him for healthy living. Mentally retarded persons may, can, will and should respond to risk with full human dignity and courage. (p. 26)

Of course, trying to determine what is a "fair share" of risk for a retarded person is itself a risky proposition. Most institutionalized retarded persons need some guidance when in the community and will continue to require occasional supervision even after they have been placed in community settings (cf. Edgerton, 1967). The alternative, of course, can be repeated experience with failure and the equally great risk that that entails. Thus, supervised apartments, sheltered workshops, and other "halfway" programs may provide retarded persons with the kind of supervised experience and exposure to both success and failure that they need to overcome patronization and learned helplessness. In short, complete integration may become too risky, whereas complete segregation can be too stultifying.

The same is probably true in the school system, which puts the special-education and the mainstreamed-classroom teacher in a difficult situation. On the one hand, the mainstreamed classroom provides the EMR child with the "dignity of risk" that is certainly essential for normal growth and development, but it also provides the child with a potential for a great deal of failure and the harmful attributional feedback that can come with it. On the other hand, the special class and/or the totally segregated environment may isolate the child from the real world and, in doing so, patronize him or her, thus preventing the child from learning from failure experiences. This obviously is a difficult situation and it is the primary reason why mainstreaming is such a complex issue. There are certainly no easy solutions.

Some encouragement is offered by the recent work of Strang et al. (1978). Recall that their research indicated that EMR children tended to have the most favorable self-images if they were exposed to two reference groups—other handicapped *and* nonhandicapped children—instead of just one or the other. In this kind of environment, retarded children are able to socially compare favorably with retarded peers with regard to their beliefs and abilities. Among peers, their "shortcomings" are less likely to become salient for them than they would among nonretarded children (cf. McAfee &

Cleland, 1965). At the same time, being in the presence of nonretarded children may serve to reduce some of the stigma associated with the label, including the expectations and attitudes that are a part of the labeling process. (See the discussion in Chapter 13 by Rosenfield and Stephan on how integration between white and minority children under supervised conditions can lead to an improvement in their attitudes toward each other.) Such a system would not be easy to implement and would, undoubtedly, create some problems of its own— problems that are difficult to anticipate right now. Nevertheless, it seems clear that a two-reference group environment, like the one described by Strang et al. (1978), can offer both the experience and the supervision that mentally retarded children need to learn, instead of "learning helplessness."

Finally, one of the most encouraging findings to come out of the research discussed here is the realization that social psychological research can be conducted with mentally retarded adults and children. Because of their intellectual deficiencies and "malleability" there has been some reluctance to conduct these kinds of opinion or attitude studies with retarded persons. There is every reason to believe that our data are valid, however, and it seems clear that these people are capable of understanding and answering sociometric and evaluation items involving the label and that they can provide us with insight into what the label means to them and what effect it has on them. Furthermore, they can provide us with invaluable information regarding deinstitutionalization and mainstreaming, including where they would like to work and go to school, and with whom they would like to live and socialize. More efforts should be made to acquire this information and, in doing so, improve service delivery systems for all retarded persons.

Notes

1. The term stigma refers to some physical or mental trait, such as mental illness or a physical handicap, which, in Goffman's (1963) words, disqualifies a person from "full social acceptance."

2. The modifications were that none of the vocabulary in the stories or questions exceeded a third-grade comprehension level, and subjects were asked to give a definition of each adjective before they gave a rating. A colored box accompanied the choices for each question. For example, the choices for the trait "Friendly" ranged from "Very friendly" to "Not at all friendly." Below the first choice was a box that was completely colored in with blue pencil; below the second a box that was two-thirds colored in; and so on. Once the four or five boxes had been explained, the subject was asked to select one of them and to indicate why he or she had chosen that one. If the justification made sense, the experimenter continued; if not, the question was repeated. After the second attempt, if the experimenter still didn't think the subject comprehended, the question was dropped and the interview proceeded. This method of visualizing the choices proved effective with regard to the validity and reliability of subjects' responses in this and subsequent studies.

13

INTERGROUP RELATIONS AMONG CHILDREN

DAVID ROSENFIELD
SOUTHERN METHODIST UNIVERSITY

WALTER G. STEPHAN
NEW MEXICO STATE UNIVERSITY

Although our society is built on ideals that stress fairness and equal opportunity for all, it is clear that these ideals are not always attained. The existence of prejudice and racial discrimination often blocks the way to true equality in our society. This chapter will examine how prejudicial attitudes are acquired and what can be done to eliminate them. In doing so, we will attempt to integrate our own findings in this area with those of other researchers. In the first section, we will discuss the nature of racial attitudes and their acquisition in childhood. This general introduction will be followed by a section that focuses on a specific topic that is relevant to the acquisition and modification of racial attitudes in children. This topic is school desegregation, one of America's most important social experiments. We will outline why desegregation was expected to modify racial attitudes and we will review the evidence concerning the effects of desegregation. Next, we will discuss factors that are related to decreases in prejudicial racial attitudes in desegregated schools. In the last section, we will analyze a set of classroom teaching techniques that have been developed to reduce prejudice in desegregated schools.

We define racial attitudes as attitudes toward socially defined racial and ethnic groups or toward members of those groups. Racial attitudes, like all other attitudes, may be thought of as having three components: cognitive, affective, and behavioral. The cognitive component consists of the processes involved in subdividing the social world into distinct groups, the sets of traits attributed to the groups (stereotypes), and the sets of beliefs concerning the groups. The affective component consists of the evaluations of members of the other groups (particularly the evaluations of the traits they possess) and the affective tone associated with the beliefs about the groups. The behavioral component is comprised of predispositions to act in a positive or negative manner toward members of a group on the basis of their group membership. These predispositions may or may not result in overt behavior. When they do result in overt behavior and the behavior is negative, we will label this behavior discrimination.

The development of racial attitudes

The first, and perhaps still the most prominent, theoretical description of the development of racial attitudes was proposed by Goodman (1952, 1964). According to this theory, the cognitive component of racial attitudes develops first, somewhere between the ages of 3 and 5. The distinctions among groups then take on evaluative connotations in the period from approximately 5 to 7 years of age. Full integration of racial attitudes (where there is consistency among the cognitive, affective, and behavioral components) occurs around the ages of 8 to 10 years. A somewhat more elaborate version of this approach has recently been proposed by Katz (1976). Her eight-stage model includes a stage prior to the emergence of the cognitive component of racial attitudes in which the child is assimilating race-relevant information. Furthermore, she de-emphasizes the distinction between the stages at which the cognitive and affective components emerge and suggests that both may emerge simultaneously. She believes that these two components become consolidated at about age 5. This consolidation is accompanied by a contrasting of differences among groups and an assimilation of perceived differences within groups. In the last set of developmental stages, the evolving racial attitudes become more elaborate and crystallize into the fully integrated attitudes as proposed by Goodman.

The evidence from studies of racial attitudes provides some support for both Katz's theory and Goodman's theory. However, before we discuss this evidence, we will briefly present an overview of the kinds of measures most often used to assess racial attitudes. The method that has been most widely used with young children is the doll preference technique developed by Clark and Clark (1947). This technique, and its many variants, uses black and white dolls, pictures, animals, or other stimuli that are presented to children. The children are then asked such questions as, "Which doll looks nice?" "Which doll looks bad?" "Which doll would you like to play with?" and "Which

doll looks like you?" The reasoning behind this technique is that the black and white stimuli represent black and white people and, thus, the children's choices can be taken as an index of their racial attitudes. Although the doll technique can be criticized on a number of grounds (e.g., Banks, 1976; Brand, Ruiz & Padilla, 1974; Katz, 1976; Stephan & Rosenfield, 1979), the results from these studies are often remarkably similar to those obtained using more direct measures of racial preferences, racial attitudes, and racial classification abilities.

One of these other, more direct, techniques of measuring racial attitudes is the Preschool Racial Attitude Measure (PRAM). The PRAM uses short stories that are read to children. The children are then asked to decide whether a black or white person displayed the traits of the protagonist. These traits may either be positive (e.g., smart, friendly, good) or negative (stupid, mean, bad). In this chapter, we will review data from both indirect and direct measures of racial attitudes.

The cognitive component of racial attitudes

Studies of the cognitive component of racial attitudes have examined both racial classification ability and ethnic stereotyping. The results of the studies of racial classification ability vary somewhat, but generally it appears that this ability begins to emerge at about 3 years of age and becomes reasonably well establied about the time children enter school. For example, Clark and Clark (1947) asked their subjects, "Give me the doll that looks like a white (colored) child." They found that for both blacks and whites, 77% of the 3-year-olds, 94% of the 5-year-olds, and 100% of the 7-year-olds responded correctly. Using the Morland Picture Interview, which requires children to make 10 of 12 correct classifications, Williams and Morland (1976) report that 16% of the black 3-year-olds and 23% of the white 3-year-olds correctly classified racial pictures, whereas 58% of black 5-year-olds and 87% of white 5-year-olds made correct classifications.

In addition to racial classification abilities, some aspects of stereotyping also appear during the preschool years. In the doll studies the children were generally asked, "Which doll looks nice?" and "Which doll looks bad?" While these questions are evaluative in nature, they do concern some specific attributes of blacks and whites ("nice" and "bad") that are part of children's and adolescents' stereotypes (Brigham, 1974; Lerner & Knapp, 1976). In response to these questions, both black and white preschool children tend to choose the white doll as looking nice and the black doll as looking bad, although whites do this more frequently than do blacks (Asher & Allen, 1969; Fox & Jordan, 1973, found this pattern for whites but not for blacks; Greenwald & Oppenheim, 1968; Gregor & McPherson, 1966; Hraba & Grant, 1970). Finally, by grade 4, children appear to have assimilated many of the characteristic traits of stereotypes of blacks and whites (Brigham, 1974).

The affective component

The affective component of racial attitudes has been extensively studied by Williams and Morland (1976) using the PRAM. Because the PRAM asks children to decide whether a white or black person possesses a positive or negative trait, the child's choices provide an index of how positively or negatively they evaluate whites and blacks. The results from a wide variety of samples that have been given the PRAM are quite consistent. At the preschool level, both blacks and whites attribute more positive traits to whites than to blacks, but whites do this to a greater degree than blacks. For early school-age children, no change in this pro-white bias has been noted for blacks, but for whites it appears that the pro-white bias decreases somewhat after the second grade. At the junior high level, whites continue to evaluate whites most positively, while blacks display a pro-black bias.

The behavioral component

Studies employing the doll technique have often included a question relevant to the behavioral component of racial attitudes. This question is, "Give me the doll that you would like to play with." The racial preferences that are expressed on this type of measure suggest a predisposition to play with children from a given group. These predispositions may or may not be related to actual intergroup behavior, a topic we will take up shortly, but the responses to this question may be taken as an index of racial preference. In responding to these questions, the general trend of the results is that whites show a high level of preference for white dolls. This preference is apparent among preschool children and does not change during the early school years (Asher & Allen, 1969; Fox & Jordan, 1973; Greenwald & Oppenheim, 1968; Gregor & McPherson, 1966; Hraba & Grant, 1970). Black preschool children also evidence a preference for white dolls, although they prefer white dolls less than white preschoolers do (Greenwald & Oppenheim, 1968, McAdoo, 1970). Early school-age black children appear to show either no preference between groups or a preference for blacks (Fox & Jordan, 1973; Gregor & McPherson, 1966). These general trends for racial preference differ from the trends for racial evaluation, but they have been supported in other studies using similar indirect measures of racial preference (Goodman, 1964; Porter, 1971; Radke & Trager, 1950; Stevenson & Stewart, 1958).

A technique developed by Morland (1962) also provides data on behavioral predispositions. This technique involves asking children whether they would prefer to play with a white or black person who appears in photographs. Williams and Morland (1976) have summarized 11 studies using the technique. Whites again show a strong preference for whites in the preschool years, and this preference does not change from preschool-age to school-age children. Black preschoolers again prefer whites, but early school-age blacks prefer blacks.

Since the research shows that white children have strong pro-white evaluations and preferences even in their preschool years while they do not develop good racial classification skills until age 5 (Williams & Morland, 1976), it would appear that whites acquire strong racial evaluations and preferences before they acquire racial classification skills. The picture for blacks is more complex. Blacks become progressively better at classifying the races with age and they show an increased preference for blacks as they get older. However, this developmental trend in preference for black playmates is not mirrored in the evaluative data in which blacks display a pro-white bias from preschool age through the elementary school years. These apparent disjunctions among the cognitive, evaluative, and behavioral components of racial attitudes raise a question about whether these three components of children's racial attitudes are actually related. On the basis of studies indicating that racial preferences among blacks and whites do not vary as a function of classification abilities, Williams and Morland (1976) conclude that "Children's awareness of racial classification has little systematic relationship to their responses to the preference . . . items" (p. 231).

Thus, these studies hint that the clear developmental progression outlined by Goodman (1964) does not exist. As suggested by Katz (1976), children may independently acquire information on the cognitive and affective components of racial attitudes. In addition, their behavioral preferences may also emerge independently of the other two components of racial attitudes. This suggests that the acquisition of racial attitudes is considerably more complicated than has generally been thought. Classification skills depend on cognitive abilities that can deal with the multidimensional schemata that are necessary to distinguish between groups. Thus, it seems reasonable to expect a clear developmental trend for this component, a trend that would follow cognitive development. Evaluative reactions, on the other hand, are acquired from socialization agents such as parents, siblings, teachers, and the media. The fact that the affective component of racial attitudes is dependent

on individual socialization experiences could account for its independence from classification abilities, which rely more on purely cognitive processes.

Although the existence of evaluative responses depends on exposure to race-specific socialization experiences, and the acquisition of classification skills depends on the development of certain cognitive skills, the development of behavioral preferences may be subject to yet a different set of acquisition processes. Behavioral preferences may be more determined by situational constraints. For example, positive feelings about other group members are unlikely to be reflected in behavioral preferences if in-group peers are opposed to interactions with out-group members. Similarly, in some families, children may be directly prohibited from playing with members of other groups despite having positive (or neutral) feelings about the group. Thus, all the components of interracial attitudes may have very different origins and, hence, may be somewhat independent.

Intergroup friendship choices

In addition to the numerous studies of children's racial attitudes that have been done in the last 40 years, a small number of studies have examined children's intergroup friendship behavior. The overall conclusions that emerge from these studies point to a developmental trend of increasingly ethnocentric friendship choices in interracial settings. For example, nursery school children appear not to discriminate on the basis of race (Porter, 1971) but, by elementary school, in-group choices do begin to emerge. Moreover, segregation by sex is more prevalent than segregation by race at the elementary school level. However, race typically becomes a more important factor in friendship choices by the end of elementary school and continues to be more important thereafter (Schofield, 1980). An indication of the high levels of ethnocentrism displayed by older school-age children can be seen in the high frequency of in-group choices that students make when they are asked to indicate who their best friends are (Gerard & Miller, 1975; Rosenberg & Simmons, 1971). For instance, in Rosenberg and Simmons' (1971) study of junior high school students, over 95% of the students' "third best friends" were in-group members. (The percentages were even higher for first and second best friends.)

The clear ethnocentrism that exists for older children in both behavior and attitudes indicates that there is a loose consistency between the components of racial attitudes and actual interracial behavior. As we will note shortly, however, the correlations between attitudes and behavior, and among the various components of racial attitudes, are never very high. This probably reflects the different acquisition processes associated with behavior and with the various components of racial attitudes.

In our attempt to analyze the different acquisition processes in intergroup behavior and the different types of acquisition processes that are associated with the three components of racial attitudes, we do not mean to imply that there is anything inevitable about these processes. The results we have presented do point to the existence of some general normative trends, but there still remains considerable variation among children in their racial attitudes. For the remainder of the chapter, we would like to focus on the causes of variation in racial attitudes. For the most part, we will analyze these causes within one context, the school. Our emphasis on the school is due primarily to the impact that schools have on racial attitudes. The belief that school experiences affect racial attitudes was clearly reflected in the testimony given by social scientists in the 1954 Supreme Court decision in the *Brown* v. *Board of Education* case on school desegregation.

School desegregation and racial attitudes

Social scientists made two types of contributions to the *Brown* decision. They testified in the individual trials, and they filed an *amicus curiae* (friend of the court) brief. The *amicus curiae* brief that was filed was written by Kenneth Clark, Isidor Chein, and Stuart Cook and was signed by 32 social scientists (Allport et al., 1953). The brief outlined the effects of segregation on prejudice and self-esteem. It stated that:

Segregation, prejudices and discrimination, and their social concomitants potentially damage the personality of all children. . . . Minority group children learn the inferior status to which they are assigned . . . they often react with feelings of inferiority and a sense of personal humiliation. . . . (Allport et al., pp. 429–430)

Some children, usually of the lower socioeconomic classes, may react by overt aggression and hostility directed toward their own group or members of the dominant group. (Allport et al., pp. 429–430)

With reference to the impact of segregation and its concomitants on children of the majority group . . . children who learn the prejudices of our society are also being taught to gain personal status in an unrealistic and nonadaptive way . . . by comparing themselves to members of the minority group. . . . The culture permits and at times encourages them to direct their feelings of hostility and aggression against . . . minority groups. . . . (Allport et al., pp. 430–434)

The social science brief was concerned primarily with prejudice and self-esteem, but it is clear from the testimony of the social scientists in the individual trials that they believed that self-esteem and prejudice affected the school achievement of minority students. These three variables—prejudice, self-esteem, and school achievement—were perceived to be interrelated in a vicious circle. White prejudice was regarded as the cause of segregation, and segregation led to low self-esteem among blacks. This, in turn, affected the black students' motivation to learn, as well as their achievement. Low self-esteem and frustration over low achievement were then turned outward in the form of prejudice toward whites. The low self-esteem and low achievement of blacks and their antipathy toward whites reinforced white prejudice, and the circle was complete.

It was reasoned that desegregation would break this vicious circle by denying an institutionalized sanction for white prejudice. If the behavior of whites was changed, their attitudes should change to be consistent with their behavior. Furthermore, in desegregated schools, the self-esteem of blacks should increase because they would no longer be stamped with the badge of inferiority represented by segregation. It was expected that these increases in self-esteem would be associated with increased achievement and reduced prejudice toward whites. The improved facilities in desegregated schools and the opportunity to interact with white students should also contribute to improvements in black achievement. Thus, intergroup contact in desegregated schools was expected to reduce the prejudices of both groups.

The empirical data collected since 1954 do not support the optimistic predictions made by the social scientists. In summarizing the results of 80 studies on the effects of desegregation on prejudice, self-esteem, and achievement, one of us recently wrote:

It is tentatively concluded that (a) desegregation generally does not reduce the prejudices of whites toward blacks, (b) the self-esteem of blacks rarely increases in desegregated schools, (c) the achievement level of blacks sometimes increases and rarely decreases in desegregated schools, and (d) desegregation leads to increases in black prejudice toward whites about as frequently as it leads to decreases. (Stephan, 1978, p. 217)

While the data indicate that desegregation did not have many of the effects it was expected to have, this conclusion must be viewed as only tentative for several reasons. First, most of these studies were done during the initial phases of desegregation programs and their results may not generalize to the long-term effects of desegregation. Also, the desegregation plans that have been studied vary from community to community, as did the age of the children studied and the ethnic composition of the schools. Because of these and other reasons (see Stephan, 1978), the long-term effects of well-planned and well-executed desegregation plans are still undetermined.

With this background, we would now like to examine the results of some of our own research in this area. In our initial study of desegregation (Stephan & Rosenfield, 1978a) we analyzed its effects on racial attitudes, self-esteem, and interracial contact. One of the limitations of many of the previous studies on desegregation is that they examined the effects of desegregation on only one variable at a time. This makes it impossible to examine the interrelationships among variables. Another important limitation of many previous studies is that the effects of desegregation were analyzed only for blacks and whites. Recently, as a result of the *Keyes* case in Denver, members of the nation's second largest minority, Mexican-Americans, have begun to be included in desegregation plans. In our study, we attempted to examine the effects of desegregation on Mexican-Americans as well as on blacks and whites. Finally, the majority of desegregation studies have employed cross-sectional designs or have used longitudinal designs with no control group. In the study we will report, members of all three ethnic groups were studied both before and eight months after desegregation. Approximately half of the students who attended the desegregated schools had previously attended naturally integrated neighborhood schools. These students had frequent opportunities for interethnic contact both before and after the court-ordered desegregation plan was implemented. For this reason, they provide a control group against which to measure the effects of desegregation on students coming from segregated backgrounds.

The data that we will present concern the effects of desegregation on sixth-grade students in a southwestern school district during the first year after desegregation was implemented (1974). The sixth grade was desegregated by creating nine schools that housed only sixth-grade students. These schools contained a racial balance between blacks and nonblacks. The Mexican-Americans were officially considered to be white. Unfortunately, this decision resulted in the formation of one sixth-grade center that contained over 95% minority students—a point we will return to later.

In 1975, there were 60,000 students in the school district—62% were white, 23% were Mexican-American, and 15% were black. There were 59 elementary schools, of which 41 were highly segregated. From the 59 schools, eight were chosen for the present study. Five of these schools were highly segregated, and three of them were naturally integrated. The students in the fifth and sixth grades of these eight schools were given a questionnaire in the spring before desegregation. Students from these same neighborhoods were then given the same questionnaire eight months after desegregation began. The sample consisted of approximately 450 students from each ethnic group.

Our sampling procedure yielded a three-factor design. The students came from two types of backgrounds (segregated and integrated), they were tested before and after desegregation, and there were three ethnic groups: blacks, Mexican-Americans, and whites. The questionnaires were administered to the children in their own schools. The measure designed to assess racial *attitudes* employed 10 sets of bipolar adjectives (e.g., friendly-unfriendly and trustworthy-untrustworthy) in a 9-point Semantic Differential format. The children were asked to rate all three groups on each adjective pair. Our index of voluntary interethnic *contact* consisted of nine items and asked how frequently the child had engaged in a variety of different types of activities with members of other ethnic groups. For instance, black children were asked how frequently they had visited the house of a white student and how frequently they called white students on the telephone. The measure of *self-esteem* was a 7-item global self-esteem scale using an agree-disagree response format. Examples of the questions are, "I wish that I were different from the way I am," and "When I meet someone new I usually think that he is better than I am."

Since each student rated all three ethnic groups, it is possible to examine attitudes toward both the in-group and the two out-groups. The results for the racial attitudes revealed two important findings. First, all three groups were highly ethnocentric, displaying more positive attitudes toward their in-group than toward the out-groups. Second, the attitudes of previously segregated blacks and whites (but not Mexican-Americans) toward all three ethnic groups were more negative after desegregation than before. The first result is consistent with a large literature that indicates that all human groups tend to be ethnocentric (LeVine & Campbell, 1972). The second result is interesting because it points to another problem with many previous studies of desegregation. Typically, most investigators only examine attitudes toward the out-group. However, we measured attitudes toward the in-group as well as toward the out-group. Had we only assessed out-group attitudes, we would have concluded that desegregation led to increases in prejudice, just as many previous investigators have concluded. The results on the attitudes toward the in-group questions indicate that such conclusions may be misleading, however. Instead, it appears that desegregation caused previously segregated blacks and whites to become more negative toward other people generally, including members of their own group. This suggests that previously found increases in prejudice that have been attributed to desegregation may not have been the result of increasing interracial antagonism, but rather may have been due to the students' experiences during the first year of desegregation. The initial phases of desegregation are often characterized by high levels of anxiety and hostility due to the opposition and conflict out of which desegregation plans arise, as well as to confusion over their implementation. These frustrations apparently result in hostility that is directed toward other people in general, not just members of ethnic out-groups.

The finding that Mexican-Americans did not display more negative attitudes after desegregation than before is at first surprising. Further investigation suggests, however, that this result may be attributable to the fact that most of the Mexican-Americans attended a "desegregated school" that contained less than 10% more members of other ethnic groups than the segregated school they had previously attended. Thus, they experienced minimal desegregation and could hardly be expected to have responded as did students who experienced the disruptions associated with more thorough desegregation.

The results on our interethnic *contact* measure revealed high levels of ethnocentrism in all three groups. In addition, desegregation appeared to have no effects on informal interethnic contact. An analysis of the relationship between interethnic contact and racial attitudes indicated that the two were significantly correlated, but only moderately ($r = .28$).

For the self-esteem measure, it was found that blacks scored the highest and Mexican-Americans the lowest. Desegregation lowered the self-esteem of blacks from segregated backgrounds but raised the self-esteem of blacks from integrated backgrounds. Thus, while the self-esteem of blacks was not generally low, desegregation did have some negative effects on it. The most likely explanation of these results is that blacks use other blacks as their social comparison group. During the initial phases of desegregation, the blacks from segregated backgrounds experienced considerable difficulty adjusting to their new school environment as indicated by the negative changes in their racial attitudes. These students may have made negative social comparisons to blacks from integrated backgrounds whose previous experiences probably enabled them to cope with desegregation more effectively. These results are also consistent with another large-scale study of the effects of desegregation on self-esteem conducted by Gerard and Miller (1975). They also found that blacks from segregated backgrounds experienced an initial drop in self-esteem. In addition, they found that black self-esteem rebounded to predesegregation levels within two years.

Overall, these results are quite consistent with previous studies of desegregation. They indicate, as have the majority of other studies, that desegregation does not reduce prejudice, increase interethnic contact, or raise the self-esteem of minority students. The ethnocentrism that was found for both attitudes and behavior indicates that by the fifth grade, children are displaying a clear pattern of in-group evaluative preference. Furthermore, the correlations between attitudes and behavior suggest that there is some integration between the evaluative component of racial attitudes and actual behavior. These conclusions are strengthened by the fact that most of these results were replicated in our second study of desegregated schools. In this study, we were primarily interested in a more thorough examination of minority group self-esteem, but we also examined racial attitudes and behavior.

Desegregation and self-esteem

There is a long-standing controversy concerning self-rejection among blacks and other minorities. This issue was central to the arguments presented by social scientists in the *Brown* trial. The results of the doll studies and other studies using similar techniques have often been cited as evidence of self-rejection among blacks. However, before one can interpret the findings that young blacks often prefer and identify with the white stimuli as an index of black self-rejection, three implicit assumptions must be made. First, it must be assumed that choosing the white stimuli implies a rejection of the black stimuli. Second, it must be assumed that the white and black stimuli represent white and black people and, thus, that rejection of the black stimuli may be taken as an indication of a rejection of black people. Third, it must be assumed that rejecting black people implies a rejection of the self on the part of black children.

There is very little evidence that directly addresses these assumptions. Indeed, studies by Williams and Morland (1976) indicate that acceptance of members of one group tends *not* to be linked to rejection of members of other groups. In fact, it appears that in-group and out-group acceptance are positively correlated, although acceptance of in-group members is higher than acceptance of out-group members. Thus, the first assumption may not be valid. Concerning the second assumption, the only strong evidence that favors it is the fact that the results from studies using the PRAM to measure playmate preferences and out-group evaluations are quite similar to the general pattern of results obtained in the doll studies. That is, both blacks and whites tend to evaluate whites more favorably, but whites do this to a greater degree than do blacks. These results suggest that it may be reasonable to regard rejection of black stimuli in the doll study as an index of rejection of blacks. Thus, there is some indirect evidence supporting the second assumption. Finally, some evidence that supports the third assumption may be found in a study by Ward and Braun (1972). They found a positive relationship between preference for black puppets and level of self-esteem among black children.

Given the tenuousness of these three assumptions and the weakness of the evidence for them, it seemed to us that a more direct approach to the issue of self-rejection among blacks was needed. In our study (Stephan & Rosenfield, 1979) we employed Rosenberg's (1965) self-esteem scale to examine the self-esteem of 350 black, Mexican-American, and white students. We then examined the relationship between self-esteem and attitudes toward the in-group and out-groups among fourth- and fifth-grade students. We also collected information on the achievement level and the social class of the students, because many previous researchers have failed to control for differences on these variables. The students were given questionnaires in a group setting along with other members of their classes. The measures of racial attitudes and interethnic behavior were modified versions of those used by Stephan and Rosenfield (1978a). They included a different set of descriptive adjectives for the attitude measure (e.g.,

mean-kind, honest-dishonest) and a wider range of contact situations (e.g., sat next to them in the cafeteria, worked on a project with them).

The results for self-esteem indicated that blacks were not significantly lower in self-esteem than whites, although the Mexican-Americans were. However, when social class and achievement levels were controlled, even this latter difference fell below significance. Thus, most of the differences in self-esteem among the three ethnic groups in our sample were apparently due to differences in their social class backgrounds and academic achievement.

The results from the attitude and contact measures supported the findings in the previous study (Stephan & Rosenfield, 1978a). All three ethnic groups had highly ethnocentric attitudes and behavior patterns. In addition, just as in the previous study, it was found that the attitude and behavior measures were moderately correlated in all three groups (mean $r = .29$).

The most intriguing finding in this study was that the self-esteem of the blacks and their ethnocentrism (an index comparing their view of blacks to their views of Mexican-Americans and whites) were positively correlated ($r = .35$). This indicates that black children who rejected blacks tended to reject themselves as well. The correlations between self-esteem and ethnocentric attitudes were not significant for whites or Mexican-Americans. Thus, these results do show support for the assumption that, among blacks, rejection of self is related to rejection of other blacks.

The results comparing the overall level of self-esteem among the three ethnic groups replicate those of our previous investigation (Stephan & Rosenfield, 1978a) that found no indication of black self-rejection. They are also consistent with a number of other studies using direct measures of black self-esteem in which blacks were *not* found to have lower self-esteem than whites, or were actually found to be higher than whites in self-esteem (Edwards, 1974; Hodgkins & Stakenas, 1969; McDonald & Gynther,

1965; Powell & Fuller, 1970; Stephan & Kennedy, 1975). When all of these studies are considered in conjunction with the small number of studies showing that blacks have lower self-esteem than whites (e.g., Deutsch, 1960; Gerard & Miller, 1975; Williams & Byars, 1968), it seems reasonable to conclude that blacks are not generally lower in self-esteem than are whites, but that Mexican-Americans often are (Coleman, Campbell, Hobson, Mood, Weinfield, & York, 1966; Stephan & Kennedy, 1975; Stephan & Rosenfield, 1978a). However, it should be pointed out that in many of the studies finding such differences, social class and achievement were not controlled.

Even though the results of Stephan and Rosenfield (1979) indicated that blacks do not reject themselves (a conclusion reached by several others who have reviewed the evidence, e.g., Banks, 1976; Edwards, 1974), there was clear support for the assumption made in the doll studies, that blacks who do reject their ethnic group also tend to reject themselves. This seems to leave us with a dilemma. If we accept the results of the studies using PRAM as evidence that black children negatively evaluate blacks, and if we accept the finding from the present study that rejection of blacks is associated with self-rejection, how do we account for the fact that the majority of studies using direct measures of self-esteem do not find evidence for self-rejection among blacks? The answer to this question appears to lie in the age of the children from whom these various sets of findings come. The PRAM data indicate that only very young black children, primarily preschoolers, show a negative evaluation of blacks. In contrast, the findings concerning self-esteem and its relationship to evaluations of blacks come from children in the later years of grade school or older.

Problems in reducing prejudice during desegregation

Although many social scientists thought that, under the right circumstances, desegre-

gation could help destroy interethnic hostility, it is clear that most current desegregation plans do not provide the right circumstances to eliminate ethnic antagonism. Allport (1954), Amir (1969), and Cook (1972) are among the investigators to systematically study the conditions that are necessary for interethnic contact to reduce prejudice. Amir (1969) points out that the degree of cooperation versus competition in the desegregated setting is an important determinant of whether or not desegregation will reduce prejudice. He based his conclusion on the results of studies that indicated that competition is likely to heighten interethnic tensions, while cooperation should tend to lessen it. Unfortunately, in most schools, competition is an integral part of the grading system, while cooperation is rarely practiced. It is not surprising, then, that the competition between whites and minorities in desegregated schools leads to interethnic hostility.

Amir (1969) also points out that interethnic contact needs to be informal and between equal-status members of the ethnic groups before interethnic relations can be improved. Desegregation rarely leads to informal, equal-status contact, however. As one of our earlier studies (Stephan & Rosenfield, 1978a) and other studies by Gottlieb and Ten Houten (1965) showed, desegregation typically does not lead to increases in *informal* interethnic contact. It is also rare that whites and minorities meet on an equal-status basis in desegregated schools. Whites usually are from higher socioeconomic backgrounds (e.g., Stephan & Rosenfield, 1979), have higher academic achievement scores (e.g., Gerard & Miller, 1975; Stephan & Rosenfield, 1979), and are accorded more status and respect by the faculty and staff of the school. These status differentials reinforce negative stereotypes of minority groups rather than destroy them, thus inhibiting improvements in interethnic relations.

The final condition that Amir feels is important for reducing prejudice is support from public officials. When public officials encourage people to resist desegregation efforts, there are likely to be racial problems and conflicts in the schools. In contrast, Pettigrew (1971) has found that where officials favor intergroup contact, interethnic relations typically improve. It is clear, therefore, that desegregation plans, as they are most often implemented, are not likely to reduce racial hostilities significantly.

Nevertheless, it is still likely that *some* students will show decreases in prejudice even though most may not. By identifying some of the characteristics that determine whether an individual will exhibit more or less prejudice, it may be possible to shed light on ways of designing desegregation plans that will be more successful.

Identifying some conditions for decreasing prejudice

Although a number of studies have examined factors that are related to individual differences in prejudice, very little research has been done to investigate the causes of *changes* in prejudice, especially within a desegregated school. Examining factors that are related to individual differences in prejudice, however, does provide a starting point for identifying variables that may cause changes in prejudice. After briefly discussing a number of these factors, we will present the results of studies that have examined how some of these factors affect prejudice during desegregation.

Situational factors

One situational factor that is a very important determinant of prejudice is informal interethnic contact. Amir (1969) discussed its importance in reducing prejudice, and both of our previous studies found that lack of contact and prejudice were related (Stephan & Rosenfield, 1978a, 1979). Although desegregation does not usually lead to overall increases in informal interethnic contact, one would expect that those students who do show increases in interethnic contact will also show decreases in prejudice.

Amir (1969) also pointed to the importance of cooperation and equal-status contact as factors in reducing prejudice in interethnic situations. Thus, although cooperative experiences may not be widespread, and although it may be unusual for whites and minorities to have equal status in the desegregated schools, nonetheless, in situations where teachers do use cooperative techniques and where whites and minorities do come together with equal status, prejudice should decrease.

Other situational factors that may help reduce prejudice include having large percentages of each ethnic group in the classroom (as opposed to "token" desegregation), desegregation of the teaching staffs, and maintaining support within the school for desegregation. Where there are large numbers of students from other ethnic groups in one's class, the opportunities for *close* contact increase, and that should decrease prejudice (St. John, 1975). Where the teaching staffs are desegregated, competent minority teachers serve as role models who contradict the negative stereotypes of minorities and undermine prejudice (Cohen, 1979). Finally, where desegregation is supported, close interethnic contact will be encouraged and rewarded.

Individual differences

A number of individual-difference variables have also been shown to be related to prejudice. For example, our earlier studies (Stephan & Rosenfield, 1978a, 1979) and a study by Trent (1957) showed that self-esteem and prejudice were related. These results support the idea that one is unlikely to be accepting of others if one does not accept oneself.

Another variable that has been shown to be related to prejudice is authoritarianism (Adorno, Frenkel-Brunswick, Levinson, & Sanford, 1950). Authoritarianism is a personality syndrome that is marked by rigidity in personality and beliefs, conventionality in values, and an inclination to be power and status oriented. A number of investigators have shown that authoritarian people tend to be highly prejudiced toward almost all out-groups (Adorno et al., 1950; Roberts & Rokeach, 1956). This prejudice is usually attributed to the harsh and threatening discipline that authoritarian people are thought to be subjected to in their childhood. The hostility engendered by this harsh discipline is then displaced onto disliked out-groups (Harding, Proshansky, Kutner, & Chein, 1968), thereby resulting in a high level of prejudice.

Two other variables, socioeconomic status (SES) and education, also have been found to be related to prejudice (e.g., Williams, 1964). One explanation for the finding that low SES people tend to be prejudiced centers around the frustrations that are associated with their low status. It suggests that the hostilities created by these frustrations may be displaced onto disliked out-groups in the form of prejudice and discrimination (Dollard, Doob, Miller, Mowrer, & Sears, 1939; Miller & Bugelski, 1948).

Parental influences

A number of parental child-rearing practices may also have an impact on children's prejudices. Researchers have repeatedly found that children's ethnic attitudes are correlated with their parents' attitudes (Epstein & Komorita, 1966a, 1966b), apparently because children tend to imitate and identify with their parents, and because their parents are very important sources of information about minority groups. However, the research done on two other parental variables—parents' authoritarianism and parents' punitiveness—is not quite so clear. One would expect that the harsh and rigid child-rearing practices of punitive, authoritarian parents would lead to hostility and anger in their children; and, since this hostility cannot be expressed against their parents, the children should displace it onto low-status groups (Mosher & Scodel, 1960). Yet the data on this point are still inconclusive. Some studies have failed to find any relationship among parental punitiveness, parental authoritarianism, and children's

prejudices (e.g., Epstein & Komorita, 1966a, 1966b; Mosher & Scodel, 1960), while others have found such a relationship (e.g., Harris, Gough, & Martin, 1950; Lyle & Levitt, 1955). These inconsistencies in the findings may indicate that parental punitiveness and authoritarianism are not very strong predictors of children's prejudices.

The next two studies that we will discuss examined the effect of many of these previously mentioned variables on prejudice during desegregation. The first study focused on parental influences and individual differences, while the second examined situational factors. Both were conducted in large urban school districts in the Southwest.

Factors affecting changes in prejudice during desegregation

Our first study (Stephan & Rosenfield, 1978b) was designed to examine how a number of factors affected *changes* in prejudice during desegregation. The following five potential determinants of prejudice were investigated: (1) the amount of close contact the students had with members of the out-groups, (2) the students' levels of self-esteem, (3) the parents' attitudes toward integration (an indication of their parents' racial attitudes), (4) the parents' authoritarianism, and (5) parents' punitiveness. Our measures of self-esteem, interethnic contact, and prejudice were the same as those used in Stephan and Rosenfield (1978a), while the measures of the parental attitudes were developed for use in this study. Each parental scale consisted of at least five items asking questions such as, "I would prefer to send my children to an integrated school" (for the parental attitudes toward integration scale), and "Most children get too much discipline" (for the parental authoritarianism scale). To measure parental punitiveness, children were asked to indicate how their parents punished them when they performed common misbehaviors.

Two hundred and thirty students in fifth- or sixth-grade classes were recruited to participate in the study two years before the segregation plan was implemented. After they filled out questionnaires (on prejudice, self-esteem, and interethnic contact), their mothers were contacted and asked to fill out the parent's questionnaire, which assessed their attitudes toward integration and their level of authoritarianism. After repeated follow-up contacts, completed questionnaires were obtained from 52% of the parents. Then, two years later (during the first year of desegregation), attempts were made to recontact all of the students whose mothers filled out the parent's questionnaire. Those contacted filled out the self-esteem, prejudice, and interethnic contact questions again, as well as questions designed to assess their parents' punitiveness. Twenty-three percent of the students whose mothers had previously completed a parent's questionnaire could not be located again, in most cases because they had left the school system. Although there was a substantial amount of attrition in this sample, the rate was no more than is typical in this kind of research.

The data from this study were analyzed by a multiple regression, with the five determinants of prejudice as predictors and changes in prejudice as the dependent variable. Because of the small number of children from whom we had completed data (65 whites and less than 40 blacks or Mexican-Americans), we decided to limit our analysis to the white children.

The results from the regression showed that 43% of the variance in changes in prejudice was explained by the five factors. The analysis also showed that changes in interethnic contact, changes in self-esteem, parental punitiveness, and parental authoritarianism were all either significantly, or marginally significantly, related to changes in prejudice. As expected, increases in interethnic contact and increases in self-esteem were associated with decreases in prejudice, while high parental punitiveness and high parental authoritarianism both were related to increases in children's prejudices. The only variable that was not related to children's prejudice was parents' attitudes toward integration.

This latter finding was surprising given the fact that previous researchers have often found that parents' and children's interethnic attitudes are related. To investigate why no relationship was found, the correlations among all of the variables were examined. This search revealed that parents' attitudes toward integration were significantly correlated with their children's prejudices when no other factors were controlled. However, when a number of partial correlations were computed, it was found that the relationship between parents' attitudes toward integration and children's prejudices was only affected by interethnic contact. In other words, when contact was controlled, the correlation between parents' attitudes toward desegregation and children's prejudices was reduced substantially and, in fact, became nonsignificant. These results suggest that interethnic contact mediates the relationship between parents' attitudes toward integration and children's prejudices. Apparently, parents who have negative attitudes toward integration exert pressure on their children to avoid contact with minorities, which, in turn, prevents the children from developing more positive interethnic attitudes.

The results of this study point to a number of areas that can lead to positive changes in prejudice during desegregation. Unfortunately, three of them involve parental attitudes (punitiveness, authoritarianism, and attitudes toward integration) and these factors are not easily changed. On the other hand, two of the determinants of changes in prejudice during desegregation (interethnic contact and self-esteem) are factors that can be influenced by various kinds of interventions. For example, even though desegregation does not often lead to actual increases in interethnic contact, it is possible to establish cooperative interethnic groups in the classroom that will lead to informal interethnic contact. In addition, at least one cooperative technique (the Jigsaw Classroom; see Blaney, C. Stephan, Rosenfield, Aronson, & Sikes, 1977) has also been shown to increase self-esteem. Thus, cooperation seems to have great potential for making desegregation work more smoothly. Shortly, we will review a series of studies designed to yield more direct insight into the benefits (and potential pitfalls) of cooperation in the classroom. But, before delving into that issue, we will examine more closely some of the other situational factors that may affect changes in prejudice during desegregation.

Classroom determinants of prejudice

After considering the results of the previous investigation, we began to realize that it may be more useful to focus on the situational determinants of prejudice in desegregated classes rather than on the personality or parental determinants of prejudice. The major reason for this change in emphasis was the fact that one usually can do little to change children's personalities or their parents' child-rearing practices. Situational factors, on the other hand, are often under the control of teachers and administrators and, thus, are good targets for interventions designed to create more positive interethnic relations.

The results of Stephan and Rosenfield (1978b), and the work of other investigators, indicate that both the classroom social structure and the classroom social climate can have a substantial impact on the prejudices of the students in the classes. For example, many previous writers have suggested that the relative status of the whites and minorities in a class (a *classroom structure* variable) will affect the prejudices of the students in the class (e.g., Allport, 1954; Amir, 1969). Furthermore, the results from Stephan and Rosenfield (1978b) suggest that cooperation (a *classroom climate* variable) may be effective in reducing prejudice in desegregated schools. Our next study (Rosenfield, Sheehan, Marcus, & Stephan, in press) was designed to test the importance of a number of classroom structure and climate variables in determining prejudice in desegregated schools.

Two classroom structure variables that we thought were important in determining prejudice were the relative statuses and the percentages of white and minority students in the classes. As in Stephan and Rosenfield (1978b), the focus of this study was on the prejudices of the white students. It was expected that, when the whites and minorities in a class had approximately the same status (that is, had approximately the same socioeconomic background and the same levels of academic achievement), many of the whites' negative preconceptions of the minorities would be undermined and, therefore, their prejudices would be reduced (e.g., Amir, 1969; St. John & Lewis, 1975). If the white students had much higher status than the minorities in the desegregated classrooms, however, this status differential might reinforce the whites' negative stereotypes of minorities and, therefore, bolster their prejudices. Thus, it was predicted that the closer the whites and minorities were on salient social status dimensions, like academic achievement and SES, the less prejudiced the whites would be.

The percentage of minorities in the classes should also affect the whites' prejudices. As minority percentage increases, opportunities for close contact increase, and that should increase interethnic harmony (Stephan & Rosenfield, 1978b). Indeed, one study has found support for the notion that interethnic friendships in whites is highest in schools that have the highest minority percentages (St. John, 1975).

The two classroom *climate* variables that were examined in this study were the amount of hostility expressed by the minorities toward whites, and the self-esteem of the students in the class. It would be anticipated that whites who meet with a great deal of hostility from minorities will become hostile toward those minorities since people tend to dislike others who dislike them (e.g., Aronson & Linder, 1965). This tendency may be especially strong during the first year of desegregation, because whites who have had little previous experience with minorities may be especially offended by the unexpected hostility from some minority students. Intergroup relations in the classroom can also be strongly affected by the level of self-esteem of the students in the class. As we showed earlier (Stephan & Rosenfield, 1978b), students who are generally more self-accepting (as indicated by high self-esteem) will also be more accepting of others. (All of these relationships are summarized in Figure 13.1.) In addition, one extra factor was investigated. Some of the children in the study were bused for purposes of desegregation. We examined the possibility that this busing may have affected their prejudices.

Data were collected in 104 different fourth-grade classes in a large southwestern school district. The ethnic composition of these classes was 55% white, 30% black, 14% Mexican-American, and 1% Asian or American Indian. Desegregation was primarily achieved by mandatory busing within specific subdistricts in the system (although some voluntary busing occurred also).

The relative statuses of the whites and minorities were measured on two dimensions: academic achievement (as measured by the *Iowa Test of Basic Skills)* and socioeconomic status (SES). These two measures were combined into one overall status dimension. To obtain a relative status measure, the statuses of the whites and minorities in each class were averaged (the students stayed in intact classes throughout the day). Relative status was computed by simply taking the difference between the status of the whites and minorities in a class.

There were two measures of interethnic relations in this study. The first was a measure of minority friendship (a behavioral measure), which asked the students to estimate such things as the percentage of their friends who were minorities. The other measure assessed the students' racial attitudes by asking such questions as "Can blacks be trusted?" and "Are Mexican-Americans O.K.?" This racial attitude measure also provided an estimate of the minorities' hostility toward whites. For each class, the minorities' attitudes toward whites (measured by these racial attitude questions) were averaged to obtain the average minority hostility toward whites for that class.

All of these measures were then averaged for all the white students in each of the classes to yield one overall measure for each variable in each class. This resulted in such measures as the average self-esteem of the whites in the class, and so on. Thus, in our analysis, each classroom was essentially one "subject."

The data from this study were analyzed by means of a path analysis. Although we will only report the basic findings from the analysis and not go into its technical nature here, path analysis is accomplished by performing a series of regressions; it yields information about both the direct and the indirect effects that various predictors have on dependent variables. We will be concentrating on the direct effects that the classroom structure and the classroom climate variables have on prejudice; that is, the effects that are not mediated by any other variables.

The path analysis showed that all of the classroom structure and classroom climate variables we have discussed were significantly related to the white students' racial attitudes and behavior (see Figure 13.1). Interestingly, the two classroom structure variables were significant determinants of minority friendship, but not of racial attitudes, whereas the two classroom climate variables were significantly related to racial attitudes, but not to minority friendship. Specifically, it was found that, as the status differences between minorities and whites decreased, minority friendship among whites increased. Moreover, as the percentage of minorities in a class increased, minority friendships in the class increased. Finally, concerning the classroom climate measures, it was found that the white students had the most positive interethnic attitudes in classes where the minorities had the least hostility toward the whites; and the whites had the most positive attitudes in the classes where they had the highest self-esteem.

It is interesting to explore the reasons why interethnic attitudes and interethnic behaviors (friendships) were found to have different causes. Our findings are not very surprising given the fact that attitudes and behavior

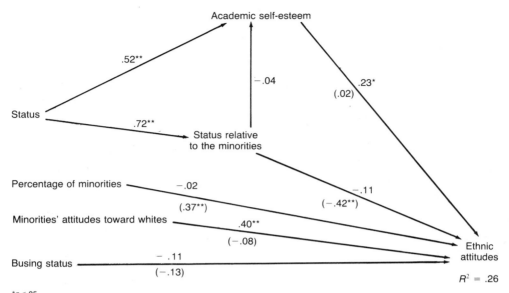

*p<.05
**p<.001
Note. The numbers in parentheses refer to the analysis using minority friendship as the dependent variable. The numbers not in parentheses refer to the analysis using ethnic attitudes as the dependent variable.

Figure 13.1. Path model for the effects of classroom structure and classroom climate on white students' prejudice in desegregated schools.

are usually only moderately related. In this sample, the correlation was $r = .22, p < .05$. Because less that 5% of their variance is shared, it is clear that they have substantially different causes. It is reasonable to expect, though, that increases in minority friendship would eventually lead to decreases in prejudice and, likewise, that decreases in prejudice would lead to increases in minority friendship. However, these changes may take longer to occur than the time span covered by the present study (our measures were taken during the middle of the first year of desegregation, so there were only a few months for changes to occur).

The findings of this study support and extend the implications of the previous study (Stephan & Rosenfield, 1978b) concerning the factors that influence interethnic relations in desegregated schools. In particular, they point to a few specific variables, which are often under the control of school administrators, that can improve interethnic relations in desegregated schools. For example,

we have shown that minority percentage is a very important determinant of minority friendship. Thus, "token" attempts at desegregation, which involve only small numbers of minorities, are unlikely to lead to positive interethnic relations in the classroom.

Improving interethnic relations by creating equal status contact in the schools may not be a simple matter, however. Our results (along with those of other investigators like St. John & Lewis, 1975) indicate that desegregation will generally be most successful when it involves mixing whites and minorities who have approximately equal status. One method of doing this, called "tracking" (e.g., making class groupings dependent on academic achievement), appears to be a solution, but, unfortunately, it has many disadvantages. For example, students in the slower classes may be labeled as slow learners, which might have negative effects on their achievement (Rosenthal & Jacobson, 1968; see also Chapter 12 by Gibbons on mental retardation). In addition, some investigators have found that tracking itself seems to have a negative impact on ethnic relations (Schofield & Sagar, 1977).

Where interventions involving the classroom *structure* are difficult to carry out, one can still consider interventions that can help make the *classroom climate* more conducive to interethnic harmony. Other investigators have discussed a number of these classroom climate factors. For example, Gerard and Miller (1975) have shown that the teacher's attitude about interethnic relations can have a powerful effect on students' attitudes. Similarly, Cohen (1979) has shown that the relative power (or powerlessness) of the different ethnic groups on the school's faculty and staff also can have a profound effect on interethnic relations. Perhaps the intervention that has been given the most attention, however, is cooperation. Cooperation creates a climate in which positive interpersonal relations are fostered and rewarded, and it may lead to close interethnic contact and higher self-esteem. Indeed, a number of studies indicate that cooperation may lead to such improvements in interethnic relations (e.g., DeVries & Edwards, 1974; Slavin, 1977; Wiegel, Wiser, & Cook, 1975). The remainder of this chapter will be devoted to studies that have examined the use of cooperation to improve intergroup relations in desegregated schools.

Cooperation

For years, it has been known that cooperation can increase liking for the people with whom one cooperates. Since the 1940s when Deutsch (1949a, 1949b) conducted his pioneering studies of cooperation, other investigators have shown that it can lead to more sharing and helping (Stendler, Damrin, & Haines, 1951), increased liking for classes (Wheeler & Ryan, 1973), and improved relations among group members (Julian & Perry, 1967; Phillips, 1956). Until recently, however, very little work had been done to investigate the feasibility of using cooperation to improve outcomes in desegregated schools. The next study we will consider (Blaney et al., 1977) was designed by a team of investigators at the University of Texas to test this possiblity.

In this study, cooperative learning groups were set up in 13 sixth-grade classrooms in seven different schools. Each class was broken down into small groups of about five students each. The course material to be covered in one part of the curriculum was then divided into five pieces (or as many pieces as there were students in the group). Each student in a group was given one and only one part of the material. It was the responsibility of each student to learn his/her material thoroughly and to teach it to the other members of the group. No other member of the group had access to another student's part of the material. Thus, even though each student was graded independently, the students in a group were dependent on one another to reach their goal of learning all the material and thereby getting a good grade. The groups were labeled "jigsaw groups" because each student in the group had only one piece of the entire "jigsaw puzzle."

The goals of this study were not just to investigate whether cooperation would reduce prejudice but, rather, to determine if it would be beneficial in achieving more general outcomes—for example, in improving liking for school, self-esteem, interpersonal relations, and so forth. To examine these questions, students in 10 interdependent classes were compared to those in three "control" classes that were taught in the traditional teacher-focused manner. Students in the interdependent classes met in their jigsaw groups three times a week for 45 minutes throughout the six weeks of the study. During this time, the students in the control classes met as they normally would. The students in all the classes were asked to fill out a questionnaire at the beginning and at the end of the study. The questionnaire assessed liking for school (e.g., "When you are in the classroom, how happy do you feel?"), academic self-confidence (e.g., "When you are in the classroom, how smart do you feel?"), and liking for the other students in the class.

The results from the study showed that many positive changes occurred in the jigsaw classes.[1] Both blacks and whites in the jigsaw groups increased in their liking for school as compared to blacks and whites in the control classes. Unfortunately, the same was not true of the Mexican-Americans in the jigsaw classes, who actually decreased in their liking for school relative to the Mexican-Americans in the control classes. This latter result is probably due to the fact that many of the Mexican-American students experienced language and communication problems when they were required to speak and teach material in English.

The findings for the Mexican-Americans were not entirely negative, however. The results for academic self-esteem show that the net effect of the cooperative experience was to improve their academic self-confidence. In fact, all three ethnic groups showed increases in self-esteem in the jigsaw classes but not in the traditional classes (see Table 13.1). This finding is important for two reasons. First, research (Scheirer & Kraut, 1979) shows that actual academic achievement may be dependent in part on how much one thinks he/she can achieve. Thus, increasing academic self-confidence should eventually lead to increases in academic achievement. Second, our previous studies (Stephan & Rosenfield, 1978a, 1978b; Rosenfield et al., in press) suggest that the higher self-esteem that results from the jigsaw groups may eventually lead to decreases in prejudice as well.

The major finding from this study was that the jigsaw groups had a beneficial effect on liking for the other students in one's group. Over the six-week period, liking for groupmates in the jigsaw classes increased more than liking for nongroupmates, and liking for nongroupmates increased just as much as did liking for classmates in the traditional classes. Thus, it is possible that more extensive use of the interdependent classroom, coupled with a system that rotates group members so that each student could interact with a variety of different groupmates, could lead to broad-based improvements in inter-

Table 13.1 Self-esteem in Jigsaw and Competitive Classes

	Pretest	Posttest
Jigsaw	20.62	21.98
Competitive	21.88	21.48

Note. From "Interdependence in the classroom: A field study" by N. Blaney, C. Stephan, D. Rosenfield, E. Aronson, and J. Sikes, *Journal of Educational Psychology*, 1977, *69*, 121–128.,

personal relationships in desegregated classrooms.

Cooperation and achievement

One aspect of the interdependent classroom that was not investigated in this initial study was academic achievement. Many teachers who were initially against the idea of jigsaw groups were opposed to it because they felt that the students did not know how to teach and, consequently, could not do as good a job as professional teachers could. Although their point is well taken, it is also true that there is some evidence concerning cooperative learning and peer teaching that indicates that other factors may compensate for the students' lack of teaching experience. For example, Dunn and Goldman (1966) found that students working under cooperative reward structures performed significantly better than those operating under competitive or individualistic reward systems. Similarly, Fay (1970) found that fifth- and sixth-grade girls learned more when they belonged to cooperative groups than when they were in competitive ones.

The research on peer teaching and cross-age tutoring shows similar beneficial effects. Experimental studies have found that these approaches lead not only to significant increases in reading skills for the tutors, but also to increases in the reading skills of the pupils (Cloward, 1967; Lippitt, Eiseman, & Lippitt, 1969; Lippitt & Lohman, 1965). These results, combined with the findings concerning the beneficial effects of cooperation on learning, led us to expect that the jigsaw technique would result in improved learning among the students, despite their lack of training in teaching.

In this study (Lucker, Rosenfield, Sikes, & Aronson, 1976) jigsaw groups were set up in six classrooms in five different schools, and five other classes in these same schools were asked to participate in the study as controls. Efforts were made to ensure that the ethnic composition in the "control" classes was similar to that of the jigsaw classes and to select "control" teachers who were highly competent and well respected.

Students in both the traditional and jigsaw classes worked for 45 minutes every day for two weeks on a curriculum that consisted of a unit on colonial America taken from a fifth-grade textbook. The material covered in both types of classes was identical. The only difference was that the material was partitioned into separate pieces for presentation in the jigsaw classes. All the students took a pretest and a posttest over the material.

A covariance analysis was performed using pretest scores and "reading level" as the covariates since both were expected to be highly related to our dependent variable— posttest score. (In the previous analyses, most of the dependent measures were attitudinal variables which were not strongly related to such factors as reading level. Thus, covariance analyses were not performed in most of the previous studies.) Because our sample of blacks and Mexican-Americans was so small, we combined them into one group.

The results from the covariance analysis are presented in Table 13.2. Students did significantly better in the jigsaw classes than in the traditional ones. This was true of both whites and minorities, but it was most marked for minorities. Indeed, the improvement for minorities was so large that, even though minorities performed significantly below whites in the traditional classes, in the jigsaw classes minority performance was equal to that of the whites. Thus, the jigsaw classroom seemed to lead to solid increases in performance for minorities without hampering the performance of the whites.

Why does the jigsaw classroom lead to such increases in performance? There are many possible explanations, but no research has yet clearly identified the source of the improvement. One possibility is that the students feel more responsibility to do their work because the entire group is relying on them, and this may lead to more time and effort being spent on homework. Or perhaps they learn more because the material is presented at a level that they can better understand. Another reason may be that the minorities who generally possess fewer school-related skills and less motivation to achieve at school than do whites (Adkins, Payne, & Ballif, 1972; Gerard & Miller, 1975; Whiteman & Deutsch, 1968) might have gained some skills or motivation from working closely with whites in the jigsaw groups. This argument is consistent with Lewis & St. John's (1972) finding that minorities who became friends with highly skilled whites performed better than other minorities. However, since Miller and Maruyama (1979) found little evidence for this "lateral transmission of values," it may not effectively explain the improvements in the performance of the minorities in our study.

Table 13.2. Adjusted Posttest Means for Whites and Minorities in Jigsaw and Competitive Classes

Dependent variable	Whites		Minorities	
	Jigsaw	Competitive	Jigsaw	Competitive
Score	64.47	62.65	64.66	57.02

Note. From "Performance in the interdependent classroom: A field study" by G. W. Lucker, D. Rosenfield, J. Sikes, and E. Aronson, *American Educational Research Journal*, 1976, *13*, 115–123.

Effects of cooperation on prejudice

Let us now return to the issue that was responsible for much of the initial interest in using cooperative groups in desegregated schools: Does cooperation decrease prejudice? The majority of studies in this area have obtained favorable results. Most notably, Wiegel, Wiser, and Cook (1975) found that cooperative interventions did lead to more positive interethnic relations. They had teachers keep track of the amount of interethnic conflict and interethnic helping that occurred in their classrooms throughout the period of their study. According to these teachers' reports, there was more interethnic helping and less interethnic conflict in the cooperative classes than in the traditional classes. In addition, Wiegel, et al. found a significant increase in the number of Mexican-American friends that the whites in the cooperative classes had. There were no substantial increases in any other combination of cross-ethnic friendship, however, and there were no decreases in general prejudice levels. These latter findings may be due to the limited duration of the cooperative experiences (three hours a week for six weeks). Perhaps a longer experience with a greater variety of groupmates would lead to more improvements in intergroup relations.

On the other hand, a careful consideration of the settings in which interethnic cooperation usually takes place leads one to wonder if there are not other factors that could inhibit the positive effects of cooperative groups. In most desegregated schools, whites have higher achievement levels than minorities (e.g., Gerard & Miller, 1975). These inequalities may place limits on the possibilities of positive changes in intergroup relations. For example, if competent white students are working together in a group with less competent minority students and the minority students cause the whites to receive poor grades, then it is possible that the white students will become more hostile toward minority students than they were before.

A study by Blanchard, Wiegel, and Cook (1975) provides some support for the idea that cooperation with less competent group members may not always lead to increased liking. In their experiment, white military personnel cooperated with each other in small groups. Sometimes one of the groupmates (who was a confederate of the experimenter) was incompetent while, in other cases, the group member appeared very competent. They found that liking for the incompetent group member was significantly below liking for the competent group member, and that this effect tended to be slightly stronger in the case of a black group member than in the case of a white group member. These results suggest that we need to look closely at the impact of competence on prejudice in cooperative groups to more fully understand its effects in desegregated settings.

The impact of competence on cooperation

We designed an experiment (Rosenfield, Stephan, & Lucker, 1979) to determine whether the negative effects of incompetence found by Blanchard, Wiegel, and Cook (1975) were limited to cooperation, or whether they occurred in competitive groups as well. If the same results were found for competition, it would be fair to say that cooperation poses no unique problems in desegregated settings. However, there is reason to believe that incompetence would have a very different impact on competitive groups as compared to cooperative groups. In cooperative groups, the more competent people help group members achieve their goals, while the less competent people sometimes hurt the chances of other group members. The opposite is true in competition. In these settings, it is the competent people who stand in the way of achieving one's goals, while incompetent people pose no threat. Thus, in competitive situations, there may be a tendency to like incompetent people more than competent ones.

To test these suggestions, we asked male college students to work in small groups with two persons who were actually confederates of the experimenter. The subjects were asked to read a section of material and take a test on it. In the competitive conditions, subjects read all the material themselves and were told that only the person who made the highest test score in their group could qualify for a prize. Subjects in the cooperative condition (which was designed to parallel the jigsaw classroom) were given only one-third of the material each and were told to share their material with each other via summaries and discussion. Either everyone in the group or no one in the group would qualify for the prize. After taking the test, subjects were given feedback about how well they and the confederates had done. In each case, one of the confederates did very well, while the other did very poorly. Subjects in the success condition were then told that they themselves had done very well on the test, while those in the failure condition were told they had done poorly.

The results showed that in the cooperation condition, incompetent groupmates were liked significantly less than competent groupmates. In the competition condition, however, there was a slight (nonsignificant) tendency for incompetent groupmates to be liked more than competent ones. The results also showed that cooperation led to more liking than competition only in the case of the competent confederate.

Because these results could have important implications for the use of cooperation in desegregated settings, we decided to reanalyze data that had been collected previously by Blaney et al. (1977). In this reanalysis, the white students' evaluations of competent and incompetent group members were analyzed. Because these evaluations were obtained both before and after the six-week period of the study, we were able to examine the *changes* in liking for classmates as a function of cooperation and competition.

The results showed that, in the jigsaw classes, liking remained basically constant for competent groupmates, but declined significantly for less competent ones. In the traditional classes, the opposite was true: Liking held constant for less competent classmates but declined significantly for more competent ones. This pattern of results held true for minority group members and white classmates.

Implications for cooperative groups

This study, along with the results of other recent investigations (Rosenfield & Roberts, 1980; Worchel, Andreoli, & Folger, 1977), all support the notion that groupmates who are perceived as hindering cooperative groups are usually disliked. On the surface, this conclusion implies that cooperation may not always be effective in reducing prejudice in situations in which minority students have substantially lower school-related skills than whites. Nonetheless, there are many situations in which cooperative groups can be effective in improving intergroup relations. For example, cooperation should reduce prejudice if the cooperative groups work on projects where the outcomes are not explicitly evaluated. Similarly, whites and minorities could cooperate on tasks that use skills in which the two groups do not differ. Also, there are some types of cooperative techniques in which the lower skilled group members do not necessarily hurt the group's performance. Two of these techniques, Teams-Games-Tournament (TGT) and Student-Teams-Achievement-Divisions (STAD), have been shown to be effective in reducing prejudice in desegregated schools—hence, they deserve special attention.

In TGT and STAD, students work together in multiethnic learning groups. Generally, they are encouraged to study together and help each other learn, but when they are tested, each student is tested individually. Unlike the jigsaw technique, each student's performance is then compared not to the class as a whole, but instead to other students in his/her "achievement division." Thus, each student's score is compared only to others who have approximately the same achievement level. Consequently, those students whose level of academic skills is low can still do very well within their achievement division. Each group's overall score is the sum of each of the group member's scores relative to the others in his/her achievement division. Thus, the poorer students are not necessarily the ones who hurt the performance of the group as a whole. This means that the blame for a group failure will not always lie with the poor students (as might be the case if their scores were not compared to those of other students at their level), and so they will not necessarily be disliked in the case of group failure.

The research done on TGT and STAD has obtained impressive results (e.g., DeVries & Edwards, 1974; DeVries, Edwards & Slavin, 1978; Slavin, 1977). All of these studies show increases in interethnic friendship choices as a result of using TGT and STAD, thus indicating that these techniques might be especially effective in improving intergroup relations during desegregation.

Attributional biases and stereotype confirmation

One final problem threatens the effectiveness of the above-mentioned techniques of reducing prejudice. It involves the way in which people process information concerning the behavior of members of the in-group and the out-group. There are a number of potential biases in the process of making attributions for the behavior of others that can lead to unfavorable impressions of out-group members. One bias comes from stereotypes. It has been found that people tend to remember events and facts that are consistent with their beliefs (stereotypes), while forgetting those that contradict those beliefs (Jones & Aneschansel, 1956; Rothbart, Evans, & Fulero, 1979). These findings imply that prejudiced whites will tend to remember events like a black doing very poorly in school, while they will forget examples of blacks who do well in school. It is easy to see that prejudices will be difficult to change if people effectively ignore events that contradict their prejudices.

Other studies indicate that ethnocentric biases also affect other cognitive processes besides memory. Research on attribution theory suggests that, when behavior is contrary to one's expectations, it is attributed to factors other than those that formed the basis of those expectations. These findings are consistent with Kelley's (1972) discounting principle and they imply that, if whites expect blacks to be lazy, but they see some blacks working hard, instead of changing their stereotype of blacks they will attribute the incident to some situational factor (e.g., there must be a very strict foreman carefully watching them work). Pettigrew (1979) has reviewed studies of this bias which he has labeled the *ultimate attribution bias*. The results of these studies suggest that people make attributions for the behavior of out-group members that are consistent with the stereotype of the out-group (e.g., Mann & Taylor, 1974; Stephan, 1977; Taylor & Jaggi, 1974; see also Chapter 12 by Gibbons on attributions made for the behavior of mentally retarded persons).

We have each conducted studies that have taken these results one step further (Greenberg & Rosenfield, 1979; Stephan, 1977). In these studies, we have examined the idea that people will tend to make derogatory attributions for the behavior of out-group members regardless of whether their behavior is consistent with the out-group stereotype. Thus, positive behaviors of out-group members may be attributed to external factors (e.g., a student helped the teacher because the teacher asked him to, rather than because he was a helpful person), while negative behavior may be attributed to that person's dispositional characteristics (e.g., a student decided not to wait for a friend because she is an impatient person not because she had to go home). If these biases are present, it is clear that people will form negative impressions of out-group members no matter how the out-group members act.

In the first study examining this possibility, Stephan (1977) studied over 700 fifth- and sixth-grade students. Blacks, Mexican-Americans, and whites answered questions about the attributions they would make for certain positive and negative behaviors performed by members of the three groups. Two examples of the questions that were asked are: "If a (e.g., white) student worked hard on a project, it would probably be because (a) he is industrious or (b) somebody made him work hard," and "If a (e.g., black) student left his baseball glove at home, it would probably be because (a) he is forgetful or (b) it was raining so they couldn't play."

The results of the study showed that Mexican-American and white students tended to make more favorable attributions for members of their own group than for members of other ethnic groups. Thus, these children saw the same behavior very differently when it was performed by an in-group member than when it was performed by an out-group member.

Our second study of attributional biases (Greenberg & Rosenfield, 1979) examined whether these unfavorable attributions for out-group members were only made by highly ethnocentric people. In this study, white male college students were asked to make attributions for the success or failure of people working on an ESP task. This task was chosen because a pilot study had shown that there were no stereotypes concerning the ESP ability of blacks and whites. Each student watched a videotape of black and white actors who either succeeded or failed on an ESP task. Then they were asked to make attributions for the actor's outcome in terms of internal factors (ability and concentration) and external factors (luck and the difficulty of the task).

The results showed that highly ethnocentric whites (as measured by a prettest) made more derogatory attributions for the blacks' performances than for the whites'. Successes by whites were attributed more to internal factors than were successes by blacks, and failures by whites were attributed more to external factors than were failures by blacks. Nonethnocentric whites, on the other hand, did not favor the whites over the blacks. Thus, the results from this study support the

implications of the previous study and indicate that it is not necessary for the behavior to be related to a stereotype for in-group members to distort its meaning. Apparently, highly ethnocentric people tend to see many of the behaviors of out-group members in an unfavorable light.

These biased attribution processes have important implications for the reduction of prejudice in desegregated schools. Because the white stereotype of minority group members is that they are unintelligent (see the review by Stephan & Rosenfield, 1980), whites may have a tendency to perceive them to be incompetent regardless of their actual behavior. Cohen and Roper (1972) have obtained results that support these notions. They found that, even when black and white group members were equally competent, the whites tended to dominate small group interactions, apparently, because both blacks and whites believed whites to be more skilled than blacks. Thus, even in situations where techniques such as TGT or STAD are used to create more positive interethnic relations, it is possible that the whites will still believe that blacks are inferior intellectually to whites.

Cohen and others (Berger, Conner & Fisek, 1974; Cohen, 1979) have recently developed a technique for dealing with these problems. The technique is based on Expectation States Theory (EST). According to EST, people develop expectations concerning the competence of others based on "diffuse status characteristics" such as race and sex. This suggestion is supported by studies showing that blacks in biracial groups make fewer comments than do whites, accept the whites' suggestions uncritically, and in general display inhibition and subordination to the white group members (Berger, Cohen, & Zeldick, 1972). Cohen suggests that this "interracial interaction disability" that results from diffuse status characteristics like race can be deactivated by specific status characteristics, such as competence on a task. However, it is not sufficient for the blacks just to equal the competence of the whites. Instead, the competence of the blacks must be superior to that of the whites before interracial interaction disability can be overcome. Thus, Cohen and Roper (1972) were able to eliminate this disability *only* when they pretrained blacks on a complex and highly technical task and then had the blacks teach the whites how to perform the task. Their results indicate that it may be necessary to actually *reverse* the stereotype before blacks and whites can work together as equals in interracial groups.

Cohen points out that the situation in which the interethnic interaction takes place is an important determinant of the success of this attempted reversal of stereotypes. She notes that, if the class and school reflect the traditional power structure of whites dominating blacks, it will be very difficult to change this stereotype. Certainly, *one* experience with *one* black who contradicts the stereotype can be attributed to chance or to the possibility that this black is an exception. However, if the white students have many experiences with many different blacks who contradict the stereotype (e.g., many competent black teachers who have a high status in the school), and if the power structure in the school reinforces the idea that blacks and whites are equal, then whites can no longer easily attribute these experiences to chance or say that all of these competent blacks are exceptions to the rule. Instead, we hope they will begin changing their stereotypes.

Augmenting the impact of intergroup cooperation

Studies of different techniques for organizing small cooperative groups have yielded a great deal of information about how to design cooperative experiences so that they will have the best chance of improving intergroup relations. One important consideration is success and failure. Failure seems to eliminate most of the positive effects of cooperation (e.g., Blanchard, Adelman, & Cook, 1975; Blanchard & Cook, 1976) and can be especially damaging to interethnic relations if the failure is blamed on less

competent members of the out-group. Thus, if possible, cooperative experiences should not end in failure. This means that the students should either cooperate on projects that are not going to be evaluated, or that goals should be established so that they are almost always attainable by the groups. Cooperation that ends satisfactorily has the best chance of improving interpersonal relationships among the group members.

Cooperative groups should also work on tasks in which students will not automatically assume that the whites are superior. If they did assume that, then the whites would tend to dominate the cooperative groups and the group's interactions would reinforce the negative stereotypes of minorities. Also, minorities would probably be disliked because they would be considered to be incompetent and therefore would be blamed for any problems that the group had in achieving its goal. Thus, the group activities should not be limited to traditional academic work, but rather be expanded to involve many tasks that are not strictly academic.

We should also point out that the power structure of the school that students attend appears to influence how competent the minority students are assumed to be. If there are few minority faculty or administrators, or if the minority staff members are in low power positions, then the structure of the school will reinforce the impression that minorities have low status and are incompetent.

Another way of improving the effects of cooperation on prejudice is to change the way the performance of the group is evaluated so that minority students will not usually be blamed for the group's problems. Techniques like TGT and STAD, which allow even poor students to help the group, will probably be more successful at reducing the whites' prejudices than cooperative techniques in which poorer students usually hurt the performance of the group. It is important to organize the groups so that the minority students do not receive an inordinate share of the blame for the group's failure.

Summary

It is clear that desegregation does not have one simple, predictable effect on intergroup relations. Instead, it has many different effects on different children depending on a variety of situational factors. The research done on these effects has yielded enough information for us to have a relatively clear idea of the kinds of conditions that can make it a more positive experience. Figure 13.2 shows a model summarizing many of the factors that determine how desegregation will affect intergroup relations. The primary factors affecting desegregation are listed below.

SCHOOL AND CLASSROOM STRUCTURE. Allport (1954), Amir (1969), and others have pointed out the importance of informal, equal-status, and cooperative interethnic contact in reducing prejudice. School and classroom structures that encourage this type of contact will help decrease prejudice. Most of these structural factors fit into two groups: those that increase informal *contact* between the ethnic groups and those that increase *respect* for minority groups. When there are a number of structural factors that increase informal interethnic contact (e.g., seating patterns which mix the ethnic groups) and when these factors negate the cultural stereotype (e.g., where there is a black principal or a number of competent, influential black teachers), the chances of decreasing prejudice are greatly enhanced. However, one must remember that, because of biases in memory and attribution processes, it may take a number of experiences with nonstereotypic behavior from outgroup members before stereotypes and prejudices can be changed.

SCHOOL AND CLASSROOM CLIMATE. The climate of a school or classroom can either be conducive to positive interethnic relations or it can very effectively inhibit them. Where teachers frown on interethnic contact, and where interpersonal relationships involve outbursts of hostility and anger, little positive interethnic contact will occur. But where the role models show interethnic harmony and encourage interethnic interaction, much more positive interethnic contact will occur.

CULTURAL ENVIRONMENT. The cultural environment can have many of the same effects as the school structure and school climate. Where the culture supports segregation and seriously threatens interethnic friendships, few children will be independent enough to have extensive interethnic contact. Similarly, if the culture downgrades minorities, it will take a concerted effort in the school to negate it. On the other hand, if the students come from an environment in which interethnic contact is supported and considered to be normal (e.g., if they come from a naturally integrated neighborhood), the likelihood of their making new interethnic contacts in school is increased.

FAMILY ENVIRONMENT. Because children are responsive to the socializing influence of their families as well as to the influence of the general culture, the examples that their families set will also influence the children. If the family supports interethnic contact through their ideas and actions, the children should be more willing to make interethnic contacts. In contrast, if they show only hostility toward out-group members, and if they display harsh and rigid child-rearing practices that engender displaced hostility in their children, the children are unlikely to develop positive attitudes toward outgroups.

INDIVIDUAL DIFFERENCES. Finally, children may differ greatly on personality dimensions that affect their interpersonal relations and, hence, their interethnic relations. Those who generally reject others, who have mainly hostile and negative relations with other people, will not be favorably disposed to out-group members and will rarely have any positive experiences with out-group members. However, those who have little hostility to displace on others and those who

School and classroom structure

Structures affecting contact
Seating patterns that mix ethnic groups
Academic and "playground" activities that mix ethnic groups
Satisfying interethnic cooperative experiences
Students come from comparable SES and academic backgrounds (where feasible)

Structure affecting stereotypes
Equal treatment of all ethnic groups within the classroom and school
Student power within the school shared by the ethnic groups
Power and status of the staff shared by the ethnic groups
Competent, responsible minority staff members
All ethnic groups respected by staff
Activities in which minorities excel are supported and respected
Students come from comparable SES and academic backgrounds (where feasible)

School and classroom climate
Good interethnic relations among staff members
Positive interethnic cooperation among students
Teachers encourage interethnic contact
Students have little interethnic hostility
Friendships stressed more than grades

Cultural environment

Environmental factors affecting contact
Live in integrated neighborhood
Support of desegregation by the officials and the populace
Set good public examples of interethnic cooperation
Eliminate any vestiges of segregation

Environmental factors affecting stereotypes
Show respect for all ethnic groups
Eliminate any vestiges of segregation
All groups should have power and status
Minorities should hold their share of important, respected public positions

Family environment

Family factors affecting contact
Support of interethnic relationships
Set examples for positive interethnic relationships

Family factors affecting stereotype
Respect for minority groups
Supportive child-rearing practices that will not result in displaced hostility

Individual differences
High self-acceptance
Low authoritarianism
High SES and high educational attainment
Little hostility in relations with others
High sociability

Figure 13.2. Factors affecting prejudice during desegregation.

generally have good relationships with others will be more likely to develop friendships with out-group members and become less prejudiced.

The number and the complexity of the factors that affect prejudice during desegregation point to the need for making informed decisions on designing the structure and atmosphere of the desegregated schools.

Armed with the knowledge of the ways to best decrease prejudice, desegregation programs can be highly successful. But where administrators reluctantly implement desegregation plans with little knowledge of how best to produce interethnic harmony, desegregation efforts may have little chance of reducing interethnic hostility.

Note

1. Again, attempts were made to ensure that improvements in the cooperative classes would not be due to the fact that those classes simply had better teachers than did the competitive classes. We made sure that each traditional teacher chosen was very well recommended and respected. In addition, we compared the attitudes of the students in the interdependent classes to the attitudes of those in the control classes at the beginning of the study. Since no differences were present at the pretest, it is unlikely that any differences that were present at the posttest were the result only of teacher differences.

14

DEVELOPING ATTITUDES TO LAW AND JUSTICE: AN INTEGRATIVE REVIEW

NICHOLAS P. EMLER
UNIVERSITY OF DUNDEE

ROBERT HOGAN
THE JOHNS HOPKINS UNIVERSITY

In this chapter we review and attempt to integrate some of the major themes in the psychological literature on how attitudes toward law and justice develop. We do not attempt to review all the relevant theories and research. Instead, we sample selectively in order to illustrate the most important themes; we refer the reader where possible to appropriate literature reviews. Inevitably in any attempt to integrate diverse areas and styles of scholarship, a set of contrasts emerge that resist easy synthesis. This is so because different research traditions raise different questions and seek different kinds of answers.

Social theorists from Comte to the present have argued that a healthy society depends on consensus about the value, legitimacy, and purpose of that society's institutions. In contemporary society law is an especially critical institution. Weber (1946) predicted, in fact, that law would become the primary means of regulating human affairs in modern industrialized societies; he thought this form of regulation would become increasingly widespread as bureaucratic organizations proliferated in all areas of social life. Following Comte, then, the big question concerns how consensus toward law and justice develops. This consensus is, of course, reflected in attitudes toward law and justice.

Psychologists have a variety of theories about the way in which consensus is produced in each generation of young people. In this chapter we consider first what can be learned from social psychology about attitudes toward law and justice. We then turn to developmental psychology to determine the origins of these attitudes. In doing so we review the fields of legal, political, and moral socialization, and we try to substantiate two broad claims. The first is that attitudes to law, politics, justice, and morality, although distinguishable, are closely related to one another. Our second claim is that people's attitudes toward law and justice largely reflect the structure of the interpersonal relations in which they take part. Our approach, which comes from the sociology of knowledge, will become more apparent after we define our major terms—attitude, law, justice, and development.

Attitude

The concept of "attitude" is one of the oldest in social psychology. According to most definitions (e.g., Secord & Backman, 1964) attitudes contain three components: beliefs, feelings, and behavioral tendencies toward some social object. The object may be a person, a group, a policy, an institution, or a value. In practice, the concept usually emphasizes at one time the emotional component and at another the cognitive or the behavioral component. Currently, the fashion in social and developmental psychology is to emphasize the cognitive aspects of attitudes. We believe it is essential to emphasize equally their affective and behavioral aspects.

The relationship between the behavioral and the other aspects of attitudes is problematic as seen by the frequent failure to find connections between people's beliefs or feelings and their actions. Along these lines we find it helpful to recall Ichheiser's (1970) distinction between "views in principle" and "views in fact." Views of the first kind refer to people's attitudes to social issues that are held in a generalized, so to speak, philosophical way. They refer to what people say they believe, feel, and ought, hypothetically, to do. Views in fact refer to what people actually do and to the beliefs and feelings that are implied by what they actually do. Most discussions about attitudes to law and justice concern peoples' views in principle.

Law and authority

Most definitions of law refer to sets of regulations devised by a centralized authority that also has the power to enforce them. The institution of law is normally assumed to be composed of rules, courts, and organized force. Consequently, attitudes to law include attitudes toward the laws themselves, toward the political process through which laws are made and revised, and toward the agencies through which laws are enforced and violations are treated.

Societies with more or less formalized legal codes have existed for centuries. At the same time, however, many societies have also managed without them (Roberts, 1979). This raises the problem of identifying what sets law apart from the other ways that communities uphold rights, punish wrongs, and exercise control over their members. The answer is that law represents a particular kind of authority.

In a still classic analysis, Weber (1947) distinguished three kinds of authority: charismatic, which depends on the qualities of a particular leader; traditional, which depends on custom and inherited titles; and legal-rational, which requires obedience to an impersonal legal order and to persons who hold positions in that order. Another feature of legal-rational authority is that authorities in particular positions are permitted only to do particular things; their jurisdiction is usually specified in rules and legal codes. Finally, legal-rational authority does not depend on a personal relationship between bureaucratic officials and those whose activities they regulate.

Legal-rational authority depends, therefore, on a particular kind of legitimacy. According to Weber,

> . . . the legitimacy of the power holder to give commands rests upon rules that are rationally established by enactment, by agreement, or by imposition. The legitimation for establishing these rules rests in turn upon a rationally enacted or interpreted "constitution." Orders are given in the name of the impersonal norm rather than in the name of a personal authority; and even the giving of a command constitutes obedience towards some norm rather than an arbitrary freedom, favour, or priviledge. (Weber, 1922–23; reproduced in Gerth & Mills, 1946, pp. 294–295)

Weber's analysis of legal-rational authority applies not just to the law but to all the various kinds of bureaucratic regulatory agencies that exist in contemporary society. Social psychologists tend to overlook the fact that many people spend most of their lives in bureaucratic organizations. They are educated in them, work in them, and often die in them. People's attitudes toward this distinctive form of authority ought to be of central concern to psychology.

Justice

Justice can be defined simply as the process by which people receive what they are due (cf. Matson, 1978). Because the state defines each person's due, justice and law are intimately connected. But there are at least four reasons why law and justice are distinct. First, it is impossible for the law to specify what each person is due in every conceivable case; nor can the state punish every "injustice" (Hogan & Emler, in press). Second, individuals can tell what is fair in cases that lie outside the jurisdiction of legal authority. Third, individual notions of justice may contradict the results of the legal process, so that people often evaluate the "justness" or fairness of legal decisions. And finally, questions of justice are somehow more universal than questions of law. In any community, disputes will arise over resources, breaches of tradition, insults, injuries—all raising questions of justice. Research by social anthropologists shows that law is only one means for settling such disputes (cf. Roberts, 1979).

Development

Psychological development is normally defined in one of two ways. In the first case, development is defined quantitatively in terms of the cumulative effects of experience. In this view, psychological development occurs in no particular order; it is simply a matter of when specific experiences happen to arise. The causes of development are external to the individual, and development itself has no end point beyond acquiring the repertoire of behavior believed to be common to most adults. This definition characterized behavioristic or learning theory models of development.

The second definition of development derives from a biological model of growth in which qualitative changes occur in a fixed sequence intrinsic to the organism. Development is therefore an inherent predisposition, the end point of which is psychological maturity. This viewpoint characterizes cognitive developmental theory. Behaviorist theories of development emphasize individual differences arising from unique learning histories. Cognitive developmental theories emphasize features that are common to all members of our species. Textbook writers most often define development so as to reflect both these views—that is, as a series of relatively enduring changes that occur in the life cycle of each person, through an interaction of intrinsic established organismic tendencies with specific environmental experiences.

Social development is complicated because it includes: (a) changes that are universal to the human species; (b) changes reflecting individual experience; (c) changes that are peculiar to particular cultures and historical periods; and (d) in all but the simplest societies, changes that are peculiar to particular groups within society. Curiously, theories of social development generally fail to distinguish among these different kinds of changes.

The social psychology of law and justice

The interrelatedness of social attitudes

Perhaps the most important lesson to be learned from the social psychological study of attitudes is that a person's attitudes regarding law, justice, morality, and politics are usually related. Moreover, individual differences in these attitudes can often be described in terms of the single ideological dimension of conservatism-liberalism. Although this dimension is commonly thought of as political, many of the issues that divide conservatives and liberals concern law, morality, and justice. There are several ways in which this point can be illustrated, one of which involves research on the covariation of attitudes.

In *The Authoritarian Personality*, Adorno, Frenkel-Brunswik, Levinson, and Sanford (1950) hypothesize that attitudes toward different social issues will be systematically related to one another; views on one issue should correlate with views on other issues. The controversy that raged around the Authoritarian Personality study after its publication all but obscured the fact that this hypothesis was confirmed. Adorno et al. were primarily interested in antisemitism, but they also developed measures of general ethnocentrism, political and economic conservatism, and an orientation they described as "authoritarian." As they defined it, authoritarianism has a strong moral component, involving uncritical obedience to authority, preference for strong leadership, rigid adherence to conventional virtues, and punitiveness toward those who ignore conventional morality or question authority. They found a correlation of +.57 between political and economic conservatism and both the ethnocentrism and the authoritarianism measures, and these latter two measures correlated .75.

Studies in America and Britain spanning 30 years have identified remarkably similar patterns of social attitudes. Time and again attitudes toward political authority, treatment of lawbreakers and deviants, the proper scope of law, social justice, and sexual morality have been found to be related. Fergusson (1939) suggested that the pattern of these relationships could be described by two underlying dimensions which he called "humanitarianism" and "religionism." The humanitarianism dimension was defined by attitudes toward war, capital punishment, and the treatment of criminals. The religionism dimension was defined by attitudes toward established religion and sexual permissiveness. Similar results were found by Eysenck (1944, 1971), Bagely (1970), and others. Ray (1973), however, concluded from a factor analytic study of several measures of social attitudes that there is only one general factor — liberalism-conservatism — underlying the domain of sociopolitical attitudes.

Measures designed specifically to assess moral attitudes also turn out to reflect this ideological dimension of liberalism-conservatism. The Survey of Ethical Attitudes (SEA) developed by Hogan (1970) to distinguish between legalistic and intuitive forms of moral reasoning is related to liberalism-conservatism (Lorr & Zea, 1977, Snodgrass, 1975). The Defining Issues Test (DIT), de-

vised by Rest (1975) to measure an abstract style of moral reasoning, is also related to this dimension. Thus, there is no clear way functionally to distinguish between domains of moral and political attitudes, because both ultimately rest on choices about human values.

This conclusion is also supported by studies wherein subjects are asked to respond to measures of moral attitudes from either a conservative or a radical perspective. Meehan, Woll, and Abbott (1979), using the SEA, and Emler, Herron, and Malone (1979), using the DIT, found that scores varied predictably as a function of the perspective taken. As Johnson and Hogan (1980) argue, these results do not mean that the SEA (or the DIT) really measure political as opposed to moral attitudes, but that there is no practical way of distinguishing between them.

Liberalism-conservatism

Findings from a variety of studes (e.g., Adorno et al., 1950; Candee, 1976; Eysenck, 1954; Hogan & Dickstein, 1972; Rest, 1975; Rubin & Peplau, 1975; Wilson, 1973) indicate that liberalism and conservatism reflect very different attitudes toward law and justice. Conservatism is associated with a preference for strict laws that are strictly enforced; that is, it is more important for the law to guarantee individual safety and security than individual rights. Thus, the purpose of law is to protect traditional values and ways of life. Nonetheless, conservatives are unwilling to extend the protection of the law to everyone, in particular to deviants or outsiders. Conservatives do not believe in using the law to create "social justice" because they regard the poor and disadvantaged as responsible for their own plight. Conservatives tend to prefer traditional or charismatic forms of authority over legal-rational authority. Finally, they prefer powerful leadership and a strong police who are free from extensive legal restrictions on their authority.

Liberals prefer laws of moderate scope.

The business of law, from this perspective, is to protect rather than restrict individual liberties. For liberals, the law ought not restrict personal freedoms such as sexual conduct, but should be used to secure justice for the "underpriveleged." Thus liberals favor legal reforms that extend the same rights to everyone, regardless of their status in society. Liberals prefer lenient treatment of offenders and emphasize reform rather than punishment. Finally, liberals dislike traditional and charismatic forms of authority; they prefer instead a carefully controlled version of legal-rational authority.

In view of the importance of the liberalism-conservatism dimension for understanding sociopolitical attitudes, it seems important to understand how these attitudes develop. What kinds of life experiences produce children, and ultimately adults, who endorse a liberal perspective, and what kinds of experiences seem to lead to a conservative outlook? The answers presently available in developmental psychology are not very helpful. The primary answer seems to be that conservatives are retarded, morally stunted, and possibly neurotic, whereas liberals are bright, morally advanced, and mature. Clearly this answer is biased and unacceptable (cf. Hogan & Emler, in press).

Normative social attitudes

The final subject from social psychology that is useful for our purposes concerns normative attitudes to justice; that is, what attitudes *do* people hold about law and justice? If central themes can be identified, they will give a focus to developmental research. Unfortunately, the literature on this topic reveals no single standard or concept of justice underlying people's attitudes and behavior. There seem instead to be numerous standards (Lerner, 1976). Nevertheless, some writers argue for the importance of a single principle: One is equity (Walster, Berscheid, & Walster, 1973); another is equality (Sampson, 1975).

Equity refers to the distribution of rewards in society in relation to some criterion of merit. The criterion might be effort, productivity, seniority, or status. There is considerable evidence that people are inclined to distribute rewards on such bases (Adams & Freedman, 1976). If people dispense rewards in these ways, then these tendencies should have consequences. For example, it has been suggested that individuals would experience distress if they were under- or over-rewarded according to the requirements of equity (Adams, 1963). When under-rewarded, they should feel anger; when over-rewarded, guilt. In either case, they should also try to restore equity by changing their own inputs. There is some experimental evidence to support this prediction (Adams & Freedman, 1976).

It also seems that witnesses will react to the inequitable (unjust) suffering of others, either by compensating the victim or by holding the victim responsible (Walster, Berscheid, & Walster, 1973). The concept of equity has also been applied to reactions to punishments (see, for example, Austin, Walster, & Utne, 1976); punishment is often seen as a way to set things right or restore equity and punishments are evaluated in this light. Finally, research on status inconsistency and relative deprivation (e.g., Pettigrew, 1967) reveals that people's beliefs about what they are due are powerfully affected by their views of their own status. In other words, people expect their rewards to be proportional to their status.

There is, therefore, evidence from a wide range of sources consistent with the idea that equity is an important standard of justice. It seems to characterize the attitude of the average person in a variety of situations. But there is more to justice than the concept of equity. Lerner (1976) points out that standards of justice vary with the situation. For example, Sampson (1975) and Leventhal (1976) reviewed several studies in which subjects preferred equality to equity. Within groups of people who must work closely together, the norm of equity can produce tension, antagonism, and disruptive competition. Finally, there are times when other considerations take precedence over justice.

Tajfel and his colleagues (e.g., Tajfel, Billig, Bundy, & Flament, 1971) show that, when individuals must divide resources between their in-group and out-group, they tend to give the advantage to the in-group and ignore equality or equity (i.e., considerations of justice).

Social psychology has little to say about our fundamental question—What attitudes toward justice (e.g., equity) are widely held in modern society? Consider equity. Although it is possible that a norm such as equity reflects a natural tendency of the human mind, it is also possible (and in our view more likely) that the equity norm reflects the values of our particular culture or social system, as Sampson (1975) and Pepitone (1976) have argued. In the absence of information regarding what attitudes toward justice are normative in modern society, it becomes more difficult to generalize about the development of attitudes toward law and justice. Consequently, we will use Weber's analysis as our starting point and assume that adults in this society are characterized by their orientation to legal-rational authority.

Developmental psychology and attitudes to law and justice

Assuming that we know what attitudes people hold toward law and justice, we turn to developmental psychology to learn how these attitudes are acquired. We will begin with a review of the relevant theories of development and related research.

Social learning

The question is how do children acquire their attitudes toward law and justice? There are two obvious answers to this question. One is that they learn by attending to what adults tell them. The other is that they learn by observation and imitation; adults consciously or unconsciously demonstrate the defining values of the society. Most theories of development emphasize learning from others, particularly parents, by observation

or imitation. They differ in their views of the conditions necessary for such learning and of the results the learning produces.

Social learning theory stresses that children learn habits by watching models. Bandura (1971) suggests there are at least four requirements that must be met in order to learn from a model. First, one must notice and pay attention to the model's behavior. Second, one must retain what has been observed, by encoding it in terms of verbal labels or by storing images in memory. Third, one must have the requisite skills to be able to reproduce the observed behavior of the model. Fourth, one must perceive the consequences of the model's actions as desirable or reinforcing.

The extent to which children learn from models is affected by two further factors. First, the characteristics of the model make a difference. Children are more likely to learn from models who are the most nurturant, powerful, or prestigious. Bandura (1974) suggests there is a difference between younger and older children in this respect. Younger children are more likely to model adults who are nurturant and/or powerful. Older children, like adults, tend to select models who have been in some way successful—usually models with relatively high status. Second, the prior experiences and acquired characteristics of the child make a difference. Those who have previously been rewarded for imitation, and those who have low self-esteem or high dependency, seem more willing to imitate.

There are five problems with the social learning theory account of socialization. First, it implies that the process of socialization is fragile because it depends on several conditions being met for a perfect outcome. Since, these conditions rarely co-occur, socialization will be, in every case, more or less imperfect and incomplete.

Second, social learning theorists maintain that a child acquires specific habits and that the strength of any one habit is not necessarily related to that of others. Since habits are acquired with respect to specific situations, conduct will be situation-specific. This view is not entirely compatible with what we know of moral conduct. For example, self-report studies of delinquency indicate that there are stable individual differences in levels of obedience to the law, and that individual dispositions to conformity generalize across situations and types of conduct (Emler, 1979).

Third, social learning theorists emphasize the nonverbal aspect of social learning—that is, learning by observation and imitation rather than by instruction. There is some justification for this; for example, children are more likely to model adults' behavior than their verbal standards (e.g., Bryan, 1975). However, this does not take into account the fact that language is one of the most distinctive features of human social conduct. Consequently, language should play an important role in human development. Within social learning theory, however, language has not yet received the consideration it merits as a major medium of socialization.

Fourth, social learning theory is concerned with the acquisition of internalized controls over behavior—self-regulatory systems. The sense of legal obligation, however, seems to imply a sensitivity to symbolic sources of control. It involves complying with the requirements, regulations, and instructions of lawful authorities. It is equally important to ask, therefore, how sensitivity to external symbolic sources of control develops and on what it is based.

Finally, despite decades of social learning research, we still do not know to what degree a child's moral attitudes are acquired by imitation of his or her parents. Hess and Torney (1967), in their research on the development of political attitudes, concluded that the family serves primarily to teach a child consensually held attitudes. This suggests that social learning in the family mainly reinforces and validates normative standards. Along these lines, other research suggests only a weak relationship between the ideological orientations of parents and their children. Mosher and Scodel (1960) found a correlation of .32 between

mothers' ethnocentrism and that of their 11 to 12-year-old children. This figure seems to represent the upper limit of the relationship between the attitudes of parents and their children. Byrne (1965) concluded that most of the variance in students' authoritarianism was a function of factors other than parental attitudes. Boshier (1973) found that conservatism in 17 to 19 year-olds correlated less than .32 with that of the same sex parent, and even lower with the opposite sex parent. Jennings and Niemi (1968) found correlations between twelfth-graders and their parents on specific moral issues, ranging from a high of .34 down to zero. Finally, Gold, Christie, and Friedman (1976), using male students, found that only one of five scales of moral-political orientation, "traditional moralism," correlated with parental attitudes—for mothers the correlation was .32, for fathers, .31.

Cognitive development

One of the weaknesses of traditional learning theory accounts of socialization is that they assume the mechanisms of learning operate in the same way throughout development. Recent formulations of social learning, however, do make allowance for the effects of the child's developing intellectual capacities (see Mischel & Mischel, 1976). Nonetheless, it was cognitive developmental theorists who first described how the structure of children's thinking changes over time. These changes are reflected in evolving attitudes toward law and justice.

PIAGET. This tradition begins with Piaget's (1932) work on the development of children's moral ideas—attitudes toward rules and justice from infancy to the beginning of adolescence. The rules Piaget examined were those spontaneously invented, recognized, and employed by children to regulate their games. The issues of justice were those that might arise between children, or between an adult and a child over the assignment of rewards or punishments.

Piaget (1932) described three phases in

children's developing consciousness of rules. Up to about 6 years, children are aware that some things are allowed and others forbidden, but they do not distinguish among natural (e.g., scientific) laws, game rules invented by children themselves, and rules imposed by adults. In the second phase, children believe game rules have some external and sacred origin and that they deserve absolute respect. The rules are regarded as immutable; they are unchanging, unalterable requirements demanding literal obedience. Children in this phase will not consider the possibility of any modification of the rules.

The third phase is marked by an appreciation that the rules of children's games are the products of mutual agreement among players themselves and that they are worthy of respect because they are based on mutual consent. At this stage children appear to understand adequately the function of rules in preventing disputes, in determining who has won and lost and, most fundamentally, in constituting the activity of the game itself. Because rules are the product of mutual consent, they can also be changed by mutual agreement. Proposed changes are accepted if all players agree that they preserve the spirit of the game as well as the abstract principle on which the game is based and which the rules exemplify. This third set of attitudes begins to emerge after about 10 years of age.

Piaget believed that this third phase is the basis for the child's understanding of the democratic process. The attitudes that emerge during this phase are, Piaget suggested, based on respect for a method—a method for resolving disagreements and making rules that Piaget called the method of cooperation. It involved the idea that each person concerned should have an equal say in any decisions to which he or she may be bound. A study by Solomon, Ali, Kfir, Houlihan, and Yaeger (1972) supports this view. They investigated 7- to 13-year-olds' views of group decision making and found that only the oldest group preferred equality of representation, but that all children prac-

ticed equality at a much earlier age. Significantly, Piaget also found that there were considerable discrepancies between children's consciousness of rules and their practice, indicating that thought tends to lag behind practice. Nonetheless, it is still a long way from the rules of children's games to the laws of the nation state.

Concerning changes in children's notions of justice and fairness, Piaget also described three phases. In the first, children believe that fairness is simply what adults or larger and stronger persons decide. Thus, in matters of punishment, children accept arbitrary severity as appropriate. In the second phase, at about 7 to 8 years of age, children begin to argue that all decisions, including those of adults, must conform to rigid standards of equality. Everyone must be treated the same. Attacks and insults must be returned blow for blow. Punishment must conform closely to the offense. All must receive equal rewards and benefits. The third phase, which emerges between 10 and 13, is called "equity," but it also seems to include the justice of need. Equity is defined by the attitude that the demands of justice must take account of individual cases. In matters of punishment this means considering extenuating circumstances as well as using punishment to restore the relationship between culprit and victim, to reform the culprit, and to compensate the victim.

Damon (1975) proposes a more differentiated sequence in the development of attitudes toward justice. He found that 4-year-olds equated fairness with their own desires. Fairness as equal treatment followed this stage, and notions of merit and deservingness appeared subsequently. Appreciation of the justice of need seemed to be yet another stage beyond this.

The sequence in which children express attitudes toward justice parallels the sequence in which these attitudes are expressed in behavioral standards. Hook and Cook (1979) note that the earliest standard practiced is self-interest; this is followed by equality, and then by what they call ordinal equity. Ordinal equity amounts to rank ordering people in terms of their relative deservingness or merit. Equity in the sense of making rewards mathematically proportional to merit seems not to be practiced until the teens.

ADELSON. The development of social attitudes depends on the development of social knowledge. Research on political socialization indicates that social knowledge is incomplete in early adolescence. Knowledge of functions of legal and political officeholders, for example, is particularly undeveloped. At the same time, children characteristically have highly positive attitudes toward these same authority figures. For instance, they express great confidence in the benevolence of political leaders, regarding them as likable and trustworthy. This generalization has held up in studies in several modern industrial democracies, including the United States, Britain, West Germany, Japan, France, and Australia (e.g., Connell, 1971, Easton & Dennis, 1969, Greenstein, 1960, 1975, Hess & Torney, 1967).

Children also display an almost total lack of insight into the nature and functioning of political and legal systems. They may believe that police officers, judges, government officials, and political leaders are benevolent, but they have not a clue about the scope and limits of their duties. Authorities and institutions are regarded in highly personalized and concrete terms. How little the 11-year-old knows is revealed in a series of studies by Adelson and others (e.g., Adelson & O'Neil, 1966; Gallatin & Adelson, 1971; Mussen, Sullivan & Eisenberg-Berg, 1977). Adelson and his colleagues show that 11-year-olds do not understand that political and legal decisions have social as well as personal consequences. Indeed, they don't understand the purpose of some government actions at all. Government, community, and society are abstractions beyond their grasp, because they think of them in terms of particular persons. They believe that laws serve the needs of particular individuals rather than the entire community. Laws are

also seen primarily as having restrictive and coercive functions. The absence of law is believed to lead to chaotic conduct. The possibility that certain laws might be difficult to enforce or widely unpopular suggests to the 11-year-old simply that they should be more rigorously and strictly enforced.

Somewhere between 13 and 15 a more abstract view of law emerges. At 13 children begin to appreciate that laws may result in social and community benefits. By 15 laws are seen as having beneficial and not merely restrictive effects. Fifteen-year-olds can conceive of internal as well as external effects arising from the absence of law—anomie, inner corruption, and personal confusion. The age of 15 also marks the appearance of the concept of amendment; here laws are seen in a more or less pragmatic manner. The 15-year-old considers what is workable as well as what is desirable and recognizes that particular laws are experiments that sometimes fail but that can be revised or amended when they do.

Yet another interesting shift of attitude occurs in this period. Younger children see conflicts between individuals and the community as conflicts between people. Consequently, they give priority to the rights and needs of the community over those of the individual. In so doing they do not appreciate that some laws may improperly infringe on individual liberties. Again, a decisive shift of attitude seems to occur between 13 and 15, with older subjects accepting both the priority of community needs over individual self-interest and the necessity for laws not to infringe on individual liberties. Older children are also more likely to stress the importance of laws guaranteeing or protecting individual rights. These trends were replicated in a later study by Brown (1974) who found an increased willingness with age to comply with laws that benefit the community but a decreased willingness to comply with laws that interfere with individual liberties.

Taken together these findings seem somewhat paradoxical. Researchers agree that younger children have highly idealized views of authorities but also highly authoritarian views of law and government, emphasizing their restrictive and punitive role. Both attitudes change in the teens. Attitudes toward formal authority become far more cynical and less trusting. At the same time, law comes to be seen in more favorable terms, with its beneficial value to the community being stressed. These apparently paradoxical changes may reflect a developing insight into the distinction between laws and the particular people who make and enforce them.

As we have seen, the distinction between political offices and the people who hold them is basic to Weber's concept of legal-rational authority. It is also clear that younger subjects do not understand this distinction (see also Furth, 1979). It is not clear whether the earlier idealization of authority reflects children's inability to understand this distinction and their tendency to personalize politics, or whether it reflects indoctrination by parents and teachers—that is, to idealize authority in all its forms. Nor is it clear whether the growing adolescent awareness of this distinction reflects an accommodation to attitudes that are common among adults, or whether it is a consequence of recognizing the distinction between the personal motives of officeholders and the formal requirements of the office.

Whatever the cause, the changes in attitudes documented by Adelson are remarkably consistent. They seem largely unaffected by social class or sex and take a highly similar form in America, Britain, and Germany. Adelson did find some interesting and significant cross-cultural differences, but the age-related effects were far more important. There are two important implications in this. First, it suggests that the changes between the ages of 11 and 18 reflect the acquisition of attitudes that are normative in Western nation states. Second, changes in these attitudes are probably a function of cognitive development and accumulation of experience. The concepts and distinctions they involve are beyond the intellectual grasp of the average 11-year-old.

KOHLBERG. A more explicit interpretation of social learning in terms of cognitive development is given by Kohlberg (e.g., 1969, 1976). Like Adelson, Kohlberg has attempted to describe the changes in social attitudes that occur during adolescence. Kohlberg, however, suggests that these changes form a sequence of discrete stages, each representing a distinct style of reasoning. He is also more concerned with the development of moral ideas than with reasoning about political or legal issues. Nonetheless, Kohlberg's conclusions show distinct parallels with those of Adelson.

Kohlberg has studied the way that people resolve dilemmas involving conflicting moral and legal requirements. His strategy has been to pose hypothetical problems and ask subjects to provide morally satisfying answers. Kohlberg has argued that the answers can be grouped into three basic types, and he has labeled these, respectively, preconventional, conventional, and principled solutions. The first type, the preconventional, appeals to the interests, fears, wants, or desires of one of the characters involved in the problem. In effect, it adopts the perspective of a particular individual. Most children under 10 and a few adolescents, Kohlberg (1976) claims, will offer solutions of this sort. Kohlberg believes that they use this type of reasoning because they do not understand that society entails shared standards of conduct. Rules and expectations are seen as external to one's self, and relations with formal authorities are interpreted in individual and personal terms.

The second type of solution, called conventional, appeals to shared standards of morality or obligations that flow from membership in society. For this reason, Kohlberg calls this the "member-of-society" perspective, and he claims it is the perspective of many adolescents and most adults. The third or principled solution is, as the name suggests, an appeal to basic and generalized moral principles that are assumed to be more basic than the moral conventions, laws, or regulations of particular societies. These nonrelative principles include considerations of overall utility, basic rights that should be upheld in any society, or universal principles of fairness and justice. Kohlberg calls this the "prior-to-society" perspective and suggests it is achieved by only a minority of adults in any society.

Kohlberg divides each of these three basic types of reasoning into two subtypes, thus producing a total of six stages. The stages are assumed to represent a sequence of development. Each stage entails a more refined interpretation of justice. The first three bear distinct similarities to those identified by Piaget (1932). What is interesting, therefore, is Kohlberg's claim that the third stage in his schema, which is the highest identified by Piaget, is still a limited view of justice. The substance of Kohlberg's claim is that children at this stage consider what is fair or right only in terms of relations between individuals. Conflicts of interest are resolved by taking the perspective of persons with whom one has personal ties or who conform to in-group stereotypes of virtue.

At Stage 4 justice is defined in terms of a formal set of community rules and regulations. Kohlberg (1976) calls this a "social system" perspective. All parties to disputes are equal members of the system; in deciding what is fair or right one takes the perspective, not of any particular individual, but of a member of the social system, a "citizen." Justice at this stage is a function, not of relationships between individuals, but of the relation between each individual and the community. Disputes are resolved by considering what is necessary to maintain the social order. In positive terms, justice is a function of appropriate rewards by society for merit; rewards are earned by complying with system requirements. This replaces the Stage 3 notion that justice is an interpersonal exchange. In negative terms, individuals do not, as they do at Stage 3, punish one another; society punishes. Punishment is no longer a means of restoring relations between individuals; it is a means of restoring the relationship between the erring citizen and his or her society. Finally, equality is no longer an interpersonal ideal; it is defined by

the uniform and regular administration of the law according to objective and impersonal standards.

The distinction between Stages 3 and 4 is consistent with our Weberian thesis that in modern society people must adjust themselves to legal-rational authority. The style of thought labeled by Kohlberg as Stage 4 marks the first appearance of the idea that a social system has a superordinate legitimate authority. The obligation to comply with legal authority is distinguished from the obligation to comply with standards of decent, considerate interpersonal behavior. The personal requirement to act virtuously or with good intentions is distinguished from the impersonal requirements of an office to discharge specified duties. These distinctions are essential to the idea of legal-rational authority.

Consequently, Kohlberg's claim that most adults in contemporary Western society are at Stage 4, is consistent with our view that the attitudes entailed by this stage are normative in societies based on legal-rational authority. Our conclusion is also supported by research indicating that this type of reasoning is not found among members of rural, preliterate societies (e.g., Gorsuch & Barnes, 1973; White, Bushnell & Regnemer, 1978). But there is a problem here. Kohlberg's research method is based on classifying the moral attitudes that people offer spontaneously. This method tends to elicit responses at the "views-in-principle" end of the attitude continuum. People's conscious views of what principles ought to guide behavior are unlikely to be the only, or even the most important, determinants of their actions. As yet, there is little evidence that the ability to spell out Kohlbergian Stage 4 concepts is related to a sense of legal obligation as reflected in actual conduct (Emler, Heather, & Winton, 1978).

The contrast between Kohlberg's Stages 4 and 5 is interesting for several reasons. (Because Kohlberg, e.g., 1978, has found no clear evidence of anyone reaching Stage 6, it can for practical purposes be excluded here.) Stage 5 is, in Kohlberg's terms, a law-making as contrasted with a law-observing perspective. Laws are chosen on grounds of social welfare and the need to guarantee individual freedoms. Individual rights are particularly important at this stage, and certain of them are seen as taking priority over law. Laws are legitimate only insofar as they have the consent of those who are bound by them. The method of cooperation that Piaget (1932) observed in older children's attitudes to game rules emerges again in this stage now with respect to civil laws.

Kohlberg's distinction between his Stages 4 and 5 resembles our distinction between conservatives and liberals. It is not surprising, then, that, among adults, the stage of moral reasoning is related to political orientation (e.g., Alker & Poppen, 1973; Candee, 1976; Emler, Herron, & Malone, 1979; Fishkin, Keniston, & MacKinnon, 1973; Fontana & Noel, 1973; Rest, 1975; Sullivan & Quarter, 1972). These studies suggest that the conventional or Stage 4 individual is likely to be ideologically conservative, whereas the postconventional or Stage 5 individual is more likely to be liberal or radical.

Kohlberg's theory provides a way of accounting for the differences between conservatives and liberals; that is, this ideological difference is based on a developmental difference in level of reasoning—those who are liberal have reached postconventional reasoning, whereas those who are conservative still reason at the conventional level. Although many psychologists may find this conclusion congenial, it is clearly politically biased (cf. Emler & Hogan, 1978).

We believe that the distinction between Kohlberg's Stages 4 and 5 confounds the structure of moral reasoning and its content, for the following reasons. Kohlberg (1971) feels Stage 4 thought has two important limitations. First, persons at this level feel no obligations to persons outside the system or to those who do not recognize its rules. Second, persons at this level recognize no rational guides to social change or the creation of laws. Stage 5 overcomes these limitations. From another perspective, how-

ever, these "limitations" are simply the values that distinguish the liberal from the conservative (see Kohlberg, 1971, p.9). Conservatives are less likely to believe that they have obligations to persons who are outside the system or opposed to its rules. They are also less likely to believe in the possibility of a rational basis for legal reform. The liberal is more inclined to see the law as an instrument for social reform and to believe that it should be used to secure social justice to protect individual rights. The conservative is less interested in individual rights than in collective security and has more confidence in what has been tested and tried—established law and tradition.

In other words, we believe that Kohlberg's developmental distinction largely reflects a difference in the ideological content of attitudes toward law and justice. If we are correct, then movement over time from State 5 to 4 should be as frequent as changes in the other direction, and our view has received some empirical support (Holstein 1976). Our view is further supported by studies in which people are asked to predict the moral responses of liberals and conservatives. If Kohlberg is correct, conservatives, who are only capable of conventional reasoning, should be unable to predict the postconventional response of radicals. We find that conservatives can predict the responses of radicals as easily as radicals can predict those of conservatives (Emler, Herron & Malone, 1979).

Cognitive developmental theories are unconcerned with the dynamic component of attitudes. They tell us what attitudes people express, but not why they care about them. Kohlberg implies that the dynamics are part of cognitive understanding. So, for example, to grasp the principle of legal obligation is also to find it morally compelling; if one understands it, one must act on it. We doubt, however, that comprehension is a sufficient motivation for compliance.

A problem with Kohlberg's theory concerns the explanation of the developmental trends he describes. In his view, cognitive development contains its own explanation.

Moral reasoning is seen as self-contained, as independent of social and cultural pressures, as obeying its own internal laws of development. The direction and pattern of development are thus dictated by dynamics inherent in psychological functioning. Again we differ. We take the view that cognitive development theories are descriptive; they describe phenomena in need of explanation. Cross-cultural research suggests that certain Piagetian cognitive operations, such as conservation and classification skills, reflect the intellectual values of the culture and that these values in turn reflect the local ecology and economy (see, for example, Dasen, 1975). If this is the case for numerical, logical, and spatial concepts, it is likely also to be true of specific moral concepts. Children would acquire those legal, judicial, and political concepts described by Adelson, Kohlberg, and others, according to his view, not as a result of spontaneous intellectual growth but because the concepts reflect important elements of the culture. The relative complexity or intellectual sophistication of specific concepts may influence the speed with which they are acquired, but the more basic question of whether or not they are acquired depends on their saliency in the community.

In the following and final section, we suggest some of the conditions that affect the development of attitudes to law and justice, with attitude broadly defined to cover both content and dynamics, views in principle and views in fact.

A role-theoretical view of socialization

The development of attitudes toward law and justice can profitably be viewed in terms of a role-theoretical model of socialization. The following three assumptions underlie our interpretation of this model. First, compliance with legal (and other) authority is overdetermined. Weber (1946) suggested at least three reasons for this. People comply much of the time because they believe they should, that is, because they see it as their duty to obey legitimate rules and authorities.

Second, each society has enough force at its disposal to compel obedience when necessary. Third, people have a deep unconscious need for guidance, order, and predictability and fear their absence.

Our next assumption is that certain prelegal attitudes are important determinants of compliance with the law. Among the most important of these are "rule attunement" and "social sensitivity" (Hogan, Johnson, & Emler, 1978; Hogan & Mills, 1976). Rule attunement refers to an individual's willingness to defer to authority, follow instructions, and obey rules in an effortless, unconflicted manner. Social sensitivity refers to an appreciation of and willingness to take account of the expectations, needs, and wishes of others (in most societies these expectations are correlated with the law). These two attitudes are formed early but continue to develop throughout life.

Our third assumption is that social learning consists largely of learning about different forms of social relationships. Relationships are, as Youniss (1979) puts it, "rule systems for interaction." Social learning is a matter of learning about the rules that structure different forms of relationships. This learning occurs through participation in social interaction. But this learning is not merely cognitive. Experiences in these relationships also shape the child's emotional responses toward the standards they entail. Putting this point differently, children's attitudes toward law and justice will reflect the kinds of relationships they have with others, the form or structure of these relationships, and their emotional reactions to them. This is a standard assumption in the sociology of knowledge—that is, that people's attitudes and beliefs reflect the patterns of social relationships in which they are embedded and live.

The first form of relationship a child lives in is characterized by a fundamental inequality of power (cf. Hoffman, 1975b). It is what Piaget (1932) called a relation of constraint, and it is the child's relationship with his or her caretakers, normally the parents. The parent-child relationship has several unique features, the most important of which is the fact that the relationship is one-sided. A parent has a social agenda and therefore can generate orderly interaction. A parent supplies the rules and the orders, and a child is expected to comply. In this respect, positions in the relationship are not interchangeable; a child cannot change places with its parents.

It is also worth noting that a great deal of the control that parents exercise takes place at the verbal level. Parents tell their children what to do and what not to do. Lytton and Zwirner (1975), for example, found that, among a sample of mothers with 2½-year-olds, verbal control was far more common than physical control. Similarly, Minton, Kagan, and Levine (1971) report that the most common interaction sequence between mothers and their 2-year-olds involves mothers telling their children to stop doing something. Cook-Gumperz (1973) found that both middle- and working-class mothers of 5-year-olds use more verbal than physical controls. Cook-Gumperz also found that verbal control often went beyond simple commands to statements of general rules and to pointing out to the child the consequences of his or her misbehavior. Finally, Hoffman and Saltzstein (1967) report that the parents of seventh-graders frequently rely on induction in disciplining their children; that is, they elaborate on reasons why the child should change its conduct.

The parent-child relationship is the model for relationships with all those persons who are stronger, larger, older, or wiser, such as older siblings, older children, other adults, and teachers. It is also likely to be the model for a child's imagined relationships with more "mythical" authority figures such as political leaders. At the same time, children's experience with these other persons can lead them to reappraise their initial attitudes toward authority, as when children begin to demand that their parents' decisions should comply with the norm of equality (Piaget, 1932).

The quality of the parent-child relationship markedly shapes a child's early attitudes toward authority— that is, rule attunement. Rule attunement, we suspect, first depends on the development of a secure attachment bond between a child and its parents (cf. Bowlby, 1969), and second on parents being warm and nurturant but at the same time authoritative in setting limits. Stayton, Hogan, and Ainsworth (1971) found that, in a sample of 11-month-old children, those who were well attached, as indicated by an independent measure, were also willing to comply with parental directives. They were attuned to parental rules in a positive way. Moreover, the mothers of these children were more warm, attentive, and responsive than were the mothers of noncompliant children.

The second form of relationship that children encounter is with peers, siblings, and others of equal power—what Piaget (1932) called relations of equality. Unlike parent-child relationships in which parents assume much of the responsibility for interaction, child-child relationships must be structured by the children themselves. Much of the structuring takes the form of games; that is, children interact largely in the context of games.

Although Piaget (1932) and others emphasize that children's social attitudes are shaped by the cooperation and mutual respect that they encounter in relations with their peers, we believe that bullying, persecution, and exploitation are also common experiences in these relationships. Frequently, a child's interests may be protected only by the intervention of adults who forcibly impose standards of fair play, sharing, and turn taking. Consequently, the experience of injustice may be more potent than the experience of cooperation in the development of attitudes toward law and justice—for example, "I only get my turn on the swing when the teacher makes the other kids play fair."

Social sensitivity (empathy, role-taking ability) is particularly important in adjusting to peer relationships. Because there are few preexisting rules for interaction on which a child can rely, successful peer play depends more on children's sensitivity to others' expectation. However, this sensitivity may well be a function of a child's relationships with its parents. If parents give their children unconditional positive (or negative) attention, it is unlikely that their children will become sensitive; for such children, parental moods and feeling carry no significant differential information.

The third form of relationship that children encounter is formal role-relationships—the prototypic relationships of the bureaucratic state and legal-rational authority. These relationships are structured according to the requirements of a position rather than the personal qualities of those who occupy that position. So, for example, the relationship between teacher and student is always much the same, as is the relationship between the coach and athlete. Two important principles of interaction in role-relationships are called "specificity" and "universality" (cf. Dreeben, 1968).

Specificity means that one should invest only limited emotion in one's formal role-relationships, because these relationships do not involve whole personalities but only specific personal qualities in certain tasks. Universality means that one should treat others who are members of the same formal category (who have the same role) in similar ways, regardless of any personal differences between them. The rules of specificity and universality have implications for the legal concepts of jurisdiction and entitlement, but to discuss those here would take us too far afield.

The competitive game is, as Mead (1934) suggested, a primary model of formal role-relationships for children. Games entail the notion of fixed roles and the interchangeability of people with respect to roles or positions in the game. Games also contain the idea that various rules and standards of conduct apply only within a limited context and time frame. An equally important model for these role-relationships is the classroom (Danziger, 1971; Dreeben, 1968. Dreeben (1968) argues that schooling plays a major part in transmitting the principles that

underlie role-relationships (specificity and universality) to children. Danziger (1971) also notes that children in school must deal with adults whose interactions with them are defined by systems of precise, written rules, "the essence of bureaucracy." Although the rules that define the scope of the teacher's authority are written down, children must deduce these rules from the teacher's actions. Here again, however, much of what the rules require is learned through verbal interaction with the teacher. Studies by Much and Schweder (1978) and Nucci and Turiel (1978) show that teachers, like parents, frequently verbalize the relevant regulations.

Initially, children tend to conceive of relationships in school in personal terms, construing the pupil-teacher relationship in much the same terms as their relationships with other adults (Furth, 1979). However, intellectual development and the increasing bureaucratization of relationships in secondary school make it likely that the role-specific nature of pupil-teacher relationships will be grasped eventually, usually in adolescence.

Experience in school profoundly shapes attitudes toward authority and bureaucratic relationships. Indeed, one can even see the school as a means for evaluating children's ability to adapt to a bureaucratic system (Danziger, 1971). This ability probably reflects a child's earlier rule attunement—a disposition that we believe underlies educability. Success in school tells adults, particularly prospective employers, that a young person is well attuned to the demands of a bureaucratic system—that he or she will observe the routine of a timetable, follow orders, obey persons with only formal authority over him or her, and persevere at tasks that are often pointless from the child's perspective. As long as children are successful in the school system, their attitudes toward social conformity are likely to remain positive. When a child starts to fail, he or she is likely to become more negative about the system and, by extension, legal-rational authority in general. Not surprisingly, a disproportionate number of adjudicated delinquents come from the ranks of those who have failed in school (Hargreaves, 1967).

The assessment of attitudes toward law and justice

We should recall that social attitudes are assessed in a social context; consequently, how people respond to attitude questions will depend on how they interpret this context. For children, it is usually the context of adult-child relationships. What children have already learned about these relationships makes them believe that there are right and wrong answers to the questions that adults pose and that they must try to get them right. Consequently, interview questions designed to assess a child's attitudes are usually interpreted by children in problem-solving terms, as tests of their ability to find the right answer. Adolescents, made self-conscious through peer interaction, increasingly interpret the problem as one of self-presentation and respond in terms of the impression they wish to create vis à vis an actual or imagined audience. There is no longer one right answer but many, and answers are chosen to suit the audience.

There are several indications of this change and several reasons for its occurrence. One indication is the documented shift in attitudes about sex-role standards (e.g., Kohlberg & Ullian, 1974). Six-year-olds have a rigid view of such standards, believing that there is a necessary connection between gender and behavior. This attitude declines steadily with age, so that by the early teens children state that adoption of such standards is a matter of preference and choice. Another indication of the shift in the way children respond to attitude questions is the decline in authoritarianism with age and the recognition that there can be different perspectives on moral issues (e.g., Lerner, 1937). Finally, research by Bronfenbrenner and others (e.g., Beloff & Paton, 1970; Bronfenbrenner, 1967) indicates that the responses of 12-year-olds to moral dilemmas vary with the subjects' expectations about who the audience will be.

As children grow older, they discover that there are no universally agreed-on answers to moral questions; they discover, in other words, a plurality of perspectives that makes single judgments relative. Because adults seem not to agree among themselves, the monolithic force of adult opinion inevitably declines. This means that children begin to realize that they have a degree of choice in their answers and, therefore, a degree of choice in how they present themselves to others. Awareness of this choice will be strongest with respect to those questions that are most hypothetical, that is, with respect to views in principle. The orientation a child adopts with respect to the liberal-conservative ideological polarity is a case in point. This orientation is never finally fixed; it is always open to modification by experience. Tendencies toward the conservative end are associated with age (e.g., Wilson, 1973) but may reflect cohort differences, whereas tendencies toward the liberal end are associated with education (e.g., Hyman & Sheatsley, 1954; Rest, 1975; Wilson, 1973) and types of occupation. These tendencies suggest that an individual's sociopolitical orientation is a function not of reasoning level but of his or her reference groups and social identity. Expressions of liberal or conservative political opinion inform the audience about a person's social alignments. As a form of self-presentaion, they indicate those groups with which he or she wishes to be identified and those from which he or she wishes to be distinguished. Newcomb's (1943) early research on friendship patterns, for example, reveals the role of reference groups in the adoption of political orientation. And research on interpersonal attraction has shown the power of ideological similarity as a basis for interpersonal attraction (e.g., Byrne, 1969).

Summary and conclusions

By now the reader must be bewildered by the variety of facts and studies reviewed in this chapter. We can summarize the foregoing material and clarify the thrust of our argument in terms of five points. First, the research literature of the last 30 to 50 years reveals certain reliable changes that occur over time in children's attitudes toward law and justice. The work of Piaget, Kohlberg, and especially Adelson spells out these changes very clearly.

Second, despite the agreement as to *what* changes occur, the *explanation* of these changes depends on one's theoretical preferences. Social learning and cognitive developmental theories provide competing explanations for the same set of developmental change data. Thus, it is not clear what these apparent developmental regularities mean because they are interpreted differently by different theories.

Third, our explanation for these changes reflects the perspective of the sociology of knowledge—that is, people's attitudes toward law and justice are largely determined by the structure of the interpersonal relationships that they find themselves in. Little children are largely involved in authoritarian or asymmetrical relationships, and their attitudes are correspondingly authoritarian. Adolescents are involved in egalitarian peer relationships. Adults are involved in bureaucratic organizations and their attitudes are characteristically different from those of children and adolescents. In this view, and for these reasons, working-class attitudes will differ from managerial-level attitudes toward law and justice, because the roles of these people in the bureaucracy are very different.

Fourth, we believe Weber's claim that rational-legal authority increasingly predominates in the modern bureaucratic state. Moreover, it is this form of control in our culture that gives the distinctive stamp to adult or "mature" attitudes toward law and justice. Thus, we regard what are called mature attitudes toward law and justice as purely relative to the primary forms of control in modern society. All of them reflect the manner in which people have accommodated to bureaucracy in adulthood; everyone must make some form of accommodation, and people will differ primarily in terms of the liberal-conservative dimension of ideology. Higher status roles tend to go with liberal or Kohlbergian Stage 5 attitudes; working-class roles tend to go with conservative or Stage 4 attitudes.

Finally, any interpretation of the major findings in developmental psychology regarding attitudes toward law and justice must give some thought to the methodology used in the research. Specifically, what is it that people do when they respond to questions about their attitudes? Most psychologists take responses to these questions at their face value, a position that we regard as indefensible. We suggest here that these responses must be interpreted in terms of "item response theory," that is, in terms of what people's motives are when they respond to attitude questions. Moreover, item response dynamics differ predictably and characteristically over time and in a way that may not be culturally bound. Specifically, younger children try to give the "right" answer to attitude questions; adolescents interpret the task in impression management terms; and adults add to impression management the perspective of their role in the bureaucracy. This brings us back to our third point—that the guiding element in impression management is the structure of the interpersonal relationships people find themselves in.

In our judgment, this role-theoretical model provides a very useful method for organizing and synthesizing existing research on the development of attitudes toward law and justice.

REFERENCES

Abraham, S., Collins, G., & Nordsieck, M. Relationship of childhood weight status to morbidity in adults. *Public Health Report,* 1971, *86,* 273.

Abraham, S., & Nordsieck, M. Relationship of excess weight in children and adults. *Public Health Report,* 1970, *75,* 263–273.

Abramson, L. Y., Seligman, M.E.P., & Teasdale, J.D. Learned helplessness in humans: Critique and reformulation. *Journal of Abnormal Psychology,* 1978, *87,* 49–74.

Adams, G.R. Physical attractiveness research: Toward a developmental social psychology of beauty. *Human Development,* 1977, *20,* 217–323.

Adams, G.R. Racial membership and physical attractiveness effects on preschool teachers' expectations. *Child Study Journal,* 1978, *8,* 29–41.

Adams, G.R., & Cohen, A.S. Characteristics of children and teacher expectancy: An extension to the child's social and family life. *Journal of Educational Research,* 1976, *70,* 87–90.

Adams, G.R., & Crane, P. An assessment of parents' and teachers' expectations of preschool children's social preference for attractive or unattractive children and adults. *Child Development,* 1980, *51,* 224–231.

Adams, J.S. Toward an understanding of inequity. *Journal of Abnormal and Social Psychology,* 1963, *67,* 422–436.

Adams, J.S., & Freedman, S. Equity theory revisited: Comments and annotated bibliography. In L. Berkowitz & E. Walster (Eds.), *Advances in experimental social psychology* (Vol. 9). New York: Academic Press, 1976.

Adelson, J., & O'Neil, R. Growth of political ideas in adolescence: The sense of community. *Journal of Personality and Social Psychology,* 1966, *4,* 295–306.

Adkins, D., Payne, F., & Ballif, B.F. Motivation factor scores for ten ethnic-cultural groups of preschool children. *American Educational Research Journal,* 1972, *9,* 557–567.

Adorno, T.W., Frenkel-Brunswik, E., Levinson, D.J., & Sanford, R.M. *The authoritarian personality.* New York: Harper, 1950.

Ainsworth, M.D.S., & Bell, S.M. Some contemporary patterns of mother-infant interaction in the feeding situation. In A. Ambrose (Ed.), *Stimulation in early infancy.* New York: Academic Press, 1969.

Ajzen, I. Intuitive theories of events and the effects of base-rate information on prediction. *Journal of Personality and Social Psychology,* 1977, *35,* 303–314.

Alker, H.A., & Poppen, P.J. Personality and ideology in university students. *Journal of Personality,* 1973, *41,* 653–671.

Allport, F.H. *Social Psychology.* Boston: Houghton Mifflin, 1924.

Allport, F.H., et al. The effects of segration and the consequences of desegregation: A social science statement. *Minnesota Law Review,* 1953, *37,* 429–440.

Allport, G.W. *The nature of prejudice.* Reading, Mass.: Addison-Wesley, 1954.

Alper, S. *Nonverbal receiving ability in preschool-age children.* Unpublished master's thesis, University of Connecticut, 1977.

Alper, S., Buck, R., & Dreyer, A. Nonverbal sending accuracy and receiving ability in preschool children. *Research Relating to Children,* 1978, *41,* 89. (Abstract)

Amabile, T.M. Effects of external evaluation on artistic creativity. *Journal of Personality and Social Psychology,* 1979, *37,* 221–233.

Amabile, T.M., DeJong, W., & Lepper, M.R. Effects of externally-imposed deadlines on subsequent intrinsic motivation. *Journal of Personality and Social Psychology,* 1976, *34,* 92–98.

Amir, Y., Contact hypothesis in ethnic relations. *Psychological Bulletin,* 1969, *71,* 319–342.

Anderson, D.F., & Rosenthal, R. Some effects of interpersonal expectancy and social interaction on institutionalized retarded children. *Proceedings of the 76th Annual APA Convention,* 1968, 479–480.

Anderson, K.A., & King, H.E. Timeout reconsidered. *Instructional Psychology,* 1974, *1,* 11–17.

Anderson, N.H. Adding versus averaging as a stimulus combination rule in impression formation. *Journal of Experimental Psychology,* 1965, *70,* 394–400.

Anderson, R., Manoogian, S.T., & Reznick, J.S. The undermining and enhancing of intrinsic motivation in preschool children. *Journal of Personality and Social Psychology,* 1976, *34,* 915–922.

Andrew, R.J. The origins of facial expressions. *Scientific American,* 1965, *213,* 88–94.

Angulo, J., & Matthews, K.A. Unpublished data, Kansas State University, 1978.

Anthony, E.J., & Gilpin, D.C. (Eds.). *Three clinical faces of childhood.* New York: Spectrum Publications, 1976.

APA (American Psychological Association). *Standards of educational and psychological tests.* Washington, D.C.: Author, 1974.

Arkin, R.M., & Duval, S. Focus of attention and causal attribution of actors and observers. *Journal of Experimental Social Psychology,* 1975, *11,* 427–438.

Arkin, R.M., & Maruyama, G.M. Attribution, affect, and college exam perfromance. *Journal of Educational Psychology,* 1979, *71,* 85–93.

Aronfreed, J. The origins of self-criticism. *Psychological Review,* 1964, *71,* 183 –218.

Aronfreed, J. *Conduct and conscience.* New York: Academic Press, 1968.

Aronfreed, J., & Paskal, V. *Altruism, empathy and the conditioning of positive affect.* Unpublished manuscript, University of Pennsylvania, 1965.

Aronson, E. The theory of cognitive dissonance: A current perspective. In L. Berkowitz (Ed.), *Advances in experimental social psychology* (Vol. 4). New York: Academic Press, 1969.

Aronson, E., & Carlsmith, J.M. The effect of the severity of threat on the devaluation of forbidden behavior. *Journal of Abnormal and Social Psychology,* 1963, *66,* 584–588.

Aronson, E., & Carlsmith, J.M. Experimentation in social psychology. In G. Lindzey & E. Aronson (Eds.), *Handbook of social psychology* (Vol. 2). Reading, Mass.: Addison-Wesley, 1968.

Aronson, E., & Linder, D. Gain and loss of esteem as determinants of interpersonal attraction. *Journal of Experimental Social Psychology,* 1965, *1,* 156–172.

Asch, S.E. Forming impressions of personality. *Journal of Abnormal and Social Psychology,* 1946, *41,* 258–290.

Asher, S., & Allen, V. Racial preference and social comparison processes. *Journal of Social Issues,* 1969, *25,* 157–166.

Astin, H.S. Patterns of women's occupations. In J. Sherman & F. Denmark (Eds.), *Psychology of women: Future directions of research.* New York: Psychological Dimensions, 1978.

Atkinson, J.W. Motivational determinants of risk taking behavior, *Psychological Review,* 1957, *64,* 359–372.

Atkinson, J.W. *An introduction to motivation.* Princeton, N.J.: Van Nostrand, 1964.

Austin, M.C., & Thompson, G.G. Children's friendships: A study of the basis on which children select and reject their best friends. *Journal of Educational Psychology,* 1948, *39,* 101–116.

Austin, W., Walster, E., & Utne, M.K. Equity and the law: The effects of a harmdoer's "suffering in the act" on liking and assigned punishment. In L. Berkowitz & E. Walster (Eds.) *Advances in experimental social psychology* (Vol. 9), New York: Academic Press, 1976.

Ausubel, D.P., & Schiff, H.M. The effect of incidental and experimentally induced experience in the learning of relevant and irrelevant causal relationships by children. *Journal of Genetic Psychology*, 1954, *84*, 109–123.

Ayer, W.A. Use of visual imagery in needle phobic children. *Journal of Dentistry for Children*, 1973, *40*, 41–43.

Ayllon, T., Allison, M.G., & Kandel, H.J. *Behavioral persuasion: A technique to eliminate chronic discipline problems.* Unpublished paper, Georgia State University, 1979.

Ayllon, T., & Roberts, M.D. Eliminating discipline problems by strengthening academic performance. *Journal of Applied Behavioral Analysis*, 1974, *7*, 71–76.

Azrin, N.H., & Powell, J. Behavioral engineering: The reduction of smoking behavior by a conditioning procedure and apparatus. *Journal of the Experimental Analysis of Behavior*, 1968, *1*, 193– 200.

Baer, A., Rowbury, T., & Baer, D. The development of instrumental contol over classroom activities of deviant preschool children. *Journal of Applied Behavior Analysis*, 1973, *6*, 289–298.

Bagely, C. Race prejudice and the conservative personality. *Political Studies*, 1970, *18*, 134–141.

Baldwin, C.P., & Baldwin, A.L. Children's judgments of kindness. *Child Development*, 1970, *41*, 29–47.

Baldwin, J.M. *Development of the child and the race.* New York: Macmillan, 1900.

Bandura, A. *Social learning theory.* Morristown, N.J.: General Learning Press, 1971.

Bandura, A. Behavior theory and models of man. *American Psychologist*, 1974, *29*, 859–886.

Bandura, A. Self-reinforcement: Theoretical and methodological considerations. *Behaviorism*, 1976, *4*, 135–155.

Bandura, A. Self-efficacy: Toward a unifying theory of behavior change. *Psychological Review*, 1977, *84*, 191–215. (a)

Bandura, A. *Social learning theory.* Englewood Cliffs, N.J.: Prentice-Hall, 1977. (b)

Bandura, A. The self-system in reciprocal determinism, *American Psychologist*, 1978, *33*, 344–358.

Bandura, A., & Mischel, W. Modification of self-imposed delay of reward through exposure to live and symbolic models. *Journal of Personality and Social Psychology*, 1965, *2*, 698–705.

Bandura, A., & Rosenthal, T.L. Vicarious classical conditioning as a function of arousal level. *Journal of Personality and Social Psychology*, 1966, *3*, 54–62.

Bandura, A., & Walters, R.H. *Adolescent aggression.* New York: Ronald, 1959.

Bandura, A., & Walters, R.H. *Social learning and personality development.* New York: Holt, Rinehart & Winston, 1963.

Banks, R.K., & Vogel-Sprott, M. Effect of delayed punishment on an immediately rewarded response in humans. *Journal of Experimental Psychology*, 1965, *70*, 357–359.

Banks, W.C. White preference in Blacks: A paradigm in search of a phenomenon. *Psychological Bulletin*, 1976, *83*, 1179–1186.

Barker, R., Dembo, T., & Lewin, K. Frustration and regression: An experiment with young children. *University of Iowa Studies, Studies in Child Welfare*, 1941, XVIII, No. 1.

Barker, R., & Wright, H. *The midwest and its children: The psychological ecology of the American town.* Evanston, Ill.: Row Peterson & Co., 1955.

Barnett, M.A., King, L.M., & Howard, J.A. Inducing affect about self or other: Effects on generosity in children. *Developmental Psychology*, 1979, *15*, 164–167.

Barocas, R., & Black, H.K. Referral rate and physical attractiveness in third-grade children. *Perceptual Motor Skills*, 1974, *39*, 731–734.

Baron, R.A. *Human aggression.* New York: Plenum, 1977.

Baron, R.M. Social knowing from an ecological event perspective: A consideration of the relative domains of power for cognitive and perceptual modes of knowing. In J.H. Harvey (Ed.), *Cognition, social behavior and the environment.* Hillsdale, N.J.: Lawrence Erlbaum Associates 1980.

Baron, R.M., & Buck, R. A Gibsonian-event perception approach to the meaning of the nonverbal communication of emotion. In *The meaning of nonverbal communication.* Symposium presented at the meeting of the American Psychological Association Convention, New York, September 1979.

Barrett, C.A., & Nicholls, J.G. Motivational factors in the intelligence test performance of Maori and Pakeha children. *Journal of Cross-Cultural Psychology*, 1978, *9*, 349–357.

Bar-Tal, D. *The formation of teachers' expectations: Attributional analysis.* Paper presented at the Annual Meeting of the American Psychological Association, San Francisco, August 1977.

Bar-Tal, D. Attributional analysis of achievement related behavior. *Review of Educational Research*, 1978, *48*, 259–271.

Bar-Tal, D. Interactions of teachers and pupils. In I.H. Frieze, D. Bar-Tal, & J.S. Carroll (Eds.), *New approaches to social problems: Applications of attribution-theory*. San Francisco: Jossey-Bass, 1979. (a)

Bar-Tal, D. *Development of causal perception of success and failure*. Unpublished manuscript, School of Education, Tel-Aviv University, 1979. (b)

Bar-Tal, D., & Darom, E. Pupils' attributions for success and failure. *Child Development*, 1979, *50*, 264–267.

Bar-Tal, D., & Frieze, I.H. Attributions of success and failure for actors and observers. *Journal of Research in Personality*, 1976, *10*, 256–265.

Bar-Tal, D., & Frieze, I.H. Achievement motivation for males and females as a determinant of attributions for success and failure. *Sex Roles*, 1977, *3*, 301–313.

Bar-Tal, D., & Greenberg, M.S. *Stability attributions of 115 adjectives commonly used to describe persons*. Paper presented at the Annual Meeting of the Midwestern Psychological Association, Chicago, 1973.

Bar-Tal, D., Guttmann, J., Kvartz, A., & Naor, V. *Evaluation of outcome as success or failure: The effect of personal variable and information*. Unpublished manuscript, Tel-Aviv University, 1980.

Baruch, D.W., & Wilcox, J.A. A study of sex differences in pre-school children's adjustment coexistent with interparental tensions. *Journal of Genetic Psychology*, 1944, *64*, 281–303.

Bassili, J.N. Temporal and spatial contingencies in the perception of social events. *Journal of Personality and Social Psychology*, 1976, *33*, 680–685.

Baumrind, D. Current patterns of parental authority. *Developmental Psychology Monographs*, 1971, *41 (1, part 2)*.

Baumrind, D. The development of instrumental competence through socialization. In A. Pick (Ed.), *Minnesota symposia on child psychology* (Vol. 7). Minneapolis: University of Minnesota Press, 1973.

Becker, W.C. Consequences of different kinds of parental discipline. In M. Hoffman & L. Hoffman (Eds.), *Review of child development research*. New York: Russell Sage, 1964.

Bell, R.Q., & Harper, L.V. *Child effects on adults*. New York: Wiley, 1977.

Bell, R.Q., Weller, G.M. & Waldrop, M.F.

Newborn and preschooler: Organization of behavioral relations between periods. *Monographs of the Society for Research in Child Development*, 1971, *36*, Nos. 1–2.

Beloff, H., & Paton, X. Bronfenbrenner's moral dilemmas in Britain: Children, their peers, and their parents. *International Journal of Psychology*, 1970, *5*, 27–32.

Bem, D.J. Self-perception: An alternative interpretation of cognitive dissonance phenomena. *Psychological Review*, 1967, *74*, 183–200.

Bem, D.J. *Beliefs, attitudes, and human affairs*. Belmont, Calif. Brooks/Cole, 1970.

Bem, D.J. Self-perception theory. In L. Berkowitz (Ed.), *Advances in experimental social psychology* Vol. 6. New York: Academic Press, 1972.

Benson, P.L., Karabenick, S.A., & Lerner, R.M. Pretty pleases: The effects of physical attractiveness, race, and sex on receiving help. *Journal of Experimental Social Psychology*. 1976, *12*, 409–415.

Berger, J., Cohen, B., & Zeldick, M. Status conceptions and social interactions. *American Sociological Review*, 1972, *37*, 241–255.

Berger, J., Conner, T.L., & Fisek, M.H. *Expectation states theory: A theoretical research program*. Cambridge, Mass.: Winthrop, 1974.

Berger, S. Conditioning through vicarious instigation. *Psychological Review*, 1962, *69*, 450–466.

Berger, S., & Kanfer, F.H. Self-control: Effects of training and presentation delays of competing responses on tolerance of noxious stimulation. *Psychological Reports*, 1975, *37*, 1312–1314.

Berkowitz, L., & Frodi, A. Reactions to a child's mistakes as affected by her/his looks and speech. *Social Psychology Quarterly*, 1979, *42*, 420–425.

Berscheid, E., Dion, K.K., Walster, E., & Walster, G.W. Physical attractiveness and dating choices: A test of the matching hypothesis. *Journal of Experimental Social Psychology*. 1971, *7*, 173–189.

Berscheid, E., Graziano, W., Monson, T., & Dermer, M. Outcome dependency: Attention, attribution, and attraction. *Journal of Personality and Social Psychology*, 1976, *34*, 978–989.

Berscheid, E., & Walster, E. Physical attractiveness. In L. Berkowitz (Ed.), *Advances in experimental social psychology* (Vol. 7). New York: Academic Press, 1974.

Berzonsky, M. The role of familiarity in children's explanations of physical causality. *Child Development*, 1971, *42*, 705–715.

Bialer, I. Conceptualization of success and failure in mentally retarded and normal children. *Journal of Personality*, 1961, *29*, 303–320.

Bigner, J. A Wernerian developmental analysis of children's descriptions of siblings. *Child Development*, 1974, *45*, 317–323.

Bingham-Newman, A.M., & Hooper, F.H. The search for a woozle circa 1975: Commentary on Brainerd's observations. *American Educational Research Journal*, 1975, *12*, 379–387.

Blackwell, L. *Student choice in curriculum, feelings of control and causality, and academic motivation and performance*. Unpublished doctoral dissertation, Stanford University, 1974.

Blanchard, F.A., Adelman, L., & Cook, S.W. The effect of group success and failure upon interpersonal attraction in cooperating interracial groups. *Journal of Personality and Social Psychology*, 1975, *31*, 1020–1030.

Blanchard, F.A., & Cook, S.W. Effects of helping a less competent member of a cooperating interracial group on the development of interpersonal attraction. *Journal of Personality and Social Psychology*, 1976, *34*, 1245–1255.

Blanchard, F.A., Wiegel, R., & Cook, S.W. The effect of relative competence of group members upon interracial attraction in cooperating interracial groups. *Journal of Personality and Social Psychology*, 1975, *32*, 519–530.

Blanck, P.D., Reis, H.T., & Jackson, L. *The effects of verbal reinforcement on intrinsic motivation*. Unpublished manuscript, University of Rochester, 1980.

Blaney, N., Stephan, C., Rosenfield, D., Aronson, E., & Sikes, J. Interdependence in the classroom: A field study. *Journal of Educational Psychology*, 1977, *69*, 121–128.

Blest, A.D. The concept of ritualization. In W.H. Thorpe & O.L. Zangwill (Eds.), *Current problems in animal behaviors*. Cambridge, Eng.: Cambridge University Press, 1961.

Blitz, B., & Dinnerstein, A.J. Role of attentional focus in pain perception: Manipulation of response to noxious stimulation by instructions. *Journal of Abnormal Psychology*, 1971, *77*, 42– 45.

Block, J. A study of affective responsiveness in a lie detection situation. *Journal of Abnormal and Social Psychology*, 1957, *55*, 11–15.

Block, J. *Lives through time*. Berkeley, Calif: Bancroft, 1971.

Blumenthal, J.A., Williams, R.B., Kong, Y., Schanberg, S.M., & Thompson, L.W. Type A behavior pattern and coronary athersclerosis. *Circulation*, 1978, *58*, 634–639.

Bogdan, R., & Taylor, S. The judged, not the judges: An insider's view of mental retardation. *American Psychologist*, 1976, *31*, 47–52.

Boggiano, A.K., & Ruble, D.N. Competence and the overjustification effect: A developmental study. *Journal of Personality and Social Psychology*, 1979, *37*, 1462–1468.

Borke, H. Interpersonal perception of young children: Egocentrism or empathy? *Developmental Psychology*, 1971, *5*, 263–269.

Bortner, R.W. A short rating scale as a potential measure of Pattern A behavior. *Journal of Chronic Diseases*, 1969, *22*, 87.

Bortner, R.W., & Rosenman, R.H. The measurement of pattern A behavior. *Journal of Chronic Diseases*, 1967, *20*, 525–533.

Bortner, R.W., Rosenman, R.M., & Friedman, M. Familar similarity in pattern A behavior. *Journal of Chronic Diseases*, 1970, *23*, 39–43.

Boshier, R. Conservatism within families: A study of the generation gap. In G.D. Wilson (Ed.), *The psychology of conservatism*. New York: Academic Press, 1973.

Bowlby, J. *Attachment and loss* (Vol. 1.). New York: Basic Books, 1969.

Boyle, D.G. A contribution to the study of phenomenal causation. *Quarterly Journal of Experimental Psychology*, 1960, *12*, 171–179.

Braine, M.D.S. Development of a grasp of transitivity of length: A reply to Smedslund. *Child Development*, 1964, *35*, 799–810.

Brainerd, C.J. Judgments and explanations as criteria for the presence of cognitive structures. *Psychological Bulletin*, 1973, *79*, 172–179.

Brainerd, C.J. Response criteria in concept development research. *Child Development*, 1977, *48*, 360–366.

Brand, E.S., Ruiz, R.A., & Padilla, A.M. Ethnic identification and preference. *Psychological Bulletin*, 1974, *81*, 860–890.

Brand, R.J., Rosenman, R.H., Jenkins, C.D., Sholtz, R.I., & Zyzanski, S.J. *Comparison of coronary heart disease prediction in the Western Collaborative Group Study using the structured interview and the Jenkins Activity Survey assessment of the coronary-prone Type A behavior pattern*. Paper read at the annual conference on cardiovascular disease epidemiology, American Heart Association, Orlando, Florida, March 1978.

Brehm, J.W. *A theory of psychological reactance.* New York: Academic Press, 1966

Brehm, J.W., & Cohen, A.R. *Explorations in cognitive dissonance.* New York: Wiley, 1962.

Brehm, S.S. The effect of adult influence on children's preference: Compliance versus opposition. *Journal of Abnormal Child Psychology,* 1977, *5,* 31–41.

Brehm, S.S. Psychological reactance and the attractiveness of unobtainable objects: Sex differences in children's responses to an elimination of freedom. *Sex Roles,* in press.

Brehm, S.S., & Brehm, J.W. *Psychological reactance: A theory of freedom and control.* New York: Academic Press, in press.

Brehm, S.S., Powell, L., & Coke, J.S. *The effects of empathy instructions on first-graders' donating behavior.* Unpublished manuscript, University of Kansas, 1980.

Brehm, S.S., & Weinraub, M. Physical barriers and psychological reactance: Two-year-olds' responses to threats to freedom. *Journal of Personality and Social Psychology,* 1977, *35,* 830–836.

Bridges, K.M.B. Emotional development in early infancy. *Child Development,* 1932, *3,* 324–341.

Brierley, D.W. Children's use of personality constructs. *Bulletin of British Psychological Society,* 1966, *19,* no.65, 72.

Brigham, J.C. Views of black and white children concerning the distribution of personality characteristics. *Journal of Personality,* 1974, *42,* 144–158.

Bronfenbrenner, U. Responses to pressures from peers versus adults among Soviet and American school children. *International Journal of Psychology,* 1967, *2,* 199–207.

Brook, C.G.S. Critical periods in childhood obesity. In W. Burland, P. Samuel, & J. Yudkin (Eds.), *Obesity symposium.* Edinburgh: Churchill Livingstone, 1974.

Broverman, I.K., Vogel, S.R., Broverman, D.M., Clarkson, F.E., & Rosenkrantz, P.S. Sex role stereotypes: A current appraisal. *Journal of Social Issues,* 1972, *28,* 59–78.

Brown, D.W. Cognitive development and willingness to comply with law. *American Journal of Political Science,* 1974, *18,* 583–594.

Brownell, K., Colletti, G., Ersner-Hershfield, R., Herschfield, S.M., & Wilson, G.T. Self-control in school children: Stringency and leniency in self-determined and exter-

nally imposed performance standards. *Behavior Therapy,* 1977, *8,* 442–455.

Brozek, J. Recent developments in Soviet psychology. *Annual Review of Psychology,* 1964, *15,* 493–594.

Bruch, H. *Eating disorders: Obesity, anorexia nervosa, and the person within.* New York: Basic Books, 1973.

Bruner, J. *The pragmatics of language acquisition.* Paper presented at the meeting of the Society for Experimental Social Psychology, East Lansing, Mich., November 1979.

Bryan, J.H. You will be well advised to watch what we do instead of what we say. In D.J. DePalma & J.M. Foley (Eds.), *Moral development: Current theory and research.* Hillsdale, N.J.: Lawrence Erlbaum Associates, 1975.

Bryant, P.E., & Trabasso, T. Transitive inference and memory in young children. *Nature,* 1971, *232,* 456–458.

Buck, R. Nonverbal communication of affect in children. *Journal of Personality and Social Psychology,* 1975, *31,* 644–653.

Buck, R. *Human motivation and emotion.* New York: Wiley, 1976. (a)

Buck, R. A test of nonverbal receiving ability: Preliminary studies. *Human Communication Research,* 1976, *2,* 162–171. (b)

Buck, R. Nonverbal communication of affect in preschool children: Relationships with personality and skin conductance. *Journal of Personality and Social Psychology,* 1977, *35,* 225–236.

Buck R. The slide-viewing technique for measuring nonverbal sending accuracy: A guide for replication. *Catalog of Selected Documents in Psychology,* 1978, *8,* 62. (Abstract)

Buck, R. Nonverbal behavior and the theory of emotion: The facial feedback hypothesis. In R. Rosenthal (Ed.), *Personal correlates of skill in nonverbal communication.* Cambridge, Mass.: Oelgeschlager, Gunn & Haim, 1979.

Buck, R. Nonverbal behavior and the theory of emotion: The facial feedback hypothesis. *Journal of Personality and Social Psychology,* 1980, *38,* 811–824.

Buck, R., Baron, R.M., & Barrette, D. *The unitization of spontaneous nonverbal behavior.* Paper presented at the meeting of the American Psychological Association, New York, September 1979.

Buck, R., Baron, R.M., Goodman, N., & Shapiro, B. The unitization of spontaneous nonverbal behavior in the study of emotion communication. *Journal of Personality and Social Psychology,* 1980, *39,* 522–529.

Buck, R., & Carroll, J. *CARAT and PONS: Correlates of two tests of nonverbal sensitivity.* Unpublished manuscript, Carnegie-Mellon University, 1974.

Buck, R., & Duffy, R. Nonverbal communication of affect in brain-damaged patients. *Cortex,* in press.

Buck, R., & Lerman, J. General vs. specific nonverbal sensitivity and clinical training. *Human Communication,* 1979, 269–274.

Buck, R., Miller, R.E., & Caul, W.F. Sex, personality and physiological variables in the communication of emotion via facial expression. *Journal of Personality and Social Psychology,* 1974, *30,* 587–596.

Buck, R., Savin, V.J., Miller, R.E., & Caul, W.F. Nonverbal communication of affect in humans. *Proceedings, 77th Annual Convention, APA,* 1969, 367–368.

Buck, R., Savin, V.J., Miller, R.E., & Caul, W.F. Nonverbal communication of affect in humans. *Journal of Personality and Social Psychology,* 1972, *23,* 362–371.

Buckley, N., Siegel, L., & Ness, S. Egocentrism, empathy, and altruistic behavior in young children. *Developmental Psychology,* 1979, *15,* 329–330.

Budoff, M., & Siperstein, G.N. Low-income children's attitudes toward mentally retarded children: Effects of label and academic behavior. *American Journal of Mental Deficiency,* 1978, *82,* 474 –479.

Budoff, M., & Siperstein, G.N. *Attitudes of EMRs toward mentally retarded peers: The effects of clinical label and academic competence.* Unpublished manuscript, University of Massachusetts at Boston, 1980.

Bullen, B.A., Reed, R.R., & Mayer, J. Physical activity of obese and non-obese adolescent girls appraised by motion picture sampling. *Journal of Clinical Nutrition,* 1964, *14,* 211.

Bullock, M., & Gelman, R. Preschool children's assumptions about cause and effect: Temporal ordering. *Child Development,* 1979, *50,* 89–96.

Butensky, A., Faralli, V., Heebner, D., & Waldron, I. Elements of the coronary-prone behavior pattern in children and teenagers. *Journal of Psychosomatic Research,* 1976, *20,* 439–444.

Byrne, D. Parental antecedents of authoritarianism. *Journal of Personality and Social Psychology,* 1965, *1,* 369–373.

Byrne, D. Attitudes and attraction. In L. Berkowitz (Ed.), *Advances in experimental social psychology* (Vol. 4). New York: Academic Press, 1969.

Byrne, D. *The attraction paradigm.* New York: Academic Press, 1971.

Caille, R.K. *Resistant behavior of preschool children.* New York: Bureau of Publications, Teachers College, Columbia University, 1933.

Calder, B.J., & Staw, B.M. Self-perception of intrinsic and extrinsic motivation. *Journal of Personality and Social Psychology,* 1975, *31,* 599–605.

Calsyn, R.J., & Kenny, D.A. Self-concept of ability and perceived evaluation of others: Cause or effect of academic achievement. *Journal of Educational Psychology,* 1977, *69,* 136–145,

Candee, D. Structure and choice in moral reasoning. *Journal of Personality and Social Psychology,* 1976, *34,* 1293–1301.

Cannon, W.B. *The wisdom of the body.* New York: W.W. Norton, 1932.

Cantor, N., & Mischel, W. Prototypes in person perception. In L. Berkowitz (Ed.), *Advances in experimental social psychology* (Vol. 12). New York: Academic Press, 1979

Carroll, J.S., Payne, J.W., Frieze, I.H., & Girard, D. *Attribution theory: An information processing approach.* Unpublished manuscript, Carnegie-Mellon University, 1976.

Carver, C.S., Gibbons, F.X., Stephan, W.G., Glass, D.C., & Katz, I. Ambivalence and evaluative response amplification. *Bulletin of the Psychonomic Society,* 1979, *13,* 50–52.

Carver, C.S., Glass, D.C., & Katz, I. Favorable evaluations of blacks and the handicapped: Positive prejudice, unconscious denial, or social desirability? *Journal of Applied Social Psychology,* 1978, *8,* 97–106.

Cash, T.F., & Derlega, V.J. The matching hypothesis: Physical attractiveness among same-sexed friends. *Personality and Social Psychology Bulletin,* 1978, *4,* 240–243.

Cautela, J. Covert conditioning. In A. Jacobs & L. Sachs (Eds.), *The psychology of private events.* New York: Academic Press, 1971.

Cautela, J., & Wisocki, P.A. The thought stopping procedure: Description, application and learning theory interpretations. *Psychological Record,* 1977, *2,* 255–264.

Cavior, N., & Dokecki, P. Physical attractiveness, perceived attitude similarity, and academic achievement as contributors to interpersonal attraction among adolescents. *Developmental Psychology*, 1973, *9*, 44–54.

Cavior, N., & Howard, L.R. Facial attractiveness and juvenile delinquency among black and white offenders. *Journal of Abnormal Child Psychology*, 1973, *1*, 202–213.

Chandler, M.J., & Greenspan, S. Ersatz egocentrism: A reply to H. Borke. *Developmental Psychology*, 1972, *7*, 104–106.

Chandler, M.J., Greenspan, S., & Barenboim, C. Judgments of intentionality in response to videotaped and verbally presented moral dilemmas: The medium is the message. *Child Development*, 1973, *44*, 311–320.

Chandler, T.A. Personal communication, 1979.

Chapman, L.J., & Chapman, J.P. Illusory correlation as an obstacle to the use of valid psychodiagnostic signs. *Journal of Abnormal Psychology*, 1969, *74*, 271–280.

Chaves, J.F., & Barber, T.X. Cognitive strategies, experimenter modeling and expectation in the attenuation of pain. *Journal of Abnormal Psychology*, 1977, *83*, 356–363.

Child, I.L. Children's preferences for goals easy or difficult to obtain. *Psychological Monographs*, 1946, *60* (4, Whole No. 280).

Child, I.L., & Adelsheim, E. The motivational value of barriers for young children. *Journal of Genetic Psychology*, 1944, *65*, 97–111.

Cialdini, R.B., & Kenrick, D.T. Altruism as hedonism: A social development perspective on the relationship of negative affect and helping. *Journal of Personality and Social Psychology*, 1976, *34*, 907–914.

Clark, K.B., & Clark, M.P. Racial identification and preference in Negro children. In T.M. Newcomb & E.L. Hartley (Eds.), *Readings in Social Psychology*. New York: Henry Holt, 1947.

Clemens, S. *The adventures of Tom Sawyer.* New York: Grosset & Dunlap, 1875.

Clifford, M.M. Physical attractiveness and academic performance. *Child Study Journal*, 1975, *5*, 201–209.

Clifford, M.M., & Walster, E. Research note: The effect of physical attractiveness on teacher expectations *Sociology of Education*, 1973, *46*, 248–258.

Cline, V.B. Interpersonal perception. In B.A. Maher (Ed.), *Progress in experimental personality research* (Vol. 1). New York: Academic Press, 1964.

Cloward, R. Studies in tutoring. *Journal of Experimental Education*, 1967, *36*, 14–25.

Coates, T.J., & Thoresen, C.E. Treating obesity in children and adolescents: A public health problem. *American Journal of Public Health*, 1978, *68*, 143–151.

Cohen, A. *Delinquent boys.* Glencoe, Ill.: Free Press, 1955.

Cohen, E., & Roper, S. Modification of interracial interaction disability: An application of status characteristic theory. *American Sociological Review*, 1972, *37*, 643–657.

Cohen, E.A., Gelfand, D.M., & Hartmann, D.P. *Developmental differences in children's causal attributions.* Paper presented at the American Psychological Association, New York, September 1979.

Cohen, E.G. Design and redesign of the desegregated school. Problems of status, power, and conflict. In W.G. Stephan & J.R. Feagin (Eds.), *Desegregation: Past, present and future.* New York: Plenum, 1979.

Cohen, S. *Social and personality development in childhood.* New York: Macmillan, 1976.

Coke, J.S., Batson, C.D., & McDavis, K. Empathic mediation of helping: A two-stage model. *Journal of Personality and Social Psychology*, 1978, *36*, 752–766.

Cole, D., King, K., & Newcomb, A. Grade expectations as a function of sex, academic discipline, and sex of instructor. *Psychology of Women Quarterly*, 1977, *1*, 380–385.

Coleman, J.S., Campbell, E.Q., Hobson, M., Mood, A.M., Weinfield, F.D., & York, R.L. *Equality of educational opportunity.* Washington, D.C.: U.S. Government Printing Office, 1966.

Colvin, R.H. Imposed extrinsic reward in an elementary school setting: Effects on free-operant rates and choices (Doctoral dissertation, Southern Illinois University, 1971). *Dissertation Abstracts International*, 1972, *32*, 5034-A.

Condon, W.S. An analysis of behavior organization. In S. Weitz (Ed.), *Nonverbal communication* (2nd ed.). New York: Oxford, 1979.

Condon, W.S., & Sander, L.W. Neonate movement is synchronized with adult speech: Interactional participation and language acquisition. *Science*, 1974, *183*, 99–101.

Condry, J., & Chambers, J.C. *How rewards change the problem solving process.* Unpublished manuscript, Cornell University, 1977.

Condry, J., & Chambers, J.C Intrinsic motivation and the process of learning. In M.R. Lepper

& D. Greene (Eds.), *The hidden costs of reward.* Hillsdale, N.J.: Lawrence Erlbaum Associates, 1978.

Conger, J.C., Conger, A.J., Costanzo, P.R., Wright, K.L., & Matter, J.A. The effect of social cues on the eating behavior of obese and normal subjects. *Journal of Personality,* 1980, *48,* 258–271.

Connell, R.W. *The child's construction of politics.* Carlton, Victoria: Melbourne University Press, 1971.

Cook, S.W. Motives in a conceptual analysis of attitude-related behavior. In J. Brigham & T. Weissback (Eds.), *Racial attitudes in America: Analysis and findings of social psychology.* New York: Harper and Row, 1972.

Cook-Gumperz, J. *Social control and socialization.* London: Routledge & Kegan Paul, 1973.

Cooper, H.M. Controlling personal rewards: Professional teachers' differential use of feedback and the effects of feedback on the students' motivation to perform. *Journal of Educational Psychology* 1977, *69,* 419–427.

Cooper, H.M. Pygmalion grows up: A model for teacher expectation communication and performance influence. *Review of Educational Research,* 1979, *49,* 389–410.

Cooper, H.M., & Burger, J.M. *Internality, stability, and personal efficacy: A categorization of free response academic attributions.* Unpublished manuscript, University of Missouri-Columbia, 1978.

Cordray, D.S., & Shaw, J.I. An empirical test of the covariation analysis in causal attribution. *Journal of Experimental Social Psychology,* 1978, *14,* 280–290.

Corrigan, R. A scalogram analysis of the development of the use and comprehension of "because" in children. *Child Development,* 1975, *46,* 195–201.

Corter, C., Trehub, S., Bonkydis, C., Ford, L., Celhoffer, L., & Minde, K. *Nurses' judgments of the attractiveness of premature infants.* Unpublished manuscript, University of Toronto, 1975.

Costanzo, P.R., Grumet, J.F., & Brehm, S.S. The effects of choice and source of constraint on children's attributions of preference. *Journal of Experimental Social Psychology,* 1974, *10,* 352–364.

Costanzo, P.R., & Woody, E.Z. Externality as a function of obesity in children: Pervasive style or eating-specific attribute? *Journal of Personality and Social Psychology,* 1979, *37,* 2286–2296.

Costanzo, P.R., & Woody, E.Z. *Parental perspectives on obesity in children: The importance of sex differences.* Manuscript in preparation, Duke University, 1980.

Court, J.M., & Dunlop, M. Obese from infancy: A clinical entity. In A. Howard (Ed.), *Recent advances in obesity research.* London: Newman, 1975.

Covington, M.V., & Omelich, C.L. It's best to be able and virtuous too: Student and teacher evaluative responses to successful effort. *Journal of Educational Psychology,* 1979, *71,* 688–700.

Cowan, P.A., Hoddinott, B.A., & Wright, B.A. Compliance and resistance in the conditioning of autistic children. *Child Development,* 1965, *36,* 913–923.

Crandall, V.C. Achievement behavior in the young child. In W.W. Hartup (Ed.), *The young child: Review of research.* Washington, D.C.: National Association for the Education of Young Children, 1967.

Crandall, V.C. Sex differences in expectancy, intellectual and academic reinforcement. In C.P. Smith (Ed.), *Achievement-related motives in children.* New York: Russell Sage, 1969.

Crandall, V.C. *Expecting sex differences and sex differences in expectancies: A developmental analysis.* Paper presented at the Annual Meeting of the American Psychological Association, Toronto, August 1978. (a)

Crandall, V.C. *Toward a cognitive-learning model of achievement behavior and development.* Paper presented at the Annual Meeting of the Motivation and Education Group, Ann Arbor, 1978. (b)

Crandall, V.J. Achievement. In H. Stevenson (Ed.). *Child psychology: Sixty-second Yearbook of the National Society for the Study of Education.* Chicago: University of Chicago Press, 1963.

Crandall, V.J., Katkovsky, W., & Preston, A. Conceptual formualtion for some research on children's achievement development. *Child Development,* 1960, *31,* 787–797.

Crawfurd, R. *Plague and pestilence in literature and art.* London: Oxford, 1914.

Cronbach, L.J. Processes affecting scores on "understanding of others" and "assumed similarity." *Psychological Bulletin,* 1955, *52,* 177–193.

Csikszentmihalyi, M. *Beyond boredom and anxiety.* San Francisco: Jossey-Bass, 1975.

Cunningham, J.D., & Kelley, H.H. Causal attributions for interpersonal events of varying magnitude. *Journal of Personality,* 1975, *43,* 74–93.

Damen, W. *The social world of the child.* San Francisco: Jossey-Bass, 1977.

Damon, W. Early conceptions of positive justice related to the development of logical operations. *Child Development,* 1975, *46,* 301–312.

Danziger, K. *Socialization.* Harmondsworth: Penguin, 1971.

Darwin, C. *The expression of emotions in man and animals.* London: John Murray, 1872.

Dasen, P.R. Concrete operational development in three cultures. *Journal of Cross-Cultural Psychology,* 1975, *6,* 156–172.

Davidson, P., & Bucher, B. Intrinsic interest and extrinsic reward: The effects of a continuing token program on continuing nonconstrained preference. *Behavior Therapy,* 1978, *9,* 222–234.

Deci, E.L. Effects of externally mediated rewards on intrinsic motivation. *Journal of Personality and Social Psychology,* 1971, *18,* 105–115.

Deci, E.L. The effects of contingent and non-contingent rewards and controls on intrinsic motivation. *Organizational Behavior and Human Performance,* 1972, *8,* 217–229. (a)

Deci, E.L. Intrinsic motivation, extrinsic reinforcement, and inequity. *Journal of Personality and Social Psychology,* 1972, *22,* 113–120. (b)

Deci, E.L. *Intrinsic motivation.* New York: Plenum, 1975.

Deets, A., & Harlow, H.F. *Early experience and the maturation of agonistic behavior.* Paper presented at the meeting of the American Association for the Advancement of Science, New York, December 1971.

Delgado, J.M.R. *Physical control of the mind.* New York: Harper and Row, 1969.

Dembroski, T.M., & MacDougall, J.M. Stress effects on affiliation preferences among subjects possessing the Type A coronary-prone behavior pattern. *Journal of Personality and Social Psychology,* 1978, *36,* 23–33.

Dembroski, T.M., MacDougall, J.M., & Lushene, R. Interpersonal interaction and cardiovascular response in Type A subjects and coronary patients. *Journal of Human Stress,* 1979, *5,* 28–36.

Dembroski, T.M., MacDougall, J.M., & Shields, J.L. Physiologic reactions to social challenge

in persons evidencing the Type A coronary-prone behavior pattern. *Journal of Human Stress,* 1977, *3,* 2–9.

Dermer, M., & Thiel, D.L. When beauty may fail. *Journal of Personality and Social Psychology,* 1975, *31,* 1168–1176.

DesLauriers, A.M., & Carlson, C.F. *Your child is asleep.* Homewood, Ill.: The Dorsey Press, 1969.

Deutsch, M. An experimental study of the effects of cooperation and competition on group progress. *Human Relations.* 1949, *2,* 199–231.(a)

Deutsch, M. A theory of cooperation and competition. *Human Relations,* 1949, *2,* 129–152.(b)

Deutsch, M. Minority group and class status related to social and personality factors in scholastic achievement. *Society for Applied Anthropology Monographs,* 1960, *2.*

DeVries, D.L., & Edwards, K.J. Student teams and learning games: Their effects on cross-race and cross-sex interaction. *Journal of Educational Psychology,* 1974, *66,* 741–749.

DeVries, D.L., Edwards, K.J., & Slavin, R.E. Biracial learning teams and race relations in the classroom: Four field experiments using Teams-Games-Tournament. *Journal of Educational Psychology,* 1978, *70,* 356–362.

DeVries, R. The development of role-taking as reflected by the behavior of bright, average, and retarded children in a social guessing game. *Child Development,* 1970, *41,* 759–770.

Dienstbier, R.A., Hillman, D., Lehnhoff, J., Hillman, J., & Valkenaar, M.C. An emotion-attribution approach to moral behavior: Interfacing cognitive and avoidance theories of moral development. *Psychological Review,* 1975, *82,* 229–315.

Dimsdale, J.E., Hackett, T.P., Hutter, A.M., Block, P.C., & Catanzano, D. Type A personality and extent of coronary atherosclerosis. *American Journal of Cardiology,* 1978, *42,* 583–586.

Dion, K.K. Physical attractiveness and evaluations of children's transgressions. *Journal of Personality and Social Psychology,* 1972, *24,* 207–213.

Dion, K.K. Young children's stereotyping of facial attractiveness. *Developmental Psychology,* 1973, *9,* 183–188.

Dion, K.K. Children's physical attractiveness and sex as determinants of adult punitiveness.

Developmental Psychology, 1974, *10*, 772–778.

Dion, K.K. The incentive value of physical attractiveness for young children. *Personality and Social Psychology Bulletin*, 1977, *3*, 67–70.

Dion, K.K., & Berscheid, E. Physical attractiveness and peer perception among children. *Sociometry*, 1974, *37*, 1–12.

Dion, K.K., Berscheid, E., & Walster, E. What is beautiful is good. *Journal of Personality and Social Psychology*, 1972, *24*, 285–290.

Dion, K.K., & Stein, S. Physical attractiveness and interpersonal influence. *Journal of Experimental Social Psychology*, 1978, *14*, 97–108.

DiVitto, B., & McArthur, L.Z. Developmental differences in the use of distinctiveness, consensus, and consistency information for making causal attributions. *Developmental Psychology*, 1978, *14*, 474–482.

Dix. T.H., Herzberger, S., & Erlebacher, A. *Using consensus information: Developmental study of Kelley's attribution theory.* Paper presented at the American Psychological Association, Toronto, September 1978.

Dollard, J., Doob, L.W., Miller, N.E., Mowrer, O.H., & Sears, R.R. *Frustration and aggression.* New Haven: Yale University Press, 1939.

Dollinger, S.J., & Thelen, M.H. Overjustification and children's intrinsic motivation: Comparative effects of four rewards. *Journal of Personality and Social Psychology*, 1978, *36*, 1259–1269.

Dreeban, R. *On what is learned in school.* Cambridge, Mass.: Addison-Wesley, 1968.

Duck, S.W. *Personal relationships and personal constructs: A study of friendship formation.* New York: Wiley, 1973.

Duck S.W. Personality similarity and friendship choices by adolescents. *European Journal of Social Psychology*, 1975, *5*, 351–365.

Duncker, K. On problem solving. *Psychological Monographs*, 1945, *58*, (5, Whole No. 270).

Dunn, L.M. *Peabody Picture Vocabulary Test.* Minneapolis, Minn.: American Guidance Service, 1959.

Dunn, R.E., & Goldman, M. Competition and noncompetition in relationship to satisfaction and feelings toward own-group and non-group members. *Journal of Social Psychology*, 1966, *68*, 299–311.

Durnin, J.V., Lonergan, M.E., Good, J., & Ewan, A. Cross-sectional nutritional and anthropometric study with an interval of 7 years on 611 young adolescent school children. *British Journal of Nutrition*, 1974, *32*, 169.

Dweck, C.S., & Gilliard, D. Expectancy statements as determinants of reactions to failure: Sex differences in persistence and expectancy change. *Journal of Personality and Social Psychology*, 1975, *32*, 1077–1084.

Dweck, C.S., & Goetz, T.E. Attributions and learned helplessness. In J.H. Harvey, W.J. Ickes, & R.F. Kidd (Eds.), *New directions in attribution research* (Vol. 2). Hillsdale, N.J.: Lawrence Erlbaum Associates, 1978.

Dweck, C.S., & Repucci, N.D. Learned helplessness and reinforcement responsibility in children. *Journal of Personality and Social Psychology*, 1973, *25*, 109–116.

Dwyer, J.T., Feldman, J.J., & Mayer, J. Adolescent dieters: Who are they? Physical characteristics, attitudes, and dieting practices of adolescent girls. *American Journal of Clinical Nutrition*, 1967, *20*, 1045.

Dwyer, J.T., & Mayer, J. *Overfeeding and obesity in infants and children.* Basel: Karger, 1973.

Easterbrook, J.A. The effect of emotion on cue utilization and organization of behavior. *Psychological Review*, 1959, *66*, 183–201.

Easton, D., & Dennis J. *Children in the political system.* New York: McGraw-Hill, 1969.

Edgerton, R.B. *The cloak of competence: Stigma in the lives of the mentally retarded.* Berkeley: University of California Press, 1967.

Edwards, D.W. Black versus white: When is race a relevant variable? *Journal of Personality and Social Psychology*, 1974, *29*, 39–49.

Efran, M.G. The effect of physical appearance on the judgment of guilt, interpersonal attraction, and severity of recommended punishment in a simulated jury task. *Journal of Experimental Research in Personality*, 1974, *8*, 45–54.

Eibl-Eibesfeldt, I. *Ethology: The biology of behavior.* New York: Holt, Rinehart and Winston, 1970.

Eibl-Eibesfeldt, I. Similarities and differences between cultures in expressive movements. In R.A. Hinde (Ed.), *Nonverbal communication.* Cambridge, Eng.: Cambridge University Press, 1972, 297–312.

Eisen, S.V. Actor-observer differences in information inference and causal attribution. *Journal of Personality and Social Psychology*, 1979, *37*, 261–272.

Eisenberg-Berg, N., & Hand, M. The relationship of preschoolers' reasoning about prosocial moral conflicts to prosocial behavior. *Child Development,* 1979, *50,* 346–363.

Eisenberg-Berg, N., & Mussen, P. Empathy and moral development in adolescence. *Developmental Psychology,* 1978, *14,* 185–186.

Ekman, P., & Friesen, W.V. Constants across cultures in the face and emotion. *Journal of Personality and Social Psychology,* 1971, *17,* 124–129.

Ekman, P., & Friesen, W.V. *Unmasking the face.* Englewood Cliffs, N.J.: Prentice-Hall, 1975

Ekman, P., Friesen, W.V., & Ellsworth, P. *Emotion in the human face.* New York: Pergamon Press, 1971.

Ekman, P., Friesen, W.V., & Tomkins, S. The facial affect scoring technique: A first validity study. *Semiotica,* 1971, *3,* 37–58.

Ekman, P., Sorenson, E.R., & Friesen, W.V. Pan-cultural elements in the facial displays of emotion. *Science,* 1969, *164,* 86–88.

Eland, J.M., & Anderson, J.E. The experience of pain in children. In A.K. Jacob (Ed.), *Pain.* Boston: Little, Brown & Co., 1977.

Elig, T., & Frieze, I.H. A multi-dimensional scheme for coding and interpreting perceived causality for success and failure events: The coding scheme of perceived causality (CSPC). *JSAS: Catalog of Selected Documents in Psychology,* 1975, *5,* 313.

Elig, T., & Frieze, I.H. Measuring causal attributions for success and failure. *Journal of Personality and Social Psychology,* 1979, *37,* 621–634.

Eliot, R.S. *Stress and the major cardiovascular disorders.* Mount Kisco, N.Y.: Futura, 1979.

Elkind, D. Egocentrism in adolescence. *Child Development,* 1967, *38,* 1025– 1034.

Elliot, R., & Vasta, R. The modeling of sharing: Effects associated with vicarious reinforcement, symbolization, age, and generalization. *Journal of Experimental Child Psychology,* 1970, *70,* 8–15.

Elman, D., Schroeder, H.E., & Schwartz, M.F. Reciprocal social influence of obese and normal-weight persons. *Journal of Abnormal Psychology,* 1977, *86,* 408–413.

Emler, N.P. *Moral character.* Unpublished manuscript, University of Dundee, 1979.

Emler, N.P., Heather, N., & Winton, M. Delinquency and the development of moral reasoning. *British Journal of Social and Clinical Psychology,* 1978, *17,* 325–331.

Emler, N.P., Herron, G., & Malone, B. *Relationships between moral attitudes and political orientation.* Unpublished manuscript, University of Dundee, 1979.

Emler, N.P., & Hogan, R. The biases in contemporary social psychology. *Social Research,* 1978, *45,* 478–534.

Emler, N.P., & Rushton, J.P. Cognitive-developmental factors in children's generosity. *British Journal of Social and Clinical Psychology,* 1974, *13,* 277–281.

Emmerich, W. Developmental trends in evaluations of single traits. *Child Development,* 1974, *45,* 172–183.

Emmerich, W., & Goldman, K.S. Structure and development of interpersonal values. In E.T. Higgins, D.N. Ruble, & W.W. Hartup (Eds.), *Social cognition and social behavior.* San Francisco: Jossey-Bass, in press.

Enos, W.F., Holmes, R.H., & Beyer, J. Coronary disease among U.S. soldiers killed in action in Korea. *Journal of the American Medical Association,* 1953, *152,* 1090–1093.

Entwisle, D.R. *Modeling young children's performance expectancies.* Paper presented at the LRDC Conference: Teacher and Student Perceptions of Success and Failure, Pittsburgh, October 1979.

Enzle, M.E., Hansen, R.D., & Lowe, C.A. Causal attribution in the mixed-motive game: Effects of facilitory and inhibitory environmental forces. *Journal of Personality and Social Psychology,* 1975, *31,* 50–54.

Enzle, M.E., & Look, S.C. *Self versus other reward administration and the over justification effect.* Unpublished manuscript, University of Alberta, 1980.

Enzle, M.E., & Ross, J.M. Increasing and decreasing intrinsic interest with contingent rewards: A test of cognitive evaluation theory. *Journal of Experimental Social Psychology,* 1978, *14,* 588–597.

Epstein, R., & Komorita, S.S. Childhood prejudice as a function of parental ethnocentrism, punitiveness, and outgroup characteristics. *Journal of Personality and Social Psychology,* 1966, *3,* 259 –264.(a)

Epstein, R., & Komorita, S.S. Prejudice among Negro children as related to parental ethnocentrism and punitiveness. *Journal of Personality and Social Psychology,* 1966, *4,* 643–647.(b)

Erikson, E.H. *Childhood and society.* New York: Norton, 1963.

Erwin, J., & Kuhn, D. Development of children's understanding of the multiple determination underlying human behavior. *Developmental Psychology*, 1979, *15*, 352–353.

Estes, W.K. Reinforcement in human behavior. *American Scientist*, 1972, *60*, 723–729.

Eysenck, H.J. General social attitudes. *Journal of Social Psychology*, 1944, *19*, 207–227.

Eysenck, H.J. *The psychology of politics*. London: Routledge & Kegan Paul, 1954.

Eysenck, H.J. Social attitudes and social class. *British Journal of Social and Clinical Psychology*, 1971, *10*, 201–212.

Falbo, T. *The attributional explanation of academic performance by kindergarteners and their teachers*. Paper presented at the Annual Meeting of the American Psychological Association, August 1973.

Farina, A., Thaw, J., Felner, R.D., & Hust, B.E. Some interpersonal consequences of being mentally ill or mentally retarded. *American Journal of Mental Deficiency*, 1976, *80*, 414–422.

Faust, I.M., Johnson, P.R., Stern, J.S., & Hirsch, J. Diet-induced adipocyte number increase in adult rats: A new model of obesity. *American Journal of Physiology*, 1978, *235*, E279.

Fay, A.S. *The effects of cooperation and competition on learning and recall*. Unpublished master's thesis, George Peabody College, 1970.

Fazio, R.H., Zanna, M.P., & Cooper, J. Dissonance vs. self-perception: An integrative view of each theory's proper domain of application. *Journal of Experimental Social Psychology*, 1977, *5*, 464–479.

Feather, N.T., & Simon, J.G. Attribution of responsibility and valence of outcome in relation to initial confidence and success and failure of self and other. *Journal of Personality and Social Psychology*, 1971, *18*, 173–188.(a)

Feather, N.T., & Simon, J.G. Causal attributions for success and failure in relation to expectations of success based upon selective or manipulative control. *Journal of Personality*, 1971, *37*, 527–541.(b)

Feingold, B.D., & Mahoney, M.J. Reinforcement effects on intrinsic interest: Undermining the overjustification hypothesis. *Behavior Therapy*, 1975, *6*, 367–377.

Feldman, J.M. Stimulus characteristics and subject prejudice as determinants of stereotype attribution. *Journal of Personality and Social Psychology*, 1972, *21*, 333–340.

Feldman, N.S. *Children's impressions of their peers: Motivational factors and the use of inference*. Unpublished doctoral dissertation, Princeton University, 1979.

Fergusson, L.W. Primary social attitudes. *Journal of Psychology*, 1939, *8*, 217–223.

Feshbach, N.D. Cross-cultural studies of teaching styles in four-year-olds and their mothers. In J.P. Hill (Ed.), *Minnesota Symposia on Child Psychology* (Vol. 1). Minneapolis: University of Minnesota Press, 1967.

Feshbach, N.D., & Feshbach, S. The relationship between empathy and aggression in two age groups. *Developmental Psychology*, 1969, *1*, 102–107.

Feshbach, N.D., & Roe, K. Empathy in six and seven year olds. *Child Development*, 1968, *39*, 133–145.

Festinger, L. A theory of social comparison processes. *Human Relations*, 1954, *7*, 117–140.

Festinger, L. *A theory of cognitive dissonance*. Stanford, Calif.: Stanford University Press, 1957.

Festinger, L, Schachter, S., & Back, K. *Social pressures in informal groups: A study of a housing community*. New York: Harper, 1950.

Field, T., & Walden, T. Perception and production of facial expressions in infancy and early childhood. To appear in H. Reese and L. Lipsitt (Eds.), *Advances in child development and behavior* (Vol. 16). New York: Academic Press, in preparation.

Filler, R.J., & Meals, D.W. The effect of motive conditions on the estimation of time. *Journal of Experimental Psychology*, 1949, *39*, 327–331.

Fine, M.J., & Caldwell, T.E. Self-evaluation of school related behavior of educable mentally retarded children: A preliminary report. *Exceptional Children*, 1967, *33*, 324.

Fishkin, J., Keniston, K., & MacKinnon, C. Moral reasoning and political ideology. *Journal of Personality and Social Psychology*, 1973, *27*, 109–119.

Flapan, D. *Children's understanding of social interaction*. New York: Columbia University Teacher's College Press, 1968.

Flavell, J.H. *The developmental psychology of Jean Piaget*. Princeton, N.J.: Van Nostrand, 1963.

Flavell, J.H. The development of inferences about others. In T. Mischel (Ed.), *Understanding other persons*. Oxford: Blackwell, Basil, Mott, 1974.

Flavell, J.H. & Wohlhill, J.F. Formal and functional aspects of cognitive development. In D. Elkind & J.H. Flavell (Eds.), *Studies in Cognitive Development.* New York: Oxford, 1969.

Foley, J.M. Effect of labeling and teacher behavior on children's attitudes. *American Journal of Mental Deficiency,* 1979, *83,* 380–384.

Fontaine, G. Social comparison and some determinants of expected personal control and expected performance in a novel task situation. *Journal of Personality and Social Psychology,* 1974, *29,* 487–496.

Fontana, A.F., & Noel, B. Moral reasoning in the university. *Journal of Personality and Social Psychology,* 1973, *27,* 419–429.

Forehand, R., Cheney, T., & Yoder, P. Parent behavior training: Effects on the noncompliance of a deaf child. *Journal of Behavior Therapy and Experimental Psychiatry,* 1974, *5,* 281–283.

Forehand, R., & King, H.E. Preschool children's non-compliance: Effects of short-term behavior therapy. *Journal of Community Psychology,* 1974, *2,* 42–44.

Forehand, R., Roberts, H.W., Doleys, D.M., Hobbs, S.A., & Resick, P.A. An examination of disciplinary procedures with children. *Journal of Experimental Child Psychology,* 1976, *21,* 109–120.

Forehand, R., & Scarboro, M.E. An Analysis of children's oppositional behavior. *Journal of Abnormal Child Psychology,* 1975, *3,* 27–31.

Fox, D.J., & Jordan, V.B. Racial preferences and identification of Black, American Chinese, and White children. *Genetic Psychology Monographs,* 1973, *88,* 229–286.

Fraiberg, S. Blind infants and their mothers: An examination of the sign system. In M. Lewis & L.A. Rosenbloom (Eds.), *The effect of the infant on its caregiver.* New York: Wiley, 1974.

Frank, K.A., Heller, S.S., Kornfeld, D.S., Spron, A.A., & Weiss, M.B. Behavior pattern and coronary angiographic findings. *Journal of the American Medical Association,* 1978, *240,* 761–763.

Freedman, J.L. Long-term behavioral effects of cognitive dissonance. *Journal of Experimental Social Psychology,* 1965, *1,* 145–155.

Freud, S. Formulations regarding the two principles of mental functioning, 1911. In *Collected Papers of Sigmund Freud* (Vol. 4). New York: Basic Books, 1959.

Friedman, M. *Pathogenesis of coronary artery disease.* New York: McGraw-Hill, 1969.

Friend, R.M., & Neale, J.M. Children's perceptions of success and failure: An attributional analysis of the effects of race and social class. *Developmental Psychology,* 1972, *7,* 124–128.

Frieze, I.H. Causal attribution and information seeking to explain success and failure. *Journal of Research in Personality,* 1976, *10,* 298–305.(a)

Frieze, I.H. The role of information processing in making causal attributions for success and failure. In J.S. Carroll & J.W. Payne (Eds.), *Cognition and social behavior.* Hillsdale, N.J.: Lawrence Erlbaum Associates, 1976.(b)

Frieze, I.H. Beliefs about success and failure in the classroom. In J.H. McMillan (Ed.), *The social psychology of school learning.* New York: Academic Press, 1980.

Frieze, I.H., & Bar-Tal, D. Attribution theory: Past and present. In I.H. Frieze, D. Bar-Tal, & J.S. Carroll (Eds.), *New approaches to social problems: Applications of attribution theory.* San Francisco: Jossey-Bass, 1979.

Frieze, I.H., & Bar-Tal, D. Developmental trends in cue utilization for attributional judgments. *Journal of Applied Developmental Psychology,* 1980, *1,* 83–94.

Frieze, I.H., Bar-Tal, D., & Carroll, J.S. (Eds.). *New approaches to social problems: Applications of attribution theory.* San Francisco: Jossey-Bass, 1979.

Frieze, I.H., Fisher, J., Hanusa, B., McHugh, M.C., & Valle, V.A. Attributions of the causes of success and failure as internal and external barriers to achievement in women. In J. Sherman & F. Denmark (Eds.), *Psychology of women: Future directions of research.* New York: Psychological Dimensions, 1978.

Frieze, I.H., McHugh, M.C., & Duquin, M. *Causal attributions for women and men and sports participation.* Paper presented at the Annual Meeting of the American Psychological Association, Washington, D.C., August 1976.

Frieze, I.H., Shomo, K.H., & Francis, W.D. *Determinants of subjective feelings of success.* Paper presented at the LRDC Conference, Teacher and Student perceptions of Success and Failure: Implications for Learning, Pittsburgh, October 1979.

Frieze, I.H., & Snyder, H.N. Children's beliefs

about the causes of success and failure in school settings. *Journal of Educational Psychology,* 1980, *72,* 186–196.

Frieze, I.H., Snyder, H.N., & Fontaine, C.M. *Student attributions and the attribution process during an actual examination.* Paper presented at the Annual Meeting of the American Psychological Association, San Francisco, August 1977.

Frieze, I.H., Snyder, H.N., & Fontaine, C..M. *Fifth graders' attributions and the attribution model during an actual examination.* Unpublished manuscript, Learning Research and Development Center, University of Pittsburgh, 1978.

Frieze, I.H., & Weiner, B. Cue utilization and attributional judgments for success and failure. *Journal of Personality,* 1971, *39,* 591–606.

Frijda, N.H. Recognition of emotion. In L. Berkowitz (Ed.), *Advances in experimental social psychology* (Vol. 4). New York: Academic Press, 1969.

Frisch, K.V. Honeybees: Do they use direction and distance information provided by their dancers? *Science,* 1968, *158,* 1072–1076.

Furth, H.G. Young children's understanding of society. In H. McGurk (Ed.), *Issues in childhood social development.* London: Methuen, 1979.

Gallagher, J.J. The sacred and profane uses of labeling. *Mental Retardation,* 1976, *14,* 3–7.

Gallatin, J., & Adelson, J. Legal guarantees of individual freedom: A cross-national study of the development of political thought. *Journal of Social Issues,* 1971, *27,* 93–108.

Gan, J., Tymchuk, A.J., & Nisihara, N. Mildly retarded adults: Their attitudes toward retardation. *Mental Retardation,* 1977, *15,* 5–9.

Garbarino, J. The impact of anticipated rewards on cross-age tutoring, *Journal of Personality and Social Psychology,* 1975, *32,* 421–428.

Garland, H., Hardy, A., & Stephenson, L. Information search as affected by attribution type and response category. *Personality and Social Psychology Bulletin,* 1975. *1,* 612–615.

Garn, S. The origins of obesity. *American Journal of Diseases of Children,* 1976, *130,* 465.

Garn, S., & Clark, D.C. Trends in fatness and the origins of obesity. *Pediatrics,* 1976, *57,* 443.

Garn, S., Clark, D.C., & Guire, K.E. Growth, body composition, and development of obese and lean children. In M. Winick (Ed.), *Childhood obesity.* New York: Wiley, 1975.

Garn, S., Cole, P.E., & Bailey, S.M. Effect of parental fatness levels on the fatness of biological and adoptive children. *Ecology of Food and Nutrition,* 1976, *6,* 1.

Gaul, D.J., Craighead, E., & Mahoney, M.J. Relationship between eating rates and obesity. *Journal of Consulting and Clinical Psychology,* 1975, *43,* 123–135.

Geer, J.H., & Jarmecky, L. The effect of being responsible for reducing another's pain on subjects' response and arousal. *Journal of Personality and Social Psychology,* 1973, *26,* 232–237.

Gelman, R. Cognitive development. *Annual Review of Psychology,* 1978, *29,* 297–332.

Gerard, H.B., & Miller, N. *School desegregation: A long term study.* New York: Plenum, 1975.

Gibbons, F.X., & Gibbons, B.N. Effect of the institutional label on peer assessments of institutionalized EMR persons. *American Journal of Mental Deficiency,* 1980, *84,* 602–609.

Gibbons, F.X., Gibbons, B.N., & Kassin, S.M. *Mental retardation and the law: Attributions of responsibility for criminal behavior of retarded and nonretarded adolescents.* Manuscript submitted for publication, Iowa State University, 1980.

Gibbons, F.X., & Kassin, S.M. *Retarded and nonretarded children's reactions to their retarded peers.* Manuscript submitted for publication, Iowa State University, 1980.

Gibbons, F.X., Sawin, L.S., & Gibbons, B.N. Evaluations of mentally retarded persons: "Sympathy" or patronization? *American Journal of Mental Deficiency,* 1979, *84,* 124–131.

Gibson, J.J. *The senses considered as perceptual systems.* Boston: Houghton Mifflin, 1966.

Gibson, J.J. The theory of affordances. In R.E. Shaw & J. Bransford (Eds.), *Perceiving, acting and knowing: Toward an ecological psychology.* Hillsdale, N.J.: Lawrence Erlbaum Associates, 1977.

Gilmore, T.M., & Reid, D.W. Locus of control and causal attribution for positive and negative outcomes on university exams. *Journal of Research in Personality,* 1979, *13,* 154–160.

Ginsberg, H., & Opper, S. *Piaget's theory of intellectual development: An introduction.* Englewood Cliffs, N.J.: Prentice-Hall, 1969.

Gjesme, T. Achievement-related motives and school performance for girls. *Journal of*

Personality and Social Psychology, 1973, *26,* 131–136.

Glass, D.C. *Behavior patterns, stress, and coronary disease.* Hillsdale, N.J.: Lawrence Erlbaum Associates, 1977.

Glass, D.C., Krakoff, L.R., Contrada, R., Hilton, W.F., Kehoe, K., Mannuci, E.G., Collins, C., Snow, B., & Elting, E. The effect of harassment and competition upon cardiovascular and catecholaminic responses in Type A and Type B individuals. *Psychophysiology,* 1980, *17,* 453–463..

Glickman, S.E., & Schiff, B.B. A biological theory of reinforcement. *Psychological Review,* 1967, *74,* 81–109.

Glucksman, M.L., & Hirsch, J. The response of obese patients to weight reduction: III. The perception of body size. *Psychosomatic Medicine,* 1969, *31,* 1–7.

Glucksman, M.L., Hirsch, J., McCully, R.S., Barron, B.A., & Knittle, J.L. The response of obese patients to weight reduction: II. A quantitative evaluation of behavior. *Psychosomatic Medicine,* 1968, *30,* 359–373.

Glueck, S., & Glueck, E.T. *Unraveling juvenile delinquency.* New York: Commonwealth Fund, 1950.

Goethals, G.R., & Darley, J.M. Social comparison theory: An attributional approach. In J.M. Suls & R.L. Miller (Eds.), *Social comparison processes.* Washington, D.C.: Hemisphere, 1977.

Goetz, E.M., Holmberg, M.C., & LeBlanc, J.M. Differential reinforcement of other behavior and noncontingent reinforcement as control procedures during the modification of a preschooler's compliance. *Journal of Applied Behavior Analysis,* 1975, *8,* 77–82.

Goffman, E. *Stigma: Notes on the management of spoiled identity.* Englewood Cliffs, N.J.: Prentice-Hall, 1963.

Gold, A.R., Christie, R., & Friedman, L.N. *Fists and flowers: A social psychological interpretation of student dissent.* New York: Academic Press, 1976.

Gold, M.W., & Ryan, K.M. Vocational training for the mentally retarded. In I.H. Frieze, D. Bar-Tal, & J.S. Carroll (Eds.), *New approaches to social problems: Applications of attribution theory.* San Francisco: Jossey-Bass, 1979.

Goldberg, S., & Lewis, M. Play behavior in the year-old infant: Early sex differences. *Child Development,* 1969, *40,* 21–31.

Goldblatt, P.B., Moore, M.E., & Stunkard, A.J. Social factors in obesity. *Journal of the American Medical Association,* 1965, *192,* 1039–1044.

Gollin, E. Organizational characteristics of social judgments: A developmental investigation. *Journal of Personality,* 1958, *26,* 139–154.

Goodall, J. *In the shadow of man.* New York: Dell, 1971.

Goodall, J. Life and death at Gombe. *National Geographic,* 1979, *155,* 592–621.

Goodenough, F. The emotional behavior of young children during mental tests. *Journal of Juvenile Research,* 1929, *13,* 204–219.

Goodman, H., Gottleib, J., & Harrison, R.H. Social acceptance of EMR children integrated into a non-graded elementary school. *American Journal of Mental Deficiency,* 1972, *76,* 412–417.

Goodman, M.E. *Race awareness in young children.* Cambridge, Mass.: Addison-Wesley, 1952.

Goodman, M.E. *Race awareness in young children* (2nd ed.). New York: Crowell-Collier, 1964.

Gorsuch, R.L., & Barnes, M.L. Stages of ethical reasoning and moral norms of Carib youths. *Journal of Cross-Cultural Psychology,* 1973, *4,* 283–301.

Gottlieb, D., & Ten Houten, W.D. Racial composition and the social system of high schools, *Journal of Marriage and Family,* 1965, *27,* 204–212.

Gottlieb, J. Attitudes toward retarded children: Effects of labeling and academic performance. *American Journal of Mental Deficiency,* 1974, *79.* 268–273.

Gottlieb, J. Attitudes toward retarded children: Effect of labeling and behavioral aggressiveness. *Journal of Educational Psychology,* 1975, *67,* 581–585.

Gottlieb, J., Cohen, L., & Goldstein, L. Social control and personal adjustment as variables related to attitudes towards EMR children. *Training School Bulletin,* 1974, *71,* 9–16.

Gottlieb, J., & Davis, J.E. Social acceptance of EMR children during overt behavior interactions. *American Journal of Mental Deficiency,* 1973, *78,* 141–143.

Gottman, J.M., & Parkhurst, J.T. A developmental theory of friendship and acquaintanceship processes. In W.A. Collins (Ed.), *Development of cognition, affect, and social relations: Minnesota symposia on child psychology* (Vol. 13). Hillsdale, N.J.: Lawrence Erlbaum Associates, 1980.

Gozali, J. Perceptions of the EMR special class by former students. *Mental Retardation,* 1972, *10,* 34–35.

Green, F.P., & Schneider, F.W. Age differences in the behavior of boys on three measures of altruism. *Child Development,* 1974, *45,* 248–251.

Green, M.L., Green, R.G., & Festa, L.I. *Sex-stereotyped tasks and attributions of success and failure.* Paper presented at the Annual Meeting of the Eastern Psychological Association, Philadelphia, April 1979.

Greenberg, J., & Rosenfield, D. Whites' ethnocentrism and their attributions for the behavior of blacks: A motivational bias. *Journal of Personality,* 1979, *47,* 643–657.

Greene, D., & Lepper, M.R. Effects of extrinsic rewards on children's subsequent intrinsic interest. *Child Development,* 1974, *45,* 1141–1145.

Greene, D., Sternberg, B., & Lepper, M.R. Overjustification in a token economy. *Journal of Personality and Social Psychology,* 1976, *34,* 1219–1234.

Greenstein, F.I. The benevolent leader. *American Political Science Review,* 1960, *54,* 934–943.

Greenstein, F.I. The benevolent leader revisited: Children's images of political leaders in three democracies. *American Political Science Review,* 1975, *69,* 1371–1399.

Greenwald, H., & Oppenheim, D. Reported magnitude of self-misidentification among Negro children—artifact? *Journal of Personality and Social Psychology,* 1968, *8,* 49–52.

Greenwood, M.R.C., & Johnson, P.R. Behavioral correlates of the obese condition. In M. Winick (Ed.), *Childhood obesity.* New York: Wiley, 1975.

Gregor, A.J., & McPherson, D.A. Racial attitudes among White and Negro children in a deep-south standard metropolitan area. *Journal of Social Psychology,* 1966, *68,* 95–106.

Grinker, J. Behavioral and metabolic consequences of weight reduction. *Journal of the American Dietetic Association,* 1973, *62,* 30–34.

Grinker, J., Glucksman, M., Hirsch, J., & Viseltear, G. Time perception as a function of weight recduction: A differentiation based on age of onset of obesity. *Psychosomatic Medicine,* 1973, *35,* 104–111.

Grinker, J., Hirsch, J., & Levin, B. The affective response of obese patients to weight reduction: A differentiation based on age at onset of obesity. *Psychosomatic Medicine,* 1973, *35,* 57–63.

Grossman, H.J. (Ed.). *Manual on terminology and classification in mental retardation.* Washington, D.C.: American Association on Mental Deficiency, 1977.

Gruder, C.L. Choice of comparison persons in evaluating oneself. In J.M. Suls & R.L. Miller (Eds.), *Social comparison processes.* Washington, D.C.: Hemisphere, 1977.

Grusec, J.E. Training altruistic dispositions: A cognitive analysis. In T.E. Higgins, D.N.Ruble, & W.W. Hartup (Eds.), *Social cognition and social behavior: A developmental perspective.* San Francisco: Jossey-Bass, in press.

Grusec, J.E., Kuczynski, L., Rushton, J.P., & Simutis, Z.M. Modeling, direct instruction, and attributions: Effects on altruism. *Developmental Psychology,* 1978, *14,* 51–57.

Guskin, S.L. Social psychologies of mental deficiencies. In N.R. Ellis (Ed.), *Handbook of mental deficiency.* New York: McGraw-Hill, 1963.

Guskin, S.L., Bartel, N.R., & MacMillan, D.L. The perspective of the labeled child. In N. Hobbs (Ed.), *Issues in the classification of exceptional children* (Vol. 2). San Francisco: Jossey-Bass, 1975.

Guttentag, M. & Longfellow, C. Children's social attributions: Development and change. In H.E. Howe, Jr. (Ed.), *Nebraska Symposium on Motivation* (Vol. 25). Lincoln: University of Nebraska Press, 1977.

Haft, J.I. Cardiovascular injury induced by sympathetic catecholamines. *Progress in Cardiovascular Diseases,* 1974, *17,* 73–86.

Hall, J.A., Rosenthal, R., Archer, D., DiMatteo, M.R., & Rogers, P.L. Profile of nonverbal sensitivity. In P. McReynolds (Ed.), *Advances in psychological assessment* (Vol. 4). San Francisco: Jossey-Bass, 1978.

Hammock, T., & Brehm, J.W. The attractiveness of choice alternatives when freedom to choose is eliminated by a social agent. *Journal of Personality,* 1966, *34,* 546–554.

Harackiewicz, J.M. The effects of reward contingency and performance feedback on intrinsic motivation. *Journal of Personality and Social Psychology,* 1979, *37,* 1352–1361.

Harding, J., Proshansky, H., Kutner, B., & Chein, I. Prejudice and ethnic relations. In G. Lindzey & E. Aronson (Eds.), *The handbook of social psychology* (Vol. 5). Reading, Mass.: Addison-Wesley, 1968.

Hargreaves, D.H. *Social relations in a secondary school.* London: Routledge & Kegan Paul, 1967.

Harlow, H.F. The heterosexual affectional system in monkeys. *American Psychologist,* 1962, *17,* 1–9.

Harlow, H.F. *Learning to love.* San Francisco: Albion, 1971.

Harper, L. The scope of offspring effects: From caregiver to culture. *Psychological Bulletin,* 1975, *82,* 784–801.

Harper, R.G., Wiens, A.N., & Matarazzo, J.D. The relationship between encoding-decoding of visual nonverbal emotional cues. *Semiotica,* 1979, *28,* 171–192..

Harris, D.B., Gough, H.G., & Martin, W.E. Children's ethnic attitudes related to methods of child rearing. *Child Development,* 1950, *21,* 169–181.

Harter, S. Pleasure derived from challenge and the effects of receiving grades on children's difficulty level choices. *Child Development,* 1978, *49,* 788–799.

Hartup, W.W. Children and their friends. In H. McGurk (Ed.), *Child social development.* London: Methuen, 1978.

Hartup, W.W., & Coates, B. Imitation of a peer as a function of reinforcement from the peer group and rewardingness of the model. *Child Development,* 1967, *38,* 1003–1016.

Hastorf, A.H., Schneider, D.J., & Polefka, J. *Person perception.* Reading, Mass.: Addison-Wesley, 1970.

Havighurst, R.J. *Developmental tasks and education.* New York: David McKay, 1972.

Hayes, C.S., & Prinz, N.J. Affective reactions of retarded and nonretarded children to success and failure. *American Journal of Mental Deficiency,* 1976, *81,* 100–102.

Haywood, H.C. What happened to mild and moderate mental retardation? *American Journal of Mental Deficiency,* 1979, *83,* 429–431.

Heald, F.P., & Hollander, R.J. The relationship between obesity in early adolescence and early growth. *Journal of Pediatrics,* 1965, *67,* 35.

Heider, F. Social perception and phenomenal causality. *Psychological Review,* 1944, *51,* 358–374.

Heider, F. *The psychology of interpersonal relations.* New York: Wiley, 1958.

Heider, F., & Simmel, M. An experimental study of apparent behavior. *American Journal of Psychology,* 1944, *57,* 243–259.

Hendrick, C., Franz, C.M., & Hoving, K.L. How do children form impressions of persons? They average. *Memory and Cognition,* 1975, *3,* 325–328.

Herman, C.P. *Possible costs of successful weight control.* Paper presented at the 9th Annual Meeting of the Association for the Advancement of Behavior Therapy, 1975.

Herman, C.P., & Mack, D. Restrained and unrestrained eating. *Journal of Personality,* 1975, *43,* 647–660.

Herman, C.P., & Polivy, J. Anxiety, restraint, and eating behavior. *Journal of Abnormal Psychology,* 1975, *84,* 666–672.

Herman, C.P., Polivy, J., & Silver, R. Effects of an observer on eating behavior: The induction of "sensible" eating. *Journal of Personality,* 1979, *47,* 85–99.

Herrnstein, R.J. Aperiodicity as a factor in choice. *Journal of the Experimental Analysis of Behavior,* 1964, *7,* 179–182.

Hervey, G.R. Regulation of energy balance. *Nature,* 1969, *222,* 629–631.

Herzberger, S.D., & Dweck, C.S. Attraction and delay of gratification. *Journal of Personality,* 1978, *46,* 215–227.

Hess, R.D., & Torney, J.V. *The development of political attitudes in children.* Chicago: Aldine, 1967.

Hibscher, J.A., & Herman, C.P. Obesity, dieting, and the expression of "obese" characteristics. *Journal of Comparative and Physiological Psychology,* 1977, *91,* 374–380.

Higgins, E.T. Role-taking and social judgment: Alternative developmental perspectives and processes. In L. Ross & J.H. Flavell (Eds.), *Development of social cognition in children,* in press.

Higgins, E.T., Feldman, N.S., & Ruble, D.N. Accuracy and differentiation in social prediction: A developmental perspective. *Journal of Personality,* in press.

Higgins, E.T., & Rholes, W.S. Impression formation and role fulfillment: A "holistic reference" approach. *Journal of Experimental Social Psychology,* 1976, *12,* 422–435.

Higgins, J.P. *The effect of verbal instruction on children's self-control.* Unpublished doctoral dissertation, University of Nebraska, 1975.

Hildebrandt, K.A., & Fitzgerald, H.E. Adults' responses to infants varying in perceived cuteness. *Behavioral processes,* 1978, *3,* 159–172.

Hodgkins, B.J., & Stakenas, R.G. A study of self-concepts of Negro and White youths in segregated environments. *Journal of Negro Education.* 1969, *38,* 370–377.

Hoffman, J., & Weiner, B. Effects of attributions for success and failure on performances of retarded adults. *American Journal of Mental Deficiency*, 1978, *82*, 447–452.

Hoffman, L.W. Early childhood experiences and women's achievement motives. *Journal of Social Issues*, 1972, *28*, 129–155.

Hoffman, M.L. Moral development. In P.H. Mussen (Ed.), Carmichael's manual of child psychology (Vol. 2). New York: Wiley, 1970.

Hoffman, M.L. Developmental synthesis of affect and cognition and its implication for altruistic motivation. *Developmental Psychology*, 1975, *11*, 607–622. (a)

Hoffman, M.L. Moral internalization, parental power, and the nature of parent child interaction. *Developmental Psychology*, 1975, *11*, 228–239. (b)

Hoffman, M.L. Empathy, role-taking, guilt, and development of altruistic motives. In T. Lickona (Ed.), *Moral development and behavior*. New York: Holt, 1976.

Hoffman, M.L., & Saltzstein, H.D. Parental discipline and the child's moral development. *Journal of Personality and Social Psychology*, 1967, *5*, 45–57.

Hogan, R. A dimension of moral judgment. *Journal of Consulting and Clinical Psychology*, 1970, *35*, 205–212.

Hogan, R., & Dickstein, E. Moral judgment and perceptions of injustice. *Journal of Personality and Social Psychology*, 1972, *23*, 409–413.

Hogan, R., & Emler, N.P. Retributive justice. In M. Lerner (Ed.), *New Perspectives on justice*. New York: Plenum Press, in press.

Hogan, R., Johnson, J.A., & Emler, N.P. A socioanalytic theory of moral development. In W. Damon (Ed.), *Moral development*. San Francisco: Jossey-Bass, 1978.

Hogan, R., & Mills, C. Legal socialization. *Human Development*, 1976, *19*, 261–276.

Hohmann, G. Some effects of spinal cord lesions on experimental emotional feelings. *Psychophysiology*, 1966, *3*, 143–156.

Hollinger, C.S., & Jones, R.L. Community attitudes toward slow learners and mental retardates: What's in a name? *Mental Retardation*, 1970, *8*, 19–23.

Holstein, C.B. Irreversibility, stepwise sequence in the development of moral judgment: A longitudinal study of males and females. *Child Development*, 1976, *47*, 51–61.

Holt, J. *How children fail*. New York: Dell, 1964.

Hook, J.G., & Cook, T.D. Equity theory and the cognitive ability of children. *Psychological Bulletin*, 1979, *86*, 429–445.

Horai, J., & Guarnaccia, V.J. Performance and attributions to ability, effort, task difficulty and luck of retarded adults after success or failure feedback. *American Journal of Mental Deficiency*, 1975, *79*, 690–694.

Horan, J.J., & Dillinger, J.K. "In vivo" emotive imagery: A preliminary test. *Perceptual and Motor Skills*, 1974, 39, 359–362.

House, W.C., & Perney, V. Valence of expected and unexpected outcomes as a function of locus of control and type of expectancy. *Journal of Personality and Social Psychology*, 1974, *29*, 454–463.

Hraba, J., & Grant, J. Black is beautiful: A re-examination of racial preference and identification. *Journal of Personality and Social Psychology*, 1970, *16*, 398–402.

Hueffer, O.M. *The book of witches*. Totowa, N.J.: Roman & Littlefield, 1973.

Hume, D. *A treatise of human nature*. Oxford: Clarendon, 1960.

Hunt, J. McV. Intrinsic motivation and its role in psychological development. In D. Levine (Ed.), *Nebraska Symposium on Motivation* (Vol. 13). Lincoln: University of Nebraska Press, 1965.

Hunter, S., Wolf, T., Sklov, M., & Berenson, J. Total cholesterol, triglycerides, lipoproteins, and the A-B coronary-prone behavior pattern in children: Franklinton Heart Study. Unpublished manuscript, 1980.

Huston, T.L. Ambiguity of acceptance, social desirability, and dating choice. *Journal of Experimental Social Psychology*, 1973, 9, 32–42.

Hyman, H.H., & Sheatsley, P.B. "The authoritarian personality": A methodological critique. In R. Christie & M. Jahoda (Eds), *Studies in the scope and method of "The authoritarian personality."* New York: Free Press, 1954.

Iannotti, R.J. Effect of role-taking experiences on role-taking, empathy, altruism, and aggression. *Developmental Psychology*, 1978, *14*, 119–124.

Ichheiser, G. *Appearances and realities*. San Francisco: Jossey-Bass, 1970.

Inhelder, B., & Piaget, J. *The growth of logical thinking from childhood to adolescence*. New York: Basic Books, 1958.

Irwin, F. Motivation and performance. *Annual Review of Psychology*, 1961, *12*, 217–242.

Izard, C.E. *The face of emotion*. New York: Appleton-Century-Crofts, 1971.

Izard, C.E. *Human emotions*. New York: Plenum, 1977.

Izard, C.E. *Emotion as motivation: An evolution-*

ary-developmental perspective. Colloquium presented at the University of Connecticut, April 1979. (a)

Izard, C.E. Personal communication, 1979. (b)

Izard, C.E., Huebner, R.R., Risser, D., McGinnes, G., & Dougherty, L. The young infant's ability to produce discrete emotion expressions. *Developmental Psychology,* 1980, *16,* 132–140..

Jackaway, R. *Sex differences in achievement motivation, behavior, and attributions about success and failure.* Unpublished dissertation, State University of New York at Albany, 1974.

Jacklin, C.N., & Maccoby, E.E. Social behavior at 33 months in same-sex and mixed-sex dyads. *Child Development,* 1978, *49,* 557–569.

Jacklin, C.N., Maccoby, E.E., & Dick, A.E., Barrier behavior and toy preference: Sex differences (and their absence) in the year-old child. *Child Development,* 1973, *44,* 196–200.

Jackson, T.W. *Life in classrooms.* New York: Holt, Rinehart and Winston, 1968.

James, W. What is an emotion? *Mind,* 1884, *9,* 188–205. Reprinted in M. Arnold, *The nature of emotion.* Baltimore: Penguin, 1968.

Jenkins, C.D., Rosenman, R.H., & Zyzanski, S.J. Prediction of clinical coronary heart disease by a test for the coronary-prone behavior pattern. *New England Journal of Medicine,* 1974, *23,* 1271–1275.

Jenkins, C.D., Zyzanski, S.J., & Rosenman, R.H. Progress toward validation of a computer-scored test for the type A coronary-prone behavior pattern. *Psychosomatic Medicine,* 1971, *33,* 193–202.

Jenkins, S.R. *"And what do you mean by success?" Fear of success and personal success goals.* Paper presented at the Annual Meeting of the Eastern Psychological Association, Philadelphia, April 1979.

Jennings, M.K., & Niemi, R.G. The transmission of political values from parent to child. *American Political Science Review,* 1968, *62,* 169–184.

Johnson, E.J., Greene, D., & Carroll, J.S. *Overjustification and reasons: A test of the means-ends analysis.* Unpublished manuscript, Carnegie-Mellon University, 1980.

Johnson, J.A., & Hogan, R. Moral judgments and self-presentations. *Journal of Research in Personality,* in press.

Jones, E.E., & Aneschansel, J. The learning and utilization of contravaluant material. *Journal of Abnormal and Social Psychology,* 1956, *53,* 27–34.

Jones, E.E., & Davis, K.E. From acts to dispositions: The attribution process in person perception. In L. Berkowitz (Ed.), *Advances in experimental social psychology* (Vol. 2). New York: Academic Press, 1965.

Jones, E.E., & deCharms, R. Changes in social perception as a function of the personal relevance of behavior. *Sociometry,* 1957, *20,* 75–85.

Jones, E.E., & Goethals, G.R. *Order effects in impression formation: Attribution context and the nature of the entity.* Morristown, N.J.: General Learning Press, 1971.

Jones, E.E., Kanouse, D.E., Kelley, H.H., Nisbett, R.E., Valins, S., & Weiner, B. *Attribution: Perceiving the causes of behavior.* Morristown, N.J.: General Learning Press, 1972.

Jones, E.E., & Nisbett, R.E. *The actor and the observer: Divergent perceptions of the causes of behavior.* Morristown, N.J.: General Learning Press, 1971.

Jones, H.E. The study of patterns of emotional expression. In M. Reymert (Ed.), *Feelings and emotions.* New York: McGraw-Hill, 1950.

Jones, R.A. *Self-fulfilling prophecies: Social, psychological, and physiological effects of expectancies.* Hillsdale, N.J.: Lawrence Erlbaum Associates, 1977.

Jones, R.L. Labels & stigma in special education. *Exceptional Children,* 1972, *38,* 553–564.

Jones, R.L. Accountability in special education: Some problems. *Exceptional Children,* 1973, *39,* 631–642.

Jones, S.C., & Panitch, D. The self-fulfilling prophecy and interpersonal attraction. *Journal of Experimental Social Psychology,* 1971, *7,* 356–366.

Jose, J., & Cody, J.J. Teacher pupil interaction as it relates to attempted changes in teacher expectancy of academic ability and achievement. *American Educational Research Journal,* 1971, *8,* 39–49.

Joynson, R.B. Michotte's experimental methods. *British Journal of Psychology,* 1971, *62,* 293–302.

Julian, J.W., & Perry, F.A. Cooperation contrasted with intragroup and intergroup competition. *Sociometry,* 1967, *30,* 79–90.

Kagan, J. *Personality development.* New York: Harcourt, 1971.

Kagan, J., & Moss, H.A. *Birth to maturity.* New York: Wiley, 1962.

Kail, R.V., & Siegel, A.W. The development of mnemonic encoding in children: From perception to abstraction. In R.V. Kail & J.W. Hagen (Eds.) *Perspectives in the development of memory and cognition.* Hillsdale, N.J.: Lawrence Erlbaum Associates, 1977.

Kanfer, F.H. The many faces of self-control, as behavior modification changes its focus. In R.B. Stuart (Ed.), *Behavioral self management.* New York: Brunner/Mazel, 1977.

Kanfer, F.H., Cox, L.E., Greiner, J.M., & Karoly, P. Contracts, demand characteristics and self-control. *Journal of Personality and Social Psychology,* 1974, *30,* 605–619.

Kanfer, F.H., & Goldfoot, D.A. Self-control and tolerance of noxious stimulation. *Psychological Reports,* 1966, *18,* 79–85.

Kant, I. Kritik der reinen vernunft. In W. Kaufmann (Ed.), *Philosophic Classics* (Vol. 2). *Bacon to Kant.* Englewood Cliffs, N.J.: Prentice-Hall, 1961. (Originally published, 1781.)

Kaplan, H. I., & Kaplan, H.S. The psychosomatic concept of obesity. *Journal of Nervous and Mental Disease,* 1957, *124,* 181–201.

Karlins, M., Coffman, T., & Walters, G. On the fading of social stereotypes: Studies in three generations of college students. *Journal of Personality and Social Psychology,* 1969, *13, 1–16.*

Karlovac, M., Feldman, N.S., Higgins, E.T., & Ruble, D.N. *The effect of consensus information on causal attributions.* Paper presented at the American Psychological Association, Washington, D.C., September 1976.

Karniol, R., & Miller, D.T. *Changes in reward evaluations in two delay contexts.* Unpublished manuscript, Tel Aviv University, 1980.

Karniol, R., & Ross, M. The development of causal attributions in social perception. *Journal of Personality and Social Psychology,* 1976, *34,* 455–464.

Karniol, R., & Ross, M. The effect of performance-relevant and performance-irrelevant rewards on children's intrinsic motivation. *Child Development,* 1977, *48,* 482–487.

Karniol, R., & Ross, M. Children's use of a causal attribution schema and the influence of manipulative intentions. *Child Development,* 1979, *50,* 463–468.

Kassin, S.M. Consensus information, prediction, and causal attribution: A review of the literature and issues. *Journal of Personality and Social Psychology,* 1979, *37,* 1966–1981.

Kassin, S.M. *Heider and Simmel revisited: Causal attribution and the animated film technique.* Invited paper presented at the Midwestern Psychological Association, St. Louis, May 1980.

Kassin, S.M., & Gibbons, F.X. *Mentally retarded adolescents' use of the augmentation principle: Perceptual versus verbal approaches.* Paper presented at the American Psychological Association, Montreal, September 1980.

Kassin, S.M., & Gibbons, F.X. Children's use of the discounting principle in their perceptions of exertion. *Child Development,* in press.

Kassin, S.M., & Hochreich, D.J. Instructional set: A neglected variable in attribution research? *Personality and Social Psychology Bulletin,* 1977, *3,* 620–623.

Kassin, S.M., & Lowe, C.A. *Kelley's attribution theory: A perceptual approach.* Paper presented at the Eastern Psychological Association, Philadelphia, April 1979. (a)

Kassin, S.M., & Lowe, C.A. On the development of the augmentation principle: A perceptual approach. *Child Development, 1979, 50,* 728–734. (b)

Kassin, S.M., Lowe, C.A., & Gibbons, F.X. Children's use of the discounting principle: A perceptual approach. *Journal of Personality and Social Psychology,* 1980, *39,* 719–728.

Katz, P.A. The acquisition of racial attitudes in children. In P.A. Katz (Ed.), *Toward the Elimination of Racism.* New York: Pergamon, 1976.

Kaye, H. Infant sucking behavior and its modification. In L.P. Lipsitt & C.C. Spiker (Eds.). *Advances in child development and behavior (Vol. 3). New York: Academic Press, 1967.*

Kazdin, A.E., & Bootzin, R.R. The token economy: An examination of issues. In R.D. Rubin, J.P. Brady, & J.D. Henderson (Eds.), *Advances in Behavior Therapy (Vol. 4). New York: Academic Press, 1973.*

Kehle, T.J., Bramble, W.J., & Mason, E.J. Teachers' expectations: Ratings of student performance as biased by student characteristics. *Journal of Experimental Education,* 1974, *43,* 54–60.

Kehle, T.J., Ware, C.L., & Guidubaldi, J. *Effects of physical attractiveness, sex, and intelligence on expectations for students' academic ability and personality: A replication.* Paper presented at the Annual Meeting of the American Educational Research Association, San Francisco, April 1976.

Keil, F. The development of the young child's ability to anticipate the outcomes of simple causal events. *Child Development,* 1979, *50,* 455–462.

Kelley, H.H. The warm-cold variable in first impressions of persons. *Journal of Personality,* 1950, *18,* 431–439.

Kelley, H.H. Attribution theory in social psychology. In D. Levine (Ed.), *Nebraska symposium on motivation* (Vol. 15). Lincoln: University of Nebraska Press, 1967.

Kelley, H.H. *Causal schemata and the attribution process.* Morristown, N.J.: General Learning Press, 1971.

Kelley, H.H. Attribution in social interaction. In E.E. Jones, D.E. Kanouse, H.H. Kelley, R.E. Nisbett, S. Valins, & B. Weiner (Eds.), *Attribution: Perceiving the causes of behavior.* Morristown, N.J.: General Learning Press, 1972.

Kelley, H.H. The processes of causal attribution. *American Psychologist,* 1973, *28,* 107–128.

Kelman, H.C. Compliance, identification, and internalization: Three processes of opinion change. *Journal of Conflict Resolution,* 1958, *2,* 51–60.

Kelman, H.C. Processes of attitude change. *Public Opinion Quarterly,* 1961, *25,* 57–78.

Kenrick, D.T., Bauman, D.J., & Cialdini, R.B. A step in the socialization of altruism as hedonism: Effects of negative mood on children's generosity under public and private conditions. *Journal of Personality and Social Psychology,* 1979, *37,* 747–755.

Kent, R. A methodological critique of interventions for boys with conduct problems. *Journal of Consulting and Clincial Psychology,* 1976, *44,* 297–299.

Kipnis, D.M., & Kidder, L.H. *How failure strikes men and women.* Paper presented at the Annual Meeting of the American Psychological Association, Toronto, September 1978.

Klaiman, S. *Selected perceptual, cognitive, personality, and socialization variables as predictors of nonverbal sensitivity.* Unpublished doctoral dissertation, University of Ottawa, 1979.

Kleck, R.E., Richardson, S.A., & Ronald, C. Physical appearance cues and interpersonal attraction in children. *Child Development,* 1974, *45,* 305–310.

Knittle, J.L. Childhood obesity. *New York Academy of Medicine,* 1971, *47,* 579–589.

Knittle, J.L. Obesity in childhood: A problem in adipose tissue cellular development. *Pediatrics,* 1972, *81,* 1048.

Kohlberg, L. Stage and sequence: The cognitive-developmental approach to socialization. In D. Goslin (Ed.), *Handbook of socialization theory and research.* Chicago: Rand McNally, 1969.

Kohlberg, L. From "is" to "ought": How to commit the naturalistic fallacy and get away with it in the study of moral development. In T. Mischel (Ed.), *Cognitive development and epistemology.* New York: Academic Press, 1971.

Kohlberg, L. Moral stages and moralization: The cognitive-developmental approach. In T. Lickona (Ed.), *Moral development and behavior: Theory, research, and social issues.* New York: Holt, Rinehart & Winston, 1976.

Kohlberg, L. Revisions in the theory and practice of moral development. In W. Damon (Ed.), *Moral development.* San Francisco: Jossey-Bass, 1978.

Kohlberg, L., & Ullian, D. Development of psychosexual concepts. In R.C. Friedman, R.M. Richart, & R.L. Vande Wiele (Eds), *Sex differences in behavior.* New York: Wiley, 1974.

Krantz, D.S., Sanmarco, M.E., Selvester, R.H., & Matthews, K.A. Psychological correlates of progression of atherosclerosis in men. *Psychosomatic Medicine,* 1979, *41,* 467–475.

Krebs, D.L. Altruism—An examination of the concept and a review of the literature. *Psychological Bulletin,* 1970, *73,* 254–303.

Krebs, D.L. Empathy and altruism. *Journal of Personality and Social Psychology,* 1975, *32,* 1134–1146.

Krebs, D.L., & Sturrup, B. *Role-taking ability and altruistic behavior in elementary school children.* Paper presented at the annual meeting of the American Psychological Association, New Orleans, September 1974.

Kruglanski, A.W. Endogenous attribution and intrinsic motivation. In M.R. Lepper & D. Greene (Eds.), *The hidden costs of reward.* Hillsdale, N.J.: Lawrence Erlbaum Associates, 1978.

Kruglanski, A.W., Alon, S., & Lewis, T. Retrospective misattribution and task enjoyment. *Journal of Experimental Social Psychology,* 1972, *8,* 493–501.

Kruglanski, A.W., Friedman, I., & Zeevi, G. The effects of extrinsic incentives on some qualitative aspects of task performance. *Journal of Personality,* 1971, *39,* 606–617.

Kruglanski, A.W., Schwartz, J.M., Maides, S., & Hamel, I.Z. Covariation, discounting, and augmentation: Towards a clarification of attribution principles. *Journal of Personality,* 1978, *46,* 176–189.

Kruglanski, A.W., Stein, C., & Riter, A. Contingencies of exogenous reward and task performance: On the "minimax" principle in instrumental behavior. *Journal of Applied Social Psychology*, 1977, *7*, 141–148.

Kuhlen, R.G., & Lee, B.J. Personality characteristics and social acceptability in adolescence. *Journal of Educational Psychology*, 1943, *34*, 321–340.

Kuhn, D., & Ho, V. The development of schemes for recognizing additive and alternative effects in a "natural experiment" context. *Developmental Psychology*, 1977, *13*, 515–516.

Kuhn, D., & Phelps, H. The development of children's comprehension of causal direction. *Child Development*, 1976, *47*, 248–251.

Kun, A. Development of the magnitude-covariation and compensation schemata in ability and effort attributions of performance. *Child Development*, 1977, *48*, 862–873.

Kun, A. Evidence for preschoolers' understanding of causal direction in extended causal sequences. *Child Development*, 1978, *49*, 218–222. (a)

Kun, A. *Perceived additivity of intrinsic and extrinsic motivation in young children: Refutation of the "overjustification" hypothesis.* Paper presented at the American Psychological Association, Toronto, August 1978. (b)

Kun, A., Murray, J., & Sredl, K. Misuses of the multiple sufficient cause scheme as a model of naive attribution: A case of mistaken identity. *Developmental Psychology*, 1980, *16*, 18–22.

Kun, A., Parsons, J.E., & Ruble, D.N. Development of integration processes using ability and effort information to predict outcome. *Developmental Psychology*, 1974, *10*, 721–732.

Kun, A., & Weiner, B. Necessary versus sufficient causal schemata for success and failure. *Journal of Research in Personality*, 1973, *7*, 197–207.

Kurtzberg, R.L., Safar, H., & Cavior, N. Surgical and social rehabilitation of adult offenders. *Proceedings of the 76th Annual Convention of the American Psychological Association*, 1968, *3*, 649–650.

Langlois, J.H., & Downs, A.C. Peer relations as a function of physical attractiveness: The eye of the beholder or behavioral reality? *Child Development*, 1979, *50*, 409–418.

Langlois, J.H., Gottfried, N.W., Barnes, B.M., & Hendricks, D. The influence of peer age on the social behavior of preschool children. *Journal of Genetic Psychology*, 1978, *132*, 11–19.

Langlois, J.H., Gottfried, N.W., & Seay, B. The influence of sex of peer on the social behavior of preschool children. *Developmental Psychology*, 1973, *8*, 93–98.

Langlois, J.H., & Stephan, C. The effects of physical attractiveness and ethnicity on children's behavioral attributions and peer preferences. *Child Development*, 1977, *48*, 1694–1698.

Langlois, J.H., & Styczynski, L. The effects of physical attractiveness on the behavioral attributions and peer preferences in acquainted children. *International Journal of Behavioral Development*, 1979, *2*, 325–341.

Lansdown, R., & Polak, L. A study of the psychological effects of facial deformity in children. *Child: Care, Health, and Development*, 1975, *1*, 85–91.

Larsen, G.Y. Methodology in developmental psychology: An examination of research on Piagetian theory. *Child Development*, 1977, *48*, 1160–1166.

Lawler, K.A., Allen, M.T., Critcher, E.C., & Standard, B.A. The relationship of physiological responses to the coronary-prone behavior pattern in children. *Journal of Behavioral Medicine*, in press.

Lazarus, R.S., Speisman, J.C., Mordkoff, A.M., & Davidson, L.A. A laboratory study of psychological stress produced by a motion picture film. *Psychological Monographs*, 1962, *76*, No.34.

Lazarus, R.S. *Patterns of adjustment and human effectiveness*, (3rd ed). New York: McGraw-Hill, 1976.

Lefcourt, H.M. Recent developments in the study of locus of control. In B.A. Maher (Ed.), *Progress in experimental personality research*. New York: Academic Press, 1970.

Leon, G.R., & Chamberlain, K. Comparison of daily eating habits and emotional states of overweight persons successful or unsuccessful in maintaining a weight loss. *Journal of Consulting and Clinical Psychology*, 1973, *41*, 108–115.(a)

Leon, G.R., & Chamberlain, K. Emotional arousal, eating patterns, and body image as differential factors associated with varying success in maintaining a weight loss. *Journal of Consulting and Clinical Psychology*, 1973, *40*, 474–480.(b)

Leon, G.R., & Roth, L. Obesity: Psychological

causes, correlations and speculations. *Psychological Bulletin,* 1977, *84,* 117–139.

Lepper, M.R. Dissonance, self-perception, and honesty in children. *Journal of Personality and Social Psychology,* 1973, *25,* 65–74.

Lepper, M.R. Intrinsic and extrinsic motivation in children: Detrimental effects of superfluous social controls. In W.A. Collins (Ed.), *Aspects of the development of competence: Minnesota symposia on child psychology* (Vol. 14). Hillsdale, N.J.: Lawrence Erlbaum Associates, 1981.

Lepper, M.R. Social control processes, attributions of motivation, and the internalization of social values. In E.T. Higgins, D.N. Ruble, & W.W. Hartup (Eds.), *Social cognition and social behavior: A developmental perspective.* San Francisco: Jossey-Bass, in press.

Lepper, M.R., & Dafoe, J. Incentives, constraints, and motivation in the classroom: An attributional analysis. In I.H. Frieze, D. Bar-Tal, & J.S. Carroll (Eds.), *Attribution theory: Applications to social problems.* San Franscisco: Jossey-Bass, 1979.

Lepper, M.R., & Gilovich, T. *Promoting generalized compliance from children with activity-oriented requests: Effects of accentuating the positive.* Unpublished manuscript, Stanford University, 1980.

Lepper, M.R., Gilovich, T., & Rest, G. *Detrimental effects of extrinsic rewards on immediate task performance vs. subsequent intrinsic interest.* Stanford University, research in progress.

Lepper, M.R., & Greene, D. Turning play into work: Effects of adult surveillance and extrinsic rewards on children's intrinsic motivation. *Journal of Personality and Social Psychology,* 1975, *31,* 479–486.

Lepper, M.R., & Greene, D. On understanding "overjustification": A reply to Reiss and Sushinsky. *Journal of Personality and Social Psychology,* 1976, *33,* 25–35.

Lepper, M.R., & Greene, D. Divergent approaches to the study of rewards. In M.R. Lepper & D. Greene (Eds), *The hidden costs of reward.* Hillsdale, N.J.: Lawrence Erlbaum Associates, 1978.(a)

Lepper, M.R., & Greene, D. (Eds). *The hidden costs of reward.* Hillsdale, N.J.: Lawrence Erlbaum Associates, 1978.(b)

Lepper, M.R., & Greene, D. Overjustification research and beyond: Toward a means-ends analysis of intrinsic and extrinsic motivation. In M.R. Lepper & D. Greene (Eds.), *The hidden costs of reward.* Hillsdale, N.J.: Lawrence Erlbaum Associates, 1978.(c)

Lepper, M.R., Greene, D., & Nisbett, R.E. Undermining children's intrinsic interest with extrinsic rewards: A test of the "overjustification" hypothesis. *Journal of Personality and Social Psychology,* 1973. *28,* 129–137.

Lepper, M.R., Sagotsky, G., Dafoe, J., & Greene, D. *Consequences of superfluous social constraints: Effects on young children's social inferences and subsequent intrinsic interest.* Unpublished manuscript, Stanford University, 1980.

Lepper, M.R., Sagotsky, G., & Greene, D. *Overjustification effects following multiple-trial reinforcement procedures: Experimental evidence concerning the assessment of intrinsic interest.* Unpublished manuscript, Stanford University, 1980.(a)

Lepper, M.R., Sagotsky, G., & Greene, D. *Self-determination, extrinsic rewards, and intrinsic interest in preschool children.* Unpublished manuscript, Stanford University, 1980.(b)

Lepper, M.R., Sagotsky, G., & Mailer, J. Generalization and persistence of effects of exposure to self-reinforcement models. *Child Development,* 1975, *46,* 618–630

Lepper, M.R., Zanna, M.P., & Abelson, R.P. Cognitive irreversibility in a dissonance-reduction situation. *Journal of Personality and Social Psychology,* 1970, *16,* 191–198.

Lerner, E. *Constraint areas and the moral judgment of children.* Menasha, Wis.: Banta, 1937.

Lerner, M. The justice motive: Some hypotheses as to its origins and forms. *Journal of Personality,* 1976, *45,* 1–52.

Lerner, R.M. *Concepts and theories of human development.* Reading, Mass.: Addison-Wesley, 1976.

Lerner, R.M., & Karabenick, S.A. Physical attractiveness, body attitudes, and self-concept in late adolescents. *Journal of Youth and Adolescence,* 1974, *3,* 307–316.

Lerner, R.M., & Knapp, J.R. The structure of racial attitudes in children. *Journal of Youth and Adolescence,* 1976, *5,* 283–300.

Lerner, R.M., & Korn, S.J. The development of body-build stereotypes in males. *Child Development,* 1972, *43,* 908–920.

Lerner, R.M., & Lerner, J.V. Effects of age, sex, and physical attractiveness on child-peer relations, academic performance, and elementary school adjustment. *Developmental Psychology,* 1977, *13,* 585–590.

Lesser, H. The growth of perceived causality in children, *Journal of Genetic Psychology*, 1977, *130*, 145–152.

Leventhal, G.S. The distribution of rewards and resources in groups and organizations. In L. Berkowitz & E. Walster (Eds.), *Advances in experimental social psychology* (Vol. 9), New York: Academic Press, 1976.

Levine, J.M. *Social comparison: A review and integration with special relevance to education*. Unpublished manuscript, Learning Research and Development Center, University of Pittsburgh, 1979.

Levine, J.M., & Snyder, H.N. *Perceived peer ability and linking in the classroom*. Unpublished manuscript, Learning Research and Development Center, University of Pittsburgh, 1978.

LeVine, R.A., & Campbell, D.T. *Ethnocentrism*. New York: Wiley, 1972.

Levinger, G. A three-level approach to attraction: Toward an understanding of pair relatedness. In T.L. Huston (Ed.), *Foundations of interpersonal attraction*, New York: Academic Press, 1974.

Levy, D.M., & Tulchin, S.H. The resistance of infants and children during mental tests. *Journal of Experimental Psychology*, 1923, *6*, 304–322.

Levy, D.M., & Tulchin, S.H. The resistant behavior of infants and children. *Journal of Experimental Psychology*, 1925, *8*, 209–224.

Lewin, K. *A dynamic theory of personality*. New York: McGraw-Hill, 1935.

Lewin, K., Lippett, R., & White, R. Patterns of aggressive behavior in experimentally created "social climates." *Journal of Social Psychology*, 1939, *10*, 271–299.

Lewis, M., & Rosenbloom, L.A. (Eds.). *The effect of the infant on its caregiver*. New York: Wiley, 1974.

Lewis, R., & St. John, N. Contributions of cross-racial friendship to minority group achievement in desegregated classrooms. *Sociometry*, 1972, *37*, 79–91.

Lickona, T. A cognitive-developmental approach to interpersonal attraction. In T.L. Huston (Ed.). *Foundations of interpersonal attraction*. New York: Academic Press, 1974.

Liebelt, R.A. Response of adipose tissue in experimental obesity as influenced by genetic, hormonal, and neurogenic factors. *Annals of the New York Academy of Science*, 1963, *110*, 723–748.

Lippitt, P., Eiseman, J., & Lippitt, R. *Cross-age helping program: Orientations, training and related materials*. Ann Arbor: University of Michigan, Center for Research on Utilization of Scientific Knowledge, Institute for Social Research, 1969.

Lippitt, P., & Lohman, J.E. Cross-age relationships—An educational resource. *Children*, 1965, *12*, 113–117.

Lipsitt, L.P., & Kaye, H. Conditioned sucking in the human newborn. *Psychonomic Science*, 1964, *1*, 29–30.

Little, B.R. Age and sex differences in the use of psychological, role and physicalistic constructs. *Bulletin of the British Psychological Society*, 1968, *21*, 34.

Livesley, W., & Bromley, D. *Person perception in childhood and adolescence*. London: Wiley, 1973.

London, P. The rescuers: Motivational hypotheses about Christians who saved Jews from the Nazis. In J. Macaulay & L. Berkowitz (Eds.), *Altruism and helping behavior*. New York: Academic Press, 1970.

Lorr, M., & Zea, R.L. Moral judgment and liberal-conservative attitude. *Psychological Reports*, 1977, *40*, 627–629.

Loveland, K.K., & Olley, J.G. The effect of external reward on interest and quality of task performance in children of high and low intrinsic motivation. *Child Development*, 1979, *50*, 1207–1210.

Lowe, C.A., & Kassin, S.M. On the use of consensus: Prediction, attribution and evaluation. *Personality and Social Psychology Bulletin*, 1977, *3*, 616–619.

Luchins, A. Primacy-recency in impression formation. In C. Hovland, W. Mandell, E. Campbell, T. Brock, A. Luchins, A. Cohen, W. McGuire, I. Janis, R. Feirabend, & N. Anderson (Eds.), *The order of presentation in persuasion*. New Haven: Yale University Press, 1957.

Lucker, G.W., Rosenfield, D., Sikes, J., & Aronson, E. Performance in the interdependent classroom: A field study. *American Educational Research Journal*, 1976, *13*, 115–123.

Luginbuhl, J., Crowe, D., & Kahan, J. Causal attributions for success and failure. *Journal of Personality and Social Psychology*, 1975, *31*, 86–93.

Luria, A. *The role of speech in the regulation of normal and abnormal behaviors*. New York: Liveright, 1961.

Lyle, W.H., & Levitt, E.E. Punitiveness, authoritarianism, and parental discipline of grade school children. *Journal of Abnormal and Social Psychology*, 1955, *51*, 42–46.

Lytton, H. Correlates of compliance and the rudiments of conscience in two-year-old boys. *Canadian Journal of Behavioral Science*, 1977, *9*, 242–251.

Lytton, H. Disciplinary encounters between young boys and their mothers and fathers: Is there a contingency system? *Developmental Psychology*, 1979, *15*, 256–268.

Lytton, H., & Zwirner, W. Compliance and its controlling stimuli observed in a natural setting. *Developmental Psychology*, 1975, *11*, 769–779.

Maccoby, E.E., & Jacklin, C.N. *The psychology of sex differences*. Stanford, Calif.: Stanford University Press, 1974.

MacDougall, R. Contrary suggestion. *Journal of Abnormal Psychology*, 1911–1912, *6*, 368–391.

MacLean, P.D. Contrasting functions of limbic and neocortical systems of the brain and their relevance to psychophysiological aspects of medicine. In E. Gellhorn (Ed.), *Biological foundations of emotion*. Glenview, Ill.: Scott, Foresman, 1968.

MacLean, P.D. The hypothalamus and emotional behavior. In W. Haymaker, E. Anderson, & W.J.H. Nanta (Eds.), *The hypothalamus*. Springfield, Ill.: Charles C. Thomas, 1969.

MacLean, P.D. The limbic brain in relation to the psychoses. In P.H. Black (Ed.), *Physiological correlates of emotion*. New York: Academic Press, 1970.

MacMillan, D.L. Motivational differences: Cultural-familial retardates vs. normal subjects on expectancy for failure. *American Journal of Mental Deficiency*, 1969, *74*, 254–257.

MacMillan, D.L. Effects of expecting success and failure on the situational expectancy of EMR and nonretarded children. *American Journal of Mental Deficiency*, 1975, *80*, 90–95.

MacMillan, D.L., Jones, R.L., & Aloia, G.P. The mentally retarded label: A theoretical analysis and review of research. *American Journal of Mental Deficiency*, 1974, *79*, 241–261.

MacMillan, D.L., & Keough, B.K. Normal and retarded children's expectancy for failure. *Developmental Psychology*, 1971, *4*, 343–348.

Maehr, M.L. Culture and achievement motivation. *American Psychologist*, 1974, *29*, 887–896.

Maehr, M.L., & Nicholls, J.G. Culture and achievement motivation: A second look. In N. Warren (Ed.), *Studies in cross-cultural psychology* (Vol. 3). New York: Academic Press, in press.

Mahoney, M.J. Self-reward and self-monitoring techniques for weight control. *Behavior Therapy*, 1974, *5*, 48–57.

Mahoney, M.J. Reflections on the cognitive-learning trend in psychotherapy. *American Psychologist*, 1977, *32*, 5–13.

Mann, J.F., & Taylor, D.M. Attribution of causality: Role of ethnicity and social class. *Journal of Social Psychology*, 1974, *94*, 3–13.

Manuck, S.B., & Garland, F.N. Coronary-prone behavior pattern, task incentive, and cardiovascular response. *Psychophysiology*, 1979, *16*, 136–142.

Marini, N.M., & Greenberger, E. Sex differences in educational aspirations and expectations. *American Educational Research Journal*, 1978, *15*, 67–79.

Mark, V.H., & Ervin, F.R. *Violence and the brain*. New York: Harper and Row, 1970.

Marston, A.R., London, B., & Cooper, L.M. A note on the eating behavior of children varying in weight. *Journal of Child Psychology*, 1976, *17*, 221–224.

Mason, W.A. The effects of social restriction on the behavior of rhesus monkeys: III. Tests of gregariousness. *Journal of Comparative and Physiological Psychology*, 1961, *54*, 287–290.

Masters, W.H., & Johnson, V.E. *Human sexual response*. Boston: Little, Brown, 1966.

Matson, W. What Rawls calls justice. *Occasional Review*, 1978, 45–55.

Matthews, K.A. Caregiver-child interactions and the Type A coronary-prone behavior pattern. *Child Development*, 1977, *48*, 1752–1756.

Matthews, K.A. Assessment and developmental antecedents of the coronary-prone behavior pattern in children. In T. Dembroski (Ed.), *Coronary-prone behavior*. New York: Springer-Verlag. 1978.

Matthews, K.A. Efforts of control by children and adults with the Type A coronary-prone behavior pattern. *Child Development*, 1979, *50*, 842–847.

Matthews, K.A., & Angulo, J. *Children's self-assessments of Type A behaviors*. Unpublished data, Kansas State University, 1978.

Matthews, K.A. & Angulo, J. Measurement of the Type A behavior pattern in children: Assessment of children's competitiveness, impatience-anger, and aggression. *Child Development*, 1980, *51*, 466–475

Matthews, K.A., Barnett, M.A., & Howard, J.A. *Children's empathic responses and the Type A behavior pattern.* Unpublished manuscript, University of Pittsburgh, 1979.

Matthews, K.A., Glass, D.C., Rosenman, R.H., & Bortner, R.W. Competitive drive, pattern A, and coronary heart disease: A further analysis of some data from the Western Collaborative Group Study. *Journal of Chronic Diseases,* 1977, *30,* 489–498.

Matthews, K.A., & Krantz, D.S. Resemblances of twins and their parents in pattern A behavior. *Psychosomatic Medicine,* 1976, *28,* 140–144.

Mayer J. Obesity during childhood. In M. Winick (Ed.), *Childhood obesity.* New York: Wiley, 1975.

Mayer, R.L. Delay therapy: Two case reports. *Behavior Therapy,* 1973, *4,* 709–711.

Mayers, B.A. Negativistic reactions of preschool children on the new revision of the Stanford-Binet. *Journal of Genetic Psychology,* 1935, *46,* 311–334.

McAdoo, J.L. *An exploratory study of racial attitude change in black preschool children using differential treatments.* Unpublished dissertation, University of Michigan, 1970.

McAfee, R.D., & Cleland, C.C. The discrepancy between self-concept and ideal self as a measure of psychological adjustment in educable mentally retarded males. *American Journal of Mental Deficiency,* 1965, *70,* 63–68.

McArthur, L.A. The how and what of why: Some determinants and consequences of causal attribution. *Journal of Personality and Social Psychology,* 1972, *22,* 171–193.

McArthur, L.Z. The lesser influence of consensus than distinctiveness information on causal attribution: A test of the person-thing hypothesis. *Journal of Personality and Social Psychology,* 1976, *33,* 733–742.

McArthur, L.Z., & Burstein, B. Field dependent eating and perception as a function of weight and sex. *Journal of Personality,* 1975, *43,* 402–420.

McCaffery, M. Brief episodes of pain in children. In B. Bergerson (Ed.), *Current concepts in clinical nursing* (Vol. 2). St. Louis: Mosby, 1969.

McCaffery, M. *Nursing management of the patient with pain.* Philadelphia: Lippincott, 1972.

McCord, W., McCord, J., & Zola, I.K. *Origins of crime.* New York: Columbia University Press, 1959.

McDonald, R.L., & Gynther, M.D. Relationship of self and ideal-self descriptions with sex, race, and class in southern adolescents. *Journal of Personality and Social Psychology,* 1965, *1,* 85–88.

McGraw, K.O. The detrimental effects of reward on performance: A literature review and a prediction model. In M.R. Lepper & D. Greene (Eds.), *The hidden costs of reward.* Hillsdale, N.J.: Lawrence Erlbaum Associates, 1978.

McGraw, K.O., & McCullers, J.C. Evidence of a detrimental effect of extrinsic incentives on breaking a mental set. *Journal of Experimental Social Psychology,* 1979, *15,* 285–294.

McLoyd, V.C. The effects of extrinsic rewards of differential value on high and low intrinsic interest. *Child Development,* 1979, *50,* 1010–1019.

McMahan, I.D. Relationships between causal attributions and expectancy of success. *Journal of Personality and Social Psychology,* 1973, *28, 108–114.*

McMillen, D.L., Sanders, D.Y., & Solomon, G.S. Self-esteem, attentiveness, and helping behavior. *Personality and Social Psychology Bulletin,* 1977, *3,* 257–261.

McNamara, S.S., Molot, M.A., Stremple, J.F., & Cutting, R.T. Coronary artery disease in combat casualities in Vietnam. *Journal of the American Medical Association,* 1971, *216,* 1185.

Mead, G.H. *Mind, self and society.* Chicago: University of Chicago Press, 1934.

Meehan, K.A., Woll, S.B., & Abbott, R.D. The role of dissimulation and social desirability in the measurement of moral reasoning. *Journal of Research in Personality,* 1979, *13,* 25–38.

Mehrabian, A., & Epstein, N. A measure of emotional empathy. *Journal of Personality,* 1972, *40,* 525–543.

Meichenbaum, D. *Cognitive-behavior modification.* New York: Plenum, 1977.

Meichenbaum, D., & Goodman, J. The developmental control of operant motor responding by verbal operants. *Journal of Experimental Child Psychology,* 1969, *7,* 553–565.

Meichenbaum, D., & Goodman, J. Training impulsive children to talk to themselves: A means of developing self-control. *Journal of Abnormal Psychology,* 1971, *77,* 115–126.

Mendelson, R., & Shultz, T.R. Covariation and temporal contiguity as principles of causal inference in young children. *Journal of Experimental Child Psychology,* 1976, *22,* 408–412.

Meyer, W., Bachmann, M., Biermann, U., Hempelmann, M., Ploger, F., & Spiller, H. The informational value of evaluative behavior: Influences of praise and blame on perceptions of ability. *Journal of Educational Psychology*, 1979, *71*, 259–268.

Michotte, A. *The perception of causality*. London: Methuen, 1963.

Midlarsky, E., & Bryan, J.E. Training charity in children. *Journal of Personality and Social Psychology*, 1967, *5*, 408–415.

Milich, R.S. A critical analysis of Schacter's externality theory of obesity. *Journal of Abnormal Psychology*, 1975, *84*, 586–588.

Mill, J.S. *A system of logic ratiocinative and inductive*. Toronto; University of Toronto Press, 1974. (Originally published, 1843.)

Miller, D.T. Ego involvement and attributions for success and failure. *Journal of Personality and Social Psychology*, 1976, *34*, 901–906.

Miller, D.T. Locus of control and the ability to tolerate gratification delay: When it is better to be an external. *Journal of Research in Personality*, 1978, *12*, 49–56.

Miller, D.T., & Karniol, R. Coping strategies and attentional mechanisms in self-imposed and externally-imposed delay situations. *Journal of Personality and Social Psychology*, 1976, *34*, 310–316.(a)

Miller, D.T., & Karniol, R. The role of rewards in externally and self-imposed delay of gratification. *Journal of Personality and Social Psychology*, 1976, *33*, 594–600.(b)

Miller, D.T., & Karniol, R. *Children's re-evaluations of rewards in a self-control situation: A test of the self-persuasion hypothesis*. Unpublished manuscript, University of British Columbia, 1980.

Miller, D.T., Norman, S.A., & Wright, E. Distortion in person perception as a consequence of the need for effective control. *Journal of Personality and Social Psychology*, 1978, *36*, 598–607.

Miller, D.T., & Ross, M. Self-serving biases in the attribution of causality: Fact or fiction? *Psychological Bulletin*, 1975, *62*, 213–225.

Miller, D.T., Weinstein, S., & Karniol, R. The effects of age and self-verbalization on children's ability to delay gratification. *Developmental Psychology*, 1978, *14*, 569–570.

Miller, N., & Maruyama, G. *Normative influence in desegregated classrooms*. Paper presented at the American Psychological Association, New York, 1979.

Miller, N.E., Barber, T.X., DiCara, L.V., Kamiya, J., Shapiro, D., & Stoyva, J. *Biofeedback and self-control*. Chicago: Aldine. 1974.

Miller, N.E., & Bugelski, R. Minor studies in aggression: The influence of frustrations imposed by the in-group attitudes expressed toward out-groups. *Journal of Psychology*, 1948, *25*, 437–442.

Miller, R.E., Banks, J., & Kuwahara, H. The communication of affect in monkeys: Cooperative reward conditioning, *Journal of Genetic Psychology*, 1966, *108*, 121–134.

Miller, R.E., Banks, J., & Ogawa, N. Communication of affect in "cooperative conditioning" of rhesus monkeys. *Journal of Abnormal and Social Psychology*, 1962, *64*, 343–348.

Miller, R.E., Banks, J., & Ogawa, N. Role of facial expression in "cooperative-avoidance conditioning" in monkeys. *Journal of Abnormal and Social Psychology*, 1963, *67*, 24–30.

Miller, R.E., Caul, W.F., & Mirsky, I.A. Communication of affect between feral and socially isolated monkeys. *Journal of Personality and Social Psychology*, 1967, *7*, 231–239.

Miller, R.E., Murphy, J.V., & Mirsky, I.A. Nonverbal communication of affect. *Journal of Clinical Psychology*, 1959, *15*, 155–158.

Miller, R.L., Brickman, P., & Bolen, D. Attribution versus persuasion as a means for modifying behavior. *Journal of Personality and Social Psychology*, 1975, *31*, 430–441.

Miller, R.L., & Suls, J.M. Affiliation preferences as a function of attitude and ability similarity. In J.M. Suls & R.L. Miller (Eds.), *Social comparison processes*. Washington, D.C.: Hemisphere, 1977.

Miller, S.A. Nonverbal assessment of Piagetian concepts. *Psychological Bulletin*, 1976, *83*, 405–430.

Minton, C., Kagan, J., & Levine, J.A. Maternal control and obedience in the two-year-old. *Child Development*, 1971, *42*, 1873–1894.

Mischel, H.N., Mischel, W., & Hood, S.Q. *The development of knowledge about self-control*. Unpublished manuscript, Stanford University, 1978.

Mischel, W. A social learning view of sex differences in behavior. In E.E. Maccoby (Ed.), *The development of sex differences*. Stanford, Calif.: Stanford University Press, 1966. (a)

Mischel, W. Theory and research on the antecedents of self-imposed delay of reward. In B.A. Maher (Ed.), *Progress in experimental personality research* (Vol. 3). New York: Academic Press, 1966. (b)

Mischel, W. *Personality and assessment.* New York: Wiley, 1968.

Mischel, W. Towards a cognitive social learning reconceptualization of personality. *Psychological Review*, 1973, *80*, 252–283.

Mischel, W. Processes in delay of gratification. In L. Berkowitz (Ed.), *Advances in experimental social psychology.* New York: Academic Press, 1974.

Mischel, W. On the future of personality measurement. *American Psychologist*, 1977, *4*, 246–254.

Mischel, W., & Baker, N. Cognitive appraisals and transformations in delay behavior. *Journal of Personality and Social Psychology*, 1975, *31*, 254–260.

Mischel, W., & Gilligan, C. Delay of gratification, motivation for the prohibited gratification and responses to temptation. *Journal of Abnormal and Social Psychology*, 1964, *69*, 411–417.

Mischel, W., & Mischel, H. A cognitive social-learning approach to morality and self-regulation. In T. Lickona (Ed.), *Moral development and behavior: Theory, research, and social issues.* New York: Holt, Rinehart & Winston, 1976.

Mischel, W., & Patterson, C.J. Efective plans for self-control in children. *Minnesota symposia on child psychology* (Vol. 11). New York: Thomas Y. Crowell, 1978.

Montemayor, R., & Eisen, M. The development of self-conceptions from childhood to adolescence. *Developmental Psychology*, 1977, *13*, 314–319.

Moore, B.S., Underwood, B., & Rosenhan, D.L. Affect and altruism. *Developmental Psychology*, 1973, *8*, 99–104.

Morland, J.K. Racial recognition by nursery school children in a Southern city. *Merrill-Palmer Quarterly*, 1962, *8*, 272–280.

Mosher, D.L., & Scodel, A. Relationships between enthnocentrism in children and the ethnocentrism and authoritarian rearing practices of their mothers. *Child Development*, 1960, *31*, 369–376.

Moss, M.K., & Page, R.A. Reinforcement and helping behavior. *Journal of Applied Social Psychology*, 1972, *2*, 360–371.

Much, N.C., & Schweder, R.A. Speaking of rules: The analysis of culture in breach. In W. Damon (Ed.), *Moral development.* San Francisco: Jossey-Bass, 1978.

Mullins, A.G. The prognosis in juvenile obesity. *Archives of Disease in Childhood*, 1958, *33*, 307–314.

Murray, S.R., & Mednick, M.T.S. Perceiving the causes of success and failure in achievement: Sex, race and motivational comparisons. *Journal of Consulting and Clinical Psychology*, 1975, *43*, 881–885.

Murstein, B.I. A theory of marital choice and its applicability to marriage adjustment. In B.I. Murstein (Ed.), *Theories of attracton and love.* New York: Springer, 1971.

Murstein, B.I. Physical attractiveness and marital choice. *Journal of Personality and Social Psychology*, 1972, *22*, 8–12.

Murstein, B.I. *Love, sex and marriage through the ages.* New York: Springer, 1974.

Mussen, P., Sullivan, L.B., & Eisenberg-Berg, N. Changes in political-economic attitudes during adolescence. *Journal of Genetic Psychology*, 1977, *130*, 69–76.

Neiberger, E.J. Children's response to suggestion. *Journal of Dentistry for Children*, 1978, *45*, 52–58.

Neisser, U. *Cognitive psychology.* New York: Appleton-Century-Crofts, 1967.

Nelson, J.F. *Personality and intelligence.* New York: Bureau of Publications, Teachers College, Columbia University, 1931.

Newcomb, T.M. *Personality and social change.* New York: Dryden Press, 1943.

Newtson, D. Foundations of attribution: The perception of ongoing behavior. In J.H. Harvey, W.J. Ickes, & R.F. Kidd (Eds.), *New directions in attribution research* (Vol. 1). Hillsdale, N.J.: Lawrence Erlbaum Associates, 1976.

Newtson, D., Engquist, G., & Bois, J. The objective basis of behavior units. *Journal of Personality and Social Psychology*, 1977, *35*, 847–862.

Nezlek, J., & Brehm, J.W. Hostility as a function of the opportunity to counteraggress. *Journal of Personality*, 1975, *43*, 421–433.

Nicholls, J.G. Causal attributions and other achievement-related cognitions: Effects of task outcome, attainment value, and sex. *Journal of Personality and Social Psychology*, 1975, *31*, 379–389.

Nicholls, J.G. Effort is virtuous, but it's better to have ability: Evaluative responses to perceptions of effort and ability. *Journal of Research in Personality*, 1976, *10*, 306–315.

Nicholls, J.G. The development of the concepts of

effort and ability, perception of academic attainment, and the understanding that difficult tasks require more ability. *Child Development*, 1978, *49*, 800–814.

Nicholls, J.G. *The development of cognitive mediation of difficulty level performances with different difficulty cues.* Paper presented at SRCD meeting, San Francisco, August 1979.

Nirje, B. The normalization principle and its human management implications. In R. Kugel & W. Wolfensberger (Eds.), *Changing patterns in residential services for the mentally retarded.* Washington: President's Committee on Mental Retardation, 1969, 227–254.

Nisbett, R.E. Taste, deprivation, and weight determinants of eating behavior. *Journal of Personality and Social Psychology*, 1968, *10*, 107–116.

Nisbett, R.E. Hunger, obesity, and the ventromedial hypothalamus. *Psychological Review*, 1972, *79*, 433–453.

Nisbett, R.E. Taste responsiveness, weight loss, and the ponderostat. *Physiology and Behavior*, 1973, *11*, 541–645.

Nisbett, R.E., & Borgida, E. Attribution and the psychology of prediction. *Journal of Personality and Social Psychology*, 1975, *32*, 932–943.

Nisbett, R.E., & Kanouse, D.E. Obesity, food deprivation, and supermarket shopping behavior. *Journal of Personality and Social Psychology*, 1969, *12*, 289–294.

Nisbett, R.E., & Ross, L. *Human inference: Strategies and shortcomings of social judgment.* Englewood Cliffs, N.J.: Prentice-Hall, 1980.

Nisbett, R.E., & Wilson, T.D. Telling more than we can know: Verbal reports on mental processes. *Psychological Review*, 1977, *84*, 231–259.

Notarius, C.I., & Levenson, R.W. Expressive tendencies and physiological response to stress. *Journal of Personality and Social Psychology*, 1979, *37*, 1204–1210.

Nucci, L.P., & Turiel, E. Social interactions and the development of social concepts in preschool children. *Child Development*, 1978, *49*, 400–407.

Ohman, A., & Dimberg, U. Facial expressions as conditioned stimuli for electrodermal responses: A case of "preparedness"? *Journal of Personality and Social Psychology*, 1978, *36*, 1251–1258.

Olds, J. Self-stimulation of the brain. *Science*, 1958, *127*, 315–324.

O'Leary, K.D., Poulos, R.W., & Devine, V.T. Tangible reinforcers: Bonuses or bribes? *Journal of Consulting and Clinical Psychology.* 1972, *38*, 1–8.

O'Leary, V.E., & Hansen, R.D. *Sex-determined attributions.* Paper presented at the Annual Meeting of the Eastern Psychological Association, Philadelphia, 1979.

Olum, V. Developmental differences in the perception of causality. *American Journal of Psychology*, 1956, *69*, 417–428.

Olweus, D. Stability of aggressive reaction patterns in males: A review. *Psychological Bulletin*, 1979, *86*, 852–875.

Oppenheimer, F. *System der Soziologie*, Tena: Fischer, 1922.

Oppenheimer, L. The development of the processing of social perspectives: A cognitive model. *International Journal of Behavior Development*, 1978, *1*, 149–1/1.

Ornstein, R. *On the experience of time.* Baltimore: Penguin, 1969.

Orr, S.P., & Lanzetta, J.T. Facial expressions of emotion as conditioned stimuli for human autonomic responses. *Journal of Personality and Social Psychology*, 1980, *30*, 278–282.

Orvis, B.R., Cunningham, J.D., & Kelley, H.H. A closer examination of causal inference: The roles of consensus, distinctiveness, and consistency information. *Journal of Personality and Social Psychology*, 1975, *32*, 605–616.

Osler, S.F., Draxl, M., & Madden, J. The utilization of verbal and perceptual cues by preschool children in concept identification problems. *Child Development*, 1977, *48*, 1071–1074.

Osler, W. *Lectures on angina pectoris and allied states.* New York: Appleton, 1897.

Paivio, A. *Imagery and verbal processes.* New York: Holt, 1971.

Parke, R.D., Hymel, S., Power, T., & Tinsley, B. Fathers and risk: A hospital based model of intervention. In D.B. Sawin, R.C. Hawkins, L.O. Walker, & J.H. Penticuff (Eds.), *Exceptional Infant IV: Psychosocial risks in infant-environment transactions.* New York: Brunner/Mazel, 1980.

Parke, R.D., & Sawin, D.B. *Infant characteristics and behavior as elicitors of maternal and paternal responsivity in the newborn period.* Paper presented at the meeting of the Society for Research in Child Development, Denver, Colorado, April 1975.

Parsons, J.E., & Goff, S. *Sex differences in achievement motivation: The influences of values, goals, and orientation.* Paper presented at the Annual Meeting of the Motivation and Education Group, Ann Arbor, Mich., 1978.

Parsons, J.E., & Ruble, D.N. *Attributional processes related to the development of achievement-related affect and expectancy.* Paper presented at the Annual Meeting of the American Psychological Association, Hawaii, August 1972.

Parten, M. Social participation among preschool children. *Journal of Abnormal and Social Psychology,* 1932, *27,* 243–269.

Passer, M.W. *Perceiving the causes of success and failure revisited: A multidimensional scaling approach.* Unpublished doctoral dissertation, University of California, Los Angeles, 1977.

Patterson, G.R. Interventions for boys with conduct problems: Multiple settings, treatments, criteria. *Journal of Consulting and Clinical Psychology,* 1974, *42,* 471–481.

Patterson, G.R. *Families* (Rev. ed.). Champaign, Ill.: Research Press, 1975.

Patterson, G.R. The aggressive child: Victim and architect of a coercive system. In E. Mash, L.A. Hamerlynck & L.C. Handy (Eds.), *Behavior modification and families.* New York: Brunner/Mazel, 1976.(a)

Patterson, G.R. *Living with children* (Rev. ed.). Champaign, Ill.: Research Press, 1976.(b)

Patterson, G.R., Littman, I., & Brown, T.R. Negative set and social learning. *Journal of Personality and Social Psychology,* 1968, *8,* 109–115.

Peevers, B.H., & Secord, P.F. Developmental changes in attribution of descriptive concepts to persons. *Journal of Personality and Social Psychology,* 1973, *27,* 120–128.

Pennebaker, J.W., & Burnam, M.A. Unpublished data, University of Texas, 1974.

Pepitone, A. Toward a normative and biocultural social psychology. *Journal of Personality and Social Psychology,* 1976, *34,* 641–653.

Pepitone, A., McCauley, C., & Hammond, P. Change in attractiveness of forbidden toys as a function of severity of threat. *Journal of Experimental Social Psychology,* 1967, *3,* 221–229.

Peraino, J.M. *Role-taking training, affect arousal, empathy, and generosity.* Unpublished manuscript, The University of California at Berkeley, 1977.

Perske, R. The dignity of risk and the mentally retarded. *Mental Retardation,* 1972, *101,* 24–27.

Peterson, R.F., & Whitehurst, G.J. A variable influencing the performance of generalized imitation. *Journal of Applied Behavior Analysis,* 1971, *4,* 1–9.

Pettigrew, T.F. Social evaluation theory: Convergencies and applications. In D. Levine (Ed.), *Nebraska symposium on motivation* (Vol. 15). Lincoln: University of Nebraska Press, 1967.

Pettigrew, T.F. *Racially separate or together?* New York: McGraw-Hill, 1971.

Pettigrew, T.F. The ultimate attribution error: Extending Allport's cognitive analysis of prejudice. *Personality and Social Psychology Bulletin,* 1979, *5,* 461–476.

Phillips, B.N. Effect of cohesion and intelligence on the problem-solving efficiency of small face-to-face groups in cooperative and competitive situations. *Journal of Educational Research,* 1956, *50,* 127–132.

Piaget, J. *The language and thought of the child.* New York: Harcourt Brace, 1926.

Piaget, J. *Judgment and reasoning in the child.* New York: Harcourt Brace, 1928.

Piaget, J. *The child's conception of physical causality.* London: Routledge & Kegan Paul, 1930.

Piaget, J. *The moral judgement of the child.* London: Routledge & Kegan Paul, 1932.

Piaget, J. *The construction of reality in the child.* New York: Basic Books, 1954.

Piaget, J. *Play, dreams and imitation in children.* London: Routledge & Kegan Paul, 1962.

Piaget, J. Piaget's theory. In P.H. Mussen (Ed.), *Carmichael's manual of child psychology* (3rd ed., Vol. 1). New York: Wiley, 1970.

Piaget, J., & Inhelder, B. *The child's conception of space.* New York: Norton, 1967.

Piliavin, I.M., Piliavin, J.A., & Rodin, J. Costs, diffusion, and the stigmatized victim. *Journal of Personality and Social Psychology,* 1975, *3,* 429–438.

Pittman, T.S., Cooper, E.E., & Smith, T.W. Attribution of causality and the overjustification effect. *Personality and Social Psychology Bulletin,* 1977, *3,* 280–283.

Pittman, T.S., Davey, M.E., Alafat, K.A., Wetherill, K.V., & Wirsul, N.A. Informational vs. controlling verbal rewards, levels of surveillance, and intrinsic motivation. *Personality and Social Psychology Bulletin,* 1980, *6,* 228–233.

Pliner, P.l. Effect of external cues on the thinking behavior of obese and normal subjects. *Journal of Abnormal Psychology,* 1973, *82,* 233–238.(a)

Pliner, P.L. Effect of liquid and solid preloads on eating behavior of obese and normal persons. *Physiology and Behavior*, 1973, *11*, 285–290.(b)

Pliner, P.L. Effects of cue salience on the behavior of obese and normal subjects. *Journal of Abnormal Psychology*, 1973, *82*, 226–232.(c)

Polivy, J. Perception of calories and regulation of intake in restrained and unrestrained subjects. *Addictive Behaviors*, 1976, *1*, 237–243.

Polivy, J., & Herman, C.P. Clinical depression and weight change: A complex relation. *Journal of Abnormal Psychology*, 1976, *85*, 338–340.

Polivy, J., Herman, C.P., Younger, J.C., & Erskine, B. Effects of a model on eating behavior: The induction of a restrained eating style. *Journal of Personality*, 1979, *47*, 100–117.

Porter, J. *Black child, white child: The development of racial attitudes*. Cambridge, Mass.: Harvard University Press, 1971.

Powell, G.J., & Fuller, M. Self-concept and school desegration. *Journal of Orthopsychiatry*, 1970, *40*, 303–304.

Price, J., & Grinker, J. Effects of degree of obesity, food deprivation, and palatability on eating behavior of humans. *Journal of Comparative and Physiological Psychology*, 1973, *85*, 265–271.

Prokasy, W., & Raskin, D. *Electrodermal activity in psychological research*. New York: Academic Press, 1973.

Raab, W., Chaplin, J.P., & Bajusz, E. Myocardial necroses produced in domesticated rats and in wild rats by sensory and emotional stresses. *Proceedings of the Society of Experimental Biology and Medicine*, 1969, *116*, 665–669.

Rachlin, H., & Green, L. Commitment, choice and self-control. *Journal of the Experimental Analysis of Behavior*, 1972, *17*, 15–22.

Radke, M., & Trager, H.G. Children's perceptions of the social roles of Negroes and whites. *Journal of Psychology*, 1950, *29*, 2–33.

Rahe, R.H., Hervig, L., & Rosenman, R.H. The heritability of Type A behavior. *Psychosomatic Medicine*, 1978, *40*, 478–486.

Raviv, Amiram, Bar-Tal, D., Raviv, Alona, and Bar-Tal, Y. Causal perceptions of success and failure by advantaged, integrated and disadvantaged pupils. *British Journal of Educational Psychology*, in press.

Ray, J.J. Conservatism, authoritarianism, and related variables: A review and empirical study. In G.D. Wilson (Ed.), *The psychology of conservatism*. New York: Academic Press, 1973.

Razran, G. The observable unconscious and the inferable conscious in current Soviet psychophysiology. *Psychological Review*, 1961, *68*, 81–147.

Read, R.H. Parents' expressed attitudes and children's behavior. *Journal of Consulting Psychology*, 1945, *9*, 95–100.

Redd, W.H. Social control by adult preference in operant conditioning with children. *Journal of Experimental Child Psychology*, 1974, *17*, 61–78.

Redd, W.H., & Wheeler, A.J. The relative effectiveness of monetary reinforcers and adult instructions in the control of children's choice behavior. *Journal of Experimental Child Psychology*, 1973, *16*, 63–75.

Reese, H.W., & Lipsitt, L.P. *Experimental child psychology*. New York: Academic Press, 1970.

Reese, H.W., & Schack, M.L. Comment on Brainerd's criteria for cognitive structures. *Psychological Bulletin*, 1974, *81*, 67–69.

Reid, J.B., & Patterson, G.R. Follow-up analyses of a behavioral treatment program for boys with conduct problems. *Journal of Consulting and Clinical Psychology*, 1976, *44*, 299–302.

Reiss, S., & Sushinsky, L.W. Overjustification, competing responses, and the acquisition of intrinsic interest. *Journal of Personality and Social Psychology*, 1975, *31*, 1116–1125.

Rest, J.R. Longitudinal study of the Defining Issues Test of moral judgment: A strategy for analysing developmental change. *Developmental Psychology*, 1975, *11*, 738–748.

Reynolds, M.M. *Negativism of pre-school children*. New York: Bureau of Publications, Teachers College, Columbia University, 1928.

Rheingold, H.L., Hay, D.F., & West, M.J. Sharing in the second year of life. *Child Development*, 1976, *47*, 1148–1158.

Rich, J. Effects of children's physical attractiveness on teachers' evaluations. *Journal of Educational Psychology*, 1975, *67*, 599–609.

Riemer, B.S. The influence of causal beliefs on affect and expectancy. *Journal of Personality and Social Psychology*, 1975, *31*, 1163–1167.

Rimm, I.J., & Rim, A.A. Association between juvenile onset obesity and severe adult obesity in 73,532 women. *American Journal of Public Health,* 1976, *6,* 479.

Roberts, A.H., & Rokeach, M. Anomie, authoritarianism, and prejudice: A replication. *American Journal of Sociology,* 1956, *61,* 355–358.

Roberts, S. *Order and dispute: An introduction to legal anthropology.* Harmondsworth: Penguin, 1979.

Robson, K.S. The role of eye-to-eye contact in maternal-infant attachment. *Journal of Child Psychology and Psychiatry,* 1967, *8,* 13–25.

Rodin, J. Effects of distraction on the performance of obese and normal subjects. In S. Schachter & J. Rodin, *Obese humans and rats.* Potomac, Md.: Lawrence Erlbaum Associates, 1974.(a)

Rodin, J. *Obesity and external responsiveness.* Paper presented at the Meeting of the Eastern Psychological Association, Philadelphia, April 1974.(b)

Rodin, J. Effects of obesity and set point on taste responsiveness and ingestion in humans. *Journal of Comparative and Physiological Psychology,* 1975, *89,* 1003–1008.

Rodin, J., Herman, C., & Schachter, S. Obesity and various tests of external sensitivity. In S. Schachter & J. Rodin, *Obese humans and rats.* Potomac, Md.: Lawrence Erlbaum Associates, 1974.

Rodin, J., & Slochower, J. Externality in the nonobese: Effects of environmental responsiveness on weight. *Journal of Personality and Social Psychology,* 1976, *33,* 338–344.

Roff, M. Childhood social interactions and young adult bad conduct. *Journal of Abnormal and Social Psychology,* 1961, *63,* 333–337.

Roff, M. Childhood social interaction and young adult psychosis. *Journal of Clinical Psychology,* 1963, *19,* 152–157.

Roff, M., Sells, S.B., & Golden, M.M. *Social adjustment and personality development in children.* Minneapolis: University of Minnesota Press, 1972.

Rose, H.E. & Mayer, J. Activity, caloric intake, and the energy balance of infants. *Pediatrics,* 1968, *41,* 18.

Rosenbach, D., Crockett, W., & Wapner, S. Developmental level, emotional involvement, and the resolution of inconsistency in impression formation. *Developmental Psychology,* 1973, *8,* 120–130.

Rosenbaum, R.M. *A dimensional analysis of the perceived causes of success and failure.* Unpublished doctoral dissertation, University of California, Los Angeles, 1972.

Rosenberg, M. *Society and the adolescent self-image.* Princeton, N.J.: Princeton University Press, 1965.

Rosenberg, M. Psychological selectivity in self-esteem formation. In C.W. Sherif & M. Sherif (Eds.), *Attitude, ego-involvement, and change.* New York: Wiley, 1967.

Rosenberg, M., & Simmons, P.G. *Black and white self-esteem: The urban school child.* Washington, D.C.: American Sociological Association, 1971.

Rosenblatt, J.S. Views on the onset and maintenance of maternal behavior in the rat. In L.R. Aronson, E. Tobach, D.S. Lehrman, & J.S.Rosenblatt, (Eds.), *Development and evolution of behavior.* San Francisco: W.H. Freeman, 1970.

Rosenfield, D., & Roberts, W.R. *The effects of success and failure upon liking for competent and incompetent members of cooperative and competitive groups.* Unpublished manuscript, Southern Methodist University, 1980.

Rosenfield, D., Sheehan, D.S., Marcus, M.M., & Stephan, W.G. Classroom structure and prejudice in desegregated schools. *Journal of Educational Psychology,* in press.

Rosenfield, D., & Stephan, W.G. Sex differences in attributions for sex-typed tasks. *Journal of Personality,* 1978, *46,* 244–259.

Rosenfield, D., Stephan, W.G., & Lucker, G.W. *Attraction to competent and incompetent members of cooperative and competitive groups.* Unpublished manuscript, Southern Methodist University, 1979.

Rosenhan, D. Some origins of concern for others. In P.A. Mussen, J. Langer, & M. Covington (Eds.), *Trends and issues in developmental psychology.* New York: Holt, Rinehart and Winston, 1969.

Rosenhan, D. The natural socialization of altruistic autonomy. In J. Macaulay & L. Berkowitz (Eds.), *Altruism and helping behavior.* New York: Academic Press, 1970.

Rosenman, R.H. The interview method of assessment of the coronary-prone behavior pattern. In T.M. Dembroski (Ed.), *Coronary-prone behavior.* New York: Springer-Verlag, 1978.

Rosenman, R.H., Brand, R.J., Jenkins, C.D., Friedman, M., Straus, R., & Worm, M. Coronary heart disease in the Western Collaborative Group Study: Final follow-up experience of 8½ years. *Journal of the American Medical Association*, 1975, *233*, 872–877.

Rosenthal, M.J., Finkelstein, M., Ni, E., & Robertson, R.E. A study of mother-child relationships in the emotional disorders of children. *Genetic Psychology Monographs*, 1959, *60*, 65–116.

Rosenthal, M.J., Ni, E., Finkelstein, M., & Berkwits, G.K. Father-child relationships and children's problems. *Archives of General Psychiatry*, 1962, *7*, 360–373.

Rosenthal, R., Archer, D., Koivumaki, J.H., DiMatteo, M.R., & Rogers, P. Assessing sensitivity to nonverbal communication: the PONS test. *Division 8 Newsletter*. Washington, D.C.: American Psychological Association, January 1974.

Rosenthal, R., & Jacobson, L. *Pygmalion in the classroom*. New York: Holt, Rinehart and Winston, 1968.

Ross, L. The "intuitive scientist" formulation and its developmental implications. In J. Flavell & L. Ross (Eds.), *Cognitive social development: Frontiers and possible futures*. Cambridge, Eng.: Cambridge University Press, in press.

Ross, L., Greene, D., & House, P. The "false consensus effect": An egocentric bias in social perception and attribution processes. *Journal of Experimental Social Psychology*, 1977, *13*, 279–301.

Ross, L., Turiel, E., Josephson, J., & Lepper, M.R. *Developmental perspectives on the fundamental attribution error*. Unpublished manuscript, Stanford University, 1978.

Ross, M. Salience of reward and intrinsic motivation. *Journal of Personality and Social Psychology*, 1975, *32*, 245–254.

Ross, M. The self-perception of intrinsic motivation. In J.H. Harvey, W.J. Ickes, & R.F. Kidd (Eds.), *New directions in attribution research* (Vol. 1). Hillsdale, N.J.: Lawrence Erlbaum Associates, 1976.

Ross, M., Karniol, R., & Rothstein, M. Reward contingency and intrinsic motivation in children: A test of the delay of gratification hypothesis. *Journal of Personality and Social Psychology*, 1976, *33*, 442–447.

Ross, M.B., & Salvia, J. Attractiveness as biasing factor in teacher judgment. *American Journal of Mental Deficiency*, 1975, *80*, 96–98.

Rothbart, M., Evans, M., & Fulero, S. Recall for confirming events: Memory processes and the maintenance of social stereotypes. *Journal of Experimental Social Psychology*, 1979, *15*, 343–355.

Rothbart, M., & Fulero, S. *Attributions of causality for important events: The profound motive fallacy*. Unpublished manuscript, University of Oregon, 1978.

Rubin, K.H., & Schneider, F.W. The relationship between moral judgment, egocentrism, and altruistic behavior. *Child Development*, 1973, *44*, 661–665.

Rubin, Z., & Peplau, L.A. Who believes in a just world? *Journal of Social Issues*, 1975, *31*, 65–89.

Ruble, D.N. *A developmental perspective of theories of achievement motivation*. Paper presented at the conference on Motivation and Education, University of Michigan, Ann Arbor, October 1978.

Ruble, D.N., Feldman, N.S., & Boggiano, A.K. Social comparison between young children in achievement situations. *Developmental Psychology*, 1976, *12*, 192–197.

Ruble, D.N., Feldman, N.S., Higgins, E.T., & Karlovac, M. Locus of causality and the use of information in the development of causal attributions. *Journal of Personality*, 1979, *47*, 595–614.

Ruble, D.N., Parsons, J.E., & Ross, J. Self-evaluative responses of children in an achievement setting. *Child Development*, 1976, *47*, 990–997.

Ruble, D.N., & Underkoffler, D. *Attributional processes mediating affective responses to success and failure: A developmental study*. Paper presented at the Annual Meeting of the Eastern Psychological Association, New York, April 1976.

Rushton, J.P. Generosity in children: Immediate and long-term effects of modeling, preaching, and moral judgment. *Journal of Personality and Social Psychology*, 1975, *31*, 459–466.

Rushton, J.P. Socialization and the altruistic behavior of children. *Psychological Bulletin*, 1976, *83*, 898–913.

Rushton, J.P., & Wiener, J. Altruism and cognitive development in children. *British Journal of Social and Clinical Psychology*, 1975, *14*, 341–349.

Rust, M.M. *The effects of resistance on intelligence scores of young children*. New York: Bureau of Publications, Teachers College, Columbia University, 1931.

Rutherford, E., & Mussen, P. Generosity in nursery school boys. *Child Development*, 1968, *39*, 755–765.

Sabatelli, R., Buck, R., & Dreyer, A. Communication via facial cues in intimate dyads. *Personality and Social Psychology Bulletin,* 1980, *6,* 242–247.

Sabatelli, R., Dreyer, A., & Buck, R. Cognitive style and the sending and receiving of facial cues. *Perceptual and Motor Skills,* 1979, *49,* 203–212.

Sackett, G.P. Monkeys reared in isolation with pictures as visual input: Evidence for an innate releasing mechanism. *Science,* 1966, *154,* 1468–1473.

Sagi, A., & Hoffman, M.L. Empathic distress in the newborn. *Developmental Psychology,* 1976, *12,* 175–176.

Salans, L.B. Cellularity of adipose tissue. In G.A. Bray & J.E. Bethune (Eds.), *Treatment and management of obesity.* New York: Harper and Row, 1974.

Salvia, J., Sheare, J.B., & Algozzine, B. Facial attractiveness and personal-social development. *Journal of Abnormal Child Psychology,* 1975, *3,* 171–178.

Sameroff, A. Transactional models in early social relations. *Human Development,* 1975, *18,* 65–79.

Sampson, E.E. On justice as equality. *Journal of Social Issues,* 1975, *31* 45–65.

Sawin, D.B., Underwood, B., Mostyn, M., & Weaver, J. *Empathy and altruism.* Unpublished manuscript, The University of Texas at Austin, 1980.

Scarboro, M.E., & Forehand, R. Effects of two types of response contingent time-out on compliance and oppositional behavior of children. *Journal of Experimental Child Psychology,* 1975, *19,* 252–264.

Scarlett, H.H., Press, A.N., & Crockett, W.H. Children's descriptions of peers: A Wernerian developmental analysis. *Child Development,* 1971, *42,* 439–453.

Schachter, S. The interaction of cognitive and physiological determinants of emotion state. In L. Berkowitz (Ed.), *Advances in experimental social psychology* (Vol. 1). New York: Academic Press, 1964.

Schachter, S. Some extraordinary facts about obese humans and rats. *American Psychologist,* 1971, *26,* 129–144.

Schachter, S., Friedman, L., & Handler, J. Who eats with chopsticks? In S. Schachter & J. Rodin (Eds.), *Obese humans and rats.* Potomac, Md.: Lawrence Erlbaum Associates, 1974.

Schachter, S., & Rodin, J. *Obese humans and rats.* Potomac, Md.: Lawrence Erlbaum Associates, 1974.

Scheier, M.F., Carver, C.S., Schulz, R., Glass, D.C., & Katz, I. Sympathy, self-consciousness, and reactions to the stigmatized. *Journal of Applied Social Psychology,* 1978, *8,* 270–282.

Scheirer, M.A., & Kraut, R.E. Increasing educational achievement via self-concept change. *Review of Educational Research,* 1979, *49,* 131–149.

Scherwitz, L., Berton, K., & Leventhal, H. Type A assessment and interaction in the behavior pattern interview. *Psychosomatic Medicine,* 1977, *39,* 229–240.

Schilit, J. The mentally retarded offender and criminal justice personnel. *Exceptional Children,* 1979, *46,* 16–22.

Schofield, J.W. Complementary and conflicting identities: Images and interaction in an interracial school. In S. Asher & J. Gottman (Eds.), *The development of friendship: Description and intervention.* Cambridge, Eng.: Cambridge University Press, 1980.

Schofield, J.W., & Sagar, H.A. Peer interaction patterns in an integrated middle school. *Sociometry,* 1977, *40,* 130–138.

Schonbach, P. Cognition, motivation and time perception. *Journal of Abnormal and Social Psychology,* 1959, *31,* 161–170.

Schucker, B., & Jacobs, D.R. Assessment of behavioral risk of coronary disease by voice characteristics. *Psychosomatic Medicine,* 1977, *39,* 219–228.

Schuster, S.O., & Gruen, G.E. Success and failure as determinants of performance predictions of mentally retarded and nonretarded children. *American Journal of Mental Deficiency,* 1971, *76,* 190–196.

Schwartz, S.H. Words, deeds, and the perception of consequences and responsibility in action situations. *Journal of Personality and Social Psychology,* 1968, *10,* 232–242.

Schwartz, S.H. Normative influences on altruism. In L. Berkowitz (Ed.), *Advances in experimental social psychology* (Vol. 10). New York: Academic Press, 1977.

Sears, R.R., Maccoby, E.E., & Levin, H. *Patterns of child rearing.* Evanston, Ill.: Row Peterson & Co., 1957.

Secord, P.F., & Backman, C.W. *Social psychology.* New York: McGraw-Hill, 1964.

Seitz, S., & Geske, D. Mothers' and graduate trainees' judgments of children: Some effects of labeling. *American Journal of Mental Deficiency,* 1976, *81,* 362–370.

Selman, R., & Byrne, D. A structural-developmental analysis of levels of role-taking in middle childhood. *Child Development*, 1974, *45*, 803–806.

Severance L., & Gasstrom, L. Effect of the label "mentally retarded" on causal attributions for success and failure outcomes. *American Journal of Mental Deficiency*, 1977, *81*, 547–555.

Shaklee, H. Development in inferences of ability and task difficulty. *Child Development*, 1976, *47*, 1051–1057.

Shantz, C.U. The development of social cognition. In E.M. Heatherington (Ed.), *Review of child development research* (Vol. 5). Chicago: University of Chicago Press, 1975.

Shapira, Z. Expectancy determinants of intrinsically motivated behavior. *Journal of Personality and Social Psychology*, 1976, *34*, 1235–1244.

Shultz, T.R., & Butkowsky, I. Young children's use of the scheme for multiple sufficient causes in the attribution of real and hypothetical behavior. *Child Development*, 1977, *48*, 464–469.

Shultz, T.R., Butkowsky, I., Pearce, J.W., & Shanfield, H. Development of schemes for the attribution of multiple psychological causes. *Developmental Psychology*, 1975, *11*, 502–510.

Shultz, T.R., & Mendelson, R. The use of covariation as a principle of causal analysis. *Child Development*, 1975, *46*, 394–399.

Shultz, T.R., & Ravinsky, F.B. Similarity as a principle of causal inference. *Child Development*, 1977, *48*, 1552–1558.

Siegler, R.S. Defining the locus of developmental differences in children's causal reasoning. *Journal of Experimental Child Psychology*, 1975, *20*, 512–525.

Siegler, R.S., & Liebert, R.M. Effects of contiguity, regularity, and age on children's causal inferences. *Developmental Psychology*, 1974, *10*, 574–579.

Silberman, C. *Crisis in the classroom.* New York: Random House, 1970.

Silverman, I. Physical attractiveness and courtship. *Sexual Behavior*, 1971, September, 22–25.

Silverstone, J.T. Psychological and social factors in the pathogenesis of obesity. In W. Burland, P. Samuels, & J. Yudkin (Eds.), *Obesity syndrome.* Edinburgh: Churchill Livingstone, 1974.

Simmons, R.G., Rosenberg, F., & Rosenberg,

M. Disturbance in the self-image at adolescence. *American Sociological Review*, 1973, *38*, 553–568.

Simon, H.A. Motivational and emotional controls of cognition. *Psychological Review*, 1967, *74*, 29–39.

Simon, J.G., & Feather, N.T. Causal attributions for success and failure at university examinations. *Journal of Educational Psychology*, 1973, *64*, 45–56.

Simpson, M.T., Olewine, D.A., Jenkins, C.D., Ramsey, F.H., Zyzanski, S.J., Thomas, G., & Hames, C.G. Exercise-induced catecholamines and platelet aggregation in the coronary-prone behavior pattern. *Psychosomatic Medicine*, 1974, *36*, 476–487.

Singh, D. Role of response habits and cognitive factors in determination of behavior of obese humans. *Journal of Personality and Social Psychology*, 1973, *27*, 220–238.

Skinner, B.F. *Science and human behavior.* New York: Macmillan, 1953.

Slavin, R.E. *Effects of biracial learning teams on cross-racial friendship and interaction.* Unpublished manuscript, The Johns Hopkins University, 1977. (Report No. 240, Center for the Social Organization of Schools)

Slovic, P. Hypothesis testing in the learning of positive and negative linear functions. *Organizational Behavior and Human Performance*, 1974, *11*, 368–376.

Smedslund, J. Psychological diagnostics. *Psychological Bulletin*, 1969, *71*, 234–248.

Smith, M.C. Children's use of the multiple sufficient causal schema in social perception. *Journal of Personality and Social Psychology*, 1975, *32*, 737–747.

Smith, T.W., & Pittman, T.S. Reward, distraction, and the overjustification effect. *Journal of Personality and Social Psychology*, 1978, *36*, 565–572.

Smith, W.F. *The effects of social and monetary rewards on intrinsic motivation.* Unpublished doctoral dissertation, Cornell University, 1976.

Snodgrass, S.R. Some relationships between socio-political ideology and moral character among college youth. *Journal of Youth and Adolescence*, 1975, *4*, 195–204.

Snodgrass, S.R. The development of trait inference. *Journal of Genetic Psychology*, 1976, *128*, 163–172.

Snyder, M., & Swann, W.B. Behavioral confirmation in social interaction: From social perception to social reality. *Journal of Ex-*

perimental Social Psychology, 1978, *14,* 148–160.

Snyder, M., Tanke, E.D., & Berscheid, E. Social perception and interpersonal behavior: On the self-fulfilling nature of social stereotypes. *Journal of Personality and Social Psychology,* 1977, *35,* 656–666.

Snyder, M., & Uranowitz, S.W. Reconstruction the past: Some cognitive consequences of person perception. *Journal of Personality and Social Psychology,* 1978, *36,* 941–950.

Snyder, M.L., & Jones, E.E. Attitude attribution when behavior is constrained. *Journal of Experimental Social Psychology,* 1974, *10,* 585–600.

Solomon, D., Ali, F.A., Kfir, D., Houlihan, K.A., & Yaeger, J. The development of democratic values and behavior among Mexican-American children. *Child Development,* 1972, *43,* 625–638.

Sorenson, R.L., & Maehr, M.L. Toward the experimental analysis of "continuing motivation." *Journal of Educational Research,* 1976, *69,* 319–322.

Spence, K.W. *Behavior theory and conditioning.* New Haven: Yale University Press, 1956.

Spock, B. *Baby and child care.* New York: Pocket Books, 1973.

Sroufe, A. The coherence of individual development. *American Psychologist,* 1979, *34,* 834–841.

Sroufe, R., Chaikin, A., Cook, R., & Freeman, V. The effects of physical attractiveness on honesty: A socially desirable response. *Personality and Social Psychology Bulletin,* 1977, *3,* 59–62.

Staffieri, J.R. Body build and behavioral expectancies in young females. *Developmental Psychology,* 1972, *6,* 125–127.

Stake, J.E. Effects of contrived information of female and male performance on the achievement behavior of preschool girls and boys. *Journal of Applied Social Psychology,* 1976, *6,* 85–93.

Staub, E. *Positive social behavior and morality, Vol. 1: Social and personal influence.* New York: Academic Press, 1978.

Staub, E. *Positive social behavior and morality, Vol. 2: Socialization and development.* New York: Academic Press, 1979.

Staw, B.M., Calder, B.J., & Hess, R.K. *Intrinsic motivation and norms about payment.* Unpublished manuscript, Northwestern University, 1978.

Stayton, D., Hogan, R., Ainsworth, M.D.S. Infant obedience and maternal behavior: The origins of socialization reconsidered. *Child Development,* 1971, *42,* 1057–1069.

Stein, A.H., Pohly, S.R., & Mueller, E. The influence of masculine, feminine, and neutral tasks on children's achievement behavior, expectancies of success, and attainment value. *Child Development,* 1971, *42,* 195–207.

Stendler, C., Damrin, D., & Haines, A.C. Studies in cooperation and competition: 1. The effects of working for group and individual rewards on the social climate of children's groups. *Journal of Genetic Psychology,* 1951, *79,* 173–197.

Stephan, C., & Tully, J.C. The influence of physical attractiveness of a plaintiff on the decisions of simulated jurors. *Journal of Social Psychology,* 1977, *101,* 149–150.

Stephan, W.G. Stereotyping: The role of ingroup-outgroup differences in causal attribution. *Journal of Social Psychology,* 1977, *101,* 255–266.

Stephan, W.G. School desegregation: An evaluation of predictions made in *Brown* v. *Board of Education. Psychological Bulletin,* 1978, *85,* 217–238.

Stephan, W.G., & Kennedy, J.C. An experimental study of inter-ethnic competition in segregated schools. *Journal of School Psychology,* 1975, *13,* 234–247.

Stephan, W.G., & Rosenfield, D. The effects of desegration on race relations and self-esteem. *Journal of Educational Psychology,* 1978, *70,* 670–679. (a)

Stephan, W.G., & Rosenfield, D. Effects of desegration on racial attitudes. *Journal of Personality and Social Psychology,* 1978, *36,* 795–804.(b)

Stephan, W.G., & Rosenfield, D. Black self-rejection: Another look. *Journal of Educational Psychology,* 1979, *71,* 706–716.

Stephan, W.G., & Rosenfield, D. Racial and ethnic stereotyping. In A.G. Miller (Ed.), *In the eye of the beholder: Contemporary issues in stereotyping.* New York: Holt, Rinehart and Winston, 1980.

Stevenson, H.W., & Stewart, E.C. A developmental study of racial awareness in young children. *Child Development,* 1958, *29,* 399–409.

Stimbert, V.E., & Coffey, K.R. Obese children and adolescents: A review. *ERIC Clearing-*

house on Early Childhood Education: Research Relating to Children, 1972, *30,* 1–30.

Stipek, D.J., & Hoffman, J.M. *Children's perceptions of the causes of failure.* Unpublished manuscript, University of California, Los Angeles, 1979.

St. John, N.H. *School desegregation: Outcomes for children.* New York: Wiley, 1975.

St. John, N.H., & Lewis, R.G. Race and social structure of the elementary classroom. *Sociology of Education,* 1975, *48,* 346–368.

Stotland, E. Exploratory studies of empathy. In L. Berkowitz (Ed.), *Advances in experimental social psychology* (Vol. 4). New York: Academic Press, 1969.

Strang, L., Smith, M.D., & Rogers, C.M. Social comparison, multiple reference groups, and the self-concepts of academically handicapped children before and after mainstreaming. *Journal of Educational Psychology,* 1978, *70,* 487–497.

Stroebe, W., Insko, C.A., Thompson, V.D. & Layton, B.D. Effects of physical attractiveness, attitude similarity, and sex on various aspects of interpersonal attraction. *Journal of Personality and Social Psychology,* 1971, *18,* 79–91.

Stunkard, A. New therapies for the eating disorders: Behavior modification of obesity and anorexia nervosa. In I. Marks, A. Bergin, P. Lang, J. Matarazzo, G. Patterson, & H. Strupp (Eds.), *Psychotherapy and behavior change 1972.* Chicago: Aldine, 1973.

Stunkard, A., d'Aquili, E., Fox, S., & Filion, R. Influence of social class on obesity and thinness in children. *Journal of the American Medical Association,* 1972, *221,* 579.

Stunkard, A., & Burt, V. Obesity and body image: II. Age at onset of disturbances in the body image. *American Journal of Psychiatry,* 1967, *123,* 1443–1447.

Stunkard, A., & Fox, S. The relationship of gastric motility and hunger: A summary of the evidence. *Psychosomatic Medicine,* 1971, *33,* 123–134.

Styczynski, L. *Effects of physical characteristics on the social, emotional, and intellectual development of early school age children.* Unpublished doctoral dissertation, The University of Texas at Austin, 1976.

Styczynski, L., & Langlois, J.H. The effects of familiarity on behavioral stereotypes associated with physical attractiveness in young children. *Child Development,* 1977, *48,* 1137–1141.

Sullivan, E.V., & Quarter, J. Psychological correlates of certain post-conventional moral types: A perspective on hybrid types. *Journal of Personality,* 1972, *40,* 149–161.

Sullivan, H.S. *The interpersonal theory of psychiatry.* New York: W.W. Norton, 1953.

Suls, J.M. Social comparison theory and research: An overview from 1954. In J.M. Suls & R.L. Miller (Eds.), *Social comparison processes.* Washington, D.C.: Hemisphere, 1977.

Suls, J.M., Gastorf, J., & Lawhon, J. Social comparison choices for evaluating a sex- and age-related ability. *Personality and Social Psychology Bulletin,* 1978, *4,* 102–105.

Suls, J.M., & Miller, R.L. (Eds.). *Social comparison processes.* Washington, D.C.: Hemisphere, 1977.

Sumner, F.C., & Johnson, E.E. Sex differences in levels of aspiration and in self-estimates of performance in a classroom situation. *The Journal of Psychology,* 1949, *27,* 483–490.

Surber, C.F. The utility of "simplification" as a developmental research strategy. *Child Development,* 1979, *50,* 571–574.

Swann, W.B., & Collins, W.A. *When persons become causes: Age and consensus as moderators of causal attribution.* Unpublished manuscript, University of Texas at Austin, 1978.

Swann, W.B., & Pittman, T.S. Initiating play activity of children: The moderating influence of verbal cues on intrinsic motivation. *Child Development,* 1977, *48,* 1125–1132.

Tagiuri, R. Person perception. In G. Lindzey & E. Aronson (Eds.), *The handbook of social psychology,* (Vol. 3). Reading, Mass.: Addison-Wesley, 1969.

Tajfel, H., Billig, M.G., Bundy, R.P., & Flament, C. Social categorization and intergroup behavior. *European Journal of Social Psychology,* 1971, *1,* 149–178.

Taplin, P. *Changes in parental consequation as a function of intervention.* Unpublished doctoral thesis, University of Wisconsin, 1974.

Taylor, D.M., & Jaggi, U. Ethnocentrism and causal attribution in a South Indian context. *Journal of Cross-Cultural Psychology,* 1974, *5,* 162–170.

Teglasi, H. Influence of situational factors on causal attributions of college females. *Psychological Bulletin,* 1977, *41,* 495–502.

Tennis, G.H., & Dabbs, J.M. Judging physical attractiveness: Effects of judges' own attractiveness. *Personality and Social Psychology Bulletin,* 1975, *1,* 513–516.

Terrell, G., & Ware, R. The role of delay of reward in speed of size and form discrimination learning in childhood. *Child Development*, 1961, *32*, 409–415.

Thaler, R., & Shefrin, H.M. *An economic theory of self-control*. Unpublished manuscript, Cornell University, 1979.

Thibaut, J.W., & Riecken, H.W. Some determinants and consequences of the perception of social causality. *Journal of Personality*, 1955, *24*, 113–133.

Thom, D.A. *Habit clinics for children of preschool age*. U. S. Department of Labor Publications, *135*, 1924.

Thoman, E. How a rejecting baby affects mother-infant synchrony. In *Ciba Foundation Symposium 33: Parent-infant interaction*. New York: Associated Scientific Publishers, 1975.

Thomas, A., Chess, S., & Burch, H.G. The origin of personality. *Scientific American*, 1970, *223*, 102–109.

Thomas, M.H., Horton, R.W., Lippincott, E.C. & Drabman, R.S. Desensitization to portrayals of real-life aggression as a function of exposure to television violence. *Journal of Personality and Social Psychology*, 1977, *35*, 450–458.

Tinbergen, N. "Derived" activities: Their causation, biological significance, origin and emancipation during evolution. *Quarterly Review of Biology*, 1952, *27*, 1–32.

Toda, M., Shinotsuka, H., McClintock, C.G., & Stech, F.J. Development of behavior as a function of culture, age, and social comparison. *Journal of Personality and Social Psychology*, 1978, *36*, 825–839.

Tomkins, S. *Affect, imagery, and consciousness: The positive affects* (Vol. 1). New York: Springer, 1962.

Tomkins, S. *Affect, imagery, and consciousness: The negative affects* (Vol. 2). New York: Springer, 1963.

Tourangeau, R., & Ellsworth, P.C. The role of facial response in the experience of emotion. *Journal of Personality and Social Psychology*, 1979, *37*, 1519–1531.

Treisman, A.M. Strategies and models of selective attention. *Psychological Review*, 1969, *76*, 282–299.

Trent, R.D. The relation between expressed self-acceptance and expressed attitudes towards Negroes and Whites among Negro children. *Journal of Genetic Psychology*, 1957, *91*, 25–31.

Trnavsky, P.A., & Bakeman, R. *Physical attrac-tiveness: Stereotype and social behavior in preschool children*. Paper presented at the meeting of the American Psychological Association, Washington, D.C., August 1976.

Turkewitz, H., O'Leary, K.D., & Ironsmith, M. Producing generalization of appropriate behavior through self-control. *Journal of Consulting and Clinical Psychology*, 1975, *43*, 577–583.

Tversky, A., & Kahneman, D. Causal thinking in judgment under uncertainty. In B. Butts & J. Hintikka (Eds.), *Logic, methodology, and philosophy of science*. Dordrecht, Holland: D. Reidel, 1978.

Underwood, B.J. Individual differences as a crucible in theory construction. *American Psychologist*, 1975, *30*, 128–134.

Underwood, B., Berenson, J.F., Berenson, R.J., Cheng, K.K., Wilson, D., Kulik, J., Moore, B.S., & Wenzel, G. Attention, negative affect and altruism: An ecological validation. *Personality and Social Psychology Bulletin*, 1977, *3*, 54–58.

Underwood, B., Froming, W.J., & Guarijuata, K.S. *Perspective-taking, temperaments, and generosity in children*. Unpublished manuscript, The University of Texas at Austin, 1980.

Underwood, B., Froming, W.J., & Moore, B.S. Mood, attention, and altruism: A search for mediating variables. *Developmental Psychology*, 1977, *13*, 541–542.

Upton, W. *Altruism, attribution, and intrinsic motivation in the recruitment of blood donors*. (Doctoral dissertation, Cornell University, 1973). *Dissertation Abstracts International*, 1974, *34*, 6260-B.

U.S. Department of Health, Education, and Welfare. *Cardiovascular profile of 15,000 children of school age in three communities, 1971–1975*. DHEW # (NIH 78-142), 1978.

Valins, S. Cognitive effects of false heart-rate feedback. *Journal of Personality and Social Psychology*, 1966, *4*, 400–408.

Valle, V.A., & Frieze, I.H. The stability of causal attributions as a mediator in changing expectations for success. *Journal of Personality and Social Psychology*, 1976, *33*, 579–587.

Van Lieshout, C.F.M. Young children's reactions to barriers placed by their mothers. *Child Development*, 1975, *46*, 879–886.

Varela, J.A. *Psychological solutions to social problems*. New York: Academic Press, 1971.

Vasta, R., Andrews, D.E., McLaughlin, A.M., Stirpe, L.A., & Comfort, C. Reinforcement effects on intrinsic interests: A classroom analog. *Journal of School Psychology*, 1978, *16*, 161–166.

Vasta, R., & Stirpe, L.A. Reinforcement effects on three measures of children's interests in math. *Behavior Modification*, 1979, *3*, 223–244.

Veroff, J. Social comparison and the development of achievement motivation. In C.P. Smith (Ed.), *Achievement-related motives in children*. New York: Russell Sage Foundation, 1969.

Vogel-Sprott, M., & Banks, R.K. The effects of delayed punishment on an immediately rewarded response in alcoholics and non-alcoholics. *Behavior Research and Therapy*, 1965, *3*, 69–73.

Vygotsky, L.S. *Thought and Language*. Cambridge, Mass: M.I.T. Press, 1962.

Wahler, R.G. Oppositional children: A quest for parental reinforcement control. *Journal of Applied Behavior Analysis*, 1969, *2*, 159–170.

Waldron, I. Sex differences in the coronary-prone behavior pattern. In T. Dembroski (Ed.), *Coronary-prone behavior*. New York: Springer-Verlag, 1978.

Walster, E., Berscheid, E., & Walster, G.W. New directions in equity research. *Journal of Personality and Social Psychology*, 1973, *25*, 151–176.

Walter, H.E., & Gilmore, S.K. Placebo versus social learning effects in parent training procedures designed to alter the behavior of aggressive boys. *Behavior Therapy*, 1973, *4*, 361–377.

Walters, R.H., & Demkow, L. Timing of punishment as a determinant of response inhibition. *Child Development*, 1963, *34*, 207–214.

Ward, S.H., & Braun, J. Self-esteem and racial preference in black children. *American Journal of Orthopsychiatry*, 1972, *42*, 644–647.

Warner, F., Thrapp, R., & Walsh, S. Attitudes of children toward their special class placement. *Exceptional Children*, 1973, *40*, 37–38.

Warr, P.B., & Knapper, C. *The perception of people and events*. New York: Wiley, 1968.

Watts, A.F. *The language and mental development of children*. London: Harrays & Co., 1944.

Weber, M. Politics as a vocation. The social psychology of the world religions. In H.H. Gerth & C.W. Mills (Eds.), *From Max Weber: Essays in sociology*. New York: Oxford University Press, 1946.

Weber, M. *The theory of social and economic organizations*. A.M. Henderson & T. Parsons (Trans.); T. Parsons (Ed.). New York: Free Press, 1947.

Weiner, B. *Theories of motivation: From mechanism to cognition*. Chicago: Rand McNally, 1972.

Weiner, B. (Ed.). *Achievement motivation and attribution theory*. Morristown, N.J.: General Learning Press, 1974.

Weiner, B. A theory of motivation for some classroom experiences. *Journal of Educational Psychology*, 1979, *71*, 3–25.

Weiner, B., Frieze, I.H., Kukla, A., Reed, L., Rest, S., & Rosenbaum, R.M. *Perceiving the causes of success and failure*. New York: General Learning Press, 1971.

Weiner, B., Heckhausen, H., Meyer, W., & Cook, R.E. Causal aspirations and achievement behavior: Conceptual analysis of effort and re-analysis of locus of control. *Journal of Personality and Social Psychology*, 1972, *21*, 239–248.

Weiner, B., & Kukla, A. An attributional analysis of achievement motivation. *Journal of Personality and Social Psychology*, 1970, *15*, 1–20.

Weiner, B., Kun, A., & Benesh-Weiner, M. The development of mastery, emotions, and morality from an attributional perspective. In W. A. Collins (Ed.), *Development of cognition, affect, and social relations: Minnesota Symposia on Child Development* (Vol. 13), Hillsdale, N.J.: Lawrence Erlbaum Associates, 1980.

Weiner, B., Nierenberg, R., & Goldstein, M. Social learning (locus of control) versus attributional (causal stability) interpretations of expectancy of success. *Journal of Personality*, 1976, *44*, 52–68.

Weiner, B., Russell, D., & Lerman, D. Affective consequences of causal ascriptions. In J.H. Harvey, W.J. Ickes, & R.F. Kidd (Eds.), *New directions in attribution research* (Vol. 2). Hillsdale, N.J.: Lawrence Erlbaum Associates, 1978.

Weiner, H.R., & Dubanoski, R.A. Resistance to extinction as a function of self- or externally determined schedules of reinforcement. *Journal of Personality and Social Psychology*, 1975, *31*, 905–910.

Weiner, M.J., & Mander, A.M. The effects of reward and perception of competency upon intrinsic motivation. *Motivation and Emotion*, 1978, *2*, 67–73.

Weisenberg, M. Pain and pain control. *Psychological Bulletin*, 1977, *84*, 1008–1044.

Weisz, J.R. Perceived control and learned helplessness among retarded and nonretarded children. *Developmental Psychology*, 1979, *15*, 311–319.

Wells, G.L. Lay analyses of causal forces on behavior. In J.H. Harvey (Ed.), *Cognition, social behavior, and the environment*. Hillsdale, N.J.: Lawrence Erlbaum Associates, 1980.

Werner, H. *The comparative psychology of mental development*. New York: International Universities Press, 1948.

Weyant, J.M. Effects of mood states, costs and benefits on helping. *Journal of Personality and Social Psychology*, 1978, *36*, 1169–1176.

Wheeler, R., & Ryan, F.L. Effects on cooperative and competitive classroom environments on the attitudes and achievement of elementary school students engaged in social studies inquiry activities. *Journal of Educational Psychology*, 1973, *65*, 402–407.

White, C.B., Bushnell, N., & Regnemer, J.C. Moral development in Bahamian school children: A three-year examination of Kohlberg's stages of moral development. *Developmental Psychology*, 1978, *14*, 58–65.

White, G.D., Nielson, G., & Johnson, S.M. Time-out duration and the suppression of deviant behavior in children. *Journal of Applied Behavior Analysis*, 1972, *5*, 111–120.

White, R. Motivation reconsidered: The concept of competence. *Psychological Review*, 1959, *66*, 297–334.

Whiteman, M., & Deutsch, M. Social disadvantage as related to intellective and language development. In M. Deutsch, I. Katz, & A.B. Jensen (Eds.), *Social class, race, and psychological development*. New York: Holt, Rinehart and Winston, 1968.

Wicklund, R.A. *Freedom and reactance*. Potomac, Md.: Lawrence Erlbaum Associates, 1974.

Wicklund, R.A., & Brehm, J.W. *Perspectives on cognitive dissonance*. Hillsdale, N.J.: Lawrence Erlbaum Associates, 1976.

Wiegel, R.H., Wiser, P.L., & Cook, S.W. The impact of cooperative learning experience on cross-ethnic relations and attitudes. *Journal of Social Issues*, 1975, *31*, 219–244.

Wiegers, R.M., & Frieze, I.H. Gender, female traditionality, achievement level and cognitions of success and failure. *Psychology of Women Quarterly*, 1977, *2*, 125–137.

Williams, J.E. Connotations of color names among Negroes and Caucasians. *Journal of*

Perceptual and Motor Skills, 1964, *18*, 721–731.

Williams, J.E., & Morland, K.J. *Race, color and the young child*. Chapel Hill: University of North Carolina Press, 1976.

Williams, R.L., & Byars, H. Negro self-esteem in a transitional society: Tennessee self-concept scale. *Personnel and Guidance Journal*, 1968, *47*, 120–125.

Willy, N.R., & McCandless, B.R. Social stereotypes for normal educable mentally retarded, and orthopedically handicapped children. *Journal of Special Education*, 1973, *7*, 283–288.

Wilson, E.O. *Sociobiology: The new synthesis*. Cambridge, Mass.: Belknap Press/Harvard, 1975.

Wilson, G.D. *The psychology of conservatism*. New York: Academic Press, 1973.

Winick, M. Introduction. In M. Winick (Ed.), *Childhood obesity*. New York: Wiley, 1975.

Winston, A.S., & Redd, W.H. Instructional control as a function of adult presence and competing reinforcement contingencies. *Child Development*, 1976, *47*, 264–268.

Winterbottom, M. The relation of need for achievement to learning experiences in independence and mastery. In J. Atkinson (Ed.), *Motives in fantasy, action, and society*. Princeton: Van Nostrand, 1958.

Withers, R.F.J. Problems in the genetics of human obesity. *Eugenics Review*, 1964, *56*, 81–90.

Witkin, H.A., Dyk, R.B., Faterson, G.E., Goodenough, D.R., & Karp, S.A. *Psychological differentiation*. New York: Wiley, 1962.

Wolf, T.M., Hunter, S.M., & Webber, L. Psychosocial measures and cardiovascular risk factors in children and adolescents. *Journal of Psychology*, 1979, *101*, 139–146.

Wolff, B.B., & Horland, A.A. Effect of suggestion upon experimental pain: A validation study. *Journal of Abnormal Psychology*, 1967, *72*, 402–407.

Wood, M. Children's developing understanding of other people's motives for behavior. *Developmental Psychology*, 1978, *14*, 561–562.

Woody, E.Z., & Costanzo, P.R. *Affect arousal and eating in obese and normal children: A test of the psychosomatic hypothesis*. Manuscript in preparation, Duke University, 1980.

Wooley, H.T. Overcoming contrariness and fears in children. *Hygenia*, March 1924, 164–169.

Wooley, O.W., Wooley, S.C., & Dunham, R.B. Can calories be perceived and do they affect hunger in obese and non-obese humans? *Journal of Comparative and Physiological Psychology,* 1972, *80,* 250.

Wooley, S.C. Physiologic versus cognitive factors in short term food regulation in the obese and nonobese. *Psychosomatic Medicine,* 1972, *34,* 62–68.

Worchel, S. The effects of films on the importance of behavioral freedom. *Journal of Personality,* 1972, *40,* 417–435.

Worchel, S., Andreoli, V.A., & Folger, R. Intergroup cooperation and intergroup attraction: The effects of previous interaction and outcome of combined effort. *Journal of Experimental Social Psychology,* 1977, *13,* 131–140.

Worchel, S., & Brehm, J.W. Direct and implied social restoration of freedom. *Journal of Personality and Social Psychology,* 1971, *18,* 294–304.

Wright, H.F. *The influence of barriers upon strength of motivation.* Unpublished doctoral dissertation, Duke University, 1934.

Wright, H.F. The effect of barriers upon strength of motivation. In R.G. Barker, J.S. Kounin, & H.F. Wright (Eds.), *Child behavior and development.* New York: McGraw-Hill, 1943.

Wright, H.F. *Recording and analyzing child behavior.* New York: Harper and Row, 1967.

Wyatt v. *Stickney.* In B.J. Ennis & P.R. Friedman (Eds.), *Legal rights of the mentally handicapped* (Vol. 1). New York: Practicing Law Institute, 1973.

Yarrow, M.R., & Campbell, J.D. Person perception in children. *Merrill-Palmer Quarterly,* 1963, *9,* 57–72.

Yarrow, M.R., Scott, P.M., & Waxler, C.Z. Learning concern for others. *Developmental Psychology,* 1973, *8,* 240–260.

Yarrow, M.R., & Waxler, C.Z. Dimensions and correlates of prosocial behavior in children. *Child Development,* 1976, *47,* 118–125.

Yates, B., & Mischel, W. Young children's preferred attentional strategies for delaying gratification. *Journal of Personality and Social Psychology,* 1979, *37,* 286–300.

Youniss, J. The nature of social cognition: A conceptual discussion of cognition. In H. McGurk (Ed.), *Issues in childhood social development.* London: Methuen, 1979.

Zahn-Waxler, C., Radke-Yarrow, M., & Brady-Smith, J. Perspective-taking and prosocial behavior. *Developmental Psychology, 1977, 13,* 87–88.

Zajonc, R.B. Attitudinal effects of mere exposure. *Journal of Personality and Social Psychology, Monograph Supplement,* 1968, *9* (P. 2), 1–27.

Zanna, M.P., & Cooper, J. Dissonance and the attribution process. In J.H. Harvey, W.J. Ickes, & R.F. Kidd (Eds.), *New directions in attribution research* (Vol. 1). Hillsdale, N.J.: Lawrence Erlbaum Associates, 1976.

Zanna, M.P., & Hamilton, D.L. Further evidence for meaning change in impression formation. *Journal of Experimental Social Psychology,* 1977, *13,* 224–238.

Zanna, M.P., Lepper, M.R., & Abelson, R.P. Attentional mechanisms in children's devaluation of a forbidden activity in a forced-compliance situation. *Journal of Personality and Social Psychology,* 1973, *28,* 355–359.

Zigler, E. Developmental vs. difference theories of mental retardation and the problem of motivation. *American Journal of Mental Deficiency,* 1969, *73,* 536–556.

Zigler, E. The retarded child as a whole person. In H.E. Adams & W.K. Boardman (Eds.), *Advances in experimental clinical psychology.* New York: Pergamon, 1971.

Zuckerman, M., Hall, J.A., DeFrank, R.S., & Rosenthal, R. Encoding and decoding of spontaneous and posed facial expressions. *Journal of Personality and Social Psychology,* 1976, *34,* 966–977.

Zuckerman, M., Lipets, M.S., Koivumaki, J.H., & Rosenthal, R. Encoding and decoding nonverbal cues of emotion. *Journal of Personality and Social Psychology,* 1975, *32,* 1068–1076.

NAME INDEX

SUBJECT INDEX